IDENTITY, CULTURE AND
GLOBALIZATION

INTERNATIONAL INSTITUTE OF SOCIOLOGY

The International Institute of Sociology is the oldest continuous sociological association in existence. It was founded in 1893 in Paris by René Worms. Early distinguished members included scholars such as Max Weber, Lujo Brentano, Enrico Ferri, Franklin Giddings, Ludwig Gumplowicz, Achille Loria, Alfred Marshall, Carl Menger, Edward A. Ross, Gustav Schmoller, Georg Simmel, Albion Small, Gabriel Tarde, Edward B. Tylor, Ferdinand Tönnies, Alexandre Tchouprov, Thorstein Veblen, Lester Ward, Sidney and Beatrix Webb, and Wilhelm Wundt.

Executive Board 1997-2001

since 1893

THE ANNALS OF THE INTERNATIONAL INSTITUTE OF SOCIOLOGY

NEW SERIES – VOLUME 8

IDENTITY, CULTURE
AND
GLOBALIZATION

EDITED BY

ELIEZER BEN-RAFAEL

WITH

YITZAK STERNBERG

BRILL
LEIDEN · BOSTON · KÖLN
2001

This book is printed on acid-free paper.

Die Deutsche Bibliothek - CIP-Einheitsaufnahme

Identity, Culture and Globalization / edited by E. Ben-Rafael with
Y. Sternberg. – Leiden ; Boston ; Köln : Brill, 2001
ISBN 90–04–12197–8

Library of Congress Cataloging-in-Publication Data

Library of Congress Cataloging-in-Publication Data is also available

ISBN 90 04 12197 8

CONTENTS

SECTION THREE

MULTICULTURALISM AND TRANSNATIONAL DIASPORAS

SECTION FOUR

THE DECLINING ACCOUNTABILITY OF THE STATE

SECTION FIVE

POSTMODERNITY

IN CONCLUSION: TOWARD A NEW AGENDA

FOREWORD

This book constitutes the eighth volume of the Annals of the International Institute of Sociology. The occasion of this volume has been the 34th World Congress of the IIS that took place in Tel-Aviv University, in July 1999 around themes implied by the title of this volume. We are also indebted to the numerous Israeli institutions of higher learning—universities, colleges and research centers—which have supported the Congress and made this project possible. While a good part of the following chapters are contributions by participants to the Congress, we have had the chance to encounter the good will of many other renowned scholars in this area who have responded positively to our invitation to participate in this project. We also want to thank cordially Dr. Joed Elich, the Senior Acquisitions Editor, Ms. Willy de Gijzel, our Unit Editor, at Brill, and the publishing house for their dedicated assistance and support all along the preparation of this book. We also want to mention with the deepest grief the decease of Jürgen Heideking who participated to the Tel-Aviv IIS Congress as a keynote speaker, and whose chapter appears posthomously in this volume thanks to the good will of his widow, Mrs. Heideking, to whom we are profoundly grateful.

GENERAL INTRODUCTION

1. ANALYZING OUR TIME:
A SOCIOLOGICAL PROBLÉMATIQUE

Eliezer Ben-Rafael and Yitzhak Sternberg

Five issues, one major question

This book is about the problématique of contemporary sociological analysis, a problématique that has dominated sociologists' theoretical writing in the last two decades and has brought about new approaches. Scholars variously emphasize distinct facets, privileging some to the detriment of others, and conducting passionate controversies with each other. In the texts that follow this chapter, these polemics can be clearly distinguished and tracked. However, what has been of importance to us in this work is less those scholarly disputes but rather the contribution made by each of the approaches involved to outlining and demarcating the space of the discussion. In this perspective, we found possible to group these diverse—and even contradictory—outlooks around a series of basic contentions. These contentions, when viewed as a whole, encompass what may be called the sociological universe of discourse about the 'newness of our time'. They do not elaborate any general theory but rather refer to a number of interlinked topics constituting a common wide 'space' of reflexion. More specifically, we analyze this universe by distinguishing five foci of discussion: (1) the delineation of relevant analytical units, reflecting on their similarity or dissimilarity; (2) the characterization of the whole constituted by these units; (3) the divisions and dynamics that develop in this reality, as a comprehensive entity; (4) the relations of power which control—or fail to control—these dynamics; and finally, (5) the general features of the reality as issuing from, or revealed by, these developments.

Regarding each of these foci, the discourse of the 'newness of our time' is articulated by discussing the pertinence (or lack of pertinence, but still serving as foci of reference) of specific concepts—some of which are brand-new, while other, older ones, receive now new meanings. These conceptualized foci, we propose, may be enumerated as follows:

(1) The comparative consideration of contemporary societies or cultures is widely discussed by referring to the notion of 'multiple modernities';

(2) The interdependence and connectedness of societies and cultures and their systemic character is debated by elaborating on the concept of 'globalization';

(3) The divisions and tensions characterizing this global world are considered by referring to the concepts of 'multiculturalism' and 'transnational diasporas';

(4) The power dimension of these developments is focused on through assessments of the question of the 'declining accountability of the State';

(5) The discontinuities of the new social reality vis-à-vis previous phases and within contemporary societies are analyzed by discussing the relevance of the concept of 'postmodernity'.

These five foci, which structure this book, are considered by scholars as referring to different features of contemporary social experience. Close consideration shows, however, that while they point to analytical distinctive phases, they may also be viewed as referring to aspects of a more or less general development involving, in varying degrees, all or nearly all societies of our world. The numerous approaches do not necessarily address all five foci—in fact, mostly they do not—but they still relate to each other in one way or another, and the authors themselves, to be sure, are well aware that they are tackling interrelated questions. It is this space of questions and attempts of—convergent and divergent—answers that outlines this universe of discourse which we speak about, namely, the 'newness of our time'. This discourse by no means stipulates simple and simplistic truth-statements. However, it is our viewpoint that the propositions which surface from all parts still give this discourse some coherence. We see one possibility to pinpoint this coherence in 'basic contentions' that we derive from the literature regarding the various foci of this universe of discourse, and which we feel reflect on the intellectual 'acquis' of these debates.

(1) *Multiple modernities*

The concept of multiple modernities figures prominently in the comparative consideration of today's societies and cultures. Sociologists who endorse this concept as a major analytical tool, view almost all existing societies either as 'modern' or 'modernizing'. In one way or another, they see them as belonging to modernity, notwithstanding the contrasts they may demonstrate vis-à-vis each other. According to this perspective, this expansion of modernity that started from Western Europe, took place over time and in different places around the world, along different patterns: Western colonialism, as illustrated by the British and French world empires; Western colonization, as in the case of America and Oceania; imperialism and the imposition of new models from the outside, as in China; cultural radiation of the West in non-Western countries, as exemplified by Japan. Everywhere modernity implements new organizational principles and cultural codes. It often completely destroys a longstanding social order, but in other instances its impact has been more moderate. In any case, modernity creates facts that can hardly be deleted by new circumstances. Even wars of independence in former colonies, or the outbreak of revolutions against local elites, leave quite intact the signs of modernity in major spheres of social activity.

In this, modernity as civilization has had a far deeper impact than the transformations brought about by the ideologies that it itself nurtures, like communism or nationalism. The communist regimes that collapsed in Eastern Europe after decades, left few prints in the structures of the new regimes and in the reconstruction of their national culture. Though, at the same time, the new forces were willing to be considered as anything except 'anti-modern'. The same is true of anti-Western nationalistic movements which gradually aligned themselves with the general aspiration for progress. The end of colonialism in the 1960s and 1970s transformed the social and political regimes of many countries, but without suppressing the drive to modernize. In practical terms, this was expressed in the adoption by the new regimes of patterns that—at least formally—widely duplicated those of Western powers, and the retention by them of modern objectives in such domains as the economy, education and welfare. Modernity instills perceptions of the individual's relation to the world, understandings of social communication, and new aspirations vis-à-vis life that, no matter how acquired, are hard to erase once they have been internalized. This, seemingly, is what Elias (1998) means by the 'civilizing process' that shapes individual experiences. These endeavors are less and less perceived as submitted to external influences—even though they turn to outside scenes like 'London', 'New York' or 'Paris' for positive references.

Furthermore, the impact of modernity is also quite different from what was achieved by the great religions—Christianity, Islam or Confucianism—in the societies which they conquered long before modernity. While both modernity and the great religions transformed the 'world-view' of human beings, world religions had answers for all questions, this-worldly and other-worldly alike, modernity had not. The answers of the great religions derived from given sets of truths which founded cosmological systems, and ended up in rules applying to every aspect of daily life. Modernity, in contrast, consists primarily of cultural codes that set people, more than ever before and regarding more areas of activity, in a relation of reflexivity to their acts and environment—including social arrangements, existing or proposed. Though, and at the same time, modernity does not necessarily (under certain versions, it may) convey precise views of the world and cosmic images, even when it proposes what many call a 'project'. By this are understood known, reflected and recognized aspirations of individual and collective actors with respect to specific spheres. In this perspective—and this is what reflexivity is all about—, actors supposedly determine their course of behavior and, consequently, the structures of their enviornment, on the basis of some 'good reasons' of theirs—whatever their criteria, values or beliefs may be. This latter notion substantiates what Boudon (2000) defines as 'rationality', and it enlightens the singularity of the modern mind. It follows that in modernity more than in any other civilization, human beings are entitled to rethink their interests, goals and purposes, and the ways to attain them. This may also (though they do not always do) elaborate velleities vis-à-vis their more general conditions of life, their vision of the 'good society', nay even the desirable 'state of the world'. By this, modernity may also induce people to contemplate, and even adopt, new truths—total, or even barbaric—and to reject choice and rationality on their behalf. This then expresses reactions to conflicts of allegiances where the loyalty to legacies seems to impose the exclusion, nay even the destruction, of the unwanted. This state of affairs derives from modernity itself, when it instills uncertainty and awakes feelings of (virtual or imagined) threats from the inside or the outside. Weber (1977) already warned that rationality tends to become anti-reflexive by achieving the status of a value of its own, and by intruding on, and getting control of, motivations and purposes. The experience of 20th century totalitarianisms shows, moreover, that there is also a possibility that leading actors rationally prefer irrationality over rationality as basis of social mobilization.

Yet, since it does not imply—at least a priori and directly—with worldviews, fundamental beliefs about the world, and general ethical codes, modernity as such does not compete—at least in a zero-sum manner—with religion that always consists of a set of ethical rules deriving from a system of assertions about the world. Modernity requests changes in life-styles, proposes new interpretations of traditional norms, and assumes a readiness to confront new challenges. In all these, modernity does have an impact on religion and traditional patterns by imposing new forms and languages. Yet by no means does it presume the end of religiosity, or replacing religious beliefs and experience. Modernity as civilization asks for new attitudes that can be equally derived from different, if not divergent, worldviews. These attitudes can be understood as implied by the agnostic philosophy of the Enlightenment era and its humanistic calling, and they can be defined as the ethics imposed by a severe image of God. This means that modernity may penetrate societies and transform them without detaching them abruptly from their traditional cultures. This also means that modernity itself assumes different forms in different contexts.

These signify that modernity and traditional religiosity are not mutually exclusive, but not that they do not find themselves in tension with each other in a diversity of areas. Modernity encourages reflexivity and the contemplation of alternative courses of action, while religiosity expects what responds to its notions of righteousness. The departure from the traditional view of reality as a priori given for the benefit of a perspective emphasizing the role of human beings in shaping their world, occasions countless discrepancies between traditional purposes and rational ends. It both follows that modernity and tradition can coexist—in one way or another—and that, consequently, the tensions between them come to constitute a lasting feature of the social reality. In the context of the diversity of local pre-modern traditions, the multiplication of modernities signifies that modern or modernizing settings differ from each other not only by the forms that modernity takes on in different societies but also according to the kinds of modernity-tradition tensions that these societies experience.

In the context of these considerations, we formulate as follows three simple and interrelated propositions that make up Basic contention #1:

1.1. Modernity expands in diverse settings, while this expansion does not necessarily eradicate existing traditional and religious standpoints and practices.

1.2. Hence, 'multiple modernities' means that modernity becomes associated with different cultures.

1.3. By the same token, modernity may represent different lasting tensions in various societies.

(2) *Globalization*

Many authors consider the universalization of modernity itself—beyond the differences that it can assume in every specific space—as a transformational process bearing its own significance and impacts. They describe this development as 'globalization'. Globalization is defined by Therborn (2000) as indicating tendencies to (1) a world-wide reach and connectedness of social phenomena, and (2) a world-encompassing awareness of actors. In other words, a global spatialization of the social reality. While there have already been examples of the conquest of, and domination over, large stretches of the world (such as the Roman Empire or the colonial expansion of the West), in our era globalization has made the globe itself, in its quasi-entirety, the relevant space of the new links that relate its various parts to each other. These links are not found only at inter-state or inter-society levels. The world-wide development of communication, cultural references and means of transportation—thanks today to the Internet, television, telephone and jet-travel—are to an unprecedented extent setting in direct relations scenes

of activity, groups and individuals from different parts of the world. Bartelson
(2000) sees here three sequences. The first sequence is transference, that is,
the intensification of interaction and exchange among social settings; the
second, resulting from transference, is transformation—that is, the emergence of changes at the level of the local system; following transformation,
the third sequence is transcendence, that is, the dissolution of the divide
between inside and outside. Featherstone and Lash (1995) discuss this evolution as the triumph of universal 'disembedding', characteristic of the 'informational order', that now embraces the planet, when the global has become
a decisive framework of contemporary social life—above the heads of the
nation-states. As asserted by Robertson (1995a), from urbanization to nationalism, we experience nowadays processes of institutionalization in which the
global influences what is meant by local—even in the absence of any formal guiding intervention.

This social experience is analyzed from most diverse and contradictory
theoretical angles. Decades ago, Wilbert Moore (1966) understood the expansion of modernity in the contemporary world as the emergence of a Parsonian
world systemic process of integration. The same developments are viewed
from a conflictual angle by Wallerstein (1974) who sees in our time a transition where the struggle of the privileged and the underprivileged has an
opportunity for engendering a new world. John Meyer and his colleagues
(1997; Meyer, 2000) share a Weberian vision and consider globalization as
a world cultural change expressed in the enactment of shared models, despite
the disparities that exist among nations regarding resources and culture. In
a similar perspective, Niklas Luhmann (1997) describes the emergence of a
global system that consists of a new single world-society where interacting
nationally-determined actors play a lesser role. Globalization, he emphasizes,
is however a variable that can exhibit varying intensity and strength in
different places or groups. Appadurai (1990; 1996) speaks, in this respect,
of 'global flows' that involve financial resources, population movements, ideas
and ideals, media, and technological knowledge. These flows may produce
random configurations by disjunctive effects, and exhibit different contours
in different spaces, depending on the perspectives of the actors—i.e., nation-
states, social movements, corporations or individuals.

Globalization, however, is also the focus of conflict analyses. Jonathan
Friedman (1995) describes a world where fragmentation is increasing, after
a phase of stable relations between hegemonic centers and weak peripheries, due to the emergence of new smaller centers out-competing and 'de-
hegemonizing' the old centers. This conflict-analysis is pursued by Fröbel
and his colleagues (2000) who show that globalization also means an international division of labor, a division that is liable to cause the closing of

factories in the West where unions are strong, and the creation, by Western capitalists, of low-wage factories in the East, where workers are generally unorganized. Bourdieu (1998) is a strong supporter of this kind of critical approach toward globalization. He sees globalization mainly as an assault against the welfare state and the high wages of workers in the West, and foresees the restoration of 'wild capitalism' aiming to retain world domination by Western economic interests. While globalization is often equated to 'americanization' and blamed for the inequities it represents, in the domain of culture, Nederveen Pieterse (1995) contends that in a globalized world, the creolization and hybridization of languages and cultures lead to 'de-authenticization'. The way is short from here to deny globalization the status of a valid concept and to see it as a secondary aspect of the very reality it is intended to account for.

It remains that even then the question of globalization, if not globalization itself, remains a focus of discussion regarding a set of processes bound to the growing interconnectedness of societies and humans in todays' world. It is in this sense that we use here the notion of globalization and that we are led to Basic contention #2:

2.1. Contemporary globalization is discussed in relation to the universal expansion of modernity and the constant strengthening of the interconnection of nations, societies and peoples.

2.2. However, these processes do not reach every spot on the globe with the same strength.

2.3. These processes, which we consider under the heading of globalization or at least in reference to it, do not preclude—and in fact nurture—old as well as new forms of conflict, exploitation and confrontation between settings and groups.

(3) *Multiculturalism and transnational diasporas*

Globalization, among other manifestations, means that the West is becoming an ever stronger lodestone for underprivileged populations in the rest of the world. As such, globalization is becoming a major factor in Western societies' development into heterogeneous populations and the multiculturalization of settings. It strengthens, in this way, the parallel development of processes stemming from the implications of democracy.

This latter aspect is addressed in the literature in a variety of manners. Cornelius Castoriadis (1997b) sees here the maturing of frictions between capitalism—which embodies rationality and is geared to mastering the environment and maximizing resources—and democracy—which allows for the manifestation of subjectivity in seeking self-expression and participation. Years ago, Ralf Dahrendorf (1959) already elaborated on this tension, specifying that it takes place between capitalist-economic exigencies, implying structural inequality, and the democratic demand for political equality, with an open-ended potential for extension to additional issues. François Furet (1981) adds that democracy may even give rise to demands for a wholesale reconstruction of society on radical egalitarian lines. This confrontation of capitalism and democracy is thematized by Alain Touraine (1992) in terms of a debate between fundamentally rival projects coexisting in Western modernity. Against this background, democracy encourages highly diverse groups to voice claims and, possibly, to enter the political game. It thus may also sustain, at least de facto, ethno-cultural groups which aspire to follow suit and formulate political exigencies. These exigencies may aim to promote a more equitable participation in society, and/or to maintain, and even to strengthen, their distinctiveness. Eventually, these exigencies may bring about a situation of multiculturalism.

Multiculturalism, as an aspect of the social order of modern and democratic societies, indicates a political, social and cultural reality, that is brought about—probably but not necessarily through confrontations—mainly by political movements, and signifies that the center recognizes the legitimate existence of diverse socio-cultural groups in society (see also Willett, 1998). Multiculturalism may exist in non-democratic societies and reflect a patrimonial relation between the center and peripheral groups. It may also constitute a de facto aspect of democratic culturally-heterogeneous societies. Our own suggestion is that nowadays, in many contemporary modern and democratic settings, multiculturalism is not only factual, but is also an institutionalized reality that represents new power relations in society. Such a development restricts the center's span of control; it endows socio-cultural actors with authority over their constituencies, as well as power vis-à-vis the center itself. This new configuration has diverse social and cultural consequences. H.D. Meyer (2000), for instance, indicates that nowadays taste is no longer the monopoly of the privileged that marks the distance separating classes and groups. In addition to the concept of taste as 'refinement', there is now a concept of taste as indicative of 'authenticity'. Multiculturalism refers to life styles, and allows new social values to emerge: it establishes legitimate alternative sources of meaning and moral authority. Taylor (1994) adds that multiculturalism emphasizes the cultural at the expense of material components of justice.

More than a few scholars insist on the conflictual potential of multiculturalism. Harvey (2000) points out to crises of identity leading, among other consequences, to racism, ethnic conflict and renewed attempts at isolationism. In the wake of these reflections, Kincheloe and Steinberg (1997) include race, gender and language under the heading of multicultural conflict. Multiculturalism, they assert, involves competing definitions of the social order grounded in divergent social interests.

In this context, Soysal (2000) recalls the paradoxes in the formation of citizenship in contemporary Western society. She observes an increasing decoupling of rights and identities, meaning that Western societies are led by their value system and political ambitions to grant more and more rights to new groups, independently from their integration in society: a contradiction that weakens the motivation to fully assimilate and get rid of all its markers. Groups, Soysal contends, may even be encouraged to multiply their particularistic claims, legitimizing them on the ground of society's universalistic democratic discourse. At this point, the discussion of multiculturalism re-joins the issue of globalization which is the direct context of the multiplication of transnational diasporas, an ever more important component of multiculturalism.

The notion of transnational diaspora indicates several interconnected phenomena. It concerns individuals who, in the context of the intense worldwide connectedness that now exists between societies, are quite easily spurred to emigrate from their (usually relatively underprivileged) countries to more fortunate ones—as 'guest workers' and 'regular' or 'illegal' immigrants. These individuals tend naturally to settle in the same cities and quarters, which eases their adaptation to their new setting. They try to comply with the pressure to adjust by learning the legitimate language and prevailing habits and customs, but their very concentration also allows them to continue to use their languages of origin among themselves and to retain aspects of their heritage. What, however, is more crucial here in the long range concerns nowadays advanced communication technologies, easy international travelling, and the general access to global mass media. In these circumstances, recently-settled immigrants in the West are able to an unprecedented extent to retain permanent ties with their relatives everywhere—in the 'motherland' as well as in other diasporas. Diaspora communities in Western societies may remain involved in networks of varying amplitude, across borders and continents, and this does by no means preclude them from to invest their best in efforts to integrate into their actual society.

Furthermore, it may be added, while democracy and globalization widely account, together, for the 'multiculturalization' of societies, so to speak, multiculturalism is also bound in a two-way relation to the notion of multiple modernities. In a world characterized by multiple modernities, individuals all over the world get to share—though not necessarily equally—some common basic notions conveyed by modernization—whether regarding aspects of the participation in the labor market, economic life, nay even forms of mass culture, politics or family life. This diffusion of modernity, under its various forms, creates elements of a common language across the borders of cultural groups. On the other hand, and by the same token, where multiculturalism exists, this means as well that in a same society diverse versions of modernity may be found among different communities. These actors, to be sure, influence each other mutually but each one's particular 'modern endeavor', so to speak, is still firstly given shape by their own ethnocultural, religious or historical orientations. In other words, the theory of multiple modernities that primarily aims to the comparative analysis of socieities does have relevance to the study of the development and dynamics of multicultural settings.

All in all, these considerations lead to the formulation of Basic contention #3:

3.1. Democracy encourages the (possibly conflictual) self-expression and self-assertion of ethno-cultural communities and tends to bring about the contemporary multiculturalization of society.

3.2. Globalization and the multiplication of modernities create favorable conditions for population movements across countries and, together with the development of multiculturalism, contributes to the emergence and multiplication of transnational diasporas.

3.3. Transnational diasporas crystallize lines of social solidarity that crosscut nations and continents and become a driving power for both the multiculturalism of individual societies, and for globalization.

3.4. The multiculturalization of society means as well that multiple modernities is to be seen as a relevant concept for its analysis.

(4) The declining accountability of the state

In the context of these developments, a major debate among contemporary sociologists concerns the extent that they remain, in one way or another, under the control of political centers which, by representing the socially powerful and influential, might, it alone, endorse them some systemic and systematic framework. In other words, the processes viewed in the above question the accountability of the state. Commentators are here again quite divided. Some are convinced that, even today, the power of the state should not be disregarded. Smith (1998), outstandingly, sees the modern state as grounded in nationalism, and by nationalism he means a form of ethnicity, generalized to the wider collective, which draws its vitality from culture and ancestry. Anderson (1991) who discusses imagined communities, is wrong in Smith's eyes, and so is Gellner (1994b) who sees nations mainly as the outcome of industrialization and state-provided schooling. It is his contention that nations are not homogeneous, but are driven to homogeneity. Other authors, however, are less inclined to downplay the state's declining power which they relate, among other factors, to globalization and multicultural-ism. For Habermas (1998), the fact that today the state shares national sov-ereignty with international bodies is a major source for the decline of the accountability of the state. Held (2000) assesses, in more general terms, that contemporary circumstances, including globalization, cause the re-configuration of political power and the emergence of new forms of governance—within states and beyond their boundaries. Philip McMichael (2000) underlines in this respect that people and governments no longer control the key deci-sions that shape their lives; Harvey (2000) pursues along this line, contending that the crisis of the contemporary state entails the decay of trade unions. According to Castells (1999), all the institutions that make up the state have been greatly harmed, entailing a crisis of the political regime's legitimacy. The nation-state is weakened by networks of money, power and informa-tion, and as a result, the life conditions of most citizens are deteriorating. This development is firstly due to the pressures set on governments by groups strengthened by the multiculturalization of society to grant them wider auton-omy and freedom of action. The notion of 'resistance-identity' indicates this tendency that emerges in communities aspiring to retain their cohesion and resisting total identification with the wider society. In some cases, 'resistance-identities' may become 'project-identities' by raising general claims vis-à-vis society on behalf of an encompassing perspective. This, however, is not the general case.

In brief, the decline of the accountability of the state, it is argued, comes up in the latter's lesser capability to implement social policies and to shoul-der its responsibility. The paradoxical character of this development, we may add, resides in the fact that such policies might have responded to the particular claims of the peripheries whose struggle for political and cultural recognition contributes most to that weakening of the state.

These considerations lead us to Basic contention #4:

4.1. The multiplication of modernities within societies, multiculturaliza-tion and globalization contribute to what is viewed by analysts as the decline of the state's accountability.

4.2. This decline of the state's accountability is not equally experienced everywhere.

4.3. Where it takes place at a significant extent, this decline necessarily influences the general effectiveness and authority of the polity.

(5) *Postmodernity*

The notion of postmodernity is another concept that emerges in scholars' debates about today's social reality—at least where the Western experience is predominant. Some scholars do not endorse this concept, and prefer different wordings, but all agree in one way or another that we can describe the contemporary era, as presenting new general features in some crucial socio-cultural respects. Without taking sides in the question of the intrinsic adequacy of the concept of postmodernity, and its relative theoretical advantages over alternative concepts, we view postmodernity as the heading under which the very newness of the reality under study is discussed.

Beyond the disagreements on the degree of discontinuity that our time represents vis-a-vis the past, and no matter which concept is used to describe it, one notes the prevailing grim and pessimistic 'mood' among scholars regarding today quality of social life. Giddens (2000), for instance, who speaks of 'late modernity', sees the newness of our time in its amplification of features that already existed previously, and defines it in terms of increased reflexivity and the disruption of taken-for-granted ways of life. Beck (1992) proposes the notion of 'risk society' to indicate the hazardous outcomes of modernity—which he calls 'bads' in contrast to 'goods'—at the present time, including phenomena such as environmental pollution, genetic engineering, and the dangers of nuclear developments. These hazards add up to the conflicts over the distribution of goods, but Beck (1996) argues that, compared to the discords of the past, none can now be held responsible for those risks. He sees these hazards in terms of 'unintentional consequences' (or 'effets pervers' according to Boudon, 1979) of modernization that incite individuals to increased reflexivity. Hence, Beck proposes to describe our condition in terms of 'reflexive modernity', that is, a stage of extreme individualization, where the major issues confronting society revolve around trust and credibility. Delanty (2000) suggests the notion of 'contested modernity' to describe the discontinuity between present and past, in order to emphasize that culture today is contested and transformative, in the context of the unprecedented development of communications. He is also ready to endorse the notion of postmodernity which, to his mind, has become—like modernity itself, capitalism, feminism and other concepts—part of our vocabulary for expressing the current condition.

In a dialectical perspective, Stuart Hall (2000) sees a basic feature of our time in the contradiction represented by globalization and collective identities. Globalization blurs the contours of collectives, and awakes two opposed reactions. A first reaction is fundamentalism which amplifies primordial identities against the universalistic significance of globalization. An alternative reaction to globalization is cultural hybridization, that expresses adjustment to this reality. Bauman (2000) then emphasizes that postmodernity consists of an era marked by pluralism, contingency and instability, where sociality is continually constructed and reconstructed, and the social structure remains fluid. Featherstone (1995) speaks of 'postmodernization' to suggest a process of implementation rather than a clear-cut social order. Candau (1998) underlines the current overwhelming tendency to assert particular identities grounded in the discourse of collective memory. He sees this search as illusionary and as a form of 'bricolage', but recognizes that these new developments take place in the context of the disappearance of encompassing identities.

Whether postmodernity is endorsed by scholars as an important tool of analysis, or only serves as a reference for discussing the newness of our time, it clearly relates to the other phases considered in the above. It refers to multiple modernities within society and multiculturalism because these trends account for the difficulties of communication that may emerge among members of same settings. It relates as well to globalization, in the measure that the latter entails new lines of solidarity cutting across societies and continents, and weakens the exclusiveness of the societal identity and culture. It also relates to the decline of the state as its major features like social fragmentation and individualization develop uncontrolled and unguided by public authority.

In brief, postmodernity—in its various wordings—primarily refers to a new reality, and it is in this perspective that we propose Basic contention #5:

5.1. Postmodernity, as a perspective on the contemporary world as well as an axis of discussion about this reality, emerges in a world described by scholars as experiencing multiple modernities, globalization, multiculturalism and the declining accountability of the state.

5.2. Postmodernity identifies the 'newness' of contemporary reality through a wide range of new or more accentuated features that include individualization, fragmentation, and fluidity of social life.

5.3. Postmodernity indicates the growing importance of particularistic identities and the decline of encompassing identities.

5.4. The growing importance of collective identities—and especially of the more particularistic ones—contrasts with the increasing blurring of the precise contours of the social boundaries delineating the relevant collectives.

In conclusion

In brief, this analysis has attempted to outline the universe of discourse of social scientists about the newness of our time. This discourse, we found, is articulated around five interconnected phases and can be summarized by corresponding basic contentions revolving around key concepts referred to—if not endorsed—by scholars from all boards (see Table 1). It is accordingly that the contributions to this book, which all deal with one or more aspects of this problématique, and in keeping with their major focus of discussion, that they are divided in the following in five sections. These sections lead to the last texts of this book which open the discussion about the contemporary concerns of sociology.

Table 1. The newness of our time: Basic contentions

(1) Multiple modernities	1.1. Modernity expands in diverse settings, while this expansion does not necessarily eradicate existing traditional and religious standpoints and practices. 1.2. Hence, 'multiple modernities' means that modernity becomes associated with different cultures. 1.3. By the same token, modernity may represent different lasting tensions in various societies.
(2) Globalization	2.1. Contemporary globalization is discussed in relation to the universal expansion of modernity and the constant strengthening of the interconnection of nations, societies and peoples. 2.2. However, these processes do not reach every spot on the globe with the same strength. 2.3. These processes, which we consider under the heading of globalization or at least in reference to it, do not preclude—and in fact nurture—old as well as new forms of conflict, exploitation and confrontation between settings and groups.
(3) Multiculturalism	3.1. Democracy encourages the (possibly conflictual) self-expression and self-assertion of ethno-cultural communities and tends to bring about the contemporary multiculturalization of society. 3.2. Globalization and the multiplication of modernities create favorable conditions for population movements across countries and, together with the development of multiculturalism, contributes to the emergence and multiplication of transnational diasporas. 3.3. Transnational diasporas crystallize lines of social solidarity that crosscut nations and continents and become a driving power for both the multiculturalism of individual societies, and for globalization. 3.4. The multiculturalization of society means as well that multiple modernities is to be seen as a relevant concept for its analysis.

(table cont.)

(4) The declining accountability of the state	4.1. The multiplication of modernities within societies, multiculturalization and globalization contribute to what is viewed by analysts as the decline of the state's accountability. 4.2. This decline of the state's accountability is not equally experienced everywhere. 4.3. Where it takes place at a significant extent, this decline necessarily influences the general effectiveness and authority of the polity.
(5) Postmodernity	5.1. Postmodernity, as a perspective on the contemporary world as well as an axis of discussion about this reality, emerges in a world described by scholars as experiencing multiple modernities, globalization, multiculturalism and the declining accountability of the state. 5.2. Postmodernity identifies the 'newness' of contemporary reality through a wide range of new or more accentuated features that include individualization, fragmentation, and fluidity of social life. 5.3. Postmodernity indicates the growing importance of particularistic identities and the decline of encompassing identities. 5.4. The growing importance of collective identities—and especially of the more particularistic ones—contrasts with the increasing blurring of the precise contours of the social boundaries delineating the relevant collectives.

SECTION ONE

MULTIPLE MODERNITIES

INTRODUCTION

The texts in Section One elaborate and specify the notion of 'multiple modernities'. *Shmuel Eisenstadt* starts his analysis by focusing on Western modernity, and the whole set of concomitant developments—structural, urban, industrial—which it represented. These developments went hand in hand with the building of the modern nation-state, national collectives and capitalist economy. All in all, these transformations were sustained by beliefs in human capability for shaping social reality—eventually towards utopias. Group interests were also recognized, as well as the diversity of interpretations of the common good. The core of modernity's program, says Eisenstadt, consisted of breaking down traditional legitimation and opening up new possibilities of political order. Intellectual antinomianism combined with aspirations to center-formation, and the consequent 'charismatization' of the center witnessed the emergence of themes like equality and freedom, justice and human autonomy, solidarity and identity. Collective identities were no longer considered as preordained, while public and private arenas were clearly distinguished. This program, however, implied numerous contradictions—between totalistic and pluralistic conceptions, or reflexivity and active construction. Ideologies now emphasized the primacy of national collectivities and the role of politics in reconstituting society. Non-European nations participated in the new program, but would reject some—or many—of its aspects. Convergence toward the West developed in realms like occupational and industrial structures, education or political forms, but divergence has been the rule in other social and cultural aspects (not to mention that in Western societies themselves, new discourses have progressively transformed the initial model). *Björn Wittrock*, in a quite similar perspective, perceives modernity as a fundamental change in traditional orientations, that develops from the underlying code of individualism—a necessary condition for the 'discovery of society' disengaged from religious representations. The modern notion of 'society' was grounded on new assumptions about what prompts human beings to act. Among other factors, it recognized the role of economic-rationalistic motivation. Individuals, moreover, were now seen as forming a systemic aggregate, imposing structural constraints upon members, in return. A major contradiction of this reality is the chasm between the overt commitment to universality and the inability to conceptualize political and social order in other than highly particularistic terms. Thus, Wittrock understands the traumas of the 20th century as endemic to the modern experience; that is, as events that have involved the violent rejection—or the overemphasizing of specific aspects—of the promissory notes both of modern and traditional institutions, in ways that remain within the frame of modern schemata. Preoccupied by the meaning of modernity in a world where it expands without erasing historical cultures, *Yitzhak Sternberg* points to the theoretical difficulty implied by the encompassing character of the notion of 'multiple modernities'. When every social reality can be viewed as pertaining to modernity, this notion inevitably encounters the difficulty of defining what remains outside its scope. This, in turn, questions its very efficiency. However, the author supports the view that sees in the concept of 'civilization' a possibility for applying necessary analytical distinctions.

Three further texts focus on major cases of cultural contextualization of modernity. *Dale Eickelman* indicates that, throughout the Muslim world, there has been a rapid growth of mass education over the past half century, which has contributed to the eroding of intellectual and physical boundaries, enabling connections across formerly impenetrable social entities. The proliferation of media profoundly influences people's attitudes to religion and political authority. Religious moderates now stress the link between Islam, reason, science, and modernity. The notion of Islam as dialogue and civil debate is gaining ground, and in fact, more than between modernists and traditionalists, clashes mainly develop among rival—more or less modernist—traditionalist groups. At the same time, market forces are reshaping economies, while a new sense of public sphere is emerging. New views of the role of religion are contributing to the creation of a civil society. All these, however, do not yet mean that the institution of liberal democracy will inevitably follow and replace the existing authoritarian regimes.

Another context of contemporary modernity is East Asia. *Tu Weiming* reminds us that East Asian intellectuals have been students of Western learning, and their commitment to Westernization has been a major factor in their societies' transformation. At the same time, however, efforts have been made to adapt what has been learned from the West to local circumstances. Under Confucian influence, East Asian modernity suggests a distinctive model which includes the assumptions that government leadership in economy is not only necessary but also desirable, that law is of essential importance but less than 'organic solidarity', and that family is the locus from which core values are transmitted to the young. Education constitutes a genuine civil religion and is expected to transfer Confucian values such as sympathy toward fellow members of the society, adherence to distributive justice, a strong public spirit, and collective orientations. The author also contends that Confucian ideals are actually best realized in a liberal democratic society.

Renato Ortiz who discusses modernity in Latin America, focuses on miscegenation which is particularly intense in this multi-racial continent, in spite of the fact that a clear hierarchy still separates the former white colonizers, the Indians and the Blacks. As another element in this picture, Ortiz recalls that—whether in its intellectualized or popular aspect—Catholicism has acted as ideological cement for the colonial social order. In this context, the nativist movements which fought for independence have reoriented the model produced by colonialism, although this has not significantly altered the oligarchic reality. The national revolutions, in turn, have replaced Spain and Portugal as references for modernity, with France, England, and the United States. But unlike Europe, Latin America has long been characterized by a dissociation between nationalism and the consolidation of modernity. Thus, in Latin America, modernity has remained 'incomplete' while tradition has been, at the same time, a source of identity and an obstacle to overcome.

The differences between 'modernities' may touch upon numberless aspects, as each case represents a particular configuration of numerous varying factors. In all modern societies, one finds a core of codes which determine, from the inside, that they belong to this world of 'multiple modernities'. *Johann Arnason*'s analysis which concludes Section One, elaborates comprehensively the historical and theoretical perspectives offered by the concept of multiple modernities. Accordingly, the paradigm of multiple modernities implies that modernity is understood as a loosely structured constellation, open to modification and redefinition, and experiencing contrasts and conflicts between different projects. But modernity everywhere tends to include features such as a progressive economy, a bureaucratic nation-state, a national identity, and the organized pursuit of scientific knowledge. This condition is common to otherwise quite different societies and cultures.

2. THE VISION OF MODERN AND CONTEMPORARY SOCIETY

Shmuel N. Eisenstadt[1]

I

Recent events and developments—especially the continual processes of globalization, and the downfall of the Soviet regime—have indeed sharpened the problem of the nature of the modern, contemporary world. Indeed, as we approach the end of the twentieth century, new visions or understandings of modernity and modern civilization, are emerging throughout the world, be it in the West—Europe, the United States—where the first cultural program of modernity developed—or among Asian, Latin American and African societies. These developments call for a far-reaching reappraisal of the classical visions of modernity and modernization. Indeed, the continually increasing processes of globalization in the contemporary world pose even more radical questions: they pose very sharply the problem as to whether the end of the twentieth century signals the end of modernity, of the modern project as it has developed over the last two centuries. Is the contemporary world withdrawing from the modern program, either in the direction of the 'end of history' or towards the clash of civilizations? The 'end of history'[2] announced the ahistorical homogenization of the world, in which the ideological premises of modernity with all their inherent tensions and contradictions have become almost irrelevant, paradoxically giving rise to multiple postmodern visions. The other direction of the end of the modern project sees the contemporary world as dominated by recession or 'retreat' to traditional, fundamentalist, anti-modern and anti-Western movements and civilizations—to use S.P. Huntington's expression 'Clash of Civilizations'— in which Western civilization—the seeming epitome of modernity—is often confronted in hostile terms with other civilizations, especially the Muslim and, to some extent, the so-called Confucian ones.[3]

---

[1] Opening address of the 34th World Congress, International Institute of Sociology, Tel Aviv, July 11, 1999.

[2] Fukuyama, 1992; Huntington, 1996.

[3] It may be worthwhile to note here that there is a certain irony in the fact that the view which promulgated overall homogenizing of the contemporary world and is seemingly very

modernity as new type of civilization

While, needless to say, both these approaches point out some very important aspects of the contemporary world, both seem to be not only incomplete but basically incorrect. In my view, what we witness in the contemporary world and what has taken place from the beginning of the modern era, have certainly not always been peaceful, and have rather often been confrontational. But whatever answers these questions provide to the problems they pose, the very intensive discussions around the interpretation of the modern and contemporary world necessitates a far-reaching appraisal of the classical visions of modernity and modernization.[4]

II

Such a reappraisal should be based on several considerations. It should be based first of all on the recognition that the expansion of modernity has to be viewed as the crystallization of a new type of civilization, not unlike the expansion of Great Religions, or great Imperial expansions in past times. However, because the expansion of this civilization almost always and continually combined economic, political, and ideological aspects and forces for far longer, its impact on the societies to which it spread was far more intense than in most historical cases.

This expansion indeed spawned a tendency—rather new and practically unique in the history of mankind—for the development of universal, world-wide institutional and symbolic frameworks and systems. This new civilization, that emerged first in Europe, later expanded throughout the world, creating a series of international frameworks or systems, each based on some of the basic premises of this civilization; and each of them rooted in one of its basic institutional dimensions. Several economic, political, ideological, almost worldwide systems emerged—all of them multi-centered and heterogeneous—each generating its own dynamic, its continual change in constant relations to the others. The interrelations among them have never been 'static' or unchanging, and the dynamic of these international frameworks or settings gave rise to continuous changes in those societies.

In the same way that the expansion of all historical civilizations had done, so did the civilization of modernity undermine the symbolic and institutional premises of the societies incorporated into it, opening up new options and possibilities. As a result of this, a great variety of modern or modernizing

close to the earlier theories of modernization and of convergences of industrial societies, also proclaims the end of modernity, of the classical program thereof.
[4] Eisenstadt, 1966; 1973; 1997b.

societies, sharing many common characteristics but also evincing great differences among themselves, developed in these contexts.

The 'original' modernity as it developed in the West combined several closely interconnected dimensions or aspects: first, the structural, organizational one—the development of the many specific aspects of modern social structure, such as growing structural differentiation, urbanization, industrialization, growing communications and the like, which were identified and analyzed in the first studies of modernization after the Second World War. The second dimension can be designated as institutional, characterized by the development of new institutional formations, the modern nation-state, modern national collectivities, new and capitalist-political economies, and a distinct cultural program that is closely related to specific modes of structuring major arenas of social life.

The 'classical theories' of modernization, of the 1950s, indeed the classical sociological analyses of Marx, Durkheim and to a large extent even those of Weber[5]—or at least one reading of him—have implicitly or explicitly conflated these different dimensions of modernity: these approaches assumed that even if these dimensions are analytically distinct, historically they still come together and become basically inseparable. Moreover, most of the classics of sociology, as well as modernization studies of the 1940s and 1950s, have assumed, even if only implicitly, that the basic institutional constellations which came together in European modernity, and the cultural program of modernity as it developed in the West, will 'naturally' be ultimately taken over in all modernizing societies. The studies of modernization and of the convergence of modern societies indeed assumed that this project of modernity, with its hegemonic and homogenizing tendencies, will continue in the West, and with the expansion of modernity, will prevail throughout the world. Implicit in all these approaches was the assumption that the modes of institutional integration attendant on the development of such relatively autonomous, differentiated institutional spheres would on the whole be similar in all modern societies.

However, the reality that emerged proved to be radically different. The actual developments indicated in all or most societies that the various institutional arenas—the economic, the political and that of family—exhibit continually *relatively* autonomous dimensions that come together in different ways in different societies and in different periods of their development. Indeed, developments in the contemporary era have not borne out this assumption of 'convergence' and have emphasized the great diversity of modern societies,

---

[5] Kamenka, 1983; Weber (1968b; 1968c; 1978); Durkheim, 1973.

modernity as multiple civilizations

even of societies similar in terms of economic development, like the major industrial capitalist societies—the European ones, the U.S. and Japan. Sombart's old question: "Why is there no socialism in the U.S.?" formulated in the first decades of the twentieth century attests to the first, even if still only implicit, recognition of this fact. Far-reaching variability developed even within the West—within Europe itself, and above all between Europe and the Americas—the U.S., Latin America, or rather Latin Americas.[6]

The same was even more true with respect to the relation between the cultural and structural dimensions of modernity. A very strong—even if implicit—assumption of the studies of modernization, namely that the cultural dimensions or aspects of modernization—the basic cultural premises of Western modernity—are inherently and necessarily interwoven with the structural ones, became highly questionable. While the different dimensions of the original Western project have indeed constituted the crucial starting—and continual reference points for the processes that developed among different societies throughout the world, the developments in those societies have gone far beyond the homogenizing and hegemonic dimensions of the original cultural program of modernity.

Modernity has indeed spread to most of the world, although it did not give rise to a single civilization, or to one institutional pattern, but to the development of several modern civilizations, or at least civilizational patterns, i.e. of societies or civilizations which share common characteristics, but which still tend to develop differently, even with cognate ideological and institutional dynamics. Moreover, far-reaching changes which go beyond their original premises of modernity have been taking place in Western societies too.

III

The modern project—the cultural program of modernity as it developed first in the West, in Western and Central Europe, entailing a very distinct shift in the conception of human agency, of its autonomy, and of its place in the flow of time—exacerbated the tensions between the constructive and destructive potentialities of the construction of social orders, highlighting the challenge of human autonomy and self-regulation and of consciousness thereof.[7]

---

[6] Sombart, 1976.
[7] The analyses of the cultural program of modernity and of its different historical experience, especially in European societies, are based on Eisenstadt (1999a; 1999b) where full bibliographical references are given.

modernity's cultural program?
• deconst'n of God-ordained, ethical cosmos
• response to decline of its legitimacy
• response which reinforces decline
VISION OF MODERN AND CONTEMPORARY SOCIETY   29
• questions givenness of transc'l visions
• stresses multiplicity

The central core of this cultural program has been possibly most successfully formulated by Weber. To follow James D. Faubian's exposition of
Weber's conception of modernity:

> Weber finds the existential threshold of modernity in a certain deconstruction:
> of what he speaks of as the 'ethical postulate that the world is a God-ordained,
> and hence somehow meaningfully and ethically oriented cosmos' . . . What he
> asserts—what in any event might be extrapolated from his assertions—is that
> the threshold of modernity has its epiphany precisely as the legitimacy of the
> postulate of a divinely preordained and fated cosmos has its decline; that moder-
> nity emerges, that one or another modernity can emerge, only as the legiti-
> macy of the postulated cosmos ceases to be taken for granted and beyond
> reproach. Countermoderns reject that reproach, believe in spite of it . . .

One can extract two theses: whatever else they may be, modernities in all
their variety are responses to the same existential problematic. The second:
whatever else they may be, modernities in all their variety are precisely
those responses that leave the problematic in question intact, that formulate visions of life and practice neither beyond, nor in denial of, it but rather
within it, even in deference to it.

> Other responses are possible: "traditionalizing" and "countermodern" responses
> among them . . . Other responses may even be more satisfying. So at least they
> seem to be, if not for most, still for man among us . . . The world is certainly
> not yet all modern. It is not likely ever to be . . . [8]

It is because of the fact that all such responses leave the problematic intact,
that the reflexivity which developed in the program of modernity went
beyond that which crystallized in the Axial Civilizations.[9] The reflexivity
that developed in the modern cultural program focused not only on the
possibility of different interpretations of the transcendental visions and basic
ontological conceptions prevalent in a society or civilization, but came to
question the very givenness of such visions and of the institutional patterns
related to them. It gave rise to the awareness of the existence of a multiplicity of such visions and patterns and of the possibility that such visions
and conceptions can indeed be contested.

Concomitantly, closely related to such awareness and central to this cultural program, was the emphasis on the autonomy of man; his or her—but
in this, in its initial formulation, program certainly 'his'—emancipation from
the fetters of traditional political and cultural authority and the continuous
expansion of the realm of personal and institutional freedom, of human

*• emphasis on emancipation from trad'l fetters
+ on personal + pol autonomy*

---

[8] Faubion, 1993: 113–115.
[9] On the Axial Age Civilizations, see Eisenstadt, 1982; 1986.

- social order as a construction of human activity
- orientation to the future

activity, creativity and autonomy. In parallel, this program entailed a very strong emphasis on autonomous participation of members of society—in the construction of social and political order and its constitution; on the autonomous access of all members of the society to these orders and their centers. The program entailed a conception of the future in which various possibilities which could be realized by autonomous human agency, or by the march of history, are opened up.

Out of the conjunctions of these different conceptions there developed the belief in the possibility of the active formation of society by conscious human activity. Within this program, there developed two basic, complementary but also potentially contradictory, tendencies about the best ways in which such construction could take place. The first such tendency was that the program as it crystallized above all in the great revolutions, and later in a sort of mirror way in the Romantic movements, gave rise, perhaps for the first time in the history of humanity, to the belief in the possibility of bridging the gap between the transcendental and mundane orders, of realizing through conscious human actions in the mundane orders, in social life, some utopian, eschatological visions. The second such tendency was rooted in the growing recognition of the legitimacy of multiple individual and group goals and interests, and of multiple interpretations of the common good.

2 basic variants
1) utopian eschatological
2) plural multiple

This shared core of the modern program also gave rise to a distinct political program. It entailed a radical transformation of the parameters and premises of the political order, of its legitimation, and of the conceptions of accountability of rulers, of the basic orientations to tradition and to authority, as well as the basic characteristics of centers, and of center-periphery relations. The central core of this political program was indeed the breakdown of traditional legitimation of the social and political order, the opening up of different possibilities of legitimation, and the contestation about the different ways in which political order should be constructed by human actors.

IV

The basic characteristics of the modern program, the combination of an open future with belief in the possibility of the active formation of society by conscious human activity, also shaped the premises of modern political order and of collective identities and boundaries. The core of modernity's political program was the breakdown of traditional legitimation of the political order; the concomitant opening up of different possibilities of construction of such an order and of contestation about the ways in which

- breakdown of trad'l legit. s
- protest + criticism as continual components
- symbols + themes of protest
- coll identities as foci of struggle
- self-perception as modern

political order should be constructed. It combined orientations of rebellion, protest, and intellectual antinomianism, together with a strong orientation to center-formation and institution-building, giving rise to social movements, and movements of protest as a continual component of the political process.[10] It entailed the combination of the charismatization of the center, or centers, with the incorporation into the centers of themes and symbols of protest which became components of the modern transcendental visions, as basic and legitimate components of the premises of these centers. Themes and symbols of protest—equality and freedom, justice and autonomy, solidarity and identity—became central components of the modern project of emancipation of man. It was indeed the incorporation of such themes of protest into the center which heralded the radical transformation of various sectarian utopian visions into central components of the political and cultural program.[11]

In parallel, the construction of the boundaries of modern collectivities and collective identities was continually problematized in reflexive ways.[12] Collective identities and boundaries were not taken as given or preordained by some transcendental vision and authority, or by perennial customs. They constituted foci not only of reflexivity but also of contestations and struggles, often couched in highly ideological terms, promulgated above all by different— above all national or nationalist—movements. Such contestations focused firstly on the relative importance of the basic components of collective identities—the civil, primordial and universalistic and transcendental 'sacred' ones, and around the modes of their institutionalization. Secondly, such contestation focused on the extent of the connection between the construction of political boundaries, defined more and more in territorial terms, and those of the cultural collectivities; and thirdly, on relations between the territorial and/or particularistic components of these collectivities and broader, potential universalistic ones. Given the strong territorial orientations of these components of collective identity, the struggles around their construction were very closely related to struggles between different states, to an extent unprecedented in comparison with 'premodern' civilizations.

Concomitantly, a highly central component in constructing collective identities was the self-perception of society as 'modern', as the bearer of a distinct cultural and political program—and its relations, from that point of view, with other societies—whether those societies claiming either to be, or to be perceived as, bearers of this program—and various 'others'.

---

[10] See Eisenstadt, 1999b.
[11] Voegelin, 1975; Seligman, 1989; and Eisenstadt, 1999a.
[12] See Shils, 1975; see also Eisenstadt and Giesen, 1995; Eisenstadt, 1998.

V

The cultural program of modernity as it crystallized first in Europe and in the Americas and later expanded throughout the world, also entailed specific visions of history and 'civilizing' vision or visions—very distinctive conceptions of the formation of man, of human personality, of the proper way whereby a civilized person is constituted, emphasizing the autonomy of man and the importance of self—or other regulation of such autonomy, and the different attributes or dimensions of human existence. Additionally, this program entailed a tendency to a combination, usually couched in strong ideological terms, of symbolic ideological distinctions and relations between different arenas of life such as family and occupation, work, and culture; between public and private realms; between different age-spans; between the sexes; between different social classes and the different spaces of social and cultural life, together with the development of very specific symbolic institutional and organizational linkages and combinations between them.

The basic components of this program were promulgated through the construction of specific narratives in all areas of cultural collectivity—the construction of history, literature which continually presented and represented the visions of the best collectivity, of 'civilized man'—and they were institutionalized through the major socializing and communicative agencies such as schools, armies and collective activities. However, they were also foci of continual contentions and struggles.

VI

The program and civilization of modernity as it developed first in the West was from its very beginning—as was the case with any great civilizational visions, for instance those of the Axial civilizations—beset by internal antinomies and contradictions and tensions, giving rise to continual critical discourse which focused on the relations, tensions and contradictions between its premises, and between these premises and institutional developments in modern societies. The importance of these tensions was fully understood in the classical sociological literature—Tocqueville, Marx, Weber and Durkheim—and was later taken up in the 1930s, particularly in the Frankfurt school, in the so-called 'critical' sociology—which, however, focused mainly on the problems of Fascism, but was later neglected in post-Second World War studies of modernization. It has recently returned to the forefront, and constitutes an ongoing continual component of the analysis of modernity.[13]

---

[13] Giddens, 1985; Joas (1996; 1999a; 1999b); Roxborough, 1999; Tiryakian, 1999.

The tensions and antinomies that developed within this program were first, that between totalizing and more diversified or pluralistic conceptions of the major components of this program—of the very conception of reason and its place in human life and society, and of the construction of nature, of human society and its history; second, between reflexivity and active construction of nature and society; third, those between different evaluations of major dimensions of human experience; and fourth, between control and autonomy.

It was around these tensions that the critical discourse of modernity developed. The most radical 'external' criticism of modernity denied the possibility of the grounding of any social order, of morality, in the basic premises of the cultural program of modernity especially in autonomy of individuals and supremacy of reason and denied that these premises could be seen as grounded in any transcendental vision. Moreover, it denied the closely related claims that these premises and the institutional development of modernity could be seen as the epitome of human creativity. Such criticisms claimed that these premises and institutional developments denied human creativity and gave rise to flattening of human experience and to the erosion of moral order; of the moral—and transcendental—bases of society, and to man's alienation from nature and from society. The more internal criticisms of this program, which often overlapped or became interwoven with the 'external' ones, evaluated the institutional development of modern societies from the point of view of the premises of cultural and political programs of modernity, as well as from the point of view of the basic antinomies and contradictions inherent in this program. Of special importance here was the multifaceted, continual and constantly changing confrontation of the program's claims to enhance freedom and autonomy with the strong tendency to control, and the continual dislocation of various social sectors that developed with the crystallization of modern institutional formations.

The tension which was probably the most critical from the point of view of the development of the different cultural and institutional patterns of modernity, and of the possible destructive potentialities thereof, has been that between totalizing, on the one hand, and more pluralistic multifaceted visions and practices, on the other; between the view that accepts the existence of different values, commitments and rationalities as against the view that conflates such different values and rationalities in a totalistic way, with strong tendencies to their absolutization.

In the cultural, ideological dimension of the modern program, the most important of those conflations of different rationalities has been the one often identified as the major message of the Enlightenment—that of sovereignty of reason—which subsumed value-rationality (*Wertrationalität*), or substantive rationality under instrumental rationality (*Zweckrationalität*) in its technocratic

totalistic ideologies ✓ s
tensions

mode, or under a totalizing moralistic utopian vision. In modern political discourse and practice, these tensions crystallized around the relations between the legitimacy of plurality of discrete individual and group interests and of different conceptions of the common good and of social order, on the one hand, and of totalizing ideologies which denied the legitimacy of such pluralities, on the other.

totalistic
=
closed
:
Jacobin
=
rev'y
:
nat'e
:
exclusionary
=
demonising

One major form of this totalistic ideology that developed in modernity emphasized the primacy of collectivities perceived as distinct ontological entities based on common primordial and/or spiritual attributes, i.e., above all national collectivities. The other such totalistic ideology has been the Jacobin one, the historical roots of which go back to medieval eschatological sources, the essence of which was the belief in the primacy of politics and in its ability to reconstitute society, and in the possibility of transforming society through totalistic mobilized participatory political action.[14] Whatever the differences between these collectivistic and absolutizing ideologies, they all shared firstly deep suspicion of open political process and institutions, especially of the representative institutions and of open public discussion, and secondly strong autocratic tendencies, as well as the tendency to exclude others and to demonize those excluded.

= grand
narrative
= logo -
centric
= anti -
plural

In the construction of collective identities and collectivities, these tensions were manifest in the contradictions between, on the one hand, tendencies to the absolutization of primordial and/or Jacobin universalistic components of collective identities as against a more open or multifaceted approach to such construction; between the closely related tendencies to homogenization of social and cultural spaces as against construction of more multiple spaces allowing for heterogeneous identities.

Closely related has been the tension between the emphasis on human autonomy, the autonomy of man, of the human person, on the one hand, and, on the other hand, the strong restrictive control dimensions, such as were analyzed among others—even if in an exaggerated way, from different but complementary points of view by Norbert Elias and Michel Foucault,[15] which were rooted in the institutionalization of this program according to the technocratic and/or moral visionary conceptions—or in other words, to follow Peter Wagner's formulation between freedom and control.[16]

All these tensions, especially that between the totalizing and more pluralistic conceptions of the constitution of human society, history and nature

---

[14] Eisenstadt, 1999a.
[15] Elias (1978; 1982; 1983); Foucault (1965; 1973; 1975; 1988).
[16] Wagner, 1994.

omnipresent within the cultural program of modernity?

and of the place of human agency in these construction; between some type of an overarching 'logocentricity', usually some 'grand narrative', and between a more pluralistic conception of the meaning of life, and of society's construction, between emphases on different dimensions of human existence, and between control and autonomy, have existed from the very beginning of the promulgation of the cultural program of modernity; and they constituted a continual component in this program's development and continual reconstruction.

VII

political programme of modernity

Tensions and contradictions closely related to those inherent in the cultural program of modernity also developed in the political arena, within the political program of modernity—closely related to the tendencies to the charismatization of the center, and to the development of the new center-periphery relations that crystallized in modern societies.

In the political arena, these tensions coalesced with those between a constructivist approach which views politics as the process of reconstructing society, and especially democratic politics—active self-construction of society as against a view that accepts society in its concrete composition; between liberty and equality, between the autonomy of civil society and the charismatization of state power; between the civil and the utopian components of modernity's cultural and political program; between freedom and emancipation in the name of some, often utopian, social vision; above all between Jacobin and more pluralistic orientations or approaches to the social and political order; and between the closely related tension between 'normal' and 'revolutionary' politics,[17] in Bruce Ackerman's formulation.

These various tensions in the political program of modernity were closely related to those between the different modes of legitimation of modern regimes, especially, but not only, those of constitutional and democratic polities—namely between procedural legitimation in terms of civil adherence to the rules of the game, on the one hand, and in different 'substantive' terms, on the other hand; and, furthermore, a very strong tendency to promulgate other modes or bases of legitimation, above all, to use Edward Shils' terminology, various primordial, 'sacred'—religious or secular—ideological components.[18]

---

[17] Ackerman, 1991.
[18] Shils, 1975.

totalistic — pluralistic
active — reflexive
equality — liberty
chais'n of state — c s
utopian — civil
vis'y — normal

VIII

All these antinomies and tensions developed from the very beginning of the institutionalization of modern regimes in Europe. As the classics of sociology were fully aware (though to no small extent it has been forgotten or neglected in modernization studies) the continued prevalence of these antinomies and contradictions also had far-reaching institutional implications, and were closely interwoven with various patterns of institutional constellations and dynamics that developed in different modern societies.

It was around these various tensions that there developed the different patterns of culture and institutions of modernity alluded to above. As these contestations emerged in Europe, the dominant pattern of the conflicts was rooted in specific European traditions, focusing along the rifts between utopian and civil orientations. Principles of hierarchy and equality competed in the construction of political order and political centers. The state and civil society were seen as separate entities by some. Collective identity—very often couched in utopian terms—was differently defined. The variety of resulting societal outcomes can be illustrated by the different conceptions of state that developed on the continent and in England. There was the strong homogenizing 'laicization' of France, or, in a different vein, of the Lutheran Scandinavian countries, as against the far more consociational and pluralistic arrangements common to Holland and Switzerland, and to a much smaller extent in Great Britain. The strong aristocratic semi-feudal conception of authority in Britain contrasted with the more democratic, even populist, views in other European countries.[19]

IX

The crystallization of European modernity and its later expansion was by no means peaceful. Contrary to the optimistic visions of modernity as implying inevitable progress, the crystallizations of modernities were continually interwoven with internal conflict and confrontation, rooted in the contradictions and tensions attendant on the development of capitalist systems, and, in the political arena, in the growing demands for democratization.

---

[19] For an illustration of some of these differences, see: Rustow, 1956; Kuhnle, 1975; Graubard, 1986.
    Thomson (1940; 1960); Thompson, 1968; Thomas, 1978.
    Beloff, 1954; Geyl, 1958; Daalder, 1971.
    Lehmbruch, 1967; Lorwin, 1971; Steiner, 1974.

Violence of crystallization

The development of modernity bore within it destructive possibilities that were voiced, somewhat ironically, often by some of its most radical critics, who thought modernity to be a morally destructive force, and emphasized the negative effects of certain of its core characteristics. All these factors were compounded by international conflicts, and exacerbated by the modern state and imperialist systems. War and genocide were scarcely new phenomena in history. But they became radically transformed, intensified, generating specifically modern modes of barbarism. The ideologization of violence, terror and war—first and most vividly witnessed in the French Revolution—became the most important components of the construction of modern states. The tendency to such ideologies of violence became closely related to the fact that the nation-state became the focus of symbols of collective identity.[20] The Holocaust, which took place in the very center of modernity, became a symbol of its negative, destructive potential, of the barbarism lurking within its very core.

These visions of the constructive and destructive potentiality of modernity became even more visible with the expansion of modernity—initially in the Americas. Indeed, the first radical transformation of the premises of cultural and political order with the expansion of modernity occurred in the Americas, where distinctive modernities emerged, reflecting novel patterns of institutional life, with new self-conceptions and new forms of collective consciousness. To say this is to emphasize that practically from the beginning of modernity's expansion, multiple modernities developed, all within what may be defined as the Western civilizational framework. It is important to note that such modernities, Western but significantly different from those common to Europe, did not develop first in Asia—Japan, China, or India—or in Muslim societies where they might have been attributed to the existence of distinct non-European traditions, but within the broad framework of Western civilizations. They reflected a radical transformation of European premises.

The tensions and contradictions in the cultural and political programs of modernity became even more viable with the expansion of modern civilizations beyond the West, beyond Europe to the Americas, and with the dynamics of the continually developing international frameworks or settings, several new crucial elements became central in the constitution of modern societies.

Of special importance in this context was the relative place of the non-Western societies in the various economic, political, and ideological

const'n + dest'n

---

[20] Giddens, 1985; Joas (1996; 1999a; 1999b); Roxborough, 1999; Tiryakian, 1999.

multiple modernities
USA
East
Sou th

international systems that differed markedly from those of Western ones. It was not only the fact that Western societies were the 'originators' of this new civilization: beyond this, and above all, was the fact that the expansion of these systems, especially insofar as it took place through colonialization and imperialist expansion, awarded Western institutions a hegemonic place in these systems. However, it was in the nature of these international systems that they generated a dynamic which gave rise both to political and ideological challenges to existing hegemonies, as well as to continual shifts in the loci of hegemony within Europe, from Europe to the United States, then also to Japan and East Asia.

But it was not only the economic, military-political and ideological expansion of the civilization of modernity from the West throughout the world that was important in this process. Of no lesser, possibly of even greater importance, was the fact that this expansion has given rise to continual confrontation between the cultural and institutional premises of Western modernity and those of other civilizations—those of other Axial civilizations, as well as non-Axial ones, the most important of which has, of course, been Japan. Truly enough, many Western modernity's basic premises and symbols, as well as its institutions—representative, legal and administrative— have indeed become seemingly accepted within these civilizations. At the same time, though, far-reaching transformations thereof have taken place and new challenges and problems have arisen.

The attraction of these themes, and of some of these institutions, for many groups within these civilizations, lay in the fact that their appropriation permitted many groups in non-European nations, especially elites and intellectuals, to participate actively in the new modern (i.e. initially Western) universal tradition, together with the selective rejection of many of its aspects and of Western 'control' and hegemony. Appropriating these themes enabled these elites and broader strata of many non-European societies to incorporate some of modernity's universalistic elements into the construction of their new collective identities, without necessarily giving up either specific components of their traditional identities (often also couched in universalistic, especially religious terms) which differed from those predominant in the West, or their negative attitude towards the West.

The attraction of these themes of political discourse to many sectors in the non-Western European countries was also intensified by the fact that their appropriation in these countries entailed a transposition to the international scene of the struggle between hierarchy and equality. Although initially couched in European terms, it could find resonance in the political traditions of many of these societies. Transposition of those themes from Western Europe to Central and Eastern Europe and to non-European settings was reinforced by the combination, found in many programs promulgated by these groups, of orientations of protest with institution-building and center-formation.

Such transposition was generated not only by the higher hierarchical standing, by the actual hegemony of the Western countries in these new international settings, but also by the fact that non-Western civilizations were put in an inferior position in the evaluation of societies which was promulgated by the seemingly universalistic premises of the new modern civilizations.

Thus various groups and elites in Central and Eastern Europe and in Asian and African societies were able to refer both to the tradition of protest and the tradition of center-formation in these societies, and to cope with problems of reconstructing their own centers and traditions in terms of the new setting. From this perspective, the most important aspect of the expansion of these themes beyond Western Europe, and of their appropriation by different groups in non-Western European societies, lay in the fact that it became possible to rebel against the institutional realities of the new modern civilization, in terms of its own symbols and premises.[21]

X

However, the appropriation of different themes and institutional patterns of the original Western modern civilization in non-Western European societies did not entail their acceptance in their original form. Rather, it entailed the continuous selection, reinterpretation and reformulation of such themes, giving rise to a continual crystallization of new cultural and political programs of modernity, and the development and reconstruction of new institutional patterns. The cultural programs that continued to develop in these societies, entailed different interpretations and far-reaching reformulations of the initial cultural program of modernity, its basic conceptions and premises. They entailed different emphases on different components of this program on its various tensions and antinomies, and the concomitant crystallization of distinct institutional patterns. Furthermore, they entailed the continual construction of symbols of collective identities; their conceptions of themselves and of their part; and their negative or positive attitudes to modernity in general and to the West in particular.

---

[21] See Eisenstadt (1999a: esp. ch. 4) and Eisenstadt, 2000.

selection reinterp'n reform'n
crystallization
const'n + reconfiguration

Such differences between modernity's various cultural programs were not purely 'cultural' or academic. They were closely related to some basic problems inherent in the political and institutional programs of modernity. Thus, in the political realm, they were closely related to the tension between utopian and civil components in the construction of modern politics; between 'revolutionary' and 'normal' politics, or between the general will and the will of all; between civil society and the state; and between individual and collectivity. Moreover, the different cultural programs also entailed different conceptions of authority and of its accountability, different modes of protest and of political activity, questioning of the modern order's basic premises, as well as various modes of institutional formations.

Of course, the preceding considerations about modernity's multiple programs do not negate the obvious fact that in many central aspects of their institutional structure—whether in occupational and industrial structure, the structure of education or of cities—as well as in political structures, very strong convergences in different modern societies have developed. They have indeed generated common problems, but the modes of coping with them, i.e. the institutional dynamics attendant on the development of these problems, differed greatly between these civilizations.

However, it was not only within Asian or Latin American societies that developments occurred which went beyond the initial model of Western society. At the same time, new modes of discourse have developed in Western societies themselves. They have greatly transformed the initial model of modernity and have undermined the original vision of modern and industrial society, with its hegemonic and homogenizing vision. A growing tendency has emerged to distinguish between *Zweckrationalität* and *Wertrationalität*, and to recognize a multiplicity of different *Wertrationalitäten*. Cognitive rationality—especially as epitomized in the extreme forms of scientism—has certainly become dethroned from its hegemonic position, as has the idea of the 'conquest' or mastery of the environment—whether of society or of nature.

XI

These different cultural programs and institutional patterns of modernity were not shaped by what was sometimes presented in some earlier studies of modernization as the natural evolutionary potentialities of these societies; or, as in the earlier criticisms thereof, by the natural unfolding of their respective traditions; nor by their placement in the new international settings. Rather, they were shaped by a continuous interaction between several factors. In most general terms, they were shaped by the historical experience of these societies in civilization, by the mode in which modernity impinged on them and in which they were incorporated into modern political, economic, and ideological international frameworks.

In other words, these programs were shaped by several continually changing factors. First they were shaped by basic premises of cosmic and social order, the basic 'cosmologies' that were prevalent in these societies in their 'orthodox' and 'heterodox' formulations alike as they crystallized throughout their histories. Second was the pattern of institutional formations that developed within these civilizations through their historical experience, especially in their encounters with other societies or civilizations.

Third was the encounter and continual interaction between these processes, and the new cultural and political program of modernity; the premises and modes of social and political discourse that were prevalent in the different societies and civilizations as they were incorporated into the new international systems and the continual interaction of these societies with these processes. Of special importance in this encounter were the internal antinomies, tensions or contradictions in the basic cultural program (and above all the political program) of modernity as it developed initially in the West—and even in the West in a great variety of ways as it became transformed with expansion and the internal changes in Western societies.

The fourth factor was the dynamics, and internal tensions and contradictions that developed in conjunction with the structural-demographic, economic and political changes attendant on the institutionalization of modern institutional frameworks, with the expansion of modernity, and between these processes and modernity's basic cultural and political premises.

It was the continual interaction and feedback between these factors that generated changes in the cultural programs that developed with them, and their continual reinterpretations, as well as the major components of their institutional formations, namely the constitution of the boundaries of their respective collectivities and the components of collective consciousness and identity of what has been designated as nationalism or ethnicity; secondly, different configurations of civil society and public spheres; and, last but not least, different modes of new modern political economies.

XII

The multiple and divergent instantiations of the 'classical' age of modernity crystallized during the nineteenth century, and above all in the first six or seven decades of the twentieth century into very different territorial nation and revolutionary states and social movements in Europe, the Americas, and, after World War II, in Asia as well. The institutional, symbolic, and ideological contours of modern national and revolutionary states, once thought to be the epitome of modernity, have changed dramatically with the recent intensification of globalization forces. These trends, particularly manifest in the growing autonomy of world financial and commercial flows, intensified international migrations and the concomitant development on an international scale of social problems such as spread of diseases, prostitution, organized crime, and youth violence. All this has served to reduce the nation-state's control over its own economic and political affairs, despite continuing efforts to strengthen technocratic, rational, secular policies in various arenas. Nation-states have also lost a part of their monopoly (that was always only partial) on internal and international violence to local and international groups of separatists or terrorists. Processes of globalization are also evident in the cultural arena, with the hegemonic expansion, via the major media in many countries, of what are seemingly uniform Western, above all American, cultural programs or visions.[22]

The nation-state's ideological and symbolic centrality, its position as the charismatic locus of the major components of modernity's cultural program and collective identity, have been weakened: new political, social, and civilizational visions, new visions of collective identity, are being developed. These novel visions and identities were promulgated by a variety of new social movements—all of which, however different, have challenged the premises of the classical modern nation and its program of modernity, which had hitherto occupied the unchallenged center of political and cultural thinking. The most important of these movements that developed in most Western countries—the women's movement and the ecological movement—were both closely related to, or rooted in, the student and anti-Vietnam War movements of the late 1960s and early 1970s. All were indicative of a more general shift in many countries, whether 'capitalist' or communist; a shift away from state and center-oriented movements to those possessing a more local scope and agenda. Instead of focusing on the reconstitution of nation-states, or resolving macro-economic conflicts, these new forces—often presenting themselves as 'postmodern' and 'multicultural'—promulgated a cultural politics or a politics of identity often couched as multiculturalism, and were oriented to the construction of new autonomous social, political, and cultural spaces.[23]

---

[22] From the vast literature on globalization, see for instance Marcus, 1993; Smolicz, 1998b.
[23] See Tiryakian, 1999.

ethnf
pm

Second, the various fundamentalist movements emerged somewhat later ②
within Muslim, Jewish, and Protestant communities, and have managed to
occupy center stage in many national societies and, from time to time, on
the international scene too. Communal religious movements have similarly
developed within Hindu and Buddhist cultures, generally sharing strong anti-
modern and/or anti-Western themes.[24] A third major type of new movement that has gathered momentum, especially in the last two decades of
the twentieth century, is particularistic 'ethnic' movements and identities, ③
seen in the former republics of the Soviet Union, in horrific forms in Africa
and in part of the Balkans, especially in former Yugoslavia.

XIII

All these developments attest to the decomposition of the major structural
characteristics and the weakening of the ideological hegemony of once-
powerful nation-states. But do they signal the 'end of history' and the end
of the modern program, epitomized in the development of different so-called
post-modernities and, above all, in a retreat from modernity in fundamentalist and communal religious movements, often portrayed by themselves as
diametrically opposed to the modern program?

A closer examination of these movements presents a much more complex picture. First, several of the extreme fundamentalist movements evince
distinct characteristics of modern Jacobinism, even when combined with very
strong anti-Western and anti-Enlightenment ideologies. Indeed, the distinct
visions of fundamentalist movements have been formulated in terms common to the discourse of modernity: they have attempted to appropriate
modernity on their own terms. While extreme fundamentalists promulgate
elaborate, seemingly anti-modern (or rather anti-Enlightenment) themes, they
basically constitute modern Jacobin revolutionary movements, paradoxically sharing—despite the obvious differences in their basic visions—many
characteristics (sometimes in a sort of mirror-image way) with communist
movements of an earlier era.[25] They share with communist movements the
promulgation of totalistic visions entailing the transformation of man and
society alike. Some claim to be concerned with the 'cleansing' of both. What
they seek is the total reconstruction of personality, of individual and collective identities, by conscious human action, particularly political action,

---

[24] Eisenstadt and Azmon, 1975; Marty and Appleby (1991; 1993a; 1993b; 1994; 1995);
Eisenstadt, 1999a.

[25] Eisenstadt, 1999a and the bibliography there.

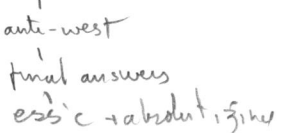

anti-west

final answers
ess'c + absolut, ziru

modernity of NSMs,
reflexive

and the construction of new personal and collective identities entailing the total submergence of the individual in the community.

Both the communist and the fundamentalist movements—mostly, but not only, the Muslim ones—are transnational, activated by intensive, continually reconstructed networks that facilitate the expansion of the social and cultural visions promulgated by these groups. At the same time, they are constantly confronted with competing visions. In all these ways, these movements and their programs constitute part and parcel of the modern political agenda. However, attempts to appropriate and interpret modernity in one's own terms are not confined to fundamentalist movements. It is possible to identify significant parallels between these various religious movements, with their apparently extreme opposites—the various postmodern movements with which they often engage in contestation, arguing about hegemony among the different sectors of society. Thus, within many of these 'postmodern' or 'multicultural' movements, there have developed highly totalistic orientations manifest among others in different programs of political correctness. Ironically, because of their great variety, their more pluralistic internal dynamics and pragmatic stance, certain 'post modern' themes have also emerged with fundamentalist movements. Beyond this paradox, these movements share an overarching concern about the relationship between the identities they promulgate and the universalistic themes promulgated by other hegemonic programs of modernity, above all the relationship between their purportedly authentic identities and the presumed Western, especially American, cultural hegemony on the contemporary scene. Significantly, concern about the erosion of local cultures due to the impact of globalization has led these movements to be suspicious of the emerging centers of a globalizing world, giving rise yet again to a continuous oscillation between cosmopolitanism and various 'particularistic' tendencies seeking authenticity.[26]

XIV

The continuing salience of the tensions between pluralist and universalist programs, between multifaceted as against closed identities, and the continual ambivalence of new centers of modernity toward the major traditional centers of cultural hegemony, attest to the fact that, while going beyond the model of the nation-state, these new movements have not gone beyond the basic problematics of modernity. They all are deeply reflexive,

---

[26] Hannerz, 1992; Marcus, 1993; Friedman, 1994; Smolicz, 1998b.

aware that there is no final answer to the tensions inherent in modernity—even if each in its own way seeks to provide final, incontestable answers to modernity's irreducible dilemmas. They have reconstituted the problem of modernity in new historical contexts, in new ways. They aim for a world-wide reach and diffusion, especially through the various media, of the movements themselves. They are politicized, formulating their contestations in highly political ideologies and terms. The problems they face, continually reconstructing their collective identities in reference to the new global context, constitute a challenge of unprecedented proportions. The very pluralization of life spaces in the global framework endows them with highly ideological absolutizing ideas, and at the same time brings them into the central political arena. The debate in which they engage may indeed be described in 'civilizational' terms, but these terms—indeed the very term 'civilization' as constructed in such a discourse—are already couched in modernity's new language, utilizing totalistic, essentialistic, and absolutizing terms. When such clashes intersect with political, military, or economic struggles, they can quickly become violent.

The reconstructions of the various political and cultural visions across the spectrum of collective identities on the contemporary scene entails a shift in the confrontation between Western and non-Western civilizations, between religions and societies, but also in the relationship of these confrontations to the Western cultural program of modernity. As against the seeming, if highly ambivalent, acceptance of modernity's premises and their continual reinterpretation characteristic of earlier reformist religious and national movements, most contemporary religious movements, including fundamentalist and most communal religious movements, seem to engage in a far more intensive selective denial of at least some of these premises. They take a markedly confrontational attitude to the West, indeed to anything conceived as Western, seeking to appropriate modernity and the global system on their own, often anti-Western, terms. Their confrontation with the West does not take the form of wishing to become incorporated into a new hegemonic civilization, but to appropriate the new international global scene and modernity for themselves, celebrating their traditions and 'civilizations'. These movements have attempted to dissociate Westernization from modernity, denying the Western monopoly on modernity, and rejecting the Western cultural program as the epitome of modernity. Significantly, many of these same themes are also espoused, though in a different manner, by many 'post-modern' movements.

While such diversity has certainly undermined the old hegemonies, at the same time it is closely connected—perhaps paradoxically—with the development of new multiple common reference points and networks—with a globalization of cultural networks and channels of communication far beyond what existed before. At the same time, the various components of modern life and culture were refracted and reconstructed in ways that transcended the confines of any institutional boundaries—especially those of the nation-state—giving rise to the multiple patterns of globalization and cultural diversification studied by such scholars as Arjun Appadurai, Ulf Hannerz, and Roland Robertson.[27]

It is this combination of the growing diversity in the continuous reinterpretation of modernity, on the one hand, with development of multiple global trends and mutual reference points on the other, that is characteristic of the contemporary scene.

XV

Within all modern and contemporary societies, new questionings and reinterpretations of different dimensions of modernity continuously developed and, in all of them, there have been continually developing different cultural agendas.

All these developments attest not to the end of history but to the growing diversification of the visions and understanding of modernity, of the basic cultural agendas of different societies' elites—far beyond the homogenic and hegemonic visions of modernity that were prevalent in the fifties. While the common starting point of many of these developments was indeed the cultural program of modernity as it developed in the West, the more recent developments have given rise to a multiplicity of cultural social formations which go far beyond the very homogenizing and hegemonizing aspects of the original version.

Nor do these processes give rise on the contemporary scene to several closed civilizations which constitute, as it were, a continuation of the historical ones.[28] It is not only, as Huntington correctly indicates, that modernization does not automatically imply Westernization. What is of crucial importance is that on the contemporary scene there occurs the crystallization of continually interacting modern civilizations in which even inclusive particularistic tendencies are constructed in typically modern ways, which attempt to appropriate from modernity on their own terms, and articulate continually, in different concrete ways in different historical settings, the antinomies and contradictions of modernity. However, it is not only that

---

[27] Appadurai, 1996; Robertson, 1992b; Hannerz, 1996.
[28] Huntington, 1996.

modernity as 'endless trial'

multiple modern civilizations have continually developed: these civilizations, which shared many common components and which continually constituted mutual reference points, have been continually developing, unfolding, giving rise to new problematiques and continual reinterpretations of the basic premises of modernity. Within all societies, new questionings and reinterpretations of different dimensions of modernity continually developed and, in all of them, different cultural agendas have developed. Such a development may indeed also lead to highly confrontation stances—especially towards the West—but these stances are promulgated in continually changing modern idioms, and may entail a continual transformation of these indications and of modernity's cultural programs.

XVI

This emphasis on the essentially modern character of all these movements and collective identities which go beyond the classical model of the territorial, national and/or revolutionary state, does not necessarily entail an optimistic view. On the contrary, they underscore not only the fragility and changeability of different modernities, but also the destructive forces that are inherent potentialities in the modern program—revealed in the most frightening way in the ideologization of violence, terror, and war. These destructive forces—the 'traumas' of modernity that brought into question its great promises—emerged clearly after World War I, became even more visible during World War II and the Holocaust, and were generally ignored or set aside in the discourse of modernity in the 1950s, 1960s, and 1970s. Lately they have reemerged again in a frightening way—in the new 'ethnic' conflicts in parts of the Balkans (especially in the former Yugoslavia), in many of the former republics of Soviet Russia, in Sri Lanka, and in a terrible way in such African countries as Rwanda and Burundi. These are not outbursts of old 'traditional' forces, but the result of the ongoing reconstruction of seemingly 'traditional' forces in a modern form. Similarly, fundamentalist and religious communal movements developed within the framework of modernity, and cannot be fully understood except within it. Thus, modernity—to paraphrase Leszek Kolakowski's felicitous and sanguine expression—is indeed 'on endless trial'.[29]

---

[29] Kolakowski, 1990.

- basically light + dark sides of modernity
- endless battle

- triumph of light side rooted in actual facts of
  diversification + its self-recognition as
  diverse

3. RETHINKING MODERNITY

Björn Wittrock

Modernity and trauma

The modern world emerged out of processes of industrialization, urbanization and political upheaval at the northwestern edge of the Eurasian landmass. It came to lead the transformation of traditional societies into modern ones. Thereby, it also deeply affected the different paths to modernity pursued in other parts of the world. These processes, so often depicted as manifestations of progress and reason, also involved immense suffering and pain for vast groups of human beings. This is equally true of the processes of conquest and domination inherent in colonialism, and the global extension of one type of modernity, namely that of Western Europe and North America. These processes resulted in societal transformations throughout the world becoming so deeply dislodged by European and North American pre-eminence as to almost remove from vision a whole range of early modernities that were evolving across the world from the fourteenth to the eighteenth centuries.

At the turn of the nineteenth century, it seemed however in the self-understanding of the intellectual, political and cultural elites of Europe and America alike, as if the crisis of modernity was about to be overcome. Thus the dangers of an unbridled market economy might be countered through well-informed social policies. The naive scientific determinism of a previous era might be overcome through an appreciation of the importance of volition and aesthetic judgment. Antiquated and inefficient bureaucracies—preoccupied, in Strindberg's famous phrase, with administering the payment of their own salaries—might be replaced by a legal-rational bureaucracy appropriate for a modern constitutional polity. World exhibitions heralded the arrival of a new era of air and light, of industrial growth without pollution, of social change linked to an appreciation of traditional values and customs, of urban growth amidst garden cities and newly invented pastoral landscapes, of global communication and movement without friction, of social development without strife, of national competition without war, of national assertiveness and international Olympic games, and of nationally important science amidst international conferences.

Germany, which had for centuries been split internally, trampled upon, exploited and conquered by mightier neighbors, had finally been united and regained some of its long-lost provinces: for the Germans, their nation could now take its rightful place in the sun and enter the world arena, not only as a major economic power and a world leader in science, but also as a political great power. If it instead chose to remain a medium-size, inward-looking European country, it would, Max Weber warned, be doomed to the status of either a province, a 'satrapy', of an Eastern despotic realm, or else to that of a junior partner of the Anglo-Saxon powers. For the British, the notion of Empire and world leadership was at its height. Russia, long regarded as hopelessly lagging behind the Western powers was undergoing a faster economic growth than that of almost any country. America, with the annexation of Hawaii and its entrance to the world arena in the wake of the Spanish-American war, and with preparations for the building of the Panama Canal under way, asserted an international position commensurate with its dramatic increase in wealth, population and educational achievement.

To liberals at the turn of the century, constitutional rule, property rights and parliamentary democracy seemed to be within reach everywhere in the civilized world. Indeed, even colonies might be elevated in due course to the status of dominions and equal partners, once they achieved the required level of maturity. It was possible to envisage a world of measured civility, personal self-control, political home-rule, with violence and uncontrolled impulses being relegated to the outer fringes of the civilized world, whether distant deserts and mountains or the inaccessible interior of persons and continents, those hearts of darkness. To the conservatives, it seemed as if the long nightmare of the Paris commune, of uprooted and enraged masses rising in armed rebellion, had subsided for good and that social order was as stable as could be. Conservative intellectuals even seemed to hold out the promise that the pernicious and divisive ideas of 1789 might be relegated to the ideological past for good. The socialists, confident with the steady growth of trade union and socialist party membership and of parliamentary representation and with the workers' international viewed as a firm guarantee of perpetual peace, proudly proclaimed that the new century was to become the century of socialism. And some utopians even spoke of the new century as the century of the child: if so, the first in the history of humankind.

Today, these expectations of a time long past cannot but evoke sadness. The tragedies of the twentieth century are of such scale that they evade our imagination, even when we are cognitively aware of them. It is today almost unimaginable to consider a time when, every day, hundreds of thousands of soldiers were sent, with the consent of their governments and the blessing of public opinion in their home countries, to their death during the major battles of the Great War. It is unfathomable how socialists and pacifists could imagine that permanent peace and universal brotherhood were just around the corner, when in fact the scale of bloodletting rapidly outstripped even the horrors of the religious and civil wars of the sixteenth and seventeenth centuries. The fear of revolution, the fear of the masses and of the revolt of the lower classes, that had alarmed conservatives so deeply and for so long, could never have presaged the ruthlessness and extent of terror that the very same Bolsheviks who had so eloquently condemned the Tsar for his policies of imprisonment and deportations would soon embark upon themselves—and on a vastly larger scale.

To read today accounts from the Great War of how Jewish inhabitants of towns and cities of Eastern Europe warmly welcomed German and Austrian troops because in ousting the Russians they brought orderliness and safety, is like reading an account from an unknown, and unimaginable world. It is even difficult for us today to read Klaus Mann's autobiographical notes, "The Turning Point", and to realize that German high culture in Prague was by and large a Jewish culture. It is painful to learn that Kafka's short stories, his tormented accounts of human trauma (and consider that most terrible story "In the Penal Colony", a story painfully difficult to read with the knowledge of the events of the 1930s and 1940s) were greeted with laughter when read aloud in literary salons in Prague in the 1920s, as hilariously humorous accounts of the frail human condition.

When Friedrich Paulsen wrote his account for the great university exposition in Chicago in 1893, he did not doubt for a moment that German science and German higher education epitomized the highest achievements of scholarship. By and large, American scholars agreed, among them Abraham Flexner, who was the most prominent of this community and remained so for decades to come. When reading Paulsen—later so much admired by educational scholars and teachers around the world, including Mao Tse-Tung—or Weber, Dilthey, Husserl, Meinecke or Hintze, it is not possible to envisage that anywhere in their thinking was the notion that, within a few decades Germany could be reduced to a heap of rubble, a devastated pariah nation, guilty of crimes beyond comprehension, or that the high culture so much admired and epitomized by all these scholars was but one step on the road to the German catastrophe.

In the inter-war period, the British, victorious in the Great War, were still active as never before with the administration of their empire, the largest in world history. The glory of the Raj was appropriately reflected in the construction of the grandiose buildings of New Delhi, and there was little to suggest that its downfall was pending. Today, even the last remnants of that empire have been ceded, and it is almost as if it had never existed. Russian empires have been broken up twice, while the suffering of the

Russian people in this century defies imagination: it is as if one trauma has overtaken another in a sequence extending over decades. Only the United States seems relatively confident in its new, if transient, role as the sole super power. Even so, in a manner recalling other empires from the Roman onwards, the American public finds its troops dispatched on war and peace missions in distant places, engaged in protracted, if not inconclusive, conflicts. Meanwhile the same public seems internally engaged in an endless debate between groups about the distribution of legitimate claims to historical mistreatment by various actions of its own state. In the meantime, the world at large seems bent on continuing to treat America and its symbols with a curious mixture of envy, awe and resentment.

Modernity and social science

In an almost obvious sense the twentieth century has been a century of trauma. These traumatic events have been captured in family memories, in private letters from those who encountered disaster, in short stories and novels, in films and works of art. However, they have been surprisingly absent from the research agenda of the social and human sciences. Instead, the core assumptions of these disciplines continue to reflect the sense of triumph and progress that obtained at the time of their own disciplinary consolidation in the late 19th and early 20th centuries. It is as if the disasters of the twentieth century had never happened, as if the major concern of social science was to understand those processes that brought growth in certain parts of the world, while leaving others behind.

It is only too easy to forget that the conceptual understanding of the modern world, as elaborated by the social and human sciences, tends, if often tacitly so, to be premised on a conception of modernization as a process of the global diffusion of Western civilization and its key institutions. Thus social scientists have long tended to describe the emergence of this modern world in terms of a dual revolution in technological and economic practices, 'the industrial revolution', and in political practices of democracy and demands for popular participation. These revolutions are seen to have been powerfully manifested in the French and American revolutions of the late eighteenth century. Key categories used to describe the emergence of this modern world are overwhelmingly created against the backdrop of the particular European path to modernity. This is equally true of broad notions such as those of the nation state or the constitutional republic as of mediating concepts, such as public sphere and civil society.

In historical perspective this should not be surprising. After all the social sciences themselves emerged as a form of reflection on the momentous trans-

(but classics not blind!)

reasons for blindness of ss

1. mod'n = western's

formations of Western societies during the processes of industrialization, urbanization and political change in the late eighteenth and in the nine- teenth centuries. These transformations were often perceived to entail an irreversible process of change, ushering in a world of modernity character- ized by economic growth. However, it was also shaped by a continuous sense of crisis and contingency. This image, captured vividly in writings of such different authors as Hegel, Saint-Simon, and later of Marx, Tönnies, Weber and Durkheim, was formulated perhaps most elegantly—and pes- simistically—by a French aristocrat in the middle of the nineteenth century. In his memoirs, written some two decades after the journey to America that would make him famous in posterity, Alexis de Tocqueville confessed he had been deeply mistaken in thinking that the sea change in social and political order inherent in the French Revolution had already ended in 1830. In 1850, he now saw this process as one of incessant and irreversible change, across all different fortunes and passions. It left behind irrevocably an old society and its sense of legitimacy, order and stability, a change that con- stituted one mighty upheaval 'that our fathers saw beginning and that we in all likelihood will not see the end of'.

Today, however, we may look back at two centuries when the social insti- tutions that became emblematic of modernity—a modern democratic nation state, a modem liberal market economy and modern science pursued in, to use the metaphor Harold Perkin, inspired by Daniel Bell, has elaborated, namely of the research-oriented university as 'the axial institution of a mod- ern society', a kind of powerhouse in a knowledge-based society—have spread as models if not always as realities, from their places of emergence in Europe to virtually all countries across the globe. In the process, however, they have often been so deeply transformed as to make the belief in a single homoge- nous modernity appear hopelessly naive. Yet, we seem woefully at a loss when we turn to the modern social and human sciences in order to find conceptual tools enabling us even to start understanding the way in which the cultural foundations of modern institutions were formed historically across different civilizations.

There are at least three basic reasons for this scholarly neglect. *Firstly*, for a long time in the nineteenth and early twentieth centuries, modern- ization seemed almost self-evidently to be identical with Westernization. The champions of triumphant European and American economic, political and cultural expansion and growth, at home and world-wide (and also its critics, such as Marx) showed little inclination to question this equivocation of modernity with the development and diffusion of the cultural program of one type of civilization. This program seemed for a long time to be com- mitted to precisely a triumphalist basic conception of its own emergence and development.

Thus to overcome this limitation, there is a need for a social science that is more open to a comparative perspective and to think through the experiences of European countries against the backdrop of the intellectual and institutional legacies of other parts of the world as well.

Secondly, in the nineteenth century, as today, there was a relative neglect among scholars to clearly bring out the role of intellectual and cultural processes in underpinning and making meaningful, indeed often constituting, the key categories of political and institutional change. It is only in recent years, for example, that scholars have systematically tried to map the deep-seated intellectual shift at the turn of the eighteenth century; what is sometimes referred to not only as a second scientific revolution, but as a momentous cultural and intellectual shift. We are really only starting to appreciate the great extent to which our most familiar conceptions of societal order, and indeed the very concepts of society, collective identities and forms of human agency, were shaped in the course of that process of intellectual, but also institutional, transformation. It is even more clear that it is only in very recent times that scholars have started seeking categories that can reflect the undeniable sense of material enrichment inherent in modernity while recognizing the other side of modernity, namely the immensely painful events that it brought in its wake. Such recognition is more deep-seated and more difficult to bring forth. It also differs from the type of account given by any classics of social science of processes of anomie, alienation, and the replacement of the attachments of an earlier and more traditional society by attachments emerging from the interactions of modern, urban-based, commercial society. Thus, the social sciences themselves were long blind to important parts of their own history, often seen as mere predisciplinary prehistory, and to the ways in which that history was intertwined with the institutional and cultural projects of modernity. There is, in other words, a strong need to link up social theory and intellectual history in a sustained effort to rethink the formation of modernity.

Thirdly, many of the key institutional features of a modern age such as the idea of a democratic nation-state did indeed emerge at the turn of the eighteenth century in forms involving dramatic ruptures with traditional forms of political and social order. This sense of rupture has however also tended to obscure, both from sight and from the field of interest, inquiries into far longer waves of change in the formation of a series of different cultural programs of modernity. Social science theory has certainly highlighted the sense of contingency inherent in modernity.

By and large, though, this has occurred within the framework of a basic conception of modernity as the unfolding of processes of increasing economic growth and public participation, as an age emerging out of the industrial and democratic revolutions, an age of mass production and mass participation. We may, however, be even more at a loss when we try to rethink the traumatic events of the last century. Present-day debates on the global development of modern societies thus coalesce around three basic stances, all of which more closely reflect the triumphant sense of late 19th century social science than the experiences of the 20th century's traumatic events.

What is needed then is a critical historical sociology that is prepared to rethink not only the formation of modernity, but also its own categories. This is necessary in order for us to arrive at a theoretically informed understanding not only of the triumphs but also of the disasters and traumas of our own age. In this respect, the contemporary debate on the emergence of a single liberal modernity and of the clashes between different cultural entities are, unfortunately, of little help. It is to this issue that the next section briefly turns.

Globalization and multiple modernities

In the contemporary discussion about the uniformity or diversity of modern societies, three positions have occupied a prominent position, outside of academic discourse as well. Thus there is *firstly* a stance that might be labeled that of *liberal historicism*. In the wake of the Soviet Union's collapse, liberal democracy and market economy, in the particular form that these institutional practices have come to exhibit in recent decades in parts of North America and Western Europe, are seen as providing the sole legitimate models of social organization. These forms will then come to be embraced, if with delays, throughout the world. Needless to say, the adherents of this view are not so naive as to assume that this type of global diffusion would entail a development towards cultural, or even linguistic, homogeneity. It would, however, mean that there would be no reason to expect any fundamental institutional innovation that could transcend these types of liberal institutional arrangements. If that were to occur, it would be unreasonable in an almost Hegelian sense, and would entail a departure from modernity, not its further development or variation. This sense has been nicely captured by the philosopher Richard Rorty:

> More important, I think that contemporary liberal society already contains the institutions for its own improvement... Indeed, my hunch is that Western social and political thought may have had the last *conceptual* revolution that it needs (Rorty, 1989: 63).

Other less sophisticated liberals have expressed far more simplistic beliefs in the coming emergence of a common global political and cultural order.

Indeed, these views tend to exhibit as many features in common with the political culture of the home countries of the authors as did Hegel's views with early 19th century Prussia.

Secondly, there is a position that focuses attention on the current array of cultural life forms and assigns each of them to a larger civilizational entity. These civilizational entities are seen to make up what almost amounts to cultural tectonic plates, that move and impinge upon each other but rarely merge or blend seamlessly into each other. At least since Toynbee, there has been what might constitute a kind of tradition in international relations research that is based on a similar view. Sometimes, as in the case of Toynbee himself and his followers, this view served as a basis for a plea for understanding and respecting a multiplicity of cultural forms.

In other cases, the inferences have tended to be more hard-nosed, so as to caution against allegedly naive beliefs that 'the others' might come to embrace the same 'Western' values as the authors do. The attractiveness of this position has largely been limited by a simple fact. To the extent that serious attention has been paid to long-term cultural developments, this position tends, as it did in Toynbee's own case, to lead to warning against a sense of cultural and societal superiority. Such a position is a much better starting point for research than for the kind of policy advice to which advocates of this program often aspired. Furthermore, for all its understanding, it tended to share with early social science a sense, even if sometimes a tacit one, of Western cultural superiority. When, on the other hand, '*cultural tectonics*' has taken on a more hard-nosed and policy-oriented character; the cultural presuppositions tend to shift from tacit to explicit. Furthermore, the position seems to suffer from an obvious weakness in terms of its policy commitment. Thus it cannot very well make sense of the fact that few contemporary political cleavages adhere neatly to the fault lines of the alleged civilization. Rather, such cleavages seem to have far more to do with state formations than large civilizational entities, especially to the extent that these are seen as more or less frozen in time in their cultural characteristics.

A *third position* is inspired by the insights provided by linguistic, philosophical and anthropological research in this century. As its starting-point, it takes the almost infinite multiplicity of historically constituted life forms, language games and speech acts. To the extent that it has tried to trace the development of such life forms or their similarities historically and comparatively, it has set the agenda for exceedingly rich research undertakings. In recent decades, however, a vastly important effort has also been made in social theory to transcend the multiplicity of individually existing life forms and language games, so as to formulate a universal pragmatic theory of

ss inability to understand c20 violence
except an residue or inexplicable eruption
or an modernity

RETHINKING MODERNITY   57

necessary features of speech acts. This theory of an ideal speech situation has proved to be of wide usefulness as a standard for assessing linguistic and institutional practices and their various deviations from the universally valid ideal situation of communicative interaction.

In a paradoxical way, this theory—elaborated against the backdrop of classical critical theory and the darkest diagnoses of modernity—has involved a remarkable transcendence of the dark dialectics of enlightenment of earlier critical theory. Instead of the cultural despair of classical *critical theory*, a vision has emerged of a *liberal utopia*, i.e. an imaginary locale where forms of power, domination and manipulation fail to exert an impact on the dialogue between human beings who engage sincerely in a common communicative life form. This analytical move simultaneously permits the realization of a multiplicity of different institutional and political practices in the modern world, and the insistence that modernity has its origins in an Enlightenment project which is universal in nature. In this analytical stance, there is but a small step between early 19th century German philosophy and late 20th century social theory, between Schleiermacher and Habermas. Thus, each of these three basic positions in the contemporary debate on multiple modernities and processes of globalization seem to fail to take sufficient account of the different cultural foundations of modernity in various parts of the world. However, they also seem to be based on presuppositions about modernity in the European context that simply do not reflect the traumatic nature of the history of Europe in the 20th century.

Clearly, however, the twentieth century has also been an age of mass destruction, mass killings and mass suffering, more so probably than any other century in the last millennium. In the self-understanding of the social and human sciences, however, these elements have rarely occupied a central position. Instead they have often been treated as atavistic, as residues of an earlier stage in the development of humankind, in a similar way as processes of collective turmoil were often seen by individualistic liberals, or as nationalism was, and largely still is, perceived by many Marxian scholars. They have also been depicted as inexplicable eruptions of dark forces lurking in the interior of individuals or societies, or at least in the heritage, if not the genes, of some groups or peoples deemed particularly murderous or savage. Sometimes mass destruction and mass killings have even been seen as an inevitable concomitant of modernity itself, as manifestations of 'the dialectic of enlightenment', to paraphrase the title of a famous book (Horkheimer and Adorno, 1972).

I shall not accept any of these accounts. Instead I shall try to outline an analysis that tries to link the study of structural transformations to that of the interpretative processes of cultural self-understanding. I shall then draw on this analysis to provide an answer to the question whether or not it makes sense to talk about multiple modernities. Clearly this term has to mean something more than the observation that decisively modem technological and economic practices exist across the world in settings that historically have exhibited, and still exhibit, customs and traditions which have vastly different origins and forms. However, judging from contemporary debates, it is far from clear what such a more precise meaning might be. Furthermore, to the extent that it might make sense to talk about a multiplicity of different institutional and cultural forms in the contemporary world, it must also be made clear why we should use the term modernity at all to describe these different forms.

My analysis will proceed in three steps. In a *first* section, I shall address the nature of the cultural and epistemic rupture in the late 18th and the early 19th centuries. This transformation was concomitant with, and helped constitute, the emergence of decisively modern institutions in the Western context. However, it has been largely neglected in the self-understanding of the social sciences, that have instead tended to focus their attention on changes in political and economic practices. The analysis of this first section will lead up to an answer to the question what, if anything, was specific—compared to other periods of cultural and institutional crystallization—to that cultural and institutional crystallization in the West that is referred to as the formation of modernity. I shall argue that it is indeed meaningful to talk about the formation of modernity as a specific event in world history.

Despite important similarities to earlier periods of crystallization, the cultural constitution of a set of new macro-societal institutions at the turn of the 18th century set the stage for a new era in world history. This is so not merely, or even mainly, because these institutions exhibit features that differ from those of previous periods; this is certainly true but only to a limited extent, and is equally true of earlier periods of major societal transformation. The major justification for the use of the term modernity has instead to do with the promissory notes of these new institutional projects and the extent to which they were based on radically new presuppositions about human agency, historical consciousness and the role of reason in forging new societal institutions.

In a *second* section, I shall try to outline how the concept of cultural trauma might help to enable an understanding of modernity that takes account of the disastrous events of the 20th century, rather than subsuming them within an all-encompassing triumphalist narrative. In this connection, I shall introduce the idea that cultural trauma might be interpreted as resulting from an irreversible violation of core components of trust and of promissory notes. The absence of such a violation of the core promissory notes of a civic institution, I shall call the minimal civic condition.

In the *third* and final section I will try to provide an answer to the question whether the notion of multiple modernities is at all meaningful in elucidating the complexities of the contemporary world and the global interconnectedness of human interactions.

The cultural constitution of modernity

There is, as already emphasized, a need for a fundamental revision of a long-standing and predominant view among social scientists and humanists, as well as in lay debates, about the formation of modernity in terms of a conjunction of a technological and political transformation—the industrial and the democratic revolutions, respectively. This traditional interpretation radically underestimates the deep-seated epistemic transformation that occurred at the turn of the 18th and 19th centuries. Despite all continuities and long-term processes of gestation, a range of recent studies suggest that there is indeed a great transition in epistemic and institutional terms at this juncture. This transition also signals a call for a radically revised self-understanding among social scientists of the history of their own disciplines. It is simply not enough to waver between a focus on the early political philosophers and legal scholars of the 16th and 17th centuries, on the one hand, and the 'classics' of social science in the period of its academic and disciplinary institutionalization, on the other. Rather, there are reasons to carefully examine the ways in which distinctively modern key concepts of an understanding of society emerge during the great transition in the late 18th and early 19th centuries.

One such shift pertains precisely to the concepts of society and history and to the new awareness of the structural and constraining nature of societal life beyond the domain of communicative interactions in the political sphere proper. Thus there is a transition to a social science that transcends the boundaries of the political sphere proper but also traces the implications and conditions of that sphere much further than the old political philosophy. Pierre Manent (1994a: 80–83; see also 1994b, 1994c, 1994d) has put forward the notion that society is a 'post-revolutionary discovery'. True enough, and as is convincingly demonstrated by Keith Baker (1994), the term 'society' undergoes a long conceptual development in the French context in the course of the 17th and 18th centuries—with a dramatic increase in the utilization of the term in the mid-18th century. It is also true that, in his critique of Louis Dumont's analysis of Western individualism and holism, Marcel Gauchet argued (this is Baker's elegant summary) that:

> Individualism was not simply a symptom of the dissolution of the primacy of the social whole, as that had been understood in traditional religious terms. It was also a necessary condition for what he once again called (following Karl Polanyi) the "discovery of society"—its discovery in strictly sociological terms, disengaged from the religious representations in which it had hitherto expressed its existence. Not until the ideological primacy of individual interests was postulated, he argued, could constraints upon these interests be discovered in the operation of an autonomous social order subject to its own laws (Baker, 1994: 112).

Johan Heilbron (1995b, 1998) has pursued an inquiry into the constitution of individual interests and the various ways in which, in the course of the 17th and 18th centuries, they were conceived as amenable to the constraints of various notions of sociability, and the socially acceptable outcomes of the pursuit of the self-interests of human beings were doomed to an existence short of true religious virtue, but at least with a prospect for a human existence beyond the borders of a Leviathan-like imposition of absolute order. However, Heilbron and many others today would agree that, even if there is a long process of gestation of the modem concept of society, the unique event of revolutionary upheaval entails that discursive controversy and poetical practice become joined in the formation of a distinctly modern era. Pierre Manent has elaborated a similar argument:

> After the Revolution, the men of the nineteenth century no longer lived merely in civil society or the state; they lived in a third element that received various names, usually "society" or "history." Regardless of what it was called, this element had the greatest authority. This "society" then was more than and different from "civil society": the latter had been created by the totality of relationships spontaneously formed by men, transformed by the desire for preservation, while the former had no explicit natural foundation. Its authority did not lie in "nature," but in "history," in the historical evolution (Manent, 1994a: 81).

True enough, Manent admits, an author such as Montesquieu granted more authority than any other 18th-century author to history understood as the development of 'knowledge' and 'commerce'. However, whereas he wanted to establish the authority of history,

> he did not feel it ... It is definitely from the Revolution that this feeling dates. More precisely, it derives from the fact that the Revolution failed to develop adequate political institutions ... The Revolution offered the original spectacle of a political change of unheard-of-scope, yet having no stable political effects,

of a political upheaval impossible to settle, of an interminable and indeterminate event (Manent, 1994a: 82).

This description of the Revolution as an irreversible and interminable process of fundamental change was formulated perhaps most clearly by one of the most well-known thinkers of the 19th century, namely Alexis de Tocqueville. Thus, in his memoirs, *Souvenirs*, written in the summer of 1850 (i.e. two decades after the journey to the New World that made him famous for posterity), he describes the Revolution as one long upheaval

> that our fathers have seen the beginning of and which, in all likelihood, we shall not see the end of. Everything that remained of the old regime was destroyed for ever (Tocqueville, 1964: 30).

In fact, Reinhart Koselleck's conception in his early work *Kritik und Krise* is quite similar. He also links the temporal duration of the process of upheaval to its spatial, and indeed world-wide, extension, as well as to its increasing intensity in terms of modernity, as a process that affects all human beings, not just, say, those in central political institutions or certain major cities:

> Das achtzehnte Jahrhundert ist der Vorraum des gegenwärtigen Zeitalters, dessen Spannung sich seit der Französischen Revolution zunehmend verschärft hat, indem der revolutionäre Prozess extensiv die ganze Welt und intensiv alle Menschen ergriff (Koselleck, 1959: 2).

However, it is also this sense of openness and contingency that serves as a forceful impetus to an examination of the structural conditions of the political body, and entails a passage from political and moral philosophy to a social science. This transition entails that five key problematiques—which today are more acutely open to reinterpretation than they have been for decades, if not for a century—are being formulated, or at least fundamentally reformulated, and are entering into the new social science discourse.

First, the whole role of historical inquiry becomes a crucial one. On the one hand, historical reasoning becomes an integral part of the intellectual transition, and even abstract reason itself becomes historicized in early 19th-century philosophy. However, on the other hand, the moral and political sciences break up into a variety of new discourses that in the course of the 19th century coalesce and are reduced to a number of disciplines. This means that the stage is set for the divergence between a professionalized historical discipline and the other social and human sciences, a divergence that we still today experience as a major intellectual divide.

Secondly, interest in language and linguistic analysis enters into all domains of the human and social sciences as a key problematique. One outflow of this is the constitution of textual and hermeneutic modes of analysis. A second one—familiar from contemporary debates on linguistic analysis and poststructuralism—is that of the relationship between text, interpretation, and consciousness. A third one is the effort to historicize language and linguistic development itself. Thereby a crucial link was provided to various collective entities such as the historic construction of notions of different peoples.

This leads to a third problematique, namely that of constituting new collective identities. If membership in a collectivity can no longer be taken for granted in terms of the life experiences of the inhabitants of a certain village or region, or of a relationship of rule between the princely ruler and his subjects, then even the most basic categories of societal existence are open to doubt.

In the late 18th century, categories such as ruler and subject are by no means irreversibly superseded—in fact they linger on in the imperial-like political entities in and at the borders of Europe for more than a century—but they are opened to doubt and, in the aftermath of the French Revolution, to the necessity of reconstitution. Categories such as 'citizen' and 'compatriot' capture some of the results of these processes of reconstitution. Robert Wokler (1998), perhaps more clearly than anyone else, has issued a strong warning against any hasty equivocation of the French revolutionary notion of a nation-state with a commitment to a truly universal conception of rights of human beings. The parallel developments in Germany and many other parts of Europe to link the constitution of collective identities to a historically constituted collectivity such as that of a linguistic group or some other cultural entity serve only to underscore further Wokler's point in this respect and to warn against an all too easy and prevalent tendency—among the self-proclaimed defenders and detractors of modernity alike—to identify the political and epistemic order of modernity with simply an extension of the Enlightenment project into political reality.

Fourthly, and as repeatedly emphasized, the whole problematique of the relationship between notions of polity, society, and civil society was succinctly and acutely reformulated in this period of transition. The fact that once again these notions are probed and fundamentally re-examined should not conceal the fact that they were indeed in many ways not just reformulated in this period, but rather discovered or even invented.

Fifthly, the most basic notion of any social and human science pertains to assumptions about what prompts human beings to act and how to interpret their actions within a broader framework. Such assumptions are at the very core of any scholarly program in the social and human sciences. At the turn of the 18th and 19th centuries the fundamental categories that we still by and large draw upon were elaborated and proposed.

Three or four such fundamental categorical conceptualizations were propounded. Each of them corresponded to a conceptualization of what 'society' was constituted by. These categories might be described as follows:

(a) *Economic-rationalistic*, with a corresponding view of society as a form of *compositional* collective;

(b) *Statistical-inductive*, with a view of society as a *systemic aggregate*;

(c) *Structural-constraining*, with a view of society in terms of an *organic totality*; and

(d) *Linguistic-interpretative*, with a societal conceptualization in terms of an *emergent totality*.

The transition from a discourse on moral and political philosophy to a social science—analyzed, for example, by Robert Wokler (1987)—in rudimentary form has already taken place in the mid-and late-1790s in France after the Revolution. It entailed a decisive shift from an agential—some would say voluntaristic—view of society to one that emphasizes structural conditions. To some extent, a similar shift occurs in economic reasoning away from a broad concern about moral and political agency towards one where, in the course of the 19th century, 'average economic man' becomes cast in a web of structural properties and dynamic regularities rather than in a moral universe of individual action.

Maybe the deep irony of this secular shift and of the rise of the social sciences is that the methodological origins are to be found in a single context, the French, where, during the revolutionary upheavals, the emphasis on agency and change was greater than had ever previously been the case, anywhere. The very concept of revolution is itself an example of a concept that is subjected to drastic conceptual change and it entails an effort not only to change a political regime but to build a new community and a new world from the very beginning. It is in reaction to this that both radicals—such as Saint-Simon and Comte—and conservatives, not to speak of reactionaries such as de Bonald and de Maistre, came to emphasize a structuralist and anti-voluntaristic conception of society.

By contrast, despite the deep influence of the French events on philosophy and scholarship in Germany, the very absence of a revolutionary transformation in the German political context was coterminous with an intellectual transformation that dramatically emphasized precisely the agential capacities of human beings. In this intellectual environment, there emerged a nexus of philosophical commitments—nicely explored in several essays by, among others, Peter Hanns Reill (1994, 1998) and Randall Collins (1987, 1998)—that involved the elaboration of a linguistic-interpretative conception of agency as opposed to a purely rationalistic-compositional one—which came

to be predominant in economic reasoning—or a structural-aggregate one—
which came to characterize sociological and statistical reasoning. Thus fundamental categories of agency and society that came to be elaborated and
refined during much of the rest of the 19th and 20th centuries, can already
be discerned in rudimentary form during the great transition. So too, however, can some of the more or less tacit, more or less explicit features that
came to affect these endeavors.

One such tacit but crucial feature concerns the abandonment of the truly
universal heritage of the Enlightenment project in favor of forms of representation and endowment of rights based on territoriality or membership in
a linguistically and historically constituted and constructed community.
Another feature concerns the curtailment, not to say abandonment, of the
earlier tradition of moral discourse even within the different conceptualization of basic agential *Denkfiguren* that were being elaborated. A third feature
has to do with the dual way in which historical reasoning came to be both
embraced and exercised—with a permanent divide between history and the
social sciences remaining until today, a divide quite unknown to previous
genres of discourse.

These three features entail a chasm between an overt commitment to
universality and the inability to conceptualize political order in other than
highly particularistic terms, a chasm between philosophical and moral discourse and modem social science, and even a chasm between history and
the other social and human sciences. The shift in epistemic and institutional
regimes that occurred at the turn of the 18th and 19th centuries did not
immediately usher in the set of disciplinary configurations in the social and
human sciences that we now all too often take for granted. This occurred
only in the late 19th and early 20th centuries—and then only in an uneven
and partial process that did not become a universal pattern of ordering until
well after World War II. However, it did entail, in a more or less rudimentary way, both the institutional form for intellectual activities and the
epistemic forms that became constitutive of the discourses on society in the
age of modernity.

The intellectual and institutional shift that occurred in this period took,
as highlighted in this section, different forms in different societies within the
European context too. However the thematic foci of the shift were similar
and the end result was the *cultural constitution of a new set of societal macro-
institutions.* In the political sphere, these institutions involved a new conception of political order as constituted and legitimated in terms of the participation
of its citizens. This is also, as already emphasized, the period when a new
conception of civil society is formulated, premised on the legitimate articulation of a discourse not only about, but also addressed to and critical of,

the official power of the state. Even if these new institutional projects were to be embattled and highly controversial in practical affairs in Europe throughout the following century and a half, they contained a new set of promissory notes. These promissory notes spelt out a set of *conceptually compelling relationships* that had to obtain for the institutional projects to be realized. These promissory notes could not, as so eloquently testified by Alexis de Tocqueville, be reversed but rather served as inevitable reference points for reformers and conservatives alike throughout the political and institutional struggles of the 19th and early 20th centuries. The traumas of the 20th century may be understood precisely as deeply painful events that have involved instances of violent rejections of the promissory notes both of modern and traditional institutions. In that sense both the so-called Great War and the Nazi experience as well as that of Stalinism entailed breaches of the trust inherent in the institutional projects of modernity that were irreversible and forced processes of cultural reinterpretation that are yet to be completed.

Cultural trauma and social theory

Scholars such as Jeffrey Alexander, Ron Eyerman, Bernhard Giessen, Neil Smelser and Piotr Sztompka have examined a series of usages of the term trauma outside of the specific psychological context in which it was once introduced into scholarly work. They have also extensively discussed the heuristic and analytical value of the concept of cultural trauma to contemporary social theory. For all their differences, these scholars seem to embrace a minimal set of presuppositions that seem useful in the present context as well. Thus, they all take issue with a lay assumption of trauma in its literal meaning of a wound, and more specifically a wound that will not heal. Trauma may of course be seen as involving lasting, maybe permanently debilitating, effects of an event, imagined or actualized in a past or in the present, often enough in a way that entails an unexpected and radical rupture. However, the indelible nature of trauma does not pertain to the nature of an event per se but to a relationship. Such a relationship may obtain between three sets of phenomena, namely firstly an event, actual, potential or simply imagined; secondly, structural properties in a personality or in a culture; and thirdly, some form of psychological or cultural articulation that may be termed traumatic under a given description.

Cultural trauma cannot, these scholars insist, be analyzed in a naively moral or naively psychological sense. This would be committing a naturalistic fallacy and disregarding the discursively constituted nature of any concept of trauma. It would also disregard precisely those processes of negotiation, interaction and exchange of instances of cognition, emotion and memory in the constitution of those states of mind and those narratives that may be termed traumatic. In the conceptual historical analysis undertaken by Neil Smelser in this context, he highlights the gradual shift of emphasis in Freudian psychological analysis.

Thus the early emphasis on naturalistic accounts of the effects of rather unambiguously describable events give way to dispositional explanations where attention is increasingly shifted to the conjunction of some external event, actual or imagined, and a set of predispositions in a given individual or in Smelser's words 'a process-in-system'. To the extent that such sets of predispositions might be systematically related to each other, it becomes possible to identify sets of psychic dynamics that might be crucial in determining behavior patterns and responses to actual or imagined events. Thus even in a classical Freudian conception, it is not possible to maintain a notion of trauma without reference to systemic properties. From this follow some important consequences.

Firstly, the systemic character entails that once the concept of trauma is transposed into the realm of sociological and historical inquiry, it cannot possibly be identified with an individual event or an individual sequence of events, no matter how dramatic or encompassing these events may be. It has to take explicit account of the nature of cultural predispositions and systemic features.

Secondly, it entails that the identification of sets of predispositions and dynamics becomes crucial. It is crucial to see that this also means that precisely because, traumatic responses are culturally constructed, they are systemic rather than arbitrary. This is exactly the point where a purely linguistic analysis will provide no leads, but has to be linked to an understanding of institutional practices and macro-societal phenomena.

Thirdly, a cultural analysis of trauma as opposed to a purely psychological account must recognize that systemic properties cannot be observed in themselves in some pure form open to observation. They are discursively articulated and inscribed in narratives that, in non-arbitrary fashion, assign signification and primacy to the different phenomena that are being articulated within the given narrative. It is these different narratives that help constitute, but also may undermine, societal practices and institutions, although the codes of institutions themselves serve precisely to secure not only the mobilization and legitimation of symbolic means but of material ones as well.

It is equally important to see that the nature of such systemic properties cannot just be representational or descriptive but must also, *fourthly*, be affective and emotional. This, incidentally, is one reason why a concept of cultural trauma tends to shed light on phenomena that have tended to be rather neglected, not only in most traditional historical sociology with its heavy emphasis on long-term processes of structural and institutional change. The same, *mutatis mutandis*, is also largely true of much of contemporary intellectual and conceptual history. Furthermore, the traumatic states that may appear in an individual or a collective concern a particular type of emotions. These emotions are related to core components of a personality and they tend to produce enduring, or indeed indelible, states of mind. As such they may take the form of explicitly formulated accounts but they may appear as vaguely sensed fears. Indelibility is then related to two further features.

Fifthly, then, there will be a pressing, insistent, even compulsive urge to engage in memorizing and conceptualizing a phenomenon that has become traumatic.

Sixthly, there is a close relationship between trauma and the core of a person's conception of selfhood or the cultural identity of a community.

Thus a traumatic phenomenon will involve a consideration or reconsideration of the very identity of a person or a cultural community. Stated in another way, the concept of trauma may be described as a conjunction of an event or a series of events that involve a fundamental violation of core components of personal and cultural identity. The effects of such a violation are indelible within the framework of the narrative in which the identity has been institutionally articulated. Such symbolic violence is rarely limited to speech acts alone but tends to be systematically linked to the institutional mobilization of non-linguistic resources and to acts of violence, not only against cultural codes, but against real living human beings with hopes and fears, memories and fragile bodies.

A delimitation of the concept of cultural trauma along these lines opens up the space for basically three types of analysis. A *first* type of analysis would be to use the concept of cultural trauma as an additional instrument in traditional historical analysis of a structural or macro-institutional kind. Thus one might argue that a study of, say, the institutional prerequisites for economic growth in Europe and America, might be linked to a study of the way in which earlier cultural codes were fundamentally broken and transcended. Or one might add an analysis of cultural trauma on to a macro-analysis of the emergence and evolution of state formations in Europe over long periods of time or of long-term processes of the growth of means of production and violence.

In all these instances, the notion of cultural trauma might be one way to link an interpretative analysis to a structural-institutional one or else to show how such structural processes in some cases did, and in other cases did not, have traumatic consequences. All of these types of analysis appear to hold promise of yielding new and interesting insights. However, all of them come close to a naturalistic position. Thereby they would risk entailing a violation of the very first presupposition in the delimitation undertaken above, namely that events in and of themselves cannot be described as traumatic or non-traumatic but only relative to a given set of cultural commitments and conceptualizations.

A *second* type of analysis might be more straightforward, namely simply to go ahead and study a range of phenomena that in either everyday language or in terms of a conception of cultural trauma, say, of the type proposed above, may be described as traumatic. This procedure would eventually produce a series of interesting case studies that could suggest fresh ways of refining, elaborating and extending conceptions of cultural trauma to new empirical domains and linking them to new theoretical formulations. It would, in other words, constitute a typical mode of articulating a theoretical idea or insight in both empirical and conceptual terms.

There is nothing much to object to in such a procedure except that it would be time consuming and ad hoc. Thus it would either depend on a highly inductivist conception of scholarly work or else it would simply rely on some standard accounts of major processes of transformations that might initiate processes of a traumatizing nature. If this were so, we would simply be back in the first case of analysis and the problems already discussed, i.e. of adding a component of cultural analysis to a standardized structural or institutional account.

A *third* type of analysis is to hold on to a restricted but clear definition of cultural trauma rather than immediately to extend and elaborate it by way of inductive articulation, as in the previous case. This third type of analysis then has to make clear what might or might not constitute a fundamental violation of core components of a cultural program. The most obvious difficulty is that the analysis requires that such components may be stated in terms that can be yielded discursively explicit. More precisely, the discursive articulation also has to make sense in terms of the discourse of a given cultural community.

Needless to say, these difficulties become formidable when the focus of analysis is one of historical-comparative research. Nevertheless—and contrary to the alternatives of accepting a naturalistic structural account of the first type or of engaging in a vast inductive exercise of the second type—this third type of analysis is conceptually much more consistent and straightforward. Furthermore, it is the only one that holds out real promise for linking cultural analysis to a macro-historical one, of forging a link between a structural and an interpretative account in a way that is potentially significant in terms of normative engagement. However, it can only do so if it limits its conceptual apparatus in the initial stage to a simple and restrictive use that provides the minimally necessary tools.

It is precisely such an analysis that may provide an understanding of the events discussed that have, in lay terms, marred the twentieth century and yet seem difficult to encompass within a traditional sociological account of the formation and development of modernity. The notion of cultural trauma might provide exactly the link necessary to overcome this disjuncture.

Cultural crystallization: the three great transformations

In the preceding two sections I have first argued that there is a need to rethink the formation of modernity by explicitly bringing into focus the discursive and cultural constitution of a range of new macro-societal institutions and practices. Thereby it is possible to highlight important features of this process that were decisively new. At the same time, however, it is only too easy to see that several of these features exhibit structural similarities with cultural reconstitution in earlier periods of institutional and cultural crystallization. There are, I think, three such major periods of deep cultural and institutional crystallization that may be discerned on the basis of scholarly works that are now available.

There is, *firstly*, that period of fundamental cultural transformation that has been labeled the *axial age.* Karl Jaspers introduced the concept in a thought-provoking book published shortly after the Second World War, later extensively elaborated by S.N. Eisenstadt and Wolfgang Schluchter (see Jaspers, 1953; Eisenstadt, 1986). Jaspers used the term axial age to refer to a series of intellectual transformations that occurred in the high civilizations around the Eastern Mediterranean, in the Indian subcontinent and in East Asia in the centuries around the middle of the first millennium BCE. These transformations were associated with dramatic increases in philosophical self-reflection and the powers of human agency. Sometimes a posited chasm between a mundane and a transcendental order—as opposed to their seamless blending into each other in traditional mythological and mystical consciousness—were seen to be linked to the emergence of new strata invested with the task of mediating between these realms.

These interpretative practices furthermore were seen to be crucial in processes of legitimating or delegitimating the power of rulers. It is important to see, however, that both in cultural and institutional terms, there is a dramatically wide array of responses to the axial age in the Eastern Mediterranean,

in the Indian subcontinent and in China. In some instances, the processes
seem to help strengthen a movement towards monotheistic religions but that
is certainly not the case either in Greece, or the Indian subcontinent—or
for that matter in Persia—or in East Asia. In some cases, the interpretative
cultural framework becomes focused on religious texts (parts of Western
Asia), in others on philosophical accounts (Greece), in others on cultural-
literary texts (the Indian subcontinent) and in other cases, e.g. China, on
political-normative codes. Thus despite the unitary term 'the axial age', the
variability in institutional and cultural forms is so large as to leave open to
question even the use of an expression in the singular to encompass these
different developments.

For Jaspers, the axial age constituted the first process of fundamental cultural 'disenchantment' *(Entzauberung)*. It signaled an irreversible transition
from *'Mythos'* to *'Logos'*. (Incidentally, it was precisely around this point of
the irreversibility of this transition that a chasm exists between Jaspers and
Martin Heidegger—his old close colleague among phenomenological philosophers in Weimar Germany. For Heidegger, but not for Jaspers, the need
to return to the Greek roots of the European intellectual tradition and to
rethink and overcome the disenchantment of modernity and an age of technology served as a starting point for his philosophical project. It also served
as a major rationale, as clearly stated in the infamous Rectoral address at
Freiburg in 1933, for his belief that the Nazi party might serve as a vehicle for such a fundamental cultural reconstitution of the European tradition
and for a basic rejection of modernity.)

Secondly, there is an analogous process of cultural reinterpretation and
restructuring during the first two centuries after the turn of the first millennium CE. I would like to introduce the term the *ecumenical renaissance* to
describe this period of cultural and institutional crystallization. In different
ways, it affected Western and Central Europe, the Indian subcontinent and
in East Asia both China and Japan. Again, as during the axial age, there
is a period that involved a dramatic surge in modes of self-reflexivity as
well as of institutional innovation or renovation directly related to these
processes of cultural reflexivity. In Western and Central Europe four interconnected processes—the so-called Papal, Feudal, Urban, and Intellectual
Revolutions of the 12th and 13th centuries—came to underpin, and indeed
to constitute, fundamentally new paths of development in European history.
Thereby they set the stage for the coexistence, within unquestioned predominance for either power, of secular and ecclesiastical power as well as
a societal situation characterized by a multiplicity of semi-autonomous guilds
and other social and intellectual groupings, including universities. Furthermore,
a set of public spheres emerged for the judicial and political assertion of

rights that had been created in the course of the feudal and intellectual revolutions. Intense contestations and violent uprisings were frequent. They
were, however, always culturally explicated and interpreted within a framework of an overarching cultural ecumene.

In Japan, there existed an analogous need as that in Europe of finding
ways of mobilizing resources in a situation of decentralization and relative
weakness. As argued forcefully already at the start of this century by Otto
Hintze, decades before Marc Bloch, this led to an institutional innovation
and to the emergence of a feudal society with the dual structure of imperial order—the *Bakufu* of the Shogun. In China, by contrast, the *ecumenical
renaissance* also saw a process of deep-seated cultural and institutional renovation. It took the form of the cultural revival of neo-Confucianism and led
to a strengthening of traditional imperial power.

Neither Jaspers nor other scholars, notably Alfred Weber, have been able
to suggest even remotely plausible hypotheses for the co-occurrence of analogous phenomena during the so-called axial age in different civilizations on
the Eurasian landmass. There might at least be a hint of such hypotheses
in the case of the ecumenical renaissance. Thus clearly across these different
civilizations, there were some important processes of cultural inter-connected-
ness, which are obvious in the relationships between China and Japan but
which might be traced in other cases as well. Furthermore, all these different
civilizations faced, to name but one possibly relevant factor, an urgent need
to design means of resource mobilization in the face of an acute threat that
affected them all, namely that of Mongolian world power.

Thirdly, there is the *formation of modernity*, the focus of this contribution.
Three features set the transformation at the turn of the 18th century apart
from previous periods of crystallization. Above all, this is the first major
period of crystallization when transformations in different parts of the world
are directly interconnected. For the other two epochal transformations, i.e.
those of the axial age and of the ecumenical renaissance, such global interconnectedness can at best be proposed in a suggestive way, but certainly
not demonstrated. Moreover, historical consciousness and reflexivity has in
this period a much more explicit focus on the nature of the public sphere
and of the state but also on the nature of scholarly and scientific practices
and institutions. In political terms, it located the public and political sphere,
rather than, say, a private or an ecclesiastical sphere, as the locales that are
necessary for transcendental reflection to be institutionally efficacious in man-
ifesting an idea of ethical life. Furthermore, this focus on the nature of the
public sphere and political order was based on ontological assumptions about
human beings of a radically new nature. Thus for the first time in history,
this idea of ethical life was premised on a radical and irreversible stance

about the principled equal rights of all human beings to participate in the macro-institutions of the public sphere and of the state. In this sense, the formation of modernity in Europe was not just another period reminiscent of the axial age or of the early emergence of a bifurcation between secular and sacred power in 12th and 13th century Europe. The discourse about language, history, agency and about societal institutions, as it was formed at the turn of the 18th century involved, as emphasized above, contesting positions concerning individual intellectual and political matters between different proponents of reform and between the advocates of different philosophical schools and political groupings. In that sense there was never, even in the most restricted Continental European setting, one single homogenous conception of modernity, much less a homogeneity of societal institutions.

Thus the 'thick', empirical, multiplicity of institutional and cultural practices after the formation of modernity cannot possibly be denied. There was, however, in epistemic terms and across all philosophical and political confrontations and divergences, a fundamental acknowledgement of the idea that agency, reflexivity, and historical consciousness might help construct a new set of institutions. These institutions were to be based on assumptions of ethical life from which no citizen could a priori be excluded and to which each citizen possessed a principled right of access. Once this stance had been taken, there was no turning back in ideational terms, no matter how long it would take during the following century for these ideas to become implemented in the political practices of different European countries.

In all three instances of cultural and institutional crystallization, the *axial age* the *ecumenical renaissance* and the *formation of modernity*, a new sense of historical consciousness, of the place of the thinking and acting self emerged. Such reflection had as its focus not solely the physical limits of personal finite existence, but in generalizable form it also brought out a discourse on ways that might bridge the chasm between the mundane and the transcendental order. Consciousness of the existence of such a chasm were in all cases also linked to consciousness about institutional practices that might serve to transcend that chasm. The discourse about such transcendence might be religious and philosophical as in the axial age, or ecclesiastically ecumenical, as in the 12th and 13th centuries in Europe, or explicitly political as in late 18th and early 19th century philosophical reflection. From the very origins of modern societal institutions there was an empirically undeniable and easily observable variety of institutional and cultural forms, even in the context of Western and Central Europe, and even more obviously so once the focus of attention shifted towards other regions of the world. However, there also emerged a set of globally relevant discursive reference points. In contrast to previous periods of crystallization, these reference points were not ecumenical in the sense that they were premised on claims to universal validity. Rather, as highlighted in the section above about the cultural constitution of modernity, they had three important features. *Firstly*, they were self-reflexive about their own cultural and institutional context. *Secondly*, they were constitutive of macro-institutions, such as a modern participatory polity, whether in the form of a nation state or a constitutional republic, that whether they were adopted or, initially often enough, rejected, became inevitable reference points on a truly global scale. *Thirdly*, they came to serve as premises for what some observers called the second scientific revolution, which involved a reconstitution of the discourses about both nature and society and the emergence of a new set of institutions for scholarly and scientific pursuits (see e.g. Rothblatt and Wittrock, 1993 and Heilbron et al., 1998). This meant that they became constitutive not only of political institutions but also of the form of modern science and its axial institution, the modem university. We seem perfectly prepared to speak about the axial age, rather than of multiple axial ages, despite much larger divergences in that period. Indeed there seems to be no valid reason to reject the notion of a 'thin' uniqueness inherent in modernity in the sense just delimited. It would be exceedingly naive and misleading to argue that there is a movement towards the global adoption of a similar set of societal and cultural practices—a vision that to most observers would appear as something of a nightmare. It would be equally misleading to deny that the formation of modernity was a deep-seated cultural crystallization that has affected all our lives throughout all countries and continents of the world and that has at its core the notions of self-reflexivity, agency and historical consciousness.

basically a big muddle
totally loses its way
seems incapable of focus

4. MODERNITY, CIVILIZATION AND GLOBALIZATION

Yitzhak Sternberg

Introduction

Any attempt to understand the contemporary social world systematically involves an implicit or explicit reliance on a specific 'philosophy of history' or *weltanschauung*, for such an attempt is based on presuppositions or arguments concerning, among other things, some major interrelated issues. First, the appropriate 'unit or units of analysis' and the delineation of the relevant boundaries. Second, the interpretation of processes and developments that the contemporary social world is part of. This involves, for example, questions regarding continuity or discontinuity, and convergence or divergence. Third, the issue of what are conceived to be the most important features for making the relevant temporal or spatial comparisons. Fourth, apprehending the relations between different contemporary societies or social groups, as well as the most important developments concerning these relations. This involves the questions of equality or hierarchy as well as those of dominance (or hegemony) and the directionality of influences. Fifth, the appropriate 'level of abstraction'; and sixth, understanding 'contemporary man'.

In what follows I will refer to several major interpretations of the contemporary social world, while making relevant comparisons between them, mainly in the light of the above mentioned issues. Of course, the differences between these perspectives are manifested in terminology, namely, in the semantics and concepts that are used.[1] However, an attempt is made here to bring these interpretations to a 'common denominator' by using the concept of 'civilization', while assuming that it may contribute to the 'comparability' of these interpretations. The emphasis will also be on what seem to me as problematic aspects in these interpretations, and suggestions for further discussion and research. In particular, I suggest here that the 'civilization' conceptualization, with its various possibilities, can be fruitful for an understanding of contemporary societies or social groups, of the differences and relations (or conflicts) between various social groups, of major processes

---

[1] On such differences of semantics and their significance, see Koselleck, 1985; Alexander, 1995; Luhmann, 1998b: 1–21.

and of 'contemporary man'; in other words, it can be fruitful in attempting to combine macro and micro levels of socio-historical analysis within the same conceptual framework.

Defining contemporary societies

There are four major contending images which attempt to understand and describe the nature and main features of contemporary societies, namely the 'industrial',[2] 'capitalist', 'modern'[3] and 'civilizational'[4] images. According to the first three images, each central concept that was indicated previously ('industrial', 'capitalist' or 'modern') symbolizes a qualitative historical discontinuity, namely, a new historical era (age or epoch) in the history of mankind—the 'industrial', 'capitalist' or 'modern' era, respectively. Furthermore, according to the adherents to each of these three images, it is actually possible to speak, respectively, of 'multiple industrial societies',[5] 'multiple capitalist societies'[6] or 'multiple modern societies' (or 'multiple modernities').[7]

And if we combine the last point with the argument concerning the appearance of a new era, then each of these three images can in fact be

---

[2] On 'industrial society' see Kerr et al., 1962; Aron, 1968a; Goldthorpe, 1971; Turner, 1975. Notions like 'information society' can be seen as 'extensions' of the 'industrial' image because they too are based primarily on the centrality of technological as well as production organization aspects in defining societal types.

[3] On 'modernity' see Parsons, 1977; Eisenstadt (1978; 1987; 2000); Germani, 1981; Berman, 1983; Anderson, 1984; Koselleck (1985; 1988); Habermas, 1987; Featherstone (1990; 1995); Giddens, 1990; Kolakowski, 1990; Turner (1990; 1994: 167–208); Heller, 1992; Osborne, 1992; Beck, Giddens and Lash, 1994; Wagner, 1994; Alexander, 1995; Kumar, 1995; Lefebvre, 1995; Luhmann, 1998b; Ortiz, 2000; Wittrock, 2000.

On 'modernization' see Eisenstadt, 1970: 289–452; Black, 1976; Parsons, 1977; Wallerstein, 1979; Germani, 1981; Bourricaud, 1987; Larrain, 1989; Beck, Giddens and Lash, 1994.

[4] On 'civilization' see Sorokin (1947; 1963); Kroeber and Kluckhohn, 1952; Bagby, 1958; Freud, 1961; Pirenne (1962; 1963); Kroeber (1963a; 1963b); Toynbee, 1965; Melko, 1969; Durkheim and Mauss, 1971; Febvre, 1973; Quigley, 1979; Braudel (1980: 177–218; 1994); Nelson, 1981; Melko and Scott, 1987; Arnason, 1988; Wallerstein, 1991a: 215–237; Arieli, 1992; Eisenstadt, 1992; Huntington (1993; 1996); Elias, 1994; Sanderson, 1995.

'Civilization' can be seen as a 'secular' term. 'Historical civilizations' are conceived as distinct, in particular, from the great religions or the 'World Religions' (in Weber's terminology). It allows an extension of the analysis spatially and temporally beyond ethnic and national groups, states etc., but not only by using the conceptualization of 'religion'. Religion can play an important part in a 'historical civilization' and hence it is even possible to speak of 'religious civilizations', but a certain 'historical civilization' can encompass several religions or be, mainly, a 'non-religious civilization'. Hence, religion, as well as other categories, can be useful as criteria for comparisons between 'historical civilizations'. See Weber, 1958; Kroeber, 1963a; Eisenstadt, 1992.

[5] See Kerr et al., 1962; Aron, 1968a

[6] In fact, Marx (1941) already spoke of 'multiple capitalist societies'.

[7] See Parsons, 1977; Eisenstadt, 2000.

interpreted in 'civilizational' or 'systemic' terms. Hence, it can be said that the proponents of each of these three images, implicitly or explicitly, talk 'civilization'—talk, respectively, about the appearance of a new 'historical civilization' in mankind's history—an 'industrial civilization', a 'capitalist civilization' (or a 'civilization of capitalism')[8] or a 'modern civilization' (or a 'civilization of modernity').[9]

Moreover, according to each of these three images, the new 'historical civilization' is described as significantly different from the previously existing 'historical civilizations' and societies. Furthermore, the new era is depicted as an era that some of its main inherent characteristics are permanent change, novelty and innovation in human life.[10] In this respect, Marx's phrase 'all that is solid melts into air'[11] aptly describes the assumptions that all three images share. It is interesting to note that, according to the 'industrial' image, one can speak of a 'post-capitalist' or 'non-capitalist' society that can still be an 'industrial society';[12] and according to the 'capitalist' image, it is possible to conceive of a 'post-industrial' or 'non-industrial' society that can still be a 'capitalist society'.[13]

Usually, however, 'modernity'[14] is charted as a wider phenomenon, with regard to institutions, processes and characteristics, than both capitalism and

---

[8] Schumpeter, the non-Marxist, devoted in his famous book *Capitalism, Socialism and Democracy* a chapter entitled 'The Civilization of Capitalism' (see Schumpeter, 1994: 121–130). There Schumpeter speaks about special characteristics of the 'capitalist civilization', such as a capitalist art and a capitalist life style.

[9] See Parsons, 1977: 215–241; Eisenstadt (1978; 2000); Germani, 1981.

[10] Change can also be manifested in a theory of recurring historical cycles; but, according to the view of the 'modern era', for example, it is not just change but also novelty and innovations that are characteristic to this era and to modernity (see Kumar, 1995). Germani even used the term 'permanent revolution' to describe this special characteristic of modernity and modernization. However, I doubt whether the term 'revolution' is still meaningful when we speak of a 'permanent revolution' in that respect. On modernity as a revolution and modernity and revolution see Germani, 1981; Berman, 1983; Anderson, 1984.

[11] See Berman, 1983.

[12] See Kerr et al., 1962; Aron, 1968a.

[13] Thus, for example, Bogdanov (1949) mentions a phase of 'commercial capitalism' which preceded the phase of 'industrial capitalism'. Furthermore, there are scholars who argue that a 'post-industrial' society can still be a capitalist society. See, for example, Touraine, 1971; Bell (1973; 1976).

[14] The terms 'modern' and 'modernity' have many meanings in the relevant literature. What is meant here by modernity is a certain type of society, the modern society that is also the most widespread and dominant society in the modern era. Hence, modernity according to this view is a 'qualitative' and a 'chronological' category. A possible alternative understanding of modernity is to conceive of it as being only a 'qualitative' and not a 'chronological' category. In that respect, see the paper of Osborne (1992), whose title, "Modernity is a qualitative, not a chronological, category" is taken from Adorno's *Minima Moralia*. On the history of the term 'modern' and on different meanings of modern and modernity, see Koselleck, 1985; Habermas, 1987; Lefebvre, 1995; Wittrock, 2000.

industrial society. Furthermore, modernity is also less 'specified' (with regard to content, time and space) than capitalism or industrial society. Hence, according to the modern image, it is possible to conceive of a 'post-industrial' or 'non-industrial' society, as well as of a 'post-capitalist' or 'non-capitalist' society that can still be a 'modern society'.[15] In certain variants of the modern image there is a further temporal and spatial extension of modernity. Phenomena, such as 'fascism', 'socialism', 'communism', 'fundamentalism' and 'postmodernity' are interpreted as, mainly, manifestations of modernity, of different aspects, or even contradictory aspects, of the modern project.[16] Hence, what can be seen as attempts to transcend modernity on the time dimension, like regenerating (or returning to) the 'pre-modern' traditions or advancing beyond modernity, are also incorporated into the project of modernity. This 'inclusiveness' is the source of the appeal and 'strength' of this image of the modern era, but is also the source of its 'weakness'. The appeal stems from the aspiration (or 'temptation')[17] to be able to explain or understand as many phenomena and developments as possible in the framework of one general theory or conceptualization.

A tendency for 'inclusiveness' can also be found in certain variants of the capitalist image (especially in certain Marxist interpretations) or the industrial image. However, because the modern image is less 'specified' and 'wider' than the industrial and capitalist images, there is also a major difference in that respect between these images. In the case of the capitalist and industrial images, it is much easier to conceive of requirements and conditions whose fulfillment will indicate the end of the capitalist or industrial society (or era). Whereas the project of modernity can be seen as bounded spatially (i.e., by the globe), though—since its beginning and ascendance—as almost unbounded with respect to time, as an endless project.

In spite of the differences between these variants of the modernity image and Fukuyama's 'end of history' thesis,[18] it is also possible to draw some parallels between them. Whereas according to Fukuyama's 'end of history' thesis, the main features of the social world have already been determined and specified, and only relatively minor developments and changes are expected to occur in the future; then, to the contrary, according to these variants of the modernity image, it is still possible that relatively significant and unpredictable developments and changes will occur. However, because of the tendency for 'inclusiveness' of these variants, it seems that all this

---

[15] See, for example, Parsons, 1977: 216–220; Arnason, 2000.
[16] See Eisenstadt, 2000. See also Giddens (1990; 1994b); Göle, 2000a.
[17] On 'temptations' in the social sciences see Wallerstein, 1995.
[18] See Fukuyama, 1992.

possible variety of changes and developments will occur within modernity, as part of the everlasting and endless project of modernity. Almost no way out of modernity can be conceived, because modernity is portrayed as absorbing all that is new and 'destroying' all that is old. Hence, the endless project of modernity can be seen as a final phase in human history and therefore as a variant of the 'end of history' theme.

According to the fourth image, the contemporary world is depicted as a world which includes several or 'multiple civilizations' (such as the 'historical civilizations' of the 'West', 'Islam' and 'East Asia'). In some variants of the modernity image, it is argued that there are several major models or civilizations of modernity, such as Europe, Latin America and the USA.[19] The view is of 'multiple civilizations' belonging to the same civilization or 'super civilization', namely, that of modernity. Hence, we actually have here an image of several 'sub-civilizations' belonging to one civilization, namely, a view of 'multiple sub-civilizations' of modernity; and not a view of 'multiple civilizations' as in the case of the fourth ('civilizational') image. Thus, of all the four images considered here, the fourth image is, indeed, the only 'multiple civilizations' image. The major civilizations which the fourth image refers to are the 'historical civilizations' that can be termed as 'pre-modern', according to the modernity image. The main dividing line is not depicted as the divide between modernity and pre-modernity (mainly, a temporal divide), but instead between historical civilizations that are conceived as 'existing' a relatively long historical time, before and after, what can be seen as the appearance of modernity (mainly, a spatial divide). In the 'multiple historical civilizations' image, then, the relation to the past is conceived as pertaining much less discontinuity than in the other three (the industrial, capitalist and modernity) images.[20] This image, *theoretically*, 'allows' the 'historical civilizations' or 'great traditions' (or 'old traditions')[21] of the 'past', as well as inter-civilizational relations, to play a far more significant role in the contemporary world and the developments over the past centuries than is acknowledged by the other three images.

It seems that some theoretical inconsistency can be found in the modernity image. Generally, this image tends to emphasize the similarities among

---

[19] See, for example, Eisenstadt, 2000.

[20] This is also a debate with regard to the appropriate place that should be given to 'tradition' in the analysis. Is all tradition 'new' or are there long-term influences of 'tradition'? Or, in other words, how far is the 'tradition' a 'new tradition'? On this issue see Shils, 1981; Hobsbawm and Ranger, 1983; Giddens, 1994b. This issue also stands at the center of the debate between 'civilizationists' and adherents to the world-system perspective. See Sanderson, 1995.

[21] On 'old traditions' etc. see Giddens, 1994b.

contemporary societies and, while doing so, also tends to stress the discontinuity with the past, with the previously existing 'historical civilizations' and 'old traditions'. Furthermore, if it is also assumed that in the modern era, these civilizations and traditions are increasingly fading away and becoming marginalized, then we have to expect that the main explanatory power in understanding not only similarities among societies, but also the uniqueness of each society and the differences and relations between societies, will increasingly be given to the specific and 'intrinsic' characteristics of modernity.

However, it can also be seen that when disciples of the modernity image *actually* analyze the unique nature and traits of particular modern societies, as well as the relations between such societies, then aspects of continuity with the 'pre-modern' past are emphasized. Thus, for example, they speak about 'Islamic modernities', 'non-Western modernities', 'Western modernity' or the hegemony of the 'West' in the contemporary world.[22] Or, in other words, they use a terminology which indicates a significant continuity with the ('pre-modern') past, a continuity of the previous 'historical civilizations' (or religions), or 'old traditions'.

Furthermore, in the several major models or civilizations of modernity variant of the modern image, the demarcation lines between different major models (or civilizations) of modernity seem to correspond to those between 'pre-modern' 'historical civilizations'. What seem to be the exceptions could be interpreted as actually being demarcation lines within the 'West', such as those between Europe and the USA,[23] and therefore not contradictory, in general outlines, to the above-mentioned correspondence. Hence, what should *theoretically* be increasingly disappearing or marginalized (the 'pre-modern' 'historical civilizations') enters the analysis (of adherents to the modern image) with almost no appropriate explanation and clarification.

It seems that the modernity image is more appropriate to understanding similarities among contemporary societies than differences and relations among these societies. With certain qualifications, the opposite can be said about the 'multiple historical civilizations' image.

Another problem of the modernity image concerns some 'moralistic' aspects of the analysis of what can be termed as the 'dialectic of modernity'. In

---

[22] See Eisenstadt, 2000; Göle, 2000.

[23] Thus, for example the unique features of the USA have been mentioned by different scholars. See, for example, Tocqueville, 1969; Huizinga, 1972; Lipset, 1996. However, the still ongoing debate is whether America should be depicted as a distinct 'historical civilization', the 'American civilization', or perhaps as being a part (or a sub-civilization) of the wider 'Western civilization'. See Hayes, 1956; Pierson, 1956; Turner, 1956; Hartz, 1964; Hofstadter, 1968; Arieli, 1992; Eisenstadt, 2000. On the general issue of 'exceptionalism' see Zolberg, 1986.

the analysis of modernity, a multiplicity of modernities as well as tensions and contradictions within modernity, are acknowledged. In that respect, among other things, the 'negative', 'pathological' or 'traumatic' side of modernity is indicated.[24] These 'negative' or 'dangerous' tendencies of modernity are mainly conceived as related to such phenomena as the Holocaust or 'Jacobinism' (or 'totalitarianism'). Thus, the 'negative' aspects of modernity are mostly attributed not to the 'major' and 'victorious' trend of modernity, but to opposing trends or to 'deviations' of modernity. These specific comparisons, as well as the tendency to identify the main 'negative' aspects as being outside the major trend, tend to diminish the possible critical outlook towards the 'mainstream' trend of modernity.

The 'postmodern' conceptualization figures prominently in the literature of recent decades.[25] There are several variants of this conceptualization. In most variants it refers to certain socio-cultural changes and to what might be seen as a postmodern 'state of mind', that are apprehended as being *within* the framework of the modernity image. Thus, for example, what is meant by postmodernity in these variants is, among other things, 'counter-modernity', 'anti-modernity', a critique of modernity, or a specific reflexivity on modernity, that are conceived as being within, and not outside, modernity.[26]

However, there is also an approach that uses the 'postmodern' terminology in order to speak of the appearance, in recent decades, of a new era and type of society in human history, namely, the 'postmodern era' (and 'postmodern' society).[27] What is manifested here is the centrality of the concept of modernity and hence the strong *substantive* connection to the modern image. This last point was among the main reasons why Albrow,[28] for example, called the new era, which in his opinion has appeared over the past few decades, as 'the global age', as something beyond modernity, while rejecting the 'postmodern' terminology for its strong substantive and conceptual connection with modernity. Moreover, acknowledging certain, or even major, recent socio-cultural changes is one thing, but arguing for the appearance and existence of a new historical era is quite another. Not every change, or even major changes, should be seen as 'epochal changes', and especially so when the latter are not adequately elaborated in theoretical terms. Accordingly, it seems to me that we still do not have enough hindsight

---

[24] See Koselleck, 1988; Eisenstadt, 2000.
[25] On 'postmodernity' see Habermas, 1981a; Giddens, 1990; Turner (1990; 1994); Denzin, 1991; Featherstone (1991; 1995); Jameson, 1991; Bauman, 1992; Jencks (1992; 1996); Smart, 1993; Hollinger, 1994; Lyon, 1994; Kumar, 1995; Castoriadis, 1997a.
[26] See, for example, Smart, 1993; Lyon, 1994.
[27] See, for example, Smart, 1993; Lyon, 1994.
[28] See Albrow, 1996.

for an assertion about the appearance, in recent decades, of a new era. Hence, for the lack of such hindsight as well as for the strong substantive connection of the postmodern conceptualization to the modernity image, the four images that were discussed here can indeed be seen as the main contending images for understanding contemporary societies.

Relations between contemporary societies or social groups

We have seen that, according to the 'multiple historical civilizations' image, inter-civilizational relations (or conflicts) exert a far greater influence on the contemporary world than is acknowledged by the other contending three images. This point was emphasized by Huntington,[29] who argues that inter-civilizational relations (or conflicts) have in fact now become the most significant ones with regard to present-day conflicts and to potential future ones. The main reasons offered by Huntington are the weakening or disappearance of other possible and potential antagonisms in the world, and his assertion that the boundaries (or 'cultural faults') between 'historical civilizations' are probably 'thicker' than all other group boundaries.

However, not enough attention is paid by Huntington to the distinction between culture, in the broad sense, and collective identity. This has implications for understanding the relations between various social groups. Thus, for example, it is possible that two social groups may become closer to each other culturally, but the conflict potentiality between these groups will not decrease and may even increase, or vice versa. What is of major importance here is how each of these groups determines itself (its 'collective identity') vis-a-vis 'others'. Moreover, what is also important, in that respect, is the degree of 'groupcentricity' (or 'groupcentrism') that accompanies these 'self' and 'other' group determinations. The greater the weight of a particular type of 'groupcentricity' in the collective identity content of a group that is manifested vis-a-vis another group, the greater too the conflict potentiality between these groups with regard to the collective identity component that corresponds to this particular type of groupcentricity.

Thus, it is possible to distinguish between different types of groupcentricity, such as 'ethnocentricity', 'natiocentricity', 'racecentricity', 'classcentricity', 'religiocentricity' and 'civilizatiocentricity' (i.e., 'Eurocentricity' or 'Westcentricity'). We also may find manifestations of several types of groupcentricity in the perceptional content of a certain group's collective identity regarding some other social group or 'others'. Therefore, in understanding

---

[29] See Huntigton, 1993; 1996.

inter-group relations, what should be considered are the group differences, the components and content of each group's collective identity, and the type or types of groupcentricity involved in these relations, as well as their relative weight in the collective identity content of each group.

Thus, for example, in understanding inter-civilizational relations and the conflict potential of such relations, we should consider the civilizational differences (i.e., cultural and other differences), the components and content of the civilizational identity and especially (with regard to the inter-civilizational conflict potential) the relative weight of 'civilizatiocentricity' in the civilizational identity content of each group involved in these relations. Hence, we should be careful 'not to bend the bent stick in the other direction'.[30] Paying attention to the influence and importance of inter-civilizational relations or conflicts (or conflict potentiality) is one thing and assuming, *a priori* and as a general supposition, that nowadays their importance is the most significant one in that respect, or that their boundaries are the 'thickest', is quite another thing.

Levels of abstraction

Moreover, a distinction should be made, in that respect, between different 'levels of abstraction', namely a more general level of abstraction and a more concrete level of abstraction. Thus, for example, in a Marxist analysis, it is possible that in a certain society several 'modes of production' can coexist simultaneously. Accordingly, a society can be defined, generally, as being a capitalist society, i.e., the capitalist mode of production is the dominant mode of production in that society. However, slavery and serfdom, for example, or other possible relations that are characteristic of feudalism, can also be found in that society, and therefore it can be said that at least three different modes of production (capitalism, feudalism and slavery) coexist simultaneously in that society.

This distinction between 'levels of abstraction' can be extended beyond the mode of production spectrum, or beyond the 'economistic' and 'monistic'[31] inclinations of Marxism, enabling other categorizations to be also taken into account in that respect. Thus, for example, a certain society can be defined at a more general level of abstraction as a 'Western society', but at the more concrete level of abstraction it could also be said that characteristics of several, or at least two, 'historical civilizations' coexist in that society,

---

[30] Bourdieu, citing Mao Tse-Tung. See Bourdieu, 1985; 1987.
[31] See, for example, Plekhanov, 1956.

although the features of the 'West' are the dominant one. Furthermore, it can be added that almost each 'historical civilization' already contains characteristics of at least one other civilization or culture, i.e., it is a 'mixed' and not a 'pure' phenomenon.[32] Other categories, such as religion, ethnicity, class, gender and race, could be included in a more concrete analysis or level of abstraction. It could open up much greater possibilities for comparisons and typologies, and thus contribute to the understanding of contemporary societies and social groups as well as the relations (and conflicts or potential conflicts) between them. However, it should be combined with the more general level of abstraction which enables us to portray the dominant characteristics and developments of a certain social group with regard to its 'internal' and 'external' aspects.

This distinction between different levels of abstraction enables us to employ a multidimensional analysis and hence not to rely only, or mainly, on an analysis of the either-or manner that tends towards 'over abstraction' and which characterizes, for example, the modern society—traditional society, or the 'West' and the 'rest' dichotomies.

'Globalization', 'modernization', 'westernization' or 'americanization'?

The process of 'globalization', and its possible impacts on the contemporary social world as well as on human life, has been much discussed lately. There are several variants of the globalization approach. According to the main variant, the essence of the globalization process can be depicted as the significant growth in the interconnectedness or interdependence of various social groups and people, as well as people's increasing awareness to this phenomenon.[33] The following discussion, unless otherwise indicated, will refer to this main variant.

As we have already seen, one variant of the globalization image proclaims that for the last several decades we have been living in the 'global age', a new historical era which goes beyond modernity.[34] Accordingly, it is impossible to speak of modernity in the 'global age', for either we are in the age of modernity or we are in the 'global age'—the two are mutually exclusive.

---

[32] See Kroeber, 1963a.
[33] On 'globalization' see Ricoeur, 1965; Featherstone (1990; 1995); Giddens, 1990; King, 1991; Robertson (1992a; 1992b); Mazlish and Buultjens, 1993; Friedman (1994; 1995); Lash and Urry, 1994; Turner, 1994; Featherstone, Lash and Robertson, 1995; Albrow, 1996; Appadurai, 1996; Hannerz, 1996; Spybey, 1996; Amin, 1997; Jameson and Miyoshi, 1998; Robertson and Khondker, 1998.
[34] See Albrow, 1996.

However, most globalization theorists do not accept the 'global age' variant, and argue instead that the contemporary social world can still be defined mainly as a modern world. But if this view of a new 'global age' in human history is rejected, is it, nevertheless, possible to speak of modernity in an age of globalization? or capitalism in the age of globalization? (terms that are used in the relevant literature).[35] What does it mean? Is it, for example, possible that we are simultaneously in the era of modernity as well as in the (or an) era of globalization? Is it then possible—and if so, in what ways and qualifications—to speak, for example, of 'multiple and/or simultaneous historical ages' in a certain historical epoch? These issues have not been sufficiently elaborated and clarified in the relevant literature, and such a clarification and elaboration is required. A possible solution is to allow for not only, or mainly, a spatial multiplicity but also for a wider simultaneous temporal multiplicity while identifying what is more dominant or significant, in that respect.

Generally, the globalization approach can be seen as an alternative to 'imperialist' outlooks, to the 'world system' perspective and to the 'civilizational analysis' approach.[36] The major contribution of the globalization approach (with the exception of the new global age variant) and of the world system perspective, can be seen as mainly related to defining and understanding relations between societies and social groups, as well as central processes of the contemporary social world. With regard to defining the nature and characteristics of contemporary societies, both approaches tend to adhere either to the modern image (mainly the globalization approach but also the world system perspective) or to the capitalist image (mainly the world system perspective). The main differences between these two approaches concern the relative weight that should be given to cultural aspects in the analysis of processes and inter-group relations, as well as the hierarchy prevailing among different social groups or societies, and the directionality of influences.

Regarding both these aspects, the globalization approach offers an alternative to the world system perspective. However, whereas giving cultural aspects a more significant place in the analysis can be seen as an 'improvement' or as a 'strength' of the globalization approach, it can equally be said that a major 'weakness' of the approach is that it does not give an appropriate place to hierarchy and inequality among social groups and societies, nor to the directionality of influences. Furthermore, it does not allow for flexibility and subtlety in these matters by posing, for example, an alternative between a one-way directionality only, or no directionality at all.

---

[35] See, for example, Amin, 1997; Eisenstadt, 2000.
[36] See Roudometof and Robertson, 1995.

With regard to issues concerning the understanding of the main characteristics and developments of the relations between different social groups (or societies) in the contemporary world—i.e. questions of equality or hierarchy as well as of dominance (or hegemony) and the directionality of influences—the globalization conceptualization can be described as a 'neutral' one. In that respect, similarities and parallels can be drawn between the concept of globalization and concepts such as 'modernization' and 'socialization',[37] in spite of all the differences between these three concepts. It is argued by the proponents of concepts such as modernization and globalization that the processes which these concepts intend to portray cannot be reduced to concepts, such as 'Westernization' 'AngloSaxonization' or 'Americanization'; or, in other words, that they are not expressing 'cultural imperialism',[38] 'one-way imperialism'[39] or one-way directionality of influences.[40] However, the alternative should not be posed in an either-or manner, as existing only between a conceptualization expressing a one-way directionality (or one-directional influences), or a 'neutral' conceptualization that does not express any directionality at all or, in other words, which expresses an almost infinite range of directionalities. In such a 'neutral' conceptualization, for example, the 'West' is de-centered conceptually and theoretically without actually being de-centered in reality.

The third alternative can be a conceptualization and theoretization that indicates and expresses directionality, but not necessarily a one-way directionality. Thus, for example, one can say it is true that modernization or globalization are not synonymous with Westernization or Americanization, but, nevertheless a concomitant acknowledgment could also be made that the Western civilization or the 'American sub-civilization' exert a far greater influence on the relevant developments and processes than other social groups, whether civilizations, religions, societies etc. Of course, the analysis can develop further by comparing different directionalities according to various spheres (i.e., economy, culture, politics) and dominant groups.

Moreover, distinctions should be made in this respect between 'directionality' and 'intentionality' of influences as well as between processes that indicate a directionality of influences and processes that attest to outcomes. Thus, with regard to the latter distinction, for example, a Westernization indicating the directionality of influences does not necessarily lead to sameness and one-to-one similarities or correspondence with regard to outcomes

---

[37] See Williams, 1977: 117.
[38] On 'cultural imperialism' see Tomlinson, 1991
[39] See Giddens, 1994b.
[40] See Abu-Lughod, 1991; Robertson (1992b; 1995a); Giddens, 1994b; Göle, 2000.

in the 'non-Western' society. Hence, for example, modernization (when indicating the outcomes) and Westernization (when indicating the directionality of influences) do not necessarily exclude each other.

It should be indicated that in the whole discussion of globalization given here, I refer, unless otherwise specified, to what can be seen as the main variant of the globalization image in the relevant literature. However, we should bear in mind that there are also other variants. Thus, for example, in certain variants globalization is conceived as connected to imperialism or some other group dominance (or hegemony). Following these variants, globalization can be conceptualized as relating to a 'higher stage of imperialism' (or a new and different stage, or unique type of imperialism in a non-evolutionary conceptualization); whereas, in other, more economistically inclined variants, globalization can be conceptualized as linked to the 'perfection' of 'free market' mechanisms. However, globalization processes are considered in these latter variants not within a conceptual framework whose main concept and theoretical interest is 'globalization'; but rather in conceptual frameworks whose main concepts and theoretical interests are 'imperialism', in general—and what was called by Fieldhouse 'capitalist imperialism',[41] in particular—in the first case, and 'capitalism', in the second case.

There are also differences between the globalization approach and the 'civilizational analysis' approach. One such difference concerns the directionality issue that was already dealt with in the comparison between the globalization approach and the world system perspective. The 'civilizational analysis' approach makes far more allowance for such a directionality, as well as for the existence of a 'dominant civilization'.

Another difference between these two approaches relates to the culture issue. Both approaches grant cultural aspects a significant place in the analysis. However, although several variants of the globalization approach take into account long-term considerations—i.e., globalization is depicted in them as a long-term phenomenon—what is characteristic of this approach (including these 'long-term' variants) is the emphasis on the influences and importance of the 'new traditions' and of the contemporary 'ideological-cultural networks' (and not the 'old traditions' or the 'great traditions', namely the traditions emphasized in the 'classical' 'civilizational analysis'). Hence, in the globalization approach, civilizational analysis is reduced to an analysis of *contemporary* 'ideological-cultural networks'[42] as opposed to the

---

[41] See Fieldhouse, 1967.
[42] See Roudometof and Robertson, 1995.

long-term 'civilizational processes' (which can be seen as distinct from, as well as connected to, 'civilizing processes') that are characteristic of the 'classical' 'civilizational analysis' approach. By doing so, one of the possible main 'strengths' of the 'classical' civilizational analysis approach, namely the considering of long-term processes (such as cycles, secular or evolutionary long-term trends etc.) is ignored or is instead seen as a 'weakness'. So, within the framework of the globalization approach, it is possible to consider long-term processes of globalization; but when it comes to the 'civilization' conceptualization within this framework, only contemporary 'networks' are taken into consideration. Hence, the attempt to incorporate civilizational analysis in the framework of the globalization approach can be seen as a manifestation of the 'retreat of sociologists into the present' which was criticized by Elias.[43]

The differences between these approaches with regard to civilizations are strongly related to the differences between them with regard to defining and understanding the main nature and characteristics of the contemporary era and contemporary societies. In that respect, the image of the globalization approach is, mainly, the "modern" image, whereas the image of the civilizational analysis approach is the civilizational (or the 'multiple historical civilizations') image—two images that differ greatly in terms of their continuity/discontinuity assumptions. Globalization processes, in the 'consequence of modernity'[44] as well as in the 'precondition for modernity'[45] variant, are conceived as connected to modernity with regard to the temporal dimension and hence are confined temporally by the pre-modernity/modernity temporal divide; whereas the civilizational analysis approach is not confined by the temporal divide between modernity and pre-modernity when considering long-term or 'civilizational' processes.

However, we have to bear in mind that the 'classical' civilizational analysis approach can be criticized as an 'over-reifying' approach.[46] Questions can be asked with regard to the coherence or cohesiveness as well as to the continuity of 'historical civilizations'.[47]

---

[43] See Elias, 1987.
[44] See Giddens, 1990.
[45] See Robertson, 1992b.
[46] See also Wallerstein, 1995.
[47] A critique on viewing 'civilizations' as integrated entities was raised, for example, by Sorokin. It is also interesting to note that Sorokin argued for the integration of what he called 'supersystems'—larger constructs than civilizations. However, the question with regard to the integration of such large 'units of analysis' as 'civilizations' should not be posed in an either-or manner, namely total or complete integration or no integration at all. See Kroeber, 1963b: 173–182.

Apprehending 'contemporary man'

In the attempt to understand the contemporary social world, the issue of understanding or defining 'contemporary man' is an important, but also a relatively neglected one. This issue has to do with the possibility of an analytical and conceptual unification of macro and micro levels of socio-historical analysis. In such an attempt, the concept of 'civilization' can be fruitful and I will suggest, in that respect, a possible analytical 'mixture' between the concept of civilization in singular and civilizations (or 'historical civilizations') in the plural, as well as some analytical and conceptual distinctions. Following Elias and Freud,[48] it can be said that in the 'civilizing process', which is a long-term process involving self-constraints and transformations in human behavior, man is departing from his 'natural situation' and becomes a 'civilized man'; i.e., he becomes restricted in his practices, thoughts and feelings by social arrangements, ways of life, manners, values and norms, namely by civilization (in the singular). Hence, a 'civilized man' is not superior or inferior to the man in his 'natural situation', but just different from him, among other things, with regard to constraints and restrictions. In each 'historical civilization' (plural) man is 'civilized', man is constrained and restricted in his behavior and thought; and therefore we can also find a 'civilized man' in each such 'historical civilization'. In each 'historical civilization', though, the constraints and restrictions on man's behavior are unique to that civilization: in other words, we have to acknowledge the existence of several or multiple 'civilizing processes'. Hence, in each 'historical civilization' we can find a unique socio-historical human type (with his specific nature and traits) that is characteristic to this 'historical civilization', namely, the specific 'civilizational man'.[49]

Moreover, the distinction between 'civilizing processes' (long-term processes which mainly concern developments in the individual's behavioral characteristics) and 'civilizational processes' (long-term processes which mainly concern the developments and characteristics of 'historical civilizations') while acknowledging and studying their interconnectedness and their possible multiplicity, could be fruitful for understanding macro and micro processes and levels of socio-historical analysis. These processes could be seen

---

[48] See Freud, 1961; Elias, 1994; Turner, 1994: 174–176.
[49] On the connection between society and personality see Sorokin, 1947; Huizinga, 1955; Weber, 1958; Freud, 1961; Kerr et al., 1962; Marcuse, 1968; Inkeles (1976; 1997); Elias, 1994; Schumpeter, 1994: 121–130.

as alternative or complementary possibilities to the globalization approach for studying and considering long-term socio-historical processes. They are also distinct from other processes that relate to the 'civilization' conceptualization, such as Westernization, Americanization etc.

Furthermore, it seems to me that analytical distinctions such as 'civilized man', 'civilizational man', 'civilizing processes' and 'civilizational processes' that are interconnected as well as relevant to important aspects of the social world and to a macro *and* micro analysis within the same conceptual framework, enable us to highlight the potential fruitfulness of a 'civilizational' conceptualization (plural and singular). Thus, for example, such a macro and micro analysis within the same conceptual framework is absent in the world-system approach and hence, at least in that respect, it seems to me that the concept 'historical civilization' is more appropriate than the concept 'historical system', suggested by Wallerstein.[50]

The attempt to understand the unique nature and characteristics of 'modern man'[51] can be apprehended in the light of what was said previously. 'Modern man' can be seen as the specific 'civilizational man' of the 'modern civilization'. However, if we adhere, for example, to the 'multiple historical civilizations' image with regard to the definition and understanding of the contemporary social world, then we expect to have several types of 'civilizational man' in this world. Hence, 'contemporary man' can be described as 'modern man' or 'homo modernicus'; as 'capitalist man';[52] as 'industrial man';[53] as 'global man' or 'homo globalicus'; or as specific types of 'civilizational or sub-civilizational man', such as 'Western man', 'homo Americanicus', 'homo Europeicus' or 'homo Islamicus'.

Moreover, what is more important is to identify the specific characteristics of each such 'civilizational man' in the contemporary world. It is not enough to declare the existence of, for example, a 'modern man' or a 'Western man'. More specific characteristics and criteria for describing, defining and understanding the 'contemporary man' are needed. Thus, for example, the following relevant (as well as other) concepts could be used: 'homo sapiens'; 'homo faber';[54] 'homo fabricatus';[55] 'homo ludens';[56] 'alienated

---

[50] See Wallerstein, 1991a; 1995.
[51] On 'modern man' see Inkeles, 1976; 1997.
[52] On 'capitalist man' see, for example, Schumpeter, 1994: 121–130.
[53] On 'industrial man' see Kerr et al., 1962.
[54] On 'homo faber' see Avineri, 1968.
[55] On 'homo fabricatus' see Habermas, 1970.
[56] On 'homo ludens' see Huizinga, 1955.

man';[57] 'one-dimensional man';[58] 'rational man'; 'godless man';[59] 'homo Hebraicus'; 'homo Hellenicus';[60] 'ideational man' or 'sensate man'.[61]

Conclusion

An attempt is made here to refer comparatively and critically to major interpretations of the contemporary social world, and more specifically, of contemporary man, societies, relations (or conflicts) between societies or social groups and major processes. The concept of 'civilization' was used as the 'common denominator' for these interpretations as well as for highlighting its possible usefulness in understanding these issues and in attempting to combine macro and micro levels of socio-historical analysis in the same conceptual framework. It is argued here that, in spite of the usually-emphasized differences between certain variants of the 'modern' image and Fukuyama's 'end of history' thesis, it is also possible to draw some parallels between them. It seems that, according to these variants, almost no way out of modernity can be conceived, because modernity is portrayed as absorbing all that is new and 'destroying' all that is old. Hence, the endless project of modernity can be seen as a final phase in human history and therefore, as a variant of the 'end of history' theme.

Attention is paid also to what seems to be an inconsistency between what should follow from the *theoretical* assumptions of the modernity image and the *actual* terminology, conceptualization and analysis of adherents to this image. It is argued, in this respect, that what should be, *theoretically*, increasingly disappearing or marginalized (the 'pre-modern' 'historical civilizations') enters the analysis (of adherents to the modern image) with almost no appropriate explanation and clarification.

It is suggested that, in understanding inter-group relations and the conflict potential of such relations, what should be especially considered are the group differences, the components and content of each group's collective identity, and the type or types of 'groupcentricity' involved in these relations, as well as their relative weight in the collective identity content of each of these groups. Furthermore, it is maintained that a distinction between

---

[57] On 'alienation' and 'alienated man' see Tucker, 1961; Fromm (1962; 1966); Josephson and Josephson, 1962; Avineri, 1968; Ollman, 1971.
[58] See Marcuse, 1968.
[59] See Kolakowski, 1990: 3–13.
[60] On the possibilities of 'homo Hebraicus' and 'homo Hellenicus' see Arnold, 1969.
[61] See Sorokin, 1947.

a more general and a more concrete 'level of abstraction' enables us to employ a multidimensional analysis and hence not to rely only or mainly on an analysis of the either-or manner that tends towards 'over abstraction', and that characterizes, for example, the modern society—traditional society, or the 'West' and the 'rest' dichotomies.

In its main variant, the 'globalization' conceptualization can be described as a 'neutral' conceptualization, and it can be said that a major 'weakness' of the globalization approach is that it does not give an appropriate place to hierarchy and inequality among social groups and societies nor to the directionality of influences. Furthermore, it does not allow for flexibility and subtlety in these matters by posing, for example, an alternative between a one-way directionality only, or no directionality at all. Moreover, the attempt to incorporate 'civilizational analysis' in the framework of the globalization approach can be seen as a manifestation of the 'retreat of sociologists into the present'.

It is argued that the concept of 'civilization' can be fruitful in the attempt to combine macro *and* micro levels of socio-historical analysis within the same conceptual framework, and some analytical distinctions are suggested in that respect.

5. ISLAM AND MODERNITY*

Dale F. Eickelman

The secular bias of modernization theory has had a significant role in deflecting attention away from the role of religious practices and values in contemporary societies, particularly in the Muslim majority world. In the early 1960s, one leading public intellectual saw the Muslim world as facing an unpalatable choice: either a 'neo-Islamic totalitarianism' intent on 'resurrecting the past', or a 'reformist Islam' which would open "the sluice gates and [be] swamped by the deluge."[1] Another suggested that Middle Eastern societies faced the stark choice of "Mecca or mechanization."[2] At the least, such views suggested an intensely negative view of the possibilities of evolution in Muslim societies and an inherent preference for militantly secularizing reformers such as Turkey's Mustafa Kemal Ataturk (1881–1938) and the Pahlavi Shahs of Iran, Reza Shah (1878–1944) and his son, Mohammed Reza Shah (1919–80). Later commentators were equally unrelenting. As recently as 1994 Ernest Gellner reiterated the view that 'Muslim society' remained the exception to the pervasive trend towards a shared culture of nationalism, with its ensuing fruit of modernity—commonly educated, mutually substitutable, atomized individuals with the potential for participating in a 'Civil Society'. In this view, civil society precludes the 'ideological monopoly' that Islam supposedly enjoins.[3]

In such formulations, Islam is merely a particularly salient example of the diminishing or obstructive role of religion and of religious thinkers in modern society. Open societies claim to respect religion and religious worship. At the same time, however, in the words of philosopher Richard Rorty, religion usually functions as a 'conversation-stopper' outside of circles of believers.[4] A slightly kinder, gentler, representation of the role of religious intellectuals in modernization theory is offered by Edward Shils. For him, intellectuals possess an 'innate need' to be in "frequent communication with symbols which are more general than the immediate concrete situations of

---

* A different version of this chapter was published in *Daedalus*, 129 (1), 2000
[1] Halpern, 1963: 129.
[2] Lerner, 1964: 405.
[3] Gellner, 1994a: 211.
[4] Cited in Keane, 1999: 12.

everyday life."[5] Although intellectual work originally arose from religious occupations, Shils writes that religious orientations in modern times attract "a diminishing share of the creative capacities of the oncoming intellectual elite." In Shils' view, among Western intellectuals in earlier periods, and Asian and African intellectuals since the nineteenth century, "the tradition of distrust of secular and ecclesiastical authority—and in fact of tradition as such—has become the chief secondary tradition of the intellectuals."[6] The notion of the sacred has shifted in his view from religious concerns to a focus on and mastery of the technological, organizational, and political skills most useful in forging a modern state in the face of congeries of supposedly primordial loyalties. The present thus belongs to the liberals and the technocrats, found primarily in the differentiated 'modern' class. Shils argues that only intellectuals attached to 'modern' values have the vision to rise above parochial identities and to attach themselves to the notion of a modern nation-state. How disconcerting to this view of modernity and the role of the nation state to see no less a committed political leader than Vaclav Havel write that "human rights, human freedoms, and human dignity have their deepest roots outside the perceptible world." On the state and its probable role in the future, Havel says that "while the state is a human creation, human beings are the creation of God."[7]

Common to all variants of modernization theory is the assumption of a declining role for religion, except as a private matter, as modernization proceeds. To move toward modernity, political leaders must displace the authority of religious leaders and devalue the importance of traditional religious institutions. 'Modernity' is seen as an "enlargement of human freedoms" and an "enhancement of the range of choices" as people began to "take charge" of themselves.[8] 'Secularization' thus refers to the fact that religions, and religious intellectuals, come to have a less prominent or influential position in modern societies. Religion can retain its influence only by conforming to such norms as 'rationality' and relativism, or by making compromises with science, economic concerns, and the state.

Paradoxically, however, it is easy to see formidable challenges to modernization theory. Of all the countries of the Third World, Iran was a society that had undergone enormous modernization prior to 1978–1979. Nonetheless, revolution ensued and not political stability, with the greatest challenge emanating from the growing urban middle classes, those who had

---

[5] Shils, 1972: 16.
[6] Shils, 1972: 17.
[7] Havel, 1999: 4–6.
[8] Madan, 1987: 747–759.

benefited the most from modernization. Moreover, it was religious sentiment and leadership, not the secular intelligentsia, that gave the revolution
its coherence and force. An Iranian political scientist, Fariba Adelkhah goes
ever further. She argues that the major transformations of the Iranian revolution took place since the 1990s, with the coming of age of a new generation of Iranians who were not even born at the time of the revolution
and who therefore had a significantly different interpretation of social context than that of the preceding generation. Adelkhah argues that a 'religious
public sphere' (*espace public confessionel*) has emerged in Iran in which politics
and religion are subtly intertwined, and not always in ways anticipated by
Iran's established religious leaders. The emergence of this public sphere has
also been accompanied by a greater sense of personal autonomy for both
women and men.[9] Likewise, Latin America offers a contrary example to the
conventional wisdom of modernization theory. In Peru and Guatemala, for
example, new networks of trust, confidence, and organizational capacities
have arisen with religious change as groups of clergy, including progressive
Catholics in Peru and evangelicals in Guatemala, contribute to creating a
social capital in which "'stability' is created from below, not imposed from
above."[10] The United States might serve as a further example.[11] Nonetheless,
it is primarily in the Muslim world that—in Gilles Kepel's evocative phrase—
we are faced with the "revenge of God."[12] In a globalized McWorld, only
the 'green menace' of 'Jihad' offers resistance. Or does it?

The return of religion

It is easy to be critical of Samuel Huntington's 'West vs. Rest' argument,
but he was one of the first political scientists to spur a more careful assessment of the allegedly clear-cut division between modernity and tradition.[13]
With more force than others, Huntington pointed out that 'tradition' is not
a residual concept but co-exists with the modern, and that a number of
traditions may co-exist in any given society—'multiple modernities' in the
words of Shmuel Eisenstadt.[14] Ethnicity, caste, and clientelism could be distinctly modern. In a word, Huntington reintroduced the concept of culture
to international relations theory. The problem with his later formulation is

---

[9] Adelkhah, 1998: 152–247.
[10] Levine and Stoll, 1997: 75.
[11] Wuthnow, 1994.
[12] Kepel, 1994.
[13] Huntington, 1993. See also Eickelman, 1997: 35–38.
[14] Eisenstadt, 1996a.

that, having reintroduced culture and religion to thinking about politics, he overstated its coherence and force. Culture became the independent variable.

The stark alternative of regarding religion as the dependent variable or regarding it as an independent variable can be avoided if, for want of a better term, we adopt an approach that can be called symbolic politics, the interpretation of symbols and the control of institutions, formal and informal, that produce and sustain them. This interpretation of symbols is played out against the backdrop of an underlying framework of the implicit values and practices embedded in a 'social imaginary'—the implicit, background understandings against which the beliefs and practices in any given society are formulated.[15] Such background understandings are common to adherents of a religion, be it Islam, Christianity, or Hinduism, although evolving doctrinal considerations are only one factor among many that contribute to the creation of this framework.

The idea of politics as a struggle about people's imaginations is a corrective to some conventional thinking. The notion of politics as centered on power relations and 'interests' does not take account of relations among individuals in a society or between societies that are based on what they think is right, just, or religiously ordained. More broadly, politics can be conceived as cooperation in and contest over symbolic production and control of the institutions—formal and informal—which serve as the symbolic arbiters of society. Politics as Leviathan is thus decisively abandoned in favor of politics as symbol maker.[16]

The role of symbolic politics in general, or 'Muslim politics' in the case of many Muslim societies, would be seen as less exceptional if the European experience with secularism was revisited. Historian Dominique Colas argues that religious discourse was a basic precondition for the rise of the early modern public sphere in Europe.[17] Strong Christian traces remain in such matters as blasphemy laws, religious holidays, and public prayers.[18] Indeed, contemporary defenders of secularism often exaggerate the durability and open-mindedness of thoroughly secular institutions, be they in the United States, Turkey, or India. In the context of the Muslim majority Middle East, the thorough-going secularism of some governing elites is associated with authoritarianism and intolerance.

Because the Muslim majority world remains feared by those who regard it as the last outpost of the anti-modern, the role of religious intellectuals

---

[15] See Taylor, 1993: 218–219.
[16] See Eickelman and Piscatori, 1996: 9.
[17] Colas, 1997.
[18] Keane, 1999: 12.

in contributing to an emerging public sphere is often overlooked. There has been a rapid growth of mass education throughout the Muslim world over the past half century.[19] In country after country since the 1950s, educational systems have vastly expanded. Even where educational expansion has not kept up with population growth, large numbers of citizens now speak a common language. Education contributes to massification, objectification, and the systematization of the religious experience, eroding intellectual and physical boundaries and enabling connections to be made across formerly impenetrable boundaries of class, locality, language, and ethnic group.

Both mass education and mass communications, particularly the proliferation of media and the means by which people communicate, profoundly influence how people think about the language of religious and political authority throughout the Muslim world. We are still in the early stages of understanding how different media—print, television, radio, cassettes, music, and the Internet—influence groups and individuals, encouraging unity in some contexts and fragmentation in others. Although rivaled by other media, the written word remains a privileged cultural vehicle for shaping religious beliefs and practices throughout the Muslim world. Books and pamphlets, including banned ones, are talked about and invoked as authority in sermons, cassettes, lectures, reviews, and conversations. In seeking to ban and confiscate them, censors only draw attention to their existence and increase their circulation.[20]

At the high end of this transformation is the rise to significance of books such as *al-Kitab wa-l-Qur'an: Qira'a Mu'asira* [The Book and the Qur'an: A Contemporary Interpretation], an 800-page book written by the Syrian civil engineer Muhammad Shahrur, as well as subsequent books elaborating his views on the role of the state, civil society, and democracy in Qur'anic thought.[21] The first book has sold tens of thousands of copies throughout the Arab world in both authorized (Damascus and Beirut) and pirate (Cairo) editions, and is widely circulated by photocopy elsewhere (including Saudi Arabia), in spite of the fact that its circulation has been banned or discouraged.

Books such as Shahrur's could not have been imagined before there were large numbers of people able to read it and understand its advocacy of the need to reinterpret ideas of religious authority and tradition and apply

---

[19] See Eickelman, 1998.
[20] Eickelman and Anderson, 1997: 6.
[21] Shahrur, 1992; 1994; 1996.

Islamic precepts to contemporary society. Yet resistance to such challenges to established authority has also been intense.

Shahrur draws an analogy between the Copernican revolution and Qur'anic interpretation, which he says has been shackled for centuries by the conventions of medieval jurists, who had mastered the craft of creating chains (*silsilas*), of traditions of authoritative learning:

> People believed for a long time that the sun revolved around the earth, but they were unable to explain some phenomena derived from this assumption until one person, human like themselves, said, "The opposite is true: The earth revolves around the sun" . . . After a quarter of a century of study and reflection, it dawned on me that we Muslims are shackled by prejudices (*musallimat*), some of which are completely opposite the [correct perspective].[22]

On issues ranging from the role of women in society to rekindling a 'creative interaction' with non-Muslim philosophies, Shahrur argues that Muslims should re-interpret sacred texts anew and apply them to contemporary social and moral issues: "If Islam is sound [*salih*] for all times and places," then we must not neglect historical developments and the interaction of different generations. We must act as if "the Prophet just . . . informed us of this Book."[23]

Shahrur's ideas directly challenge the authoritative tradition of Qur'anic exegesis (*tafsir*) and Islamic jurisprudence (*fiqh*). The subtitle of his first book—"a contemporary interpretation"—uses the term *qira'a*, which can mean either reading or interpretation, rather than the term *tafsir*, which directly evokes the established conventions of traditional Islamic learning from which Shahrur advocates a decisive break. For many Muslims and established men of religious learning, Shahrur argues that traditional disciplines of learning such as *tafsir* have implicitly acquired an authority equal to that of the Qur'an itself, except that the juridical tradition says little about tyranny, absolutism, and democracy.[24] Such ideas are at the center of an emerging social imaginary.

 · Because Shahrur's ideas pose such basic challenges to existing authority, he has been attacked in Friday sermons in Damascus and elsewhere, even though one leading legal scholar, Wael Hallaq, recently wrote that Shahrur's efforts to reformulate Islamic jurisprudence are the 'most convincing' of all contemporary thinkers.[25] These commentaries on Shahrur are all the more

---

[22] Shahrur, 1992: 29.
[23] Shahrur, 1994: 23. As popular as Shahrur's views are in some circles, it severely underestimates the ability of *madrasa*-trained religious scholars to adapt their version of authoritative religious learning to new contexts. However, most observers agree *madrasa*-trained scholars are losing their audience and former authority.
[24] Shahrur, 1994: 23.
[25] Hallaq, 1997: 253.

noteworthy because his notion of disseminating his ideas is almost as formally rigorous as Kant's notion of 'public' contained in his essay on the Enlightenment, in which the idea of 'public' is the words of a writer appearing before readers without the help of authoritative intermediaries such as preachers, judges, and rulers. With the exception of a study circle in Damascus, his primary means of communication is the book, an unadorned means of persuasion that appeals to a growing educated middle class and continues to represent the pinnacle of knowledge to others.

Shahrur is not alone in attacking both conventional religious wisdom and the intolerant certainties of religious radicals and in arguing instead for a constant and open re-interpretation of how sacred texts apply to social and political life. Another Syrian thinker, the secularist Sadiq Jalal al-'Azm, for instance, does the same. A debate between al-'Azm and Shaykh Yusif al-Qaradawi, a conservative religious intellectual, was broadcast on al-Jazira Satellite TV (Qatar) on May 27, 1997. For the first time in the memory of many viewers, the religious conservative came across as the weaker, more defensive voice. A similar debate took place in December 1997 on the same program between Nasir Hamid Abu Zayd and the Egyptian religious thinker, Muhammad 'Imara. Such discussions are unlikely to be rebroadcast on state-controlled television in most Arab nations, where programming on religious and political themes is generally cautious. Nevertheless, satellite technology and videotape render traditional censorship ineffective. Tapes of these broadcasts circulate from hand to hand in Morocco, Oman, Syria, Egypt, and elsewhere.

Other voices also advocate reform. Fethullah Gülen, Turkey's answer to media-savvy American evangelist Billy Graham, appeals to a mass audience. In televised chat shows, interviews, and occasional sermons, Gülen speaks about Islam and science, democracy, modernity, religious and ideological tolerance, the importance of education, and current events. Because he regards Turkish nationalism as compatible with Islam, Gülen has the pulse of a wide spectrum of religiously minded Turks.[26] Religious movements such as Turkey's Risale-i Nur appeal increasingly to religious moderates, and in stressing the link between Islam, reason, science, and modernity, and the lack of inherent clash between 'East' and 'West', promote education at all levels and appeal to a growing numbers of educated Turks. One need not visit Turkey to learn more about the movement, for its Website is available in English and Turkish.

Iran's Abdukarim Soroush argues that a proper understanding of Islam

---

[26] Aras, 1998; Eickelman, 1998.

enjoins dialogue, a willingness to understand the opinions of others, adaptation, and civility. Indonesian and Malaysian moderates make similar arguments.[27] To the annoyance of more conservative clerics, Soroush has captured the religious imagination of Persian speakers in Iran and abroad, and his work, in translation and on the Internet in several languages including Turkish, Arabic, and English, has a reach far beyond Iran.

Not all religious books are aimed at highbrows. Mass schooling has created a wide audience of people who read but are not literary sophisticates, and there has been an explosive growth in what a French colleague of mine, Yves Gonzalez-Quijano, calls generic 'Islamic books'—inexpensive, attractively printed texts intended for such readers.[28] Some of these books address practical questions of how to live as a Muslim in the modern world and the perils of neglecting Islamic obligations, and not all appeal to reason and moderation. Many have bold, eye-catching covers and sensational titles such as *The Terrors of the Grave, or What Follows Death*,[29] while other, more subdued works offer advice to young women on how to live as Muslims today. Often based on the sermons of popular preachers, Islamic books are written in a breezy, colloquial style rather than the cadences of traditional literary Arabic, and are sold on sidewalks and outside mosques rather than in bookstores. While Egyptian Nobel Laureate Naguib Mahfouz is considered successful if he sells 5,000 copies of one of his novels in a year in his own country, Islamic books often have sales in six figures.

As a result of direct and broad access to the printed, broadcast, and taped word, more and more Muslims take it upon themselves to interpret the textual sources—classical or modern—of Islam. Much has been made of the 'opening up' (*infitah*) of the economies of many Muslim countries, allowing 'market forces' to reshape economies, no matter how painful the consequences in the short run. In a similar way, intellectual market forces support some forms of religious innovation and activity over others. In Bangladesh, women's romance novels, once a popular specialty distributed in secular bookstores, now have Islamic counterparts which are distributed through Islamic bookstores, making it difficult to distinguish between 'Muslim' romance novels and 'secular' ones.[30] The result is a collapse of earlier, hierarchical notions of religious authority based on claims to the mastery of fixed bodies of religious texts. Even when there are state-appointed religious authorities—as in Oman, Saudi Arabia, Iran, Egypt, Malaysia, and some of the

---

[27] Vakili, 1996.
[28] Gonzalez-Quijano, 1998: 171–198.
[29] al-Tahtawi, 1987.
[30] Huq, 1999.

Central Asian republics—there no longer is any guarantee that their word will be heeded, or even that they themselves will follow the lead of the regime.

Religious intellectuals in the emerging public sphere

Thinkers such as Muhammad Shahrur are redrawing the boundaries of public and religious life in the Muslim-majority world by challenging religious authority. The replacement they suggest implies a constructive fragmentation. With the advent of mass higher education has come an objectification of Islamic tradition in the eyes of many believers, so that questions such as "What is Islam?" "How does it apply to the conduct of my life?" and "What are the principles of faith?" are foregrounded in the consciousness of many believers and explicitly discussed. These objectified understandings have irrevocably transformed Muslim relations to sacred authority. Of crucial importance in this process has been a 'democratization' of the politics of religious authority and the development of a standardized language inculcated by mass higher education, the mass media, travel, and labor migration. This has led to an opening up of the political process and heightened competition for the mantles of political and religious authority. Without fanfare, the notion of Islam as dialogue and civil debate is gaining ground.

A new sense of public is emerging throughout Muslim-majority states and Muslim communities elsewhere. It is shaped by increasingly open contests over the use of the symbolic language of Islam. New and accessible modes of communication have made these contests increasingly global, so that even local issues take on transnational dimensions. Muslims, of course, act not just as Muslims but according to class interests, out of a sense of nationalism, on behalf of tribal or family networks, and from all the diverse motives which characterize human endeavor. Increasingly, however, large numbers of Muslims explain their goals in terms of the normative, globalized language of Islam. Muslim identity issues are not unitary or identical, but such issues have become a significant force. It is in this sense that one can speak of an emerging Muslim public sphere and a reconsideration of the role of religion in 'modern' societies elsewhere.

This distinctly public sphere exists at the intersections of religious, political, and social life and contributes to the creation of civil society. With access to contemporary forms of communication that range from the press and broadcast media to fax machines, audio and video cassettes, from the telephone to the Internet, Muslims, like Christians, Hindus, Jews, Sikhs, and protagonists of Asian and African values, have more rapid and flexible ways of building and sustaining contact with constituencies than was available in earlier decades. The asymmetries of the earlier mass media revolution are being reversed by new media in new hands. This combination of new media and new contributors to religious and political debates fosters an awareness on the part of all actors of the diverse ways in which Islam and Islamic values can be created. It feeds into new senses of a public space that is discursive, performative, and participative, and not confined to formal institutions recognized by state authorities.

Just as there is general scholarly recognition that there are multiple paths to modernity,[31] there is a practical awareness of multiple claimants to the task of staging virtue, including a public engagement in the name of religion. In this respect, print or other media direct consciousness to and craft certain models of civility, membership within a community, and citizenship within a nation, all resting on more or less mutual packages of commitments and expectations.[32] As in Hinduism and Christianity, the real 'clash of civilizations' in the modern era is not, as Hefner says, "between the West and some homogeneous 'other' but between rival carriers of tradition within the same nations and civilizations."[33]

Publicly shared ideas of community, identity, and leadership take new shapes in such engagements, even as many communities and authorities claim an unchanged continuity with the past. Mass education, so important in the development of nationalism in an earlier era,[34] and a proliferation of media and means of communication have multiplied the possibilities for creating communities and networks among them, dissolving prior barriers of space and distance and opening new grounds for interaction and mutual recognition.

Two cautions, however, are in order. The first is that an expanding public sphere need not necessarily indicate more favorable prospects for democracy, any more than 'civil society' necessarily entails democracy. Authoritarian regimes are compatible with an expanding public sphere, although an expanded public sphere offers wider avenues for awareness of competing and alternate forms of religious and political authority. Nor does civil society necessarily entail democracy, although it is a precondition for democracy.

The proliferation of the means of communication in today's global society, with its rise of mass education and a proliferation of means of communication, is increasing the power of religious intellectuals in much of the

---

[31] Eisenstadt, 1996a: 396–426.
[32] Salvatore, 1997: 55–56; Salvatore, 1998: 87–119.
[33] Hefner, 1998b: 92.
[34] Gellner, 1983: 28–29.

Muslim majority world. Increasingly, these intellectuals have become a transnational elite. Acquiring such a global presence may diminish the importance of cultural traditions, but it increases disparities of class. Mobility increases for a small segment of the elite with globalization but it increases polarities with the more localized rest. As a consequence, religious intellectuals like Iran's Abdokarim Soroush become more in tune with Edward Said, but at the risk of losing touch with the local majority.

In the present era, to paraphrase the Sorbonne-educated Sudanese religious intellectual Hasan Turabi, an *'alim* or religious intellectual is as likely to be an engineer or doctor as a religious scholar.[35] Even the idea of Islamic law, the *shari'a*, once a matter entrusted to specialists, now involves large numbers of people—and not just a scholastically trained religious elite—who debate its meaning and application.[36] Just as the new media have blurred the line between public and private, so has the modern era blurred the assumed hard and fast line between religion and politics.

The prevailing secularist bias of prevalent theories of society have alternatively marginalized religious forces and religious intellectuals or have demonized them. I have emphasized trends in the Muslim world because they have been characterized as especially resistant to 'modernity'. Yet they can be seen as open as those of any other civilizational religion. We live in a world in which an Islamic leader such as Fethullah Gulen meets popes and patriarchs, advocating diversity and tolerance in the public sphere more than many of his secular counterparts, and yet at the same time arguing that Islam is thoroughly compatible with an enlightened Turkish nationalism. Far from compromising the public sphere, religious movements and religious intellectuals in the Muslim majority world can advocate compromise and a mutual agreement to persuade by words rather than by force. Religious intellectuals may claim strong links with the past, but their practice in the present conveys significantly different ideas of person, authority, and responsibility.

[35] al-Turabi, 1983: 245.
[36] Vogel, 1999. See also Bowen, 1999: 80–105.

6. 'CONFUCIAN' EAST ASIA AND MODERNITY*

Tu Weiming

In an attempt to reconsider modernity both as a historical phenomenon and as a conceptual framework, I wish to raise three sets of issues: (1) traditions in the modernizing process, (2) the relevance of non-Western civilizations for the self-understanding of the modern West and (3) the global significance of local knowledge.

While each one of these issues is immensely complex, and the interaction among them layers the picture with ambiguities, a discussion of them together will hopefully show new possibilities emerging in this creative confusion, and show that we are at a critical juncture for moving beyond three prevalent but outmoded exclusive dichotomies: the traditional/modern, the West/the rest and the local/global. Our effort to transcend these dichotomies has far-reaching implications for the development of an ethic for the global community. I would like to focus my attention on the rise of East Asia as exemplifying this mode of thinking.

Whether or not Hegel's philosophy of history signaled a critical turn which decidedly relegated Confucianism, together with other spiritual traditions in the non-Western world, to the dawn of the Spirit, the common practice in cultural China of defining the Confucian ethic as 'feudal' is predicated on the strong thesis of historical inevitability implicit in the Hegelian vision. The irony is that the whole Enlightenment Project as captured by the epoch-making Kantian question, "What is Enlightenment?" was actually an affirmation that cultural traditions outside the West, notably Confucian China, got it right even without the benefit of revelatory religion. What happened in the 19th century when the dynamics of the modern West engulfed the world in a restless march toward material progress was definitely not the result of a straightforward working-out of the Enlightenment Project. On the contrary, the Enlightenment Project was thoroughly undermined by the unbound Prometheus, symbolizing an unmitigated quest for complete liberation. While the demands for liberation from all boundaries of authority and dogma characterized the Enlightenment Project, the modern West, to the rest of the world, was also characterized as conquest, hegemony and enslavement.

* A different version of this chapter was published in *Daedalus*, 129 (1), 2000.

Hegel, Marx and Weber shared the ethos that, despite all its shortcomings, the modern West informed by the Enlightenment mentality was the only arena where any true difference for the rest of the world could be made. The unfolding of the Spirit, the process of historical inevitability or the 'iron cage' of modernity was essentially an European predicament. Confucian East Asia, the Islamic Middle East, Hindu India, or Buddhist Southeast Asia was on the receiving end of this process. Eventually, modernization as homogenization would make cultural diversity inoperative, if not totally meaningless. It was inconceivable that Confucianism or, for that matter, any other non-Western spiritual traditions could exert a shaping influence on the modernizing process. The development from tradition to modernity was irreversible and inevitable.

In the global context, what was assumed by some of the most brilliant minds in the modern West to be self-evidently true turned out to be parochial. In the rest of the world and, arguably, in Western Europe and North America, the anticipated clear transition from tradition to modernity never occurred. As a norm, traditions continue to make their presence known in modernity and, indeed, the modernizing process itself is constantly shaped by a variety of cultural forms rooted in distinct traditions. The recognition of the relevance of radical otherness to one's own self-understanding of the 18th century seems more applicable to the current situation in the global community than the inattention to any challenges to the modern Western mindset of the 19th century. It seems that, toward the 21st century, the openness of the 18th century as contrasted with the exclusivity of the 19th century may provide a better guide for the dialogue of civilizations.

In light of the controversial hypothesis of the 'coming clash of civilizations',[1] the need for civilizational dialogues and for exploring a global ethic is more compelling. Among the Enlightenment values advocated by the French Revolution, fraternity, the functional equivalent of community, has received scant attention among modern political theorists. The preoccupation with fixing the relationship between the individual and the state, since Locke's treatises on government, is of course not the full picture of modern political thought, but it is undeniable that communities, notably the family, have been ignored as irrelevant in the main stream of Western political discourse. Hegel's fascination with the 'civil society' beyond the family and below the state was mainly prompted by the dynamics of the bourgeoisie, a distinct urban phenomenon threatening all traditional communities. It was a prophetic gaze into the future rather than a critical analysis

---

[1] Huntington, 1996.

of the value of community. The transition from *Gemeinschaft* to *Gesellschaft* was thought to have been such a rupture that Weber referred to 'universal brotherhood' as an outmoded medieval myth unrealizable in the disenchanted modern secular world. In sociological terms, the Kantian vision of the kingdom of ends is merely a philosophically imagined utopia.

The upsurge of interest in community in recent decades in North America may have been stimulated by a sense of crisis that social disintegration is a serious threat to the well-being of the Republic, but the local conditions in the United States and Canada, precipitated by ethnic and linguistic conflicts, are generalizable throughout the highly industrialized, if not postmodern, First World. The advent of the 'global village' symbolizes difference, differentiation, and outright discrimination as well as integration. The conflict between globalizing trends, including trade, finance, information, migration, as well as disease and localism rooted in ethnicity, language, land, class, and religious faith makes the task of exploring global ethics painfully difficult.

The revival of Confucian teaching as political ideology, intellectual discourse, merchant ethics, family values, or rhetoric of protest in industrial East Asia since the 1960s and socialist East Asia more recently, is the combination of many factors. Despite tension and conflict rooted in primordial ties (particularly ethnicity, language, cultural nationalism, and life-orientation), the overall pattern in East Asia is integration based on values significantly different from the Enlightenment mentality of the modern West. Evidently, East Asian intellectuals have been devoted students of Western learning for more than a century. In the case of Japan, the samurai-bureaucrats learned from Dutch, British, French, German and, in recent decades, American learning, the superior knowledge of Western science, technology, manufacturing industries and political institutions. The Chinese scholar-officials, the Korean *yangban*, and Vietnamese literati, in a similar way, acquired knowledge from the West to build their modern societies. Their commitment to substantial, comprehensive, or even wholesale Westernization enabled them to thoroughly transform their economy, polity, and society according to what they perceived, through firsthand experience, as the superior modus operandi of the modern way. This positive identification with the West, and active participation in a fundamental restructuring of one's own world according to the Western model, is unprecedented in human history. However, East Asia's deliberate effort to relegate its own rich spiritual resources to the background, for the sake of massive cultural absorption, enhanced the need to appeal to the native pattern to reshape what they had learned from the West. This model of creative adaptation following the end of the Second World War helped them to strategically position themselves in forging a new synthesis of Enlightenment rationality and Confucian humanism.

For a proper appreciation of China's modern transformation, a historical note seems in order. An unintended consequence of Matteo Ricci's
introduction of Catholicism to China and the Jesuits' China experience in
the seventeenth century was the Chinese intellectual contribution to the
Enlightenment in Europe. Through missionary reports, intellectuals in France,
England, Italy and Germany became aware of the humanistic splendor of
Chinese civilization. Montesquieu, Voltaire, Quesnay, Diderot, the philosophers, the physiocrats, and the Deists were fascinated by Chinese world
view, cosmological thinking, benevolent autocracy, and secular ethics. While
the vogue for things Chinese that overwhelmed Eighteenth-century Europe
was more a craze for chinoiserie than a quest for philosophical insight,
Confucian China was an intellectual challenge to the self-reflexivity of some
of the most brilliant Western minds. Unfortunately, the effects of the Enlightenment mentality, especially in its nineteenth-century Eurocentric incarnation,
on China and her self-perception as a developing modern state, has been
devastating.

The modern West's dichotomous mode of thinking (spirit/matter, mind/
body, physical/mental, sacred/profane, creator/creature, God/man, subject/
object) is diametrically opposed to the Chinese habits of the heart. Informed
by Bacon's knowledge as power and Darwin's survival through competitiveness, the Enlightenment mentality is so radically different from any style
of thought familiar to the Chinese mind that it challenges all dimensions of
the Sinic world. The Enlightenment faith in instrumental rationality fueled
by the Faustian drive to explore, know, subdue and control, made spectacular progress in science, technology, industrial capitalism, nation-building,
democratic polity, legal systems, educational institutions, multinational cooperation, and military hardware. As the international rules of the game,
defined in terms of wealth and power, were superimposed on China by
gunboat diplomacy, Chinese intellectuals countenanced the inevitability of
Westernization and acted accordingly.

The sense of urgency that prompted Chinese thinkers of the May Fourth
(1919) generation to advocate wholesale westernization as a precondition for
cultural survival was disorienting and self-defeating. The deliberate choice
to undermine rich spiritual resources and to embark on a materialist path
to save the nation, led to revolutionary romanticism and populist scientism.
The demand for effective action and demonstrable results was so compelling
that the life of the mind was marginalized. As a consequence, there was little room for reflection, let alone meditative thinking. For philosophy, the
outcome was disastrous. In this regard, the modern fate of Chinese intellectuals was much worse than their Indian counterparts. While centuries of
colonization did not break the backbone of Indian spirituality, the semi-

colonial status prompted the Chinese intelligentsia to reject in toto and by choice all the spiritual traditions that defined China's soul. We have only just begun to see indications that the Chinese thinkers are recovering from this externally imposed and internally inflicted malaise.

With all of its boundless energy and creative impulse, the Enlightenment mentality is incapable of reflecting on things at hand, oblivious to the 'holy rite' of human-relatedness, and ignorant of self-cultivation as an art of living. The collapse of the former Soviet Union may have destroyed the Chinese Communist faith in the inevitable historical process precipitated by the revolutionary vanguard in the strategy of class struggle for universal equality. However, the assumption that human beings are rational animals, endowed with inalienable rights and motivated by their self-interest to maximize profit in the market place, is a persuasive, if not inspiring ideology in the People's Republic of China. Market economy, democratic polity, and individualism, perceived by Talcott Parsons as the three inseparable dimensions of modernity, are likely to loom large in China's intellectual discussion. The Enlightenment mentality is alive and well in cultural China. Many young scholars strongly believe that the basic intellectual problem in the tragic history of China's modernization was that national sentiments to save the nation overshadowed the need for a deep understanding of the Enlightenment. This lamentable outcome made China's march toward modernity painfully tortuous.

The assumption is that the concerted effort to learn from the West was frustrated by the burning desire for national survival. As a result, the time was too short and the space too limited for Enlightenment ideals such as liberty, equality, rationality, and due process of law to grow and flourish in the Chinese intellectual soil. It may have taken centuries for science and democracy to become fully established in Western Europe and North America, but the Westernizers and, by implication, the modernizers, had only a few decades to try to transform China in the spirit of science and democracy. However, some of the difficulties lay in the ambiguity of the Enlightenment mentality itself as well. The Chinese Westernizers and modernizers, seasoned in the Enlightenment mentality, were all committed political activists with a passion to save China from the dark history of backwardness, its own feudal past.

The Confucian tradition, having been marginalized as a distant echo of the feudal past, is forever severed from its imperial institutional base, but it has kept its grounding in an agriculture-based economy, family-centered social structure, and paternalistic polity which have been reconfigured in a new constellation. Confucian political ideology has been operative in the development states of Japan and the four Mini-Dragons (Taiwan, South Korea, Hong Kong, and Singapore). It is evident in the political processes of the People's Republic of China, North Korea, and Vietnam. As the demarcation between capitalist and socialist East Asia begins to blur, the cultural form that cuts across the great divide becomes distinctively Confucian in character. Economic culture, family values, and merchant ethics in East Asia and in Cultural China have also expressed themselves in Confucian terms. It is too facile to explain these phenomena as a post-modem justification. Even if we agree that the Confucian articulation is but an afterthought, the apparent fit of Confucian capitalism (network capitalism), Confucian democracy (soft authoritarianism), and Confucian group spirit with emerging East Asian economy, polity and society suggests, among other things, the transformative potential of Confucian traditions in East Asian modernity.

Specifically, East Asian modernity under the influence of Confucian traditions suggests a distinctive model:

(1) Government leadership in market economy is not only necessary but is also desirable. The doctrine that government is a necessary evil and that the market in itself can provide an 'invisible hand' for ordering society is antithetical to modern experience West or East. A government that is responsive to public needs, responsible for the welfare of the people, and accountable to society at large, is vitally important for the creation and maintenance of order.

(2) Although law is essential as the minimum requirement for social stability, 'organic solidarity' can only result from the implementation of humane rites of interaction. The civilized mode of conduct can never be communicated through coercion. Exemplary teaching as a standard of inspiration invites voluntary participation. Law alone cannot generate a sense of shame to guide civilized behavior. It is the ritual act that encourages people to live up to their own aspirations.

(3) Family as the basic unit of society is the locus from which the core values are transmitted. The dyadic relationships within the family, differentiated by age, gender, authority, status, and hierarchy, provide a richly textured natural environment for learning the proper way of being human. The principle of reciprocity, as a two way traffic of human interaction, defines all forms of human-relatedness in the family. Age and gender, potentially two of the most serious gaps in the primordial environment of the human habitat, are brought into a continuous flow of intimate sentiments of human care.

(4) Civil society flourishes not because it is an autonomous arena above the family and beyond the state. Its inner strength lies in its dynamic interplay between family and state. The image of the family as a microcosm of the state and the ideal of the state as an enlargement of the family indicate that family stability is vitally important for the body politic and a vitally important function of the state is to ensure organic solidarity of the family.

Civil society provides a variety of mediating cultural institutions that allow a fruitful articulation between family and state. The dynamic interplay between the private and public enables the civil society to offer diverse and enriching resources for human flourishing.

(5) Education ought to be the civil religion of society. The primary purpose of education is character-building. Intent on the cultivation of the full person, school should emphasize ethical as well as cognitive intelligence. Schools should teach the art of accumulating 'social capital' through communication. In addition to the acquisition of knowledge and skills, schooling must be congenial to the development of cultural competence and appreciation of spiritual values.

(6) Since self-cultivation is the root for the regulation of family, governance of state, and peace under Heaven, the quality of life of a particular society depends on the level of self-cultivation of its members. A society that encourages self-cultivation as a necessary condition for human flourishing is a society that cherishes virtue-centered political leadership, mutual exhortation as a communal way of self-realization, the value of the family as the proper home for learning to be human, civility as the normal pattern of human interaction and education as character-building.

It is far-fetched to suggest that these societal ideals are fully realized in East Asia. Actually, East Asian societies often exhibit behaviors and attitudes just the opposite of what is indicated by the supposed salient features of Confucian modernity. Indeed, having been humiliated by imperialism and colonialism for decades, the rise of East Asia, on the surface at least, blatantly displays some of the most negative aspects of Western modernism with a vengeance: exploitation, mercantilism, consumerism, materialism, greed, egoism, and brutal competitiveness. Nevertheless, as the first non-Western region to become modernized, the cultural implications of the rise of 'Confucian' East Asia are far-reaching. The modern West, as informed by the Enlightenment mentality, provided the initial impetus for worldwide social transformation. The historical reasons that prompted the modernizing process in Western Europe and North America are not necessarily structural components of modernity. Surely, Enlightenment values such as instrumental rationality, liberty, rights-consciousness, due process of law, privacy, and individualism are all universalizable modern values: but, as the Confucian example suggests, 'Asian values' such as sympathy, distributive justice, duty-consciousness, ritual, public-spiritedness, and group orientation are also universalizable modern values. Just as the former ought to be incorporated into East Asian modernity, the latter may turn out to be a critical and timely reference for the Western way of life.

If Confucian modernity definitively refutes the strong claim that modernization is, in essence, Westernization or Americanization, this does not mean that the rise of East Asia augurs the advent of the Pacific Century, symbolizing the replacement of an old by a new paradigm. The answer is likely yes. But the idea of a kind of reverse convergence, meaning that the time is ripe for Western Europe and North America to look toward East Asia for guidance, is ill-advised. While the need for the West, especially the United States, to transform itself to become a learning, as well as a teaching, civilization is obvious, what East Asian modernity signifies is pluralism rather than alternative monism. The success of Confucian East Asia in becoming fully modernized without being thoroughly Westernized clearly indicates that modernization may assume different cultural forms.

It is thus conceivable that Southeast Asia may become modernized in its own right without being either Westernized or East Asianized. The very fact that Confucian East Asia has provided an inspiration for Thailand, Malaysia, and Indonesia to modernize, signifies that Buddhist and Islamic and, by implication, Hindu forms of modernity are not only possible but highly probable. There is no reason to doubt that Latin America, Central Asia, Africa, and indigenous traditions throughout the world all have the potential to develop their own alternatives to western modernism.

We must pause at this juncture to reflect on what has just been said. The neat conclusion, as the result of our commitment to pluralism, may have been reached prematurely. Any indication that this is likely to happen, a sort of historical inevitability, betrays simple-minded wishful thinking. We do not have to be tough-minded realists to know the likelihood of this scenario occurring. If the 'first world' insists upon its privilege to overdevelop, if industrial East Asia forges ahead with its accelerated growth, if the People's Republic of China immerses herself in the 'four modernizations' at all costs, what shape will the world be in fifty years from now? Is East Asian modernity a promise or a nightmare? One wonders.

The current financial crisis notwithstanding, the rise of Confucian East Asia into the most vibrant economy the world has ever witnessed in the last four decades has far-reaching geopolitical implications. Japan's transformation from an obedient student under American tutelage to the single most powerful challenger to American economic supremacy compels us to 'look at the sun' with utter seriousness. The 'reform and open' policy of the People's Republic of China since 1979 has propelled her to become a gigantic development apparatus. The Tiananmen tragedy of 1989 gave the impression that Beijing is brutally oppressive. While the collapse of the Berlin Wall and the disintegration of the former Soviet Union signaled the end of international communism as a totalitarian experiment, socialist East Asia (mainland China, North Korea and, for cultural reasons, Vietnam) seems to be in the process of reinventing itself in reality, if not in name. With thousands of political dissidents in the West and a worldwide network that supports Tibet's independence, China's radical otherness is widely perceived in the American mass media as a threat. The assumption that, since China has been humiliated by the imperialist West for more than a century, revenge may have been her principal motive force for restructuring world order seems self-evident. Memories of the Pacific theater of the Second World War and the Korean War, not to mention the Vietnam War, give credence to the myth of the Yellow Peril. The emigration of wealthy Chinese from Southeast Asia, Taiwan, and Hong Kong to North America, Australia, and New Zealand further enhances the sense of crisis that there is a Chinese conspiracy to rearrange power relationships in the global community.

The rise of 'Confucian' East Asia—Japan, the Four Mini-Dragons, mainland China, Vietnam and possibly North Korea, suggests that despite global trends defined primarily in economic and geopolitical terms, cultural traditions continue to exert shaping influences in the modernizing process. Although, genetically, modernization originated from the West, it has already assumed cultural forms so significantly different from those in Western Europe and North America that, empirically, we must entertain alternatives to Western modernism. However, the rise of 'Confucian' East Asia signals that modernization may assume different cultural forms. It does not indicate that Western modernism is being eroded, let alone replaced, by East Asian modernism. The claim that Asian values, rather than Western Enlightenment values, are more congenial to current Asian conditions and, by implication, to the emergent global community in the 21st century, is highly problematical, if not simple-minded. The challenge ahead is the need for global civilizational dialogue as a prerequisite for a peaceful world order. The perceived clash of civilizations makes the dialogue imperative. The paradox, then, is our willingness and courage to understand 'radical otherness' rooted in the primordial ties of concrete living communities as an irreducible step toward true communication, without which basic trust and fruitful mutuality between us and them can never be established, and the global community, indeed communities, will remain disintegrated and dangerously conflictual.

If we assume, as dictated by the East Asian example, that traditions shape the modernization process and, in a substantial way, define the meaning of being modern, what is the status of the claim that modernity must be conceived in terms of three inseparable dimensions: market economy, democratic polity, and individualism? Surely, the case at hand enhances the conviction that market economy, as a powerful engine of modernization, is a constitutive part of modernity.

It is worth noting, however, that the market economy, as it has been practiced in East Asia, is not at all incompatible with strong and comprehensive government participation. Political leadership often provides necessary guidance for a functioning market. In both domestic coordination and foreign competition, economically sophisticated government officials are often instrumental in allowing for the smooth functioning of the system and for creating an environment for healthy growth. Collaboration between officialdom and the business community is the norm in East Asian societies and the pervasive and fruitful interaction between polity and economy is a defining characteristic of East Asian political economy. The authority of the government in adjudicating economic matters may take different forms—direct management (Singapore), active leadership (South Korea), informed guidance (Japan), passive interference (Taiwan), or positive non-interference (Hong Kong)—but the presence of the government in all weighty economic decisions is not only expected but also desired by the business community, as well as the general public.

The universal applicability of democratic polity notwithstanding, East Asian manifestations of the democratic idea strongly suggest that democratization as a process is not necessarily incompatible with bureaucratic meritocracy, educational elitism, and particularistic social networking. The western democratic experience itself has been significantly shaped by traditions of pragmatism, empiricism, skepticism, and gradualism as in the English case; anti-clericalism, rationalism, culturalism, and the revolutionary spirit as in the French case; and romanticism, nationalism, and ethnic pride as in the German case; and the continuous presence of a strong civil society as in the American case. The Confucian faith in the betterment of the human condition through self-effort, commitment to family as the basic unit of society, and to family ethics as the foundation of social stability, trust in the intrinsic value of moral education, belief in self-reliance, work ethic, and mutual aid and a sense of an organic unity with an ever-extending network of relationships, provide rich cultural resources for East Asian democracies to develop their own distinctive features.

It is true that the Confucian rhetoric, as in a discussion of Asian values, may be used as a strategy for criticizing the indiscriminate imposition of Western ideas on the rest of the world. The new agenda to broaden human rights from exclusive emphasis on political and civil rights to include economic, social, and cultural rights may very well be perceived of as a strategic maneuver engineered by Asian leaders to divert attention from blatant human rights violations by authoritarian regimes in East Asia. While there is an obvious need for East Asian societies under the influence of Confucian culture to free themselves from nepotism, authoritarianism, and male chauvinism, democracy with Confucian characteristics is not only imaginable but may also become practicable.

East Asian intellectuals are actively involved in probing the Confucian tradition as a spiritual resource for economic development, nation-building, social stability, and cultural identity. The echoes of the iconoclastic attacks on Confucius and Sons still reverberate, however, in the halls of academia and in the corridors of government throughout Japan and the Four Mini-Dragons. Paradoxically, the Confucian personality ideals (the authentic person, the worthy, or the sage) can be realized more fully in a liberal democratic society than either in a traditional imperial dictatorship or a modern authoritarian regime. East Asian Confucian ethics must creatively transform itself in light of Enlightenment values before it can serve as an effective critique of the excessive individualism, pernicious competitiveness, and vicious litigiousness of the modern West.

Intellectuals in the Confucian world have been devoted students of Western learning (Dutch, British, French, German, and American) for more than a hundred years. As they became seasoned in the 'universal' discourses exclusively informed by the Enlightenment mentality of the modern West, they began to raise challenging questions by drawing on their own indigenous spiritual traditions. The transvaluation of Confucian values, as a creative response to the hegemonic discourses of Western Europe and North America, seems a natural outcome of this intercultural communication. Part of the impetus came from a critical awareness among Chinese intellectuals that Cultural China is no longer an agrarian society with its vast majority statically wedded to the land. For it is also one of the most dynamic migrant communities in the world.

With more than 36 million ethnic Chinese overseas, primarily in Southeast Asia and throughout the world, it is impossible to relegate the most enduring and dominant ethical system to the background by consigning it to either the 'feudal past' or the 'agrarian present'. Chinese encompass not only the largest farming population but also one of the most enterprising merchant classes in the emerging global community. If we assume that Confucian culture still matters and that its values are still cherished, or at least unconsciously upheld by the Chinese people, the form of modernity that the Confucian tradition helps to shape should be relevant to the rest of the world in understanding the human condition. On the contrary, if Confucian ethics can no longer provide guidance for action in Chinese society and if Confucian values are neither relevant nor crucial to Chinese economic behavior, there is an urgent need to inquire what ethical thinking can provide a strong enough moral basis for the Chinese to take an active part in the global stewardship so essential to world peace.

The matter is immensely complicated by the decision of the political leadership of the People's Republic of China (PRC), through the 'reform and open' policy, to join the restless march toward modernity narrowly defined in terms of wealth and power. Already, an internal migration of more than 100 million people has occurred within the PRC mainly from the countryside to the cities, especially those along the southeastern coast where economic development has been most vibrant. As the tidal waves of commercialization begin to overwhelm the Chinese interior, the pressure of migration will be greatly enhanced.

In the perspective of 'Cultural China', a second migration, as contrasted with the first migration of millions of Chinese from the Guangtong and Fujian provinces to Southeast Asia in the nineteenth century, is underway. Chinese with substantial financial resources in Southeast Asia, for reasons of political security, economic opportunity, cultural expression, or education for their children, have begun to emigrate to Australia, Canada, and the United States in the last two decades. The number will be greatly increased as residents of Hong Kong and Taiwan join the process. In the United States, ethnic Chinese from South Vietnam and students from the PRC in recent years have literally altered the landscapes of Chinatowns and international student communities throughout the country. On the other hand, it should also be noted that, in recent decades, there has been a steady flow of highly qualified professionals in science and engineering returning from North America to industrial East Asia.

If we broaden our scope to include both industrial and socialist East Asia, the presence of Japanese, Korean, and Vietnamese communities throughout the world further enhances the need to understand Confucian ethics.

I would like to interject, at this junction, a paragraph from Edwin Reischauer's prophetic statement made in 1973 and subsequently published as "The Sinic World in Perspective" in the Foreign Affairs:

> The peoples in East Asia ... share certain key traits, such as group solidarity, an emphasis on the political unit, great organizational skills, a strong work ethic, and a tremendous drive for education. It is because of such traits that the Japanese could rise with unprecedented speed from being a small underdeveloped nation in the mid-nineteenth century to being a major imperial power in the early twentieth—and an economic superpower today ... And now her record is being paralleled by all the other East Asian units that are unencumbered by war or the economically blighting pall of communism—namely, South Korea, Taiwan, Hong Kong and Singapore, which, like Hong Kong is essentially a Chinese city-state. Throughout the non-East Asian countries of Southeast Asia, Chinese minorities remain so economically and educationally dominant as to cause serious political and social problems. One cannot but wonder what economic growth might be in store for Vietnam, if peace is ever

achieved here, and for China and North Korea if their policies change enough to afford room for the economic drive of which their people are undoubtedly capable.[2]

If we maintain that Confucian ethics is an underlying East Asian value, two qualifications are required. First, the implicit designation of East Asia as 'Confucian' in the ethico-religious sense, is comparable to the validity and limitation of employing 'Christian', 'Islamic', 'Hindu', and 'Buddhist' in identifying geopolitical regions such as Europe, the Middle East, India, or Southeast Asia. The matter is confounded by the religious pluralism of 'Confucian' East Asia. However, it is not at all difficult to imagine that Shintoist or Buddhist Japan, shamanist, Buddhist or Christian Korea, and Daoist or Buddhist China are all constitutive parts of the East Asian spiritual landscape. Second, Confucian ethics so conceived is not a simple representation of traditional Confucian teaching. Rather, it is a way of conceptualizing the form of life, the habits of the heart, or the social praxis of those societies which have been under the influence of Confucian education for centuries.

As we are confronted with the issue of a new world order in lieu of the exclusive dichotomy (capitalism and socialism) imposed by the superpowers, we are easily tempted to come up with facile generalizations: 'the end of history',[3] 'the clash of civilizations', or 'the Pacific century'. A far more significant line of inquiry is to address truly fundamental issues confronting the global community: are we isolated individuals, or do we each live as a center of relationships? Is moral self-knowledge necessary for personal growth? Can any society prosper or endure without developing a basic sense of duty and responsibility among its members? Should our pluralistic society deliberately cultivate shared values and a common ground for human understanding? As we become acutely aware of our earth's vulnerability and increasingly wary of social disintegration, which critical spiritual questions should be asked?

Since the Opium War (1939), China has endured many calamities. Prior to 1949, imperialism was the main culprit, but since the founding of the PRC, erratic leadership and faulty policies must also share the blame. Although millions of Chinese died, the neighboring countries were not seriously affected and the outside world was, by and large, oblivious to what actually happened. Since 1979, China has been rapidly becoming an integral part of the global economic system. More than 30% of the Chinese economy is tied to international trade. Natural economic territories have

---

[2] Reischauer, 1974
[3] Fukuyama, 1992.

emerged between Hong Kong and Quangzhou, Fujian and Taiwan, Shandong and South Korea. Japanese, European, and American as well as Hong Kong and Taiwanese investments are present in virtually all Chinese provinces. The return of Hong Kong to the PRC, the conflict across the Taiwan Straits, the economic and cultural interchange among overseas Chinese communities and between them and the motherland, the intra-regional communication in East Asia, the political and economic integration of the Association for Southeast Asian Nations, and the rise of the Asia-Pacific region will all have a substantial impact on our shrinking global community.

The revitalization of the Confucian discourse may contribute to the formation of a much needed communal critical self-consciousness among East Asian intellectuals. We may very well be at the very beginning of global history rather than witnessing the end of history. And, from a comparative cultural perspective, this new beginning must take as its point of departure dialogue rather than clash of civilizations. Our awareness of the danger of civilizational conflicts, rooted in ethnicity, language, land, and religion, makes the necessity of dialogue particularly compelling. An alternative model of sustainable development, with emphasis on the ethical and spiritual dimensions of human flourishing, must be sought.

The time is long-overdue to move beyond a mindset shaped by instrumental rationality and private interests. As the politics of domination fades, we witness the dawning of an age of communication, networking, negotiation, interaction, interfacing, and collaboration. Whether or not East Asian intellectuals, inspired by the Confucian spirit of self-cultivation, family cohesiveness, social solidarity, benevolent governance, and universal peace, will articulate an ethic of responsibility as Chinese, Japanese, Koreans, and Vietnamese emigrate to other parts of the world, is profoundly meaningful for global stewardship.

S.N. Eisenstadt and W. Schlucter observe in the Daedalus issue on 'early modernities':

> Theories of modernization and of modernity, as formulated in the fifties and sixties, were based on the assumption of convergence. It was believed that modernization would wipe out cultural, institutional, structural and mental differences and, if unimpeded, would lead to a uniform modern world. While minor differences would remain, according to these theories, primarily due to the persistence of premodern factors, in the long run, they would fade away.[4]

In the eighties when the economic dynamism of East Asia was exceptionally strong, the thesis of reverse convergence was either clearly articulated

---

[4] Eisenstadt and Schluchter, 1998: 2.

or strongly implied by several theoreticians of modernization. The ideas of 'Asian values', 'network capitalism', and 'the Asia-Pacific century' were in vogue for more than a decade. The financial crisis of the summer of 1997 prompted a new discourse. Since authoritarianism and crony capitalism were identified as the main reasons why the Asian financial institutions had suffered from lack of transparency, public accountability and fair competitiveness, the arguments for reverse convergence have lost much of their persuasive power. As the economies of Japan and Korea begin to recover, East Asia will probably reemerge as an important reference for Western Europe and North America. It seems that as "the multiplicity of modern societies around the globe is obvious" and that "the claims to cultural supremacy of any single one of them may appear only a demonstration of arrogance,"[5] mutual referencing among societies is inevitable and the dialogue of civilizations is both desirable and necessary.

---

[5] Wittrock, 1998: 38.

7. LATIN AMERICAN MODERNITY*

Renato Ortiz

I would like to begin my reflection on a cautionary note. It is not easy to speak of Latin America as if describing it as a geographic continent sums up its totality. Strictly speaking, perhaps it is more prudent to speak of Latin Americas. First, there are substantive differences in relation to the actual process of colonization, which led a country like Brazil to be distinct from the others of Hispanic tradition. One cannot ignore the multiplicity of regions nor the diversity in indigenous traditions found by the colonizers, for example, nomadic peoples of the Brazilian jungle or structured civilizations with states and hierarchy of class in Aztec Mexico or in Incan Peru. However, I believe that it is possible to treat the question of modernity from a more generic point of view, highlighting certain features common to this manifest diversity; features that once again, when positioned historically, diverge in the construction of each country's national destiny.

The first aspect that must be stressed in any discussion is the connection with the past; more precisely, the constitution of the forms of social organization and sociability constituted during the colonial period and the crises of independence. That is, modernity will emerge from the previous step, from a tradition socially shaped, from a historical synthesis developed in contact between the colonizer, the indigenous peoples, and in the case of many countries, from the work of African slaves. What can be highlighted as a common element in this process of social formation that predated the first steps of the industrial revolution?

The conquest of Latin America signified the disaggregation of indigenous societies. Social and physical disaggregation—because all the demographic projections, independently of the contact situation, whether of Spanish or Portuguese domination—show a drastic decrease in indigenous populations. In Brazil, the estimates oscillate between five to ten million indigenous people at the time of discovery, a number that has been reduced today to only 200 thousand. In Mexico, during one century of Spanish control, the indigenous population was reduced from 25 million to one million.

The old forms of social organization are therefore replaced by those implanted by the colonizer. Yet, we are not talking about 'pure' forms, Spanish

---

* A different version of this chapter was published in *Daedalus*, 129 (1), 2000.

or Portuguese: the mixture is intense, resulting in a miscegenated population and an intermediate class of mixed race. Miscegenation is accentuated
with the arrival of African slaves to work in the mines, plantations and
domestic service. In a certain way, looking at the past of the Latin American
societies, a discussion about post-modernity, in its aspect of cultural plurality, seems to me completely inappropriate. As Nestor Garcia Canclini points
out, the process of miscegenation is a constituent part of these societies and
has little to do with the flexibility of capitalism or the decline of high culture (its mixture with popular cultures resulting from industrial cultures, as
some post-modern analysts would affirm).[1]

Miscegenation is broad and generalized but does not take place by chance.
There is a clear hierarchy separating the colonizer, Indians and Blacks. This
signifies that Latin America is profoundly marked in its history by the institutions of slavery and servitude, discrimination made legitimate and blessed
by the Catholic religion. Whether in its intellectualized or popular aspect,
Catholicism acts as ideological cement for the colonial social order.

The nativist movements and those of independence at the end of the
18th century and the beginning of the 19th in some way reorient the social
and cultural model produced by colonialism. The ideas of the Enlightenment,
liberalism, the evolutionary thinking of Comte, confront the existing conservatism and traditional Catholicism. Personalities such as Sarmiento and
Bolivar, attentive to what was happening in Europe, believed that only the
education of the popular masses could lead to an effective transformation
in Latin American societies.

Yet, these ideas are not imposed alone; they are translated, adapted in
accordance with the local interests and conveniences. Perhaps the most eloquent example of the distance between the principles of the Enlightenment
and the oligarchic reality is the introduction of the Declaration of the Rights
of Man in the Brazilian Constitution of 1824. The universality of democratic
ideas clashes entirely with the demands of a slave society. Or, as Roberto
Schwarz says, liberalism is an 'idea out of place' that acts as a legitimating
element of the oligarchic rule.[2] So a State and juridical system are created
that restrict political and economic participation to the dominant elite at
the same time that the servile relations, formed from the colonial period,
are preserved.

The rupture from Spain and Portugal reorganizes the administrative politics and juridical structures of each country. Bolivar's dream intended to

---

[1] Canclini, 1989.
[2] Schwarz, 1977.

make Spanish America politically unified, but in reality the interests of local sectors prevail. From the old colonial organizations arise national States. The national revolutions, in turn, redefine the parameters for Latin American societies; Spain and Portugal, old metropolises, are no longer the reference. This is substituted by another, the modernity of some European countries. France and England, and at the end of the century the United States, embody a new type of social organization.

It is necessary to make clear that it is not so much the special national specificity of these countries that counts but a realization of modernity as a form of social configuration. If Paris can be seen as 'the capital of the 19th century', as Benjamin considers it, it is not so much because of its 'Frenchness' but by the fact that, as a city, it experiments with new social relations. Paris is a place of modernity. In this sense, an urban reform in Buenos Aires and in Rio de Janeiro, inspired by Haussmann's model, reveals less an 'imitation of French taste' than really a frustrated attempt to promote modern urbanism. Within this perspective the debate about Europeanization versus Americanization, intense among Latin American intellectuals at the turn of the century (see, for example, the writings of Rodó),[3] reflects not only a preference for this or that country, for Europe or for the United States, but above all a vision that takes different realizations of modernity as models to be followed. In this movement, the redefinition of Spanish and Portuguese parameters are put aside because they are countries that still remain in the periphery of modernization of the European continent. The references to the old metropolises become rarer and rarer.

As in Europe, the 19th century in Latin America is the century of nations, yet, if in countries like England, France and Germany, the emergence of the nation is intimately associated with the consolidation of modernity, in the Latin American case we have a disassociation of these two movements. During the 19th century the dream is the Industrial Revolution but it only will become concrete in the 20th century when Latin American societies effectively modernize. In this sense, there is a distance between the ideal and the undeniable reality. Each country, in picturing its national identity has as an obligatory reference what is happening in Europe (part of it, to be more precise) or in the United States. The image reflected in the mirror will thus always be distorted. Basically, what is being sought does not yet exist.

A comparison with Japan is clarifying on this point. The Meiji revolution wants also to modernize the country and the reference point is exactly

---

[3] Rodó, 1991.

the same—the 'Western' industrialized world. But the lag in relation to modernity is perceived from tradition. The Japanese want 'Western' technology and science but administered by 'Oriental' morality.[4] Stated another way, the Tokugawa past (or better, part of it) is valued while the articulating element of modernity is being constructed. Confucionist values, filial piety and asceticism, come to be considered as the interior ground on which to build a specific Japanese modernity. In Latin America the dominant elite sees the mixed tradition as an obstacle, a brake, something to be overcome. Thus, the inevitable contradiction between the fixed ideal and the undeniable reality.

This contradiction is manifested in various ways. Perhaps the most visible is the opposition between civilization and barbarity, which cuts across different aspects of social and cultural manifestations. One example is the repression of popular religiosity. Considered as popular belief, the fruit of ignorance (Afro-Brazilian cults, indigenous religions, messianic movements that 'must' be punished by arms—Antonio Conselheiro and the Contestado in Brazil), they affirm the barbarianism that exists in the majority of the population. Another example is Carnival in Brazil. While the Carnivalesque form imported from Europe, such as the Venetian Carnival, was associated with the idea of lights, of spiritual enrichment, the popular Carnival was repressed as a potential source of disturbances.[5]

The peripheral modernity, as Beatriz Sarlo argues, could therefore be expressed only as a simulacrum of European modernity.[6] This unconvincing imitation of what was happening 'on the outside', had as its counterpart the impossibility of modern institutions taking root in Latin America. Political life, the legal institutions, and the capitalist economy were seen as incompatible with the traditional legacy. Travelling to lands so strange and hostile, they lost their initial objectives. There is, then, in Latin America, above all at the end of the 19th century and the beginning of the 20th, a profound pessimism in relation to modernity.

It is a moment in which there is a proliferation of racial interpretations that, in a fatalistic way, try to understand the destiny of the Latin American nations. In Brazil, Silvio Romero, Nina Rodrigues, Euclides da Cunha try to define the Brazilian as a mixture of three races: the Black, the Indian and the White. Combining 'racial theories' with the influence of the environment (geographic determinism is an important reference for the intellectuals of this epoch), they succeed in forging a national identity that is

---

[4] *The Cambridge History of Japan; the nineteenth century*, 1989; Eisenstadt, 1996a.
[5] Queiroz, 1997.
[6] Sarlo, 1988.

problematic.[7] This not only happens in Brazil. Jorge Larrain shows us how, in Hispanic Latin America as well (for example, in the writings of Sarmiento and Ingenieros) the racial problem is seen in identical terms.[8] Given this racial mixture, the white world sees itself diminished by the threat of 'inferior races' (Indians and Blacks). Racial interbreeding, miscegenation, is in this sense a problem and not really a virtue, as it will inevitably contribute to the degeneration of the indisputable qualities of White civilization. From this comes the recurring argument to promote European immigration (Italians, Germans, etc.), at the end of the 19th century. It is justified as being a therapy for containing racial contamination. Civilization and progress could only be reached with a 'whitening' of the society as a whole.

The racial, in truth racist, theories associated with the determinism of location permitted each Latin American nation to imagine its own national identity. In each place, differentiated by its specific geography (abundance of rivers, land locked, influence of tropical climate, existence of pampas, etc.), racial mixture gives rise to a particular 'people'. This thinking, strongly influenced by the European ideas of the 19th century, the interpretations of Gobineau, evolutionism and Social Darwinism, evidently ended in an impasse. Given the atavistic problems, modernity becomes incongruent.

This negative vision starts to change at the beginning of the 20th century. Octavio Ianni observes that the concepts of the 'cosmic race' of Vasconcelos (Mexico) and of 'racial democracy' of Gilberto Freyre (Brazil) denote exactly this movement of change.[9] The exaggerated fantasies of the authors who introduce such concepts—Vasconcelos believes that a 'cosmic race' of Latin Americans would be the first 'synthesized race in the world'; Gilberto Freyre thinks that mixed-race Brazil is a harmonious acculturation of peoples and cultures living in the same territory, that are of little importance for our discussion. These notions, as imprecise as they might be (and containing much ideology), invert the negative relation existing before. Racial mixture is valued as positive.

This reorientation of Latin American thought corresponds to profound transformations in society: agrarian reform (Mexican Revolution) and an effective project of industrial revolution, urbanization, rationalization of the State system, redefinition of the notion of work (in a servile society, work cannot be considered as having any value). A process that now takes on economic development as a goal to be achieved (constitution of national

---

[7] See Ortiz, 1985.
[8] Larrain Ibánez, 1996.
[9] Ianni, 1993.

markets that signifies the implementation of a policy of import substitution).
Within this context manifestations of popular culture, previously seen as
signs of barbarianism, are redefined as national 'roots'; that is, they are valued as potential symbols in the construction of a national identity (for example, the emergence of the Samba, considered until then as music of the
Blacks, as an 'essential' element in the Brazilian identity). Additionally, the
cultural manifestations that evolved around the new means of communication, principally the radio and the cinema, reinforce this sentiment of nationality. Melodramas, radio soap operas, films, little by little come to be
expressions of identities of each country, each place.[10] There is a movement,
as Jesus Martin Barbero demonstrates, that is intimately connected with the
populism of the 1930s, 1940s and 1950s, because the national State, to be
constructed as such, has to seek in popular culture the appropriate elements
for its own legitimization.[11]

However, valuing modernity as positive does not signify obtaining it. The
Latin American dilemma consists of the process of its realization. The national
States have to construct what they do not yet possess. In this sense, what
is desired can only be found in the future. In Latin America modernity is
always a project (in the Sartrean sense of the word), a utopia, something that
belongs to the future. For this reason Latin American modernity is different
from European. In the countries already industrialized, modernity poses the
question of the artistic form as an adjustment to transformation of society.
What is intended is the construction of an artistic language that is in harmony with the changes found in day to day life (electric light, street cars,
railroad systems, automobiles, cultural effervescence of the metropolis, etc.).

In Latin America it is exactly these elements of modernity that are lacking. Modernism exists but without modernization, which leads the participants of these movements (Mexican muralists, Brazilian painters and writers)
to join the political process of the construction of a national identity. It is
in the political sphere that artistic inspiration can finally find the appropriate ground for its manifestation. In this way, the 'modern' is announced in
the arts, but its effective realization is dislocated on the temporal level. We
can say the same of the developmentalist theory (in vogue in the 1950s with
CEPAL). When its spokesmen affirm that 'without an ideology of development there is no development', what is being reiterated is that the modernization project was prior to the existing underdevelopment. The expectations
were therefore postponed in time.

---

[10] See Ford, 1985; on the same issue, Canclini, 1994.
[11] Barbero, 1998.

This way of thinking about modernity has some implications. The first of these is that Latin America did not construct a tradition of criticism in regard to modernity. The modern is seen as having intrinsic value, a goal to be attained. In this sense, an ambiguity is nourished in regard to tradition. It is simultaneously a source of identity and an obstacle to be overcome. The modern will be, in principal, this overcoming element.

Another implication relates to the supposed dualism of Latin American societies; as an example—Populism. In the view of many authors it would be a kind of conjunction of distinct temporalities.[12] On the one hand, the popular classes, recently constituted in the urbanization process, do not yet have the psychosocial conditions or a cultural vision compatible with democratic behavior. On the other hand, urban-industrial society does not have the political institutions capable of incorporating the popular masses within the framework of representative democracy. Populism would therefore be a compromise solution, a phenomenon of 'transition'. I highlight the term as it has a decisive influence in various analyses about Latin American politics (for example, 'democratic transition'). But transition to where? Evidently for something that is delineated in the future. It is not just by chance that the modernization theory, elaborated in American universities in the 1950s and 1960s, had great repercussions in Latin American studies. The teleology that it encompassed, its idea of steps (see Rostow) fit with the expectation of a temporal lag in Latin American 'backwardness'. It presupposes in this way that modernity is accomplished in phases of development that implies accepting that it possesses a direction, the realization of the actual pattern in the society of Western Europe and the United States. The question that is then raised is how to understand the Latin American problem not as a detour, or a delay, but as Martin Barbero considers it, "a difference that is not summed up in 'backwardness'".[13] This implies admitting the existence of a certain originality in the process of the realization of Latin American modernity.

This necessarily leads us to rethink the notion (often more implicit than explicit in sociological analysis) of the referential standard of modernity. I don't believe that the gradual abandonment of the concept of modernization and its replacement with modernity was fortuitous. Modernization implies an action directed to some place. It has an origin, a reference point and a direction. It is this direction that is now in question. When Eisenstadt talks of 'multiple modernities' what he wants to say is that the modernity matrix

---

[12] Ianni, 1975.
[13] Barbero, 1998.

is historically realized in different forms.[14] In each place it is renovated and differentiated. However, if this is true, we have to disassociate the matrix from its place of origin—Europe—or the 'West', as some would have it. If it is possible to say, as Weber does, that modernity was born in the 'West' (we know that this is an interminable discussion) we must then add: modernity is not, by its nature, western. The matrix should not be confused with its historical realizations. Europe is only the first chronologically, but neither the only one nor the best formed. The theme of 'backwardness' can then be replaced, as the question is no longer thought of in temporal terms. In making comparisons, these differential modernities should be taken as a starting point, not an uncertain future in which all will be reflected (in this sense the notion of post-modernity also seems inadequate, as it assumes a passage of time that historically does not manifest itself in the same way in the reality of existing societies).

If in the 1930s, 1940s and 1950s, modernity was still a project to be constructed, starting in the 1970s and 1980s many complained that it had already been achieved. The impact of the First and Second Industrial Revolutions is felt and in some countries like Argentina, Brazil and Mexico creates national markets of considerable dimensions. Nestor Garcia Canclini points to some facts that indicate a structural change in Latin American countries:[15] more widespread and more diversified economic development; consolidation and expansion of urban growth begun at the beginning of the 20th century; increase in the market of cultural goods; introduction of new communication technologies, particularly television; and advances of progressive political movements.

These transformations are visible when you look at the examples in the sphere of cultural industries (Televisa in Mexico, Globo in Brazil). They redefine the relationship vis-à-vis traditional popular culture, promote consumption of industrialized goods, and introduce new life styles, which signify the emergence of new patterns of sociability and cultural legitimacy. The cultural industry, by its strength and extension, becomes a locus of socialization that now enters into competition with other loci—the family, religion, life in rural regions, etc. It is modern in its configuration (rationalization of time and technique) and in its diffusion (products offered: soap operas, comic books, women's magazines, men's magazines etc.), and contrasts with the idea of a rural, oligarchic, 'backward' Latin America.

Certainly, many of the prior problems still exist: poverty, marginalization

---

[14] Eisenstadt, 1994.
[15] Canclini, 1989.

of the popular classes with respect to educational and health services, and regional inequality. However, what interests us in this discussion is that we can say that a 'tradition of modernity' is constructed in Latin America.[16] In truth, when speaking of tradition we normally think of things from the past, preserved in memory and practice. Immediately, what comes to mind are terms like folklore, historical patrimony, as if these expressions conserve the marks of an older time that extends to the present. Tradition and past are identified and seem to radically exclude the new, identified as modern. Rarely do we think of the traditional as a set of institutions and values that, even though products of recent history, are imposed on us as a modern tradition, a way of being, tradition as norm, although tempered by its image of movement and rapidity. However, as anthropology teaches us, tradition is everything that is inserted in daily culture. In this sense, throughout the 20th century a tradition of modernity is constructed in Latin America; it contains the patterns and references, technical and social, which orient individual conduct and aspirations. Modernity became therefore something present, an imperative of our times, and no longer a promise dislocated in time: problematic modernity, controversial, but without doubt an integral part of day to day life (TV sets, automobiles, airports, shopping centers, restaurants, cable television, advertising, etc.). It is within this new context, atop this modern tradition, in conflict with local traditions, that a new movement begins: globalization. What had been redefined internally in the process of the constitution of nation states is once more put in check.

Globalization introduces new parameters to the discussion. Modernity and nations are social configurations that historically emerge together. The first rises with the Industrial Revolution, but its material form of existence is expressed in the nation. The second, in its turn, is affirmed through the development of its 'modernity'. The nation is not only a 'historical novelty' (to use Hobsbawm's phrase), but a new type of social organization rises and develops in its interior. Globalization signifies that modernity is no longer confined to national frontiers, it becomes world-modernity. The link between nation and modernity will therefore crumble. Metaphorically, I would say: it is possible to be modern without being national. In this case, multiple modernities will not just be a historicized version of the same matrix, they are connected to an integrating tendency that de-territorialized certain 'items' in order to group them as globalized units. Nationally produced differences are now partly cross cut by the same process. For example, the rise of de-territorialized identities (the universe of consumerism with its life styles) that

---

[16] See Ortiz, 1988.

escape the boundaries imposed by the different modernities of each place.[17] They approximate social groups distant in space but close in patterns of consumption, taste and personal inclinations. The problem that is raised, therefore, is to understand how this movement of globalization cuts across traditions of modernity existent in Latin America.

There are still implications of a political nature that are worrisome. Nation and modernity were movements that utopically accompany each other in the Latin American context. The time lag between them could, in princi-pal, be resolved through the idea of a 'national project', that is, the capa-bility of the nation state to construct this modernity. To the extent that modernity and nation become disjunctive terms, the very idea of a national project enters into crisis. The autonomy that the Latin American nation states had (or imagined they had) in the consolidation of their collective destinies no longer can be sustained. This occurs within a worrisome frame-work, because world modernity builds upon differences and inequalities. Only a post-modern idealism can imagine affirming, purely and simply, that difference is a synonym of plurality and democracy. The construction of nationalities was problematic in Latin America, but at the moment that the very idea of nation enters into crisis (this does not mean to say disappears) we reach the end of the 20th century without having been able to reverse the situation of pre-established domination. The affirmation of differences has, therefore, to be qualified since, in the context of a globalized world, there is order and hierarchy, and if some pluralism exists, we must con-sider it as a 'hierarchized pluralism'.

[17] Ortiz, 1997.

8. THE MULTIPLICATION OF MODERNITY

Johann P. Arnason

The enduring variety of modern cultures and societies is easier to observe than to theorize. The growing interest in distinctive patterns or configurations of modernity may, however, be seen as an attempt to reorient a debate long dominated by visions of unity, and as a first step towards proper recognition of diversity. Among the programmatic formulations in this vein, S.N. Eisenstadt's concept of 'multiple modernities' would seem to be the most pertinent. If we want to explore the issues that arise in connection with the new approach, the first questions to be considered have to do with preliminary bearings: in the current intellectual context, the case for a more pluralistic understanding of modernity must be stated against dominant fashions as well as persisting traditions.

Changing directions

To speak of multiple modernities is, by definition, to reject some widespread views of the contemporary world, but the critical implications differ from case to case. The idea of an ongoing and innovative pluralization of modernity is obviously incompatible with postmodernist positions, and it gives a specific twist to the critique of postmodernism: those who consigned modernity to the past based their claims on misguided notions of a uniform pattern embodied in a whole historical epoch.[1] This line of argument might enable us to account for the spread as well as the heterogeneity of postmodernist currents (they could be seen as responses to structural shifts or tensions in modern societies, drawing on a common language, yet reflecting the dynamics and demands of different situations). But for this line of argument to be pursued in earnest, we would first need to explore the problematic of multiple modernities in a more systematic fashion than has so far been done. As for the more recently fashionable notions of globalization or a global age, sometimes defended as better answers to questions

---

[1] On the conflation of substantive and epochal understandings of modernity, cf. Yack, 1997. The paradigm of multiple modernities may be seen as an attempt to escape conflation without severing the connection between the two aspects: the substantive meaning of modernity is contested, and the conflicts between rival interpretations take place in historical settings.

132   JOHANN P. ARNASON

raised by the postmodernists, the objections must be stated in more nuanced terms.[2] The idea of multiple modernities rules out the notion of globality as a general condition characteristic of a new epoch, but it would—if developed in appropriate ways—be capable of linking up with the analyses of those who take a more pluralistic view of global transformations. If the changes in question are the outcome of different and often divergent processes, which interact in varying combinations, it may be possible to show that the multiple configurations of modernity involve corresponding modes of globalization—or at least to raise the question whether they do so.[3]

For present purposes, however, demarcation from current alternatives is less important than the break with established traditions: the emerging paradigm of multiple modernities has so far mainly taken shape in explicit contrast to some basic assumptions of earlier modernization theory. Four aspects of this critical turn will be central to the following argument.

First and foremost, the new approach contests the widely shared but often implicit view of modernity as a uniform, unambiguously structured and self-contained pattern in progress towards full realization and harmonious integration (Parsons is the most obvious example of theorizing in this vein, but similar premises were taken for granted by many authors who did not feel obliged to spell them out). If the idea of multiple modernities is to make sense, we can only think of modernity in general as a loosely structured constellation, open to modifications and redefinitions, selective appropriations and contextual adaptations. In other words, the idea of differentiation—always central to modernization theory, inasmuch as it dealt with the increasingly autonomous development of different structural or institutional components—is now extended to overall configurations of modernity. This does not mean that we can do without any common denominator, but we can no longer try to impose a general definition prior to historical and comparative exploration of the varieties of modernity. The question of unity and diversity remains on the agenda, but with a significant twist to their relationship—a twist towards greater recognition of diversity—and with a clear awareness that no balanced account can be given without a historical analysis of the different trajectories of modernity.

Second, the notion of one main current of modernization—of the kind Parsons has in mind when he describes the succession of vanguard societies and their paradigms, from northwestern Europe to the other side of the

---

[2] On the idea of a global condition as a more plausible version of postmodernity, cf. Albrow, 1996.
[3] Cf. Especially Held et al., 1999.

Atlantic—becomes as questionable as the corresponding one of a 'main pattern' of modernity. This is not to deny that specific visions and dynamics of modernization may prevail over others—to a greater or lesser degree, and in a more or less definitive fashion. But the idea of multiple modernities serves as a warning against building such developments into basic concepts: they should, rather, be explored and explained at the historical level. To mention only the most topical case, it is beyond dispute that we are currently witnessing a sustained effort—backed up by economic, political and ideological forces—to impose a hegemonic model of modernization. According to the advocates of the model in question (variously described as Anglo-American, neo-liberal or global-capitalist), this is a matter of modernity finally coming into its own; but if we think in terms of multiple modernities, the first task is to examine the historical background and the likely historical limits to this turn of events. The starting-point is a multiplicity of modernizing dynamics and strategies, together with changing patterns of interaction between them; a shift in favour of one dominant model should be analyzed in that context.

Third, we are casting doubt on the idea of a unifying project of modernity, even if it is—as in the version defended by Jürgen Habermas—set against its incomplete and one-sided embodiments in the practices and institutions of modern societies. The paradigm—or the interpretive hypothesis—of multiple modernities suggests that we should focus on the contrasts and conflicts between different projects of modernity, some of which may represent more effective, more rationalized or more normatively grounded syntheses of the underlying multiplicity than others. Moreover, the issue of multiplicity resurfaces at another analytical level: if modernity is characterized by multiple cultural orientations in more or less open conflict with each other, every comprehensive project is faced with the problem of balancing or reconciling these rival claims. Pioneering insights into the problematic of modern values and cultural spheres in conflict can be found in the work of Max Weber, but his treatment of this topic is as fragmentary and unfinished as the rest of his work; the question of second-order conflicts between attempts to defuse or overcome first-order ones is one of the issues that have to be considered if his analyses are to be taken further, and it has an obvious bearing on the history of global rivalry between alternative visions of modernity.

The last point to be noted is less directly related to the critique of a previously dominant paradigm. The idea of multiple modernities raises new questions about the civilizational status of modernity. Such issues were not on the agenda of mainstream modernization theory, and they were left untouched by its most prominent critics. But if modernity exists and unfolds in multiple forms and directions, it is at least a plausible hypothesis that long-term legacies of the kind which we associate with distinctive civilizations will be among the differentiating factors. Eisenstadt has developed this line of reasoning with convincing results. But if, on the other hand, it makes some sense to speak of modernity as a condition common to otherwise diverse societies and cultures, it clearly cuts across civilizational boundaries. Modernity would thus seem to be a civilizational formation *sui generis*—we might say that it appears as both more and less than a civilization among others, more due to its unprecedented global thrust and less in view of its contextual dependence on pre-existing civilizational premises, and that this ambiguity merits more attention than it has hitherto received. Here we are, in short, dealing with a theme that belongs to the unarticulated background rather than the explicit framework of earlier modernization theory (a tacit understanding of modernity as a triumph of civilization in the singular is often reflected in arguments which make no formal reference to civilizational perspectives), and it can only come into focus after a comprehensive change of direction.

The above comments do not amount to more than a preliminary sketch of reconsiderations in progress; the idea of multiple modernities has, in other words, been briefly elucidated as a keyword for new interpretive orientations in a field still overshadowed by a strong but restrictive tradition of theorizing. We should now move on to the second and more extensive part of the discussion: an exploration of ways to structure and develop the problematic that we have tried to demarcate in tentative terms. Three approaches to this task—the genealogical, the structural and the hermeneutical—will be distinguished. But the analytical contrasts summed up in these labels should not obscure the point that the three lines of thought can be seen as complementary, even if their effective coordination has so far left much to be desired.

Genealogical perspectives

A genealogical approach would focus on four main themes: a) the *sources*, i.e. the historical backgrounds and contexts of modern formations, with particular emphasis on civilizational preconditions; b) the *patterns*, i.e. the constellations of modern structures, institutions and cultural frameworks, which take shape in different settings, and which constitute the most salient reason for speaking about multiple modernities; c) the modernizing *processes* which unfold within and between these constellations, and which differ in regard to levels of dynamism, overall directions, and the relative weight of

various trends; d) the *self-interpretations* grounded in or grafted onto structurally and historically different experiences of modernity.

(a) As for the sources, it seems clear that we can still speak of a particular and privileged relationship between modernity and an older Western
civilization, even if recent research may have shown that this relationship
was less exclusive than both historians and theorists tended to assume. If
modernity is nevertheless to be understood and theorized as a new civilizational formation, we must deal with a double question: what were the
specific characteristics which enabled the European ancestor civilization to
mutate into a more radically new and incomparably more dynamic form,
and on what basis can we draw a historical boundary between Western
European antecedents and their modern sequel?

There seems to be growing agreement among historians that a new civilization emerged in western Europe[4] in the eleventh and twelfth centuries AD.
Paradoxically, the consensus on this point is accompanied by doubts and
debates about some of the interpretive constructs previously used to describe
medieval Western Europe (cf. especially the ongoing controversy around the
idea of a 'feudal revolution').[5] If there is a widely shared (however tentative) view of the specifics of this new civilization, it can probably be summed
up in two points. First, the exceptionally pluralistic character of the new
formation is beyond dispute, and there are several sides to this pluralism.
The emerging Western European civilization drew on multiple traditions—
indirectly (but importantly) on Greek and Jewish sources, more directly on
Roman and Christian transformations of these two seminal legacies, as well
as on the heritage of the Germanic ethnies that had conquered the western part of the Roman empire, and on elusive but significant inputs from
the peripheral regions of the northwest.[6] Furthermore, Western Europe developed in interaction with two other more advanced heirs to the legacy of
late antiquity, the Byzantine and the Islamic civilization. It was also marked
by an internal pluralism of power structures: a changing balance between
landowning military elites, monarchies, urban communities and a church
with claims to universal authority shaped the dynamics of medieval society.
At the same time, the region was split between multiple political centers,
and their mutual rivalry proved conducive to sustained processes of state
formation. Finally, the attempt to impose a comprehensive and definitive

---

[4] Cf. Moore, 1997; and also Bartlett, 1993.

[5] For the most recent round of the debate on the feudal revolution, cf. the contributions
in *Past and Present*, 152 (1996) and 155 (1997).

[6] For little known speculations on the role of the northern and northwestern periphery,
cf. Borkenau, 1981.

orthodoxy was from the outset confronted with heterodox currents, strong enough for historians to have seen this epoch as the first chapter in the history of European dissent.

Second, the expansionist drive of the new civilization was evident from the beginning, and this factor played a major role in its internal development. There was, of course, nothing unique about this expansionist turn as such; but some specific features stand out in contrast to the long-term dynamic of western Christendom's most threatening rival. Western European expansion—directed towards the northern, eastern and southern periphery—seems to have interacted with the centers of state formation in a more constructive way than its Islamic counterpart. At the same time, it was too multi-central to be harnessed to empire-building; the unified empire of early Islam has no parallel in the post-Roman history of the West, and the much later achievements of regional empire-builders in the Islamic world (Ottoman, Safavid and Mughal) were only emulated on the European periphery, whereas the core domain was never controlled by an imperial center. Last but not least, the Western European pattern of expansion seems to differ from the Islamic one in that there were more signs of an incipient difference and tension between religious and political forces involved in the process; this trend can be seen as a first indicator of the incomparably more massive separation of secular expansion from religious connections that was to gather momentum during the modern epoch. The medieval phase was still articulated and legitimized in predominantly religious terms (the crusades and the myth that survived them are the most obvious example), but on some occasions, the spread of power structures and the civilizational frameworks attached to them seems to have developed a dynamic of its own and at more or less overt odds with stronger versions of the primacy of religion. The conflict between the papacy and the Sicilian kingdom under Frederick II, the defeat of the German Order by the Polish-Lithuanian Commonwealth, and the trade and state-centered strategies of Venetian empire-building are cases in point.

In view of this background, it would seem plausible (without excluding other perspectives) to link the mutation of a Western regional pattern into an increasingly global modern one to a major shift in the relationship between pluralism and expansion. From the sixteenth century onwards, pluralism within the West took a significant turn: the consolidation of the 'new monarchies' eliminated some key actors and components of the medieval world, but it also paved the way for innovative forms of interaction. The states that became central to the early modern history of Western Europe operated, coexisted and competed within a broader field of economic, political and cultural forces which had an ongoing transformative impact on both intra-state and inter-state structures. At the same time, this new constellation was—as a result of the early modern take-off of European expansion—projected into a global arena where both interstate competition and the divergent dynamics of economic, political and cultural change unfolded in ever-widening dimensions.

(b) This interpenetration of two sets of processes—those internal to the original Western context and those induced by the broadening of historical horizons—is crucial to the understanding of our next thematic complex: the varying patterns or overall configurations of modernity. To speak of multiple modernities is not to suggest that we should return to a self-contained history of each variant. Rather, the crystallization and diversification of patterns is to be analyzed in relation to a broader context; long-term background developments, global constellations and interpretive as well as strategic responses to both these sets of circumstances interact and combine in different ways. The differentiating processes take place in a setting of increasingly global interdependence. A first major distinction has to do with the contrast between Western and non-Western forms of modernity: even if we accept that 'early modernities' emerged as a result of relatively autonomous processes in separate parts of the world, it still seems indisputable that the non-Western cases—some of which were more clear-cut and resilient than others—did not, in the longer run, evolve alongside the more expansive Western ones. The idea of multiple modernities is by definition a move towards more balanced understanding of non-Western patterns, but it does not downplay the crucial importance of responses to or reinventions of the ascendant Western models. Historical originality may be manifested in selective and innovative appropriation, rather than in self-contained development.

Comparative analysis of the patterns of modernity is still a strikingly underdeveloped part of the sociological field. Here I can only briefly outline a few lines of inquiry that have at least been adumbrated in recent work. First, the relationship—and the level of compatibility—between more or less reconstructed traditional components and more or less adapted modern elements varies from case to case; as is well known, Japanese modernity has figured prominently in debates on this issue. The questions to be considered include both the legitimizing and the critical uses of traditions, and we must allow for rediscoveries of temporarily sidelined traditional sources as well as the ongoing adaptation of more permanent aspects. Second, existing patterns of modernity are not ipso facto coordinated or coherent wholes; their levels of cohesion should be seen as a matter for comparative and historical analysis. To stay with the example just mentioned, it would be difficult to deny that more cohesive patterns of modernity emerged in Japan than in the Islamic world. Third, it has been suggested that different patterns of modernity could be compared with regard to the relative importance of differentiation and integration, and that one of the cardinal errors of earlier modernization theory was a tendency to assume a constant balance between these two aspects; once again, Murakami Yasusuke's analysis of Japanese modernity as characterized by a primacy of integration is a case in point.[7] It would, however, seem more appropriate to pose the problem not only in terms of relative weight, but also in regard to different relationships between differentiation and integration, as well as different forms of these twin dynamics. As I have tried to show elsewhere, such perspectives can be applied to the Soviet variant of modernity.[8]

But the question of forms and levels of integration is also inseparable from the problematic of conflict: Göran Therborn draws attention to the exceptional importance of civil conflict in the history of European modernity: from the High Middle ages to the twentieth century (with peaks in the seventeenth and the first half of the nineteenth century), the contests between tradition and innovation, as well as between alternative paths of innovation, "were largely and typically decided by . . . one form of internal conflict or another".[9] Other parts of the world developed other patterns of conflict. In East Asia, the region least affected by Western domination, the crucial phase of advanced modernity was marked by interstate conflicts, including those which involved a shared legacy and territory: wars between Japan and China, between rival successor states to the Chinese Empire, and between the two post-colonial Korean states transformed the regional power structures during the first half of the twentieth century. And as is now becoming increasingly clear, these conflicts were submerged rather than overcome by global bipolarity during the second half. In the case of the Islamic world, it seems appropriate to speak of a prolonged external conflict with another civilization perceived as technologically superior but lacking religious legitimacy.

Finally, patterns of modernity may be more or less capable of all-round changes that give rise to a sequence of forms. Peter Wagner's pioneering work on the mutations of Western modernity can be read in this vein.[10] As Wagner argues, restricted liberal modernity (dominant during the first two-thirds of the nineteenth century) and organized modernity (similarly central to much of twentieth-century history) represent two very different configurations, separated by a phase of crisis; the second type was succeeded by another

[7] Cf. Murakami, 1987.
[8] Arnason, 1993.
[9] Therborn, 1995: 22.
[10] Cf. Wagner, 1994.

crisis (Wagner speaks of a "cultural revolution against organized modernity"), and it is still a very open question whether a more advanced version of liberal modernity will in due course crystallize. From this point of view, the failure of the Soviet model can perhaps be seen as a matter of inability to match Western self-transformations: the Communist version of modernity proved capable of effective competition with the West in important fields for some time, but incapable of developing into a matrix of new modernities.

(c) Our interpretation of modernity stresses the interconnections and the overlap between patterns and processes, but some themes and questions are best understood in relation to the latter aspect. Assumptions about the essential similarity and homogeneity of modernizing processes reflect a focus on supposedly uniform structural-functional imperatives inherent in modernity as such; multiple forms and directions become more visible if we take institutional frameworks and cultural orientations into account. Here the idea of multiple modernities may serve to clarify, synthesize and re-focus insights that have emerged within modernization theory as well as in the work of historians and sociologists less identified with the mainstream. Some starting-points for a typology of modernizing processes should at least be briefly noted.

We can, to begin with, analyze the different types of modernizing processes with regard to the specific areas of social life where they have the most focused and far-reaching impact; this applies, in particular, to transformations centered on the economic, political or ideological levels, even if the dynamics at work depended on a broader spectrum of factors and conditions. This point of view becomes more relevant if we see the inaugural revolutions of modernity as key episodes and culminating phases of more long-term processes. It is now generally accepted that the industrial revolution in late eighteenth-century Britain was such a turning-point in an unfolding interaction of historical forces which favoured the take-off of an unprecedentedly expansive capitalist economy. At roughly the same time, a very different historical breakthrough took place in the trans-Atlantic part of the British Empire; if we follow recent accounts of the American secession (especially Michael Mann's analysis), it is mainly on political grounds that this successful colonial rebellion can be described as a revolution and as the beginning of a distinctive path to modernity. Most importantly, "the constitution as rule of law—and not as elsewhere the state or sovereign parliament"[11] became the focus of collective identity and the foundation of political culture, and this institutionalization of a new vision of political order

---

[11] Mann, 1993: 161.

had momentous consequences for all domains of social life. On the other
hand, reinterpretations of the French Revolution suggest—although the
debate is far from over—that this uniquely controversial episode is best
understood as the crystallization of an exceptionally ideologized mode of
transformation, prepared but not pre-programmed by the Enlightenment;
the ideological projects that emerged and clashed in the course of the revolutionary upheaval were at first centered on the political sphere, but could—
as later experience was to show—acquire new meanings in other contexts,
most notably in the economic sphere.

But it is also possible to compare different constellations of modernizing
processes with regard to the overall shape of relationships between the various dimensions of development. The figurational sociology of Norbert Elias
and his followers, developed in conscious opposition to mainstream modernization theory, has drawn attention to the importance of state formation
processes—not as an ipso facto determining factor for all other developments, but as a particularly central and therefore revealing component of
a broader network. State formation presupposes and stimulates transformative processes throughout the social environment of the power center, and
the varying outcomes of such interconnections are reflected in different trajectories of modernization. This angle of comparative analysis merits more
systematic use than has so far been attempted. But it is also worth noting
that the dynamics of state formation may take a turn which obstructs or
overburdens other paths of development. Two very different cases may be
briefly mentioned. The early modern history of Spain—very much a part
of the overall European configuration of early modernity—was arguably
shaped by an overstretched project of state and empire-building which led
to the atrophy or reversal of other modernizing trends, and thus ultimately
to irreversible decline.[12] On the opposite margin of the European world,
the Russian sequence of sometimes partly successful but always to some
extent counterproductive state-centered revolutions from above—and ideological projects devised to maximize their impact—raises fundamental questions about the continuity and discontinuity of modernizing processes.

A further line of comparative analysis has to do with dominant strategic
goals of modernizing projects. In a very general sense, control and mobilization may be seen as complementary aspects of all the initiatives in question: the modernization of power structures entails the expansion of control,
but the mechanisms of control are superimposed on an expanding spectrum
of forces mobilized for the purposes of development. The distinction between

---

[12] Cf. Perez Diaz, 1998a.

the two aspects is, however, particularly relevant to the understanding of the most radical conflict between alternative paradigms of modernity. For socialist critics, the most serious flaw of capitalism was the maintenance of obsolete forms of control (those associated with private property), no longer compatible with the achieved levels of mobilization (the growth of productive forces), and the task was to construct a new order where the two functional imperatives would be fully reconciled. In the context of policies pursued by Communist regimes (drawing on the Socialist tradition in a selective fashion, and in changing combinations with other sources), this search for an alternative to capitalism translated into attempts to maximize control and mobilization at the same time.

(d) To treat self-interpretations of modernity as a separate side to our problematic is to presuppose that they are neither reducible to more basic factors nor identical with operative projects; they are, in other words, neither 'superstructural' by-products of material dynamics, nor transparent expressions of an underlying logic. Here I can only briefly indicate what seems to me to be the most promising starting-point for a comparative analysis of self-interpretations: it has to do with tensions within, versions of and responses to liberalism. If it is the case that a "renewed emphasis on the liberal foundations of social order"[13] has been a salient characteristic of the most recent phase of modernity, this should be seen as a return to the mainstream of self-interpretation (together with some new questions about it), rather than a definitive self-rediscovery. To cut a long story very short, the core content of liberalism might be defined as an interpretation of modernity which tends to impose mutually homogenizing images of capitalism, democracy and science (all these institutional complexes are more or less explicitly seen as manifestations of a self-correcting rationality open to empirical tests and criteria), and align them with the imaginary signification of the autonomous and sovereign individual. The insoluble problems associated with the latter notion (the social dimensions of autonomy and sovereignty can never be collapsed into individual projects) give rise to revisions and divergent reinterpretations: more sophisticated models of economic man are developed in response to the critique of classical utilitarianism, but visions of the individual as an active citizen can also cast doubt on the whole tradition of theorizing autonomy in terms of strategic rationality. More generally speaking, the conflicting interpretations of autonomy reflect the tensions between liberal premises and the historical field on which they are superimposed.

---

[13] Wagner, 1994: 137.

The problematic of the underlying patterns reappears in dissonances between economic, political and cultural liberalism.

This view of the history of liberalism—as an ongoing contest of homogenizing and re-differentiating trends—may be a useful antidote to current fashions. The last two decades have been characterized by a major political and ideological resurgence of market-centered and fundamentally economistic modes of thought; they are commonly subsumed under the category of neo-liberalism, although retro-liberalism might seem a more apposite term.[14] The approach suggested above should help to put such shifts in a proper perspective. But it also throws light on countercurrents, especially the socialist and nationalist responses to and critiques of liberal modernity. They relate to the liberal tradition in diverse and changing ways. Selective but significant references to key elements of the liberal tradition play an important role in their history (socialist choices could, in some noteworthy cases, be presented as logical conclusions from properly understood liberal premises); on the other hand, the critique of liberalism gave rise to counter-projects which in the most pronounced cases developed (or were incorporated) into alternative visions of modernity.

Further questions for comparative analysis have to do with variations in the relationship between liberalism and its more or less assimilable or marginalizable rivals, due to different civilizational settings. Premodern intellectual and political traditions vary in regard to the degree and direction of their impact on the articulation of modern self-images. A systematic study of such connections is one of the most promising paths towards a more pluralistic understanding of modernity.

Structural dynamics

The structural approach is perhaps best introduced as another perspective on one of the themes already envisaged from a historical angle: the patterns of modernity. Instead of focusing on their concrete historical variety and theorizing parallels as well as contrasts, the structural line of argument would shift the emphasis towards their basic components and explore the possibilities of variation prefigured at this level. Our main concern would, in other words, be with the constitutive elements of the modern constellation, the interconnections between them, and the differentiating dynamics built into this context as such.

---

[14] This term was suggested by Bernard Yack.

Before going on to spell out some implications of this analytical strategy, a terminological point should be noted. In contemporary social theory, the notion of structure tends to shift between broad and narrow meanings; it seems difficult to do away with this ambiguity, and it depends on the context whether it is preferable to use the concept in a flexible or a restrictive sense. For present purposes, a broad definition is more useful: the term 'structural' does not refer to the particular theoretical perspectives that have been applied by structuralist schools of thought (self-styled or not), nor does it have the specific meaning which Eisenstadt has in mind when he distinguishes between structural and institutional aspects of society in general and modernity in particular (in the latter context, structural aspects have to do with fundamental uniformities in the dynamics of modern societies, such as industrialization, urbanization and bureaucratization). Rather, I am referring—in a very general sense—to trans-subjective dynamics operating within relatively constant frameworks, and therefore distinguishable from the projects of self-defining actors as well as the contingencies of history. From this point of view, the structural components of modernity incorporate both institutional and cultural aspects, and as I will try to show, the paradigm of multiple modernities differs from the Parsonian model in making this content explicit, instead of tacitly conflating cultural and istitutional patterns with a systemic logic. Moreover (and no less importantly), the Parsonian assumption of a finite and closed list of basic components is rejected. The analysis now begins with an open-ended spectrum of constitutive forces, and the question of closure (more precisely: forms of closure) becomes an issue for comparative analysis.

The proposed line of inquiry can draw on one particularly important and still under-used classical source. Max Weber's discussion of socio-cultural spheres with divergent logics and in more or less acute conflict with each other has in recent years attracted more attention than it did during the heyday of modernization theory, but the most influential readings (such as the Habermasian one) have filtered it through very restrictive frames of reference.[15] Although a detailed interpretation of Weber is beyond the scope of this paper, a few remarks on his argument may help to clarify the tasks of a structural analysis.

Weber's account of the plurality of cultural spheres ('world orders' or 'life orders' as he also likes to call them) suffers from a persistent failure to draw clear boundaries between modern and premodern conditions. It seems clear that he wants to theorize a constellation that is particularly characteristic of

---

[15] The key texts are Weber, 1970a; 1970b; 1970c.

advanced modernity, but has to some degree been prefigured by developments within some traditional civilizations (his first and most extensive treatment of the subject suggests, for example, that Indian cultural patterns were much more conducive to the differentiation of spheres than Chinese ones). If we concentrate on the modern part of the problematic, it may be convenient to distinguish several categories of spheres. Weber discusses the most material and directly formative forces of the modern world (the economic and the political sphere); the increasingly dominant and unquestioned interpretive framework which undermines, transforms or marginalizes all others (modern science); the traditional guarantee of unifying meaning which survives in more or less mutant and minimized forms (religion); and the distinctively modern attempts to develop innerworldly substitutes for religion (the aesthetic and the erotic sphere). In all cases, an interpretive horizon, grounded in specific activities and areas of social life but reaching beyond them in a more or less articulate fashion, is crucial to the delimitation of a sphere. The level of institutionalization varies from case to case, and some spheres are by definition resistant to institutional constraints. Finally, the autonomous logic of a specific sphere may not exclude inbuilt conflicts between rival interpretations, models and projects; Weber's account is, admittedly, rather perfunctory on this point, but it can at least be argued that his critiques of socialism (as a misguided synthesis of trends inherent in the economic and political structures of modern societies) and of some cultural interpretations of science show a certain sensibility to interpretive conflicts as expressions of autonomy.

The question of divergent trends within a common sphere seems a useful starting-point for post-Weberian reflections on the same problematic. If we limit the discussion to three indisputably fundamental components of modernity, a corresponding spectrum of trends and counter-trends can be mapped out and linked to the agenda of structural analysis. The capitalist economy, the bureaucratic nation-state and the organized pursuit of scientific knowledge are integral parts of the modern constellation, and they also function as sources of models and visions that are projected beyond the boundaries of their respective spheres and become frames of reference for more comprehensive conceptions of modernity. Both national (or regional) variants and successive phases of modernity differ in regard to the relative weight of the three factors; at another level, each of the three spheres may be more or less directly prioritized by dominant ideologies or modes of thought.

Inasmuch as the specific logics of the different components can affect both the operative structures and the self-representations of modern societies, it seems appropriate to describe them as divergent modernities (multiple modernities are, by contrast, varying combinations of the components in question). The dimensions of divergence are particularly evident in the global arena: the worldwide diffusion of the capitalist economy, the bureaucratic state and the scientific mode of knowledge gives rise to very different processes and trajectories. But there is another side to the category of divergent modernities. Each of the spheres mentioned above is also contested from within. Alongside the mainstream of an expanding capitalist economy.

Ideological constructs (and strategies based on them) project a selective interpretation of the capitalist dynamic beyond its more complex structural framework and present themselves as alternatives to or perfected versions of historical capitalism. The classic example of an alternative model is, of course, the Marxian vision of communism, which generated a whole cluster of traditions. Following Castoriadis and Bauman, Marxism may be described as a capitalist counterculture: its key theme is the liberation of the productive forces from the capitalist framework, within which they have undergone revolutionary changes but remain limited by particular interests and obsolete forms of economic power. The future society of abundance and free development is an imaginary variation of existing capitalist patterns.

As for the political sphere, the bureaucratic nation-state—combining new modes of identity with new mechanisms of control—is central to all accounts of modern history, but so are the democratic transformations which unfold within its boundaries and give rise to aspirations which go beyond them— in the double sense of aiming to minimize or even abolish the state as an institution, and overcoming the limits of the state as a territorial unit. Visions of such kinds are not confined to one side of the political spectrum. Images of self-regulating society liberated from the state include the utopias of council democracy and generalized workers' control, but also the project of radical free-market liberalism; in the global arena, it is now a commonplace that revolutionary internationalism has given way to the elitist phantasms in quest of a borderless world. It should, however, be added that the radical anti-statist trends have been less important in clear-cut forms than as malleable ingredients of projects which maintain a more ambiguous overall stance. The socialist tradition is an exemplary case in point. It owed much of its original strength and appeal to the promise of a new society that would eliminate not only the market (that part of the project drew on the capitalist counterculture mentioned above), but also the state; in long-term practice, however, socialist visions of the future proved adaptable to various kinds of statist strategies.

Modern science may at first seem much less open to conflicting interpretations and more systematically oriented towards universal standards than the modern economy or the modern state. But philosophical accounts of science are notoriously controversial, and they reflect different cultural perspectives on the methods and results of scientific progress. There is also a cultural angle to the economic and political conflicts which have been discussed: alternative images or definitions of wealth and power are counterposed to those embodied in dominant institutions. If we take this cultural context into account, the interpretive field around modern science becomes more comparable to the other spheres; and although it remains true that the mainstream of modern science has not been accompanied by alternative models on the same scale as have the modern economy and the modern state, the foundations and limits of unified norms for scientific inquiry remain a matter of permanent debate. More importantly for present purposes, scientific progress has from the outset been faced with countercurrents which cast doubt on its claims to represent a triumph of rationality and an end to the mirage of a meaningful world. The conflicts between Enlightenment and Romanticism—and the recurrent attempts to overcome them—are at the center of cultural modernity.

More specifically, the romantic tradition—defined, in a very broad sense, as the quest for new sources of meaning to counter the perceived destruction of meaning by cognitive progress—is capable of reorientations and metamorphoses which have affected the self-constitution and self-understanding of modernity in various ways. With reference to the above reflections on the civilizational background to modernity, three aspects of this problematic should be briefly mentioned. Romanticism has, as is well known, been a key factor in the construction of national identities; its specific contributions vary from case to case, but it is never absent from the field. As a result of the emergence and proliferation of national identities within the Western world, an older civilizational identity has become less prominent, its links to ongoing historical processes more problematic, and its very existence more open to doubt. Although detailed comparisons are beyond the scope of this paper, it may be noted in passing that the relationships between civilizational and national identities in the Islamic, South Asian and East Asian worlds have developed in ways very different from the West. On the other hand, romantic motives and concerns played a major part in kindling the interest in other civilizations that has been such a major theme in modern Western culture, even if efforts in this direction could later take both ideological and critical turns which obscured the original sources. The role of intercivilizational encounters—and their interactions with global power structures—in the history of modern culture is still inadequately understood (the fashionable lambasting of 'Orientalism' has probably done more harm than good). Finally, the romantic attitude at its most extreme is reflected in radical traditionalism: the rejection of modernity as such and en bloc in the name of reinterpreted traditions or an idealizing vision of tradition in general. The influence of this current is not limited to its most uncompromising—and therefore marginal—ideological expressions. Traditionalism serves, among other things to articulate and at the same time misrepresent the projects of fundamentalist movements. As Eisenstadt has convincingly argued, their thoroughly modern strategies—aiming at a comprehensive reconstruction of society—are filtered through discourses which proclaim unconditional allegiance to traditions.[16]

The divergent but variously balanced trends discussed above should suffice to illustrate the inbuilt diversity of modern transformations. To conclude this part of the argument, some further conceptual distinctions—and corresponding lines of inquiry—may be suggested. Multiple modernities, in the sense proposed here, are the different configurations of the diverse components of modernity—with more or less selective emphasis on some of them—that prevail within geopolitical boundaries (state, regions or civilizational areas). The concept of alternative modernities is best used in a more restricted sense: with reference to patterns or projects which define themselves in explicit opposition and as global or at least regional alternatives to the pattern perceived as dominant, i.e.—in the first instance—the more or less ideologized Western one. The most important alternative modernity was, of course, the Soviet model, but more qualified cases would include Japan and/or the East Asian developmental state in a more general sense. It may be useful to think of alternative modernities in terms of a continuum: as a more or less pronounced or articulate aspect of multiple modernities. And as the Japanese case shows, the strength of this aspect can vary from phase to phase within the same pattern. The last point leads to a further category. Successive modernities are, on this view, the forms which follow each other within a pattern circumscribed by regional or civilizational boundaries. As noted above (with reference to Peter Wagner's sociology of modernity), the Western trajectory can be theorized in terms of such a succession, whereas the Soviet model proved incapable of changes on that scale. It must, however, be added that the very different but still in some ways incomplete path of transformation in China complicates the picture. For a balanced view of exits from the Soviet model, a systematic comparison of East European and East Asian trajectories would be needed.

---

[16] S.N. Eisenstadt, 1999a.

Hermeneutical horizons

The third and last approach, which I propose to call hermeneutical, is best introduced in connection with the question of unity in diversity. For all its emphasis on mutations and multiplications, the present argument still assumes that the formations in question are in some sense variations on a common theme, offshoots or elaborations of a shared pattern which we can treat as a defining characteristic of the modern world. It is, moreover, impossible to define this overarching constellation without confronting its self-definitions and the question of their common ground. Here we encounter a crucial difference between theories of modernization and theories of modernity: as long as the focus is on the dynamics and processes of change, without much explicit concern for the underlying premises, the conceptual framework will tend to stress structural aspects and factors. This was a constant feature of mainstream modernization theory, and when culture was brought back in, it tended to appear as another structural component, albeit with some par-ticular privileges—as it did, for example, in Parsons' account of the cyber-netic hierarchy. But when—at a later stage—the issue of modernity as a condition came to the fore, as a result of the perceived need to reexamine things taken for granted in the first phase of modernization theory, a more significant cultural turn was inevitable. Modernity is—whatever else may be said of it—a self-defining, self-interpreting condition: the very use of the term 'modern' implies a reference to the self-description of an epoch which demarcates itself from the past, claims to differ from it in significant ways, and envisages further movement away from it. In that sense, one can speak of a hermeneutical opening, i.e. an acceptance of the confrontation with pre-existing cultural orientations. This constitutes a permanent task inher-ent in the very proposal to theorize modernity.

It might be argued that a hermeneutical anchoring in self-descriptions was already achieved—even if not fully articulated—by classical social theory. There are obvious connections between the self-images of the Enlightenment and the classical images of society and history, and the interpretive frame-works built on this basis were capable of further conceptual refinement: that applies, for example, to the understanding of moral patterns in society, as it developed from Durkheim to Parsons, or the analysis of rational patterns in history, as it unfolded from Marx to Habermas. But the conceptions of modernity that emerged in this context were of the kind that I have been proposing to criticize. They centred on emphatic ideas of unity, on definitive, unifying and unambiguous principles used to demarcate modernity and to chart its course. If the problematic of multiple modernities entails a break with this frame of reference, it remains to be seen whether we can find an alternative hermeneutical line to link up with.

The first step that suggests itself is a more abstract formulation of the hermeneutical premises. The link to the self-understanding of modernity might be maintained in the most general sense, without taking on board any of the specific contents which had been more or less explicitly incorporated into classical theory. In this way, a self-demarcating definition as such, prior to all concrete alternatives, would serve to stake out the historical field for a post-classical theory. Two examples should suffice to illustrate this line of argument. In an essay which recapitulates extensive work on the subject, Reinhard Koselleck points out the unconvincing results of all attempts to date the origins of modernity in terms of a technological, economic or political breakthrough; all historical boundaries are blurred, and the problem becomes even more obviously insoluble if we try to synchronize changes in different domains. Parallel developments are always disrupted by the 'non-contemporaneity of the contemporaneous' (die Ungleichzeitigkeit des Gleichzeitigen). From this point of view, the various historical interpretations—those who focus on sixteenth-century innovations as well as those who emphasize the two revolutions at the end of the eighteenth century—all run into the same difficulties. For Koselleck, the only way out is a reflexive turn: the question of the origins of modernity is refocused on the structures of consciousness which explain both the irrefutable sense of radical novelty and the insoluble problems encountered when this subjective perspective is short-circuited with historical realities. If the problem is posed in such terms, there can be no doubt about the main landmark. The "concept of a new time in an emphatic sense"[17] is an invention of eighteenth-century thought, and its two most momentous implications are the perception of an ongoing acceleration of history and the idea of an open future. Historical analysis can show that the translation of this new consciousness into global structures and everyday practices is a very uneven long-term process, but the temptation to equate a new horizon with a whole historical epoch will also have to be given its due: an illusion can become a real historical force.

In explicit agreement with Koselleck's focus on the eighteenth century, but with a very different agenda for the analysis of modernity, Göran Therborn also proposes a cultural definition of modernity as "an epoch turned to the future, conceived as likely to be different from and possibly better than the present and the past."[18] The diffusion and dominance of

---

[17] Koselleck, 1987a: 278.
[18] Therborn, 1995: 4.

this new attitude—the discovery of a new, this-worldly future—then becomes
a matter of empirical research. The cultural opening to the future combines
with other factors in different settings, develops at an uneven pace in various parts of the world, and affects the multiple domains of social life in
correspondingly diverse ways.

The importance of eighteenth-century shifts in cultural interpretations of
historical time is not in dispute. But a hermeneutical approach to the problematic of modernity cannot rest content with an observable change of self-
image and leave the rest to historical and comparative research. Rather,
the reference to the cultural self-definition of an epoch should be taken as
a starting-point for further reflections along hermeneutical lines. If hermeneutical understanding involves—by definition—an effort to surpass the self-
understanding of actors and authors, and to distinguish levels of implicit
meanings behind the explicit ones, the same applies—mutatis mutandis—to
the understanding of socio-cultural patterns in history. The conceptual innovations of the late eighteenth century (and, as Koselleck would add, the first
decades of the following one) drew on a cumulative history of action, thought
and experience in different areas of life. Koselleck's own account refers to
'criteria' of novelty that were separately discovered and developed from the
sixteenth to the eighteenth century, but could only be synthesized and coordinated at a higher level of historical consciousness.[19] Charles Taylor's distinction between interpretation and articulation (admittedly not always clearly
stated) may be relevant to this issue: a broad, loosely knit and unevenly
unfolding complex of interpretive trends (in the sense of meanings at work
and in the making within practical contexts) was articulated at the level of
interconnected concepts which in turn opened up new horizons for historical change. In short, the ambiguous and uncoordinated transformations that
preceded the eighteenth-century mutation are not simply a background to
the leap into cultural modernity; it would seem more plausible to theorize
them as earlier phases of the same process. The demarcation from the past
and the discovery of the future presuppose a historical experience of movement beyond traditional boundaries, and the paths of this prehistory are
diverse enough to justify the plural concept of early modernities.[20] Within
that framework, some turning-points loom larger than others. Most obviously, the sixteenth century—marked by changes to the internal structure
of European civilization, as well as to its geopolitical position—represents a
new beginning.

---

[19] Koselleck, 1987a: 281.
[20] Cf. *Daedalus*, 1998.

On the other hand, the sequel to the eighteenth-century crystallization of cultural modernity has—to say the least—proved difficult to explain in terms of the ripening or realization of a project. The Enlightenment had a long-lasting historical impact, but it did not redesign the course of global history. Hermeneutical perspectives may help to avoid over-rationalizing visions of past or possible progress, without losing sight of the cultural orientations that continue to affect the dynamics of modern societies. More specifically, the hermeneutical notion of effective history (Wirkungsgeschichte) highlights the plasticity and historicity of meaning in ways that seem germane to the modern transformation: interpretive constructs and frameworks have a logic and an efficacy of their own, but they acquire new meanings and develop in new directions as their potential is selectively realized in changing contexts. The complexity and ambiguity of such interconnections is particularly evident with regard to the most important political landmark in modern history. Recent and ongoing work on the French revolution has led to a twofold revision of traditional views. In contrast to the reductionistic models that dominated the field for a long time, cultural and ideological preconditions of the revolution are now taken more seriously, but the discontinuities due to unforeseen transformations of ideas in action have also been brought into focus. The latter point relates most directly to the emergence of the nation-state as the unanticipated but unavoidable framework for the practical implementation of revolutionary visions.[21] In conjunction—and sometimes in competition—with the nation-state, other aspects of the modern constellation play a similarly transformative role. Briefly, the history of cultural modernity is made up of multiple contextualizations, and seen from that angle, it lends itself to the two analytical perspectives outlined above: the genealogical and the structural. But to underline the particular importance of a hermeneutical approach, even if it calls for combination with the other two, one further aspect should be noted. The hermeneutical theme par excellence is the conflict of interpretations, broadly understood as a permanent presence of rival orientations within a shared frame of reference. There is an obvious way of linking this notion to the sociological tradition: although the idea of modernity as defined by a constitutive conflict—a conflict built into its core, but capable of taking different directions in changing circumstances—did not figure prominently in the mainstream, it has been defended and developed by both classical and contemporary authors. Among the classics, the most salient example is Max Weber's vision of

---

[21] The debate on the ideological context of the French Revolution was reopened by Furet, 1981; on the nation-state as heir to the revolution, cf. Wokler, 1998.

modernity as characterized by a permanent tension between the expansion of rational apparatuses and the affirmation of individual autonomy and creativity. A brief survey of contemporary variations on this theme may take us one step further.

Contemporary accounts of a central modern conflict differ from Weber in that they refer more explicitly to perceived or potential tensions between capitalism and democracy. Capitalism appears as an embodiment of rationality (or of an imagination masking itself as rationality), geared to mastery over the environment and to the maximization of resources; democracy as an expression of subjectivity in quest of self-determination and participation. Such interpretations always have to do with the underlying cultural orientations at work on both sides, rather than with formal rules or functioning institutions. It seems clear that this perspective can be adapted to a broad spectrum of political positions. A representative radical version can be found in the work of Cornelius Castoriadis, who equates the spirit of capitalism with a vision of the unending expansion of rational mastery, and the other side of the 'dual institution of modernity' with the project of autonomy understood as radical democracy. For Castoriadis, a society committed to autonomy would downgrade the pursuit of wealth and power, so as to avoid the instrumentalization of its core value.[22] The reformist point of view is perhaps best exemplified by Ralf Dahrendorf's account of 'the modern conflict'[23] between the democratic demand for political equality, with an open-ended potential for social extension, and the capitalist primacy of economic liberty, inevitably accompanied by structural inequality. On the conservative side, the most interesting arguments have been put forward by François Furet and Martin Malia: for them (irrespective of disagreements on other points), capitalism and democracy are interconnected aspects of the bourgeois world, but democracy can take a subversive and self-destructive turn when its logic gives rise to extreme demands for a wholesale reconstruction of society on more egalitarian lines.[24] Finally, we can perhaps distinguish a fourth version, where the conflict between rationality and subjectivity is thematized with a view to understanding a new constellation which has changed the terms of debate between rival projects; against that background, the very idea of a political alternative must be reexamined. This seems to me to be the main thrust of Alain Touraine's *Critique de la Modernité*.[25]

---

[22] This is a recurrent theme in Castoriadis' writings; for a particularly forceful statement, cf. Castoriadis, 1997b.
[23] Dahrendorf, 1988.
[24] Malia, 1994; Furet, 1995.
[25] Touraine, 1992.

A closer look at Touraine's work will help to link the hermeneutics of modern conflicts to problems discussed in the preceding sections of this paper. His synthesizing concepts of rationality and subjectivity retain a link to ideas traditionally associated with the developmental logics of capitalism and democracy, but aim to cover a much broader field. Although he proposes no clear and detailed definition of rationality, it seems clear that he has in mind a very broadly understood combination of cognitive and purposive activities (it is worth noting that this approach implicitly questions the Habermasian distinction between strategic and communicative rationality: a better understanding of the overarching *telos* of communication may be seen as a prescription for more effective pursuit of that goal). Only a very inclusive notion of rationality can bring together images of society as a planned order, visions of sovereign individuals in pursuit of their interests, and models of human nature as a force to be released from traditional constraints.[26] As for subjectivity, the antagonistic and subversive other of modern reason, Touraine's account of it includes not only social movements and *aesthetic* countercultures (Rimbaud's *Season in Hell* is mentioned as a key text in the history of modern subjectivity), but also—and more provocatively—intellectuals at odds with modernity, whose critique of dominant forms of subjectivity is more explicit than the counter-paradigms on which it is based (this applies, inter alia, to Foucault and the Frankfurt School). Against this background, the definition of the subject as "the will of an individual to act and to be recognized as an actor"[27] seems too narrow: in fact, Touraine's analysis goes beyond the domains of action and recognition and refers to a broader spectrum of formative ideas in modern culture. The issues of self-determination, self-expression and self-exploration appear as variations on a common underlying theme.

If the central conflict of modernity is redefined in these inclusive terms, it can no longer be identified with any pure or paradigmatic forms. The general interpretations of the opposite sides only make sense as common denominators of open-ended sets of trends in different areas of social life and phases of modern history. By the same token, the covering concepts are open to further interpretation in light of new or previously neglected experiences. The ideas of rationality and subjectivity are perhaps best understood as complementary and equally incomplete self-images of modernity, drawing on multiple sources and developed at a particular historical juncture; they highlight and sum up a bifurcation of reflexivity which manifests

---

[26] Touraine, 1992: 24.
[27] Touraine, 1992: 242.

itself in diverse ways across the whole range of modern cultural patterns. This line of argument allows us to relativize the idea of a central modern conflict without losing sight of its merits: all accounts of conflicting principles must be seen as interpretive constructs, imposed on a field of interconnected but also divergent rivalries, and therefore always in need of further contextualization. Touraine's revised analysis of modernity (significantly different from the conceptual framework used in his earlier writings) is, as I have suggested, the most ambitious and innovative restatement of an older set of ideas; it should, in other words, be read as a new but by no means final move in an ongoing interpretive process, rather than a general and complete theory. It includes some sustained and fruitful attempts to link the problematic of rationality and subjectivity to the analysis of historical actors and processes in specific contexts; among the 'fragments of modernity' examined from this point of view, the nation-state, the enterprise and the consumer are of particular importance. On the other hand, Touraine's critique deals primarily—almost exclusively—with advanced Western modernity, and a broadening of horizons beyond this domain would bring other aspects of the background problematic to the fore. It remains to be seen how extensively the hermeneutical framework—centred on the conflict-ridden relationship between rationality and subjectivity—would have to be modified in response to more systematic study of non-western modernities. But the questions to be confronted in that field would also take us back to structural and historical perspectives on the varieties of modernity. The internal logic of the hermeneutical approach thus leads to a combination with the other analytical strategies sketched above. For present purposes, this is my case; more substantive conclusions would require a much longer preamble.

SECTION TWO

GLOBALIZATION

INTRODUCTION

In Section Two, *Alex Inkeles* discusses the expansion of modernity through-out the world, emphasizing the 'convergence' of societies everywhere, which in itself promotes the consolidation of the globe into one system. Inkeles cites, in this respect, Parsons' assumption that the industrial, democratic, and educational revolutions established the modern era. Many societies come to exhibit similar types of organization, occupational distribution, national constitutions, forms of government and so on, in spite of cultural differences that leave their prints on social development. The resulting convergence is influenced by, and itself influences, globalization.

Aysegul Baykan and *Roland Robertson* discuss the notion of spatialization by focusing on how spaces are defined, contested and articulated into power and identity systems. The case which they study is Anatolianism, which opposed Turkish history outside Anatolia and in Islam, while the Kemalist narrative of the modernization project turned to the West for models of what a 'civilized' nation looks like. Another form of Western-influenced glob-alization is illustrated by the case of democratization in Africa. *Benyamin Neuberger* contends that the aspiration to political modernity was already a component of the fight for decolonization which in most cases ended with the establishment of states that formally adopted the Western democratic model. These regimes collapsed in the 1960s in the context of pre-colonial and colonial sequels, material conditions, ethnic divisions, and weak national identification in the populace. However, in the 1990s, a powerful renewal of aspirations for democracy in dozens of African countries brought about new, relatively free elections and the re-establishment of a multi-party sys-tem. Underlying this transformation were not only the accumulated hatred of corrupt tyrants and economic collapse, but also the influence of Western models and of global trends engendered by the termination of the Cold War and the consequent decline of Africa's geopolitical assets. On the other hand, and beyond the mediated interconnectedness of local and outside scenes, as illustrated by Anatolianism and democratization in Africa, *Abram de Swaan* shows how globalization also operates directly, through one of its most crucial and complex manifestations, that is, the expansion of world languages. Among the 4,000 distinct languages spoken in the world, only a few are highly demanded by learners and benefit from a relatively central status across societies. English, moreover, is at the 'galactic center' of our world, reflecting and shaping the global economic, political and cultural reality. As shown by the case of Algeria's language policy, however, glob-alization may also be embedded in conflictual processes. In *Mohamed Benra-bah*'s chapter, a former colony is described, hostile to the perpetuation of its former metropolitan cultural and linguistic influence. In a drive to bring back Algeria into the Arab world and Islamic culture, Arabization was imposed by declaring classical Arabic the only language to be used in all spheres. This policy, however, encountered the sharpest opposition from a variety of groups that were especially close to French culture or to their own vernaculars, whether Arabic on non-Arabic. Citing Gellner, Benrabah says that the North African knows in his heart not only that God speaks Arabic, but also that modernity speaks French. In practice, Arabization is doomed to limited success in a globalizing world. In a comparative per-spective, *Jerzy Smolicz* then considers the higher-education systems of four different societies—the Philippines, Poland, Australia and Iran, and perceives convergences as well as divergences. Among other features, it is under the influence of common references that higher education is open in these four societies to an ever-growing number of students. At the same time though, access to specific institutions is becoming more and more selective. This means an increasing quality gap between relatively few elite universities and numerous middle-of-the-road or even sub-standard institutions. While this development itself—that is, the growing privatization of higher education— is linked with globalization processes, the responses found in each country to the public issues raised by this kind of development strongly depend on the particular educational traditions of each society.

Alain Touraine proposes at this point a general view according to which globalization actually means the triumph of economic forces which are more and more organized at the world level, while the state and other political, legal or social agents are of a limited capacity of intervention. This is above all the triumph of capitalism in context of the fall and disintegration of other patterns of economic and social life. The new technologies, however, that are produced transform our conception of time and space. In many different parts of the world new actors, individual and collective, are asking for new rights consisting essentially of the claim to combine one's partici-pation to the economic world with the defense and reinterpretation of one's cultural heritage. We thus live now in a world where orientations and atti-tudes are more strongly defined than social and political movements, leaving a wide empty space between the economic system and culture. The new movements are farther and farther from transforming themselves into new political parties, and this explains the new importance of civil society in a time when conflicts mainly oppose new cultural orientations and the logic of capitalism. This conflictual perception of globalization is still radicalized in *Johan Galtung*'s perception. In his chapter, he equates the practice (at least so far) of globalization with Americanization. A model that deeply contradicts what he understands by 'equitable globalization'. The latter, he contends, is the process whereby all genders, generations (also future), races, classes, nations, states and regions pull together and cooperate in a participatory and equitable way to produce a world with better livelihood for all. Instead, what we now have is 'Americanization', or at best, 'Westernization', dominated by a small group of people in a small group of countries using the term 'globalization' as a cover-up. Equitable globalization may find an instructive model in the Swiss example. In Switzerland, four nations cooperate in producing a country with its flaws, but also a remarkable co-existence within and peace without, in addition to direct democracy and well-being. It is the author's aspiration that the United Nations would be capable of developing this kind of diversity within some unity for the whole world. A confederation of many cultures within a meta-culture that accommodates rather than excludes.

9. CONVERGENCE IN SOCIETAL SYSTEMS[1]

Alex Inkeles

Although Parsons' work is replete with references to the convergence of *theories* about social systems, he did not, so far as I know his work, address the idea of convergence in actual *institutions* and in *entire societies* until near the end of his career. The vehicle for this venture was a pair of books which Parsons wrote for the series called Foundations of Modern Sociology which I edited for Prentice Hall. Parsons produced two books for the series, one titled *Societies: Evolutionary and Comparative Perspectives*, published in 1966,[2] and the second on *The System of Modern Societies*, published five years later in 1971.[3] The two volumes, thoroughly edited, were combined in a single book by one of Parsons' devoted and admiring students, Jackson Toby, in order to make the material more accessible to a wider audience. That project, which had Parsons' personal approval, resulted in a book under the title *The Evolution of Societies* published in 1977.[4]

Perhaps because it was written as textbook, this work seems to have been systematically neglected both by followers and critics of Parsons' theories. Toby saw Parsons' two volumes, as 'a masterpiece', a judgment in which I concur. Taken together the two volumes present a magisterial sociological summary of the evolution of human society ranging from the primitive, through the archaic societies such as ancient Egypt and Mesopotamia, continuing with historic empires such as the Roman, and so moving through history until the emergence of the system of modern societies. The scope is daring, and the quality of the exposition high. More critical, from the point of view of sociological history, is that this is probably the only place in which Parsons more or less systematically set out his theory of social evolution. In this work Parsons formulates a theory of social change which Toby finds 'logically more compelling than Weber's'.

---

[1] Presented at the International Conference "A Legacy of 'Verantwortungsethik': Talcott Parsons' *Structure of Social Action After Sixty Years*", Heidelberg U. 26–27.6, 1997. An earlier version of this chapter appeared in Barber, Bernard and Gerhardt, Uta (eds.) *Agenda for Sociology: Classic Sources and Current Uses of Talcott Parsons' Work*, Baden-Baden: Nomos, 1999. We thank the publisher for his permission to publish this text here (Note of the editors).
[2] Parsons, 1966.
[3] Parsons, 1971.
[4] Parsons, 1977.

Parsons' views on societal evolution and convergence

As the first element I present extracts from *The Evolution of Societies* which, taken together, succinctly sum up Parsons' position with regard to the issues I will address in the main body of this paper. In examining these extracts two points should be kept in mind. Parsons sought to establish what he saw as the main line of the evolution of human societies. Evolution does not necessarily lead to sameness. Indeed the history of evolution in nature seems above all else to be a story of endless, even explosive, differentiation of life forms. Yet it is notable that in this same context Parsons also explicitly used the term 'convergence' to mean the tendency for societies in the modern era to become more alike. There is a resolution of this apparent paradox, which I reserve for a later point in my exposition, in order to permit the reader to move on to an appreciation of Parsons' position.

Major social processes shaping the modern world

In his analysis of the modern era, which he dated from roughly the 18th century, Parsons identified a set of revolutions, and other major social processes, as the main agencies of change leading to the emergence of what we know as modern societies:

> The industrial revolution further differentiated the economy and the democratic revolution further differentiated the polity from the societal community. Unless modern societies were to be torn apart by these differentiating tendencies, integrative processes were necessary . . . this chapter will undertake to set forth the kinds of factors capable of integrating modern societies: the legal system, the extension of citizenship, market systems, bureaucratic organizations, and associational organizations (Parsons, 1977: 174–175).

> The industrial revolution shifted economic organization from agriculture and the commerce and handicrafts of small urban communities; it also extended markets (Parsons, 1977: 182). The democratic revolution stimulated efficient administration, the industrial revolution the new economy. Weber saw that in a later phase the two tend to fuse in the bureaucratization of the capitalist economy (Parsons, 1977: 182–183). The educational revolution is as characteristic of modernity as the industrial and democratic revolutions have been . . . Secular disciplines have become institutionalized in the system of higher education based on the universities . . . One aspect of this revolution is the spread of basic education . . . a feature of the educational revolution has been the continuous extension of the education of the population beyond literacy (Parsons, 1977: 190).

Main emergent characteristics of modern societies

Parsons argues that the result of these revolutionary influences was the emergence of the first modern societies in history. He delineated the main characteristics of these historically emerging modern societies as follows:

- Monarchies survived only where they have become constitutional.
- Aristocracy still twitches but mostly in the informal aspects of stratification systems—nowhere is it structurally central.
- There are still established churches, but only on the less modern peripheries . . . the trend is toward separation of church and state and denominational pluralism.

> The emergence of full modernity thus weakened the ascriptive framework of monarchy, aristocracy, established churches, and an economy circumscribed by kinship and localism to the point where ascription no longer exercises decisive influence. Modern components had already developed by the eighteenth century, particularly a universalistic legal system and secular culture . . . Further developments in the political aspects of community emphasized the associational principle, nationalism, citizenship, and representative government. In the economy differentiated markets developed for the factors of production, primarily labor. Occupational services were increasingly performed in employing organizations structurally differentiated from households. New patterns of effectively organizing specific functions arose, especially administration (centering in government and the military) and the new economy (Parsons, 1977: 182–183).

Parsons affirms the idea of convergence

Parsons saw the three major revolutions, and the related social forces they unleashed, as producing an unequivocal effect, namely that of causing all the nations of the world to be much more alike in their social structure. The following series of statements from Parsons' exposition should leave no doubt as to his position:

> The system of modern societies, though originally European, has been extended to the entire world . . . increasingly, all contemporary societies share the same general ideas and values . . .[5]

---

[5] At this point Parsons added the important qualification: "but even in an interdependent world, societies are not carbon copies of one another; they play different roles in the world community."

I believe that the United States is a model for other countries in structural innovations central to modern societal development. The United States is extending the organization of social life in individualistic, decentralized, and associational directions (the historic roots of which can be traced to the feudal period in Europe). Comparable patterns of individualism, decentralization, and associational pluralism also characterize closely related societies, Canada and Australia. *Other societies will necessarily adopt these features as they move toward modernity* (Parsons, 1977: 215, italics supplied).

This is what I mean when I speak of a system of modern societies: extension of a common culture to all societies yet different societies playing differentiated roles within the world community (Parsons, 1977: 216).

The modern system has extended beyond the Western cultural areas, however. European influence has pervaded the rest of the world through trade, missions, settlements and acquisition as colonies (Parsons, 1977: 226).[6]

The imperialist phase of Western society's relation with the rest of the world was transitional. *The trend toward modernization has now become worldwide.* The elites of most nonmodern societies accept aspects of the values of modernity, especially economic development, education, political independence, and some form of democracy. Though the institutionalization of these values is uneven and fraught with conflict, the trend toward modernization in the Western world will probably continue. We cannot expect a clear outcome of the contemporary post-imperialist ferment for a considerable time. But the burden of proof rests with those who argue that any major part of the world will settle into a non-modern pattern of society during the next couple of centuries, although the variations within the modern type will probably turn out to be very great (Parsons, 1977: 226, italics supplied).

There is a convergence of sociocultural development such that nearly all societies reflect to varying degrees the industrial revolution, the democratic revolution, and the educational revolution. It is therefore only a slight exaggeration to say that all contemporary societies are more or less modern (Parsons, 1977: 229, italics supplied).

Expressing a view quite unorthodox at the time, Parsons suggested that we should not make too much of the variation from the older European patterns which nations such as Communist Russia manifested. Instead, he proposed "the value content of these ideologies should be regarded as specifications of the more general Western value pattern of instrumental activism rather than as departures from it." Finally, he concluded "... *the societies of the world have grown similar to one another, have formed one modern culture ...*" (Parsons, 1977: 229, italics supplied).

---

[6] Japan was discussed by Parsons at this point, with emphasis on the strains caused by modernization.

What do we mean by convergence?

The simplest and least ambiguous meaning of convergence as a social science concept is provided by its geometric form. If a social phenomenon can be plotted as a line on a chart, then convergence can be said to exist if the trajectory of two or more lines brings them closer and closer over time. The social units under study can be said to have converged if the plotted lines actually meet at some point. The field of demography is replete with illustrations of this phenomenon. For example, in a set which includes industrialized and industrializing nations, birth rates and the proportion of the population which is over 65 will tend to converge. It is, of course, not necessary to plot lines on a chart to assess convergence, the advantage of this approach being mainly as a concrete visual demonstration. The same phenomena can be dealt with by working directly with various rates, proportions, absolute numbers, and the like, and there is a simple index which can be used to express the degree of convergence which any such time series manifests.

The matter becomes more complicated when the phenomena under observation cannot readily be described in more or less precise quantitative terms. In that case, we are reduced to describing convergence in statements of a much more imprecise and essentially qualitative nature. Such statements may be exceedingly broad, as when Parsons asserted that "the nations of the world have grown similar to each other." Obviously, this will seem to many observers much too general to be satisfying, and they will insist on much greater specificity. However, even the next degree of specification may still be at a rather general level, as in Parsons' assertion that as they enter the modern era virtually all societies undergo institutional differentiation leading to the greater separation of political, economic, and religious functions in institutions specialized to perform those functions.

Still greater concreteness is provided by specifying the particular institutional complexes which come over time to be more widely installed in some set of nations under observation. It should be noted that in numerous ways these more structural types of change, and the transformation of institutions such as schools, can actually be expressed in quantitative terms, and their analysis therefore also be conducted by means of statistical procedures.

What is the evidence for convergence?

Some features of contemporary societies which Parsons saw as converging on a common model seem so obvious that few efforts are made systematically to document them. For example, there is not much disposition to challenge his assumption that in more and more societies "occupational services are increasingly performed in employing organizations structurally differentiated from households", or his assertion that in matters of social placement, increasingly after the 18th century "ascription no longer exercises decisive influence." In any event, most research on convergence issues has focused on the more concrete level of specific institutions and institutional complexes, and on studies of popular attitudes and values. Among the many studies which document the tendency for the world's major nations, and in particular the industrial nations, to adopt similar institutional forms, and for their populations to develop similar attitudes and values, we note the following, stressing that the list is not remotely exhaustive but is rather purely illustrative.

Williamson and Pampel document the diffusion of systems of social security for the aged across nations and time.[7]

John Boli has shown how strikingly alike are the basic structure and content of national constitutions, especially as they have evolved over time.[8]

Aaron Benavot and his and associates have shown that over time the basic school curriculum in most nations in the world has experienced near universal standardization such that the subjects covered and even the time allocated to different subjects have become striking alike in nation after nation.[9]

Francisco Ramirez and his associates reveal the progressive granting to women of the right to suffrage, so that this condition is now nearly universal.[10] The widespread adoption of fairly standard features of government mandated retirement schemes in industrial and industrializing countries is documented by Inkeles and Usui.[11] In Asia, in countries with political and economic systems as different as those of Communist China, Taiwan, and Japan, attitudes and values can be shown to be moving in common directions, similar to those earlier observed in the process of modernization of Western nations. For example arranged marriages, previously standard, are now exceedingly rare, couples meet at school or work rather than at the initiative of parents, and love is increasingly the prime motivation in the selection of a mate.[12] Huntington[13] and Diamond[14] insist on the spread of democratic government to more and more countries.

---

[7] Williamson and Pampel, 1993.
[8] Boli, 1987.
[9] Benavot et al., 1991.
[10] Ramirez et al., 1997.
[11] See Inkeles and Usui, 1989.
[12] See Chapter 13 in Inkeles, 1998.
[13] Huntington, 1991.
[14] Diamond, 1996.

The Comparative Charting Group has carefully measured a series of major characteristics of six advanced countries in Europe in order to ascertain whether or not these national societies are following common or separate paths of development. Through dozens of familiar indicators, ranging from infant mortality to the speed of internal transportation, they found these nations "drew closer together, erasing most of the previously existing differences among themselves."[15]

Theoretical orientations of efforts to explain convergence

Parsons thought of his analysis as being guided by an evolutionary perspective. Just as in nature, he argued, more complex forms of life evolve from more simple forms, so also in the social realm societies evolve from less to more differentiated forms. Such a model is, however, purely descriptive. It does not tell us anything about the mechanisms which drive the process from one condition to another. In the case of early forms of the theory of evolution in nature this gap was filled by positing the influence of a struggle for scarce resources which led to the survival of the fittest, and hence to the perpetuation of the characteristics of the survivors. Parsons did not, at least as I read him, suggest a similar model to explain what he saw as societal evolution. Indeed, I do not find him proposing any systematic theory to explain the evolutionary process he posited. He did say that "the United States is a model for other countries in structural innovations central to modern societal development", but he did not explicitly specify a model of diffusion or imitation. Rather he simply assumed other societies will "*necessarily* adopt these features as they move toward modernity." (Parsons, 1977: 215, italics supplied)

Other social scientists who have presented more detailed evidence on the facts of societal convergence have generally been more explicit in specifying the theory which either guided them to search for, or which in their view explained the drive towards, the convergence they sought to document. We note briefly, some of the main lines of theoretical analysis.

Diffusion and imitation theories. It has become almost a cliché to stress how far the modern world has linked individuals everywhere in one vast worldwide communications network which freely transcends national boundaries. Hollywood is often identified as at the center of this web, its dream factories disseminating worldwide images of interpersonal relations, ideas about

---

[15] The quotation is from Caplow, 1998. A full account of their findings is found in Langlois et al., 1994.

the good life, fantasies about love and riches, models of intrigue and violence, standards of dress and criteria of beauty whose homogenizing influence is pervasive and world wide. The radio, and even more television, are also often seen as clever spiders manipulating different strands of this net which is perceived as having ensnared the great majority of humankind. The energy to operate this vast machinery, the theory holds, derives ultimately from the business interests of multi-national corporations, who, to sell their products, rely on powerful advertising campaigns. The symbols from those advertisements create a common world culture, made concrete in the specific use of the standard cigarettes, soaps, clothing, razors, and other goods, modest or luxurious, used by the populations of most of the world's countries.

This theory is attractive, and can surely be anecdotally verified by almost everyone. In my own case, on recently visiting a modest provincial city in Finland I was startled to discover all the adolescent boys wearing their baseball-type caps with the brim at the back just as did the boys in the provincial town in California in which I lived. There is absolutely no direct connection between these communities. One must assume the youngsters in both countries saw the same movies and watched either the same TV programs or at least programs initiated at some common source. Nevertheless, systematic evidence to establish the role of mass communication in the convergence of popular tastes is not, to my knowledge, extensive, and the connection, seemingly obvious as it may seem, is not easily definitively proved.

Worldwide elite cultures. A variant form of the diffusion theory has been heavily relied on by John Meyer and his associates to explain the high degree of uniformity they have found in various features of national school systems.[16] This uniformity is noted in the general organization of their curricula and in even the detailed allocation of emphasis *within* different elements of the curriculum such as that devoted to science. To explain this uniformity Meyer and his associates argue that a worldwide elite culture has developed which defines what is at least minimally required of any nation in order not to be seen as backward or underdeveloped. In this culture there are certain standards of what is expected of a modern nation which are shared by the several sets of elites who control power and shape different institutions in nation states. For the sake of preserving national prestige in the system of nation states, these elites strive to adopt and closely follow whatever is the standard set either by important international agencies or by the most prestigious or powerful nations. As a result of their sharing this

---

[16] The basic theoretical and empirical foundation for this approach was laid down in Meyer and Hannan, 1979. A more current exposition of the basic idea and a detailed application will be found in Meyer et al., 1992.

world wide elite culture, and despite greatly varying local conditions and national needs, the officials with the power to do so impose an externally generated standard curriculum on their respective national school systems.

Again at the anecdotal level I can testify from personal experience that there are indeed situations which unambiguously validate the model guiding the investigations of Meyer and his associates. If you were to examine the official sanitary codes embodied in legal regulations of most countries in Latin America in the 1960s and 1970s you would discover that despite the great difference in the size, wealth, economic development and degree of Europeanization of those countries, their official health codes were surprisingly similar, often containing almost exactly the same wording. Through first hand contact I quite accidentally discovered the source of this remarkable congruence. An expert in health law whom I met while doing research in Chile told me that as a consultant to the Pan American Health Organization, known as PAHO, she was assigned periodically to visit the Minister of Health in all the Latin American countries, and to display to each of them what the councils of that international organization had identified as the latest standard regulations which every self respecting country should adopt. Not wishing to be seen as backward and benighted, the several ministers each in turn agreed, usually with only some small modification, to incorporate the latest standard into their respective national sanitary code. Of course, this made the health codes remarkably uniform from country to country, quite without regard to the appropriateness of the regulation or the degree of its actual enforcement in practice.

John Meyer and his associates present some anecdotal evidence of their own in support of their theory as it applies to school curricula. However, to give greater credence to their assumption about the influence of external centers on domestic policy, the followers of this theory offer some systematic statistical correlations. These involve, on the one hand, the degree of connectedness a country has with international agencies and, on the other hand, the degree to which it has conformed to the international standard in the organization and content of its school curricula. They find the correlation positive and statistically significant, and interpret that as confirming their hypothesis.

World system theory. At first glance the world system theory elaborated by Wallerstein and his school would seem to be a challenge to convergence theory.[17] World system theory argues that ever since the 16th century the

---

[17] His theory, and the evidence to support it, are laid out in three volumes. Of most relevance to the discussion here is the last: Wallerstein, 1989. For an accessible and sympathetic summary of the work of this school see Shannon, 1989.

entire world has been organized as one capitalist system which is fixedly divided into two distinct tiers, one composed of states in the so called 'Center', with all the others constituting the 'Periphery'. States in the center dominate and control the world system, and determine the division of labor within the system as a whole. Individual states may move in or out of the center, and more rarely out of the periphery, but the basic structure of the system is assumed to remain fixed.

This notion of the fixity of the system would seem to place the Wallersteinian theory in opposition to the assumption that individual nations will converge on a common structure or structures. Indeed, the theory does deny the possibility of such convergence, but only as applies to the convergence of states in the core with those in the periphery. So far as regards the states within the periphery, however, one version of the theory argues that their common condition as weaker states, and the influence of the policies which the center imposes on them, creates in the peripheral states a number of common features which make them more alike despite what might otherwise be true given their distinctive histories and unique cultures. These common features around which the peripheral states are convergent include: dependency on the core, especially economically, but also politically and culturally; surrender or loss of true national autonomy in most matters, but especially in the freedom to develop one's own economic pattern of development; subordination to the needs of international capital, including acceptance of production roles determined by that source rather than by national preference or natural advantage; and the hollowing out of indigenous national culture as the needs for the expansion of the international market force the substitution of locally made goods and ideas by products disseminated from the periphery or from other elements within the worldwide capitalist market.

Technological imperatives and structural-functional theory. To some extent in the Meyer model, and almost exclusively in the Wallerstein model, the pressure toward convergence is seen as *externally driven*, or even imposed, on many nations. An alternative view, which I favor, while not denying either the fact of imitation or the influence of powerful nations, gives more emphasis to processes internal to nation states and their populations. This approach assigns a greater role to local policy initiative, and stresses processes of adjustment and adaptation which are spontaneous responses to certain institutional arrangements associated with industrialization and 'modernization'.[18] The model makes the following assumptions:

---

[18] A full scale empirical test of some of the main assumptions of the model will be found in Inkeles and Smith, 1974. The theory of convergence is further elaborated at a general level, and illustrated in several empirical investigations in Inkeles, 1998.

Either in response to the requirements of industrial production, or independently as a way of maintaining national autonomy and power, or as a response to domestic demand, governments undertake or facilitate the transformation of national systems of communication and transportation, of the educational system, of banking and commerce arrangements, and of other institutions which are newly introduced or made over to increase their effectiveness, efficiency and competitiveness.

Once a commitment to modernization is made, certain technical imperatives assert themselves. There are, after all, some common and compelling technical features of running an air line which do not permit of much variation without generating high costs in equipment, money, and ultimately lives. Such measures are not adopted because they are fashionable, but because the failure to do so can have direct practical consequences. The result is that nations come to have broadly comparable arrays of institutions organized along increasingly common lines.

In this process they do not necessarily lose basic cultural features. For example, there is no reason why they must shift from Hinduism to Christianity, or from Chinese to English, or from a common law to a civil law tradition, since the technical imperatives built into the operation of most institutions in most cases do not make any of these cultural features less suitable than any other. In analogy to evolution in nature, the societies involved in this change process undergo 'convergent evolution'. Thus, faced with a habitat rich only in hard to crack nuts, different species of birds will all adapt by developing beaks of a similar kind suitable to cracking the hard nuts. They thus become alike in a notable feature without otherwise ceasing to be of different and distinct species.[19] And, of course, this structural convergence need not be limited to a single feature of social structure, but can occur in several, making the units in question seem more and more alike without thereby making them of the same species.

Looking at the popular level this model assumes that living in institutional environments which are highly similar from nation to nation stimulates

---

[19] For an example involving lizards, see *Science*, Vol. 279, 27 March 1998, p. 2043. Anole lizards were introduced into four different islands in the Greater Antilles and then evolved in various ways. DNA evidence indicates the original lizards coming to each island were genetically different, "but similar evolutionary pressures shaped them into similar ecomorphs." For example, whatever their species of origin, anole lizards living in tree tops have large toe-pads and short legs, while those that live on the ground have long strong hind legs. The lizards on each island are more closely genetically related to other lizards on the same island, but in physical form the similarities follow not from genetic origin but from the nature of the habitat, so that lizards in a similar habitat have similar physical form even though they live on different islands and have different origins.

attitudes and values which are broadly comparable from one national population to another. In this process of homogenization, education in modern schools plays a particularly critical role. It inculcates skills, values and
expectations which are more or less common across nations. Especially in
the case of women, education, particularly when combined with paid employment, induces much more independence and autonomy. In these circumstances women no longer accept having their parents select their mate but
insist on making their own choice; they marry later and have fewer children; and they divorce more often. None of these processes are imposed
from without, least by international capital or hegemonic world powers.
They certainly may be influenced by models provided in the movies and
on television. But I believe they are best understood as spontaneous and
parallel adaptations to new sets of standard social conditions which have
the effect of increasing the convergence of national populations on more
common marriage and family patterns.

Some common misconceptions, misperceptions, and misunderstandings

So complex a process as convergence is bound to generate failures of communication above the already high average characteristic of the social sciences. No doubt some of the difficulties are caused by those who advance
the theory and seek to mobilize evidence in support of it. Their statements
may be too imprecise and lack proper specificity, their claims too global
and sweeping, their evidence thin, often anecdotal, and not compelling as
proof of their assertions. For their part, critics of the theory manifest their
own form of imprecision, often attacking claims the convergence analysts
did not actually make, and ignoring the caveats and reservations with which
they qualified their assertions and conclusions. And some critics seem often
to dismiss evidence in support of the theory on *a priori* grounds simply
because it seems to run counter to their intuition or to the assumptions of
the theories they hold. Experience suggests that in this kind of situation attempting to allocate guilt and responsibility is not productive. Instead, I
hope that communication can be improved by identifying, and perhaps
clarifying, some of the most common misconceptions, misperceptions, and
misunderstandings.[20]

Similarity, even uniformity, is in itself not proof of convergence. Social systems and
institutions which seem very much alike, even identical, across nations did

---

[20] The issues raised and resolutions proposed in the next section are more fully discussed
in Inkeles, 1998.

not necessarily get that way as a result of becoming more alike over time. They may well have been alike from their beginnings.

Moving in the same direction, or changing at the same rate, does not necessarily produce convergence. A frequent tendency of social systems is to change in the same direction, and/or at the same rate, as others in some defined cohort of nations. Thus, all the nations of Europe might experience a two percent rate of economic growth over a long span of time. Such patterns may be of great importance, but they represent *parallel* and not convergent change. In itself parallel change does not produce convergence. If the base on which a common rate of change is differentiated from the start, as for example in a division into rich and poorer countries, the parallel change, important as it may be in itself, ensures the maintenance of a structure of differentiation rather than a process of convergence.

'Converging' and 'converged' should not be confused. Two institutions or two rates may be coming to be more alike over time, and this may justify stating that they are, in the span of time specified, converging. But to be in the *process* of converging is not the same as to have actually met at a truly common point, that is, to have converged. Those who support the theory often prejudge the question, assuming that clear cut evidence of strong convergent movement is tantamount to ultimate unity. On the other hand, critics assume that because they can identify persistent differences, that proves that the entities in question have not converged, even when the analyst did not commit the error of presuming the ultimate outcome and was careful to specify the limits of the available evidence.

Evidence of convergence in some elements within an institutional complex, such as that constituted by a culture's marriage and family patterns, cannot be assumed to mean a comparable process of change in most, let alone all, elements of the given complex. Thus, in many countries on the Pacific Rim the proportion of marriages which were 'arranged' dropped within the span of 50 years from close to 80 percent of all marriages to a mere 10 or 15 percent, but at the same time the commitment to the principle of filial piety in those same populations remained virtually unchanged at very high levels.[21] Those advancing the idea of convergence may easily slip into the error or assuming that striking evidence of change in one element is an almost certain indicator that other elements of a given institutional complex have changed in equal degree. For their part, critics of the theory often make the mistake of assuming that pointing to elements of a complex which have not changed disproves the fact of convergence in some other element of the same complex which has converged.

---

[21] See chapter 13 in Inkeles, 1998.

Even less justified is the assumption that convergence within any one institutional complex, however pervasive, is proof of the likelihood of convergence in other different institutional complexes. Marriage and family attitudes and practices may converge dramatically, but religious beliefs or styles of political leadership may continue to be highly differentiated across nations and populations. For example, Thomas Metzger argues that despite the many indications of modernization and even Westernization on Taiwan, 'the mode of discourse', especially among Chinese intellectuals whatever their political orientation or their position with regard to modernization, remains distinctive from that of Western intellectuals.[22]

All statements about convergence must be recognized as time bound. Rates of change either toward convergence or toward differentiation are rarely uniform over time, but rather tend to be discontinuous depending on various world conditions. Thus, a long term movement for the nation states of the world to adopt some form of democratic politics has proceeded in at least three distinct waves. In the period from 1917 to 1945 the trend was in the opposite direction, with many nations which had previously adopted democratic systems abandoning them in favor of various forms of authoritarian government. After a new surge in the creation of electoral democracies after 1945 there was another period of retrogression in the late 1950s and throughout the 1960s. The tide then shifted, and a period of intense movement to adopt democratic forms of governance between 1974 and 1990 brought about a near doubling of the number of democratic states in the world. Although somewhat slowed thereafter, the trend continued, and by 1996 electoral democracy had become the predominant form worldwide, accounting for 62 percent of all national governments. Obviously, how one reads the evidence for a convergent tendency in national governance world-wide would depend heavily on whether one was looking at the data for one or another time period, or was, instead, assessing the trend over the entire span of two centuries.

Convergence is neither inevitable nor universally welcome. There is no reason to believe that convergence is an uncaused cause. It comes about only because and if certain conditions are met. Even when the necessary conditions seem to be met, whether convergence occurs or not is a matter of probability and not a matter of certainty. To a significant degree national policy can slow down and inhibit, if not entirely prevent, the process of convergence in particular national settings. The experience of Maoist China, Castro's Cuba, and of North Vietnam, in the Communist camp, of Burma as a

---

[22] Metzger, 1988; 1991.

hybrid form, and of India in the category of more democratic states, all in varying degree illustrate the way in which national policy can inhibit or prevent tendencies towards convergence with some international standard. Islamic and Christian fundamentalism, and some extreme forms of Jewish Orthodoxy must, at least in part, be understood as a reaction to the experience of, or perception of, certain forms of attitude and value convergence, a convergence favoring individualism, self-determination, self-expression, free thinking, and other qualities of the modern liberated personality. By the effectiveness of their action on followers and on governments these orthodoxies inhibit, and in some cases even reverse, the tendency of peoples in many parts of the world to follow an increasingly common style of popular living and thinking.

Conclusions

Misconceptions, misperceptions, and misunderstandings apart, one must take a stand on the underlying issue. I think the world is experiencing a process of convergence in institutional structures, in associated cultural assumptions and practices, and in individual attitudes and behavioral orientations which is wide in scope, deep in penetration, and profound in its implications for how human existence will be conducted. As Talcott Parsons (1977: 229) expressed it: "There is a convergence of sociocultural development such that nearly all societies reflect to varying degrees the industrial revolution, the democratic revolution, and the educational revolution." More recently Thomas Metzger sought to capture the essence of this process by reference to the widespread institutionalization of three markets: the market of goods and services, the market of consent and power, and the market of ideas.[23] Many parts of the world have experienced Parsons' three revolutions in only modest degree, and many societies have only partially and imperfectly institutionalized Metzger's three essential free markets. Moreover, even in those societies which have most advanced the three revolutions and institutionalized the three markets, the process of social change is continuous. The forms around which social action converges are not fixed, but are rather constantly changing and evolving. Convergence is therefore never an end state, but is rather a continuous process. It is always proximate, and can never be final. That makes its study a formidable challenge to the theoretical sophistication and methodological acumen of the social sciences.

---

[23] Metzger, in press.

10. SPATIALIZING TURKEY

Aysegul Baykan and Roland Robertson

In this chapter, we invoke the theme of spatiality in order to cast more light on the much-debated issue of the contested making of modern Turkey. Our argument centers on the general proposition that the disputed narrative of the birth of the Turkish Republic in the early 1920s, following the crumbling of the Ottoman Empire, may be far more adequately approached and rendered by a direct encounter with spatial practices and disputes. More specifically, this chapter is on how space changed conceptually in articulating the meaning of the new nation-state's territory. We are also interested in how contestations over these definitions have evolved to this day.

Spatiality and the problem of modernity

In recent years, the issue of modernity has been given much attention. Much of this has arisen in response to the fading of the debate about postmodernity. To put it very simply, the debate about postmodernity became particularly extensive during the 1980s but was greeted sceptically by many comparative and historical sociologists, on the grounds that there was little empirical understanding of modernity. More specifically, some began seriously questioning whether it was sensible and meaningful to talk about a single, amorphous modernity. The latter idea of modernity-in-general had been propagated by those proclaiming that modernity was dead—or at least, dying fast—in the face of the rise of non-foundational epistemologies and the proliferation of small, as opposed to grand, narratives.

Thus, for various reasons, the thesis that we are now in postmodern circumstances has been challenged from several different perspectives. Here we will mention only those challenges that have a direct bearing upon our specific empirical concerns in the present chapter. First, and probably most important, there has been a shift toward the delineation and typification of different forms of modernity, a shift that has involved a *spatial* turn, in the sense that modernity had been, for the most part, previously considered as merely a stage in a *single* diachronic process. And even though sociological and philosophical interest in modernity in recent years has eschewed concern with modernization, as that term was used in the so-called modernization theory of the late 1950s to early 1970s, this interest nonetheless has been temporal in the sense of casting modernity as part of a chronological sequence in the history of social formations. The spatial turn of which we have spoken involves a focus upon the variety of modernities in different regions and civilizations of the world—without, it should be said, denying for a moment that these spatially distributed modernities each have a history and can indeed be treated diachronically so long as their spatial distribution is fully recognized. Thus, in fact, the emphasis placed here on the spatial dimension is intended to rectify an overemphasis on the temporal dimension, to the detriment of spatiality. Moreover, even though we have said that spatially focused modernities each have a history, this should not be interpreted as meaning that these histories are unrelated. Far from it. Not merely are the histories of different forms of modernity closely intertwined, the very idea of their spatial and 'inter-spatial' relationships considerably affects the ways in which we construe their histories. This is where the well-known theme of contested collective memory *in the historical sense* intersects the much less explored issue of collective memory *in the geographical sense*. It is now readily admitted that collective historical memories are constantly manipulated and constructed. However, we are only in the *relatively* early stages of recognizing that what is true of history is also true of geography (Soja, 1989; Robertson, 1995a; Lewis and Wigen, 1997).

The second main challenge to the strong postmodernity thesis has arisen from the still-growing debate about globalization. Considered comprehensively and multidimensionally—as opposed to economistically—the globalization debate has largely subsumed and relativized the debate about postmodernity. More precisely, the sociological and anthropological articulation of the theme of globalization (coming well before the usage of that term to denote global capitalism, bureaucratically sustained, paradoxically, by such organizations as the IMF, the WTO and the World Bank) has shown that much of what the postmodernists have said can be 'grounded' in the process of globalization. Understood to mean basically the two-fold development of reflexive global consciousness, on the one hand, and rapidly intensifying global interconnectedness, on the other, globalization may be seen as the producer of multiple narratives and, not least, an increasing sense of the salience of space. In other words, the idea of globalization inherently carries with it a sensitivity to socio-geographical fluidity, as well as to the contested nature of global, or world, history.

There is a third relevant challenge to the strong postmodernity argument, namely that associated with the ideas of reflexive modernization and detraditionalization (Beck, 1992). Since, however, elaboration of these concepts has to a fair degree gone hand in hand with the valorization of globalization as the axial sociological principle of our time, there is little need to dwell upon these issues in the present context (Beck, 2000b). Suffice it, then, to say at this point that the notions of reflexive modernization and detraditionalization have been closely bound-up with the proposition that we are presently in a phase, globe-wide in reach, in which the idea of tradition has been destabilized—in the sense that traditions have been greatly relativized. The greatly flourished notion of the invention of tradition is relevant here, for it echoes Marx's well-known theme of 'the nightmare of tradition'. Thus detraditionalization—as well as its opposite, reflexive modernization—is an *extension* of modernity; but an extension which in and of itself has been partly responsible for the recent spatial turn. As we have said, it is the concern with globalization which is the core phenomenon with respect to the spatial turn, but the themes of reflexive modernization and detraditionalization are most proximate precipitants of the explosion of interest in spatiality. This, in the sense that both attenuate the idea of a single, temporally-defined modernity (Robertson, 1995a, 1995b, 2000).

The Turkish experience in spatiality

In discussing issues of citizenship, Salzmann (1999) shows the diversity of the problems encountered by the Ottoman Empire during the nineteenth century, such as the dilemma between already established systems of societal organization and the demands of the times and of the superpowers. However, the primary problem was that of constituting a centralized state which could enforce a uniform relationship between the state and individual subjects. This was after "more than a century of decentralized rule that had encouraged a wide variety of 'vernacular' political systems (socially, economically, and organizationally specific or spatially contained relations of power)" (Salzmann, 1999: 38). The vernacular, with its peasants, traders, guild members, and so forth, resisted the local hierarchical structures and the new centralized and standardized norms and rules. The land ownership and tax collecting claims, the rights to rent and fiefs would in the face of the new rules of basic rights and universal citizenship disrupt the centuries old conventional constitution of the rights of the confessional groups, the *millets*.

> The meaning of citizenship was continually reshaped by discussion and contention between majority and minority; between individuals, semiautonomous bodies, and an emerging legal and public sphere. These discussions were never contained within the state's territorial boundaries. The great powers, international institutions and lobbies, as well as post-Ottoman nation-states—the

empire's phantom limbs—continued to influence the debates about rights as well as the content of an Ottomanist identity (Salzmann, 1999: 56).

It is Salzmann's contention that, unresolved claims to citizenship other than merely nationalist, imperialist claims, within the diverse nature of the Empire, played a significant role in the matching of individuals to borders after 1918.

For the leaders of the new post-Ottoman state, the re-territorialization of the area within the borders defined by the so-called *Misak-i Milli* (specifically, a National Pact dated 1920) had to be constituted through the political principle of republicanism. The idea was implicit in the constitution of 1921, although not in its name (Ozbudun, 1987). This is an important issue, because the definition of the new state was not constituted by a synchronic concept of a 'Turkish nation', mapped on a territory with the collective memory of the complexity inherited from the Ottoman Empire. The dynamics of the space would resist a totalizing ideology as the general principle that would subject the lived practices of that space to itself as an empty given. The memory of the Ottoman past, with contestable claims to Ottoman citizenship, as Salzmann (1999) argues, would possibly accept Republicanism but not the ideological character of the Pan-Turkism of the Young-Turk era. Writing in 1963, Tachau innovatively stated that neither in the 1920s nor even in the 1960s was there a clear and acceptable interpretation of what a Turkish national identity implied. To understand the Turkish war of independence after the First World War, the burdens Anatolian Muslims faced *vis-à-vis* unfavorable economic conditions on the one hand, and military obligations on the other, do not need to be presented here. But it is essential to follow Tachau's line of thought to note the collective encounter of the people of the occupation by foreigners and the narrative of the love of fatherland in resisting it.

The desire for the 'mother'-land (as in Turkish) need not to be taken as a synonym for a desire for a 'nation', let alone a nation-state. The collective memory of that motherland crosscuts singular definitions of ethnicity, religion, language, and so forth. The mutual coexistence of the *millets* of the Ottoman Empire implied that they constituted a collective political space. 'Places' were made and shared, even if not the particular communities, as the collective 'home'-land. With the rise of the nation-state ideology, cultures and communities became considered as spatially territorialized singularly. The emphasis on an overlapping space, territory, identity, and the state, overlooked the complexity of place-making (Gupta and Ferguson, 1997; Herb and Kaplan, 1999; Baykan, 2000).

Let us take Salzmann's argument on the difficulty of constructing state-citizenship relationships in the Ottoman Empire a step further. We believe he is right in arguing that claims to citizenship were instrumental in matching individuals to borders, in the sense that there was also the problem of matching a territory to the idea of the state. Western Empires, for example, ruled over territorial spaces of 'colonies'. The Ottoman Empire, viewed as the 'sick man' by the major West and Central European powers would be stripped of its 'empireness' in the 1920 Sèvres agreement by having all of its territories taken away, except for a minute area in the middle of Asia Minor. It is difficult to claim that identification of the Empire as Turkish in its later stage had a territorial basis, although Anatolia was originally defined as such (as Turchia) by the Western Crusaders during the eleventh century (Guvenc, 1994: 23). On the other hand, the discursive space of 'Ottomanism' was intended to contain the diversity of identities within the given territorial space and within the legitimacy of state-citizenship relations.

Duara (1996: 152) argues that

> we will need to break with two assumptions of modernization theory. The first of these is that national identity is a radically novel form of consciousness... The second assumption is the privileging of the grand narrative of the nation as the collective historical subject. Nationalism is rarely the nationalism of the nation, but rather represents the site where very different views of the nation contest and negotiate with each other.

According to Duara (1996), people of different communities had different cultural identities that they defined in relation to each other, and in relation to the state, in the form of political self-awareness, but this was not the same as the modern nationalisms of the nation-state (cf. Robertson, 1998). Looking from Duara's perspective, we can argue that the complexity of different identities of the Ottoman Empire prevents us from seeing them as cohesive historical subjects with a perfect match between an essential culture, territory, and national identity, in the process of realizing themselves within a nation-state. Ottomanism failed to become an effective ideology, not because it was not 'modern', but because it did not find a referent for its 'Others' in the practical everyday lives of particular places and within the 'vernaculars' of existing communal relations. Similar to the idea of the national subject, a collective historical consciousness was intended by Ottomanism. Yet, the lack of legitimacy of such an historical subject, that was an imperialist enterprise, made it unrealizable.

Under these circumstances, the intellectual-discursive territorialization of Turkey's space, mapped as a new state, and the 'people' who belonged to it, attracted some to the movement of Anatolianism (*Anadoluculuk*). According to Tachau (1963), although it was not very significant in numbers of membership or in its longevity and power, Anatolianism was the counterpoint to Pan-Turkism. We can trace the origins of this movement to 1918 at which time the necessity of matching the Turkish culture to a homeland and thus to Anatolia was underlined. One of the founders of Anatolianism, Hilmi Ziya Ulken (1979) states that, against the dominant ideologies of Ottomanism, Islamism, and Turanism (Turan as the home-land of all Turkic people), there had emerged a movement of narrow Turkism or Turkeyism (*Turkiyecilik*). Ulken (1979) narrates how, based on Henri Lichtenberger's "*Richard Wagner, Poete et penseur*", he had started a movement which recognized Anatolia as the source of Turkish culture and between 1918 and 1919 had brought out the periodical "*Anadolu*", in handwritten form for twelve issues, together with Resat Kayi (Ulken, 1979: 470). Later, in 1919, as a Political Science student, Ulken wrote a book with the title, "*Anadolunun bugunki Vazifeleri*" (Present duties of Anatolia) which he could not get published.

Nevertheless, this cultural movement, according to Ulken, spread among students and, in the hands of Mukrimin Halil, became a new ideology. From that point on, the movement would separate into two different directions, one as 'cultural Anatolianism', the other as 'ideological Anatolianism'. The latter's approach was more political in nature and adopted Monroe's doctrine that America belonged to Americans (Ulken, 1979: 471). In 1923, Ulken and his friends published the new "*Anadolu*" for ten issues. There, he recounted the works of his friends as an alternative consciousness to Ottomanism, Turanism, and Islamism, in the form of 'homeland-ism' or 'country-ism' (*memleketcilik*). They basically opposed the specificity of Turkish History, traced to origins outside Anatolia and to Islam. Ulken (1979: 473) argues that theirs was a 'concrete' concept of nation, being constituted with reference to the accumulated cultures of the Anatolian people and their folkloric and lyric mythologies, as opposed to the abstract forms of the other ideologies listed.

Reading these issues of *Anadolu*, Ustel (1993: 52) claims that, although the issues of language, literature, folklore, and education were covered within the articles, the dominant themes were nationality and national history. Ustel shows that the desire to start Turkish History with the history of Anatolian Turks, led some members of the journal to argue that the authoritarian regimes of the Sultanate and the Committee of Order and Progress were colonialist in nature *vis-à-vis* the Anatolian folk. However, more interestingly, for example, according to Ziyaeddin Fahri, one of the contributors, the real problem was the lack of a national culture (and its scientific and philosophical formulations) deriving from Anatolia. His claim was that, the concept of culture (*hars*) of the group of Turks, as formulated by the famous Ziya Gokalp, was not acceptable, since it defied the complexity of cultures as found in Anatolia. He emphasized the need for a 'national' culture which would unite all minorities and ethnic groups in the body of the (Anatolian) nation (cited in Ustel, 1993: 53–54).

The inflation of the movement into populism and peasantism in the early periods of the Republic need not be discussed here. But among the several reasons for its demise, as discussed by Tachau and Ustel, is that it was not founded within the leading administrative-elite structures of the early Republic, which were motivated by more radical reform movements. The official narrative account, as set by the Turkish History Thesis in the early 1930s, would trace Turks to Central Asia. The path chosen by the state at that date can also be accounted for by the prevalent articulations of cultural, political and economic realities of the world order. The cultural milieus of Fascism and Nazism provided such histories which eventually became totalizing state policies and set examples for similar models in other parts of the world. Turkey found herself in the position of opposing such regimes and their imperialist aims, on the one hand, and on the other, cooperated, imitated, and/or participated in institutional and cultural encounters, especially with Italy, in re-organizing her own institutions (Baykan and Barlas, 1999). However, although Italy from the early days of the Republic interpreted the Turkish transition as that of the 'Anatolianization' of Turkey, and helped to organize various cultural institutions, departments in Turkish universities, and the official history conference during the thirties, she was secretly critical and sceptical about Turkish claims to a Mediterranean region and to claims of a larger Turkic History (Baykan and Barlas, 1999).

Copeaux (1998) offers more perspective on Anatolianism by examining the works of other literary figures of a later period, such as Halikarnas Balikcisi and Sabahattin Eyuboglu. He argues that, the emphasis on the given 'earth' (*toprak*), territory that is, as a multicultural construction found as a home to include not only the cultures of antiquity and of Greeks but also the history of the Kurds and the Alevis. For Copeaux, however, this understanding of Anatolia as the joint earth and origin of all culture is objectionable because, in its intention, it also posits Anatolia as a container within a political narrative which resists appropriation by Greeks. Furthermore, the narrative is also silent on the Armenians, children of the same earth. In short, from within today's critical discourse, it can be argued that Anatolianism also saw space as a passive container, as an origin in thought rather than as praxis, and was essentialist in nature. Nevertheless, it provides the grounds in which we can start looking into the narratives of space and deconstructing the discourses of nationalisms and identities that come with it.

The search for a national space

The quasi-official, or Kemalist, narrative of the Turkish modernization project is well known. Claiming to distance themselves from the backwardness
of the trappings of the Ottoman Empire and Ottoman Turkism, Kemal
Ataturk and his political allies turned to the West for models for what a
'civilized' nation should look like, the standard of 'civilization' possessing a
globally widespread significance at that time (Gong, 1984). The theme of
civilization had become increasingly worldwide during the later years of the
nineteenth century and the first twenty years or so of the twentieth century.
This theme had particular relevance for much of Asia; resulting from the
attempts by powerful Western nation-states—such as Britain, France, Germany
and the USA—to impose specific behavioral practices on Asian societies or
regions. However, actual or potential societies in Asia developed civilizing
projects, partly in order to fend off the Western powers by acquiring Western
techniques and ideas, and partly in order to become respected members of
international society (Robertson, 1992b: 115–128).

In situating Ankara as the capital, the National Assembly produced a
bifurcated conception of the new nation-state. On the one hand, the choice
of Ankara, in conventional terms an obviously pre-modern city, symbolized
the so-called Anatolian essence of the new nation. On the other, Istanbul
was the repository of some of the very Western practices and ideas that
were considered essential for strengthening the new Turkish nation-state.
The need to appear to distance the new country from many of the features
of Ottomanism was, however, a crucial consideration; quite apart from the
fact that the wars of independence from the occupying victorious powers at
the conclusion of the Great War of 1914–1918 and the demise of the Ottoman Empire had largely taken place in Anatolia. Furthermore, until 1922,
Istanbul was under the occupation of British, French, and Italian forces.

According to Keyder (1999), Istanbul has been the quintessential world
city for most of her fifteen hundred year history. It was the biggest market
between India and Western Europe and had also been the bureaucratic seat
of Empires. Not only did the city interconnect trade routes but it was also
a big consuming city. Nevertheless, the great diversity of Istanbul did not
provide a united, articulated population in the manner of a 'civil society'
because ultimately the disarticulated corporatist groups were governed and
transformed into a system by the centralizing logic of the Empire. Con-
sequentially, it was against the interest and beyond the power of the corporatist groups to build the city's infrastructure and articulate it to the emerging
modern global system (cf. Robertson, 1992b). The physical space of the various groups reflected the place-making of the symbolic order of the respec-

tive groups. This brought into sight (and site) the divisions between various ethnic groups who were perceived as extensions of the Western powers by the local Muslim population, who were physically set apart from the new urban encounters. Keyder explains how it was the Republican refusal of the city that led to her marginalization to both westernization and the high culture of Islam:

> The formation of the nation-state might have been expected to draw new protective boundaries and recuperate Istanbul's fracture in the name of nation building. A nation, after all, is an attempt to accommodate the global within what is considered the local. However, this was not to be because of two reasons, both due to the peculiarity of the nationalist vision championed by the republican elite. One, the kind of modernization represented by the actual experience of the Ottoman empire, and especially of Istanbul, was considered to be inauthentic because it was compromised by the nature of its adherents. In other words, since the westernized population was mostly non-Muslim, they could be dismissed as an excrescence, and even a parasite over the "real" nation; thus they fell outside the purview of the local. This drawing of lines also meant that the Muslim fellow travelers could be dismissed as compradors, not only inauthentic but also in bad faith. Second, according to the modernist republican cosmology, the local itself was also suspect because it was compromised by its adherence to Islam and, therefore, to obscurantism. In the ideal version, the local had to be fiercely irreligious, embodying all the virtues of tradition without its vices: ready and willing to be injected with positivism and progress (Keyder 1999: 9–10).

Being the essence of Anatolia may have been the narrative form that prescribed Ankara as a symbolic qualifier. However, following Keyder's point of view, it is easy to see why, originally, the city in its physical space and way of life of the actual occupants had a limited relationship to the space of the new ideas of republicanism, progress, and civilization. Once Ankara became the capital, foreign planners and architects were invited to build a 'modern' city. The physical space of the 'modern' accompanied new communication structures, administrative and educational institutions, foreign embassies, and public spaces for various social events such as ballrooms, concert-halls, theatres, restaurants, hotels, large boulevards, and so forth. The folk, symbolically contained in the old town within the fortress, stood as a sign of the past and the people of the Anatolian countryside who moved to the city were spatially and culturally distanced from the new (Nalbantoglu, 1997). The local was removed, rejected, and problematized within the narrative of the 'rural', and even when in the late 1960s more than fifty percent of Ankara's population was living in squatter housing, the space of the vernacular remained transparent to or outside the sight of the modern perspectives (Nalbantoglu, 1997).

The preceding discussion should not lead us to think of the political sphere of the state as the counterpoint to society; as in a state-society binary, whereby agency and historical dynamics are attributed entirely to the state and society is the effect of state actions. The modernist imaginary of the state is not reducible to the consciousness of the leaders and the elite. It cannot be contained and limited simply by the political space of the governance. Grounding social transformation in general and nation-state making in particular on spatial praxis forces us to look once again into the concept of 'society'. Just as we take space to be a real practice which needs to be explained in its own right, dismantled into its different fragments, layers, and internal contradictions, as well as external ones, society similarly has a complex nature. It should not be a totalized and transparent concept, encouraging us to think that the meaning of what the concept refers to, when used with a qualifier such as Turkish, is an ontological given.

This was clear, we believe, to the reformists of the interwar period because instead of encountering a given Turkish society, they worked to make one. The performative role of the state in making the 'modern' republic during the twenties and thirties can be understood by way of taking into account the making of a new generation through new practices of modernity, particularly as lived in newly-established heterotopia, spaces such as 'people's houses' and 'village institutes', and in new economic spaces such as factories.

> Heterotopia are places of Otherness, whose Otherness is established through a relationship of difference with other sites, such that their presence either provides an unsettling of spatial and social relations or an alternative representation of spatial and social relations . . . This Otherness has to do with different modes of ordering rather than simply with a contrast between order and resistance. Heterotopia do not exist in themselves . . . It is the heterogeneous combination of the materiality, social practices and events that were located at this site and what they came to represent in contrast with other sites, that allow us to call it a heterotopia. Heterotopia exist when the relationship between sites is described by a difference of representation defined by their modes of social ordering (Hetherington, 1997: 8).

The generation of the Republic educated in modern spaces came of age with the cultural imprint of the 1920s and 1930s. In the early 1920s, the population was less than thirteen million, of which approximately 84 percent lived in rural areas. According to the State Statistic Institute's figures, the entire urban population, including large cosmopolitan cities like Istanbul and Izmir, was around two million. The exodus of the non-Muslim population accounted for the dramatic reduction in the cities' populations and the cultural diversity that the Ottoman Empire was accustomed to. These numbers are indicative of the range of the population effected on day to day basis by the new state's culture of modernity. In narratives of modernization, we come across two seemingly contradictory viewpoints, the view which posits the policies of the state as alien and hostile to the body of the society, and the historical narratives of coming of age in modern spaces of various cities where one could listen to music and read the classics of literature at People's Houses and Village Institutes and go for promenades in public spaces with family members. The fact is that the process, not of being but of becoming, needs to be analyzed. Everyday realities changed from one day to the next. The new policies in health care and investments in infrastructure and the 'heterotopia', constituted an engagement in praxis, a historical dynamic, which cannot be taken as fixed points in time. The population increased rapidly and the periphery became interwoven into the links that tied various places to the center in a similar manner:

> Still largely unexplored by critical studies of architectural history is the transformation of provincial towns under the modernizing agenda of the young republic, the construction of public buildings symbolic of the administrative and ideological apparata of the new regime (*hukumet konagi* and *halkevi* in particular), complete with the formal square (*humet meydani*) and the municipal park (*belediye parki*) with their inevitable Ataturk statues, the characteristic prototype buildings for communication, transportation and education which were crucial to the dissemination of the Republican ideology and for connecting the provinces to the center of authority in Ankara (*istasyon, PTT, okul*), and finally, new residential districts for the modernizing bureaucratic elites, typically in proximity to railway stations (*istasyon mahalleleri*). The share of construction industry production values in the national expenditure budget shows an increase from 37% in 1923 to 78% in 1929, until slowed down by the world economic crisis (Bozdogan, 1994: 39).

There were local differences among the languages spoken, religions practiced, and produce raised. More than a million migrated to the new nation from far-flung former territories of the Empire. As a new generation of children were growing up in the modern imaginary of the new Republic, adults were facing the hardships of the postwar era, many with the pains of dislocation. Their villages and towns were frequently restructured and disrupted. In this process, many cities lost their prewar characteristics that had been defined by cultural, ethnic, and religious differences. They were subjected to modernist mappings that carved into their everyday lives. Nevertheless, the differences lived transgressively in their private spaces as they also lived side by side within the same public spaces. The everyday experiences, the contradictory locations in 'modernity' and 'tradition', the multiple languages spoken and religions practiced, and bodies as the sites of these different maps and memories that define particular identities, together drew the contours of the pockets of spaces not figured inside the conventional modernist space.

The narratives of testimonials, autobiographical stories and oral histories—clearly legitimate sources of information—today present us with a history of the cities where they grew up (Margosyan, 1995, 1996; Ceyhan, 1996). For example, Margosyan's childhood was spent in the southeastern city of Diyarbakir, in the *Gavurmahallesi*, the neighborhood of 'the infidels'. From this neighborhood, he remembers the peddlers selling their goods in Kurdish, the Armenian artisans hammering their iron, schools taught in Turkish and parents speaking in many languages. In his narratives, the use of home space, the neighborhood streets, the courtyards, the shops and the public space of the larger city are presented to the reader through the eyes of an Armenian child growing up in Diyarbakir in the 1940s. The multi-vocality, the gendered nature of the quotidian practice and the layering of cross-cultural encounters, through the experiences of his neighborhood, tell us the stories of a city. People traveled to this city from long distances, a time recorded to memory as that of the *tehcir* (deportation), and for a new understanding of time (of the new nation), all carved into the child's mind as the collective memories of his community. The collapse of a house roof, the travels of a father, the dual names they carry (Muslim and Armenian) also give us clues as to the hardships and complexities undergone by the adults of this protective world of the child. At the same time, these children participated in the processes of the making of the universal subject of Turkish citizenship, as they were educated in and participated within the public space of the modern heterotopia discussed above.

One of these public spaces, People's Houses (*Halkevleri*) are especially important, for they often played the role of the middle ground between these local cultures and the center's civilizational mission (Ozturkmen, 1994). The categories of the activities were: Language, History and Literature, Fine Arts, Theater, Sports, Social Assistance, Public Classes and Courses, Library and Publishing, Village Development, and Museums and Exhibitions. Initially, there were fourteen of them in various cities across Anatolia. By 1939 there were already 373, and the numbers of the People's Rooms, the local branches especially in rural areas, reached 4371 by the end of 1949 (Ozturkmen, 1994: 163). There was much demand from every city and every region to have their own People's House and there was always competition among them to show the extent of public involvement. Contemporary intellectuals wrote on issues pertaining to all areas of interest, from philosophy to economy, or from health care to tourism in the official journals of these institutions. However, more significantly, local research and intellectual activities also found their ways into these publications:

Despite the lack of consistent methodology, members of the People's Houses became pioneer fieldworkers who pursued faithful research and collected material in their own localities and neighborhoods That the result of their work were published in the periodicals of other publications of the People's Houses not only legitimized that activity in the eyes of the public but helped in the construction of a 'national genre repertoire,' fed by, and circulating through, different parts of the country. What is now called the 'Turkish national culture' follows, in large measure, the generic structure laid out by the People's Houses in the thirties and forties (Ozturkmen, 1994: 164–165).

We may, once again, note the Anatolianization of local differences, the production, communication, and distribution of folklore as a collective definition, abstracted from their local use and made into a fragment of a general body of shared meaning systems, where they could be appropriated and re-appropriated in various forms, such as, to give an example, by the musical genre of Anatolian rock. After the multi-party system came into effect in 1946, People's Houses became the target of the Democratic Party's criticisms for their organic link to the single-party regime of the Republican People's Party, and they were closed when the Democratic Party came to power in 1950.

The marker of the 1950s was the emergence of new, regionalist, clientelistic relations from within different local origins and with small-town economic interests (Gunes-Ayata, 1994). These were the consequences of the state-planned economy of the 1930s and the economy of the Truman doctrine and the Marshall plan during the post-1945 years. A newly developing bourgeoisie, growing concentration of land in the hands of wealthier peasants, competing interest groups, regional differences, and de-peasantisation constituted the dynamic elements of the society. These groups contested the Republican Party's vision of modernity, bringing to power in 1950 the Democratic Party. The pro-West and pro-US politics, participation in the Korean war, a growing commodification of consumer culture (together with relaxation of import restrictions in the early 1950s) went side by side with the liberalization of the cultural domain, whereby religion was used as an item of value for the state to distribute downward along clientelistic lines in return for votes.

By 1960 it had become obvious that the rule of the Democratic Party opposed the interests of the civil servants and intellectuals, as well as the disenfranchised populations cut off from traditional patron client lines. Those who grew up inside the Republican heterotopia identified with a secularist and modern etatism but faced increasing autocratic limitations to their space of action from the regime. The Democratic Party was using the majoritarian system for its own benefits to limit the rights of the opposition, as there was no separation of powers to keep its power in check. Meanwhile, those who were more readily identifiable as the petit-bourgeoisie of towns, tied to the state in particularist interests—their particularity defined via an ideology of politicization and problematization of 'tradition' and 'religion'—, gained from the state.

The 1960 coup led to a new constitution with separation of powers and political differentiation. However, the dominant narratives on social conflict were not primarily focused on the theme of secularism and the state as would be the case in a couple of decades. The distribution of resources between an expanding national bourgeoisie, the landowners, and the growing segments of the population (whose earnings were based on either wages or on erratic earnings coming from the informal and marginal sectors) plus the rural poor, became problematic especially with the economic crisis of the 1970s. These groups clashed not at the level of rights for cultural expression or for individual rights, but in terms of opposing interests expressed through a political-narrative of left and right, or on identities picked up from a range of narratives, as 'the progressivists and/or the Westernists' versus 'the traditionalists'. These categories were not always economic classifications based on opposing class interests, but also referred to competition for access to resources based on clientelistic lines. To put it differently, value codings of identities have been catachrestical, always shifting (Spivak, 1989). Being Western could mean being 'anti-imperialist', in which case traditionalists stood in favor of close relations with the West or with the United States. The negotiation between concept metaphors of secularism versus religiosity, under different political articulations, have taken value codings *vis-à-vis* other issues of value. These themes divided the country around a right-left dispute, but mostly in competition for the government that ultimately decided on the distribution of resources between different vertical lines of interests.

The weakening of the left after the coup in 1980 and the rise of the populist center-right can be framed by such a shift in the perceived value of these positional spaces. The closing down of political parties and the curtailing of union rights after 1980 helped to set up the environment for drastic changes in the organization of the economy. The initial period of military rule and the rewriting of the new constitution were the building blocks for a globalized economy and the liberalization policies of the new government. The period is marked by the relative decline of the share of industry in the national economy in favor of the service sector with declining wages and increasing inequities in the distribution of income. These changes resulted in new structurations at the level of the spatial organization of cities like Istanbul. With fast urbanization and increased population, a new, young generation was born and raised for whom life's meanings are written on an urban-scape with alternative, different, and unconnected patterns of practices (Baykan, 1999). In the world-cities of Turkey everyday production and consumption of work and culture extend from the limits of uncertain jobs for the sub-contractors for global companies and street vendors to high executive positions of international banking, Latin American soap operas to Islamic fashion shows, jazz festivals to arabesque concerts, new squatter areas, to gated suburbia. In the political sphere, a fragmented electorate has emerged which moves between various populist parties, the majority of which are right of center. These parties contest for the control of the resources of the state, a power which has become especially important due to the access it provides to the gains inherent in the process of privatization. Nevertheless, this new 'society' of the shrinking middle class and an increasing urban and rural poor, living right on the axis of global-local fault line have lost the benefits of a state-run economy, but seek access to power and identity within the exchange value of culture's meaning-making processes. This kind of organizing of society's interest groups runs counter to the horizontally distributed interest groups of a civil society. However, the seeming break-up between the state and realities of a spatially organized politics of socio-cultural practices has been interpreted as the newly emerging civil society as against the state. Therefore, the usual (Islamic) society—(Kemalist) state duality has become re-appropriated through, once again, a totalizing approach to these categories.

Concluding comments

Any discourse on Turkey will be begging the question unless it deals with the problematical place of the 'East' of Eastern Turkey (although usually separated from narratives on the East, Eastern parts of the Black Sea with the port city of Trabzon can even be included in here), and how the region has come to engage with the social and historical space of Turkey in general. This area of Turkey is a space of cultural, economic, and political contestation. The cities of Trabzon, Erzurum, Van, Mardin, Diyarbakir were heterogeneous cities where the Bakhtinian carnival took residence until the tragedies of World War I. In Mann's (1987) terms, each of these cities occupied a space within a different map of economic, ideological, political, and military sources of power. Their trade routes went to Russia, Asia, and the Middle East. The cultural links of the Pontus Greeks of Trabzon and the Armenian nationalist movements reaching over to Russia, the Sufi fraternities and Kurdish tribes over to Iran, Baghdad or Syria, they were contested spaces of the political games of the Russians, the French, the British, and the Italians. The religious sectarian interests worked and practiced there in hundreds of independent schools for each minority group, or in Sufi orders, paving the way for new ideas for nationalist movements. Despite its military presence and its administrative rule, the relation of the Ottoman state to this space was often ineffective. The entire character of these places were changed after the war. Turkish history books narrate the triumphant victory in Izmir on the Aegean coast. However, there is scant information on how and when the Russians left Erzurum or Trabzon after years of occupation. The residues of the collective memories are slowly being forgotten or replaced by new ones.

Economic underdevelopment, insurgent nationalism, and tribal-populist clientalisms are some of the more contemporary narratives to identify the problematic zoning of this region. Nevertheless, it is not difficult to claim that, overall, Eastern Turkey does not occur in the collective imaginary of Turkish society, except an acquaintance with it through watching television news programs on the current state of the PKK (the illegal Kurdish separatist organization) or hearing accents on the streets of cosmopolitan cities such as Istanbul where people from Eastern Turkey migrate in large numbers. We do not imply that any one group is particularly ascribed a geography in Turkish society. What we are trying to present is how spaces are defined, contested, made, and articulated into systems of power and identity. The process of homogenization of culture over the space of Anatolia has taken different paths into new spaces. Some view Istanbul as a global space, others view Turkey in general as an Islamic space (the West for example in considering Turkey for membership in the European Union). These definitions will be contested many times as encounters among different agencies and their practices of different social, political, and cultural orders will reflect back on to struggles over space.

11. DEMOCRACY AND DEMOCRATIZATION IN AFRICA

Benyamin Neuberger

In the 1990s there was much talk in Africa about democracy and democratization. In Africa—as indeed everywhere else—democracy means either 'thin' or 'procedural' democracy, based on a multi-party system, free elections and parliamentary opposition, or a liberal 'thick' democracy which, in addition to institutions and procedures, stresses limited government, basic freedoms, the rule of law and a political culture of moderation, non-violence, compromise and tolerance.

We call the transition from dictatorship to democracy 'democratization'.[1] Democratization starts when the authoritarian regime begins to disintegrate. Throughout the transition period it may combine democratic and authoritarian ingredients. The end point may be the constitution of a democracy of the procedural or liberal variety (e.g. South Africa). Sometimes, democratization does not end with democracy but with a return to authoritarianism (e.g. Burundi), a slide towards anarchy (e.g. Somalia) or the consolidation of a 'mixed' system (e.g. Senegal).

In Africa we have seen three 'waves' of democratization, two major and one minor. The first wave of democratization—decolonization—was fought for democratic goals and values: national self-determination, free elections, 'one man, one vote', NIBMAR ('No Independence Before Majority Rule'), freedom of the press, basic liberties and 'equal pay for equal work'.[2] In the late 1950s and early 1960s this wave resulted in the establishment of independent states, presidential or parliamentary governments, democratic constitutions and multi-party elections. In the late 1970s there was another 'minor' democratic wave, when Ghana, Nigeria and Upper Volta (Burkina Fasso) returned to civilian multiparty rule, Senegal abandoned its one-party-system and Zimbabwe became independent without outlawing the European 'Rhodesian Front' (RF) and the 'Zimbabwe African People's Union' (ZAPU) opposition parties.

The 1990s saw the third wave of democratization, which brought about elections and a change of government in dozens of African countries. The

---

[1] For a general analysis of democratization in Africa, see Bratton and Van de Walle (1997: 1–60, 97–158), Joseph (1997) and Ottaway (1997).

[2] On the democratic dimension of anti-colonial nationalism see Neuberger (1986: 11–18) and Neuberger and Keren (1997: 89–102).

first wave collapsed in the 1960s and ushered in the creation of one-party
dictatorships or military governments (or both at the same time). The short
episode of the second wave was over when Nigeria's Muhammed Buhari
(in 1983), Ghana's Jerry Rawlings and Upper Volta's Thomas Sankara (in
1979) staged military coups. What were the reasons for the failure of democracy in the 1960s and 1970s? What were the reasons that, in dozens
of African states, civilian and military dictators seized power, that in the
late 1980s a limited form of multi-partyism continued to exist only in seven
out of fifty states—The Gambia, Senegal, Mauritius, Botswana, Zimbabwe,
Namibia and South Africa? There is no single cause or explanation for the
failure of democracy in the 1960s and 1970s. One explanation is the non-
democratic historical heritage—both pre-colonial and colonial. Africa's pre-
colonial systems—contrary to the romantic notions of 'African democracy',
'rural democracy' and the democratic 'village palaver'—were largely autocratic and personalistic, and were not based on any balance of power of
institutions. It was basically 'palace politics'—the politics of fear, intrigue,
rumors, suspicions and uncertainty. Some of the features of postcolonial
regimes can be traced directly to their pre-colonial origins. The tendency
of postcolonial presidents to declare themselves 'presidents for life' is a glar-
ing example of the force of pre-colonial personalism. Pre-colonial sultans
and chiefs were also mostly 'rulers for life'. The autocratic nature of the
pre-colonial regimes characterized mainly pre-colonial traditional African
states and not segmentary stateless societies. Certainly the heritage of Africa's
pre-colonial states is more relevant for its postcolonial states than the heritage of its stateless societies.

The colonial heritage was no less authoritarian. Colonial government was
not responsible government. Colonial governors, provincial and district com-
missioners and *commandants de cercle* concentrated in their hands political,
legal, police and military authority. In essence—especially in the periphery—
colonial rule was military rule. In all the colonies, government was centralistic, etatistic and heavy-handed. Compulsory labor was one of the 'normal'
features of colonialism. Certainly, colonial regimes varied from the relatively
liberal British to the brutal Portuguese, but none was democratic. True,
there was last-moment democratization in the 1950s, but that was too little
and too late to create a semblance of a democratic tradition, even in the
British colonies.[3]

The socio-economic conditions were certainly not conducive to sustain
democratic governments. In African societies millions of people struggle daily

---

[3] On the colonial heritage, see Young, 1998.

with the problems of malnutrition and hunger, basic shelter and water supply, disease and a low life expectancy. Life is a daily struggle for survival and democracy and civic liberties appear as a 'luxury' for the rich—Europe and America who can afford it. African societies are highly polarized between a very rich few and the masses of the poor, and since Aristotle we know that, in such societies, democracy is highly unlikely.[4]

Another major reason often cited for the failure of democracy is the ethnic factor. Most African states are not nation-states, neither ethnic nation-states nor civic nation-states. Most states consist of dozens of ethnic groups—in many of them there is not even a majority nation. Unlike the 'classical' 19th and 20th century East European state, in the typical African State all ethnic groups are minorities. There is thus no overarching territorial identity in the African state, no national consensus usually regarded as vital for any functioning democracy. Modernization gaps between different regions frequently overlap with ethnic cleavages. In almost all African states, poor and non-modernized regions and ethnic groups face relatively developed regions and ethnic groups. The lack of cross-cutting cleavages makes for increased polarization, while democracy demands moderation and compromise. Competition for power becomes 'ethnicized' by ethnic parties, ethnic politicians and ethnic elections. Ethnic politics very often implies that elections are decided by ethnic statistics and demography. Elections thus become meaningless, for they give no chance to ethnic minorities. In the 1960s ethnicity was also seen as a major separatist danger, which had to be suppressed at all costs—also at the 'cost' of democracy—in order to maintain a state 'une et indivisible'.[5]

Another obstacle to the consolidation of democracy in the 1960s was the ineffectiveness of the African state. Much has been written about Africa's 'soft state' and about the 'withdrawal of the state'.[6] A precondition for a stable democracy is an effective and legitimate state. In the 1960s Huntington remarked that democracy cannot work when all output (government, bureaucracy, municipalities, police) and input institutions (parties, unions, voluntary organizations) are weak and rudimentary. The tasks African states have to deal with—state creation, nation building, distribution and participation—are in inverse relationship to their capabilities. Such states are certainly not likely candidates for democratic government. Ironically, it is the weak African state which is highly centralistic. Malawi's President Hastings Banda used to say: "Nothing is not my business. Everything is my business". The etatist

---

[4] On class polarization in Africa, see Sklar (1979) and Diamond (1987).
[5] On ethnicity and the postcolonial state, see Neuberger, 1999.
[6] On the 'soft state' in Africa, see Azaria and Chazan, 1987.

centralism, espoused both by left-wing 'radical' and right-wing conservative regimes prevented the growth of a non-bureaucratic bourgeoisie which would have been vital for democratic progress.

Economic dependence on the whims of the international commodity markets has made Africa's monocultural economies highly vulnerable. Huge price fluctuations led to the sudden fall of economies and living standards—a situation which any democratic regime would have found difficult to survive. In some of the African colonies the anti-colonial struggle was fought by radical—revolutionary guerrilla forces—not by liberal-democratic movements. That was certainly the case in Angola, Mozambique and Guinea-Bissau, which established a one-party dictatorship immediately after independence. In the 1960s we even witnessed the rise of an African one-party-state ideology which became dominant in all of Africa. The pragmatic-conservative ideologues of the one-party-state, like Houphouet Boigny, Kenyatta, Senghor and Banda, declared multi-partyism to be a luxury at that state of Africa's development and argued that necessities of planning, development and modernization and the dangers of 'tribalism' and separatism demanded a strong one-party state. The radical 'leftist' ideologues regarded the one-party state as representing the 'will of the people'. They also argued that Africa as a supposedly 'classless society' needed no multiplicity of parties, whose function in Western society is to represent class interests. In all of Africa, democracy was tainted from the beginning. It was associated with the West, and the West was associated with colonialism and imperialism.[7]

While the causes for the downfall of the democratic systems in the 1960s were clear to all, many found the strong wave of re-democratization of the 1990s quite surprising.[8] The fact that this wave is still with us after a decade is even more significant, for we know that the second 'minor' wave of the late 1970s collapsed within a few years. Indeed, democratic progress in the 1990s was dramatic. While between 1960 and 1990 there was only one democratic change of government, in 1991–1993 alone the incumbent rulers of Benin, Zambia, Cape Verde, Sao Tomé and Principe, Mali, the Central African Republic, the Malagasy Republic, Niger, Lesotho and Burundi were voted out of office. In the following years the same happened in South Africa, Malawi, Sierra Leone and Congo Brazzaville. In Benin and the Malagasy Republic, the newly elected rulers were again voted out of office after four years in government.[9]

---

[7] On Africa's One-Party-State Ideology see Neuberger (1971, 1974).

[8] For a general discussion of the 'third wave', see Kunz (1991), Chazan (1992), Klein (1992), Ndue (1994) and Bratton and Van de Walle (1997: 159–232).

[9] On some African countries that experienced a change of government by elections, see Cowan (1992), Decalo (1997), Gervais (1997), O'Toole (1997) and Matlosa (1999).

In addition to changes of government by elections, there were multi-party elections in most other African countries—including Kenya, Cameroon, the Ivory Coast, Ethiopia, Angola, Mozambique, Nigeria, Ghana and Namibia. While before 1990 there was an opposition in Parliament in only seven states (The Gambia, Botswana, Mauritius, Zimbabwe, Senegal, Namibia and South Africa), in the 1990s there was some opposition representation in all of them.

Some of Africa's worst tyrants disappeared from the political scene in the 1990s. Rwanda's Habyarimana was assassinated, Liberia's Doe and Equatorial Guinea's Macias were executed, Ethiopia's Mengistu Haile Mariam and Congo's Mobutu fled from their countries and Malawi's Banda and Sierra Leone's Yosef Mommoh were voted out of office.

All African countries had more varieties of freedom in the 1990s—more press freedom, more freedom of speech and more freedom of assembly, more freedom of movement and more freedom of political organization. With the notable exception of Uganda's Musoveni, during the 1990s nothing was written any more in favor of the one-party state. The one-party state ideology which was dominant in the 1970s and 1980s simply evaporated. Rulers, politicians, intellectuals and students who had hailed the one-party state became overnight supporters of multi-party democracy. Tanzania's Nyerere who sincerely believed in 'one-party democracy' and wrote numerous books and articles in its favor in the 1960s said later on in the 1990s that "it is not God's wish that there should be only one-party".[10]

The 'democratic wave' of the 1990s was a surprise for many 'Afro-pessimists'. Just as it was important to understand the causes of the rise of the one-party-state and the military regime in the 1960s and 1970s, it is similarly important that we understand the rise of democracy in the 1990s. One major reason for the downfall of the authoritarian regimes was the accumulated hatred and disgust of Africa's tyrants and oppressors.[11] History shows that oppressive rule always ends in a call for liberation and liberty. An oppressive rule may gain partial legitimacy and political support if it is instrumentally effective—succeeding in war, advancing education or making for rapid development and modernization. Africa's dictators—whether Marxist or conservative, civilian or military—were all total failures in economic and social development. The 1980s were regarded in almost all African states as the 'lost decade'—a decade of declining GNP, per capita income, investments and foreign aid, a decade of rising debt, capital flight, poverty and hunger. The Structural Adjustment Programmes (SAP) imposed by the World

---

[10] Nyerere, 1998.
[11] On the nature of Africa's dictators, see Bratton and Van de Walle (1997: 61–96) and Chehabi and Linz (1998: 3–48).

Bank and the International Monetary Fund (IMF)—devaluations, a cut in food subsidies, privatization, a reduction of the bureaucracy and liberalization of trade—may have been economically sound in Holland or Norway but in Africa they brought more unemployment, more poverty and more hunger. The SAP led to food riots (e.g. in Zambia, Liberia, Kenya), which accelerated the destabilization of the authoritarian regimes. The SAP needed a 'strong state', but in effect it further weakened the state and the regime.

Economic failure in the 1960s was one reason for the fall of democratic regimes raising hopes that 'strong men' would solve the problem. In the late 1980s and early 1990s the economic catastrophe was attributed to the dictators, and popular rage was directed against them. The economic collapse of the 1980s was partly caused by the deteriorating terms of trade, by drought, desertification and shrinking arable lands, as well as by high birth rates and population density. High military expenditures and corruption on an unprecedented scale also contributed to the economic collapse. Some corruption was legitimate in the eyes of the population, but the theft of billions by Africa's 'kleptocrats' led to disillusionment and widespread cynicism. The 'wabenzi' (people with Mercedes Benz cars), the 'ventriotes' (rhyming with 'patriots'), the 'big men with tummies', were hated throughout Africa. Economic decline also led to rising crime, growing disease and declining education. In 1990, 13 of the 21 states with a lower per capita income than in the 1960s were in Africa.

Events in Eastern Europe also had an impact on Africa. Africans became aware of Gorbachev's *glasnost* and *perestroika* in the Soviet Union. They saw the success of Poland's 'Solidarity' and of Havel's 'velvet revolution'. They also saw the execution of Ceaucescu and the fall of the Berlin Wall. Gabon's Omar Bongo noticed that "the wind from the East had shaken the coconut palms". Some of the coconuts—Ethiopia's Mengistu, Somalia's Barre, Liberia's Doe, Malawi's Banda and Zaire's Mobutu—indeed fell (though the coconut Omar Bongo, remains in place . . .).

The end of the Cold War in the late 1980s also played a role in launching Africa's democratization wave. Overnight, radical Marxist dictators lost their Soviet patron—there was no more Soviet aid, no security assistance, no military experts. The West had also no more reason to back 'its' tyrants—Mobutu, Doe, Moi, Banda. Both superpowers abandoned 'their' clients. Some succeeded in holding on to their power, but others were toppled by their people, by bullets or ballots.

The end of the Cold War led to the decline of geopolitical and geostrategic considerations in the African policy of the Great Powers. While Russia completely withdrew from Africa, the Western World showed greater readiness to apply pressure for Africa to democratize. The World Bank announced a change in its policy in the late 1980s. Before that the dominant World Bank and IMF philosophy was that economic growth would lead to democratization. In 1989 the World Bank Report said: "The root cause of weak economic performance in the past has been the failure of political institutions". By the late 1980s 'good governance', democracy and respect for human rights were seen as preconditions for economic growth. Accordingly the Bretton Woods institutions applied pressure on the African states to move towards democracy if they didn't want to risk losing WB/IMF support. The US—especially under Clinton's presidency—assisted those states that were ready to liberalize their political regimes (e.g. South Africa, Ghana, Senegal) while halting all aid to 'rejectionist' dictatorships (e.g. Mobutu's Zaire, Abacha's Nigeria and Eyadema's Togo).[12] France followed suit with the announcement of the La Baule Declaration (1990) by President Mitterand, that tied development aid to democratic progress. Mitterand declared that there is no 'dévelopement sans démocratie'. Great Britain formulated the Hurd Doctrine (named after Foreign Minister Douglas Hurd), that made any aid conditional on progress in the spheres of human rights, accountability, pluralism, and the rule of law.

Another explanation for democratization attributes internal pressure to democratize to the 'ripening' of a civil society composed of churches, student associations, teachers' unions and professional organizations of lawyers and journalists. According to this 'civil society theory' such groupings play a crucial role in organizing demonstrations for democracy, in mobilizing international pressure and forming an alternative leadership.[13]

Finally there is the 'domino theory'. In the 1960s the chain of military coups d'état, that in state after state abolished multi-partyism was explained by the domino theory. In the 1990s it worked the other way—states imitated each other by promulgating multi-partyism, holding elections, liberalizing society and even deposing long-serving dictators.

Democratization in Africa in the 1990s was real, but is far from being a completed success story. While the 'Afro-optimists' see the wave of democratization in the 1990s as a 'second liberation', 'Afro-pessimists' see the changes of the last decade as largely episodic and cosmetic, arguing that basically we are back in the early 1960s.[14]

---

[12] On the US policy of democratization, see Moss (1995), Gordon (1997) and Barkan and Gordon (1998).

[13] On the 'civil society theory' see Fowler (1993), Bratton (1994), Harbeson (1994) and Monga (1995).

[14] On the 'Afro-pessimist' perspective, see Ihonvbere (1993), Kanté (1994), Ihonvbere (1996a), Ihonvbere (1996b), Creevey (1997), Heilbrunn (1997), Mundt (1997), Takougang (1997), Turner (1997) and Chabal and Daloz (1999: 17–30).

The 'Afro-pessimists' stress the large scale manipulation and fraud in many of Africa's 'free' elections. It is certainly true that in many states the opposition was suppressed (e.g. in Ethiopia), that it had no access to the electronic media (e.g. in Senegal and the Ivory Coast), that the election results were falsified (e.g. in Cameroon). In Togo, hundreds of thousands of voters were expelled from the country in order to reduce the potential opposition vote. In some other countries (e.g. Mauritania, Ethiopia), the major opposition boycotted elections which they regarded as a mere farce. For these very reasons the opposition very often contested the election results (e.g. in Angola, Togo, Ivory Coast, Cameroon and Nigeria in 1999). In 1993 even the Nigerian government did not recognize the election results (which were unfavorable to its presidential candidate).

Despite democratization, many of Africa's dictators and military rulers (e.g. Ghana's Rawlings, Uganda's Musoveni, Burkina Fasso's Compaore, Gabon's Bongo, Togo's Eyadema, the Ivory Coast's Houphouet-Boigny and later Bedie, Cameroon's Biya, Guinea's Conté, Equatorial Guinea's Nguema and Kenya's Moi) stayed in power—some of them by 'winning' questionable elections. In Benin and the Malagasy Republic former military dictators (Kerekou and Ratsiraka), who had lost power in the first democratic elections (in 1991–1992), were returned to power in the second elections (in 1996). In Nigeria General Obasanjo, another former military ruler who was in power in the late 1970s, was elected president in 1999. Another fact to which the 'Afro-pessimists' point is that some of the democratic 'new men' had been part and parcel of the old power structure. Zambia's president Frederick Chiluba who had led the MMD (Movement for Multiparty Democracy) to power in 1991 after waging a campaign for democracy and against Kenneth Kaunda's tyranny, was himself the boss of the workers' union which had been an integral part of Kaunda's power establishment. The same is true for Malawi's president Bakili Muluzi who defeated the autocratic 'president for life' Hastings Kamuzo Banda in 1994. Muluzi had been for years secretary-general of the Malawi Congress Party, Malawi's only party in Banda's one-party state.

Although the human rights situation has certainly improved in most African states, it is still a far cry from Western liberal-democratic standards. In many African states, administrative detention, the imprisonment of journalists (e.g. in Ethiopia), the expulsion of opposition leaders (e.g. in Burkina Fasso) and the opening of fire on demonstrators (e.g. in Kenya) show how far Africa still has to go. According to what is known, almost all regimes continue to be neo-patrimonial, corrupt and personalistic. Nor does the very low turnout in elections (between 20% to 40%) augur well for Africa's democracy. It shows that the politics of an urban elite, lacking any meaningful roots in the countryside, still dominates the political scene.

Another indication for 'Afro-pessimism' is the persistent power of ethnicity. Parties are still to a large extent sociologically—if not ideologically—ethnic parties or coalitions of ethnic groups. In that sense they are not very different from the 'one-party tribes' of the 1960s. Voting is very often strictly ethnic voting. Thus KANU won the elections in 1993 and 1998 because of the Luhya, Kamba, Griama, Masai, and Kalenjin vote, while Kenya's two largest ethnic groups, the Kikuyu and the Luo, overwhelmingly voted for the opposition. In Malawi, the vote in 1994 and again in 1999, created a three-party system representing the ethnic divide between Tumbuka, Tonga and Chewa. The same traditional ethnic divide could be seen in elections in Angola, Benin, Cameroon and Ghana. Even in post-Apartheid South-Africa, Africans, Coloreds, Indians and Whites continue to vote differently (although in this case the ANC managed to overcome, to a large extent, the ethnic cleavage within the African majority). Not only is ethnicity as strong as ever but in a number of states democratization even increased ethnic tension, leading to bloodshed and civil war. The most shocking cases are Rwanda and Burundi. In Rwanda 'liberalization' led to the rising strength of the opposition parties (both Hutu and Tutsi) and even to the inclusion of the opposition in a Government of National Unity based on the Arusha Agreement between the Habyarimana Government and the *Front Patriotique Rwandais*. The same agreement ignited fears among the ruling Hutus about the 'Tutsi danger'. To deal with this 'danger' the extreme wing of the ruling party planned and executed a 'final solution' to the 'Tutsi question', in which almost one million people were slaughtered. In neighboring Burundi, democratization led to the election of the first Hutu president, Melchior Ndadaye, elected in April 1993 by the Hutu majority in free elections. As a reaction to that truly democratic election the Tutsi dominated army assassinated the elected President (in October 1993) and in effect returned to power—at first indirectly and in 1996 directly by a military take over of the former military dictator, Pierre Buyoya. A Hutu-Tutsi civil war has raged all over Burundi since October 1993, and hundreds of thousands have been killed on both sides.

Other examples of ethnic violence erupting as a result of democratization are the Issa-Afar war in Djibouti, the fighting between the quasi-ethnic clans in Somalia and the violent struggle for power in Congo Brazzaville. In order to stay in power, incumbent governments sometimes invite 'spontaneous' ethnic violence and 'ethnic cleansing' by mobilizing ethnic support against the opposition parties. We saw this in Kenya before elections in

1993 and again in 1998 when the pro-government Kalenjin and Masai attacked the Kikuyu and Luo in the Rift Valley, and also in Mobutu's Zaire, which encouraged ethnic cleansing of the Baluba from Shaba Province by exploiting the traditional Lunda-Baluba rivalry. The wholesale expulsion of tens of thousands of Ewes from Togo is another example of the same phenomenon—increased ethnic violence because free election might topple both the ruling dictator (e.g. Togo's Eyadema and Kenya's Moi) and the dominant ethnic group (e.g. Kabre in Togo and Kalenjin in Kenya).

Another disturbing phenomenon is the army's return to power in some African countries. Certainly Africa of the 1990s will be an Africa with far fewer military coups and military regimes than Africa of the 1970s and 1980s, but hopes that the return to civilian rule of the 1990s was irreversible did not materialize. We saw the army in Nigeria canceling free elections and staying in power (in 1993) as well as successful military coups d'état that toppled elected governments in Niger (1996), The Gambia (1996), Burundi (1996), Sierra Leone (1997) and Congo Brazzaville (1997). Additionally, there were attempted coups d'état in Mali (1996) and the Central African Republic (1996).

The precarious state of democracy and democratization in the late 1990s shows that some of the conditions which led to the downfall of democracy in the 1960s have not changed much. The economic situation is still catastrophic. Although there was positive growth in the 1990s, as opposed to negative growth in the 1980s, this seems to have resulted from the rising prices of Africa's primary products (e.g. coffee, cocoa, cotton) and not from real structural change. Industrial growth in the 1990s was less than 1%. Africa's share in world trade continues to decline—3% in 1990, 2.5% in 1996. Private investment in the whole of Africa ($5.0 billion in 1995) is less than in Thailand or Argentina, and most of it goes to few countries (South Africa, Nigeria, Ghana, Angola). Africa's debt is staggering ($223 billion in 1996) and the interest on its debt consumes 20% of its foreign exchange earnings. Africa's dependence on aid is without any proportion to any other area in the world—11% of the GNP as opposed to 1.2% in the Middle East, 0.7% in Asia and 0.4% in Latin America.

Africa is by far the poorest continent, with millions of people dying every year of hunger, AIDS and other diseases. As we have seen, the ethnic question remains as important as it was during the 1960s. Events in Eastern Europe—the breakup of the USSR, Yugoslavia and Czechoslovakia and the numerous ethnic wars in the former Yugoslavia and Soviet Union may have even transformed illegitimate African 'tribalism' into legitimate 'ethnicity'. Indeed, the 1990s witnessed the first successful secessions in Africa, in Eritrea and Somaliland.

Africa is far from having a stable democratic political culture and African politics is still, to a large extent, 'politics of the belly'. It seems that the movement for democratization was—as in Russia—more a movement against dictatorship than a movement for democracy. We also know, again, as in Russia, Romania, Serbia, Slovakia and other former communist states,—that some of the 'new' elites are basically the 'old' elites. This means that very often the collapse of dictatorship is not necessarily followed by the consolidation of democracy.

Interesting questions still remain open. What is the real connection between economic liberalization and democratization? Does democratization follow economic liberalization, or vice versa? What is the linkage between development and democratization? Are the prospects for democracy better in relatively developed countries or in countries whose economies—though underdeveloped—are rapidly growing? Is ethnic heterogeneity an obstacle to democratization, or can it contribute to democratization—through federalism for example? What is more important for democratization—internal or external pressure? Can democracy be imposed by outside powers? Can it be imported? Is it possible to further democracy by constitutional engineering—by federalism, proportional representation, national unity governments or the prohibition of ethnic parties? What is the importance of tradition? Can it serve democracy—as traditional assemblies, consultation, participation, competition, accountability and decentralization seem to suggest in Botswana—or not, as the autocratic legacy seems to suggest in Rwanda, Ethiopia and Northern Nigeria? Does democracy have a better chance where there is more of a 'Western' impact? What importance should we attribute to the quality of leadership? Does it matter if we have a Mandela or a Mobutu, a Nyerere or a Moi, a Senghor or a Bongo?

All in all, there are more questions than answers. It's too early to celebrate the second democratic liberation.[15] It's too early to say if there is light at the end of the tunnel. Maybe there is another tunnel at the end of the tunnel. Nevertheless, in the long run there will be democratic light at the end of the autocratic tunnel.

---

[15] On the uncertain future of democracy in Africa, see Decalo (1992), Clapham (1993), Hawthorn (1993), Lancaster (1993), Young (1996), Bratton and Van de Walle (1997: 233–267), Clark (1997), Owusu (1997), Chabal (1998) and Wiseman (1999).

12. A POLITICAL SOCIOLOGY OF THE WORLD LANGUAGE SYSTEM*

Abram de Swaan

The dynamics of language spread[1]

The languages of the world together constitute a global system held together by multilingual people who can communicate with several language groups. The position of each language in this system may be characterized by its 'communication value' (Q), the product of its prevalence and its centrality. Languages represent a very special class of economic goods, they are not only collective goods, they also display network effects: such non-excludable communication networks may therefore be called 'hypercollective goods'. All texts, recorded or memorized, together constitute the accumulated cultural capital of a language group, once again hypercollective in character. The special characteristics of languages, language groups, and their accumulated textual capital help to explain the dynamics of language acquisition, conservation and abandonment. These concepts will be used to analyze the options confronting authors and users of texts in the relatively small or large language groups: the former may stick with the restricted language, learn the larger one or find a translator; the latter may wait till the others learn their large language or they may use translators.

The emergent world language system

There exists a dynamic world system of languages, held together by multilinguals, people who speak more than one language and can therefore communicate with one language group or another, and as the case may be, translate for third parties. Of course, the distribution of these multilinguals is by no means random, nor is it constant. The formation of the world

* This chapter was published in *Language Problems and Language Planning*, 22 (1 & 2), 1998. We thank the publisher, John Benjamins Pub. Co. for the permission to reproduce this chapter here (Note of the editors).

[1] Special thanks are due to the members of the working group for sociogenetic and psychogenetic studies, especially Geert de Vries, and to Johan Heilbron and Johan Goudsblom, for their comments on an earlier version.

language constellation comes from demographic processes first, when children adopt the language of the family they are born in. But beyond that,
its structuration results from students' foreign language acquisition and some
languages are much more in demand than others. As a matter of fact, the
system displays a very strong structure: a hierarchical or nested pattern of
connections.

There exist at least 4,000 distinct languages (depending on varying estimates and definitions of what constitutes a distinct language rather than a
dialect, regiolect or sociolect).[2] A small number of these languages, some
140, is especially interesting because each of them is spoken by at least one
million people.[3] Together they comprise 90% of the world's population.
Among these 140 languages there are some that are especially in demand
by foreign language learners. Not only because many other people speak
the language as their mother tongue, but also because quite a few people
who themselves speak another mother tongue have opted for this one as
their second language. As a result, such a language allows people who each
speak a different idiom to communicate in this third, intermediary, language. Such a language I have called a central language, 'central' in proportion to the percentage of multilinguals in that particular (sub)system of
languages, whose repertoire contains that language:[4] e.g. in some subsystem
of languages, say the language constellation of the peoples of the former
Soviet Union with its many nations and tongues, not only is Russian still
the most widely dispersed language, but more importantly in this context,
almost anyone who speaks more than one language speaks Russian either
as a first or as a foreign language. In other words, not only is the prevalence of Russian very high, but what matters here, its centrality is also max-
imal: it is part of (almost) every multilingual repertoire. In other words: the
ex-Soviet language constellation was and is held together by Russian (Turkish
and English now play increasingly important roles).[5] Some languages do not
number all that many speakers: their 'prevalence' within the given (sub)sys-
tem is relatively low. Nevertheless, most multilingual speakers in that (sub)sys-
tem have the language in their repertoire, and accordingly it is quite central:
this was the case of Latin in medieval Europe: with a relatively low number of speakers, its centrality was very high, since a major proportion of
speakers who were competent in more than one language spoke Latin.

---

[2] Cf. Crystal, 1987: 284–285.
[3] Cf. Crystal, 1987: 284–285.
[4] Cf. De Swaan, 1988: 69 sqq. The definition has been slightly revised, since.
[5] Cf. Kreindler, 1993.

A language that is highly central with respect to a subsystem may be peripheral on the next system-level. For example, Netherlandish is central within the language constellation of the Low Countries, where Frisian, Sranan Tongo, and Samami speakers, if they know another language, and almost all of them do, are competent in Netherlandish. The same is true—albeit to a lesser degree—of Antillians speaking Papiamentu as their maternal language (although some of them speak Spanish or English as an additional language, rather than Netherlandish). But at the next higher system level, the European constellation of languages, Netherlandish is quite peripheral: Europeans outside the Low Countries rarely if ever choose to learn it as a foreign language. Its prevalence puts it in the middle ranks, 27th in the world ranking list, 6th in the European Union, but its centrality in the EU is minimal.[6]

It is English that holds the nations of the European Union together, just as Arabic links the many North African and Middle Eastern peoples of the Koran, or Malaysian in its different versions connects the inhabitants of South East Asia. There are about a dozen languages in the world that serve as central languages at this (sub)continental level. Some do not count many speakers, but function nevertheless as languages of wider communication with high centrality: Swahili, for example. Some languages have a very large number of speakers, but are hardly central in the sense that few people have learned them as a foreign language: e.g. Japanese. The situation with Chinese, the most frequently spoken language in the world, with over a billion speakers, is somewhat unclear, as it is not known how many people acquired it in school as a foreign language, and how many learned it at home as their mother tongue. Much depends on how the differences between local versions of Chinese and the pothongua standard language are evaluated.[7] Finally, although very few people outside China learn Chinese, the language is spread across the globe by many millions of emigrants.

This dozen or so (sub)continental languages may be compared to so many suns, the centers of their respective solar systems, each of them surrounded by a ring of planets, the national languages for which they serve as the central medium. The 'national' languages in their turn serve as the central language in a planetary (sub)system with a number of moons: local or tribal

---

[6] Laponce (1984: 61, 72) ranks it 27th according to the number of speakers, and approximately 12th according to its 'economic importance'. Its 'Q-value' (see below) in the European Union around 1991 was in fact 0.007; cf. De Swaan, 1993b: 251. Only 1% of the citizens of the European Union reported that they were able to speak Dutch, although it was not their mother tongue; cf. *Eurobarometer* 44, 1996: 94.

[7] Cf. Barnes, 1982: 264 esp.; De Francis, 1984.

languages spoken by people who use the national language as their means of wider communication. In this constellation of moons circling planets, and planets turning around suns, one language is at the galactic center, in the midst of a dozen solar systems: this center of the linguistic galaxy is, of course, English. It is English that allows Arabs to talk with Russian speakers, Francophones with Chinese, Japanese with Spanish speakers or Lusophones with Malaysians. Below this global level, in several (sub)continental subsystems, English functions as a sun for the national planets: in most of Europe, in East Africa, and in India where it competes with another language for subcontinental communication, Hindi.

The galactic metaphor is of course no more than a telling expression for a hierarchical or multiple nested structure. But the multiplicity and complexity of the world's constellation of languages does reveal a surprisingly strong and simple order. In first instance, this order is the result of demographic distribution and of patterns of foreign language acquisition. But more often than not, the choice for a foreign language has been dictated by political authorities, and usually it is imposed through the school curriculum.

Communication potential of a language (repertoire)

A language's prevalence and its centrality both provide a partial indication of its utility to those who use it.[8] Therefore a suitable indicator of its worth, also to foreign language learners, is its 'Q-value': the product of its prevalence and its centrality in a given (sub)system of languages.[9]

Imagine a country with a great variety of language communities. Say, it was once colonized, and the language of the former occupiers is still in use. There is one major indigenous language and a number of native languages of more restricted diffusion. Only a tiny minority of European descent (say 3%) still speaks the former colonial language, 'K', as its mother tongue; almost no one in this group knows any of the indigenous languages. The largest language group, the mother tongue speakers of language 'A', comprise 35% of the population. The other language groups are all much smaller. Only a small percentage of the inhabitants (say 20%) have learned

---

[8] Coulmas (1992) contains an almost encyclopedic and also most eclectic discussion of economic aspects of language use. The author deals at length with the notion of the value of a language, defining its value-in-use as a function of the number of its speakers, later adding half a dozen of other components, among which is the number of those who have acquired it as a foreign language (pp. 83–90).

[9] See De Swaan (1993b) for further details, empirical results on the European Union, and for a more general expression.

any second language at all. Imagine that 10% percent of the entire population attended high school and learned the colonial language 'K' there.
Another 10 percent learned an additional indigenous language in day to
day interaction. As a consequence 20% of the population is bilingual (speakers of more than two languages are ignored here). Assume, moreover, that
the most widely spread language, 'A', has been acquired as a second language by 2% of all inhabitants. The total prevalence of the former colonial language is 13%: three percent mother tongue speakers plus ten percent
high school graduates. The prevalence of the indigenous language 'A' is
almost three times as large: 35% percent mother tongue speakers, plus two
percent who acquired it as a second language, makes 37 percent in all.

Mere prevalence provides only a partial insight in the importance of a
language in a language constellation. Much also depends on the functions
of a language in connecting different language groups. In the present example, 20% of the population speaks more than one language and may therefore perform mediating functions. Ten percent of the population, or one
half of all multilinguals, speak 'K' (almost all of them high school graduates). Accordingly, its centrality equals 0.5. The largest indigenous language,
'A', is spoken as a second language by only 2% of the population, or by
one tenth of all bilinguals; its centrality is 2/20 or 0.10. The Q-value of
any language is obtained by multiplying its prevalence and its centrality for
a given language. In the case of the former colonial language 'K' this results
in a Q-value of (0.13).(0.5) = 0.065. For the largest indigenous language,
'A', the outcome is (0.37).(0.10) = 0.037. The superior Q-value for 'K', the
ex-colonial language, reflects its 'strategic importance', which would have
been obscured if only the prevalence of the respective languages had been
taken into account. The example depicts a constellation that is quite characteristic of many multi-ethnic societies in the period before and after decolonization, up to the very present.[10]

Similarly, in the European Union, German is most prevalent as a mother
tongue. English is most prevalent when speakers who acquired it as a foreign language are included along with native speakers. Moreover, since the
vast majority of European multilingual speakers have English in their repertoire, the centrality of English is much larger than that of German, or of
French for that matter. As a consequence, the Q-value of English in the
constellation of the European Union (since 1991) was 0.50, that of German
0.12. French did score a Q-value of 0.19, since its relatively high centrality

---

[10] For descriptions of an actual instance of such a constellation, cf. De Swaan 1991b; cf.
also Laitin (1989a; 1992).

as the 'second' second language makes up for the relatively low numbers of its native speakers.[11]

In order to understand the evolution of these language constellations and to predict their future course, it is necessary to analyze why people choose to learn one language rather than another. Most importantly, perceptions and expectations of other people's language choices play a role in their own choice: if most Europeans expect that almost no one will want to learn French as a foreign language, French loses much of its appeal as a second language learned for purposes of wider communication. If, on the contrary, most people expect English to become the medium for wider communication almost everywhere in the world, that perception itself is sufficient reason to learn English.[12]

The approach so far assumes that individuals freely choose which languages to learn and aim at achieving a repertoire with a maximum communication potential (Q-value). But these individual decisions may have the aggregate result of weakening the position of some other language, e.g. because fewer and fewer people still want to learn it as a second language, or even because people do no longer bother to use it or even to teach it to their children as their first language, a fate which befell Irish and many other peripheral languages. In such a case, a collective defense of the language by its remaining users may be the only way to protect it against erosion by another language.

Languages as 'hypercollective goods'

From an economic point of view, languages may be compared with industrial standards and with certain supply networks. In the first place, they require an investment. Although children learn their mother tongue apparently with very little conscious effort,[13] mastering additional languages requires hard albeit often rewarding work—an investment of time and, as the case may be, tuition money. When consumers make a choice between appliances that conform to one among several competing standards, e.g. VHS, VR 2000 and Betamax for video recorders, they acquire a stake in either sys-

---

[11] Cf. De Swaan, 1993b: 250–251.

[12] Such a self-fulfilling prophecy presently is being realized in Europe, where an increasing number of high school students choose English rather than French among the foreign languages offered in the curriculum, cf. *Eurobarometer* 34, 1991; see also *Eurobarometer* 44, 1996. On the competition between English and French, see Flaitz, 1988.

[13] Cf. Pinker, 1994.

tem by the very act of buying a VCR machine. When people subscribe to one newspaper among many, or subscribe to one among a number of competing telephone companies, electricity suppliers, garbage collection services and so on, they acquire a vested interest in one particular service network among its rivals. Their commitment to one language, standard or network depends in the first place on the expected net benefits of the one they opted for minus the expected net benefits of the next best option plus the costs of switching to that alternative. Changing newspapers hardly involves any costs, switching banks may cause some expense, opting for a new word processor requires considerable retraining, adopting a different language demands major adaptation efforts. And, of course, any change in familiar habits is a mental sacrifice in itself. Language loyalty is an extreme case of consumer loyalty.

Whenever anyone learns a given language, opts for appliances with a specific standard or subscribes to a particular supply network, the person by doing so increases the utility of that language, standard or network for all other speakers, consumers, or subscribers who are already using it. There are several reasons for this: in supply networks the constant costs of the infrastructure are shared by a greater number of users. Of course, the same effect occurs with all commodities that can be manufactured at a lower cost per unit as production volume increases: these are straightforward economies of scale. When prices are decreased accordingly, these benefits accrue to new purchasers, and in the case of networks, in the course of time, they profit the old subscribers too. In the case of languages no such effect operates. They are not produced by anyone: they are simply there, freely available in live conversations. Languages may be acquired, and in so doing will be made accessible, at some expense through language courses, books, newspapers, tv or radio programs and so on. Since these may be distributed at quickly decreasing marginal costs to growing audiences, the spread of languages indirectly does generate economies of scale.

There is a second reason why people will opt for the winning alternative in a competitive situation: since they have a vested interest in the language, the appliance, the network, they will chose the alternative that is most likely to survive. This will guarantee them the availability of spare parts, accessories and repair shops in the future, and in the case of languages, the continued supply of texts in the particular idiom. A third and closely related effect has to do with the reputation of large brands: people assume that large suppliers will manage the manufacturing process more carefully and will be more willing to take back defective products or compensate for damages than smaller brands, precisely because the good reputation of the brand is such a valuable asset to the supplier. This is especially germane in the case of service providers such as banks or telephone companies. But it is irrelevant for the spread and maintenance of languages.

A fourth effect occurs in the case of standardized consumer appliances that function with specific kinds of information carriers ('software'), such as personal computers, televisions, record players, CD, CD-i, or CD-ROM players, tape, cassette, DAT, DCC and video recorders and so on. The larger the market share of a given standard, e.g. PAL-SECAM in television, the greater the number and variety of programs and recordings supplied for machines conforming to that standard. And this in turn increases the value of these appliances to their users.[14] In this case there is a close correspondence with languages: the more speakers there are, the more readers, and therefore the more authors and the more texts they produce.

The features mentioned so far are known in the economic literature as 'external network effects' and they operate in every kind of network as a special sort of economies of scale.[15] But there is an additional reason why the value of certain networks may increase for its users as new subscribers join them—a reason that is more specific to the phenomena under discussion. In some networks, such as telephone systems, as the number of connections grows, every individual user may communicate with a larger number of other subscribers. This effect does not occur in all supply networks. It is absent in the case of sewage, gas, electricity, or TV-cable systems which deliver a centrally supplied commodity or service to their users, but do not also connect them with one another. On the other hand, it does operate in telephone or postal delivery systems and in electronic mail networks such as Internet: *it is typical of those networks that serve the function of connecting the subscribers with one another: i.e. transport and communication networks.*[16] In these cases every new extension increases the number of potential connections for all existing users. Precisely this effect operates in the case of languages that gain new speakers: for every speaker of the language, the number and variety of possible conversation partners or correspondents increases with each new speaker added. However, the great difference between languages and

---

[14] Cf. Kindleberger, 1983.
[15] E.g. Katz and Shapiro, 1986.
[16] Kindleberger (1983: 377) remarks with respect to standards of measurement: "In fact they are a strong form of public good in that they have economies of scale. The more producers and consumers use a given standard, the more each gains from use by others through gains in comparability and interchangeability." Accordingly, it may be argued that these standards create commununication networks with respect to some measurement. Kindleberger presents as examples a.o. measures of time, and of value (i.e. money). Language remains entirely unmentioned! It is, however, referred to in passing by Blankart and Knieps, 1991.

all the other examples is that languages are not produced, or owned, or marketed: they exist as free goods.[17] Clearly, the external network effects occur independently of the fact that languages are free goods: communication networks such as telephone or e-mail systems do produce these effects, even though they are someone's property and are inaccessible without permission and, usually, a subscription fee (i.e. these networks are 'excludable').

Languages exist, they are the product of human creativity, but they are the creation of no one in particular and they are nobody's property. Anyone making the effort to learn them is free to speak or write them. But does that make languages collective goods? The question cannot be answered without defining the collectivity with respect to which languages may or may not be collective.[18] This collectivity can be no other than the category of people who are actual or potential users of the language, i.e. all those persons who belong to the language system or subsystem under consideration. If a language is to be considered a collective good in the strict sense, four conditions must be satisfied:

(1) It is impossible, on technical or economic grounds, to exclude anyone from enjoying the collective good.[19] On the whole, natural languages are completely accessible for anyone making the effort to find a textbook or an instructor (or even a patient conversation partner). Even the most secluded regimes, like Albania or North Korea, did not attempt to prevent outsiders from learning their language, although they much obstructed any attempt to practice it by denying entry to visitors.[20]

(2) The collaboration of many, but not of all those concerned is required to bring about the collective good or maintain it. Since natural languages already exist, what matters here is maintenance: a language can survive

---

[17] There are invented languages, the 'artificial' languages such as Volapuk, or Esperanto (cf. Eco, 1993), and computer codes called 'languages,' such as FORTRAN, C or BASIC. Since their value is so much dependent on their spread, the inventors tend to leave the languages at the free disposal of everyone, while textbooks or courses on diskettes etc. may be sold for a price.

[18] Cf. Olson, 1965: 5. Cf. also De Swaan, 1988: 5.

[19] Admittedly, there are secret languages and codes that allow to exclude outsiders; interestingly enough, in these cases the main assumption of the present theory, that languages increase in value, the greater the number of their speakers, does not apply. On the contrary, a secret, including a secret code or language, does not meet the second condition, ruling out vetoes: one traitor can 'give it all away'.

[20] Domestic attempts at exclusion do occur, e.g. the Turkish government's effort to prevent Kurds from using or learning their language. Since language acquisition mainly occurs in the bosom of the family, such policies are notoriously costly in human terms and in policing efforts. Unless they are coupled with physical deportation or even annihilation, as in Nazi-Germany and in the Soviet Union under Stalin, they remain mostly ineffective.

defection by some speakers and therefore the survival of a language does not depend on any particular speaker defecting, i.e. no speaker has a veto.

(3) For the collective good to be brought in existence or maintained, the efforts of a single person are not sufficient. No one can create or salvage a language on his own.[21] (If one person could decide, this would again make the language's fate dependent on a single person's veto.)

(4) Finally, the collective good's utility to its users does not diminish as new users are added.[22] Languages certainly meet this condition and satisfy an even stronger requirement.

In conclusion, natural languages satisfy the definition of a collective good. Moreover, a language's utility does not just remain equal as its speakers increase in number. It actually *increases*. A language will therefore be called a *hypercollective* good. All non-excludable transport and communication networks share this property of hypercollectivity.[23] This remarkable property— utility increases with an increasing number of users—also characterizes transport and communication networks that do not constitute collective goods, but joint or common goods, i.e. networks that allow to exclude some people and therefore to exact a user's fee for connection, such as road, rail, telephone and computer networks; accordingly, these may be called *'hyper-common'* goods. Since in the case of hypercollective goods, entry nor exit can be controlled, stampedes may occur, either toward or away from them. As the number of their users grows, so does their utility. In the case of a language, its Q-value increases, and at each higher value level new categories of users may find it profitable to join, when their particular 'tipping point' has been reached.[24] The expanding language more attractive to the speakers of yet another repertoire, until every speaker in the system would be better off by adding this language rather than some other, at which point,

---

[21] There is some evidence that languages that have come into existence in the relatively recent past, e.g. creole languages, were indeed 'created' by a relatively small number of people, possibly very young children, in a very brief span of time; cf. Pinker, 1994: 32–39; cf. also Mintz and Price, 1992.

[22] For many collective goods, there is a limit to this condition: when too many people want to enjoy them at the same time, 'crowding' occurs. But no such effect manifests itself in the case of languages, they can not be 'overused'.

[23] Gatherings where the main purpose is the pleasure of mutual encounter and where access is free, constitute another example, although at some point crowding may occur (while initially it is part of the pleasure): neighborhood parties, demonstrations, fairs etcetera; it is also a latent characteristic of markets, shopping malls and so forth.

[24] Schelling (1978: 99–102) discusses this notion of 'tipping' as it applies to neighborhood migration. Laitin (1993: 229–231) adopts this concept of a 'tipping game' for the analysis of foreign language learning.

it would become part of the repertoire of every speaker in the (sub)system.[25] Since multi-language systems are quite stable, there must be some force working for inertia: the costs of expanding one's repertoire, i.e. the expense and the effort of learning an additional language in relation to the expected benefits.

Conversely, an outward stampede, the cumulative desertion of a language, may result when an increasing number of speakers of that language becomes fluent in another language and a dwindling number of speakers remains that can be addressed in this idiom only. Of course, the two processes— the stampede towards the expanding language and the stampede away from the imploding language—may reinforce one another, especially when expectations about the numbers of converts to the one language and deserters from the other begin to play a part in the choices of language learners. The costs of language acquisition can slow down these cumulative effects. Moreover, people may neglect to use their language, but they can not so easily erase it from their memories. Definitive desertion occurs only when the next generation no longer learns the parental language. Finally, collective measures may be adopted to discourage people from abandoning their language, but such initiatives evoke all the dilemmas of collective action. In the following, this chapter will discuss the choices that present themselves to the users of the smaller and the larger languages, especially those users who specialize in producing texts: the authors. Should they favor free exchange of texts, either in original or translated version, or should they favor protectionist policies; should they learn to read and even write in foreign languages, or should they pay for translation; should they abandon their mother tongue or maintain it so that their collective cultural capital will remain accessible? Will these dynamics result in the conservation of the original language, produce a stable equilibrium of diglossia, or lead to the transition from one language to the other? The preceding theoretical analysis will serve to elucidate these questions.

The unequal exchange of texts

Languages define areas of communication. Beyond these limits, exchange of cultural practices and products is restricted to the degree that they depend

---

[25] Church and King (1993) have shown that in a system of two languages, learning costs being equal, and individual gains increasing with the number of users, all efforts will be directed towards learning the language that had more users to begin with, unless quite outlandish learning cost curves are assumed.

on language: the visual arts cross much more easily than, say, poetry. For language-dependent cultural practices to transcend linguistic barriers, some degree of bilingualism among the public is required, or the efforts of specialized bilinguals, i.e. translators. Languages tend to both insulate and protect the language-dependent cultural elites in their domain: on the one hand, what they produce does not on its own transpire to the outside world; on the other hand, the cultural production in other languages cannot penetrate and compete directly in their domain, it requires local competence in these different languages, or translation from them. This insulation operates more intensely for the less widely spread languages. As a result, the corresponding cultural elites are faced with a dilemma: opt for a more widely spread, second language and compete with many more producers on a much larger market, the 'cosmopolitan strategy'; or, opt for the less widely spread language and compete with only a few others for a much more restricted public, the 'local' strategy. Thus, say, Surinamese, Frisian or Antillian authors face a dilemma between Sranan, Frisian or Papiamento on the one hand, and Netherlandish[26] on the other. Dutch authors, in turn, have had to confront the choice between Netherlandish and English.

The case for remaining with the smaller language, or adopting it, is on the whole more developed and advanced more explicitly than its opposite, the choice for the large language. The arguments most commonly advanced are: (1) the small idiom is threatened, it may even disappear if people abandon it in increasing numbers: 'language death'—the metaphor of the extinction of a threatened species, a theme that has preoccupied sociolinguistics for some time now;[27] (2) the closely related, but more general argument that indigenous cultural practices and products will not survive unless the language in which they are embedded continues to be spoken and understood; (3) the struggle against linguistic hegemony and cultural imperialism as they are fostered by adoption of the more widely spread language.[28] The case for choosing the larger language, on the other hand, remains mostly implicit and the choice often appears like tacit desertion of the cultural heritage. And yet, it is not all that hard to mobilize the canons of universalism in its support.[29] Can the positions in this discussion, the options for one or

---

[26] 'Netherlandish' and 'Dutch' are here used as synonyms, denoting the language spoken in the Netherlands and Flanders (i.e. the Flemish part of Belgium). Its spelling and vocabulary are standardized under the auspices of the joint 'Taalunie'.

[27] Cf. Dorian, 1989; 1998; Hindley, 1990; the brief contributions on 'Endangered Languages' in *Language* 68(1) [March 1992]: 1–42; and Uhlenbeck, 1994.

[28] Cf. Phillipson, 1990.

[29] The most vivid and interesting discussions occurred in India and in anglophone Africa. Cf. for the latter, Omotoso (1994: 28): "If the cultural imperialists imposed their languages

another language-dependent cultural practice be analyzed in terms of a different debate: one that does not focus in the first place on matters of culture, identity and group solidarity, but rather on the political sociology of language in the context of a transnational language constellation? That is what this chapter sets out now to accomplish. This former part began with a broad sketch of the evolving world language system.[30] The next section presented an index for the communication potential (Q-value) of a language within this system. The third section defined languages as 'hypercollective goods', since they represent not only a category of collective goods, but also display network effects.

This section begins with a description of the dilemmas confronting authors (and other providers of language-dependent cultural products) who must decide whether to address a relatively restricted audience in their native tongue or compete in an acquired language for a much larger public. The next section is devoted to the issue of free or restricted exchange of texts in the divergent contexts of languages with either high or low Q-value. The theory of free exchange and the theory of collective goods both revolve around a dilemma. Under conditions of free exchange there is a choice for authors between being a small fish in a big pond or a big fish in a small pond. When the collective good of language conservation is at stake, there is a choice whether or not to join one's peers in an effort to maintain it as a separate small pond. The final section discusses what happens when authors switch to the dominant language, while competence in that language spreads among speakers of the original, indigenous language: at some point the domestic language may begin to be abandoned and the collective, accumulated stock of texts in that language will become increasingly

---

in the past, why have these Africans now, either as individuals or as states, not gone back to the restoration of their own languages? Or are the imperialists still at work?". Omotoso heaps special scorn on Ngugi wa Thiongo, a Gikuyu author who after much international success declared that he would no longer write in English but in his native language only. Omotoso 'could only smile and wonder for how long this decision would hold.' Wa Thiongo's Gikuyu writings were rightaway translated into English and from there in other languages. Cf. Ngugi wa Thiongo, 1986. Omotoso quotes Caliban from Shakespeare's *The Tempest* (I,2):

You taught me language; and my profit on't
Is, I know how to curse: the red plague rid you
For learning me your language.

Osotomo then (p. 33) cites the Nigerian novelist Chinua Achebe on English: "I have been given this language and intend to use it." Kwame A. Appiah (1992: 60) comments: ". . . few things, then, are less native than nativism in its current forms."

An early, frank statement in favor of europhone languages from a Nigerian minister visiting India in 1953 is quoted in Whiteley (1971: 189): "We are not keen on developing our own languages with a view to replacing English. We regard English as a unifying force." For two authoritative and opposing voices from India, cf. Kachru, 1986 and Dua, 1994.

[30] See De Swaan, 1993a; 1993b.

inaccessible. Under these conditions, 'hypercollectivity' operates against survival of the language community and its collective cultural capital, resulting
in a stampede towards the dominant language at the expense of the indigenous idiom.

Texts as commodities in international exchange

Once, a measure for the value of a language, its Q-value, has been defined,
and the distinctive character of languages (and other non-excludable communication networks) as hypercollective goods has been established, two new
and related issues present themselves: under what conditions do authors and
speakers prefer free exchange of language-dependent products, or texts, and
when will they choose to protect their community from linguistic exchange?
And, secondly, under what conditions will they resort to collective measures
to protect their language community? In other words, how does the theory
of free trade *vs.* protectionism apply to language-dependent cultural exchange,
and, what can be said on the collective aspects of the dilemmas of language
loyalty *vs.* language defection? The first issue is discussed in this section, the
second in the next.

In the international exchange of language-dependent culture goods, i.e.
texts, transport costs play a minor role, decreasing to almost zero for their
transmission with modern means of electronic communication. In this respect,
texts are the international commodity *par excellence*. What makes foreign texts
costly is the expense of translation. In the most straightforward case, interpreters or translators produce a version of the text in the domestic idiom.
The costs of their specialist services may in many respects be compared
with those of transportation, and even the concept of distance has some relevance: 'distant' languages are generally harder to learn, requiring greater
investment on the part of translators. But quite often, many members of
the domestic public can do without translation services, as they are themselves
competent in the foreign language. Such competence did not come without
cost, in terms of time and effort spent in acquiring foreign language skills.
Mastering a foreign language is in some respects comparable to purchasing
a second home or opening a branch office in another country: it allows one
to operate on two national markets, and thereby save transportation costs
and duties while residing abroad, just as polyglots can save themselves translation costs, once they have made their linguistic investment.[31]

---

[31] The advantage of learning a highly central language may not reside so much in the
opportunities it presents to communicate with speakers of some third language who are also

Very much like transportation costs and excise duties, the costs of translation or foreign language learning function as a barrier protecting indigenous authors, i.e. domestic producers of texts in the local language. As a consequence, a language community in which competence in a foreign language (especially in one with higher Q-value) is relatively scarce provides authors with a natural 'protective' barrier. Their captive audience finds itself restricted to domestic or translated texts, very much like consumers who must either buy goods produced domestically or pay transport costs and import duties. A somewhat chauvinistic public may not mind too much, preferring texts with a strong *couleur locale*, just as it prefers the flavor of domestic bread, wine or beer to outlandish alternatives.[32] Let us pursue the argument by concentrating on one kind of—highly specialized—language users: the authors. Their most advanced language skills, and for literary authors, moreover, their 'style', represent their major if not their only investment capital.[33] They may be thought of as simple-minded entrepreneurs, out to maximize their audience.

For authors whose native tongue is a rather peripheral language (i.e., one with a low Q-value), there may be advantage in using it, if theirs is a mostly monolingual audience. They need not make the—very costly—investment of learning another language to such perfection that they can publish in it. They are assured of a public that can not turn elsewhere, while their foreign competitors find themselves hampered by the costs of translation, quite forbidding in small language communities. Probably, native authors are best protected in societies where most people can understand and read the standard version of the domestic language, i.e. elementary education is widely spread, while few citizens have attended secondary school and therefore fluency in other, larger, languages is rare: there is a wide audience for texts in the indigenous language and only a small public has access to alternatives in foreign languages. This is probably the case in China, in parts of the Indian Hindi belt (even though illiteracy there still stands at a staggering

---

fluent in the central language, but to read translations that have been made into it from a multitude of other languages.

[32] Hoskins and Mirus (1988) take as their central concept the notion of 'cultural discount', i.e.: "A particular programme rooted in one culture, and thus attractive in that environment, will have a diminished appeal elsewhere as viewers find it difficult to identify with the style, values, beliefs, institutions and behavioural patterns of the material in question." Cf. also Biltereyst (1992: 533): "A country-by-country analysis shows that own-language drama is successful"; and on p. 536: "the popularity matrix—in those countries is dominated overwhelmingly by domestic and US fiction, with a clear stress on home made drama. Fiction from other countries is virtually non-existent."

[33] One must not, of course, underestimate the value of 'an unhappy childhood: a writer's goldmine' according to Conolly, 1961.

80%),[34] in Egypt, Indonesia and in the Philippines. Indeed domestic language newspapers, indigenous radio or television programs and popular songs with lyrics in the local idiom flourish in these countries.

The consumers of language dependent culture, on their part, stand to gain most from the most varied supply of texts, accessible at the lowest cost. Understanding a text in their native language for them requires neither translation, nor foreign language skills. But the supply of domestic texts is necessarily limited in the smaller language communities. Even many large societies miss out on many textual genres (e.g. scientific publications, mass entertainment productions).[35] Domestic authors can not easily satisfy the local demand for these texts, since they can not supply them single-handedly, as such genres require a very costly, extensive and finely branched production network: academic departments, or a film and music industry. Thus, if the consumers wish to extend their options, they must gain access to foreign texts.

On the other hand, the authors are faced with a restricted market for their texts: the local audience that understands the domestic language. Especially in the smaller language communities demand may not be sufficient to sustain more than a few authors in the more specialized genres, such as novels, poetry, literary and historical essays. Unless the authors accept to diversify their activities, e.g. take a job on the side as most literary writers in the smaller language communities do, they will be prompted to seek access to larger markets and try to publish in a more widely spread language. The author then has two options: (1) learn a foreign tongue with high Q-value well enough to compose texts in it, a major and high risk investment; (2) find a foreign publisher who will commission a translation into the high-Q language; this, too, requires a considerable and risky investment—on the part of the publisher. But the potential gains are proportional: a chance of large circulations in a much larger market.[36]

Mastering a foreign language to such perfection that one can compete with native authors is a rare feat, but it has been accomplished, not only by Conrad and Nabokov, or Ionesco, Cioran and more recently Kundera, but also by Jan de Hartog and in the unstylish realm of social science—by me and many others. The other option, to have the texts translated, comes

---

[34] Cf. Prasad, 1979: 22.

[35] In 1980 almost two thirds of all chemical and almost three quarters of all medical articles were published in English; adding five other languages would account for well over 90% of publications in these fields; cf. Laponce, 1984: 66–68. Except in the USA, television entertainment is for a very large part imported, and imports come overwhelmingly from the United States; cf. Varis, 1984; Biltereyst, 1992: 523.

[36] For statistics on translations from Netherlandish, cf. Heilbron, 1995a.

at considerable cost. Translation of say, a 300 page book at present rates costs approximately 17,000 US dollars; that implies, at an expected circulation of 2000 copies—certainly not too conservative an estimate—an addition of $8.50 to an average store price of, say, $25 per copy. The median first printing of a novel on the English language market is certainly not larger than of a novel on the Dutch market. This makes translation costs higher than average expected royalties. For films, translation costs tend to be much lower, but voice-over is again quite costly: it is routinely required by audiences in large countries who tend to despise subtitles, which are almost metaphorical for the snob-appeal of exotic movies.[37] In other words, for authors whose native language is understood by a relatively restricted audience there is the low-risk, low gain strategy of publishing in the mother tongue for a domestic public, and the high-risk, high profit strategy of seeking publication in a widely spread language. The two, however, are not mutually exclusive: one can become a small fish in a big pond, remaining all the while a big fish in a small pond. It demands making an effort and taking a risk, and more often than not it requires good connections with foreign publishers and *literati*, i.e., it takes transnational social capital.

The users of texts in the more peripheral languages who want to transcend the limitations of domestic supply equally face two options: pay for translation, or, learn the language with the higher Q-value. The first option implies continual payment of the current costs of translation. The second represents an investment in learning the more widely spread language, a considerable investment in terms of time, effort and money which, moreover, requires some maintenance, i.e. regular reading and viewing of products in the foreign language. Once a text is translated, however, the expense does not increase with the size of the text's circulation. Marginal costs are nil. Therefore, translation costs of texts that achieve a very large circulation, or that remain in demand for a long time, tend to become insignificant: products of mass culture and products of classic culture may be translated at very low cost per consumer, e.g. a TV-serial like Dallas, or a volume of the complete works of Shakespeare. Readers and listeners with specialized interests, be it in science, high literature, or any other specific field of language-dependent culture, will find that translations may appear with much delay, in erratic fashion, of low quality or at high prices, if at all. They may find it more useful to invest in learning the high-Q-language, thus avoiding to pay for translation and increasing their access to products in

---

[37] On the aversion of dubbing and subtitles among English speaking television audiences, cf. Hoskins and Mirus, 1988: 500.

that language. Interestingly enough, the rarer translations of foreign texts are, the more it pays for consumers to invest in learning the larger language.[38] Moreover, the smaller the peripheral language in question, the more likely it is that translations from the larger language will remain rare and inadequate. Finally, in Western Europe and the US almost all foreign language learning occurs in secondary school and the vast majority of the relevant age cohort does indeed attend full daytime education at that level.[39] As a result, the investment is compulsory and the effort is made at the very start of one's career as a consumer of language-dependent cultural goods. In other parts of the world, secondary school attendance is much lower. It is up to the parents to send their child to a school where foreign languages are offered, or it depends on the adult individual's decision to take private language courses. Whether foreign language learning is compulsory or not, in all cases the motivation to invest an added effort of one's own, i.e. the motivation to learn a foreign language, is increased when appealing cultural products are not widely available in translation into the peripheral language. The incentive for publishers to translate texts in the more peripheral language decreases if more potential readers and spectators are also fluent in the more central language.[40]

In conclusion, restrictions on the translation and dissemination of foreign language-dependent products paradoxically will increase motivation among the public to invest in foreign language learning, an effect that may even be reinforced by a gain in prestige of such foreign products.

Protectionism and free trade in cultural exchange

There is, however, one *caveat*: authors have reasons to be worried by foreign competition, but in the long run so does their public which may come

---

[38] A similar effect operates in the multinationalization of firms; cf. Carnoy (1993: 71): "The greatest pressure on automobile firms to become global, however, is still protectionism—the power of national political aims imposing themselves on comparative prices." Since duties and other trade restrictions make it more costly to import or export, "the general effect will be to increase the costs of using external markets relative to multinational control" (p. 60). I.e., it will more likely pay to open a branch office or subsidiary plant in the protectionist country.

[39] In 1990, 93% of young people in Europe speaking some foreign language had learned it at secondary school, cf. *Eurobarometer*, 1991.

[40] There is a countertendency: as the cultural elites, fluent in the foreign language, are familiar with these foreign texts and performances, their prestige may convince others that these products are indeed desirable and the demand for translated versions may increase accordingly among those sections of the public that have not learned the foreign language. The relative impact of the two tendencies is a matter of empirical investigation.

to fear that indigenous authors will be forced out of the field through the impact of translated and imported texts. Concern may grow that in the long run this will lead to a general erosion of the mother tongue and of domestic culture in general, i.e. in the terms of this analysis, to an overall depreciation of the original investment in mastery of the mother tongue. In other words, the consumers' short-term preferences in the long run may damage their collectively accumulated cultural capital. This is of course a very familiar argument, both in the debate on the protection of national cultures and in the discussion on the protection of domestic 'infant' and 'essential' industries, such as armaments or nutrition. Also, given the low marginal costs of translation of foreign texts, the familiar arguments from international trade theory about 'dumping' may well apply in the case of cultural exchange. Television and movie conglomerates in the very large language communities may export comedies and old films at negligible rates, preventing the small countries at the receiving end from developing a domestic entertainment industry that can compete—even if only internally—with foreign imports. American film and TV-producers, especially, have engaged in 'dumping' by supplying their products abroad at marginal cost or less. In the realm of the arts and sciences, moreover, a vast part of the foreign products have been subsidized at home. Under the terms of classic trade theory this might provide an argument in favor of protection against 'cheap' imports, but it is rarely invoked in the case of high art and science, as they appeal to a quite restricted public only.[41] As a result, the producers in the small language area may advocate restrictive policies, such as tariffs and quotas for foreign cultural commodities. In fact, this proposal crops up whenever European cultural policy is on the agenda and came again to the fore during the GATT negotiations between the US and the European Union.[42] Producers may petition the government to impose tariffs or quotas on cultural imports, a practice that has been adopted by the French government for television, films and popular music broadcasts, and again the argument against 'dumping' plays a major role.

Although most of these arguments have some substance, in the case of quotas and outright prohibition they do limit consumers' freedom of choice, an especially contested outcome in the realm of texts and culture in general,

---

[41] For an even-handed but skeptical discussion of the defense of protective trade measures, cf. Bhagwati, 1988.

[42] Import quotas on foreign films and TV-productions were strenuously propagated by the French and only recently dropped by the EU in favor of production subsidies for domestic films and television productions. Cf. "EU ministers pick funding over quotas", *International Herald Tribune*, June 22, 1995. Cf. also Forrest, 1994.

where freedom of expression and information are at issue. The less inva-
sive policy of imposing tariffs on foreign imports still taxes consumers in the
sensitive realm of cultural participation. Moreover, such policies are commonly justified as protecting merit goods, in this case expressions of high
culture. Thus, the French campaign for quota on American cultural imports
(mainly movies and TV-series) in the European Union did identify 'European'
with 'high' and 'American' with 'low' culture. However, foreign provenance
does not of itself imply low cultural standing, nor does domestic origin guarantee high artistic prestige. At second sight, there are additional considerations against the restriction of foreign cultural imports. First, limiting the
access to foreign language-dependent products may work to increase their
scarcity value and their prestige, their 'snob' appeal and curiosity value, and
thus, perversely, increase demand. This, of course, is what happened with
American culture under the Nazi regime and with Western culture in the
former Soviet Union, and it may have fed the immense popularity of Disney
and Hollywood in France.

Secondly, the 'couleur locale' and 'domestic cultural value' arguments also
cut both ways: indigenous authors and performers may come to rely too
much on domestic practices and facile imitations; as a consequence their
products may end up being considered 'homely' and boring. Finally, authors
and performers may pressure the government into granting subsidies for
domestic products, also to improve their competitive position vis-à-vis foreign imports. This is standard practice in the European film industry, and
less visibly so, in the production of TV-comedies and documentaries. Domestic
literature and the arts are routinely subsidized. In classical trade theory,
government subsidies on exports are an accepted argument for protective
barriers by the importing country. However, in this case such counter-mea-
sures are hardly considered. European books, songs and films that have been
subsidized at home hardly represent a threat for domestic producers in the
US, or elsewhere for that matter.[43]

At this point a second revision of classical foreign trade theory is in order.
Many cultural products clearly can be considered 'merit goods', i.e. products that when consumed by individuals, generate positive external effects,

---

[43] The situation is entirely different for the former French, Spanish, Portuguese and British
colonies, especially in Africa, where the former colonial language remains the most central
(but usually not the most prevalent) and cultural commodities in the ex-colonial language
actually prevent the emergence of cultural (including scientific) production in the indigenous
language. On the other hand, the former colonial language in many countries remains the
only medium of nation-wide communication and therefore also facilitates exchange on a
translocal level. On the concomitant dilemmas see a.o. the literature quoted in the opening
section.

or favorable consequences for others who do not themselves purchase or use them. In more sociological terms, a small audience for indigenous poets may keep poetry in the domestic language alive, stimulate poets to go on writing in that language, maintain and reinforce interest in the poetic heritage etcetera. This may be a good reason to subsidize poets and poetry books, and even people who do not themselves read poetry may agree to such grants since they want to be part of a culture in which poetry survives. Merit goods may be defined accordingly, as commodities that one agrees others should be using. The prestige of high art and high tradition may radiate towards people who themselves have no part of them. This also applies to international exchange: people who travel and work abroad have a collective interest in the international prestige of their culture, even if they themselves are no consumers of it. The 'merit goods' argument is of course the mainstay in the case for cultural subsidies. There is another, less widely spread argument: cultural producers must make a relatively very large, high risk, individual investment that pays off only in the long-term. During their formative years they often find themselves living in poverty with only a small chance of ever becoming successful. Under such conditions, producer subsidies seem justified (although this implies an argument to tax 'windfall profits' reaped at a later stage and age.)

In the preceding section, arguments have been borrowed from the theory of international trade, the theory of collective goods, the theory of merit goods, and the theory of cultural capital. Together they can support the case for a free trade policy with regard to cultural exchange—no tariffs, no quota—and for a policy of domestic subsidies to producers of high culture. These grants should support especially risky—i.e. advanced, initially contested—forms of expression, because of a probability estimate of their future 'merit' as cultural goods. In both policies, what is at stake is the contribution of both foreign and domestic cultural products to the collective cultural capital of the society concerned. The same case can not so convincingly be made for subsidies to the producers of 'mass culture', in so far as they are not considered to generate positive external effects, or to contribute to the collective cultural good.[44]

---

[44] I am well aware that this is, or should be, a most controversial consideration, since the substantive criteria of cultural 'merit', or contribution to collective cultural capital, can in no way be inferred from generally accepted principles. Nevertheless, there is an empirical finding that deserves mentioning in this context: both Pierre Bourdieu (1979: 33–34) and in a replication study, Van Calcar and Koppen (1984) found that people who are not at all interested in or knowledgeable about 'high culture' agree that it is more meritorious, or in the present terms, that other, 'better educated' persons should participate in it. This is an aspect of what Bourdieu calls 'cultural hegemony'. Cf. also De Swaan, 1991a.

The collective aspects of language, and of culture in general, will again be the subject of the next section. But before embarking upon the discussion of that topic, the third and the fourth party in unequal cultural exchanges need to be briefly characterized: the producers and the consumers of language-dependent cultural goods in the widely-spread language. The treatment can be brief, since their position is rather straightforward and most privileged. By definition, the users of a language with high Q-value profit from the position their language occupies in the encompassing constellation of languages. Their advantage is a clear case of what economists would call 'location rent'.[45] Without any effort on their part, the 'communication value' of their language increases, as others learn it as a foreign language. The tremendous advantages of this position may be seen when looking at the exports of language-dependent cultural goods from the US and England. This privilege does not accrue by birthright alone through the gift of the native tongue, it can be acquired: quite a few writers, many singers and actors, legions of scientists and scholars have made the effort to acquire fluency in English and reaped the rewards that go with it. Nor does it come solely with a position in Babylon, the anglophone metropolis: an astonishing number of writers from peripheral societies where English is prevalent in one form or function, e.g. India and the Caribbean, have gained a worldwide stature through their mastery of English prose. Success with an audience that has English as its mother tongue very frequently also brings recognition by a globally dispersed public that has acquired English as a foreign language, and next, translation into the many languages that are linked to the web of English by the most numerous cohorts of translators and interpreters.[46] Not only the rents from linguistic capital enter the equation, as a special kind of cultural capital, but also the rents from social capital based on network position in the international web of cultural exchange.

The authors in the large languages have little to fear from foreign imports: translation costs operate as a small but protective impediment, equal to the translation costs the other way round (as symmetric as transportation costs for that matter), and the effort demanded from foreign authors who wish to acquire the required fluency to produce English language texts serves as another, rather formidable, protective barrier. Moreover, even though foreign born authors enter the English language market either directly, or through translation, the increase in foreign consumers who have mastered the language is even faster, making any measure of domestic producer protection

---

[45] Cf. Muth, 1968.
[46] Cf. Heilbron, 1995a.

rather superfluous.[47] It goes without saying that under these conditions, the US is well advised to support free cultural exchange across the globe, even if it has to do so unilaterally.[48] The cultural prestige adhering to English language exports is commensurate with the position of the language and the culture in the global network of cultural exchange. Such prestige is not only a function of the worldwide distribution of the culture but also of the global military, political and economic hegemony of America—and formerly of England.[49] The position of cultural consumers who are native speakers of the central language is as privileged as that of the producers, if not more so: competition from abroad brings the consumers only more variety in supply, while they need not fear at all for the survival of their domestic culture. On the contrary, each day, all over the world, tens of millions of students are busy learning English, in the process improving their own position in the world language constellation and, unbeknown to them, improving the value position of all other English speakers, while native anglophones may not even realize what enviable blessing is bestowed upon them by the sheer accident of their mother tongue and the learning efforts of unknown myriads of foreign students.

Monoglossia, polyglossia, and heteroglossia

The users of a language share it as a hypercollective good. But having constituted a language community over a long period of time, centuries, maybe millennia, they also maintain together the accumulated collective cultural capital of texts recorded or memorized[50] in that language. Just as every addition of speakers profits all others, every new text increases this accumulated cultural stock. In principle, a language community should be ready to subsidize new speakers to join its ranks, since they increase the Q-value of its language for all its members. Language courses for recent immigrants

---

[47] For brevity's sake I have limited this discussion to the case of English; however Arab—a growing international language community—and French, a stagnant one at best, would provide interesting cases on their own.

[48] This again is a tenet of classical international trade theory since David Ricardo and John Stuart Mill; cf. Bhagwati, 1988: 24–33.

[49] Nevertheless, economic, political and military dominance do not always translate into cultural hegemony: the former Soviet Union tried hard to introduce its language and culture in the satellite countries, without much success, however. Young East Europeans swear that they know no Russian, even after six to nine years of intense instruction (cf. Vogel, 1994).

[50] En Afrique, chaque vieillard qui meurt est une bibliothèque qui brûle [In Africa, every old person who dies is a library burning], Hompate Ba, quoted in Diongue, 1980: 53.

are indeed routinely subsidized in Israel and European Union countries such as the Netherlands. For the same reasons, it would be rational for the British or the American, or for that matter the French or German governments to sponsor courses abroad in their respective languages. But many students there are willing to pay for textbooks and tuition anyway, since they want to improve the Q-value of their repertoire by adding a widely spread language. Governments in developed countries, on their part, indirectly do subsidize foreign language instruction by financing secondary education. This, too, is rational both for the individual who acquires a repertoire with higher Q-value, and also for the collectivity, since the language grows in value as its centrality increases with a gain in multilinguals in its ranks, e.g. students who have learned a foreign language. In other words, speakers of a language profit from the foreign language learning efforts of other speakers of the same idiom without any effort on their own part: they gain opportunities to find interpreters between that foreign language and their own and this is reflected in the increase of the term C_i in the expression for Q_i. The same applies to speakers of that foreign language, again without activity on their side, since its Q-value also grows with the increase of its multi lingual speakers. Where hypercollectivity prevails, language learning is a no-loss game, with benefits for all concerned. The gain comes at a cost, however: the expense and effort of language learning itself.[51]

Polyglossia,[52] the co-existence of several languages in one society, be it often in distinct social domains, need not damage anyone in terms of the present argument. However, under certain conditions it may lead to the abandonment of one idiom, often the low-Q indigenous language, in one domain after another by a growing number of speakers. Gradually at first, but at an increasing rate, the original language is deserted, the language community in its entirety begins to tilt towards the new language like a ship making water and leaning over ever further until it capsizes. A stampede out of the indigenous language and toward the imported tongue ensues. This is the phenomenon called 'language death' or 'language extinction' in the literature. Clearly, it is difficult not to depict the process as a tragic loss. The metaphor of death or extinction conjures up the image of a lost species. A biological species, however, may be saved by safeguarding the environment where it finds its niche. For a language to survive, a considerable number of people must maintain their speech and maybe their ways of life

---

[51] The effort in itself need not be a sacrifice, as is more often the case with human labor and effort, it may be pleasurable for its own sake.

[52] The term is a variation on an expression coined by Ferguson (1959): 'diglossia'.

against the inroads of a changing social environment—a rather more formidable task.

As an increasing proportion of the speakers in the original language community becomes bilingual, the added Q-value of being fluent not only in the exogenous but also in the indigenous language begins to diminish, since more and more people who speak the domestic language can also be reached in the foreign one, until no one is left who speaks the domestic language only and competence in it no longer adds to one's Q-value.[53] Children may now learn the new language at an ever earlier age, with increasing facility, and they may even adopt it as their mother tongue instead of the original language. From an individual perspective this is entirely rational. Only the costs of language learning and the emotional costs of abandoning one language for another will delay the transition towards the dominant foreign language. Once the great majority of the original language community has become bilingual and diglossia is well-nigh complete, heteroglossia sets in: the original language no longer adds much to the value of individual repertoires (i.e., less than its 'maintenance' costs) and it will increasingly be abandoned, as the other language takes over.

However, at this point other considerations may become predominant: with the surrender of the indigenous language the collective cultural capital becomes increasingly inaccessible and either the constituent texts must be translated into the dominant language, or this endogenous collective cultural stock is lost and the individual cultural capital predicated on that collective hoard must be written off. (Of course, the new speakers of the hegemonic language in the process acquire access to the collective cultural stock of that language community.) Since it usually does not pay for anyone on his own to translate endogenous texts into the hegemonic language, a collective effort must be made by the members of the language community in dissolution. But whoever speaks and acts for this disbanding language community will most likely prefer to salvage it, not by translation of its heritage, but by preventing desertion of its members in the first place:

---

[53] The prevalence, $P\{i,j\}$ for a two-language repertoire $\{i,j\}$ is defined as the proportion of all speakers in the language constellation S who have either the language i, or the language j, or both in their repertoire. When all j-speakers have learned the language i, $P\{i,j\}$ = Pi. Equally, $C\{i,j\}$ is defined as the proportion of *multilingual* speakers who have either i, or j, or both in their repertoire. Unless there are speakers of a third language in the constellation who also speak j, but not i, or speakers of j who also speak some third language, but who do not speak i, which is rare in the actual constellations under study, it is the case that $C\{i,j\}$ = Ci.

As a result: $Q\{i,j\}$ = $P\{i,j\}.C\{i,j\}$ = Pi.Ci = Qi. Competence in the language j no longer adds to a speaker's Q-value.

a collective effort must be made to maintain the idiom, even if only as a second language. There will be pressure upon adults to continue to use it, and upon children to go on learning it as their parents did.[54] Clearly, a community with an effective coordinating agency, e.g. a political authority of its own, is in a much better position to impose its policies than a collectivity that must rely on voluntary compliance.[55]

Authors, i.e. all producers of texts, have a larger stake in the original language and in the conservation of its cultural stock than others, because of their costly investment in language skills and in knowledge of the texts. Moreover, for them the switch to the dominant language as a full means of expression requires a much larger effort than for those who only speak, hear and read it. And, finally, if and when the domestic language is maintained by a sufficiently large audience, this provides the authors with a protected market for their texts, and provides them with an added interest in maintaining the original language. Thus, unless they make up their mind to become cosmopolitans, venturing into the high-Q language community, authors will feel compelled to defend the domestic language. Translators and interpreters, too, have a vested interest in slowing down the spread of the dominant language and in preventing the desertion from the original language, so as to maintain a clientele for their services. It should therefore come as no surprise that specialized producers and translators of texts are among the first to defend the domestic language, together with politicians who wish to preserve their local support base and community leaders or clergymen who do not want to see their congregation disband as its unifying language evaporates. The 'tipping point' in the transition from diglossia to heteroglossia comes when for those who speak both the indigenous and the exogenous language the costs of maintaining the local language begin to outweigh the latter's dwindling additional Q-value. That occurs when a considerable majority of the community has already become bilingual. Once desertion sets in, parents no longer teach the language to their children and no longer make an effort to speak it 'correctly' themselves. If the language is to survive at all, individual language maintenance is no longer enough. Young adults must be pressured into the much larger effort of learning what used to be their mother tongue but has by then become 'the language of their elders'.

---

[54] It is customary to argue that no one is individually motivated to contribute an effort towards this collective objective. However, in this case also, many of the activities required are not just a 'sacrifice' but are also rewarding in themselves, e.g. admonition, rebuke, scandalization and even demonstrating, rioting and terrorist attacks. Negative informal sanctions quite often are a pleasure to apply. Cf. De Swaan, 1988: 5.

[55] Cf. Laitin, 1987; 1989b.

In general, the gains that speakers may reap from addition of new users of their language find their counterpart under obverse conditions in the increasing losses that the remaining speakers suffer once others begin to desert. Since language is a hypercollective good, and cultural stock constitutes a collective good for the language community, language maintenance raises problems of collective action and confronts individual language users with the concomitant dilemmas: it would indeed make sense for everyone separately to maintain the original language if many others could be counted on to act likewise. However, since one cannot be sure the others will do so, in each individual case maintenance of the original language appears not worth the effort. In such situations people often publicly profess their allegiance to the collective heritage, while privately they neglect their inherited language and their cultural inheritance, while ensuring the career prospects of their children by making sure they will become proficient in the dominant language.[56] On the whole, when the language community also constitutes a state, its government can avert a stampede out of the national language, even when a high degree of diglossia prevails. It can do so by safeguarding the domains of domestic politics, national culture, education, law and so forth as the preserve of the indigenous language and by preventing the exogenous language from usurping all prestigious functions.[57] Thus, while some European countries, e.g. the Netherlands, Luxembourg and Denmark are rapidly approaching a state of universal multilingualism and pervasive diglossia with English (with well over 80% of the population competent in English), there are at present no signs of abandonment or neglect of the indigenous language. Rather, each language functions in a series of distinct social domains, and even if switching between the two is frequent, the one hardly encroaches upon the other.[58] If there is no reason for alarm, there is cause to remain alert: English may make inroads into new speech domains and the indigenous language may loose additional functions that carry high prestige. But so far an equilibrium of diglossia has proved quite stable.

---

[56] No one has depicted these dilemmas more starkly than David Laitin, 1992; 1994.

[57] Languages that are spoken by a community that is coterminous with a state, I have called 'robust languages' which derive both their durability and their distinctiveness from the protection of a permanent and well-demarcated state; cf. De Swaan, 1993b: 252.

[58] The public is much concerned with the appearance of foreign, mostly English, loan words in the vocabulary. But such additions to the lexicon leave the 'hard core' of the language, its grammar and pronunciation, mostly unaffected; cf. Hagège, 1987: 27–89. The resilience of many European languages is demonstrated by the adoption of English terms, such as 'delete' or 'save' in computer speech, which are then declined according to the rules of the borrowing language, e.g. in Dutch: 'Ik heb de file geseeft'—i.e., 'I saved the file.'

Discussion

Although linguists, and sociolinguists especially, have produced an enormous number of most informative studies on the social determinants and functions of language, and macrosociolinguists have made a specialty of research into language planning, the rivalry and accommodation between language groups has so far received limited attention. The political sociology of language is still in its initial stage. And economists, on their part, have rarely studied language per se, and as a result some of the most remarkable economic characteristics of language have gone unnoticed. Sociolinguists have looked into the costs and benefits of multilingualism, translation and so forth—most notably Florian Coulmas—but they did not apply economic theory. The political economy of language is only just emerging. The political economy and political sociology of language departs mostly from individualist premises, but in the process it produces a collectivist perspective, built around the notions of the Q-value of a language repertoire, of a language as a hypercollective good, and of remembered or recorded texts as collective cultural capital. Nor do the rationalist premises prevent the inclusion of cultural values per se. On the contrary, communication with other language users, access to texts (or language-dependent cultural commodities), access to a collective cultural heritage are defined as the relevant cultural interests.

The present approach starts out with the description of a coherent and structured language system, global in scope at its most encompassing level. Within this structure, choices for one language or another may be explained with the concept of Q-value, a combined index of a language's prevalence and its centrality. Language-dependent cultural goods percolate through this system as texts, transcending language barriers directly to multilingual users, or indirectly through the mediation of translators. Producers of texts may opt for the domestic market, the 'local' strategy, or try their chances in a more prevalent and central ('high-Q') language for a larger market, the 'cosmopolitan' strategy. Authors in the indigenous language may seek production subsidies. They may also demand protective measures, like producers of other commodities, against foreign dumping, as an 'infant industry', or as producers of 'merit goods'. At the core of the analysis is the notion of the effects of individual language choices upon other language users: the concept of hypercollectivity. Initially, the expansion of a language community seems to benefit everyone, but there may come a point where multilingualism spreads so widely through the smaller, more peripheral language community that the indigenous language is in danger of massive abandonment. It is at this point that state protection may help to safeguard the national language, robust as it is; but languages that must function without such shelter may indeed be threatened by a stampede of deserters.

The global language system is one aspect of a world system that so far has been described mostly as a world economy of division of labor, trade and finance, or as a constellation of states and international agencies precariously held together by intertwined national interests and international law. More recently the earth has been recognized as one ecological system, and in the recent past there has been a surge of interest in the dialectics between local and cosmopolitan cultures within a global culture system. The world language system is most closely connected with this global system of cultures, but it reveals a strongly coherent and ordered structure of its own. As such, the emerging world constellation of languages may be related to the economic, political, ecological and cultural aspects of the world system in a new approach to the study of transnational society.

13. LANGUAGE AND MODERNITY IN ALGERIA

Mohamed Benrabah

Introduction

Language policy in Algeria, known as Arabization, is a centralized governmental decision. It has been imposed since the independence of the country in 1962, and in a systematic way after the military coup in 1965. Even though no official attempt has been made to evaluate language planning in this country, most observers agree upon the fact that Arabization in Algeria is a total failure. Let us first illustrate this failure and then try to give a tentative explanation for this lack of success.

Unforeseen development

In June/July 1998, Algeria hit the headlines with events related to the language issue. On August 5th 1998, the Law on Total Arabization was imposed: as from this date, Classical Arabic was to be used in all spheres of public life, with the exception of higher education, for which the deadline was July 2000. Ten days earlier, on July 25th, a leading Algerian singer, Matoub Lounès, was assassinated by an armed group. What caught the world's attention was the uprising that took place in the Kabylie region. Rioters burnt or destroyed symbols of central authority such as banks, headquarters of political parties, etc., and, most strikingly, all public sign-posts in Arabic leaving untouched scripts in Berber and French. It was just another opportunity for the Berber-speaking community to show its refusal to accept the language policy imposed by the authorities. In Algeria, Berber unrest with linguistic claims as its background has been a recurrent phenomenon for the last two decades. In fact, this illustrates the failure of Arabization as a tool of nation building.

Arabization has also failed as an instrument of language shift. Algerian Arabic speakers have not changed their linguistic behaviour in their day-to-day interactions by adopting Classical Arabic. During a meeting organized by the Higher Council for the Arabic language in March 1999, for example, the Secretary of State for Culture declared: "In the street, people use all sorts of languages except [Classical] Arabic, this is not the normal state of things at all." This State official also suggested that Classical Arabic should be "imposed in the heart of society, in streets, public places and inside homes" (Bendaoud, 1999: 5). The mother tongues (Algerian Arabic and Berber) are maintained by the populations as a reaction against this imposed centralized language policy.

What is more, French, the language of the 'ex-colonizers' against which Arabization was implemented in the first place, has never been as present and thriving as it is today. As an illustration, it is worth mentioning the status of that language among Algerians. In 1996, fifty-two candidates sat for the French 'Baccalauréat' exam (Simon, 1996: 1). All these examinees, who had followed a French curriculum in an Algerian secondary school in Algiers (the former 'Lycée Descartes' renamed 'Lycée Bouamama'), were sons and daughters of military generals, ministers, Secretaries of State and high officials. Hence, more and more Algerian parents have come to view this 'elite closure' (Myers Scotton, 1993) as unfair and have started to invest sometimes substantial sums of money in the French educational system so as to allow their offspring to sit for the French 'Baccalauréat'. In May 1999, the total number of candidates who sat this exam rose to four hundred, with half of them coming from the Lycée Bouamama (Sadki, 1999). More-over, the Arabization of the national educational system (at primary and secondary levels) has led to a disastrous situation: two presidents, the late Mohamed Boudiaf and Abdelaziz Bouteflika, described it as 'sinistrée'.

These three illustrations clearly show how Arabization has failed in its attempt to impose the aims it set out to fulfill in the first place: (1) language shift by making Algerians adopt Classical Arabic; (2) eradication of the mother tongues (Berber in its various forms and Algerian Arabic in its various forms); (3) eradication of the former colonizers' language, French, which is often the native tongue of certain Algerians. Arabization has not been successful for a number of reasons, two of which are, to our mind, of paramount importance. On the one hand, there is the authorities' refusal to recognize Algeria's perennial linguistic and cultural diversity and, on the other, a denial of the population's thirst for modernity.

Linguistic pluralism

After independence, Algerian authorities embarked on building a nation based on the French Jacobin model. Linguistic and cultural unification was imposed with a deliberate refusal of reality that was characterized by plu-ralism and diversity. As an illustration, one can mention the different con-quering groups that settled in North Africa. In addition to the Berbers, the original settlers of the region, this area attracted the Phoenicians, the Romans, the Vandals, the Byzantines, the Arabs, the Spaniards, the Turks and the French, in that order. Almost all these invaders influenced the linguistic make-up of the region. For instance, at the lexical level and besides Arabic patterns and morpho-syntactic structures, one can find in present-day Algerian Arabic, words such as *rfissa* and *barkukas* (two traditional dishes) from Latin, *boukraj* ('kettle') and *braniya* ('aubergine') from Turkish, *kanasta* ('basket') and *essekouila* ('school') from Spanish, *miziriya* ('poverty') and *kamyoun* ('lorry') from French. Finally, Algerian contains a large number of words of Berber origin: in the North West of the country, Algerians use, for example, *aghlal* for 'snail' and *ajreuj* for 'strainer'.

From the above-mentioned (invading) groups, three have had a significant impact on present-day Algerian linguistic panorama. First, Berber, which used to cover the entire area, is still found in a number of places, despite all subsequent conquests. It has survived in different forms: 'Kabyle' is spoken mainly in the mountains on the North coast, east of the capital Algiers; 'Shawia' in the Aurès region situated slightly to the south and east of Algiers; 'Tamashek' is the mother tongue of the Tuaregs who live deep south in the Sahara desert. As a result of urban expansion during colonization and after independence, Berber-speaking subjects can be found in substantial numbers in certain cities and towns.

In places where Berber died out, it is Arabic that has replaced it. The first Arab invasion took place in the 7th century and mainly influenced urban inhabitants. It was in the 11th century that rural populations started adopting Islam and the Arabic language under the influence of Bedouin tribes coming from Arabia (the Banu Hillal). During the Turkish reign (1529–1830), Islam and linguistic Arabization continued to spread. While Classical Arabic remained the language of religion, a new type of Arabic was born as a result of language mixing: various Middle Eastern Arabic varieties brought by soldiers who were in contact within camps and with the local Berber language. It is this Berber substratum which gives the North African varieties of Arabic their identity which differs from the Middle Eastern varieties the substratum of which is Aramaic.

Up to 1830, education was closely related to religion and based on the holy book, the Koran. All schools were attached to mosques (or other religious institutions) and financed by private donors or religious institutions. After invading in 1830, the French imposed schools financed by the state to spread their language. The indigenous populations viewed this offer with suspicion and skepticism: they considered this as a way of stripping them of their faith. And the occupying forces' actions reinforced them in this belief: the French army expropriated lands owned by religious institutions which used to finance the traditional educational system. The result was resistance and 'cultural ossification'. Parents preferred their children to remain illiterate rather than lose their faith. The European civilian settlers were pleased by this attitude because they feared the end of colonization as a result of educating the local populations in French.

Language and modernity

Resistance lasted until the 1920s, though in 1910, despite the opposition of the civilian settlers, the French government imposed enrolment for military service for all Algerians. 173,000 joined the French army and 119,000 Algerians emigrated to France to replace the French workers who had been conscripted. As soldiers and immigrant workers, Algerians became aware of the benefits that they could gain from going to French schools: learning French could only improve their socio-economic position. When back home, they started claiming a French education for their children. Thus, French was not imposed upon Algerians but rather 'assumed' by them. Unconsciously, they started to acknowledge the French language as 'cultural capital' (i.e. knowledge, skills, educational qualifications, etc.).

The 1920s also witnessed the emergence of the nationalist movement which had gradually grown among immigrant workers who had gained political awareness through contact with their French colleagues in trade unions. But the nationalist movement also grew in towns and cities in Algeria which had simultaneously recorded an important growth in urbanization. In 1830, for example, less than 5% of the total population lived in towns and cities, and the country was a vast rural area entirely devoted to agriculture and nomadism. By 1906, 16.6% of the population lived in towns and cities and, by 1926, the urban population reached 20.2%. In 1830, ideas such as 'nation' and 'nationalism' were unknown to Algerians: the country consisted of 516 tribes, out of which only 206 accepted allegiance to the Ottomans. The remaining tribes were either completely independent or semi-independent (Harbi, 1994: 226). Group membership was solely based on adherence to a tribal structure and/or the larger Muslim (pan-Islamic) community. The denomination 'Algeria' itself had not existed until it was coined and decreed by the French in 1839. After the Second World War, the French language was to become an instrument for freeing the country.

During colonization, Classical Arabic was the language that carried 'symbolic capital' (i.e. honor, religion, etc.). Apart from the fact that, right from the start, the Berbers had never managed to dissociate religion from the (sacred) language, there was another factor which enhanced its prestige during the French occupation. The basis of French ideology (one language-one nation, one nation-one language) could not allow the existence of a rival, Classical Arabic. It therefore relentlessly persecuted this language until a ministerial decree signed on March 8th 1938 declared it a 'foreign language'. Of course, this enhanced its status as a 'martyr-language' and a strong symbol for resisting colonialism.

At the moment of independence—as a result of 132 years of French presence and cultural mixing—Algeria was "already in phase with significant forms of modernity" (Bessis, 1995: 234) such as ideas of 'nation', 'democracy', 'social justice', 'secularism', etc. This is what Ernest Gellner (1973: 19) says about the importance of the causal factor in the growth of North Africa's national consciousness:

> . . . the agent of modernity in North Africa was initially France. I believe the impact of French culture in North Africa to be profound and permanent. In his heart, the North African knows not merely that God speaks Arabic, but also that modernity speaks French.

After the military coup in June 1965, the new regime used Islam and the Koranic language as tools for gaining legitimacy (Grandguillaume, 1995: 9–11). Arabization at any cost was imposed without the consent of the majority. Among all Arabic-speaking countries, Algeria was certainly the least prepared national community for this kind of language planning. The significant lack of means was simply an enormous handicap because French colonialism had eradicated almost all traditional structures that had existed before 1830. In schools, Arabization imposes teaching methods as well as contents of manuals which are meant to debilitate the new generations and expropriate them of their past (e.g. teaching the hatred of Berber ancestors, encouraging collective amnesia), of their language or languages (e.g. teaching linguistic guilt complex, linguistic simplification) and so on. Arabization has actually turned out to be an instrument in the hands of totalitarianism for social control. Far from being a linguistic process, language planning in Algeria has become a process for the Islamization of society.

Expropriation of modernity

Yet most important of all is the fact that the population has become aware of its leaders' insincerity. As stated above, for reasons of social reproduction ('elite closure'), political elites and their allies register their offspring in bilingual or French educational institutions but impose a monolingual Arabized/Islamized school tailored for the people's children. As early as 1981, John P. Entelis (1981: 208) warned about

. . . the mediocre and incomplete nature of much of the educational process [and if it] continues unchecked [a] 'third' generation of disillusioned and economically 'unabsorbable' counter-elites, as described by Waterbury and Zartman for Morocco, may emerge.

Here are Waterbury and Zartman's remarks (quoted in Entelis, 1981: 208):

> The fact that these [third generation counter-elites] often tend to be semi-educated, traditionalist school-leavers, trained only in Arabic and more hostile than frustrated in their feelings toward modernization, suggest that their reaction will be neo-traditionalist . . . Islamic, populist, and Qadhafite. It will be one of cynical radicals, suspicious of any leadership . . . intolerant, impatient, and embittered over being excluded from the public benefits that private [and public] corruption make appear inexhaustible.

Algerian elites have also encouraged cultural dislocation by not incorporating peacefully the French dimension of the Algerian national identity. An Algerian Francophone author writes:

> In 1962, Algerians got independent but have not been liberated. They have come to realise this within an accumulation of frustrations. Furthermore, France is more present than ever in the mind of every Algerian; however, nobody has ever tried to integrate this aspect peacefully (Tengour, 1995: 77).

Moreover, in the field of corpus planning, the authorities have resorted to what Grandguillaume (1983: 31) calls 'Arabization-translation' which is nothing more than straightforward borrowing from French. 'Modernizing' Classical Arabic in this way is seen by the population as an illegitimate way of expressing modernity. Consequently, many Algerians consider Arabization/Islamization as a means of expropriating from them the right to acquire modernity.

This point may be taken into account for a paradoxical state of affairs: despite a systematic attempt to implement Classical Arabic against French (and the mother tongues), there are nowadays far more Algerians who are competent in French than in 1962. Despite a drop in standards due to poor teaching methods, the total number of French-speaking Algerians which was 49% in 1993 (with a total population of 27.3 million) is estimated to reach 67% in 2003 for an estimated population of 47 million (Rossillon, 1995: 91). To understand this seemingly paradoxical result, one must take into consideration the population's linguistic representations and attitudes towards the languages that are in competition. In other words, 'national' language and identity "as formulated by its official champions [do] not necessarily coincide with the actual self-identification of the people concerned" (Hobsbawm, 1990: 134). In fact, elites in countries like Algeria tend to lose contact with the realities of their society with which they can no longer communicate.

Conclusion

Arabization in Algeria has produced a divided society. On the one hand, there are intolerant, traditionalist monolinguals lacking a sense of national belonging and supporters of a trans-national (Arab) Islamic 'nation'—they despise Algeria as a nation. On the other, one finds another group of people who resist this language policy as a tool of homogenization and standardization. These are Algerians who do not want to be shackled by monolingualism. They are attached to the idea of nation-building in the modern sense and to an Algerian national community marked by its perennial pluralism. Among them, one can mention those who create linguistically and artistically in their mother tongue. The Berber uprising in April 1980 was preceded by an unprecedented explosion in artistic creativity (music, theatre and literature) in the Berber language. The musical phenomenon called RAI sung in Algerian Arabic is another expression of this resistance.

RAI goes back to a traditional form of Bedouin music born in the southwest of Algeria (Oranie) in the early 20th century and modernized in the 1970s. At the beginning, the lyrics were mainly concerned with alcohol, sex and love; that is to say, topics banned by traditionalists and amplified by 'official' conservative institutions such as school, TV and radio. What is more, RAI—which has become international—often adopts and adapts most of its lyrics from the Algerian cultural heritage known as *Eshi'r el-Melhun* written in Algerian Arabic. It, therefore, praises this heritage. The word RAI itself means 'opinion'—'my opinion as an individual against your opinion'; 'my opinion against that of the traditional social group which refuses individual autonomy'; 'my opinion against that of those who have power (i.e., the regime)'.

As advocates of Algerianess, RAI singers have become one of the targets of those segments of the Algerian society who prefer a trans-national 'nation' and consider music as unacceptable. After the assassination of Cheb Hasni in October 1994, many artists fled the country causing a short decline of RAI singing. A year later, however, it thrived again and has increased exponentially ever since. Cheb Mami, a well known international RAI singer, had been in exile since 1989 and after a ten year absence from his country, he sang in front of 100,000 of his countrymen in July 1999. When hearing him sing *bladi hiya el djazajr* ("My home country is Algeria"), the audience was entirely devoted to Cheb Mami's cause (Metaoui, 1999: 24). As to the question of the Arabic language in Algeria, Cheb Mami declared on a French TV channel (ARTE) on June 1st 1996:

> We do not speak Classical Arabic in the street! There is language mixing . . . They always identify themselves with the Saudis and the Kuwaitis, while we are Algerians!

RAI singers thus represent the component parts of a society that yearns for a clear break with the social and political past of their country. They are proponents of a conception of modernity on one's own terms, those of the Algerian population. Instead of Arabization, what is required is a policy that is likely to be more appropriate to the reality of the country, a policy of Algerianization.

14. GLOBALIZATION AND PRIVATIZATION IN HIGHER EDUCATION

Jerzy J. Smolicz

Although globalization is not a phenomenon of our time alone and was apparent, for example, in the classical epoch under the aegis of the Roman empire, the current situation is unique because of the rate of cultural interchange and the 'compression' of cultures under the impact of mass communication technologies. The economic, political and cultural aspects of globalization have been much discussed already, but the educational repercussions have been slower to emerge. This paper aims to discuss the transformation of higher education systems through 'privatization'.

Under the impact of globalizing market forces, there has been a general trend towards the reduction of per capita public funding to higher education despite the continuing increase in student enrolments. Although the administrative procedures adopted have varied from country to country, in terms of their outcomes, these changes can be regarded as essentially a series of privatization measures, achieved through the transfer of a proportion of the costs to the community, either by state universities imposing fees, or new private institutions being established. The objective of this paper is to analyze the process of such privatization in the higher eductaion systems of Poland, Iran, Australia and the Philippines in order to examine the transfomation pathways which have been adopted within the framework of each country's differing national tradition, and the way the changes have affected the quality of education being offered to students.

Emerging commonalities and 'multiple modernities'

The shifting of responsibility for the funding of higher education to students and their families, as well as other outside government sources, can be regarded as a form of 'privatization'. This may result in the creation of 'private', 'independent', 'church' or other non-government institutions (which can be considered *independent privatization*), or take the form of directly imposing fees upon students when they attend formally state-funded colleges and universities (which may be labeled *public privatization*). The ideology underpinning this transformation has been summarized by Boumelha (1998: 37) as the assumption that "education is a private matter of individual choices and personal benefits" gained by graduates for the employment market. Behind this view stands the model of education that "devolves the responsibility for the common good to the aggregate of atomized individual choices". This approach breeds a spirit of competition among the different higher education sectors, driving institutions towards the supposed rewards and incentives of the market place and away from the traditional concept of an academic community of scholars dedicated to the pursuit of learning.

A common feature to be observed in all the countries under study was the desire of the four governments to compensate for diminished per capita funding by retaining, or even increasing, the state's influence or control over the institutions. Another outstanding characteristic of recent developments has been the widening quality gap between the relatively few elite universities, on the one hand, and the more numerous middle-of-the-road, mediocre or even sub-standard institutions designed for the mass market.

While this paper focuses on the commonalities associated with the impact of globalization, another possible approach would be to examine the way in which privatization in each of the countries has followed a related but, nevertheless, distinct pathway. Such distinctions could be viewed from the perspective of each country's unique history and culture and its current political and economic realities, in order to examine the extent to which these educational transformations provide support for the sociological concept of 'multiple modernities' (Eisenstadt, 1996a, 1996b; Ben-Rafael, 1998; Ishitsuka, 1998). While acknowledging the potential inherent in the hypothesis of multiple modernities, with its belief that the globalization process encounters a response that reflects each culture's unique forms of adaptation to change, the elaboration of this interpretation of privatization falls beyond the scope of this paper. There is little doubt, however, that the two phenomena are complementary and interactive, in the sense that emerging commonalities of globalization in the university sector serve to evoke responses which are characteristic of the educational traditions of each country.

Historical and cultural background

Even though the four countries studied are geographically and politically diverse, there are certain cultural and historical resemblances among them. For example, both Poland and the Philippines are overwhelmingly Catholic, with their Catholicism deeply influenced by the counter-reformation epoch of Trent and its aftermath throughout the XVII and XVIII centuries (de la Costa, 1961; Halecki, 1966: 316–349; Davies, 1996: 469–576). Even today, student attitudes to family and religion observed in the two countries show similar trends, and in both societies the Catholic church plays a leading role in education, including the tertiary sector. Although Iran, as a prominent member of the Islamic civilization, belongs to another religious heritage, recent history shows that monotheistic religions, such as Islam and Christianity (at least in their more traditionalist forms), can at times, present a common front, as happened in the case of the United Nations population conference in Cairo. It is also clear that religious leadership plays an important role in the education of all three countries (Smolicz, 1990b, 1993).

In the case of Poland and Australia, both countries are heirs to the European tradition of the university, which the Philippines also shares through both its Spanish and American derived heritage. Poland and Iran, on the other hand, have both experienced revolutionary change in their societies, which has deeply affected their higher educational sectors. Most recently (1989) Poland has undergone a democratic political transformation and a profound shift away from state dominance to market economy, while Iran has gone through the trauma of the Islamic Revolution of 1978–79 and a shattering war with neighboring Iraq, which ended only during 1988–89. One could also add that both Poland (under General Jaruzelski) and the Philippines (under former President Marcos) experienced periods of martial law during much of the 1980s, which had a similarly negative and stagnating effect upon university education in both countries (Szczepanski, 1978, 1983).

Research approach

The common observation point for this particular study was provided by Australia's need to establish criteria for assessing the tertiary qualifications of immigrants who enter the country and whose degrees need to be judged as objectively as possible. Although the assessment has been carried out within the framework of the Australian university standards and norms, it can be regarded as attuned to generally accepted expectations of higher educational institutions. An internationally acknowledged outcome of these concerns has been the publication of "Country Education Profiles", a series of concise and authoritative reviews of the education systems of over eighty countries, together with evaluations of their higher educational institutions in terms of their academic performance and professional status (National Office of Overseas Skills Recognition, 1992–1996).

The author's investigations in the Philippines, Iran and Poland, were carried out, at least in part, within the framework of the Australian National Office of Overseas Skills Recognition (NOOSR). This facilitated access to the leaders of the higher educational sector in the countries concerned and enabled the gathering of a variety of demographic, academic and socio-economic data in relation to both students and staff. It does not follow that such access was invariably easy, since the educational sectors in the countries concerned have proved sufficiently heterogeneous to have built up mutual rivalries that hinder communication. Considerable effort was required to research both the state institutions and the plethora of private universities and colleges, which have been established in Iran, Poland and the Philippines, in both the metropolitan and country areas. It should be noted that the analysis of the findings are entirely those of the author, and quite independent of any government authority in the countries investigated or any assessment of their educational systems in Australia.

The Philippines

The Philippines' university system has been developed upon the United States' model, despite the country's vastly different cultural, political and economic setting. The non-government sector has traditionally been the dominant one, with over 85% of Filipino tertiary students being educated in religious or other 'private' ('sectarian' or 'non-sectarian') institutions, which rely on fees and endowments for their existence—with no governmental support whatsoever. This private sector is extremely diverse, with fewer than a dozen relatively high fee-paying universities serving the elite. Several hundred other institutions have attuned themselves to provide for students from a variety of income levels, ranging from middle class to those with very modest means who work at nights to enter what are sometimes called 'diploma mill' universities or colleges at the bottom of the academic ladder. As one of the most distinguished Filipino educational leaders put it

> It is always possible for students to find some tertiary institution and get a four year diploma. It helps the massive unemployment problem in the country. Filipinos themselves know the pecking order among universities and the relative quality of the degrees concerned (Gonzales, in Smolicz, 1990a: 7).

This 'quality diversity' was documented in NOOSR's 1991 study of the then 700 odd higher educational institutions in the Philippines (National Office of Overseas Skills Recognition, 1995a). Ultimately, the institutions were evaluated into four broad categories on the basis of their academic standing, in such factors as research activity, qualifications of the staff and the 'track record' of graduates, as well as the quality of their teaching and learning environments, including their library resources, equipment and building facilities. Other features examined included the entry requirements, fee structure, degree of autonomy, the extent to which their courses were accredited and the performance of their graduates in the professional board examinations which determine the right of graduates to practice in their chosen profession (Smolicz, 1990a).

To some extent the NOOSR categories reflect the division between metropolitan Manila and the 'outside regions' (or provinces), as well as the distinctions between social strata and ethno-linguistic groups (Smolicz and Nical, 1997). It is significant that among the eight universities that were placed in the first or highest category, as many as seven were private, most of them run by the main religious orders of the Catholic Church (Jesuits, De La Salle Brothers, Dominicans and Opus Dei). Although the Philippines Government does not provide any financial support, it subjects private universities to controls through its Commission of Higher Education (CHED). They need to obtain prior permission from the Commission, for example, for the introduction of new subjects or an increase in fees (generally limited to a fixed percentage of the previous fees).

The state sector is also very diverse, with one university—the University of the Philippines (UP)—playing a unique and dominant role, through its powerful Board of Regents and institutional safeguards to protect its independence, even in course structure from the controls of CHED. The great competition among students to gain places at the UP, together with decreased government funding for education, can be held responsible for the introduction of fees which are currently being charged for those UP students who come from higher income families. The UP system has expanded over the years to some half a dozen locations situated in the provinces outside Manila. Although these are all linked federally, each sets its own standards and takes responsibility for its own degrees. Other state universities (generally labeled as 'State Colleges') are accorded a much lower prestige rating and their standards are below many of the elite private institutions.

Most of the recent expansion of tertiary education in the Philippines has been in the private sector, making the Filipinos a nation with one of the highest scholarization ratios in Asia. In fact, over the past eight years the number of institutions claiming higher educational status has climbed from some 700 to over a thousand. A recent survey commisioned by the National Youth Commission has shown that, in spite of economic difficulties, Filipino youth appear to be optimistic about the future and eager to grasp the educational opportunities that are being offered to them (Sandoval, Mangahas and Guerrero, 1998).

Australia

Australia, with still only a very limited private tertiary sector, can be regarded as occupying a place at the other end of the spectrum from the Philippines.

Originally, Australian universities were funded by the various states, which in 1901 formed the Australian Federation. Funding continued to be primarily a State government matter until World War II, when Federal (Commonwealth) Government began to provide funding for the sector's expansion—a process which culminated in 1974 when the Commonwealth accepted full funding responsibilities, at the same time as it abolished tuition fees. While the provision of the central source of funding accelerated the expansion of the higher education system, it also led to a creeping increase of government control of the universities and a corresponding diminution of their traditional autonomy. The full effect of this became apparent by 1990 when the 50 colleges of advanced education, with a greater or lesser degree of 'persuasion', were amalgamated with the 20 universities to form the "Unified National System" of 45 higher educational institutions, mostly labeled as universities (Mackenzie, 1995: 43). By 1995 the number of government-funded universities had stabilized at 36 large self-accrediting and publicly-funded universities (National Office of Overseas Skills Recognition, 1995b).

A great surge of student enrolments during the eighties led to the government decision to cut public funding to universities. This was achieved by the 1988 introduction of what has been referred to as 'public privatization' which, in Australia's case, involved recovering from students some of the costs of higher education tuition, under the Higher Education Contribution Scheme (HECS). (Repayment of these charges is deferred by most students, until they are earning an income above a specified level.) The decision to charge fees breached the short-lived free higher education ideology which had prevailed from 1974. The process of fee payment has continued, with subsequent governments increasing the proportion of average tuition fees to be repaid by students, as well as decreasing the level of income at which repayment is demanded of former students. (The proportional increases to be repaid have become particularly large in medicine, science and engineering.)

Since 1994, when student enrolments reached just under 600,000 (a rise of 70% since 1980), universities have been actively encouraged to charge fees for postgraduate degrees, with no regulation of the level of fees charged. In this way the process of 'privatization' has been extended until at present the vast majority of postgraduate coursework degrees at the Diploma and Masters level have been excluded from the HECS scheme and the students concerned required to pay fees, even though Australian residents are being charged at a lower rate than international students. The most recent 'concession' granted to universities has been permission to enroll undergraduate full-fee paying students who have 'just missed' a 'subsidized' place, up to the limit of a quarter of the number of students accepted on merit criteria under the HECS scheme. This move has clearly opened the way for fee paying Australians to enter state universities. Under the impact of the economic downturn, the number of people paying full fees is likely to grow, as universities are subjected to a reduction in funding through fewer subsidized (HECS) places. Although the number of international students exceeded 46,000 in 1994, the continuing upward trend in these enrolments, especially from Asia, remains in doubt due, to the economic crisis in that region.

At this stage it is expected that most students using the full-fee pathway will be applying to high prestige universities and entering prestige faculties, thereby further increasing the quality disparities in what is officially a unified university system. The widening of the 'academic quality' gap has been steadily increasing, as the so-called 'Group of Eight' universities (Melbourne, Monash, Sydney, New South Wales, Queensland, Adelaide, Western Australia and Australian National University) have succeeded in securing close to two thirds of the country's research funding, while those at the bottom of the 36-university ladder receive less than 1% each.

A recent survey, funded by the Australian Research Council (ARC), which sought the views of staff at three universities with different academic profiles, identified several concerns over the way recent changes to higher education have affected teaching and research. Overall the survey found a rapid and pessimistic change of opinion about the quality of students in the 1990s. The report states that universities, especially the Group of Eight traditional research universities, "continue to prefer excellence in student selection but are under pressure to fill (HECS) government-funded places". In consequence, the segmentation of the university sector is being deepened as the Group is "determined to capture the higher ground at the expense of the other universities" (Taylor et al., 1996). The belief prevailing in Australian universities, according to the ARC survey, is that higher education has been increased at the expense of excellence—a finding also confirmed in the poll of the National Tertiary Education Union (Richardson, 1998: 35).

These studies reflect a growing disenchantment with the reforms of former Minister, John Dawkins, who was responsible for introducing the Unified National System (UNS). According to one vice-chancellor, Michael Irving, the amalgamations between universities and colleges have left Australia with an "under-resourced, [functionally] homogeneous system whose quality of teaching and research has been compromised by government intervention". In consequence, the UNS experiment can be regarded as an "expensive failure which is likely to be replicated as technical and further education seeks to emulate universities" (Healy, 1998: 35). Irving's criticisms were echoed by the ARC study which found that universities were attempting to acculturate former college members into a 'research culture', for which they were ill prepared. In addition, a recent Australian National University study showed that while research quantity had remained constant, its quality had declined. This resulted in the Group of Eight standing even further apart from other members of UNS and claiming that scarce research funding had been spread too thinly.

These divisions within the Australian higher education sector have been exacerbated by deregulation and increased 'private provider' competition. Early privatization initiatives, such as Bond University (founded by a formerly successful entrepreneur), a small Catholic university run by the Dominicans (Notre Dame) and off-shore campuses developed by some universities for international students were on a relatively new scale. In July 1998, the 142 year-old Melbourne University was the first to give rise to a private local off-shoot in the form of Melbourne University Private (MUP), which was approved by the state government as a bridge to new private-sector investments in universities. MUP has been designed primarily to cater for the post-graduate market in government and industry and among international fee-paying students.

As in the case of private universities in Poland and Iran (to be illustrated in subsequent sections), MUP is destined to rely heavily on the staff of the parent Melbourne University working under consultancy contracts. Officially this private 'spin-off' from an elite state university has been established to strengthen endangered traditional university values, through the provision of what has been described as a "live, face-to-face interactive experience" for private students, as well as to supply new jobs and greater revenue. What is certain is that such developments will further deepen the divisions within the ranks of Australian universities, which the National Unified System, introduced but a decade ago, was supposed to have homogenized.

In this way, the Australian and Filipino higher education systems show convergence in a number of important ways, such as increased government controls and limitations of funding for the growing student population. Similar features can also be observed in Polish and Iranian higher education, although the rate of increase of student numbers in Iran, and to a lesser extent, Poland has been particularly spectacular and proportionally exceeding the Australian rate of growth.

Poland

Under Communist rule, Poland possessed but one private university, the Catholic University of Lublin, which was established before World War II and remained the only non-government tertiary institution in Central and

Eastern Europe until the collapse of the communist regimes over 1989–1991 (National Office of Overseas Skills Recognition, 1992; Smolicz, Wozniak, Smolicz, Secombe & Uszynska, 1993). After the enactment of a law in 1990 permitting the establishment of non-government higher educational institutions in Poland, their number increased to 16 in 1992 and to over 120 in 1997. These newly established bodies already cater for over 100,000 students, or more than 10% of the total tertiary student enrolments. This represents a growth rate of 63% over the first four years of their existence (Smolicz, 1997).

The rise has occurred most rapidly in areas that were neglected under the communist rule and which have been most vigorously developed by the private sector. For example, since 1990, enrolments in Social Sciences have risen five-fold, those in Business Studies and Marketing threefold and those in Law and Education two to threefold. Over twenty institutions are in some way involved in the in-service or pre-service training of teachers. This stress on the acquisition of additional pedagogical qualifications is partly caused by the requirement for all teachers to complete their higher educational studies if they are to retain their jobs—a situation which in the near future could lead to oversupply on the educational market.

The rapid growth of the non-government sector of higher education, after over forty years of repression of all private initiatives in education, has gained for Poland the label of 'a little America in the heart of Europe'. The new institutions have filled a niche within an underfunded and overcrowded educational market, which has been expanding rapidly to meet the needs of the fledgling market economy. The founders of these institutions, all of them non-profit making, were mainly associations, foundations, educational co-operatives, trade unions, school communities and corporations, as well as groups of individuals made up of experienced university academics, who perceived a need which was not being met by the frequently outdated structures established under the former regime. The founders included, for example, fellows of the Polish Academy of Science and professors from the University of Warsaw and other long established universities.

One of the outstanding features of the growth of the non-government sector is the way it has run counter to the former communist government's centralization of education in the large cities. Although Warsaw continues to act as a magnet for all new educational ventures (with over 30 new establishments), several new institutions have been created not only in the larger cities such as Cracow and Poznan, but also in small country towns which were previously quite distant and isolated from the mainstream educational developments. In a few cases these new provincial centres have acquired an international reputation.

Since the newly established private sector was obviously incapable, on its own, of providing staff at the academic level required to achieve accreditation, it has made use of academics employed at the State institutions. Academics themselves, because of the low pay at State universities, almost invariably have been anxious to secure additional employment, frequently holding two 'full time' appointments, one of which is held to be 'primary'. The 'primary' place of appointment is normally held at an established state institution, which provides the prestige, while the non-government position secures additional pay, at a higher rate than the State.

While recognized institutions officially frown on the practice of double or even treble appointments, they are helpless to forbid it in the face of the poverty of academics, especially those with large families. Since many new institutions are being established in country towns formerly without any academic base, staff members are obliged to travel long distances each week, a situation detrimental to their performance, especially their research endeavour (Pelczar, 1996).

While the greatest innovation is clearly taking place in the private sector, the state sector has also been dramatically affected by the liberalization of the political system and the market economy. In 1997 this consisted of 97 institutions, divided into universities and other higher educational institutions, with specialized functions (e.g., Engineering, Medicine, Agriculture or Music). This large and unwieldy group has been challenged by decreased government spending on education and increased pressure on entrance quotas. The effects exerted by this kind of 'market economy' were particularly profound, amounting to 'shock therapy', following the stagnation of the pre-1989 period, brought about by the imposition of martial law in 1981.

There is little doubt that competition from the private sector has also played a significant part in stimulating the state sector. The latter did not respond through the imposition of partial fees on all students (as in Australia), but through fees being imposed on selected groups, particularly part-time, night-time and external students. Hence 'free' higher education, traditionally offered in Poland, is now limited only to that fraction of students who are able to pass very highly competitive examinations for 'day' study places. The extent of competition for the 'day' or 'free' places at the prestigious universities, such as Warsaw, is shown by the number of applicants sitting entrance examinations at that university in 1997–12 candidates for each place in Management Studies, Economics and Sociology; 10 candidates for a place in Computing, 9 for Psychology, 8 for Law—with the latter faculty offering an equal number of places in its 'evening' classes for fee-paying students. The designation 'evening studies' also has frequently been illusionary, since this label is being applied to classes held virtually any time in the afternoon or evening. Students missing out on university entrance examinations now have the opportunity of joining the 'evening' classes at the state universities or of entering private sector higher education institutions—their enrolment in both cases being dependent on their ability to pay fees. The differences in the academic standards achieved by full-time, as opposed to part-time or external students, are very significant, especially in the case of the non-government sector.

Iran

Iran has witnessed a dramatic escalation in the demand for higher education among its fast-growing population. The increase in student enrolment in the private sector has been particularly spectacular, so that both the size of the increase and the rapid rate of growth, have far outstripped the similar expansion of non-government higher educational institutions in Poland.

While the imperial government of Iran encouraged university education, there was only a small number of students receiving higher education at universities in Tehran until the early 1950s. Rapid increase followed until 1971, although student enrolment stood at under 70,000 during 1969–70. This grew each year up to 1978–79, when enrolments reached 175,675. Further increase was arrested by the Islamic Revolution when, for a period of time, all universities were closed (since students were regarded as the most radical element in the country and a possible danger to the newly established order, as they had proved to be with the previous one). The numbers fell until 1982/3 when they stood at 117,148, almost down to the level prevailing in 1972/73. From then on, there followed a rapid increase, with pre-revolutionary levels being exceeded in 1987/88, when the student numbers reached 204,862. State university enrolments subsequently escalated to 312,072 in 1990/91 and up to 576,070 in 1996/97 (Institute for Research and Planning in Higher Education, 1997).

Even such a significant increase in the State higher education system, however, has been eclipsed, in terms of percentage growth, by the unprecedented explosion of the private sector, which virtually from scratch, grew in the post-revolutionary period to reach the record number of 550,000 students in 1996/97. The Iranian tertiary education system as a whole, both State and private, has grown approximately tenfold since 1982, to reach over 1,100,000 students in 1997. Growth in the numbers of students has resulted in an increase in the number of graduates and of teaching staff (from over 5,700 graduates in 1982 to over 80,000 in 1997, representing a fourteen-fold increase; and from some 9,000 teaching staff in 1982 to about

40,000 in 1997, a four-fold increase only) (Institute for Research and Planning in Higher Education, 1997). Mansouri (1998) estimates that over the last ten years, the number of students has jumped almost five-fold from approximately 250,000 to nearly 1.2 million.

This expansion has to be understood in the context of Iran's continued very high birth rate, still one of the highest in Asia (4.27). This did not decline by 1995 in the way it did in countries such as Indonesia (2.63) or Thailand (1.74). In fact, while projections for the next 20 years in countries such as Japan and Korea indicate a significant population decline in the university age bracket (18–27), in the case of Iran there is likely to be a very large expansion (Hugo, 1998; Sabagh, 1998).

The pressures exerted upon Iranian universities by the growing demand for higher education among the Iranian population became even more severe after the end of its war with Iraq. Unable to provide for this demand through a further increase of the State universities, the Islamic government turned to its own religious establishment for help.

According to official sources, the 'Free' (sometimes translated as 'Open') *Azad Islamic University* first established in 1981, some two years after the Islamic Revolution, by leading religious leaders (Ayatollahs), including the current religious leader Ayatollah Khamenei. It remained small, however, until the end of the Iran-Iraq war which devastated both these Islamic countries for over eight years. When a large mass of demobilized and unemployed soldiers flooded the university market, a substantial number of them were rewarded with a place at the Azad, with scholarships provided to cover the fees. In this context, the Azad has not been 'free', either in the financial or the academic sense, because it has remained under orthodox Islamic control and dependant on indirect government support for its survival and development. Following the Islamic Revolution the new leadership never appeared fully convinced of the loyalty of the State universities, with the result that Azad found particular favour among the more conservative factions of the religious establishment. Although formally responsible to the Minister of Higher Education, the Azad has relied, ever since its inception, on its religious connections to by-pass ministerial guidelines which attempted to control and slow down its incredibly fast expansion.

Such an expansion clearly raises the question of the quality of instruction that students receive in an institution which (with over half a million students) can be regarded as one of the largest universities in the world. The university is governed by Central Management under a President which oversees its 'units' or 'branches', which by 1998 reached a total of 114, scattered throughout the country. Despite its geographical spread, it remains financially and administratively centralized, with its branches in the capital providing the greatest concentration of academic talent and infrastructure. Of the five branches in the capital, the Tehran branch (together with the Tehran Medical Branch) represents the nucleus of the original system and can be regarded as the nearest in academic standing to the better State universities.

The evaluation of this highly distinctive type of privatization of higher education differs widely, depending upon the sources that one relies upon, although personal observation can help in estimating their reliability (Smolicz, 1998c). Information from within the Azad is difficult to acquire and is largely based upon oral sources. It claims to have hired some of the best State university professors through its higher salary offerings. As a result Azad views its standards as being the 'same' as those in the State system, with the advantage that it has a high percentage of mature students who are 'better motivated' because of the "wealth of experience that they bring with them" (Barandan, 1998). Although its fees would be regarded as moderate to low by international standards, they are far from easy to meet for many Iranians. As a result, most of the students are either working, financed by their parents, or under contract to some government ministry. Such a contract system with sympathetic sections of government ministries seems to have been, and continues to be, one of the most important pillars of support for Azad.

It is generally assumed that the initial capital for Azad was provided by government grants, which enabled the new university to engage in large scale building operations and the hiring of large premises. Currently various ministries sign contracts with Azad, and pay their employees' fees, in order to help them to upgrade their qualifications. Under this system, government public servants are almost invariably assured of ultimate success in their studies, as well as of the promotion, which is linked to the gaining of additional qualifications.

A much harsher light is thrown upon Azad by officials from the Ministry of Higher Education, who are prevented from intervening to correct what they perceive are its many failings. An example of such a 'failing' is provided by the way Azad succeeded in gaining recognition for its degrees on par with the State system. The Azad leadership waged a systematic campaign which, it was claimed, only gained the approval of Majlis (or Parliament) after a number of its members were granted Azad's own law degree—on the grounds of the parliamentarians' self-evident expertise as legislators.

Azad's status in the eyes of the intending students may be observed at the time of the annual universities' entrance competitions (or 'Konkur'), with candidates who gain highest scores opting for the top State universities, such as Sharif University of Technology, Esfahan University of Technology, Tehran

University, or Medical Tehran University in the first instance (Institute for Research and Planning in Higher Education, 1996). Of some 1,200,000 school leavers competing for university places no more than 10% can be admitted to the free places at the State universities. Those who fail to get places but are determined to pursue their studies and have the money to pay for them sit for the 'Konkur' organized by the Azad University. The elite branches of Azad in the capital, particularly its Tehran Branch, which have the ability to secure the services of those State university professors in the city, are those that most students seek to enter.

The question upon which there is no agreement is whether Azad, for all its alleged failings, fulfills a useful social function in society by admitting at least a portion of the high school students who otherwise have 'nowhere to go', due to the very high youth unemployment in Iran. According to an internationally renowned physicist, turned educationalist, Reza Mansouri (1998: 10), however, the admission of young people to university studies in Azad merely delays the time of reckoning by four or more years. He comments caustically that

> the quantitative developments are worrisome (. . .) [and that] the arguments made by some policy makers that the economic development of the country necessitates the increase in the number of students is certainly an imprudent and primitive one.

Researchers at the Institute of Research and Planning in Higher Education also point to the dysfunctional aspects of the Iranian private sector. Instead of regarding Azad as solving the problem of providing greater educational opportunities and helping with youth unemployment, it is seen as an institution that compounds or even creates new dilemmas. In their view, Azad has insufficient resources and staff to cater for such vast numbers of students. Hence, many leave the university not adequately trained but having sacrificed their own, or their family's resources to pay for this type of private education.

One explanation of the uncontrollable growth phenomenon has been provided by Farjadi (1998) who lists the factors which explain what he calls "the excess demand for higher education". These include the relatively low cost of the private sector; unemployment among young people competing for higher education places; and the phenomenon described as 'diploma-disease', a term used to explain the desire for a university degree, in the belief of the economic rewards awaiting graduates. Such misguided aspirations, it is claimed, contribute to the inflated parental demands for university education for their children, causing families to strain all their resources to achieve this end. The dominant role of the public sector in the employment of graduates results in pressures being put on the government to keep increasing bureaucratic structures in order to swell the number of public servants required. The democratization of the electoral process for the Majlis has meant that each member of parliament has been subjected to demands from his or her constituents, who press for a university in 'their village'.

The rather precarious present condition of the majority of Iranian universities appears to have been characteristic of the history of the higher education system in Persia. [The country changed its name from Persia to Iran only in 1935 (Frye, 1975).] While information on pre-Islamic higher education in Iran is very limited, medical schools have existed in almost all historical periods. Following renewed development during the earlier periods of the Islamic era, higher educational institutions were eventually converted to religious schools, with natural science replaced by theology. The flourishing medieval Islamic colleges of the earlier epoch can, therefore be regarded as 'non-reproductive', since the sudden sprouts of excellence in a particular institution at an earlier period ended in decline, with no sustainable continuity among any of these original ancient seats of learning (Mansouri, 1998). The current spasmodic and erratic upsurge could be interpreted as yet another of these episodes, representing a sacrifice of quality for the sake of satisfying demands for quantity.

Issues of quality control assurance

In all the countries in this study, the question of academic standards in teaching and research is of vital significance. This applies both in relation to the mushrooming number of private higher educational institutions and the parallel growth of the government funded universities which are often based upon former teachers' colleges or technical institutes.

With its long established private sector, *the Philippines* has evolved both a formal and informal system of quality control for its institutions. The informal system is based upon the reputation that universities enjoy among the public, both on account of their perceived social status and their 'track record' in ensuring good employment prospects for their graduates. With regard to the formal system of evaluation, the system of *accreditation* has come to acquire an increasingly important role for private tertiary institutions. The unusual aspect of the system is that it is not compulsory, but self-imposed and voluntary. It was pioneered by the Philippine Accrediting Association of Schools, Colleges and Universities (PAASCU), and virtually all significant Catholic institutions now enjoy some degree of accreditation from this body. Of the other two accrediting bodies, one represents the accreditation branch of the 'non-sectarian' association of colleges and universities. The other body is a grouping of mainly Protestant universities and colleges (Smolicz, 1990a).

The system of accreditation is still incomplete in the sense that only subjects and disciplines have been accredited at this stage, rather than universities and colleges as a whole. It would also appear that the Catholic sector applies its quality control in a particularly consistent manner, with teams of external visitors making at least two visits to an institution that has requested accreditation, and a series of periodic tests at subsequent dates. The three accrediting agencies are federated to form the Federation of Accrediting Agencies of the Philippines (FAAP). There exists Congress legislation which provides support and recognition for the accreditation process, but many aspects of this legislation still remain unfulfilled.

The main benefits of accreditation, apart from increasing the prestige of the university concerned in the eyes of prospective parents and students, is a reduction in the supervision of the institution's programs by the Commission for Higher Education (CHED), since accredited subjects can undergo a series of internal curriculum changes without prior reference to and approval from CHED.

Another important feature of the Philippine method of quality control, which can provide a valuable indicator of the worth of a given degree at a particular university, is to be found in the requirement for all graduates to pass a *professional board examination* before being allowed to practice in their profession. This applies currently to all the 'professions', including medicine, nursing, teaching, engineering, forestry, dietetics, architecture, medical technology, dentistry, law accounting, business management, etc. Only the study of arts and sciences *per se*, (which does not attract a great number of Filipinos in any case) appears to lack this type of extra screening test, since it relates to no particular profession.

Hence, successful completion of a professional degree does not signify the opening of gates into the practice of the profession—but merely permission to sit for the examination that is set by the board of a particular discipline. Except in the case of the teaching profession, these examinations are conducted by professional licensing boards that come under the orbit of the Professional Regulation Commission (PRC). The examinations are conducted independently of the universities by the boards of examiners whose members are appointed by the President of the Republic on the recommendation of professional associations.

The results of these examinations are almost invariably regarded as representing the 'worth' of a particular university in the subject concerned. The lists of successful candidates are published in the daily press, with 'top-notchers' accorded the distinction of having both their rating and their universities announced publicly. Top ranking universities take success in such examinations almost for granted, expecting almost all their students to pass. But the less successful, especially provincial universities, advertise their success in particularly good years. Hence scrutiny of the results of board examinations forms an important criterion of the proficiency of its graduates, as well as the esteem in which a particular university is held in the community.

The situation in *Australia* stands in contrast to the Philippines, since universities are empowered to accredit their own programs. Programs which are designed to meet the registration or membership requirements of various professions must be approved by the professional bodies concerned, but graduation from an accredited course of study satisfies the requirements for admission to membership of the profession. At the same time, professional bodies, such as the Institution of Engineers, accredit all engineering programs leading to a Bachelor of Engineering degree and, by occasional inspections, attempt to ensure that professional standards are maintained.

A major change since 1989, however, has occurred in the evaluation of university research, with a government initiative towards a more competitive allocation of research funds by identifying national priorities in research. Such allocations have favored the previously identified Group of Eight sandstone universities which have emerged as an elite entity in the supposedly unified system. The regular publication of unofficial guidelines on relative university performance in teaching and research has also demonstrated increasing inequalities within Australian higher educational institutions.

In *Poland* the government has officially exercised control over the registration of new tertiary institutions, both academically, through the General Council for Higher Education and politically, through the Ministry of Higher Education (Pelczar, 1996). These bodies have determined a set of academic standards which must be reached for the purpose of licensing the institutions to grant degrees, which at this stage have been limited to the Licentiate (equivalent to Bachelor degree) or the more advanced Magister degree (at the level of an Honors or Masters degree). An institution is only reviewed at a subsequent date if it wishes to be upgraded from the level of granting Licentiates only, to one of granting Magister degrees. The fact that as many as 120 new institutions of varying quality have succeeded in getting accredited in less than a decade shows that the system is not yet fully effective in ensuring satisfactory measures of quality control.

The qualifications of academic staff have been used as the yardstick in accrediting new institutions. The rules in this regard are less demanding for institutions applying to grant the Licentiate only, than for those claiming the right to grant the Magister degree, a prerogative so far limited to less than a dozen institutions. The rules specify the number and rank of the academic staff employed by the institutions: four senior academics (at habilitated doctor level) are needed for granting a Licentiate and as many as eight are required for those awarding Magister degrees.

Staff qualifications are easier to determine and evaluate across institutions in Poland than in countries such as Australia, where each institution awards its own higher degrees and dispenses its own professorial titles. Poland has retained a centrally controlled system for the academic ranking of university staff members and has evolved a three-tier system of higher degree titles, namely those of doctor (PhD), habilitated doctor and professor, used in the sense of the highest academic title, rather than just a position in the employment hierarchy (Smolicz, Wozniak, Smolicz, Secombe and Uszynska, 1993). The habilitation procedures are complex and Faculty Boards of only the most established research-oriented universities can initiate a proposal for such an appointment, which ultimately needs to be reviewed by the Committee for Academic Degrees and Titles, which either approves or disapproves the decision of the Faculty Board of the particular university. So far, none of the non-government institutions is qualified to award a doctorate, let alone initiate habilitation procedures. The centralized control of academic qualifications of staff is one means of safeguarding the standards of the 'newcomer' institutions against national standards based upon international comparisons.

An unofficial quality review of Polish tertiary institutions, conducted annually by *Wprost* (1996–98), as well as the evaluation undertaken by the author (Smolicz, 1997), selected 12 Polish higher educational institutions as operating at the level of first-class international universities. The universities of Warsaw, Cracow and Poznan are invariably singled out for inclusion in the elite list. Also included are other famous Warsaw higher schools specializing in Technology (Politechnika), Medicine and Economics. However, for the second successive year two private colleges, both specializing in Business Studies and Management, have made the first dozen list, one in Warsaw and the other 'in the provinces'. In their area of economics/business/management, these two colleges appear at the top of the rankings together with only one state institution.

Overall, on the basis of the existing material, there were some 30 institutions, out of the 120 existing in the private sector in June 1997, that could be regarded as generally granting Licentiates at levels expected of good state sector institutions. This suggests that in Poland the newly emerging private sector has already found a niche for itself and been able to reach, in at least some instances, good academic levels.

In contrast to the other three countries, Iranian universities lack procedures that could ensure some general measure of quality control, especially in relation to the private sector. The State universities, just like those in the Philippines and Australia, vary greatly in quality, so that with the help of research staff at the Institute of Research and Planning in Higher Education, it was possible to distinguish among universities classified as 'outstanding', 'very good' and 'good', with the remaining described as "average, to below average" (Smolicz, 1998c). The Institute's influence resides in the developmental and supervisory role which it may exercise on behalf of the Ministry of Higher Education.

The private Azad sector is formally subject to ministerial guidance and supervision. In practice, however, its uncontrollable growth has occurred in spite of the Institute's warnings about the inability of the Azad to maintain even a modicum of academic quality, especially in its branches outside the capital. Some of the latest country branches have been established in small towns, at great distances from the nearest library. They fill 'vacant spots' in the country's educational map, and can be regarded as adaptations of the long established Islamic tradition of a village teacher, who had another occupation, such as a blacksmith, but in his spare time gathered together a group of students, who literally sat at his feet to learn the Koran. Some of the small Azad country branches appear to have been built upon that model, with the assumption that a room, a blackboard, and a part-time teacher will suffice to satisfy the aspirations of students and their parents. Such an Islamic tradition cannot be despised, but it does not satisfy the country's current needs for well qualified graduates.

An awareness of the need for quality improvements in higher education through accreditation is already evident in the State sector at least, as shown by Abbas Bazagran (1998), who has developed an accreditation model, involving both self and external evaluation, based on a pilot study of the medical science and health services. Such pilot research projects, reported at international conferences, are still a long way from developing the type of accreditation procedures that are taken for granted in the Philippines.

Conclusions

A common concern which occurs when reviewing both the *Iranian* and *Polish* expansion is the question of how the newly established institutions have been able to find academic staff of appropriate caliber. The answer for both of these countries is very similar: the senior staff at least comes overwhelmingly from the state universities. By keeping academic salaries at a level below the country's average wages, and often below those provided for skilled manual laborer or secretaries, the governments concerned have been virtually obliging academics (particularly those with families) to seek additional income, thus providing relatively cheap and readily available labor for the supposedly independent fee-charging institutions.

In this way the governments have achieved a double saving effect, by avoiding the creation of extra places at universities, as well as saving money on staff salaries. Although the effect on academic quality, including teaching, but particularly on reduced research output and diminished or peripheral supervision of research theses, has been very serious, no prohibition on the acceptance of additional work has been possible. In this way governments may have been saving money on student fees, general university expenditure and academic salaries, by sacrificing the academic standards of their universities and colleges and reducing the caliber and potential of their graduates.

The situation in the Philippines is somewhat analogous, with a proportion of staff seeking additional employment in a variety of educational institutions and agencies. In a highly feminized profession, especially in faculties such as Education and the Humanities, women are also made to rely on their husbands' business or professional enterprises as the means of being able to 'afford' to teach at a university. This type of situation is likely to occur even at the elite private colleges where the academic salaries are also low by western standards. Educational leaders have commented that the 'double employment' situation, although officially only temporary because of the transition to market economy, will be difficult to reverse, once people have become used to this type of supplementary income (Pelczar, 1996).

The effect of government frugality in cutting back university funding, accompanied by the often indiscriminant expansion of student numbers (partly in response to electoral pressures) has been deleterious, across a range of countries as different from each other as the four investigated in this paper. It has affected students' families and their available resources, but also forced many into part-time employment, diminishing the time that can be devoted to studies. The effect on staff in countries such as Poland and Iran has been particularly unfavorable, including health and family life. The quality of academic teaching has suffered in diminishing student contact, especially with senior staff, who often appear intermittently and whose lecturing standards may lose much through constant repetition and lack of new material update. More obviously, one has witnessed a decrease in the standards expected in the supervision of theses and examining, with Poland's 'open defense' of PhD theses at times unearthing the absence of both. Although Australian academics have not suffered to the same extent, the recent 'downsizing' perpetrated on Australian academics in more than one Australian university has cut deeply into the heart of education, especially in the humanities and social sciences.

The greatest sufferer in this regard has been academic research—particularly strikingly demonstrated in the case of Iran. According to Reza Mansouri (1998: 10),

> A five-fold growth in the number of students within a decade and the inflation in the number of universities, fields of education, particularly in post-graduate studies, should be compared to the nearly fixed number of faculty members, particularly those possessing PhD, or with the number of scientific papers published by Iranian scientists in international journals.

Mansouri (1998: 10) further notes that, since the academic standards were below the international levels before the 1996 inflation in student numbers, it may be assumed that it has decreased even further. He adds that, "there are still university students among the presidents of the universities and colleges", and he quotes the example of one scientific department of Tehran university, which "has accepted approximately 70 students for PhD, whereas its faculty has failed to publish even five international papers in the same year". It can be estimated that the number of research publications in the sciences and humanities before the Islamic Revolution (1978) stood at approximately 500 papers annually. This fell to some 200 papers immediately following the Revolution, to recover to the present level of some 500 papers once again. According to Mansouri, this represents one paper annually per 81 staff members, so that even a hundredfold increase in research output would still be insufficient to reach an acceptable level.

While Iran stands at the extreme end of the four countries under consideration there has also been an obvious decline in Poland, with the former Rector of Warsaw University and a world renowned physicist claiming in 1998 that his former university colleague and current Minister of Finance was 'murdering' Polish higher education, through budgetary cuts. Although the Philippines appears more stable, because of its long-established elite private universities and its single privileged government-funded university, the general standards of tertiary education have been falling there, too, as testified by the Education Office of the Philippines Congress (Congressional Commission on Education, 1991). The privatization trends and public spending cuts are already perceptible in Australia in discouraging student demand in vital areas and leading to demoralization of academic staff who feel they may be subjected to dismissal at the whim of 'strategic plans' developed under the newly emerging rule of market managers (Department of Employment, Education and Training, Higher Education Division, 1993). In Iran the lack of soundly educated graduates, well-grounded in their disciplines, is compounded by the increase in under-educated mass-market graduates, who are likely to swell the numbers of the unemployed.

This study showed that while higher education is becoming open to an ever greater number of students, the move to privatization tends to favor those who can afford the fees involved. The defects revealed in the functioning of the privatization measures, especially in relation to the caliber of graduates produced and the research quality and output of academic staff, demonstrate the danger of placing the fate of universities at the mercy of the market-driven forces of globalization. Both the Philippines, with its tradition of private enterprise in higher education and voluntary accreditation and Poland, with its tradition of university procedures for ensuring the maintenance of academic staff standards appear, at this stage, to have in place more effective means of controlling the quality of privatization expansion than those countries without such safeguards. The Australian expansion of higher education, on the other hand, has occurred without reference to formal safeguards in, for example, professorial appointments, which can be made by each new institution at its own discretion and in the absence of any national or international control mechanisms. Overall, the study highlighted that while each country has responded to the demand for expansion in the higher education sector by deployment of globalization driven privatization, the rate and manner of these responses have reflected their particular culture and heritage in education.

15. THE NEW CAPITALIST SOCIETY

Alain Touraine

There are many ways to describe the economic transformations which characterize the end of our century. In the decade between 1989–1999, many scholars defined the changes in terms of globalization. More recently, we have heard about the 'new economy'—sometimes referring to the new information technologies in general, sometimes to the Internet alone—and claims that it is a new industrial revolution. These rather specific interpretations do not exclude two more general ones: the first is the idea that the 'information society' is a new type of society, comparable in importance to the 'industrial society'. The second insists, quite naturally, on the concept of capitalism, which is now much more widely used than a generation ago, and is more elaborated than the vague notion of market economy. This perspective generally criticizes State intervention in economic life, though its direct attacks against the Welfare State and public schools are less frequent. This diversity of analyses does not indicate a confusion of ideas, but, on the contrary, expresses the awareness that major changes in economic life have occurred and that the predominant post-war economic pattern, with its emphasis on industrial production, national policies, rationalization, and productivity, no longer pertains.

Any analysis of globalization, whether as an ideology and as an actual trend, must, first of all, consider the place of globalization in this vast, multidimensional representation of 'global' change. Initially, globalization had a rather narrow meaning: the incorporation of new areas into world trade. Some analysts and international organizations speak of new industrial countries or emergent economies. It is difficult, however, to view South Korea, Hong Kong and Singapore as recently important economic centers. On the other hand, Malaysia, Mexico, Brazil and—why not—Poland and Turkey can be considered emergent economies. But it is difficult to regard them as important enough to define a global process of change. Moreover, between 1994 and 1999, several emergent economies have been hit by serious economic crises, whether short term, as in Korea, Mexico and Brazil, or long lasting, as in Thailand, Indonesia and Argentina, which raise questions about the new economies. Russia is a different case in point. Even if the crisis of the ruble was the most dangerous monetary crisis of the decade, it is not globalization but the extreme weakness of the Russian State that explains this brutal devaluation. A similar weakness accounts for the fact that Latin America has seen the flight of large amounts of national and foreign capital from insecure and speculative investments back to Wall Street and other central financial markets. There are many more reasons to regard this narrow concept of globalization as unconvincing.

The importance of the concept of globalization does not lie in its describing a major aspect of economic reality. Its weighty symbolic value comes from the fact that it has acquired a much wider meaning, actually a 'global' one. The concept conveys the idea that worldwide markets (commercial and financial), new information technologies, transnational corporations, and the hegemony of the United States all pertain to the same general transformation. These processes have resulted in the fact that no political power is now able to control a worldwide economic system.

Hence, I regard this integrated view of global change less as an intellectual hypothesis than an ideological construction. It is difficult or impossible to show that all these developments are interdependent and participate in a unified global trend. The network society, to use Manuel Castells' term, has made real-time worldwide communication easier, but it cannot be considered the main cause of globalization. Transnational corporations, for their part, have been highly active for many years, especially in oil, food, automobiles, and chemical products; and the international role of Ford, Sony and Unilever cannot be taken as an effect of information technologies. Similarly, American hegemony is not a consequence of new technologies; it is a direct effect of the US victory in the Cold War. Last but not least, the fantastic increase in capital movement far exceeds the growth of international trade, so that it must be understood in itself.

The notion of 'global' change, which is not merely geographic, but postulates a new interdependence of all economic trends and, even more importantly, their independence from any kind of institutional or national control, is unacceptable. Information technologies create a new type of society or, at least, a new industrial revolution, new structural problems, and new actors and conflicts. But a new type of society cannot be described only by the process of modernization which it undergoes, just as the industrial society could not be described only by industrialization. Capitalism, socialism, world dependency and even colonization are all patterns of modernization. On the other hand, the industrial society and the information society are types of societies. It is true that industrial society and capitalist society are often treated as synonymous; but this is gainsaid by the fact that we know of industrial non-capitalist societies and of capitalist non-industrial societies.

The real meaning of the concept of globalization is that it supports a strictly capitalist view of the world, from which are excluded many social and political actors, and especially the State. One may certainly assume that this capitalist ideology is unrealistic, especially in countries where the State controls half the GNP. In fact, globalization is more acceptable as a 'geographic expression' than as an economic or political reality. What most directly undermines the capitalist representation of the world is not cultural diversity or identity politics, however; it is not even the nation-State, which has not in and of itself been an enemy of free international trade or transnational corporations. It is the 'social' State that poses the greatest challenge to the capitalist representation of the world, because its intervention in the economy responds to social demands, which are supported by political parties, generally leftist ones, or by unions, on behalf of the interests of wage-earners—albeit sometimes against economic rationality.

It is nowadays quite common to think badly of over-protective laws and regulations and, even more so of neo-corporatist policies. However, few people in European countries or in countries like Canada, Israel or Australia, want to eliminate the Welfare State; most people in these countries, for example, oppose a 'dual' health system, where excellent facilities for the rich go hand in hand with deficient public hospitals for the poor. Reference to globalization, however, generally implies a negative attitude towards all kinds of State intervention. There are everywhere powerful movements which aspire to eliminate the 'State-controlled' economy and the national and State companies which adapt with difficulty to international markets, and it is not only liberal intellectuals who criticize the poor management of public companies and public services. These criticisms imply that parliaments should have no right to pass laws that respond to social demands rather than to profit-making strategies. In fact, however, there are many different kinds of public companies and not all of them depend directly on government decisions or corporatist rules. Similarly, we know how different public universities may be: some have considerable autonomy, others almost none. But the ideology that permeates all references to globalization goes beyond specific criticisms to condemn, and to urge eliminating, all State intervention from the economic and social life. This blanket condemnation reveals the vagueness and arbitrariness of the idea of globalization, even if it has positive features—particularly the awareness that the post-war model of State-led national reconstruction is no longer rational.

Part of the concept of globalization is the claim that economic growth basically depends on the elimination of national barriers and the free circulation of goods, capital, ideas and—why not—manpower. This idea, however, was more widely accepted a decade ago than it is today. Between 1989 and the mid-nineties, it was the prevailing ideology, expressed by the Washington Consensus. Only a few short years later, however, the first

Congress of Economists for Development defended diametrically opposite ideas in their meeting in Washington, in which some authors of the Washington Consensus also participated. Most of the economists in the Congress now emphasized the importance of non-economic factors in economic growth. They accepted the idea that the more advanced a national economy is, the more important non-economic factors are to the nation's economic growth. Initially, an economic system needs capital and labour—that is, direct economic factors. Then, as has been demonstrated in numerous national cases, growth must become self-sustaining. This requires not only better infrastructure but also education, a spirit of innovation, the elimination of privilege, and, more broadly, everything we include in the expression 'the will to grow', a notion that is often associated with national consciousness. We are accustomed to add to this image of self-sustaining growth the even more complex notion of sustainable growth, which takes into account the need to protect the society from a large range of risks, such as pollution, the destruction of the environment, technological catastrophe, civil war, urban chaos, and so forth. These risks are not directly economic: they are more directly related to the political capacity to make long-term decisions and, very often, to resist organized social interests. Above all, and quite elementarily, if we ask economists to name the most important factor in economic growth, most of them will answer: education. These points are so well known and have been so widely discussed in the last twenty or thirty years that we may be surprised to hear so many statements describing globalization as a pure market economy associated with the disempowerment of the nation-State.

Furthermore, if we consider all the major national economic crises of the last two decades, it is easy to discern, beyond the important role played by the volatility of national and international speculative capital, the responsibility of the nations' economic and political leaders. The Japanese banking system was responsible for the 'bubble' which burst and brought Japanese economic growth to a halt for ten years despite the enormous liquidity the government poured into the market. The Korean shaebols piled up vastly unreasonable debts. The Russian government, or its inability to govern, was the main cause of the dangerous crisis of the ruble in August 1998. The Brazilian government, prior to the 1999 crisis, was spending more than its total revenues on salaries and retirement pensions of public service workers. After these crises, which shook the world-economy, major international financial institutions began to revise their policies, which had contributed to the crises, especially in South-East Asia. Their leaders began to express new ideas, which could sound self-critical. The President of the World Bank declared that social goals were more important than direct economic targets. The Executive Director of the International Monetary Fund repeatedly asserted that priority should be given to strengthening the nation-State and rescuing local and regional cultures threatened by the triumph of international—actually American—culture. The Interamerican Development Bank, which spends much more than half its budget on educational and other social investments, went so far as to dedicate its 1999 meeting entirely to the subject of culture.

These observations, among other factors, make it impossible to define globalization in terms of the unification of the world's economic life. Globalization rather consists of an ideology that stands in opposition to the post-war model of State-led national reconstruction programs. To describe what happens to societies nowadays, we must, instead, distinguish various changes which are not necessarily associated with one another. The primary change, as already noted, is the rapid emergence of the information society. Yet while the ability to transmit information in real time facilitates the movement and speculative uses of capital, the contemporary hyper-development of financial capitalism can by no means be explained by purely technical causes or by the development of financial mathematics. Similarly, the growth of world trade is certainly the most visible and real aspect of globalization, but it has not transformed international economic life and, in fact, has been going on for a long time. Those who attribute major importance to the new emerging economies are wrong, for capital has become disappointed with the economic crises in these economies and has often gone back to New York and London. In the context of the enduring weakness of the euro and the slowdown of Japanese economic growth, the world economy appears, more than ever, to be trilateralized or even integrated around the dollar. Moreover, though we often speak of global companies acting in the main free economic zones, these companies have been powerful actors for a long time. Finally, American hegemony is much more the outcome of the American victory in the Cold War and the disintegration of the Soviet system than of any economic transformation. This hegemony is now particularly visible in cultural industries, such as films, television and the Internet, and in the enormous and accelerated concentration of capital in this sector, where superpowerful companies have been formed. Though few if any countries have been able to resist the overwhelming control of this market by American companies, the tendency to American hegemony need by no means be termed globalization. These observations lead, indeed, to the unambiguous conclusion that there is no mega-trend, no unified process toward a world situation defined by the formation of worldwide networks or even by an integrated worldwide economic system.

The only real, that is, non-ideological, meaning of globalization is that it

proclaims—correctly—the decline and, in some cases, the disappearance of
State-led national policies, especially since the end of the Soviet Empire.
But the genuine significance of the concept of globalization is that it transforms this negative conclusion into a positive one: the triumph of capitalism—of the internal logic of economic interests, especially those of capital
owners, without interference by any kind of social voluntarism, ideology, or
political projects. Globalization means the triumph of economic forces that
are increasingly organized at the world level, while political, legal and social
agents retain very limited if any capacity to intervene at this level at all. It
would be more than superficial to consider globalization a new stage in the
internationalization of economic activities. During World War II, the entire
world participated in the conflict that opposed Germany, Japan, and their
allies, to the US, Britain, the Soviet Union, and their allies. This certainly
was a global conflict. The 1929 market crash was also a global phenomenon, albeit a more limited one, whose consequences were felt in most parts
of the world. But, today, when so many people speak of globalization, they
refer not to the internationalization of economic, political and cultural
processes, but to the triumph of capitalism. This is what gives the concept
of globalization much greater importance than what it would have as a
purely geographic notion. It is strange to observe that, with no explanation
or proof, the concrete reality of globalization is generally believed to require
cutting social security benefits, and to justify privatization and the increasingly unequal distribution of non-economic services such as education and
health. A liberal view of economic life, the idea that social action should
be eradicated or at least transformed into rational economic activity, leads
to an erroneous interpretation of reality. We see today, almost everywhere,
the triumph of capitalism—practically, politically and intellectually. Capitalism
has probably never reached such an apex before. This assertion is not a
value judgment, for capitalism has triumphed with the decline and disintegration of alternative patterns of economic and social life. But it is no less
obvious that while this point seems descriptive, it also represents ideological thinking and has become part of a system of power. This understanding is by no means extreme. It is based on the visible hegemony of capitalism
and its neo-liberal ideology. We may also add here that while the Cold
War was creating the false image of two competing economic, social and
ideological systems, the Soviet system was never a real economic alternative. Imposed on a large part of the world by military power, it never was
genuinely competitive with the Western world.

  Yet even if we recognize the concept of globalization as an expression of
pure capitalism and even if we accept the idea that some countries are today aiming at purely capitalist control of social change, there is still no rea-

son to identify capitalism with a new system of productive forces. It is true that very often in the past, 'industrial society' and 'capitalist society' were considered synonymous. But this confusion has never been acceptable, no more a century ago than it is today. A mode of production and a process of modernization are two different things—just as the construction of empires by armies is fundamentally different from the type of society, whether rural, commercial or industrial, that develops within this mode of modernization. Whenever people speak of globalization, they express the idea that the growth of financial networks and the development of new information technologies are two aspects of the same phenomenon, though actually they are not. Manuel Castells, who has described the new networks and analyzed them in depth, states very clearly that the new productive forces that these networks control do not in themselves determine the political and economic organization.

Take the United States as an example. We may express serious doubt even about the characterization of the United States as a capitalist country. After so many of salience, the notion of globalization is giving way to the idea of the 'new economy'—a rather vague term which sometimes designates the Internet and its ramifications, and sometimes the information society as a whole. Whatever the designation of the society, the rapid development of productive forces in the United States is not necessarily explained by the triumph of capitalism in this country. European countries, moreover, are becoming aware that they lag behind the United States in the utilization of new technologies, and that Ireland, Finland and Israel are more completely involved with the new technologies than are the main European industrial countries. The superiority of the United States does not reside in its more globalized economy, but in the fact that it has rapidly created a widely-used new technology that has deeply transformed the prevailing methods of management and resource allocation. It is only very recently, not before 1996–98, that Western European countries have become conscious of their technological lag and are beginning to try to catch up. But even if they make major progress in the coming years, it will be difficult for them to keep abreast with the United States.

The new technologies were not produced solely by the market economy. The Internet was created by European scientists, then supported by the Pentagon; its rapid diffusion has been the outcome of the American entrepreneurial spirit, by no means only the direct consequence of the logic of financial capitalism. Some universities, for example, Stanford, have played a major role in this technological development, especially the Silicon Valley. Neither technological developments nor entrepreneurship are products only of capitalism. What is more, in most countries, the rapid adaptation to the new economy requires not only a new purely capitalistic process of development, but also State intervention.

Intellectuals and politicians constantly analyze the new technologies which have transformed our conceptions of time and space, and attempt to predict their social and cultural effects. They are particularly preoccupied with the social control of information, and more than a few of them fear that new forms of domination may arise. The American media speak of the new divide which will separate those who control and use the new technologies and those who do not. It is increasingly clear that when we speak of the new technology it is impossible to speak of new 'productive forces' without considering new 'social relations of production'. We have come a very long way from the superficial view of the new economic and technological transformations, which insists only on the growing internationalization of exchanges.

I mention these fundamental, long-term, problems here not to deal with them practically but in order to clarify the significance of the fact that public attention is focused today less on the information society and the new economy than on globalization as such. At the center of this public attention is capitalism and its apparent world-wide victory. This means that instead of the primary question, 'who are the local and national actors who might resist globalization?' we must ask: 'who can oppose the victorious neo-capitalism with a different view of social organization and social change?' The activists who made it impossible for the World Trade Organization to meet normally in Seattle and who disrupted the IMF meeting in Prague.

This situation is new. During the long post-war period, when the State prevailed over private capital, political and ideological problems were more conspicuous in the public arena than economic and social issues. The decline in the political and ideological orientation of public opinion and of socialist, social-democratic, and communist parties began only in the seventies. Today, this decline is visible at all levels. This includes the social sciences where the study of strategies, rational choices, and resource mobilization has gained ground at the expense of the study of social and political movements. It also includes leftist political parties, which have accepted, more or less rapidly, the central role of the market economy. Recently, moreover, supporters of a so-called 'third way' have expressed their acceptance of market rules with much greater clarity than they formulated their reform programs. Extreme ideological and political disorganization characterizes the countries and regions where Soviet, Chinese, or Cuban influence had formerly been strong. For example, in Latin America it is impossible to name a single 'leftist' regime, with the possible exception of Venezuela, which is now in the midst of a rapid process of change. F.H. Cardoso in Brazil and R. Lagos in Chile, who represent moderate regimes on the continent, are sharply criticized by leftist groups. Most Andean countries are in the hands of dictators or the army or are led by conservative governments. Mexico, which has liberated itself from its corrupt clientelist, one-party system, is today trying to implement a progressive liberal economic program which would eliminate corruption. In other countries, guerrillas have disappeared, leaving behind a severe political crisis. The same can be said of Africa, with the exception of South Africa.

Some readers may consider this brief description too extreme and too pessimistic. On the contrary. I believe that the point should be stated in a radical manner. Russia and China have both joined the capitalist world, and no country or political group in the world is trying to disseminate a 'socialist' view of social change. Obviously, no leftist party or government has been able to elaborate new ideas. The vacuum is visible in both social theory and political action. We observe the resistance of old ideas and, in particular, calls for State economic intervention, but we do not observe the birth of many new intellectual currents or political forces. Those of us who devote our time to the search for new intellectual and political orientations know well that the still powerful desire for continuity with the post-war period is pointless. We know we must accept the present hegemony of a purely capitalist view of the world as our starting point. Hence, the basic question is whether or not it is today possible to propose an alternative view. Or, must we just accept as given that, for a longer or shorter period of time, the whole world constitutes a totally capitalist environment?

From this perspective, we must consider, or reconsider, the question: who today are the potential or actual actors—actors who are not simply agents of the capitalist process? A preliminary answer is that today's actors are no longer social actors; they are not classes, political parties, occupational groups or communities; they are defined first and foremost by the nature of their association with the holders of economic power. We suggest the possibility of a different representation of social action. First of all, we are able to counter the liberal view with a variety of approaches which all assert the major importance of social actors. These approaches share three main orientations: (1) support for rational choice, which is actually part of neo-liberal ideology and capitalist practice; (2) advocacy of political influence on society and economy ; and, lastly, (3) the creation of institutional guarantees for political, social, and cultural rights, which, historically, have preceded, and are foreign to, capitalist logic. Together, these three orientations may sustain 'social efficiency', even though this efficiency is bound to involve more complex choices, entailing more frequent conflict. A society in which these orientations are dominant favors the emergence of actors, that is, individuals and groups, who are able to transform their environment and, thus, to introduce more innovation. It is this general perspective on the 'good' society, rather than the traditional call for State economic intervention, that may be the genuine, dynamic alternative to neo-liberalism.

The first orientation, support for rational choice, is inherent in capitalist logic. We find here two main behavioral principles, which are much the same as the two principal goals of capitalism: namely, consumption and competition. This orientation assumes that people tend to act according to the logic of self-interest or, more generally, of pleasure, with no attempt to build up an integrated and meaningful life experience. With this behavior, they respond to stimuli that serve and are manipulated by the power holders. Yet, even if we accept this assumption, there is still no reason to identify the positive attitude toward the information society as favorable, as such, to power holders.

Of the three orientations, the creation of institutional guarantees for political, social, and cultural rights, is the most important, because this orientation directly opposes the logic of capitalism. This orientation is reminiscent of the political movements that fought for political rights in the eighteenth century and of the various labour movements which attained social rights in industrial societies. Moreover, we see today that in many parts of the world, new actors, both individual and collective, are claiming new cultural rights. They aspire to combine their participation in the economic world with the retention or reinterpretation of their cultural heritage and cultural projects. The strength of these new movements re-establishes the role of political action and endows actors with the capacity to make choices, to feel free, and to take responsibility for their own experience. One may, moreover, distinguish between what is commonly called identity politics—through which individuals and groups strive to protect social attributes, like sex, age, craft, creed, ethnicity or religion—and the demand for cultural rights, which is best defined as the defense of the 'subject'.

We live in a world where orientations and attitudes are more strongly defined than social and political movements. This does not mean that political parties can be defined without reference to social interests, but rather that organized action is no more than one possible expression of people's attitudes or orientations. Superficially, identity politics may seem to correspond to organized action, but more careful observation reveals that political groups, directed mainly towards seizing power, often mobilize cultural resources such as religion or national identity without necessarily identifying with them, even as they articulate them. The contrast, in this respect, between the current situation and the situation in the industrial society is striking. In the industrial society, organized social actors were tightly linked with political parties. Everyone spoke of social class and of left-wing or right-wing parties—meaning parties that were closely associated with social classes. Some parties called themselves working-class parties; in Sweden, one party called itself a bourgeois party. In contrast, today there is a wide gap between powerful economic systems and cultural-political orientations. Political parties and organized social movements are so weak that cultural orientations are commonly designated with no relation to economic conflicts.

The road we have followed may appear to lead us very far from the classical definition of our problem: how can actors resist globalization? Can the nation-State survive this process, which seems to create powerless states that can control only a small part of their economic production and exchanges, while multinational corporations control an ever larger part of their activities? Is this 'political void' going to last or is it a temporary phenomenon, characteristic of a social transition that will end with the formation of new organized political forces? Regarding this last question, while such a reconstruction is certainly possible, I believe that the present situation is still more likely to become more extreme. This does not mean that we are experiencing a process of depolitization or a decline of interest in public affairs. It does mean that political and social participation is less and less directly oriented to the control of the State. At the beginning of modern times, we saw an almost total identification of organized social action with political goals, driven by the collective will to attain State power. This identification has been decreasing for a long time.

Today, there is practically no organized women's movement; and the defense of minorities is generally in the hands of small associations or NGOs. Ecologists have attained a sizable political representation in Germany and France, but almost everywhere, there is a sharp conflict between the 'realo' wing, to speak like the Germans, which tends to represent the educated and repressive urban middle class, and the 'fundi' wing, which retains the character of an anarchist social movement. Similarly, we observe that new cultural and social movements are more and more remote from the ideal of transforming themselves into new political parties. What is new here is that these agents are agents of deep and lasting cultural change, despite the feebleness or even absence of their instruments of political action. In relation to this reality, one observes the new importance of public opinion, the media and informal leaders, and, more generally, of civil society as a whole. The media are particularly important in advancing many of the new cultural orientations, even though they are widely used for advertising, political influence, or simple economic projects.

In brief, if we recognize that the idea of globalization is a superficial expression of capitalism, we also understand that present-day conflicts are not between organized forces but mainly between the logic of capitalism and new cultural orientations. Such conflicts cannot be dealt with primarily at an institutional level, be it national, continental, or worldwide, because they directly resist the capitalist process of modernization with new forms of protection for human rights.

16. AMERICANIZATION VERSUS GLOBALIZATION

Johan Galtung

Globalization = Americanization (at least so far)

In his famous book *Blowback: The Costs and Consequences of American Empire*[1] Chalmers Johnson describes how

> computer and telecommunications technologies radically lowered transaction costs while increasing the speed and precision with which finance capitalists could transfer money and manipulate currencies on a global scale. The managers who controlled these funds began to encourage investment anywhere on earth under the rubric of "globalization", *an esoteric term for what in the nineteenth century was simply called imperialism.*[2] (italics ours)

The term caught on and people everywhere seem to believe that there is such a thing going on; how else to explain the frequent use of the term? So let me try a definition:

> Globalization is the process whereby all genders, generations (also future), races, classes, nations and states and regions pull together and cooperate in a participatory and equitable way to produce a world with better livelihood for all.

The problem is that there is no such project in the world today. We have a male-middleaged-white-upper class-Western project, particularly from OECD countries and then even more particularly from the USA, to run the world.

A more descriptive term than 'globalization' would be 'Americanization'; a somewhat more generous term would be 'Westernization'. But even those terms only locate the process nationally/geographically and do not touch the other dimensions of gender/generation/race/class. The whole process is dominated by a small group of people in a small group of countries using the term 'globalization' as a cover-up, turning those who use that term in an unreflected way a part of the cover-up. The USA today runs the world militarily and politically, to a very large extent culturally; the little sharing there is can be found in the economic field with some other OECD countries.

To get straight to the point, let us use Switzerland as an example. There are four identities based on culture (identity can also be based on gender,

---

[1] Johnson, 2000.
[2] Johnson, 2000: 204–205.

generation, race, class) inside one country with the German culture being by far the strongest; yet we cannot talk about germanization of the Swiss. We can certainly talk about 'switzerization' as the result of that tetra-cultural interaction over the centuries. But that type of super-identity over and above the four constituent parts is neither the result of melting pot processes, grinding them, melting them down to homogeneity with the original identity gone forever, nor the result of the stronger driving out the weaker. In Switzerland we are dealing with a case of genuine evolution, adding a layer of identity on top of the constituent identities through cooperative processes, not Darwinian evolution of the competitive 'survival of the fittest' type (whether that happens by eliminating them or melting them down in a pot lined with the ingredients of the dominant identity, like language, myths).

It may be worth while looking at some of the mechanics of that process in Switzerland, since 'germanization' is obviously what would correspond to americanization and 'switzerization' what would correspond to globalization.

What Conflicts Are Switzerland the Solution Of, and How?

[1] Peripheries that find each other: better be together at the top of the European water tower than peripheries of Salzburg (Archbishop)/the Habsburgs, Milano, Paris, Frankfurt/Berlin.

[2] Neutrality to prevent disintegration: as Austria, Italy, France and Germany often were at war, participation would split Switzerland and turn them against the country. Neutrality as a contract was the solution. With all four neighbors members of the EU and three (soon four?) members of NATO, this argument for neutrality is decreasingly relevant, armed neutrality yielding to good relations with all parties, hosting meetings, active peace-making. The country is not member of the EU or of the UN.

[3] By and large a doctrine of defensive defense: located between four major powers the military doctrine combines being non-provocative with strong. Short-range 'Raumverteidigung', not only at the border—focusing on stationary military capability (guns mounted in mountains) and short range army, navy and air force combined with militia-type armed forces, locally based.

[4] To root the army locally military service is compulsory and soldiers keep their gun at home and practice regularly. After 4 months training the units reconvene 2 weeks/year over 20 years.

[5] Linguistic identity is protected by peaceful coexistence between four language areas: German (70%), French (25%), Italian (4%), Rhetoromanisch (1%). All 4 are official languages and learning another official language is required for all.

[6] For the groups to be equal Switzerland was a confederation till 1848 and federation from 1874, with foreign affairs, security and finance decided centrally, and the rest locally.

[7] The 7 member cabinet represents not only the regions but also the political groupings (Zauberformel, the magic formula). It is accountable to the people, not to the parliament it already mirrors.

[8] In Switzerland peasant revolts were relatively successful, leading to a pattern of local decision-making; direct democracy. Switzerland with 1/1000 of the world population had 60% of the national referenda (on specific issues) in the 20th century.

[9] To make democracy local, cantons could not be too big. There are 23 cantons (3 of them are divided in two half-cantons), making a total of 26—Rhetoromanisch in 1, Italian in 1, French in 4 completely and 2 partly, and German in the rest.

[10] To root democracy in the people the people can initiate a referendum (with 100,000 signatures) demanding a vote within two years. For the vote to become law it has to be supported by at least 50% of the people and 50% of the cantons.

In other words, a carefully worked out balance to ensure that each identity can be preserved, yet at the same time creating an overlayer of identity based on precisely the success of those efforts. As the Swiss exercise has gone on for quite some time the generations are certainly cooperating; a weak point was (is?) inter-gender cooperation on an equitable basis—and inter-race was (is?) precarious as evidence by the efforts to limit/eliminate immigrants of color (not mentioned explicitly, but underlying the many 'initiatives').

Maybe we should add to this a distinction between shallow and deep culture, and refer to the latter as the 'collective subconscious', 'collective memory' or 'mentality'—all those assumptions that are normally not verbalized but somehow taken for granted within a culture. Thus, the constituent Swiss nations are very willing to learn the other languages, at least passively, and to pick up food habits. But deep culture is not in the cultural exchange, meaning things like (here very stereotypically indicated) German urge to germanize others, particularly those in the East; French sense of superiority, Italian sense of estheticism as a way of life.

Not only do the others not imbibe such perspectives with their intake of the other languages; they may not be present or only in a diluted form. After all, Switzerland is based on three *periphery* cultures and one local peasant culture.

Let us then try to formulate some basic hypotheses relating the three concepts brought together in this book.

First, cultures and identities are like truths. They may be competitive, one driving out the other (like Lavoisier's experiments were interpreted as the death blow to the phlogiston theory); in which case there is an obvious threat even if acquiring the dominant culture may be an explicit goal. But they may also be cooperative, complementary (like the wave perspective and the particle perspective on light); in which case they may coexist peacefully and respectfully under an overlayer of a meta-culture housing them all (like Niels Bohr's daoist interpretation of reality). To help build that Swiss meta-culture was a major challenge to the Swiss. Today the Europeans in the European Union are now trying to do exactly that, successfully or not. The task is formidable.

Second, 'globalization' is seen here as an effort to build a world meta-culture *sui generis*, not by superimposing one culture on others. As pointed out, there is no such process going on with, say, the English/Chinese/Hindi/Russian-speaking trying to evolve, together, a shared meta-culture. Instead we find 'americanization' deliberately or not pushing out (parts of) other cultures, and not only among elites but in entire nations. The hypothesis is that this will be for and against America, welcomed by some, submitted to by others and creating deep resistance reinforcing existing identities by still others.

The problem: Americanization, with the US deep culture

Here is A synoptic sketch of the US deep culture:

A. *The Chosenness-Glories-Traumas syndrome (historical)*

   I. *Chosenness (in the USA from the 17th–18th centuries)*[3]
      A chosen, covenanted people, under God, with rights and duties.
      A sacred land, God's New Cana'an, transgression is a sacrilege.
      US citizens and lives of a higher kind than other peoples.[4]
      US national (vital) interests are of a higher kind.
      US as final arbiter, the hegemons' hegemon, the world center.
   II. *Glories (coming out of the US 18th–19th centuries)*
      Melting pot, the US as a multi-cultural/ethnic country.
      Trinity: Judeo-Christianity/Free Market/Independence-Democracy.
      Bringing the Trinity to pagan/unfree/non-democratic countries.

---

[3] The themes under this heading are essentially East Anglia-Puritan-New England-Yankee themes, so the general hypothesis is that their ethos overpowered the other tribes from England so brilliantly analyzed in *Albion's Seed* (Fischer, 1989): the Pennsylvania Quakers from the Midlands, the Virginia Gentlemen from Devonshire and the common people from the English-Scottish-Irish border regions, in the Appalachians. Maybe it took a Civil War to wipe out the influence of the Virginian Founding Fathers (no Mothers)?

[4] Thus, the 'noble savages' of early Puritan thinking became 'Children of Satan' and Rev. Cotton Mather, minister of Boston, started sending the Indians small-pox infested blankets.

Manifest Destiny in North America, the Americas, the World.
USA is invincible/ superior; God is behind/ USA is right.[5]

III. *Traumas (suffered in the US 19th–20th centuries)*
Immigrant traumas suffered before and after 'New Beginning'.
Genocide/ structuro-culturocide on Native Americans/ Hawaiians.
Enslaving/ commercializing/ exploiting/ repressing Africans.
War of Independence before/ after Declaration of Independence.
The Civil War for/ against Secession.
The Wars Not Won (in a sense Korea, Viet Nam).

B. *The Dichotomy-Manicheism-Armageddon syndrome (biblical)*

DICHOTOMY: *US 'two-ness' in general, us or them, for or ag'in*
MANICHEISM: *God vs Satan, Good vs Evil*
ARMAGEDDON: *Violence as the final arbiter*

C. *Repression-projection mechanisms (presumably timeless)*

Repression/ denial of Self's violence; Self seen as peaceful.
Projection of violence on Other; denial of Other peacefulness.
This program or code has a name: *patriotism*.[6] At the individual level
it is better known as *megalomania/ paranoia*, and *machismo*.

A genealogy has been indicated for the 21 constituent archetypes, starting
with timeless mechanisms of repression and projection. As peace is conceived of as a virtue, and violence as a vice, the latter is denied in Self and
the former in Other. With the priorities reversed RP mechanisms would
also have been reversed; with *yin/yang* perspectives[7] realism might prevail in
both images. The mechanisms serve to organize the universe, and will work

---

[5] This includes the emphasis on *winning* the Cold War, not only being one party witnessing the other party collapse/implode. A good effect (break-down of the Soviet Empire)
has to have its cause in the good party, the USA, e.g., by forcing them into an arms race
they could ill afford, or a technological race they could not win. But winning in a war goes
beyond merely defeating the enemy; there should also be an element of changing the enemy.
If Russia should backtrack into socialism the winners in this sense would be defeated; hence
the obvious prediction that the USA will do anything possible to prevent a Communist party
victory in the presidential elections in Russia 16 June 1996.

[6] Some might feel that 'chauvinism' or 'jingoism' would be more appropriate terms. But
in the US case conscious affirmation of such points pass for patriotism. Of course, such syndromes do not only apply to nations and countries, but also, for instance, to gender ('male
chauvinism'), race (indeed), class; maybe also to generation; in short to all the fault-lines in
human society.

[7] In other words, also seeing the evil in self and the good in other, not being limited to
the good in self and the evil in other. And in addition the good in whatever is evil and the
evil in whatever is good, and so on, *ad inf.*

with extra ease if that universe is already seen as Self/Other dualist settings for repression/projection.

The Pilgrim Fathers of the Plymouth Colony, Massachusetts Bay (Mayflower, 1620), were partly (35 of 102) Select Puritans, reading the Bible and the Chosen People/Promised Land archetypes as written for them. As there was no Cana'an on the Eastern side of the Mediterranean the Jews evidently had not made it (Reverend Cotton). The other chosenness archetypes can be seen as logical satellites, as variations over the theme of US exceptionalism.[8]

A covenanted country got started under the real founder of what later became the United States of America, John Winthrop I (from 1630). The colonists who founded Jamestown, Virginia earlier (1609) seem to have been more ordinary colonizers,[9] less burdened by puritan chosenness. The Quakers, who under William Penn established the 'Holy Experiment' in Pennsylvania (1681) also labored under blossoming CMT-complexes, but *chosen for peace* (George Fox was the first conscientious objector, to Cromwell's armies, in 1651). However, there is little doubt as to what was dominant and what was recessive.

The following centuries created glory myths based on facts and foibles, reality and virtual reality. The themes are well-known; they all give more content to the chosenness, more flesh on the bones. In a sense they flow from the chosenness. If you are chosen, in a promised land, how can you be somebody else's colony, even if (or precisely because) that was where most immigrants came from? Later others came, well traumatized, blended in a melting pot that obviously had an Anglo-Saxon, even WASP lining, filled with chosenness. Over time the ideology solidified as *Judeo-Christianity* (the hyphen came later, and also serves to marginalize Islam among the Abrahamic religions, and also all other religions); *Free Market and Enterprise* (meaning the freedom to create property and to use property to create more property); *Independence and Democracy* (meaning free choice among alternatives, by secret ballot).

The Trinity gains significance through negation: countries that are Muslim

---

[8] I once witnessed a debate between two US presidential candidates, George Bush and Michael Dukakis (July 1988), where Bush pointed at his opponent without looking at him, saying approximately the following: "And he believes the United States of America is an ordinary country somewhere on the UN roll call list between Albania and Zimbabwe. Whereas I tell you, this is a most exceptional country . . .". Like William Jefferson Clinton, on the occasion of that major US use of violence against Self, the Oklahoma bombing 19 April 1995, referring to Lincoln's words about the USA as the last, best hope for humankind.

[9] Meaning grabbing land, cheating and stealing, killing if necessary, but maybe less in the name of God. Their myth may have been more El Dorado, hoping for gold in North America, eventually settling for tobacco, cotton and slaves.

or entertain other faiths including professing atheism or being pagan; countries with other economic systems including professing socialism or being economically primitive-traditional; countries with other political systems, including professing authoritarianism or being politically primitive-traditional. One of the three may qualify for the position as the Evil Other, the ground being prepared by the almost timeless syndrome in the subconscious, the DMA. From that notion flows missionary commands to bring Judeo-Christian faith, Free Markets and Democracy to others, starting with the pagans and the primitive/traditional, going on to the more recalcitrant, with one Armageddon[10] after the other, emerging invincible. A drama.

This mighty crusade could not, and cannot be enacted without encountering resistance, as others might be of a (very) different opinion. Those who came to the shores of America were already traumatized, by political repression or economic exploitation, sometimes also direct violence. They had been persecuted and/or steeped in misery. All of them had horror stories from Europe's countless upheavals produced by gender, generation, caste/class, nation, country contradictions, with emerging State and emerging Capital. Those who left were neither clergy, nor aristocracy, but common people with their women, true believers, with *ressentiment*. They fought each other like hell, including intense labor-management violence.[11]

They inflicted unfathomable sufferings on Africans, Native Americans and Hawaiians, the Blacks, Reds and Browns. The traumas are still felt as lasting 'post-traumatic stress disorder'.[12] But here the reverse trauma suffered by evil-doers, is in focus, the mix of guilt having inflicted mega-violence on Other, and the nightmarish fear that 'one day they will come back and do the same to us as we did to them'. The *exemplar* would be Nat Turner's slave revolt in 1831, with 70+ rebels killing 59 whites.[13]

---

[10] The homologue of the Rapture being, of course, the visa and subsequent emigration to the USA

[11] The archetype would be the 'bomb-throwing anarchist'. I am indebted to R. Rubenstein for this important point, see his *Comrade Valentine* (Rubenstein, 1994) for deep insights in anarchism and bomb-throwing.

[12] PTSD. This point is very well made by George, 1995.

[13] Nat Turner was a Native American bondsman. After the revolt was suppressed education, movement and assembly of slaves were forbidden. No doubt reading and writing could challenge the system of slavery. But it also challenged something more basic: the dogma that Blacks were incapable of acquiring such skills being illiterate as a race, not as a person or a nation. The dogma of white superiority was at stake. Kolchin (1993: 156) makes the very important observation that the slaves did not succeed like the Haitian insurrection, initiated in 1804 by Toussaint l'Ouverture, or to some extent the Russian massive peasant wars. "The waves of repression that followed each insurrection, conspiracy, and rumored conspiracy simply reinforced what was obvious to most slaves: under existing conditions, armed revolt was folly" (*ibid.*). But the successful revolt of the underdog might have liberated the oppressors

The War of Independence and the Civil War constitute an interesting combination. Struggle for independence/freedom for the country and democracy for the people, from illegitimate rule (engendering the trauma of being attacked by one's own kind, the British) is right; secession from legitimate rule is wrong and has to be repressed. Thus it was wrong of Britain to use force against the USA, but right of the North to do the same against the South. According to the victorious North, that is.

Let us try some recent media articulations to make a point.

Chosenness requires its articulation, but not too often. The sentiment should not be trivialized. A statement late August 1995 by Colin Powell, at that time still a possible presidential candidate, may cross that fine line. According to a report from the New York Times Service[14] "he got a round of applause by declaring that America had been established by divine providence to lead the world". What has been established by divine providence should not be taken lightly. Moreover, such statements are exclusive, applying only to America, not to 'America, like to any other country'. The statement may be interpreted not only as a license to lead the world, but as a duty to do so.

One small example of what this projection onto the center of the world stage means, again from the New York Times Service,[15] is the description of O.J. Simpson as "the most famous defendant who ever lived". Some people might have seen Jesus Christ as a good candidate for that position, at least in the Christian world, perhaps with Alfred Dreyfus as another candidate for the last one hundred years. But they both suffer from a major shortcoming: they are neither Americans, nor contemporary, narrowing 'who ever lived' in space and time.

How the USA, as center of the world, treats even friendly countries, was revealed in Austria in January 1996.[16] The USA had planned using nuclear land mines in Salzburg, Austria, on top of having maintained 79 secret weapon depots after Austria had been declared a neutral country in 1955. The US ambassador had to apologize to the Austrian heads of state and government. A sensation in Austria; not reflected in US media.

There is something deeply pathological about this deep culture, not saying by that the West, or the whole world for that matter, has not also pro-

---

from some of their trauma. The successful repression comes at a very high psychological price. The brutal repression of all efforts by the Reds and the Blacks and the Browns set the pattern for the glory of being invincible, and the trauma of revenge, some day.

[14] *International Herald Tribune*, August 31, 1995. In other words rather recent; not a 19th century quote.

[15] *International Herald Tribune*, October 10, 1995.

[16] *Der Standard*, January 27–28, 1996.

duced other pathological cultures. A top military person is tapping what he knows is a reservoir of positive feelings, the basic national myth, and reaps applause. Some status is needed to invoke God; Colin Powell had that status. A journalist is so taken in by the OJ case that the commentary gets a little out of hand. The USA, a superpower, behaves like one, depositing arms wherever they may come handy against another superpower, probably with the connivance of some local military and politicians. What else is new, what's the issue? Apart from US reaction if others had behaved that way?

The issue is not concrete action; nobody was hurt. The issue is the absence of reaction, protest. Such examples of verbal and physical action might one day add up to something quite significant: a US C-in-C thinks he has God's mandate, the USA is the only center in the world, Salzburg is obliterated. The kind of material out of which a quick consensus can be made.

In short, this is essentially a colonialist, imperialist deep culture. The world has been through this kind of exercise before: the Roman Empire, other Western imperialisms (Habsburg, Spanish, Portuguese, Dutch, English, French, Belgian, German, Russian to mention some, maybe Zionist), non-Western empires (Omayyad, Abassid, Persian, Ottoman, Han, Japanese—Inca, Aztec, etc.). There have been lesser versions of the same referred to as 'nation-building' as when a Center tries to engulf others militarily, politically, economically and culturally and make them peripheries.[17] But so far only the Christians and the Muslims tried to colonize the whole world.

The responses to Americanization: welcome, submit, resist

And they did not manage, in spite of the clear wish to do so, for instance in the Papal Bull (Alexander VI) *Inter Caetera* of 3 May 1493 dividing the world in two parts, Christian and Pagan (being discovered and to be discovered), giving the former very extensive rights and duties over the latter.

Let us first try to answer one obvious objection. OK, the idiom of globalization is American culture, with some kind of basic English, certain fast foods, the CNN version of what happens in the world, US popular culture particularly in music, all of them highly attractive, embraced by billions, more successful than Christianity can ever hope to be. Can't one just leave it at that shallow level, does one have to embrace the deeper level as well, with all its imperial aspects? Does one really have to buy into the whole collective memory, the history and the deep history?

---

[17] Thus, Germany was and is run from Berlin with a heavy Prussian accent; Indonesia is run by Java; Great Britain by London with surroundings; France by 'le monstre' Paris; etc.

The answer is yes and no. Of course it is possible to be just a victim of a closed local market outcompeted by some transnational company, or of mysterious diseases due to genetically manipulated food, and hardly able to formulate in any kind of English the impact of 'globalization'. But chances are that the more culture you imbibe, the more deeply it settles—at least that is a reasonable hypothesis. And with that might come a feeling well absorbed into the guts: better be in the Center than in the Periphery, better be on the sending than on the receiving side. And that is probably a major reason in addition to economic rationality why so many people in the colonies try to get to the 'mother country': be in the Center, in some years your offspring may even invade your own country.

Under americanization the whole world becomes an empire with the Center in the IMF-World Bank-WTO-Pentagon-State Department-NYSE complex; each country a colony. But, as mentioned above, in the economic sphere, there is some sharing with some other OECD countries; some will be less colonized than others. And in the cultural sphere two countries stand out having an identity almost if not quite identical:

- England, and to some extent all the other parts of the British Isles, as 'mother country'; and
- Israel, as another major embodiment of the Jewish-Christian (hyphenated) lateral of the Abrahamitic triangle.

They would be parts of the Center, but not really the center of the Center.
   What follows from these assumptions?
   [1] *Welcome the americanization.* The soil is well prepared. Think of the work the British Council and related aspects of British imperialism did around the world to prepare people for the Chaucer-Shakespeare-Milton tripos; only to find them welcoming enthusiastically such 3Ms as Mickey-Madonna-Michael (Jackson). There will be a feeling of basic compatibility between own self-image and the US superiority complex. And this may translate into being a local little center of americanization, if only as the proud owner of very recent CDs. Or it may translate more than ever into the yearning for the Green Card, the entry ticket to the Center, not only where the action is but from where the action, all action, emanates.

So the prediction is more immigration into the USA than ever, more than they may even appreciate—much like the reverse trend that has taken place in other Western empires.

Again the Swiss example is instructive. There is no major cross-cultural internal migration because there is no clear center in Switzerland—Bern does not play that role. Switzerization is a way of feeling at home where home is, not a way of becoming German. A major achievement, it seems.

[2] *Submit to americanization.* The new culture comes as an overlayer, taken on as a matter of course or necessity, unreflected, unresisted. This may happen where the local or national culture is weak in comparison to the exposure to US culture. Thus, the best speakers of American English in Europe are probably the citizens of smaller nations, like the Nordic countries, Be-Ne-Lux—and Switzerland for that matter. There is less material for resistance. The local/national culture may function like a dark hole (in the universe)—only absorbing, emitting nothing. Sad, but not unrealistic in many quarters.

Special attention should be given to the countries recently defeated by the USA, during the Second World War (Pacific War in Asia): Germany and Japan, and to a lesser extent three more countries that also had sinned by committing fascism: Italy, Spain and Portugal. In all these countries, but particularly the first two, America took on God-like features as omnipotent, omnipresent and omniscient and equally importantly: benevolent, as proved by the fact that they were forgiven for their sins. One would expect the general mode to be receptive out of sheer habit by now, seeing americanization of the globe as the continuation of what is happening in defeated countries anyhow. Isn't it better to submit without having to be defeated first? Or, if not submit, at least not resist divine forces openly?

[3] *Resist americanization.* This will be the general reaction, and probably more deeply and more extensively so the more americanization there is in domain (geographical and social space) and scope (depth). Forces give rise to counterforces.

In the first run we are thinking of the excluded abrahamitic religion, Islam. But Orthodox Christianity, Hinduism, Buddhism and Confucianism will also continue and deepen their resistance, particularly when they find each other in Eurasia, increasingly feeling the pincer movement as NATO expands westward and AMPO (the US-Japan security system, with Taiwan and South Korea as de facto members) expands westward. These are dramatic, macrohistorical changes happening right now, before our eyes, with close to 50% of humanity caught by the pincer. The resistance in Latin America and Africa will probably be much less given that there is less material with which to build effective resistance. On the other hand, the Spanish and Portuguese speaking countries in Latin American do not carry the burden of a fascist past because their countless military dictatorships were for, not against the United States.

But to this should be added resistance based on class rather than nation. With the gap between rich and poor increasing so dramatically that up to 100,000 die every day of hunger in a system with its center of gravity in the Washington-New York axis the resistance from below will add to the lateral resistance from other cultures. If for each person dying from avoidable misery there are, say, ten persons who care sufficiently to feel anger then the potential for revolt is rather potent. The problem with any system with a center is that aggression will be directed precisely against that center.

The USA can probably not be beaten militarily. But it can be beaten spiritually, like communist Soviet Union and *apartheid* South Africa recently simply by no longer believing in their *project*. Americanization is a structure in process in search of a soul; with no soul, no inner faith, no real will, it becomes as vulnerable as all its predecessors.

There is an interesting party political expression of this. The two parties (or the two right wings of the single American party as Gore Vidal expresses it) both protect the wealth of the corporations and the US elites through exploitation (huge differences in hourly wages between high and low), the difference being that the Democrats seem to want to exploit all over the world whereas the Republicans are more home-oriented and careful and feel the necessary exploitation can be done at home. The former position is known as 'global responsibility' in the local political jargon, the latter as 'isolationism'. The sense of global mission among the Democrats will engender enthusiastic 'globalization'; the lack of faith, the spiritual backlash is likely to show up first among Republicans who will start talking about military withdrawal from abroad and then about military engagement only when attacked.

However this may be, the responses to Americanization do not spell out an attractive world, and certainly not one worthy of the epithet 'globalization'. There will be cultural corpses along the road, cultures not able to mobilize enough identity to stand up. There will be cultures driven into exile in their own country with a thick overlayer of US plebeian culture—the patrician version as usual being reserved for certain elites in the Center. And there will be intense resistance, fight. War.

What might globalization look like?

The answer, of course, is not in the idealistically sounding definition given above, but by referring to something empirically existing or at least potentially existing.

Imagine the name was not Switzerland, but, say, United Nations of the Alps, with four members. The four nations cooperate in producing a country with its flaws (money-laundering, suppression of women, a high level, of self-righteousness), but also a remarkable co-existence within and peace without, in addition to direct democracy and well-being.

Would the United Nations of the whole world be capable of doing the same? Today there is no other possible carrier of a project of that magnitude where everybody would find a place, feel reasonably at home, except, that is, those who want to run the global game in their own name.

Take as an example a research project, any one, of UNESCO. Irritatingly inefficient, could be done much better in a think tank in the Center? Maybe, but only if one forgets to figure into the equation the value of researchers of different nations trying to pull together to create a truth in which more than one corner of the world can feel at home.

The United Nations have not yet done to the world what Switzerland has done to that part of the Alps: diversity within some unity. A confederation of many cultures within a meta-culture that accommodates rather than excludes. A thing like that cannot be imposed from above by fiat, like the Soviet Union tried in defining *sovjetskij tchelovjek*, Soviet Man, for all. It has to grow organically like it did in Switzerland. Give the UN some time and we are on the road to an equitable globalization.

SECTION THREE

MULTICULTURALISM AND TRANSNATIONAL DIASPORAS

INTRODUCTION

Jürgen Heideking opens Section Three by exploring the unique type of modernity exemplified by North American society. His analysis focuses on the nature of this primary case of contemporary Western multiculturalism. America, Heideking remarks, has become the most liberal, democratic and commercially-minded nation in the world. For this same reason, Americans have been engaged since the Revolution in a continuous debate over the nature of government and society. The United States underwent sharp tensions between the desire for 'republican harmony' and the legitimation of diverging interests. The reality of an immigrant society worked against the desire for a homogeneous nation state. A 'civil religion' rooted in Puritan utopian beliefs served, in this context, as an alternative to European-type ethnic and religious homogeneity, and accounts for the American society's development into a foremost example of a multicultural social order.

Elihu Katz analyzes democracy through a global view by revealing the impacts of different kinds of media on social organization. The printed press, he shows, was the launching pad for participatory democracy by crystallizing public opinion. Then came the radio, which displaced the newspaper as the medium of national integration. The radio started bringing politics inside the home, and television completed the job, in addition to enhancing the role of personality and of personal image at the expense of ideology, in the crystallization of political attitudes. But television, Katz contends, has now become a multi-headed monster pulling in all directions. Privatization and commercialization have exacerbated the segmentation of society. At the same time, the contemporary 'globalist' tendency means that today's blockbuster programs captivate the whole world. The nation-state is now ignored, and the newer media—multi-channel television, satellite broadcasting and, above all, the Internet—undermine the polity itself. The Internet, in particular, enables ongoing conversations among networks of individuals beyond national references, and reinvigorates the cultural networks of so-called 'deterritorialized communities.' Multiculturalism and ethno-cultural diversity challenge society to define guidelines that can both deal with the diversity and define a common frame of reference. Although the majority of societies consist of different ethno-social entities, *Bernard Spolsky* who analyzes types of language policies throughout the world, shows that this crucially relevant issue is hardly dealt with by centers in a consequential manner.

Turning now to transnational diasporas, *Stanley Tambiah* points out that the last 25–30 years have witnessed unprecedented migratory movements across countries. Even after achieving economic and educational integration, diasporic communities still strive to maintain their social and religious distinctiveness. Many diaspora populations aspire to maintain a dual perspective on their existential circumstances. This kind of attitude involves multiple pools of memories and subjectivities, both context-bound and interpenetrating. In interacting with their home communities, diasporas provide the best illustration of 'cultural hybridization', 'creolization', and 'eclecticism'. *Eliezer Ben-Rafael* pursues this discussion about the new diasporas and their circumstances. Among other factors, he underscores the role of inter-state relations which often prevent countries that are sensitive to their international status from hermetically closing themselves off to immigrants. Moreover, the governments of the immigrants' countries of origin may seek to retain a 'patronizing' role over their citizens living abroad. In return, diaspora communities often become lobbying forces, in their adopted country, on behalf of their homeland's interests or those of communities established elsewhere but linked to their diaspora. Here, the variety of the sociological situations is allied with a richness of sociolinguistic phenomena. Different languages come into contact, reflecting and concretizing identity processes that find expression in linguistic changes, the creation of inter-languages, and the formation of a diversity of bilingualism. Such linguistic developments specify the twofold aspects of multicultural reality when seen globally—the diversity of cultural groups pertaining to the same society, and the diversity of communities pertaining to the same diaspora. *Michal Bodemann* focuses on the specific example of the new Jewry in Germany. He analyzes the development of this case of diaspora, noting the role played by collective memory, the quality of the group's leadership, and its institutional composition. Bodemann also points out the importance of this diaspora's territorial and home orientation, as a reflection of globalization processes. However, he also sees the nation-state as playing a role of its own in shaping the group's social condition. In this, Bodemann joins the discussion of the next section regarding the power, control capability, and interests of states for both confronting socio-cultural fragmentation in society and retaining autonomy of action vis-à-vis the supra-national, in a globalized universe.

17. THE DISCOURSE ON MODERNITY IN THE UNITED STATES*

Jürgen Heideking

Introduction

In recent years we have witnessed renewed interest in comparative transatlantic studies intended to further our understanding of the similarities, differences, and mutual influences between 'modernizing' societies in Europe and the Americas since the late 18th century. The sharp distinctions of the past seem to have given way to a more complex picture of an 'Atlantic civilization' characterized by different 'paths' to modernity which created a pattern of 'multiple modernities' in the western world. While 'consensus' historians of the 1950s and 1960s emphasized the 'conservative nature' of the American Revolution, Gordon S. Wood in his latest book claims that, from early on, the United States acted as the 'avant-garde' society of Western civilization. At the beginning of the 19th century, in his view,

> Americans had become, almost overnight, the most liberal, the most democratic, the most commercially minded, and the most modern people in the world. And this astonishing transformation took place without industrialization, without urbanization, without railroads, without the aid of any of the great forces we usually invoke to explain 'modernization'. It was the Revolution that was crucial to this transformation. It was the Revolution, more than any other single event, that made America into the most liberal, democratic, and modern nation in the world.[1]

In a similar way, Charles G. Sellers and others have advanced the thesis that the American people were the first to create a modern civil society, which affected and transformed all aspects of life from family relations to cultural productivity.[2] Although much empirical research has been done over the last decade, a number of general questions need to be more systematically explored. In this paper I would like to raise two of these more general questions, namely:

---

* A different version of this chapter was published in *Daedalus*, 129 (1), 2000.
[1] Wood, 1992: 6–7.
[2] Sellers, 1991.

a) how did those dramatic changes occur that so rapidly catapulted the United States into such a leading position?;

b) what were the specific qualities and characteristics of American modernity that set the United States apart from advanced European states such as England and France?

To give more than just tentative answers to these questions would require a much better understanding of simultaneous historical developments on both sides of the Atlantic and of mutual influences in the Atlantic world in the 18th and 19th centuries. That western European societies also underwent rapid change during this time has been shown by historians such as Paul Langford and H.T. Breen. According to Breen, an 'impressive fiscal-military state' emerged in England already during the 18th century. In order to be able to compete with the continental European powers, England instituted a modern banking system, a complex government bureaucracy, and a strong military establishment. At the same time, the political decision-making process was being centralized in the Westminster Parliament. In parallel with growing commerce and trade, a politically articulate middle class rose to participation and began to change the tastes, manners, and modes of thinking. All this went hand in hand with intense feelings of English patriotism and the construction of a 'British' national identity. From a stable 'mixed and balanced government', as it was still described by Montesquieu, Great Britain evolved into a modern parliamentary system, a dynamic nation state, and a powerful colonial empire.

Similar observations were made in the case of France, where the revolutionaries endeavored to install a powerful, centrally governed and centrally administered nation state. Further to the east, Prussia and Austria undertook 'modernizing' reforms in order to keep pace with their western rivals. Seen from the vantage point of the ruling European elites, the revolutionary and post-revolutionary United States did not appear as particularly advanced or 'modern', but rather as a 'young', 'unfinished', 'backward', and even 'uncivilized' country. Most Americans didn't strive to imitate the British or the French in setting up an 'impressive fiscal-military state' but, on the contrary, defined their own collective identity in reaction to negatively perceived European 'models'.

We should be careful, however, not to homogenize American history after independence and in the early national period. It is important to understand that, beginning with the Revolution, Americans were engaged in a continuous 'grand debate' over the construction and development of their own government(s) and society (or societies). One of the first 'high points' of this debate was the struggle over the ratification of the US Constitution in 1787/88, when Alexander Hamilton remarked that it seems to have been reserved to the people of this country, by their conduct and example, to decide the important question, whether societies of men are really capable or not, of establishing good government from reflexion and choice, or whether they are forever destined to depend, for their political constitutions, on accident and force.[3]

This debate raged through the whole period of the French Revolution, pitting Federalists against Jeffersonian Republicans, and later it was carried on by Whigs and Jacksonian Democrats in the framework of what has been called the 'second American party system'. Overlooking the time from the Revolution to the Civil War, one can speak of an ongoing 'discourse of modernity' in the light of American historical experience, involving different ideologies (or variants of republican ideology), different material interests (especially agrarian versus commercial), different political concepts (a strong national government versus 'states' rights'), and different visions of the future (a consolidated, commercial-capitalist 'empire' versus a confederation of small, homogeneous republics).

Another important and often overlooked aspect of this debate was a continuous critical examination of European 'models' of modernity, especially Great Britain and France. The American version of modernity, therefore, resulted from struggles and compromises between different programs, projects, and visions advanced by various groups of the social elite and later by national parties. From this perspective, the Civil War may be seen as part of this debate, when the internal contradictions were finally resolved in a violent way.

Although the emerging American market economy acted as an integrative force, at least three distinct societies emerged during the first half of the 19th century: a capitalistic, free-labor, and immigrant society in the North and Northwest; a plantation and slave-holding society in the South and Southwest; and a still unsettled 'frontier society' in the Far West. Only by taking this complex historical background into account can we attempt to identify and define the distinctive features of United States modernity.

My general thesis is that most of the aspects which we today regard as particularly 'modern' resulted either from the rejection of European models by the majority of American citizens, or from the practical inability of the United States to measure up to European standards of modernity. The basic fact is that the United States did not develop into an 'impressive fiscal-military state' of the British model, nor into a centralized nation state envisaged by the French revolutionaries. Instead, the outcome of the American

---

[3] Hamilton, 1961: 3.

'discourse of modernity' before the Civil War was a decentralized federal union, a unique 'partly national, partly federal' republic (James Madison in Federalist No. 38), a federal system on a continental scale, but centered more on the states than on the national government. While many Europeans were still looking down on the United States as a kind of 'irregular', underdeveloped country, Alexis de Tocqueville recognized the enormous potential as well as the inherent dangers of the 'American experiment' with popular sovereignty and democratic self-government.

In the following, I would like to highlight five aspects which seem to me to characterize American modernity in the early Republic, which set the United States apart from most European countries, and which—as it later turned out—gave the Americans a 'head start' on the road to modern 'civil society'.

1) *The emergence and cultivation of peculiar American 'constitutionalism'*

The concept of a written constitution and declaration of rights was already embedded in American colonial history; during and after the Revolution it was further developed on the state and federal level toward a kind of 'constitutional patriotism' helping to integrate the diverging political and social forces.

This constitutionalism was especially useful because it helped to temper the original radical-republican concept of popular sovereignty, enshrined in some of the first state constitution of Pennsylvania. Whereas radical republicans favored direct participation, strict majority rule in small, homogeneous 'commonwealths', and the preponderance of unicameral legislatures in a 'simple' system of government, the US Constitution of 1787/88 established the principles of 'checks and balances', of limited and representative government, and the rule of law backed by a strong, independent judiciary. If one looks at the constitutional debate of 1787/88 as a first critical discourse on modernity, then the outcome favored the more liberal, progressive, 'British' vision of the Federalists over the partly conservative, partly radical republican vision of the Anti-Federalists.[4] In the view of the founders, their 'complex system of government' was better suited to protect the rights of minorities and to assure a steady, energetic administration. These basic tenets of American constitutionalism were soon accepted by most citizens, although the tensions between a radical, community-based ideology and a more liberal, individualistic world view continued well into the 19th century. In gen-

---

[4] Heideking, 1988.

eral, Europeans found it difficult to understand the almost religious admi-
ration or even 'worship' of the constitution, and they didn't view American
constitutionalism as particularly 'modern'. Especially the idea of a limitation
of power stood in contrast to the desire of European rulers and reformers
to create strong, efficient systems of government.

2) *The continuous search for a 'federal balance' between centralizing and
decentralizing or particularistic forces*

For Europeans, progress and 'modernization' meant first of all centralization of state power, in order to overcome the various traditionalist and particularist forces of the 'old regime'. In late eighteenth-century Europe,
republics and republican confederations such as Switzerland and the United
Netherlands were considered by most people as relics of the past, not as
future-oriented models. According to Montesquieu's "De l'esprit des lois,"
a large or 'extended' republic could only exist as a loose confederation of
independent states. Internally, the small sovereign republics would guarantee participation and political liberty to their citizens, and externally the
confederation would preserve the peace and defend the common interests.
In America, such a solution was favored by the anti-Federalists, but James
Madison strongly disagreed with both Montesquieu and the radical republicans at home:

> The uniform conclusion drawn from a review of ancient and modern confed-
> eracies, is, that instead of promoting the public happiness, or securing public
> tranquility, they have, in every instance, been productive of anarchy and confu-
> sion; ineffectual for the preservation of harmony, and a prey to their own dis-
> sentions and foreign invasions . . . I most earnestly pray that America may have
> sufficient wisdom to avail herself of the instructive information she may derive
> from a contemplation of the sources of their misfortunes, and that she may
> escape a similar fate by avoiding the causes from which their infelicity sprung.[5]

The opposite alternative, however, of concentrating all power in a national
government was even less attractive to the majority of Americans. Consequently,
the Philadelphia Convention established neither a loose Confederation of
small republics nor a unitary nation state but, as Madison called it in *The
Federalist*, a "partly federal, and partly national" government.[6] European observers had great difficulty in seeing anything 'modern' in this solution, and
even many Americans considered it as somewhat irregular.[7]

---

[5] Madison, 1990: 1029, 1031.
[6] Madison, 1961: 257.
[7] See, for example, Warren, 1986: 272–291.

In contemporary understanding, sovereignty had to be firmly placed in one hand or in one single institution, and could not be divided between the nation and the states. Some people predicted that the federal government would in time 'swallow up' the state governments, while others foresaw that the states would soon reduce the central government to a mere shadow. But this system of federalism had a number of advantages, which were already clearly understood and described by Tocqueville in the 1830s: there existed probably no better way to take into account the regional diversity of the United States, especially the differences between North and South, but also the problems of a constantly westward moving frontier. The federal government could concentrate its attention on relatively few national questions, avoiding excessive bureaucratization and keeping expenses and taxes low. In an even more important way, the new federalism strengthened the energy and independence of local and state governments, and it fostered the individualism and self-reliance of the American people who didn't always look for help to a distant national government. From the nineteenth-century European point of view, however, this new type of society appeared hardly 'modern' because it seemed to defy the order, regularity, and authority of the emerging modern nation state.

3) The tension between a desire for 'republican harmony' and the acceptance of diverging interests

Earlier than most other countries, the English colonies in North America and the independent states after 1776 had to come to terms with a wide variety and a vigorous defense of material, political, and religious interests. These interests were represented in the colonial assemblies and later in the state legislatures, where groups of delegates soon began to form factions and parties. This development collided with a general republican belief in the harmony of interest and in the necessity for a virtuous people to work together for the common good. During the War of Independence, this concept of a homogenous, harmonious polity had inspired efforts to exclude all 'non-patriots' from political participation by way of test oaths or pledges of allegiance, and even to remove them as 'Tories' and 'traitors' from the community. In the late 1780s, however, the diversity of interests manifested itself again, and it became even more pronounced by the rapid expansion of a free press in the various states, as well as by a widely shared conviction of the vital importance of 'public opinion' in a republican society. While therefore most Americans remained ideologically committed to the vision of republican virtue, consensus and harmony, the post-war political and economic reality was characterized by a diversity of interests and by political competition at all levels of society. In the early 19th century this tendency became even stronger as a consequence of the widening of the franchise (achieved through state constitutional reforms) and the growth of voter participation.

Beginning with the debate over the ratification of the US Constitution in 1787/88, more and more voices publicly defended and legitimized party politics, thereby moving the people closer to a pluralist understanding of the political process. Public life in the American states and on the federal level was neither individualistic nor collectivist, but became rather group-centered as state factions coalesced into broader coalition movements and highly articulate national parties such as Whigs and Democrats. Viewed from the other side of the Atlantic, this turbulent political life again defied order and regularity and threatened the authority of the state. In reality, however, the continuing tension between republican ideology and liberal-democratic self-government proved to be productive, and from our present perspective, the early acceptance of political pluralism in the United States must be seen as an important, distinctive element of American modernity.

4) *The evolution of citizenship from republican exclusiveness to democratic universality*

The process of party formation was accompanied by a changed under-standing of the concept of citizenship in a republic. As outlined above, the American revolutionaries started with a relatively narrow, exclusive notion of republican citizenship. The first state constitutions defined citizenship as a privilege by tying it to such conditions as a 'permanent stake in society' (meaning landed property), loyalty to the government, and the payment of taxes. This republican exclusiveness continued after the Revolution, albeit in a moderated form, when Federalists such as John Adams praised the 'natural aristocracy' as chosen leaders of the people, and when Southern planters and plantation owners preserved the 'deferential society' of colonial times, and even strengthened their elitist, paternalistic rule. Nevertheless, the 19th century witnessed a continuous, although uneven, move in the direction of democratic universality. Long before Andrew Jackson's 'Era of the Common Man' in the 1830s and 1840s, most states had already instituted white male suffrage, and even the wave of nativism which greeted the new immigrants from Europe in the 1840s and 1850s did not change the liberal natural-ization law. In stark contrast to most other countries, every newcomer to the United States could claim citizenship after only five years of permanent residence.

Despite many legal and practical restrictions, and despite continued exclu-siveness and 'white supremacy' in the post-civil war South, the United States achieved the broadest suffrage and the highest rates of political participation of all comparable countries in the 19th century. The fact that this development occurred mostly before the beginning of industrialization helps to explain why most Americans—in contrast to their European contemporaries—didn't perceive capitalism and democracy as mutually exclusive but tried to adapt their political strategy of representing and defending group interests in the existing framework of republican government to changing circumstances.

5) *The peculiar relationship between federal government, state governments, and society*

This final point concerns the early development of what is now being called the American 'civil society'; for our purpose, it seems useful to distinguish three elements and treat them separately:

a) *The military sphere and the problem of public order*
For Americans the fear of 'standing armies' was part of their colonial heritage and republican belief system. After the War of Independence, an intense debate took place between the advocates of a strong national military establishment, led by Alexander Hamilton, and the defenders of the traditional system of state militias. The resulting compromise, laid down in the US Constitution, provided for a small professional army and navy, while leaving the militias—as the only military reserve force—almost completely under the authority of the state governments.

Not only most European observers, but also many American military experts considered such a system as antiquated and inefficient. Nevertheless, it proved adequate to deal with the various national threats and crises in the late 1790s (the 'Quasi-War' with France), in 1812–14 (the second war against Great Britain), and in 1846–48 (the war against Mexico), as well as with the constant danger along the Indian frontier. The reasons for preserving the state militias were more of a political than of a military nature. The militia system implied the right of the people to bear arms, as it was guaranteed in the second amendment to the Constitution. This, in turn, limited the 'coercive power' of the national government and, in more general terms, the 'monopoly of power' (*Gewaltmonopol*) of the state in North America. Whereas in Europe, this 'monopoly of power' was seen as a necessary condition for modern state-building, Americans decided against a strong, permanent military establishment, and even against strong police forces on the state level. Especially in frontier regions, the lack of 'police power' and the easy availability of weapons had serious disadvantages and sometimes even created a climate of violence and vigilantism. On the other hand, however, this fragility of state authority never really threatened the stability of the political system as a whole, and the absence of a powerful standing army and an influential officer corps protected and even consolidated the supremacy of the political leadership.

b) *The economic sphere and the emergence of a 'market society'*
The public debate over the best way to foster economic development was even more vigorous than the argument over achieving internal and external security, and it continued right through the Civil War and into the 20th century. The history of the early 19th century was marked by the competition of two concepts: on the one hand, a kind of national development program, first advocated by Alexander Hamilton in his "Report on Manufactures" of December 1791, and later championed by Henry Clay and the Whig party in the form of the 'American System'; on the other hand, a kind of state mercantilism preferred by many small entrepreneurs from the rising middle class, by state politicians interested in strengthening their power base, and on the national level by the leader of the Democratic party, Andrew Jackson, who remained attached to the values of Jeffersonian (agrarian) republicanism, but who first of all wanted to limit the political influence of the east coast's business and banking elite. In this contest, Jackson and the Democrats generally prevailed, with the consequence that 'internal improvements' (mainly infrastructural measures such as building roads, bridges, canals, and railways) were planned, financed, and executed at the state level often by private corporations holding charters from state legislatures—without the involvement of the federal government. The only influence that could be exercised by Congress and the national government in the economic field was based on their land ownership in the western territories and on their right to lay tariffs on imported goods.

This peculiar and constantly contested balance of power in economic relations resulted (1) in strengthening the states which became laboratories for economic experimentation, and (2) in vitalizing the private sector by encouraging the establishment of hundreds of business corporations, interest groups, and other 'voluntary associations' (their effectiveness was already vividly described by Alexis de Tocqueville in "De la democratie en Amerique"). A more centralized 'American System' might have improved the regularity and steadiness of economic development; but the combination of decentralized state mercantilism and private enterprise obviously provided a solid basis for an expanding market economy and an independent, almost self-regulating civil society.

c) *The religious sphere, the separation of church and state, and the construction of a 'civil religion'*

Religious diversity was already a hallmark of the English colonies in North America, and the enforcement of intellectual or spiritual conformity never got a realistic chance in the New World. During the Revolution, freedom of conscience and the free exercise of religion were guaranteed in state constitutions as well as in the first amendment to the US Constitution. The process of strictly separating the political and the religious spheres began in 1785 with Virginia's Bill for Establishing Religious Freedom (originally drafted by Thomas Jefferson) which made all churches equal before the law and declared direct financial support to any denomination illegal. It also outlawed religious requirements for political and civil offices. In the early nineteenth century, all the other states followed suit, although some of them in a rather reluctant and piecemeal way. While in Europe (and Latin America) the trend assumed the direction of privileged state churches with limited toleration for members of other religious groups, in the United States religious denominations had to compete for members on an equal basis, and in the process became just another form of 'voluntary associations', enriching (and sometimes troubling) the life of civil society. Instead of impeding or even stifling religious activities (what many Europeans expected to happen under such conditions), this 'free market situation' fostered awakenings and mass conversions, especially in the western parts of the country and it brought forth numerous reform movements, from temperance to abolitionism. The strong presence of women in these religious reform movements has often been noted as another distinctive trait of American society in the 19th century.

The decision for a separation of church and state must be seen as part of a broader movement toward ethnic, religious and cultural diversity and pluralism in the United States. Although newcomers often encountered heavy pressures to conform to and assimilate into the dominant social and cultural norms, the reality of an immigrant society worked against the desire for a homogeneous nation state. In Europe, nationalism was often identical with enforced homogeneity and the repression of ethnic and religious minorities. American society was not completely resistant to this danger, but the advantages of diversity were recognized there much earlier. Extremely important, in this respect, was the development of an interdenominational 'civil religion' as an alternative to (or a kind of 'ersatz' for) European-type ethnic and religious homogeneity. This civil religion was rooted in the Puritan past with its utopian visions of the colonies as the 'new Jerusalem' and the settlers as a 'chosen people' who would play a central role in God's order of salvation. With the separation from England and the founding of the United

States, and against the background of growing religious diversity, civil religion became an essential element of American collective identity. The nationwide celebrations on the occasion of the adoption of the Constitution in 1788 and George Washington's first inaugural address of 1789 attest to the fact that the 'nationalizing' potential of civil religion was immediately recognized by the political and intellectual leaders of the founding generation.[8]

The symbols, rituals, and ceremonies of civil religion helped to 'sanctify' and legitimize the new political order, and to commit the American people to the basic principles and values of republicanism and constitutionalism embodied in the Declaration of Independence and the Constitution. In this way, the founders succeeded in establishing a secular, progressive political order without alienating the people from the religious sources of their common historical experience. American civil religion, while constantly changing and adapting to new circumstances, kept the original Puritan vision alive by demanding, as Robert Bellah has called it, "an understanding of the American experience in the light of ultimate and universal reality."[9] Despite the ever-present danger of propagandistic abuse, this must be seen as an original and effective response to the needs of an immigrant nation as well as to the dilemmas created by the interdependence of modernization and secularization since the Enlightenment.

Conclusions

Although this is just a broad outline of a very complex problem, the observations made above seem to justify the conclusion that the now widely admired 'American modernity' resulted to a large extent from a deeply engrained resistance against structures, institutions, values and norms that were considered by many Europeans as the essence of modernity. Another factor was the practical inability to conform to European projects and visions of modernity, first of all the fragility of central state authority in a vast, expanding federal republic, which, in turn, strengthened the forces of local self-government as well as the 'intermediary institutions' and voluntary associations of the emerging civil society. The Americans, it seems, created a 'modern' society because they—contrary to many Europeans—did not or could not aim at establishing a centralized, homogeneous, powerful sovereign

---

[8] Heideking, 1994; cf. Gebhardt, 1990.
[9] Bellah, 1967: esp. 18. For similarities and differences in the religious legitimation of western forms of national identity and nationalism, see Hutchinson and Lehmann, 1994; Krakau, 1997.

nation state. Their process of state formation produced a limited, federal government for a strong, diverse and pluralistic civil society. Only today can we fully recognize that this—partly voluntary, partly forced—decision for constitutional limitations and for national integration through democratic pluralism and civil religion was decidedly 'modern', progressive, and future-oriented.

18. MEDIA TECHNOLOGIES, SOCIAL ORGANIZATION AND DEMOCRATIC POLITIES[1]

Elihu Katz

In their zeal to discover the persuasive powers of mass communication, students of media effects have given far more attention to their content than to their technologies. They have also paid little attention to the social situations in which the media are received, i.e. to the fact that books and the internet typically are read in isolation, that turn-of-the-century newspapers were read in cafes, that television is (or used to be) viewed in families, that films are viewed with friends, that it takes two to telephone and at least ten to read the Torah.[2]

It is thanks to Harold Innis (1950) and Marshall McLuhan (1964)—one an institutional economist, the other a classicist—that we were reminded, in mid-century, to look to the effects of media technologies on social organization (cf. Carey, 1967 and Katz, 1998). They were not the first to note that media of communication (and transportation) may exert a determining influence on the structure of society; rather, it was their effort to theorize this relationship that attracted attention.[3] McLuhan was interested in· how media technologies constrain the mental processing of information which, in turn, affects both personality and social institutions; according to McLuhan, the linearity of print, for example, induced straight-and-narrow thinking, rational-legal and asocial personality, and, in turn, structures such as assembly lines and railroads. Innis, for his part, distinguished between portable media that conquer space and monumental media that span time; the former establish empires, the latter reinforce religious traditions. These theories—overly deterministic, especially in McLuhan's work, often oblivious to the power of those who control the media—succeeded in directing attention to media effects on social institutions rather than on opinions and attitudes of individuals.

---

[1] This is one of a series of overlapping papers seeking to develop appropriate concepts for treating the social implications of new media technologies. Previously published papers include Katz, 1992; Katz, 1996; Katz, 1998.

[2] For an early discussion of what is now incorporated as an aspect of 'reception' media and cinema studies, see Freidson (1953). For inspiration, see Simmel's discussion of the significance of numbers in Wolf (1950).

[3] David Riesman et al. (1950), for example, suggested that print and television were related, respectively, to 'inner-directed' and 'other-directed' personality types and cultures.

This paper proposes to review some thinking about media technologies and social organization. It will blithely ignore all of the warnings about technological determinism in order to make the point that students of social organization and social change would do well to ponder the influence of the media of communication, absent their messages, their owners, and their organizational forms. Of course, this is an impossible task because technologies do not have their own way; they are harnessed by humans. There is no intrinsic reason why radio should have been organized on a nation-wide basis in most countries, rather than on a municipal basis or on the basis of interest groups such as a church or a trade union. There is no reason why television should have been established as a public monopoly in one country and opened to competition in another. To talk of national television as if this form were technologically determined is obviously wrong. Or, to talk of television as if it were incapable of provoking rational discussion—as Postman (1986) contends—is to walk into the same technological trap. With the reader's permission, we shall do so nevertheless.

The prologue that now follows relates a series of illustrations drawn from different epochs. These are meant to exemplify ways in which media technologies bear on social organization. Because the concept 'diaspora' has been revived lately, in connection with post-modernity, the first example deals with the Jewish diaspora and its medium, the Book or the Scroll; the last example returns to the question of contemporary diasporas. In-between, we draw on examples from the Egyptian empire and its media, from the Protestant Reformation, and from the closing of the American frontier. None of these has direct bearing on democratic polities, however. The rest of the chapter then shifts to modern nation states, and examines the succession of media—newspaper, radio, television, internet—which have contributed so much to their making, and unmaking.

Some examples of how media influence social organization

Since diasporas are fashionable again, it is worth thinking back to the question of how the dispersed Jewish people held together for almost two millennia. The answer is that the Book—the Old Testament—held the people together. Everywhere they moved—East, then West—the medium of the Jews was the Torah and the library of commentaries it generated. In every Jewish community, scripture was (and is) read publicly in synagogues and market-places from hand-written parchment scrolls in the presence of at least ten persons. These readings are in weekly portions such that the five books of Moses are completed in a yearly (or tri-annual) cycle. Its relevance is expounded in sermons. It establishes the sabbath and holidays. It is a refresher course in the myths, heroes, and places of collective memory. It is a rule book of behavior, a constitution. It preserved the Hebrew language, requiring literacy of every Jewish (male) person. It invited new scholarship and exegesis, and gave status to those who were most proficient, rewarding achievement in learning. It generated an interactive network of scholars whose Questions and Answers criss-crossed the seas. In two words, it was a portable homeland.[4] Deterministic? Probably not. But functional theory is not enough to explain it.

Contrast this with Innis' (1950) analysis of ancient Egypt. The people lived along the banks of the Nile, and were periodically inundated, says Innis, until it became evident that a centrally-controlled system of dams would solve the problem. This led to the establishment of a bureaucratic Kingdom which used the river as a medium of transportation on which to float hieroglyphic messages on papyrus to direct officials at their stations up and down the river. Employing these media of space, the Pharaohs soon consolidated their centralized empire and sought to further it both in space (by conquest, partly through the expansion of written language) and in time (pyramids and monuments). *Empire and Communication* is how Innis describes his case studies of the interaction of media and organization.

An even more famous example is the effect of movable type and printing on the individualism of the Protestant Reformation (Eisenstein, 1979). Print made it worthwhile to translate the Bible into the spoken languages of Europe, and commerce invited the printers to sell it to the newly literate. These developments 'disintermediated' (Katz, 1988) the parish priest and his monopoly on the Word of God. Protestant decentralization and sectarianism displaced the Catholic Church in many places, and if Weber is right, led to the spirit of capitalism. There is no use quibbling about whether print directly 'caused' this change—of course it didn't—but one cannot imagine how it could have happened otherwise. The technological attributes of the printed page—ease and speed of distribution, exactness of reproduction and durability—also led Elizabeth Eisenstein to connect print to the rise of science (astronomers could share their observations with speed, accuracy and fixity).

James Carey (1967) attributes the economic integration of the United States to the telegraph. More than the railroad, which also overcomes distance, the telegraph adds instaneity to the equation. It allows a stockbroker

----

[4] Katz and Adoni (1973) have elaborated on this. See also Scholem (1973) for an example of the traffic of emissaries in the diaspora during the time of the false messiah, Shabbetai Zevi.

in San Francisco to bid on the New York stock exchange without being penalized by distance.

Newspaper and nation

Following this world tour of examples of the interaction of communication media and social organization, let us turn to consider media and democratic polities. Benedict Anderson (1991) suggested that the nation is a mental construct—an imagined community—which is united by the simultaneity of reading the newspaper in a shared language. Before Anderson, political scientists and sociologists—Gabriel Tarde, for example—remarked on the shared experience of newspaper reading, and the way in which newspapers mark the boundaries of a nation-state.

Tocqueville ([1835] 1969), Bryce (1891), Tarde ([1901] 1989), Habermas ([1962] 1989) all dwell on the agenda-setting role of the press. For Habermas, as for Tarde, the press is the launching pad for the process of participatory democracy, where conversation takes up the agenda proposed by the press, public opinion arises from conversation, and opinion leads to both collective and individual action vis-à-vis government and the market. But Habermas' 'bourgeois public sphere' is too rarified to be true. Cafes and coffeehouses seem unlikely places for the kind of rational and rule-bound deliberations Habermas attributes to assemblies of the newly-empowered merchant class standing up to the powers-that-be. Schudson (1997) rightly objects that this kind of policy-oriented 'political talk' is too formal to be called conversation.

Gabriel Tarde ([1901] 1989) is closer to the mark.[5] As an observer of the Parisian 'public sphere' at the end of the 19th century, Tarde saw democracy in action in the cafes, coffeehouses and salons. But this was conversation as we know it—informal, open, rambling, non-instrumental—which, nevertheless, percolated considered opinions about public affairs. In Tarde's view, the press was a kind of menu placed on the cafe table, to guide conversation. Conversation everywhere followed these guidelines of public and private talk, as it traveled from cafe to cafe, and congealed into one or two opinions. Tarde's interest in interpersonal exchange led him to see how opinions were clarified in the course of conversation, and his interest in

---

[5] Tarde's essay, "La Conversation," is a founding document for the study of mass communication and public opinion; it is included in Tarde ([1901] 1989). As criminologist, lawyer, judge and social psychologist, Tarde interested himself in the networks of social interaction, and especially in crowds and publics.

diffusion (Tarde, [1880] 1903) led him to speculate on how opinion was aggregated like snowballs. More often than not, it was the newspaper that reported the distribution of aggregated opinion and used it to put what Tarde called a 'brake on government', and what we think of as social control by the press in its role as watchdog. Aggregate opinion also affected individual choice—how to vote, how to buy, and so on. In short, it was Tarde who most clearly hypothesized a linear relationship among press, conversation, opinion and action, where the press set an agenda (based on government and parliament), offered it as a menu to cafes and salons, which, in turn, percolated considered-opinion, which aggregated into public opinion, and stimulated action.

But Tarde is interesting not only as a functional theorist. He is even more interesting as a technological theorist, and a sociologist of institutional change. His observation about the role of the press—not its content—in national integration has already been noted. Continuing this thought, Tarde goes on to show how the press displaced that other source of national integration, the king. Until the press, says Tarde, the king was the only one who knew what was happening in different places in his realm, thanks to his spies and bureaucrats. Now the press knew, too, and could tell village A what was happening in village B and vice versa. Gradually, says Tarde, this process undermined the king, and unseated him.

At the same time, Tarde notes that the sense of community that pervaded the nation in the wake of the press, also made its way into the national assembly which, theretofore, had given its delegates the right to dissent from any proposition that seemed inappropriate to their particular regions. The national spirit—the imagined community—that accompanied unification, thanks to the press, gave a big push to majority rule, says Tarde. Here, then, is another example of media affecting social institutions. The newspaper unified the nation, unseated the king, introduced majority rule.

Note again that this argument proceeds on two levels: the level of individuals, small groups, collective behavior—the microdynamics of democratic functioning—and the more macro level of institutions. At both levels, the media played a central role.

Radio, television and democracy

Let us take Tarde's model into the twentieth century, and examine radio, television and the internet—the three major successors to the newspaper—from the point of view of their relationship to democratic societies at both micro and macro levels.

Radio displaced the newspaper as the medium of national integration. Even in nations with national newspapers—and many had only a city-based press—the simultaneity of radio, the immediacy of its transmission, and its accessibility to the less literate gave radio a major advantage. Because of the (then) shortage of broadcasting frequencies, radio stations had to be licensed everywhere and, in response, had to establish their independence of government (as the private press had done much earlier).

The institutionalization of radio took two forms: there was the US model, exported to most of South America and parts of Asia, and the British model which was adopted throughout Europe and most of the countries colonized by Europe. The American model licensed multiple stations which were privately owned and financed by advertising. These formed themselves into several (not many) national networks, and attracted huge audiences both severally and together.

The British model was based on the explicit rejection of its American counterpart (A. Briggs, 1961); it viewed the airwaves as public property and vested authority in a public broadcaster. The charter granted the BBC a monopoly of the airwaves, the right to raise a fee from all users, and provided for its independence both of government and commerce. The idea that a quasi-tax could support a powerful medium that would be critical even of government itself was a great social invention. Cardiff and Scannell (1987) show how the newly-established BBC acquainted the various regions and provinces with each other's voices, invented traditions for celebrating civic and religious holidays together (that is, nationally and pluralistically), and democratized access to the royal family and to government (the King's Christmas message, for example).

At one level, then, radio was an important instrument of enfranchisement. Yet, we should look to questions of technology and place to sort out the institutional effects of the establishment of radio. The first thing to note is that radio began to move politics inside the home. If early newspapers were sold on the street and delivered to cafes and coffeehouses to fuel conversation, radio became part of the domestic domain. True, the democratizing salon—meeting place of old and new classes—was also a living room; but when it functioned as a salon it was a quasi-public place. In the era of radio, the living room was just a family room.[6] True, the politics of the living room also began to give women political status, but the radio family was probably further removed from politics than the newspaper reader. Lazarsfeld and Merton (1948) remarked on the 'narcotizing dysfunction' of

---

[6] See, for example, S. Briggs, 1981.

radio news which gave its listeners the illusion of being politically involved.

But a far more drastic effect of broadcast technology was to allow national leaders direct access to the people over the heads of parliament. Both Hitler and Roosevelt used radio in this way. Hitler simply dismissed the parliament and spoke directly to large throngs in the streets and stadia, and, via the newly-established radio, to people at home. Mutatis mutandis, Roosevelt instituted the fireside chat which he used to persuade a dubious citizenry and an even more dubious legislature to support his New Deal and his decision to join the Allies in the War. He did so by 'disintermediating' the Congress. Structurally speaking, then, we can say that just as Tarde sees the press as displacing the monarch, we may view radio as a first step towards establishing an 'imperial presidency', at the expense of the legislature.

What radio began, television continued. In the same sense that radio disintermediated the parliament, it is appropriate to suggest that television disintermediated the political party. Television completed the job of moving politics into the home, while also enhancing the role of personality and of personal imagery at the expense of political ideology. Whereas radio, like newspapers, still made it possible to read or listen selectively to one's own side, television made it almost impossible to ignore the other side. Everywhere that television has diffused, and by now that is everywhere, the format of pre-election Presidential Debates has followed.[7] One sees—and favors—one's own side, but one also notices that the other man is almost as acceptable, and that there isn't much difference between the parties either—because they are both vying for 'everybody'. Party affiliation became increasingly weak in the era of television: the precinct captain, and his favors, were soon gone. And, gradually, primary elections have become more important everywhere (including primaries open to non party-members) and the influence of party chieftains and smoke-filled rooms is in decline. Political conventions have become uninteresting, and television—especially commercial television—has been quick to show its disinterest in what were once major 'media events'.[8]

Thus, television also contributed ambivalently to democratic societies. In its final report card, one can say that it took over radio's role as the medium of national integration in a big way, and dispatched radio to its new role as everyman's 'companion'. Like radio, television was organized in national networks and supplied nations with shared images, interests and tastes. Its homogenized middlebrow culture went a long way to creating the kind of

---

[7] See Kraus (1962) and subsequent debate reports by Kraus.
[8] See Russo, 1983.

classlessness which the Frankfurt School (Horkheimer and Adorno, 1972) perceived as the ultimate blow to class-consciousness. The American Thanksgiving is an example of how television pervades holiday ritual, offering parades, football games, and culinary advice as ceremonial prescriptions to the vast majority of Americans.[9] Live television events—from Sadat's visit to Jerusalem and the Pope's to Poland, to the Watergate hearings and the funeral of Diana—changed the order of things. At its best, TV's investigative journalism excelled; one cannot easily forget the independent voice of the BBC in the British-French-Israeli Suez Campaign or television's influence in Vietnam and Bosnia.

On the other hand, television's cultivation of imagery reminds us of Habermas's perception that the decline of the bourgeois public sphere was followed into the 20th century by a new 'representative public sphere' in which the charisma and regalia of absolute monarchs would return in the guise of public-relations agencies which wrap themselves around political and industrial leaders, their ministries and corporations. PR blind us to what goes on inside these organizations and overwhelms rational-critical deliberation. The Falklands and the Gulf War show us, symbolically, how the public relations of Governments have learned the lessons of keeping television journalism off the battlefield. And, the home has indeed become the locus of most informal political talk: it is possible that such talk feeds back into the political system—but it is also possible that this is a much diminished politics of participation.[10]

The new media technology and the nation-state

But television, as we knew it, is dead or dying. From the medium, par excellence, of national integration, it has become a multi-headed monster pulling in all directions.[11] The new technologies, especially satellite and cable, have erased any memory of crowded airwaves, and make possible the hundreds of channels now reaching us at home. Governments have been unable to resist the temptations of privatization and commercialization and have opened the airwaves to almost any group willing to pay for a broadcasting franchise. The primary victims (apart from the public) are the public broad-

---

[9] On broadcasting and holidays, see Handelman and Katz (1990), and Cardiff and Scannell (1987).

[10] Currently, there are raging debates over the nature of participatory democracy: how it works (or doesn't), how and whether it ought to work, etc.

[11] See Gitlin (1998) and Katz (1996).

casters in the British tradition, who have had to make way for commercial competition that undermines their popularity and their (admitted) paternalism in matters of culture and politics. The commercial celebration of the customer being right has displaced the more tutorial public broadcast. The license fee is in jeopardy; people say—as they have done since the introduction of the earliest commercial channels—that they don't watch the public broadcaster, so why should they pay the tax?

The price of multi-channel broadcasting is not simply in the changing standards, but in the segmentation of society. The channels striving to attract everybody are now being joined by specialist channels that cater, potentially, to any interest group that is willing to patronize their advertisers. While it hasn't happened yet, not everywhere, the signs are evident that the pluralism of classic radio and television—in which there was a homogenization or melange of tastes on the same channels (over the already-noted objections of the Frankfurt School, which saw such amalgamation as a hegemonic effort to eradicate class-consciousness) is on its way out, and the multi-culturalism of segmented channels is well on its way in. This means that television is rapidly losing its role as the medium of national integration, and that the groups and interests which constitute society are no longer visible to each other. Only now does it become clear that a single, monopoly public television channel—which gave voice to pluralism, and was truly independent of government and commerce—can be *more* functional to democracy than the supposed competition of multiple channels that are increasingly segmented by interests and ethnicities.

It seems indisputable that television, as we knew it, is waning as the medium of national integration. It resembles nothing so much as a middle-sized video store, offering choice of programs and films on request. Someday soon, it will be possible to order one's program or film by computer, for direct broadcast to the home.

Indeed, it may be said that the new video technology has two tendencies. One might be labeled 'tailoring' in the sense that channels and programs and even newspapers can be delivered, as in be-spoke tailoring, to suit the exact measurements of the individual consumer. Tailoring can also be made to suit segmented groups—as zoot suits once did, or hasidic garb, or bikinis. The other technological tendency is 'globalism', in the sense that there are certain blockbuster programs that captivate the world—whether media events like Diana or the Pope, or soaps and sitcoms like 'Dallas' and 'ER'. Note that both of these tendencies—call them teleologies—ignore the nation-state! Tailoring falls short of the nation, globalism reaches beyond it.

Looking at the media technologically, then, and in terms of the social conditions of their reception, it becomes possible to look beyond the functional

ways in which the media empower individual citizens in democratic polities, fuel conversations and feed back public opinion to government and legislature. The technologies of the media direct us to look at a different order
of effect on institutions. It is in this sense that Tarde noted that the technology of the newspaper—apart from its content—unseated the king, and
that we, in the same tradition, can observe that radio reinstated him, so to
speak, by allowing the leader direct access to the people over the heads of
the parliament, and that television undermined the political party, creating
some of the same conditions we used to associate with 'mass society', that
is, a society without intermediary organization (Kornhauser, 1959). Taking
one more step in the same direction, it is possible to suggest that the newer
media—multichannel television, satellite broadcasting and, above all, the
internet—are undermining the polity itself.

The internet is the epitome of the new media technologies. Its potential
is mind-shattering, but it is very unlikely to succeed television as a medium
that can rally a nation. In fact, there is no medium in sight to perform the
kind of national integration that the press, radio and television have performed heretofore. Rather, the internet seems geared to follow-up conversations among networks of individuals, in the way that conversations responded
to the agenda of press and broadcasting—except that there may be no consensual national agenda and perhaps even no nation!

Another mission of the internet, as it seems to be developing, is to rein-
vigorate the cultural networks that used to be called 'diasporas'. It seems a
great irony that diasporas are reemerging in the twenty-first century. The
Jews may have returned to their homeland, but the Jewish diaspora persists, and even competes. So does the Palestinian diaspora, and the diaspora of Mexican immigrants to the United States, and Turkish guest-workers
in Germany, and many other cultural groups who are wandering the world
as immigrants, indentured servants, and foreign workers. Most of these
groups are not easily assimilated: partly because the host country doesn't
want to incorporate them, partly because they have their own doubts, about
whether to remain, but partly because the great new wave of media technologies provide a steady supply of the culture and the language they left
behind. Far stronger than the Goethe Institute, or the Dante Aligheri Society
or the British Council, satellite television and the internet are the agents of
what Appadurai (1996) calls 'de-territorialized' communities.

How the nation will respond to these centrifugal tendencies is not at all
evident. 'Media events' may reconvene the nation now and then, but even
that's not self-evident in that it depends on the pooled resources of broad-
casters and the pooled will of citizens. The newspaper may be reinvigorated
in its new role of commentator and speculator on what is likely to happen.

But if we take media determinism seriously, it seems most likely that new transnational associations—diasporas and groups with global interests—may become increasingly strong at the expense of the nation state. And if students of the internet are correct in their predictions, the whole of these networks of communication will be operated for commercial gain, and advertisements will interrupt even the reading of the Torah.

19. LANGUAGE POLICY, PRACTICE AND IDEOLOGY

Bernard Spolsky

A meaningful analysis of language policy (defined precisely as an attempt by someone who has or claims authority to influence the language practice or ideology of others) requires a clear differentiation between policy, practice and ideology. It further demands a recognition of the differences between what might be called 'thick' policy—cases like France where there is a long history of complex and detailed policy making—and 'thin' policy—cases like the United States and Great Britain where there have been only minor attempts at intervention in language practices. This paper will survey some cases on the thick and thin ends, and then try to place Israeli language policy on the continuum.

My concern in this chapter is to contribute to the understanding of a model for the description and explanation of language policy. To do this, I start with a number of terms and suggested working definitions. The first is *language practice*. The language practice of a community is what Hymes (1967; 1974) calls its ethnography of communication, or Gumperz (1968; 1971) talks about as the linguistic or speech repertoire of a speech community, namely its habitual pattern of selecting among the varieties that make up its linguistic repertoire. An even broader but perhaps more useful concept of Community of Practice has been proposed to include not just language practices (Holmes and Meyerhoff, 1999). The language practice may be conceived of as a multi-dimensional matrix where varieties (with all their complexities) are allocated according to the situations, interlocutors, and topics for which they are used. In other words, for each domain (to take the concept and term developed by Fishman: Fishman, 1972) and set out by him in the study of the New Jersey Barrio (Fishman, Cooper, and Ma, 1971). It is at this level that the processes analyzed by de Swaan (de Swaan, 1998a; 1998b) for the dynamics of language spread (an economic model recognizing languages as 'hypercollective goods' with properties which account for the diffusion of language with high Q or 'communication values').

The second is *language ideology*. Language ideology, according to Silverstein (1979), is a set of beliefs "about language articulated by the users as a rationalization or justification of perceived structure and use." In his use of the term, Silverstein is particularly concerned about beliefs about language structure. Schieffelin, Woolard, and Kroskrity (1998) present a number of valuable studies of language ideologies. My use of the term comes more from Dorian (1998), who refers in particular to the post-French Revolution Western European 'ideology of contempt' for anything but the standard national language as one possible language ideology. I use the term then to designate a community's consensus on what value to apply to each of the language varieties that make up its repertoire. Put simply, language ideology is not unlike language policy with the policy-maker left out, what people think should be done. Language practice, on the other hand, or the ethnography of communication is what people actually do. It is at this level that one will consider the "accumulated cultural capital of a language group" which, de Swaan points out, is lost if a language is lost, and the identity value of a language that provides a counter-force to the Q value and accounts for resistance to language shift.

With these two concepts defined, I propose to define *language policy* as an attempt by someone who has or claims to have authority over others to modify in some way their language practice or ideology. The importance of this definition is to restrict language policy to cases where there is a clearly identifiable agent arguing for or attempting to impose a specific policy decision. Linguistic hegemonies, then, are by this narrower definition issues of practice (the effect of Q values) or ideology (the desire preserving a culture or an identity) rather than policy, which applies to clear explicit efforts to modify the beliefs and behaviours of others.

Following general sociolinguistic practice, language policy can be broken down into a number of major classes of activity (Fishman, 1973; Rubin et al., 1977). A policy concerning language *status* may take the form of laws or regulations determining the permissible or required languages in certain situations. Proclaiming an official language is status policy or planning. A policy concerning *corpus* sets out the approved forms of a language. Preparing official lists of approved spellings or terms or grammatical rules, or new lexicon is corpus planning or policy. A corpus policy goes beyond general statements ("speak English" or even "speak correct English") to quite specific regulations ("don't say 'ain't'" or "spell 'honor' without a 'u'"). A policy concerning language *acquisition* or education sets requirements or situations or opportunities for learning a desired or required language or variety of a language (Cooper, 1989: 33). An approved foreign language curriculum for public schools is an example of language acquisition or education policy or planning (van Els, 1992; 1994). A sub-category of acquisition is a policy concerning the *diffusion* of a language beyond national boundaries. An office in a country's government (like the Goethe Institute in Germany or the British Council in England) charged with supporting and encouraging the teaching of the country's national language in other countries is engaged in diffusion planning or policy (Ammon, 1992; Kleineidam, 1992).

As well as asking what a policy is, one may obtain a finer taxonomy by asking *who* makes the policy (such as the writers of a constitution, the state or its agencies, various levels of government, various parts of an educational system), *who* are the people expected to follow the policy (such as citizens, speech communities, government officials, majorities or minorities, teachers or pupils), *why* the policy was made (such as unifying the nation, expressing ideology, providing for ease of communication, maintaining or changing identity or dominance), *how* the policy was made (such as by law or regulation or persuasion), and *what (if any) was the effect* of the policy (Spolsky and Shohamy, 1999). As de Swaan points out, a language defended by a government is especially "robust."

Attempts to describe language policy and study its structure are made difficult by the complexity of the possible patterns. As Ferguson (1977: 9) put it,

> All language planning activities take place in particular sociolinguistic settings, and the nature and scope of the planning can only be fully understood in relation to the settings.

In the search for a more parsimonious model, Lambert (1995) suggests that the four types of language policy activity discussed above are most likely to be found in association with particular types of *ethnic composition of a society*. He distinguishes three types of countries that are defined by their overall linguistic mix. The first type are countries that are linguistically *homogeneous*. Such countries, like Japan or Russia or the United States, do of course contain linguistic minorities, but the minorities are perceived to be small and insignificant, and are geographically or socially marginalized. The second type are *dyadic* (or triadic) countries, which include two or three relatively equal ethnolinguistic groups. Prototypical examples are Switzerland, Belgium, Fiji, Canada. The third group are *mosaic* societies, countries like Nigeria and India and Papua New Guinea, which contain a large number of ethnic groups. More than half the countries of the world, Lambert notes, have five or more substantial ethnic communities. There are, Lambert points out, important interactions between his typology and the kind of language policy. The homogeneous (or monolingual) countries usually assume that issues of status planning have already been decided. They put a great deal of emphasis on a normativistic type of corpus planning, pay some attention to acquisition planning, and are sometimes politically motivated to develop a diffusion policy. The second and third type of country is usually locked into debate over status planning, but as this gets settled, the other three kinds of activity may also become important.

Lambert's typology of countries raises certain problems, in that he treats it as based on the actual linguistic situation within the country. In earlier models, Fishman (Fishman, Ferguson, and Das Gupta, 1968; Fishman, 1969) had suggested that the important condition was not so much the language situation as clusters of language attitudes. Fishman's approach has value in its ability to treat perception and policy as distinct from observable reality, and in its distinguishing actual situations from ideologies or beliefs about them. Fishman classed countries according to the number of *Great Traditions*, or national ideological identities, that they recognized. In one cluster, he placed countries with a single Great Tradition, which of course corresponds to Lambert's homogenous country. The homogeneity in Fishman's view is a matter of belief rather than fact. Another cluster consisted of countries that recognized two or more Great Traditions, and corresponding to each, two or more national languages. A third cluster, corresponding to Lambert's mosaic countries, had no single Great Tradition, and thus recognized the importance of a number of languages.

There are other distinctions I wish to consider in this paper. They concern the 'how' rather than the 'why' of language policy, namely the way that a policy has been promulgated and in what form it is available. The first is the issue of explicit and implicit language policies. In the simplest case, the policy is expressed in written legal documents—a national constitution, published laws, cabinet or government documents or regulations. To find out what the policy is in the cases of an explicit written and published policy is relatively straightforward, although there will be cases of ambiguity or even conflicts that may require judicial interpretation. The task of the student is made much more difficult when the policy is nowhere spelled out in published laws and regulations, but needs to be pieced together from an analysis of language practice and then shown to have been the result of definite but not necessarily written decisions of policy makers.

The second is the location and scope of a policy. Roughly speaking, a policy may be national or federal, or regional (made at provincial or state levels) or local, public or private, and intended for all or a selected group of people under the authority of the policy-making body.

The third is the issue of what I might call the relative thickness or thinness of the policy. A 'thick' policy is one that appears in repeated laws and regulations, with agencies designated to carry out the functions. A 'thin' policy is one that appears only occasionally, in a few isolated and even unrelated byways of regulation making.

Without for the moment going into the issue of reasons for language policies, it appears to be general that language practice and language ideology have an important effect on language policy, in that if there is a uniform language practice and a consensus language ideology, there is likely to be only a thin (and probably) implicit language policy. Similarly, even if language practice is complexly multilingual, if there is a consensus on language ideology (such as the attitude to the value and use of each of these varieties), local policies are likely to be what it needed. If there is complexity in practice and differences in ideology, there will likely be attempts by the ideologies to develop strong explicit policies to modify practice in their direction.

In the rest of this chapter, I wish to discuss some cases of thick and thin policies, and then attempt to characterize Israeli language policy on the same dimensions. It is appropriate to start with one of the oldest and most elaborate central governmental efforts to determine language policy, the case of French, basing my analysis on the excellent recent study by Ager (1996; 1999). The first formal documents setting out policy are Articles 110 and 111 of the Edicts of Villers-Cotterêts, issued by François I in 1538. This required that French (rather than Latin) should be used in law courts in all regions under the rule of Kings of France worked also against the status of the many regional languages that came under French jurisdiction for the rest of the millennium. In the 17th and 18th century, the establishment of the French Academy provided a body that worked for the standardization of the language around the prestigious regional variety selected as standard (Cooper, 1989). The next major steps were those taken by the Revolutionary governments. A report by Abbé Grégoire having shown in 1794 how few Frenchmen spoke or understood the language, a decree passed in that year backed up the law passed a year earlier requiring all public instruction to be in French by appointing teachers of French in all areas where other languages (Breton, German, Basque) were spoken. The decree further required French to be used for all official acts, public and private. Separate decrees were issued converting private schools into public (so requiring the use of French), banning German in Alsace, attacking regional languages, and enforcing the use of French in schools and in official business. These 1694 laws were continually applied by the courts throughout the 19th century, and French Ministers of Education considered the replacement of the regional languages by French to be their major task. Nonetheless the regional languages survived. Four of them, Basque, Breton, Catalan and Occitan were allowed to be taught as optional extras by the Deixonne Law of 1951, but a ministerial circular putting the law into effect was only issued in 1969. Corsican was added in 1974. In the 1970s, under de Gaulle, new institutions were added to encourage French and *francophonie*. Some efforts to improve the status of regional languages took place in the 1970s and 1980s, but formal support only came with the Mitterand government, since when a number of ministerial circulars have recognized and provided some encouragement for regional languages. With these languages in very weak positions but still surviving and even reviving (see Jones, 1998 on Breton), the

French government is working slowly to conform with the European Community's position in favor of regional and minority languages. The most recent affirmation of the role of French was the Toubon Act, passed in 1994, and requiring the use of French in five domains: education, employment, audio-visual media, commerce and public meetings (including congresses). Since then, there have been a number of important ministerial circulars. One required all civil servants to use French. Another required them to use French in dealings with foreigners living in France, at international meetings, when dealing with international organizations, and when on missions. A 1998 circular detailed how French officials at European Community meetings must not only speak French in public and informal meetings but require that all documents be presented in a French version.

While the need for the constant reassertion of the primacy of French may be seen as a sign not just of insecurity (Ager, 1999) but also of the slowness with which language policies work, it does provide the student with ample evidence of the development of policy. Others are much harder to trace. Historians have found traces of discussion of language policy in the discussions leading to the adoption of the US Constitution, but no explicit policy emerged and language issues emerged only at the State level. As a result, there was room at the State level for some recognition of French in Louisiana and Spanish in New Mexico.

But the need to develop explicit national policy was for a long time avoided by the steady growth of a consensual ideological acceptance of the primacy of English. Presumably encouraged by the natural ambivalence of immigrants to the language of the country they have left and their relative powerlessness at least until they have acquired competence in the language of their new land, there were only small pockets of resistance to the shift to English that seems to have occurred without the need for explicit wide scale policy. There were however local policy decisions in line with the national ideology in cases where local practice appeared in conflict—the banning of bilingual education in the xenophobia of the years after the First World War as well as in present-day California, for instance (Ruiz, 1994; Ricento, 1996).

All of this leads one to suspect that, logically, the absence of formal language policy may be the result of consensual ideology of existing language practice. Explicit policy, either central or local, will appear only when ideology and practice are not in harmony. This helps explain Fishman's remark, in his review of a new edition of Schiffman (1996), about the failure of French policy: the very fact that French language policy remains so prominent is a sight that it is working against a set of ideologies and practices that it continues to fail to effect.

Similarly, the absence of Israeli language policy is a sign of a general consensus of ideology about the importance of Hebrew that did not conflict with non-obtrusive language practices. Only when the recent weakening of Zionist and related Hebrew ideologies have raised some people's fears has there been an effort to proclaim a pro-Hebrew policy. A combination of strong ideology, personal practice and local policies was needed in early days (say until 1913) to bring about the unique revernacularization and revitalization of Hebrew, but by 1920, the weight of the increasing Q or communication value of Hebrew was strong enough that, bolstered by 10 years of ideological campaigning, most Jewish immigrants were persuaded to add Hebrew to their repertoires. By 1948, the 'robust' support of government helped the 'stampeding' communication value to overcome the language practices of the massive immigration. While there are concerns to be noted with the newly competing Q value of English (in Israel as throughout the world), there are no signs yet that a situation has developed where there is need for renewed policy activities in support of Hebrew.

20. VIGNETTES OF PRESENT DAY DIASPORA*

Stanley J. Tambiah

Transnational movements of people and their implications

Under the label transnational movements I should ideally deal with three flows: the flow of people through transnational migrations; the flow of capital in our present time of multinational capitalism; and the flow of information over vast distances in the context of modern developments in communication. The three flows of people, capital and information are dynamically related and interwoven, and together generate some intensified effects that are said to be distinctive of our so-called 'postmodern' world. For example, the three processes in combination test and breach the autonomy, sovereignty and territorial boundaries of extant nation states hitherto considered as the primary units of collective socio-political identity and existence. They also intensify and sharpen socio-cultural diversity in what are called plural societies, which are becoming a common global condition, and pose for them the challenge of multicultural coexistence, tolerance and accommodation. It is striking that the last twenty-five to thirty years or so have witnessed an unprecedented movement of people within countries, from South to North and East to West. Certain expansionary, even explosive, economic developments in certain parts of the globe, and recent political upheavals have both caused two kinds of population movements—voluntary migrations and involuntary displacements which for some purposes we should keep separate and for others consider together. Both voluntary migrants and displaced refugees who make transnational passages and are relocated in other countries may be labelled as forming diaspora communities, and the dynamics and patterns of their involvement in transnational experiences and interactions will be the main subject of this essay. During the period 1965–85 the size of international migrants, (both voluntary and displaced refugees) proportionately to their total populations, was of much larger significance to the developed countries than to the developing ones. It is notable that by 1985, Europe and Northern America were hosting the largest concentrations of international migrants, amounting to 23 million and 20 million

---

* A different version of this chapter was published in *Daedalus*, 129 (1), 2000.

respectively. In Northern America, the United States alone hosted 16.5 million migrants.

Stages and forms of incorporation

An important issue integral to the viability of plural societies is the policies and institutional arrangements by which immigrants are variably incorporated into the host country.

It is possible to distinguish three broad types of migrant incorporation that can also serve us as measures or yardsticks. They are assimilation, exclusion and integration. A fourth category is multiculturalism which intersects with integration but highlights issues relating to the recognition of difference within plural societies while holding them together as viable polities.

Assimilation may be regarded as largely a one-sided process by which the migrants are expected to take the initiative of adapting themselves to the host society with the aim of becoming indistinguishable from the majority of society. It is consistent with policies by which the State leaves outcomes largely to market forces. The most famous example of this is the stereotype US ideology of the melting pot. Exclusion involves the participation in or incorporation of migrants only into selected and marked-off sectors of the host society. Migrants are denied access to other areas, mainly through legal mechanisms. The Gulf States and Japan (which according to a UN report is the archetypal closed society) are striking examples. Exclusion in a negative sense favours the formation of enclaves of ethnic groups experiencing a deep sense of discrimination and liminal existence.

Integration, the third type of incorporation involves positive two-way processes of mutual accommodation between migrants and their host society. Successful integration in liberal countries has been enabled by active State policies in the areas of housing, employment, education and language training, access to health and social services, and by equal opportunity and affirmative-action legislation. Successful integration and incorporation is, of course, not instantaneous but is achieved over time and usually becomes evident only with the second generation. In terms of timing, three stages could be distinguished: first, participation in the economic or labour market areas; followed by access to social services, education and housing; and finally, a fuller social and cultural incorporation, climaxed by access to citizenship.

The concept of multiculturalism is much commented upon these days by theorists, such as Charles Taylor and Will Kymlicka[1] and by activists. In

---

[1] See Taylor (1994) and Kymlicka (1995).

this presentation I have in mind a situation in plural societies where the immigrant populations, although they have gained substantial, even equal rights in most spheres of life, are motivated to constitute themselves as 'ethnic' communities that are distinguishable from the host population. What is both problematic and intriguing is that the processes and measures that facilitate integration with the host society can at the same time work side by side with and in tension with the processes and concerns that engender particularizing ethnic group formation. Such formation is buttressed by support from migrant associations and networks pursuing special interests, and concerned with the maintenance of their distinctive cultural, religious and familial practices, and with the teaching and maintenance of their own mother tongues. It is becoming increasingly evident that a number of present day diasporic communities, even while becoming economically and educationally integrated, may strive to maintain their social and religious distinctiveness. Thus multiculturalism as a project and goal is intimately related to what are termed 'identity politics', and in Charles Taylor's language, to 'politics of recognition' and 'politics of difference'.

The culture and political life of diaspora communities

The term 'diaspora' seems to be in high fashion these days, and its popularity courts the danger of inordinately stretching it. James Clifford has appropriately called it "a traveling term, in changing global conditions."[2] Diaspora in earlier times "described Jewish, Greek, and Armenian dispersion [but] now shares meanings with a large semantic domain that includes words like immigrant, expatriate, refugee, guest worker, exile community, overseas community, ethnic community."[3] In the face of these multiple as well as fluid connotations it would be wise not to strive towards a tight, inclusive definition embracing general criteria. William Safran has attempted a kind of ideal type representation of diaspora as expatriate minority communities, dispersed from an original 'center' to at least two 'peripheral' places; they maintain a memory or myth about their original homeland, they believe they are not, and perhaps cannot, be fully accepted by their host country, they see the ancestral home as a place of eventual return and a place to maintain or restore. The collective identities of these diaspora communities are importantly defined by this continuing relationship with the homeland.[4]

---

[2] Clifford, 1997: 244.
[3] Clifford, 1997: 245. He is quoting from Tölölian, 1991: 4–5.
[4] Safran, 1991.

Clifford once again appropriately remarks that the most questionable feature of this ideal type construction is the thesis of a strong attachment to and a desire for a literal return to a well-preserved homeland—a requirement that does not accord with large segments of even the Jewish historical experience, let alone other well-known diaspora communities. The philosopher Charles Taylor's plea for the recognition of the worth of multiculturalism in our time is informed by this modern, or if your prefer, postmodern, condition: that all societies are becoming increasingly multicultural, while at the same time becoming more porous. Their porousness means that they are more open to multinational migration; more of their numbers live the life of diaspora, "whose center is elsewhere."[5] By this expression "whose center is elsewhere" Taylor presumably is suggesting that diaspora communities though located abroad still have their primary concerns turned towards their 'home countries' of origin. Such primary orientation may apply to some diaspora but there are many for whom such a strong imputation may not apply. Some theorists even go so far as to assert that diaspora communities find themselves in a 'deterritorialized' situation and state of mind. These characteristics are truer of diaspora communities in their earlier stages of existence than in their later stages, especially in those contexts in which the host societies permit them to stay for long periods with chances for alien residence status and eligibility for access to the social and educational and other services available to regular citizens.

I have problems with the term 'deterritorialization' that is promiscuously used in certain circles. Many diaspora populations who are variably on the path of integration rather than stuck in the state of exclusion, temporary residence and deterritorialization, may actually cope with the concerns of a 'dual territorialization', and possibilities of a dual or even triple perspective on their existential circumstances involving multiple pools of memories and subjectivities both context bound and interpenetrating. They face the problem of securing their existence in the new host societies; at the same time, they feel the need to create and maintain relationships with their home communities. (They are involved in yet a third network of lateral interconnections transcending the borders of both the state of origin and of resettlement that I shall address shortly.) We need to know better than we do today how diaspora communities placed in different host environments voluntarily form, or are constrained to form spatial and social enclave communities; how they coalesce to deal with discrimination and prejudice when they face it; how they develop their economic niches and specialize in the

---

[5] Taylor, 1994: 63.

businesses and services in which they are competitive, and how in time they become effective voting banks when they become eligible to participate in local, state, and national politics, and generate their own politicians, mediators, and political bosses. The time may come when such immigrant communities are officially recognized as 'minorities' who on that basis may enter the arena of national politics.

While they are developing their milieu in the host society, there is evidence that diasporas are simultaneously in considerable interaction with their home communities of origin—sending remittances as well as seeking investment capital, returning to marry homeland brides or husbands, sponsoring new migrants, making periodic returns home to indulge in nostalgia, to build new or refurbish old family seats and alleged ancestral homes, to do the same for churches and temples, to sponsor and finance local festivals, to go on pilgrimages and to make conspicuous, pious, merit-making gifts. And in turn they may invite cultural groups, musical and dramatic ensembles and troupes, and charismatic holy men and women to visit their settlements abroad so as to authenticate their cultural and ethnic identity and pride, and to exhibit the high culture of their home countries from which they are spatially distanced. A matter of much contemporary concern is their direct participation in effervescent affectively charged ethnonationalist movements, and religious revivals and fundamentalist causes that are erupting in their home countries. Such participation has been labelled as nationalism or ethnonationalism at a 'distance'. But this 'distance' is only a partial truth, and to explicate the immediacy of this participation we have to consider the implications of the modern information and communication revolutions.

Let me now consider another major feature of diasporic communities. Although associated with a 'homeland' (country or region within a country) of origin, and although situated in another country of migration, these two frames—country and state of origin and host country and state—do not by any means cover or exhaust another aspect of the lives of diaspora. Migrants and immigrants of similar origins are distributed and situated in many diasporic locations, such that they are interconnected especially by modern media and travel in a transnational transactional arena focused on their own preoccupations and interests. The actors in this arena, be they individuals, families, groups, business enterprises, for whom for certain purposes national and state boundaries as such are irrelevant or secondary, constitute crisscrossing and intersecting networks that Hannerz has dubbed "the global ecumene."[6] Thus the ability and incentives of kin and friends and co-religionists,

---

[6] Hannerz, 1996: 6–7.

and ethnic associates, to circulate between these sites, and to exchange money and goods and information, and to conclude marriage contracts and exchanges, poses for anthropologists the task of mapping this extended sprawling and yet connected social world. Thus transnational connections linking diasporas need not be articulated primarily through a real or symbolic homeland. Decentered, lateral connections may be as important as those formed around a teleology of return. Now it is foolhardy to think, given the multiplicity and variety of diaspora throughout the world, that it is possible to suggest general ordering principles regarding their orientations. However, it may be possible to suggest two kinds of positionings between which most contemporary diasporas have to negotiate and operate.

On the one hand, many modern diaspora groups—be they Sikhs in Vancouver, or Sri Lankan Tamils in Toronto, or Blacks in London balancing their Caribbean and Afro-American backgrounds with British affiliations— do not by and large actually expect to return for good to their societies of origin, though they may have strong connections with events and people there. They usually harbour nationalistic or patriotic longings and sentiments at a distance and may materially support home causes from a distance.

On the other hand, these same groups, to use James Clifford's words, "may wax and wane in diasporism, depending on changing possibilities— obstacles, openings, antagonisms, and connections—in their host countries and transnationally."[7] Many migrant groups stereotyped in negative terms as Blacks, Browns, Hispanics, Turks, Algerians by large segments of the host societies will inevitably have to struggle to be accepted by their hosts, and therefore in turn will always pose issues of accommodation and incorporation with, and resistance to, the hegemonic and discriminatory attitudes and policies of their hosts. But beyond the two positioning mentioned above, there is the third imperative of the need of diaspora communities to reproduce and maintain themselves over time through effecting marriages between persons located elsewhere in other diaspora communities or in their societies of origin, through sharing cultural knowledge and receiving visiting priests, artists, and public figures, and also sharing and fusing assets to extend their businesses, and professional interests. These lateral links and networks between diasporas that have little to do with state affiliation, have been greatly facilitated by modern transformations in communication technology.

---

[7] Clifford, 1997.

Towards multiple modernities

The perspective I have outlined which focuses on diasporic communities in terms of three frameworks—in terms of their evolving relations with their host societies, of their continuing relations with their societies of origin, and of their interconnecting global relations with other spatially dispersed diaspora communities of their own kind—has now to come to terms with certain cultural processes mentioned in recent writings. Examples are 'hybridization' (Rushdie), 'creolization' (Hannerz), and 'eclectisicm' (Lyotard; Harvey). These labels aspire to characterize the ways in which we and our contemporaries, facing increasing exposure to transnational influences, selectively incorporate them and synthesize them with our varied roots of origin, senses of our past, distinctive migration histories, preexisting practices, and new encounters in our places of destination, both short term and long term. The term 'hybridization' we may attribute to Salman Rushdie who characterized one of his famous novels thus:

> The *Satanic Verses* celebrates hybridity, impurity, intermingling, the transformation that comes of new and unexpected combinations of human beings, cultures, ideas, politics, movies, songs. It rejoices in mongrelization and fears the absolutism of the pure. Mélange, hotchpotch, a bit of this and a bit of that is how newness enters the world.[8]

According to some commentators the multiplicity of choice and the rich variety of diverse experiences which run together in simultaneity is a postmodern condition in general.[9]

Lyotard echoes this same sentiment when he remarks:

> Eclecticism is the degree zero of contemporary general culture: one listens to reggae, watches a western, eats McDonald's food for lunch and local cuisine for dinner, wears Paris perfume in Tokyo and 'retro' clothes in Hong Kong.[10]

Colourful as is the term 'hybridization', flashy the term 'eclecticism', and demoralizing the term 'deterritorialization', they do not help us answer what a persistent anthropologist will ask: in these cultural mixings and exchanges what ingredients, what mechanisms, what valuations are the dominant strands that produce the distinctively local flavor, the distinctively local syncretic patterning and social orderings, as well as the creative innovations? Diaspora communities of different origins, backgrounds and orientations will inevitably vary in their accommodative and innovative responses, and my readers will,

---

[8] Rushdie, 1992: 394.
[9] See for example, Harvey, 1989.
[10] Lyotard, 1984: 76.

I am sure, agree that substantive ethnographic accounts of some depth are preferable to fragmentary illustrations served up in some current programatic writings. So let me conclude by providing three strikingly different vignettes to drive home the point that there are multiple patterns of modernity, not frozen but in process, that can bloom in our time of intensified transnational processes.

A theoretically interesting formulation that can be illustrated ethnographically can be entitled, following S.N. Eisenstadt, 'multiple modernities in an age of globalization'. The classical theories of modernization developed in the fifties tended to view the following components of Western civilizational experience as constituting a single interrelated package of universal relevance: industrialization, urbanization and technically advanced communication media; capitalist market economy; the formation of modern nation states and national collectivities; and an accompanying cultural program and patterning. It was assumed that these institutional and value constellations will 'naturally' and inevitably take root in all modernizing societies.

Today we know that the assumption that the convergence of these components will create a uniform world has not been borne out. We know that these and other components can in different societies meet and combine in different ways during different phases of their transformations. Granted that some form of economic development, creation of greater wealth and its redistribution, with accompanying technological linkage, is a common program and aspiration in most contemporary societies, it is quite evident that these societies can and do engender multiple civilizational patterns on the basis of selective choices, while sharing certain common modernizing goals.

In sum, we should explore the possibility of 'multiple modernities', and I propose to provide some vignettes to illustrate this proposal. My first vignette describes the religious orientations and activities of certain South Asian Indian suburbanites of primarily middle class status living in Massachusetts, USA, who are also fully in control of Western scientific and modern commercial skills. I describe how the members of this overseas diaspora community are not so much fixated on their roots in a particular region in India and with eventual return to their homeland (though they do make visits to their regions of origin and frequently find their spouses there), as with recreating the religious and cultural bases of their lives in their new locations. A focal point of this recreation is building a Hindu temple in classical Indian architectural style, a task accomplished by successful negotiations with local state authorities.[11]

---

[11] This sketch is taken from Diana Eck's Pluralism Project at Harvard University.

My second vignette deals with the quite different proclivities of a single Cantonese lineage, initially located in the New Territories, a border zone separating the Communist regime of mainland China from the British colony of Hong Kong.[12] The members of this lineage became dispersed, settling in different parts of the world especially the major cities of Europe and North America, and now run some 400 plus successful restaurants in Europe alone. The distinctively Chinese aspect of this affluent diaspora is that their ancestor tombs and shrines are permanently and immovably located in their original village in the former New Territories, and the lineage members (now several thousand strong and many of them belonging to the fifth generation since the original dispersion) have to return there to conduct their ancestor worship. The unanticipated development that has intensified their annual return to their once marginal village is that, after the unification of Hong Kong with mainland China, the land there held in lineage trusts has become prime real estate worth billions. The fortunes of corporate capitalism have conspired to generate an intensification of ancestor worship among this already affluent diaspora, and there are good reasons for the emergence of this form of modernity that is a happy marriage between corporate capitalism and ancestor worship based on filial piety.

My third vignette is about the Daudi Bohras, a denomination of Ismaili Shias, numbering some one million residing in over fifty countries around the world, but concentrated in India, Pakistan and East Africa. They are well known as a successful business and mercantile community. Their largest concentrations are in the Western Indian states of Gujarat and Maharashtra, with the seat of the religious hierarchy located in Mumbai. The distinctive features of the life of this dispersed community orchestrated by a highly centralized and regulative religious hierarchy centered in Mumbai are that in respect of religious life there is a strictly enforced and accepted conformity in terms of both orthodoxy and orthopraxy (no alcohol, no non-halal food, a public dress code for men and women, endogamy, contribution of tithe from earnings, etc.) combined with the use of the most modern communication media to transmit transnationally homilies and rituals by 'radio relay', couriered video-cassette, and (soon) by closed circuit satellite television broadcast. Again in the conduct of their business, while disallowing usury and sponsoring no interest credit unions for depositing savings, the Bohras expertly employ computers, internet and websites, and the most 'rational' forms of business accounting etc., to maximize business efficiency and success. And

---

[12] This illustration is taken from James Watson's long term study of the members of the Man Lineage whose ancestral village is located in the former New Territories.

yet again, they run their *madrasas* in a way that combines Islamic teaching with the teaching of modern science and professional skills, and they have a very high literacy rate for men and women, far exceeding any other community in Pakistan or India. Committed to parallel Islamization and modernization, to orthodoxy/orthopraxy and the marvels of modern long distance communication, steadfastly avoiding political violence and professing to be a closed group and preferring dissidents to break away than remain, enthusiastically adopting advanced scientific technology selectively, resorting to top-down enforcement of conformity and at the same time initiating innovation and coordinated change, the Bohras present an unusual composite photograph of an alternative modernity suited to a self-conscious minority situated in a wider arena of diversity and recognized difference.

A discussion of transnational processes and multiple modernities that powerfully engender pluralist interactions of peoples and cultures may serve as a corrective to Samuel Huntington's gothic vision of a world bifurcated by a clash of exclusivist civilizations. Huntington, and certain other conspicuous political prophets of doom in the United States, have asserted that the end of the Cold War will inexorably be succeeded by a new 'clash of civilizations' divided by primordial deep faults of language, religion and culture, and that the Western bloc, led by the United States and Western Europe, should retreat into isolationism to protect its interests.

In reviewing the expansionary phase of global capitalism, together with its unequal and uneven effects, especially in the 1970s and 1980s, it makes sense to say that many parts of the globe were becoming porous and interactive as a result of massive population movements, large movements of capital, and accelerated exchanges of information, and thereby also becoming more pluralistic and multicultural. The current economic downturn and contraction—let us hope that it will not last long—is also a grim reminder of the magnitude of that interrelatedness, and the deadly effects of reversing it and reverting to exclusivism and nationalistic chauvinism.

21. THE TRANSFORMATION OF DIASPORAS: THE LINGUISTIC DIMENSION

Eliezer Ben-Rafael

Studying diasporas: the sociolinguistic dimension

Today's literature of ethnicity is strongly focused on the notion of 'transnational diaspora' as one of the major factors that account both for the internal diversity of societies and new lines of resemblance among them. Diaspora means the dispersion in different countries of groups of a same origin that remain in contact with each other and with their homeland (Van Hear, 1998). A range of authors view this phenomenon as recent and as bringing out a new concept of ethnic identity, the importance of which is such that it concerns not only the evolving of groups but also the social order itself (Soysal, 1994; Baubock, 1994; 1998). Another group of researchers contends, on the contrary, that it speaks of a well-known condition that is everything but new and which hardly indicates any essential identity-related differences between the contemporary cases of diasporas and those of the past (Portes and Rumbaut, 1996; Guarnizo and Smith, 1998). It is the contention of this chapter that these transnational diasporas effectively represent a new phenomenon in the realm of collective identity and identity dilemmas, comparatively to types of diaspora that prevailed in previous epochs, and that this is best captured when studied in a comparative perspective through characteristic patterns of bilingualism.

One knows, in a general manner, how varied, at any epoch, the phenomenon of ethnicity may be. Some groups successfully transplant themselves from one corner of the world to the other, integrating their new environments 'painlessly', so to speak and, within one or two generations, becoming indiscernible components of the society. On the other hand, one also knows that integration may imply cultural difficulty, exclusion and political conflict (George, 1984). In the same society, different groups may undergo different experiences according to their demography, human capital, symbolic resources, and the attitudes that the absorbing setting and culture have towards them. In a general manner, resentment about poor conditions where individuals see themselves confined by their environment, the advantages they expect from the articulation of collective power, or profound attachment to parochial legacies may motivate groups to keep to markers of distinctiveness and to fight for the right to remain distinguished (in both senses of the term). Moreover, in the same group, major differences in collective identity may appear among fellow-ethnics according to class conditions, education or personal endeavors—better-off members of the group, for instance, have more contacts with out-groups and tend to emphasize their ethnic identity less than others do. Anyway, some members are closer to assimilation outside the group, and others may still be firmly anchored in their community or stand somewhere between total assimilation and determined retentionism. The actual formation of an ethnic group takes place, and the continuity of its identity is ensured, only as far as there are people in the group who reject total assimilation as an option, and want to remain distinct—even though the group itself may experience thorough transformation and become unrecognizable in comparison to what it happened to be in earlier generations. 'Ethnicization'—or the elaboration of an ethnic identity—when it occurs, means that individuals bestow—whether or not in unanimous terms—expressive meanings to their endeavors as members of the group, demand from themselves loyalty to putative kinsmen and feel allegiance to symbolic distinctiveness (Lal, 1983). The same group experiences ethnicization differently, if at all, in different societies, according to specific cultural influences, power relations or other circumstances. It may thus undergo diverse kinds of transformation of looks and outlooks, challenging in varying degrees the models proposed, or imposed, by the environment.

Yet contemporary societies, and this applies at least to democratic settings, are, more often than not, unable to oppose, in the long run, a core of people determined to openly express an attachment to a singular identity, in particular when these people draft power from within their group by convincing influential milieus of fellow-ethnics to identify with the 'collective cause'. Another condition is gaining strategic political advantages by articulating assets with competence, in front of the major rival forces of the national scene. Democracy is, in this respect, a particularly favorable context for ethnicization as the political scene is exposed to the eyes of all, and is theoretically open to anyone. Once politically organized—whether as parties, constituencies within parties or interest groups—ethnics may then draw from the center resources that will enhance their capability to express themselves and their motivation to do so. The cultural singularity of groups may then even become a recognized aspect of the society itself, which signifies a development of society toward institutionalized multiculturalism. From now on, the group enjoys the right of expressing its identity as an aspect of its participation in the setting and, in wider terms, as a structural characteristic of the setting itself.

This is the kind of evolution that immigration often contributes to modern and democratic societies. What is new in this era of globalization, according to the literature of the field, is that today, once 'installed in their ethnicity', so to speak, individuals are also likely—much more than in the past—to remain in permanent contact, as a part of their 'normal endeavor', with people of 'their kind' elsewhere and, mainly, with their original homeland. These aspirations assumedly find support in the unprecedented headway achieved by technologies of communication, transportation and media which delete distances and allow immigrants and offspring to move from one country to another and retain permanent links—by phone talk or other forms of direct interchange, updated real-time information, frequent visits—with the 'homeland' or fellow-ethnics in other countries. One adds here that in one way or another the contemporary world is also composed of complex networks of international obligations and commitments, which in itself favors immigration and prolongs the responsibility of governments over nationals outside the 'homeland'. Governments capitalize politically on their diasporas and with the help of cultural and social activity aimed at their immigrant citizens, they often act in target-societies as factors of 'ethnicization'. As for the ethnics themselves, their insertion in the target-society, to be sure, will make them 'different' from their brothers, relatives and friends left behind. However, in terms of emotions and some aspects of their identity, they may still feel that they belong to the same 'breed'. They may also aspire to share the feelings of power, solidarity and cultural continuity warranted by diaspora ties, and discover gratification in the retention of such contacts—in spite of the cultural difference now separating them from the people of their kind elsewhere.

To the extent that this effectively occurs and differentiates nowadays diasporas from previous cases, one may also contend that the notion of a transnational group does not just describe the very fact of dispersion of a given group over the world, but also indicates a structured whole where components interact, significantly and meaningfully, despite their dispersion. In this, it might then be asserted, transnational diasporas constitute a major factor of social transformation in contemporary societies.

It is our own contention that the comparative study of language and characteristic patterns of bilingualism in diasporas may offer an answer to this question, one that goes beyond the simple description of behavioral syndromes, and delves into the identities standing behind these syndromes. Sociolinguists, indeed, have shown how far languages reveal the forces behind the dynamics of social divisions. Ardener (1989) has elaborated on the role of language in ethnocultural experiences as relating surface and deep structures. Fishman (1989) has extensively analyzed the major importance of language in processes of symbolization and cohesion of groups and societies.

Linguistic activity as outlined by Edwards (1988), simultaneously translates group allegiances into behavior, and builds up collective identification. Linguistic variation is associated with social identity, and linguistic markers identify cleavages (Garmadi, 1981; Myers Scotton, 1983). A group marker (Goffman, 1973; 1972) may consist of a linguistic system, or only in a limited register of tokens and ready-made expressions, perhaps even a small number of linguistic characteristics, or just an accent. In any case, a linguistic marker includes individuals in an identifiable category, excluding anyone else (Gumperz 1987). Stating who stands in and who stands out, it points out to 'contrastive self-identities' (Fasold, 1987) made up of those people who are determined to remain a distinct community (Milroy, 1989). Thus, with the help of sociolinguistic tools, the following aspires to evince if—and if so, how far and to what extent—contemporary 'transnational diasporas' are different from other kinds of diaspora.

To confront these issues, we will follow widely discussed types of diasporas that present different models of relations between the ethnic group and the rest of the society. These models are found in Western societies, up to now and ever since the beginning of modernity, but they were predominant, as forms of ethnicity and diaspora, at different and specific epochs. We will view these models, à la Weber, as ideal-types that draw out sets of related principles that should be reflected, with more or less emphasis, in a variety of empirical realities. This means that we can by no means speak of these categories in too strongly exclusive terms when it comes to precise empirical cases. Because cases that respond to different ideal-types may indeed exist concomitantly, they cannot but influence each other. This being said, we will consider the best illustrations of the various categories and try to go beyond their mere descriptions in order to get to the essential singularity as it can be read in characteristic patterns of bilingualism.

With the support of sociolinguistic research (see Beebe and Giles, 1984) and generalizing the scope of notions like subtractive and additive bilingualism, one may speak of subtractive multiculturalism as opposed to additive multiculturalism. Subtractive multiculturalism refers to individuals who tend to leave their original culture while acquiring the culture that is dominant in the society and assumedly represents the collective personality of the society. Additive multiculturalism means that the acquisition of the dominant culture does not prevent the retention of some faithfulness to one's particular heritage. Even then, though, as a result of the very exposure to the dominant culture, the cultures of specific groups may evolve into *intercultures* articulated by *interlanguages*. These notions differ from the concepts of bi-culturalism and bilingualism widely used by social scientists to describe the simultaneous participation of individuals to two—or more—different cultures and languages. Indeed, they emphasize that, in addition to their capacity to find themselves in different cultures and use, at their will, different languages, individuals also tend to some extent to amalgamate the cultures and languages that they control into new cultural repertoires and linguistic codes. In other words, the notions of intercultures and interlanguages designate cultural and linguistic patterns that are shaped by composite intermingling sources. One thinks here especially of individuals who control both the legitimate language and their own original vernacular, and who not only alternate between these codes from one speech situation to another, but also use them, at their convenience, within the same discourse. What is more, we also know from language-in-contact theory (Myers Scotton, 1983; Gumperz 1987) that even when the original vernacular is more or less abandoned and the legitimate code has become predominant, within the group's community life, this original language may still influence—through calques, borrowings or styles of speech—the way individuals use the legitimate language. This signals the desire of people to express collective allegiances by retaining selected markers. Such markers vary in intensity of use and their systematic character, according to situations and locutors, but as such, they give shape to a sort of interlanguage indicating a more general process of the emergence and crystallization of an interculture. This latter notion applies to the integration of originally alien symbolic sets into one whole, the disparate elements of which do not exclude one another but, on the contrary, may appear conjunctively in the same modes of behavior. In brief, the study of this area of issues focuses on the extent that groups remain, vis-à-vis the dominant culture, *culturally—and to a varying extent, linguistically—contrasting entities*, or on the contrary, are submitted to processes of *acculturation*, or even of *assimilation*. Acculturation means becoming increasingly less different from those who best represent the dominant culture, and assimilation means that acculturation comes to include social identity (Ben-Rafael, 1994).

The enclave

A first syndrome is the enclave—in Jewish terms, the ghetto or the shtetl. This model was prevalent among minority groups before and during early modernity, and it is still exemplified by so-called 'fourth-world' communities like Gypsies, Amerindians, Aborigines or Haredi Jews. According to this syndrome, in-groups live in special quarters or regions as half-foreigners.

They are almost ignored by mainstream society and they themselves form a quite closed circle, turned in on themselves. This does not prevent them from developing relations with kin and fellow in-groups elsewhere—in the same society or further away, beyond national borders. They may be in contact with remote communities sharing their primordial identity, the belief in a God and a Bible, a language, and/or symbolic ancestors. In this model, individuals may get up in the morning, go to work, attend social meetings or religious rituals, receive guests from the outside world, go to a show and still not meet anyone that is not a fellow-member of the group or taste food that is not typical of the group. The relation to society is carried out at the level of economic life by peddlers, small entrepreneurs engaged in tourism, or clerks who encounter out-groups on a regular basis by working outside their community. At the political level, this group-society relation is conducted by notables who play the role of brokers on behalf of the group.

When considering speech activity and its linguistic aspects, it appears that people in this model speak in their own vernacular most of the time. This vernacular may convey a literature of its own and written journalism as well as an oral saga. Many within the community are monolingual, with only a restricted register of words pertaining to the society's legitimate language. Hence, language which is here a 'perfect' marker of the group and its boundaries (Hechter 1975; 1978), excludes the group from direct participation in activities pertaining to mainstream society that take place in the dominant language. By all means, this sociolinguistic syndrome sets the enclave in contrast with the rest of the society (Gumperz, 1967; Fishman, 1967), with the exception of in-between individuals. Peddlers or public clerks know better than others the language of 'non-groups' (the '*goy*', the '*franji*' or the 'white') as they meet with them more intensively than others. Their acquisition of the legitimate language, however, is additive and does not entail the loss of the group's vernacular as their allegiance to their community remains unquestioned. The same is true of the elite elements within the group, who are bilingual at a high level of competence and who act as buffers between the community and the authorities. This model of elite bilingualism recalls, in fact, the social diffusion of world communication languages—English, French, German, Spanish or Russian—in third-world countries, where the ones who learn and control these languages are figures who, using their status and power, serve as brokers with international centers.

At any rate, the vernacular of the community represents its principal linguistic assets and conveys its diaspora experience; it binds it to a real or virtual 'homeland' and to other diaspora communities. It attests to diaspora solidarity which accounts for the travelling of ethnics from one community to another, paying visits to relatives and friends, and seeking social opportunities. Eventually it also favors intra-diaspora politics or displacements to faraway communities of dignitaries, priests, money-collectors, teachers or artists. Last but not least, it also favors the circulation among communities of cultural and symbolic objects—books, artistic works, recorded music or narratives.

A good example is offered by the French-speaking Québecois during the early modernization of Canada (Lijphart, 1977; Lemieux & Hudon, 1975). Québecois were then a widely rural group dominated by notables and dignitaries sustained by the Catholic Church. These individuals controlled the English language and served as brokers with the English-speaking elite. This did not prevent the Québecois from developing, on the other hand, an intense French-Québecois cultural life, as well as maintaining and amplifying their relations with French-speaking groups throughout Canada—outside Quebec—and in the USA—down to Cajun country.

All these replicated the Eastern European Jewish diaspora where, for centuries, well-structured communities led a life of their own, under the leadership of their religious elites, alienated from the Polish, Russian or Rumanian society. Yiddish, the Jews' vernacular, and the Biblical Hebrew used in the religious academy were the only widely-known languages. Since many Jews were tradesmen and had contacts with non-Jews, quite a few individuals had command of basic Polish, Russian or Rumanian. Merchants who dealt with non-Jewish customers regularly, and the notables who, were the community's brokers vis-a-vis the Authorities, were the principal good bilinguals. This accounts for Yiddish's local coloration that distinguished groups of Jews from each other. Gypsies throughout Europe, Germans in Eastern Europe, or North American Indians are all examples which may be linked to this type of syndrome.

In brief, and focusing on what the language activity reveals, the condition here is one where the parochial language is an individual's first language (L1) and the national language, when known at all, is the second language (L2). As a rule, expressions and words of L2 find way to L1 as borrowings, under the influence of the environment. But, all in all, and this influence notwithstanding, this syndrome indicates that the community is collectively a part of society, that is, as a specific and distinct segment, but not through the individual adhesion of its members to the national setting. Hence, it is more than plausible that the commitment of individuals goes primarily to the community, and that their attitude toward the national or societal identity is less asserted, if not frankly alienated.

The symbolic-ethnic diaspora

A second syndrome of diaspora widely discussed in the literature, is the symbolic-ethnic diaspora. It has prevailed in modern societies ever since the last decades of the 19th century and up to the mid-20th. These societies share an ambition to constitute nations unified by culture and language, and to integrate on this basis any new group of immigrants. Here immigrants become members of the society as individuals, that is, citizens. As nationals, they are expected to primarily identify with the nation and to internalize its norms and values. They are proposed—if not imposed—'to be like others' and turn a 'new page'. They may even be invited to change their names.

Not every absorbing society shares the same enthusiasm for integrating newcomers indiscriminately, and some are more prone than others to allow a degree of pluralism and diversity, by refraining from requesting thorough cultural conformity to mainstream models (Tabory and Lazerwitz, 1983; Van den Berghe, 1978). The classic example distinguishes between American pluralism and French republicanism. In the US, as is well-acknowledged, groups are freer to retain symbols and elements of culture to mark their collective identity, while in France, in contrast, the dominant ideology insists on the urge for national uniformity and the total acceptance of the French language and '*civilisation*'. In both societies, however, the newcomers, whose social insertion primarily depends on their individual efforts, acquire the dominant culture and language, and generally tend to 'forget' their own— whether Italian, Yiddish or German. On the other hand, many ethnics do not always completely assimilate into the mainstream culture and continue to display a kind of 'symbolic' secondary allegiance. Thus, the difference between the USA and France mainly concerns the pace and scope of these processes which depend, in fact, not only on the dominant culture's attitudes but also on the groups' own velleities, as well as on demographic, political or economic circumstances. Hence, all other factors being equal, boundaries are less precise where members are scattered throughout social hierarchies, or concentrated at upper levels—than when, on the contrary, ethnics are numerous in lower classes and thus experience isolation.

In the area of language (Hechter, 1975; 1978), this syndrome means in any case that social boundaries are also far less linguistically clear-cut than in the enclave model. Giles and his colleagues (Giles et al., 1977) speak of upward convergence to designate the abandoning of ethnic languages for linguistic assimilation into society. However—and this is the upwardly divergent model—the dominant group in the social setting may then be willing to protect its distinctiveness from ethnics by increasing its linguistic assets. It does so by amplifying its use of complex linguistic patterns, or acquiring prestigious foreign languages—English, French or others—and making them markers of special status by keeping them out of reach of subordinate groups. Still quite unusual in modern settings, in some cases downwardly divergent groups may then reject subordination by struggling for the preservation of their own languages concomitantly with their 'bilingualization'.

Anyway, and contrarily to the enclave model, it is the acquisition of the national legitimate language that is the general rule in cases of symbolic-ethnic groups. Community linguistic markers mainly consist of limited registers of L1 inserted in L2, when L2 is used among ethnics (Garmadi, 1981; Myers Scotton, 1983). Confined to a secondary role, L1 is completely or partially lost, and bilingualism is most often subtractive at the benefit of the national language. This is the case even in a society more tolerant of pluralism, such as the USA, where institutions like educational or religious frameworks structure the community and convey to the public place elements of the group's cultural and linguistic legacy. This pattern reflects the individualistic orientation of the predominant mode of integration in society, and the lesser role granted to communities. In more than a few cases acculturation, which is always there, is followed by total assimilation (Myers Scotton, 1983; Bell, 1983; Beebe and Giles, 1984; Street and Giles, 1982); in many others, it is followed by partial assimilation and the profusion of 'in-between' endeavors.

Urban Italo-Americans, for instance, enjoy America's tolerance of pluralism and gather around a 'little Italy' which comprises typical restaurants and groceries, in a linguistic landscape where Italian words and expressions play a role. Yet very few third- or fourth- generation American-born Italians still know Italian beyond sparse linguistic elements. The majority has no contact with anything 'from Italy'. At the same time, when it comes to French Italians, the picture is 'the same but more' as almost all signs of Italian culture have vanished from the public's eye, following the total and rapid assimilation of the formerly thriving 'Rital' community. The notion of 'Italian' has here become just a detail of personal biographies (Faidutti-Rudolph, 1964). In these cases, the meanings of diaspora are clearly at their weakest. Groups which integrate into their respective society and see the principal aspect of their collective identity in their national label, care little for fellow in-groups elsewhere. Only those who retain some symbolic allegiance to their ethnicity and some familiarity with its legacy remain sensitive to the ethnic plight, and respond to calls of ethnic organizations.

Transnational communities

Still, as already mentioned, when it is a question of a democratic regime, ethnics may be induced to join the many actors who raise support from specific constituencies and enter the political game—even where the dominant culture condemns ethnic politics. Thus, in Jacobinian France, one finds recently arrived North African Muslims and generations-long French citizens like Corsicans who give open expression to their symbolic ethnic identities, and exploit opportunities offered by the political conjuncture. Gradually, and at first through local politics, symbolic ethnicity inserts itself in this way into the socio-political reality taking advantage of the means and resources that democracy offers whoever is capable of mobilizing a constituency.

The political success of some ethnic groups may, to be sure, awake other groups and instigate them to take part in politics in one way or another. Such processes may be powerful enough to imprint themselves in far-reaching changes of the social order. Above all, they push society toward multiculturalism; that is, toward a stage where factional exigencies are salient legitimate issues, increasing the incoherence, tension and fragmentation that the conjunction of singular exigencies implies for the polity.

As already discussed here, such developments have occurred in several modern settings during the latter decades of the 20th century, in a context also marked significantly by processes deriving from globalization. This concomitance of multiculturalization and globalization is viewed by scholars as the actual background of the third syndrome of diaspora elaborated by leading work in the field, namely, the transnational diaspora. Soysal (1994) and Baubock (1994; 1998) propose paying special attention to the outcomes of the development of the welfare state which grants benefits to residents, independent of their civil status and their social integration. These circumstances, it is strongly acknowledged, weaken the urge for immigrants to engage in thorough acculturation, let alone assimilation. On the other hand, globalization accounts for the capability of groups who still remain distinct entities in their society of adoption, to avoid discontinuing relations with relatives, family, friends and colleagues left behind or living elsewhere. The technological transformation of the three Ts—Transport, Telephone and Television—have minimized the time, meaning and cost involved in geographical distance. Last but not least, international commitments, as we already know, have made embassies and consulates of countries of origin active actors in the community life of diaspora groups who, in return, are very often ready to use their political power to lobby locally on behalf of their homeland's interests.

What is now to be derived from these new traits of modern societies is that, at the level of the private individual, the basic experience of this kind of diaspora means nothing less than 'dual homeness'. That is, the fact of having two homelands—the original and the new. Which home is then given stronger relative emphasis in the identity of individuals may, of course, vary among ethnics from class to class or from milieu to milieu among the people of the same community. The response to this question may also vary within the same diaspora, from one community to another. But none of these alter the basic 'dual-homeness' condition.

This syndrome, too, is best illuminated by studying language activity. This activity, indeed, is the best index, in our understanding, for measuring the special features of this kind of social reality. As soon as a transnational group is involved in activities that set it in relation with its original homeland or with diaspora communities elsewhere, it creates and opens a field of language activity where original vernaculars remain, or become again, pertinent. This activity may involve the circulation from diaspora communities to the original homeland and back of written, broadcast or oral messages containing significant information, political statements, ideological positions, emotional expressions or symbolic and artistic productions. As a whole, they represent a volume of communication conveyed by parochial vernaculars which are here both tools of transfer and symbols of identity. However, this does not prevent ethnics from also acquiring the languages prevailing in their actual society and use them in the endless daily speech situations which involve no ethnic aspect. In other words, ethnics experience here additive bilingualism where each language which they know is relevant to another circle of interaction.

It is in this perspective that one understands the reality of contacts between legitimate languages and vernaculars. Though the two categories of language are used in different areas of activity, they are known, retained and used by the same people, for recurring situations. This kind of intense linguistic contact, that is, a contact that takes place in the minds of individuals, thus accounts for the richness of sociolinguistic phenomena like code-switchings, borrowings and calques in both L1→L2 and L2→L1 directions. The scope of these linguistic—mainly lexical—phenomena, which appear principally in speech situations involving an ethnic dimension, may even engender genuine interlanguages as additional reflections of how far ethnics have not become just bilingual by their linguistic knowledge, but also by their living with two or more languages (Penalosa, 1981; Heller, 1988).

Russian immigrants to Israel since the late 1980s are a good illustration of this syndrome. Characterized by a high level of education and professionalization, many have found jobs that are equivalent, or almost equivalent, to their former positions (Lerner, 1993; Raday and Bunk, 1993). The group as a whole undergoes acculturation by rapidly acquiring Hebrew and initial elements of the Israeli Hebrew culture (Ben-Rafael et al., 1997). These immigrants probably come to feel more Jewish here than they did in their country of origin. Their past under a Marxist-Leninist regime explains the fact that only 10% of them are religious, and only half of them possess any knowledge of Judaism. Their aspiration to form and remain a distinct community finds expression in their political crystallization into several parties which participate on their own behalf in Israel's public life. As a rule, Russian Jews have retained ties with friends and relatives in Russia, and they also keep contact with the German or American Russian-Jewish communities which have been formed in recent years. Diasporic tourism develops, helping to consolidate this new Russian-Jewish diaspora. Estimates show that about 20% of Russian Israelis make annual trips to their home cities, and over 40% visit Russia every 2–4 years (Remennick, forthcoming).

In the realm of linguistic activity, these diasporic orientations explain why many Russian Jews in Israel are strongly attached to their original language and are determined to retain it and transmit it to the young. This aspiration also accounts for the success of Russian newspapers, magazines, cultural centers, large-scale happenings and many other cultural or social activities where the Russian language is predominant. Scores of writers continue producing works in Russian, aimed at both Russian-speaking Israelis and the Russian-speaking world. On the other hand, Russian also becomes unavoidably tainted with Hebrew, through numberless borrowings and innovations: a development that only expresses the influence of Israeli life and the 'bi-culturalization', so to speak, of Israeli Russian Jews. They themselves speak with humor about their 'Hebrew Russian', and sometimes with mixed feelings and derogatorily about their 'cultural hybridism'.

Other examples of transnational diasporas are the North African immigrants in France (Todd, 1994), in Holland or Germany, the Turks who settled in Germany and Holland, or Mexicans and Puerto Ricans in the USA. In all these cases, one finds a similar retention of the original language concomitantly with the acquisition of the legitimate language; an insertion in the new society conjunctively with activities oriented toward the original homeland and other groups of the diaspora. As a rule, original languages play an important role in these activities as the language of gatherings, festivals, celebrations and prayers. In more than a few cases, they remain the language spoken at home. This language is in permanent contact with the legitimate language and is profoundly influenced by it, leading to the creation of interlanguages like Israeli Russian, French Arabic or German Turkish. These additive bilingualisms and interlanguages express how far the people involved endeavor to maintain a dual culture as well as the intermingling of cultures.

Conclusion

In conclusion, we have recalled three major ideal-types of diaspora, as described by the literature and which are reported as prevailing syndromes of different stages of modernity. We are then able to show the essential differences that characterize these types with respect to their prevailing patterns of bilingualism (see Table 1).

Considering the linguistic patterns attached to each of these models, we may now also distinguish the major and different identity dilemmas that stand behind each of them and which, when seen side by side, indicate the nature of their differences:

- The *enclave's* major dilemma, as transpiring from its pattern of bilingualism, revolves around the question, not of the identification with the community which is taken for granted, but on the contrary, with the national society, that is, for a Polish Jew: 'how much Polish?', and for an American Indian, 'how much American?'.
- The *symbolic-ethnic group's* major identity dilemma, questions, in contrast, not the identification with the national society that is taken for granted, but with the community. That is for a French Briton, 'how much Briton?' or for an American Italian, 'how much Italian?'.
- The *transnational group's* basic identity dilemma in this kind of diaspora is how to consider the two identities: 'how much Turk *and* how much German?', or 'how much Moroccan *and* how much Belgian?'.

At this point, we must recall that by now the transnational diaspora, during these decades of the shift of centuries, is gaining an ever greater saliency. This process, most plausibly, has impacted on several groups that until recently responded to other syndromes. Beyond their own community affairs, for instance, a symbolic-ethnic diaspora such as the the Irish in the USA has become more and more concerned with, involved in, and in strong contact with, the problems of its original homeland, i.e. Ireland. This transnationalization of a symbolic-ethnic group has been influenced by the example of American Jews who recently have been perhaps the most articulated instance of transnational diaspora.

They have mobilized their power for the sake of the interests of Israel, their symbolic homeland at the same time as building up and intensifying

Table 1. Models of diaspora in different contexts

Model	Context	Sociological features	Sociolinguistic features
Enclave	Early modernity	community in margins of society; retention of contacts with diaspora	dominance of L1; L2 influences; bilingualism of brokers and elites
Ethnic group	Modernity	members integrate society individually; the group represents a second identity; selected symbols show varying commitments	community dominated by L2; L1 elements serving as markers in speech involving ethnic aspects
Transnational diaspora	Globalization	members experience dual homeness; retention of links to fellows elsewhere	L1 and L2 used in different areas; language contacts marked by code-switching, borrowings and other linguistic innovations

their community structures. Moreover, they have devoted—with greater or lesser success—an ever larger place to the study of modern Hebrew in their community educational framework. In another relevant case, in the Province of Quebec there has been renewed interest and feeling of responsibility, at least culturally and linguistically, for Francophones all over Canada, and even in the USA as far south as Louisiana's Cajun community where one finds Québecois teachers of French. On the other hand, in France itself, the transnational Muslim North African diaspora could well be a reference for many half-assimilated Jews who have recently become more active on behalf of their community and diaspora affairs. Among new related phenomena, one can even include the stronger public saliency of Catholic congregations in numerous countries, in the wake of incessant—and yet always impressive—papal mass gatherings across the world. Here, however, it is not a question of diffusing a common language but a not-less elaborated set of religious symbols and messages which also facilitate international intercommunity communication. In this sense, one may now speak of a new Catholic transnational diaspora in the making throughout the world—in secular, non-Catholic and non-Christian societies.

All in all, transnational diasporas effectively appear to represent a new phenomenon in the field of collective identity, when set in a comparative perspective with the types of diaspora that prevailed in other eras. The context of this development is the encounter of multiculturalism and globalization—that is, the socio-cultural diversification of the very societies that were the cause, by their encompassing influence, of the overwhelming trend toward uniformity prevailing throughout the contemporary world. Hence, while these societies were diffusing their languages throughout the world, other languages or vernaculars were, and still are, penetrating them, conveyed by cohorts of new immigrants whose allegiances to their new homes were not, *ipso facto*, to necessarily delete their affinity to their original homeland. In the final analysis, while different diaspora groups engender the diversity of the society which they share, it is according to their singular development that the different groups of fellow-ethnics diversify their common diaspora.

The study of the new bilingualism shows the extent, greater than ever before, in which these dynamics set the shared and the different in intimate relation.

22. ETHNICITY COSMOPOLITANIZED?
THE NEW GERMAN JEWRY

Y. Michal Bodemann

Introduction

In recent years, under the onslaught of theories of postmodernism and post-structuralism,[1] a powerful two pronged argument has impacted upon conventional approaches to the sociology of ethnicity and nation. The first of these arguments, following Fredrick Barth (1969), has insisted on the constructed, invented and imagined nature of nation and ethnos (Hobsbawm and Ranger, 1983; Anderson, 1991), whereas the second strand, largely incorporating the first, is arguing that globalization, the new media, international mass migration and travel have fundamentally transformed the nature of nation and ethnos by 'deterritorializing', 'transculturalizing', 'transnationizing' these 'ethnoscapes' into numerous diasporic and hyphenated communities (Appadurai, 1996).

With human rights superseding nation-state based international law, nation-states, it is claimed, have suffered a "political and constitutional loss of power", with national sovereignty undermined (Beck 2000a: 80, 84); it is argued, that nation states are on their "last legs" (Appadurai, 1996: 19), have been seriously weakened and in its course, ethnicities have been transformed into post-national and transnational risk communities that are affectual and can virtually be assumed or discarded at will (Beck, 2000b: 92,98). Ethnic groups, it is said, are constituted, in part, by construction of memory, memory, however, that is boundary-transcending (Beck, 2000a: 99), and these national or ethnic identities therefore appear as 'landscapes of memory' (Beck-Gernsheim, 1999). In this paper, I will briefly discuss these arguments, will sketch the development of the new, post-War Jewish community in Germany and will then ask how these new debates around nation and ethnicity can be made to apply to the case of German Jewry.

These current arguments around nation and ethnicity are by no means entirely new, however; it might indeed be argued that inherently univesalistic

---

[1] This paper should be seen as part of an ongoing dialogue with Elisabeth Beck-Gernsheim and Ulrich Beck. I wish to thank both of them for a lively interchange and stimulating discussions.

ideas about processes of globalization have been with us for some time; indeed, in terms of the world at the time, medieval Catholicism with its widespread use of Latin, Islam with Arabic, were indeed 'catholic', universalist and global movements that allowed vigorous communication between scholars and theologians throughout the world known at the time. Also, as far back as 1848, Marx and Engels arrived at a surprisingly similar diagnosis about the effects of globalization in their own time, at the onset of industrialization: The relations of capital, they wrote in a celebrated passage of the Communist Manifesto, have swept away

> all fixed, fast-frozen relations, with their train of ancient and venerable prejudices and opinions . . . (10) . . . modern industrial labour, modern subjection to capital, the same in England as in France, in America as in Germany, has stripped him of every trace of national character . . . (18) In place of the old local and national seclusion and self-sufficiency we have intercourse in every direction, universal independence of nations . . . The intellectual creations of individual nations become common property. National one-sidedness and narrowmindedness become more and more impossible, and from the numerous national and local literatures there arises a world literature. (Marx and Engels, 1959: 11)

Later on, the idea of the constructed and imagined nature of ethnos and nation began to take off from Marx' ideas as well: as part of the superstructure, ethnic and national belonging was seen by Marxists as being superstructural, largely ephemeral and a product of economic relations; moreover, in the course of the development of capitalism, the "peoples without history", as Marx and Engels saw them (Rosdolsky, 1964), presumably without independent economic bases, were to disappear and in Europe only the major *Kulturnationen* such as Germany, France and Britain would survive. Marxist theorists, then, saw ethno-national belonging fundamentally as a product of economic conditions. One of the most resolute theorists in this regard was the Belgian Trotskyist Abram Leon. In his book on the "Jewish Question" (Leon, 1970), Leon argued that the Jewish people's survival, through the vicissitudes of two millennia of Jewish history, can be explained by their presumed constant economic role in the sphere of circulation, as a stratum with a particular economic outlook and organized in ethno-national terms, as a 'people-class' therefore, whose system of ideas, religion etc. was determined by their particular economic role; in a communist society, Leon and other Marxists, including in particular Lenin, argued, very much in the dismissive mode of Marx himself, that these capitalist and pre-capitalist conditions would come to an end and consequently, ethno-national solidarities would evanesce into mere folkloristic reminiscences.

We should not forget, however, that at the height of European nationalism, no less a theorist than Max Weber himself stressed—albeit in a highly differentiated manner—the imagined/constructed elements in ethno-national belonging. Accusing Weber of being a primordialist (Appadurai, 1996: 14, 145 and passim) is thus clearly unjustified, as a quick perusal of his writings on nation and ethnos, especially in his *Economy and Society*, would amply show. In contemporary sociology and history, such distinguished Marxist oriented sociologists and historians as Eric Hobsbawm, Benedict Anderson or Edna Bonacich have, in various directions, pursued this economic reductionist approach to the phenomena of national, ethnic and racial relations; not infrequently, ethno-national identities are being viewed as entirely epiphenomenal; as feelings that can be 'whipped up' at will (Bonacich, 1980).

The turn from the 19th to the 20th century, the pinnacle of European chauvinist nationalisms was also, however, the nadir of European ethnicity; the classical example might be French and German Jews who felt nothing but unconditional patriotism for their country and/or who denigrated or even denied their Jewish heritage. Among the sociologists, Emile Durkheim in France and Georg Simmel in Germany might fit into these categories, not to speak of many Jewish socialists, Rosa Luxemburg above all, who not only rejected her Jewish heritage but as a labour leader, also considered national distinctions, such as between Germans and Poles, as largely irrelevant. It is telling, therefore, that Stalinism at first at least, persecuted the Jews not as Jews or Zionists, but as 'Cosmopolitans', well aware of many Jews' dismissal of their own ethno-national background. In the US, the earlier idea of the melting pot corresponds to that view of ethnicity as an epiphenomenon. Nationalist sentiments, on the other hand, might even be intertwined, paradoxically, especially in sectors of the educated bourgeoisie, with strands of cosmopolitanism. Max Weber, Thomas Mann, and numerous other scholars and writers, not to speak of the higher nobility throughout Europe, might at times even combine chauvinist sentiments with a cosmopolitan outlook. Nationalism and ethnic consciousness by no means must go in tandem, therefore, and any examination of the writings of Carl Schmitt who advocated an ethnically homogeneous state that distinguished clearly between friend and enemy and that required the "excretion or annihilation of heterogeneity" (Schmitt, 1979: 14).

Postmodernist positions tend to differ from these earlier cosmopolitan or de-ethnicized attitudes particularly in one regard, however: they do recognize the role of ethno-national belonging or ethnic cultures at least to some extent, but at the same time, also cast them off an absolutist pedestal: both Beck and Appadurai speak of deterritorialization and transformations of territory into symbolic spaces (Appadurai 1996: 21 ff.; Beck, 2000a: 98) or virtual communities and neighbourhoods by means of electronic mediation; Beck speaks of constant shifts between de- and re-localizations, and de- and re-nationalizations (Beck, 2000a: 98) which in turn may be based upon the emergence and "invention" of "boundary-transcending layers of memory". In the same vein Beck-Gernsheim speaks of Germans, Jews and others as 'landscapes of memory' (Beck-Gernsheim, 1999), and societies are ethnically contingent, ethnic groups being mixed together like in a salad bowl (Beck 2000a: 99). How does all that fit with one particular case, that of the Jewish minority—and its surprising revival—within the German nation-state, within Europe, and in relation to Israel and other Jewish diasporas throughout the world?

Post-war German Jewry

Within given migrant or ethnic communities, demographic fluctuations alone might sometimes reveal changes in the character of these communities and their socio-cultural, economic and political structures. This can certainly be shown for the case of post-War German Jewry. In the early post-War years, the Jewish population in Germany fluctuated heavily, from a few thousand to up to as many as 250,000 people. This was largely due to the influx of Jewish Displaced Persons who were housed in camps throughout the Western occupied zones of Germany. Subsequently, and for nearly forty years onwards, the Jewish population in West Germany began to stagnate around 25,000 to 30,000 members; of these, about 5,000 to 6,000 had settled in West Berlin, the former center of German Jewish life. Indeed, this post-war demographic stagnation did not consist in the figures alone; the entire structure of the community, its religious orientations and the role of Jews in German society itself seemed rigidly cemented by community control through authoritarian leadership and bureaucratic patronage. The appearance of such rigid authoritarianism by itself was a clear indication of the structural weakness of the community: there were an insufficient number of qualified, educated individuals who could have involved themselves in Jewish community life and who could have checked the authoritarian instincts of the few.[2]

In this climate and for most of these forty years, critical voices of particular individuals and of entire groups such as the Jüdische Gruppen, inspired by the student movement, were savagely attacked by Jewish leadership or, at best, ignored. In the GDR, despite the minute Jewish population of about 400 in the late 1980s, the situation developed on quite similar, even more

---

[2] I have described the evolution of German Jewry in more detail in Bodemann (1996a). See also especially Brenner (1997) and Burgauer (1993).

accentuated tracks. Only in the 1980s, the East German regime began to discover the Jews as a useful tool of foreign policy and of its professed anti-fascist ideology (Bodemann, 1996a: 100 ff.; Offenberg, 1998). In both East and West, this stagnation slowly began to break up in the 1980s, but only after the Wende, the collapse of the Wall, was that cast really broken.

Since 1989, total community membership in Germany has more than doubled, from less than 30,000 to over 70,000, and in reunited Berlin from under 6,000 to 11,000 in 1999. To these figures, for the case of Berlin alone, we should add an estimated six to nine thousand individuals of Jewish origin not registered with the community; for all of Germany, we would, accordingly, arrive at a figure of over 100,000 Jews and individuals of Jewish origin which, after all, is already one fifth of the figure of 1933. Indeed, some communities such as Düsseldorf today have as many members as they did in 1933.

In East and West Germany, the Jewish population stagnated demographically for almost forty years, and the organized community stagnated similarly in its entire structure. Its institutions were immobilized and turned into an empty shell of mere political representation, and the Jews let themselves be instrumentalized for political goals, in East Germany to the point of abject self renunciation. Mario Offenberg, secretary of the small neo-orthodox Congregation Adass Jisroel in Berlin has characterized this leadership poignantly as 'state-and-memorial-site Jewry'. The explanation for this development is quite straightforward. When Robert Weltsch, the German Zionist leader, returned to Berlin in 1946 for a visit, he wrote back to his friends in Palestine: "It smells of corpses here, of gas chambers and torture chambers. The remnant of Jewish settlements in Germany must be liquidated as quickly as possible. Germany is no soil for Jews."[3]

The communities at the time saw themselves largely as temporary structures, 'Liquidationsgemeinden', communities set up for the sole purpose of temporarily harbouring and caring for individuals that were to leave Germany shortly thereafter, preferably for Palestine. Few considered life in Germany as a promising future.

As a consequence, and even when that 'liquidation' did not come to pass, the Jews in Germany were bound up inside their communities in a corset of bureaucratic patronage, having to contend with, or accepting, an aging and monolithic leadership and a diminishing number of people in the younger generation. The community questioned and rejected its own legitimacy and many thought of themselves as living on 'packed suitcases'; these suitcases

---

[3] Weltsch, 1946.

were often very literally packed, even where, after some time, they were put behind a staircase and were collecting dust. Into the 1980s, Jewish authors published books such as, "This is not my country" (Fleischmann, 1982), "In the home of the henchman", "Stranger in one's own land" (Broder and Lang, 1979), and a magazine of these imaginary exiles called itself "Babylon". These Jews imagined themselves, and sometimes, in fact, might have been, exiles in the classical sense: they were sojourners, the type of strangers whom at the turn of the century, Georg Simmel, Berlin sociologist par excellence, would have termed as those who come today and leave again tomorrow, expressed here in the very metaphor of the packed suitcase.

Yet ironically, during the long and lonely journey of these Jews through post-War Germany, from re-establishing the communities at war's end to the founding of the two German states and the Cold War, from rearmament and the economic miracle, the student movement and Ostpolitik to the memory wars of the late 1970s and 1980s and to unification, a second development remained largely unnoticed: soon, the Jews in Germany, and the Jewish Displaced Persons in particular, had begun to form an armed cocoon shielding themselves against an alien and hostile world, the world of their murderers and tormentors, a world that they rejected and that rejected them. Within that cocoon, Jews married and raised children, established nursing homes and schools and a large web of personal social and economic relations and more complex communal institutional structures. It is my contention that this armed cocoon was the precondition for a renascence of Jewish life in Germany; when the cocoon began to burst in the mid-1980s, it had created the institutional preconditions for a new vitality of Jewish life beyond the stagnation of the previous forty years.

There have therefore been marked changes in the past fifteen years. Although we cannot know today whether the wheel could not be reversed tomorrow, and some of my own lingering doubt notwithstanding, I would be prepared to argue that today, German Jewry is the most dynamic Jewish diaspora in Europe and worldwide. Apart from the dramatic growth of the communities, the change is apparent, for example, in the fact that the Berlin community whose past two leaders were well over seventy years of age, is now being chaired by a 50-year old, and that one half of all 21 members of the Repräsentanz, the community council, are just around 50 years of age, and only three over 60. This youthfulness, of course, and a jump over more than an entire generation, is directly due to the ravages of the Shoah.

This abrupt generational change has also produced entirely new interpretations of one's own life and identity that, only a few years ago, would have been sharply rejected by the previous gerontocracy. These include statements such as the following, made by a university student and candidate at the last council elections two years ago:

> . . . as a Jewish community we [are at] a point where we have to look straightforward into the future, and where we can no longer look into the past. With the enormous Jewish immigration . . . great opportunities have opened up to the Jewish community of Berlin . . . Judaism can not be lived in humility, but [should be lived] in joy—not in order to defend our Jewish identity, but in order to celebrate it.

Only a smaller number of Jews in Berlin would go that far today, and turn away so radically from their past; and yet, the rupture between Jews and Germans, based upon that past, is ever more clearly being suspended, as in this statement of a younger candidate:

> The community must open itself. The fact that Berlin has changed fundamentally cannot pass us by without leaving a trace. The community cannot place itself at the margins. It must participate in the societal life of this city. It is part of this society and also has to be part of it.

We must here remember that only about ten years ago, members of even this community council were vigorously opposed to the immigration of Russian Jews to Germany. Today, on the other hand, this affirmation of Jewish life in Germany goes so far as in the case of this elderly candidate, who reminded her readers of her own fate as a former emigre, who had to live "so many years abroad . . . in a foreign country", and who is therefore concerned about a "warm acceptance of the new community members". In earlier years, it was an outright embarrassment to many Jews having to live in the land of the perpetrators; today, however, Norma Drimmer, member of the council executive, wishes that the "Jewish community may become a lively center which could take on a key function for the Jewish communities of Europe." Within these interpretations and in contrast to the priorities of previous years, the Shoah and Israel, while still being critically important, nevertheless have moved into second row.

Even in the official self presentation, this change becomes noticeable. In the post-War period, the Berlin Jewish community still had its own monthly paper, *Der Weg*, which went out of existence in the early fifties, with the beginning of the years of stagnation—although it then still appeared pro forma for some time as a page in the *Allgemeine Wochenzeitung der Juden in Deutschland*, published in Düsseldorf. Only in 1984, a small monthly bulletin, the *Kulturspiegel*, was being published once again. Five years later, this was turned into the *Berlin-Umschau*, and since the beginning of 1998, a glossy and colourful new monthly publication appeared in its place, the *jüdisches berlin*. Within 15 years, then, the community at first presented itself as a 'mirror', relating back unto itself; as the *Umschau*, it began 'looking around', taking more clearly note of its environment, and now with the new name it sees itself, in the affirmative, as a part of Berlin.

In one of its first issues, we find on the cover page a suitcase from Russia on a street in Berlin—a direct reversal of the metaphor of the packed suitcase of the earlier years: it is an arriving Jewish suitcase, not one that is about to leave the country. A few issues later, we see on the cover page a shofar blown by a young man, far above Berlin—an image inconceivable only a few years earlier. Originally, the *Kulturspiegel*'s masthead was dominated by a large sketch of the community center, as an emblem of the administration and of the Jewish social life hidden inside; later, in the *Berlin-Umschau* this emblem was shrunk substantially and now in the new *jüdisches berlin* it has moved entirely into the background, as a tiny icon. Clearly, a community that firmly sees itself as a part of Berlin stands in contradiction to a fortress, as it was seen in earlier years.

In this last decade, not only the representation of the community towards the public, but especially its inner life has been intensified in dimensions that earlier were entirely unimaginable. For example, a look at the calendar of events of fall 1997 compared to just ten years before indicates that by the fall of 1997, community events had quadrupled, concurrent with a doubling of the membership. Theatre, art and computer groups have shot up, new egalitarian forms of the religious service, folklore and tradition groups have emerged and notably, thanks to the Russian immigrants, a club of veterans of the Great Patriotic War has been set up. This development, often described as a 'renaissance', is especially due to three elements.

The most obvious one, first, is indubitably demographic, the immigration of East European Jews to Berlin and to the rest of the republic. Even if it is too early to tell today whether this is a long term development or merely a short efflorescence that will collapse without its necessary nutrients, this intensification of Jewish life is due unquestionably to a very high degree to this new immigration of largely highly trained, highly educated and motivated immigrants. The new vitality due to this immigration, of course, has not only revitalized the Jewish community alone, but is also an immense contribution to the cultural and economic life of Berlin and Germany as a whole. Indeed, the German authorities may have been unwise not to have encouraged the emigration of Russian Jews to a much greater degree and much earlier; the immense benefits of this immigration with its highly trained and motivated individuals are palpable in Germany today as is the case, albeit in entirely different dimensions, in Israel and even North America. Here was, and still is, an opportunity which the German authorities have missed.

A second reason for this renascence that should not be overlooked is the continuous public financial and, within specific limits, political support given to the Jewish community. In 1998, for example, of its 47 Million DM budget, the community receives from the City Senate and from other public sources 44 Million. These funds are earmarked especially for schools and kindergartens, money that, however, would also be made available to non-Jewish institutions; approximately 3 million Marks are raised through the community's own membership taxes. There can be no doubt, furthermore, that the Jewish community, from the question of immigration and building permits to cultural programming such as street festivals, has been enjoying the special sympathy of the Berlin Senate; even recent conflicts such as that concerning the Jewish Museum can not hide that fact. The Muslims, with well over 100,000 faithful in Berlin alone, have not received any comparable concessions. This political support is closely connected to the fact that in Germany Judeophile milieux have developed together with a wide ranging interest in Jewish culture and Judaism. How else can we explain the fact that an exhibit such as "Jüdische Lebenswelten" some years ago, an exhibit on this small ethno-religious minority, had drawn over 300,000 visitors?

A third, and very important reason for this new dynamism are the structural changes within the community—on one hand, what the historian Michael Brenner has termed the emergence of a secular, Jewishly educated stratum and on the other, within this stratum, the new role of women. The women are pushing for reforms in the area of ritual practice, they have been developing, jointly with like-minded men, egalitarian forms of religious service and have become involved ever more visibly in the various organizational spheres of the community. Here as well, today's Jewish community is markedly different from its years of stagnation when only older males determined the politics and the public life of the community. Next to the Russian immigration, nothing will affect the Jewish community as much, and enrich it as much, as this advancement of the women and of the new intellectual stratum in the public terrain of the community.

What could the contours be that are emerging from this astonishing reemergence of Berlin Jewry and of the German Jewish community at large—contours that as little as a dozen years ago were still unimaginable? Internally, the monolithic, asphyxiating control of community affairs, and largely within a culturally, if not religiously orthodox environment, have disappeared. The diverse interests and orientations, this new plurality can never again be brought under one hat as had happened in the past. The authoritarian role of former Jewish leaders such as Werner Nachmann, Heinz Galinski, or even of the late Ignatz Bubis have long since become anachronistic. The momentum is moving away from authoritarian structures towards a spectrum of leadership that is located somewhere between oligarchical and democratic rule. No doubt, in Berlin at present, Andreas Nachama is the principal, elected, representative of the community. Yet who could deny that inside and outside the community today, there are also other authoritative Jewish voices? The voices for example, of Mario Offenberg, secretary of the neo-orthodox congregation Adass Yisroel; György Konrad, president of the Akademie der Künste; Julius Schoeps, historian and director of the Moses Mendelssohn Zentrum in Potsdam; Gary Smith, director of the American Academy; Michael Blumenthal, former secretary of the treasury in the Carter administration in the US, and Director of the Jewish Museum, and now even the European office of the American Jewish Committee in Berlin are being listened to in Jewish affairs. As a natural consequence of this new Jewish normalcy in Germany, internal conflicts will increase within this multipolarity as well—but what would a vibrant Jewish community be without internal contradictions?

Towards the outside, in relation to the Berlin public, the political strength of the community, paradoxically, has been weakened on account of its current resurgence, and for two reasons. For one, by virtue of the plural differentiations and the newly competing political poles in the Jewish community, the monolithic nucleus has disappeared: with this new institutional diversity, the various Jewish representatives simply do not always share identical interests and perspectives, and for this reason as well, Jewish interests are not as effectively brought across as in the previous decade. The controversy concerning the Jüdische Museum, where the community originally could not obtain control in its very own affairs, is an example of this loss of power. In Heinz Galinski's, the community's long term leader's, time, these machinations would have been hardly imaginable.

The second reason has to do with the increasing distance from the Holocaust. The cynical remark from within the Berlin Senate that Andreas Nachama's problem is that he does not have a tattoo on his arm is quite to the point: the current generation of German politicians is no longer being impressed by references to the German past. This disappearance of a monolithic Jewish politics, however, the diffusion of power, surely does not mean that in the future, the relations of German politicians to the Jewish community will become easier. Since from now onwards, there is no longer a single Jewish representative with whom one could negotiate, it will also be more difficult to reach political agreements.

What consequences does Berlin as the new capital have for the Jewish community? It is remarkable, first of all, that the Russian-Jewish influx to Berlin coincides with the decision to move the capital from Bonn to Berlin. A Western capital without ethnic diversity as was the case with Bonn, was still conceivable, but a capital that would also want to be a metropolis and be cosmopolitan, similar to London, Paris, New York and Washington, will not be able to function without ethnic division of labour. This means, for countries in the West, that a Jewish presence here is a sine qua non.

Up until 1989, the Jewish political centers were Düsseldorf, Frankfurt, and initially Munich as well; for the small Jewish community in East Germany, it was of course East Berlin; with unification, the particular identity of the East Berlin community was extinguished. The Jewish leadership in the times of the Bonn Republic came, as a rule, from western Germany; Galinski remained the fly in the ointment from Berlin. All of this has now changed. Jewish institutions, most notably the Zentralrat offices, have returned to the historic Jewish sites in the center of Berlin, have occupied the lieux de mémoire which so far had been the locales of the small East Berlin community. With that return, however, an historically unprecedented centralization has set in that will profoundly transform Jewish life in Germany at large.

It has often been said that the memory of the Shoah in Germany is slowly coming to an end and that, in particular, the concrete to be poured for the construction of the Holocaust memorial in Berlin will extinguish this memory at last. Yet Jewish history is irrevocably inscribed into the memorial landscape of this city. This memory, with or without artificial memorials, will be perpetuated and even be strengthened as long as Berlin is capital and as long as German national identity remains an issue in some form. With today's renascence of German Jewry and its emergence out of its armoured cocoon, Jewish life in Germany might at some point again be taken for granted, by both Jews and Germans. Once this point has been reached, the distortive imaginations of Jewry by their environment may be corrected in favour of real-existing German Jewry; and only then will the dominant Jewish self perception, that of being a stranger in one's own land, finally have become a thing of the past.

In summary, then, this account of the Jewish community in Germany, largely conceptualized before the rest of this paper was written, really does not speak to the arguments of the postmodernists, and most accounts of ethnic groups at least in North America have not addressed their arguments either. How does postmodernism explain, for example, the survival of this community in its ethnic cocoon in previous decades, and its current revival and opening to the surrounding society? This makes one wonder, at the very least, how important these arguments really are in the appearances of ethnicity today; moreover, the case of the new German Jewry shows very clearly (a) that so far, the nation-state has by no means been on its 'last legs' as far as its role vis-à-vis ethnic minorities is concerned: in Germany, for example, the state very largely has defined the nature and role of the Jewish community;[4] (b) that a community's memory is always relational, and, while invented or transformed (Beck, 2000a: 99), it is local and not simply congruent with that of ethnic groups in other national contexts, nor could it be easily translated into these contexts: Dutch, or Austrian Jewry, for example, not to speak of American Jews, remember the Shoah differently from German Jewry—a 'reflexive cosmopolitanism' (Beck, 2000a) is clearly ruled out in this regard; (c) that the role and make-up of ethnic leadership is crucial to the community survival. Afro-American ethnic institutions, for example, cannot be fully understood without recognizing their leadership, with Louis Farrakhan on one hand and Jesse Jackson on the other, nor can German Jews be understood without the late Ignatz Bubis and his successor as chair of the Central Council of Jews in Germany, Paul Spiegel. Such leadership, however, and the ethnic institutions they represent, are locally constituted and cannot be translated into transnational contexts, even where they begin to form international associations such as the World Jewish Congress, the Congress of overseas Italians or an international council of aboriginal groups.

Ethnic groups and ideological labour

So far, I have provided a brief historical overview and a sketch of the Jewish community in Germany and in particular in Berlin today. How does the case of this community relate to the questions posed at the beginning? One first terminological issue should be cleared up in this regard. When I speak of an 'ethnic group' I mean that group of individuals that, in a census for example, describe themselves as belonging to that group. When I speak of an 'ethnic *community*' such as the Jewish community, I mean the entirety of actors' activities that are being realized within the institutional web established by Jews in Germany. Often, the postmodern discussions, as e.g., Appadurai, ignore the institutional structures undergirding ethnic communities and their networks.

These webs, then, should not be seen in terms of an organization chart with clear levels and hierarchies but rather as an assembly of more central and more peripheral, even partly antagonistic or rivalling, nodes that define

---

[4] This is the point made by Elisabeth Beck-Gernsheim (1999), an account including Nazism's role in the categorization and classification of racial groupings. Such classificatory policies have a crucial role in shaping ethnic identity.

themselves in Jewish terms. It may include a Jewish gay/lesbian study circle and a Lubavitch Sunday school as well as a predominantly Jewish group dealing with racism and interreligious relations in a given city. This community may not include persons of Jewish origin who may well define themselves as Jews, belonging to the Jewish ethnic group, but who are dissociated from any of these webs. This may not exclude their potential membership at a later date: they might begin to belong to it whenever they see fit to join or rejoin any part of the web of activities within the community. Beck-Gernsheim (1999) has correctly pointed to this diffuseness of the idea of ethnic belonging. This diffuseness has to do with the characteristic absence of legal charters such as established by Apartheid or the Nürnberg laws; ethnicity is not defined through passports and genealogical tables. While it is in flux at the fringes, however, in its core it is sustained by its institutions, its leaders and functionaries.

One issue, as far as that 'community' is concerned relates to the argument of the ethnic 'salad bowl'. It is readily apparent here that ethnic groups are not politically, economically and socially 'neutral' and therefore do not function according to the salad bowl principle in societies; instead, ethnic groups are very much defined by the state they find themselves in. In a recent paper, Helmuth Berking has pointed out that, in the US, for example, in the framework of affirmative action programs, "race and ethnicity related data" are being produced that, in fact, help create, or strengthen, ethnic groups (Sassen, 1999b; Berking, 2000). These ethnic groups, however—Whites as opposed to Latinos, Latinos and Asians, Asians and Afro-Americans—are categories sui generis, creations of particular nation-states such as the US and not present in these terms even in neighbouring Canada. In Israel, similarly, the two major national groups, 'Arabs' and 'Jews', have each been differentially constructed as 'Beduins', 'Palestinians' or 'Druse'; and Jews likewise have been structured in an array of diverse ethno-religious sub-groupings.

In Germany in turn, Jews and the Jewish community have had bestowed upon them privileges that differentiate this group markedly from other minority groups. In Germany, Jews are exempt from military service; in contrast to the Gypsies, (the Sinti and Roma), restitution payments to Jewish survivors of the Shoah have been more comprehensive; at a more informal level, the minute Jewish community has far greater visibility in German society than other, numerically much larger ethnic groups such as the Turks, and Jewish culture is granted much higher public and private attention— and financial support—than, for example, Turkish or Greek cultural activities. As in the US and elsewhere, each one of these ethnic groups occupies one or more distinct socio-political locations within German society.

I have described this role of minorities in states as 'ideological labour' (Bodemann, 1990): by this I mean the ideological location of ethnic minorities within given states. Let me illustrate this for the case of usury in medieval Europe: the Church forbade its faithful to be taking interest for credit. This function was taken on primarily by the Jews instead. This particular economic function, however, carried with it a distinct ideological connotation: the Jews' 'sinful', un-Christian, activity made Catholic values visible, reaffirmed the Jews' attribute as 'killers of Christ' and marked the boundaries between Christianity and its enemies. In the US, similarly, Afro-Americans are constructed as impulsive, instinct driven, violent and lazy and thus at variance with the puritanical values of white America. Their ideological labour is defined in terms of crime, and represented as such in the media, in the criminal courts and prisons where Blacks are massively overrepresented.

In Germany today on the other hand, the ideological labour assigned to, and assumed by Jews concerns their central role as guardians of two segments of German national memory: the glorious German-Jewish past, from the Bismarck era to the end of the Weimar Republic, when Germany was at the height of its political and cultural might in Europe, and the catastrophe of Nazism that destroyed it all. It would be highly unusual, for example, to have any issue related to Nazism or related to contemporary racism in Germany not being commented upon in the media by the one or other prominent Jew. It is important to see, moreover, that despite European integration, to this day, ideological labour has remained nation-state specific, dependent on particular national discourses: in France, Britain or Switzerland, ideological labour performed by Jews—as that of other minorities—is quite distinct from that performed in Germany.

In terms of ideological labour, while Turks in Germany are the representation of the total other in relation to Germanness—'oriental culture', the scarf, and Islam[5]—the ambiguous status of the Jews accentuates these ethnic boundaries: they are both 'like us', and they are strangers: 'like us', because their outward behaviour, their speech, habits and looks cast them as Germans, whereas their 'exotic' religious practices, their role as Holocaust victims or their ties to Israel cast them as the other.

---

[5] This construction of the other is nicely illustrated in the case of a cover page of Der Spiegel, 1997. This cover, a photo collage, showed, under the cover "Dangerously Alien: The Failure of Multicultural Society", a young Turkish woman holding a Turkish flag, in an ominously threatening context, together with pupils in a religious Islamic school and armed young men, obviously portraying Turks. This woman, "Yasemin K." recently won a libel suit against Der Spiegel. Far from demonstrating at a militant Turkish rally, the woman actually had demonstrated for German-Turkish reconciliation in Germany after the anti-Turkish pogrom in Solingen on 29 May 1993. See to this Süddeutsche Zeitung, 2000.

The question of diasporic public spheres

What about the idea of "transnational culturalist movements", "diasporic public spheres" (Appadurai, 1996: 147) where the idea of 'home' becomes irrelevant, and where ethnic groups without central geographic locus hover as diasporas throughout the continents? What about the idea of reflexive cosmopolitanism, de- (and re-) and de-ethnicization, of de-localization in societies and the ideal of a cosmopolitan society (Beck, 2000a)? Looking at the case of German Jewry, at first glance, much seems to speak for this range of arguments. Here was a scattering of highly heterogeneous elements—German Jews, Jews from various countries in Eastern Europe—that after the Shoah and over the years were being moulded into a Jewish community partly of its own doing, partly on account of obvious German political interests: a flourishing Jewish community would be a prime showcase for a denazified and democratic Germany.

These Jews, then, seemed de-localized and perhaps de-ethnicized as well: their home environment in Eastern Europe had been obliterated, had become a 'vanished world', and even German Jewish emigrés returned to a world that was not the world, and often were not the homes they had left when they escaped Nazi persecution. Having lost their local roots and their old ethnic networks—Jewish friends, relatives, Jewish social organizations, synagogues and in these synagogues, forms of religious service they may have been attached to from childhood, their de-ethnicization may appear to have set in even well before any of these issues had been debated. At the same time, their links with other diasporas—Jews in Palestine, in North and South America, would seem to suggest the salience of the idea of a Jewish diasporic public sphere.

All these beginnings notwithstanding, however, we can observe that this scattering of diverse Jewish elements after the war, returnees and former Displaced Persons from Poland, Hungary or Rumania gradually developed into a new, relatively homogeneous Jewish community that considered itself as such, all the internal cultural differences notwithstanding. Moreover, while virtually all of these Jews had lost what they might have called their home, and feeling in Germany as 'strangers in their own land', it only took a few years for them to construct Israel as their—however imaginary—home.[6] As with the land issue in the case of the Palestinians, (Appadurai, 1996: 21,

---

[6] Thus, the New Year's Message of the Central Council of Jews in 1950 contained the following passage: "Our first greetings for the New Year therefore go to the responsible men of our government in the holy Land, the admirable figure of President Professor Weizmann and the dynamically creative Prime Minister Ben Gurion . . . (Quoted in Bodemann, 1996a: 184).

161), the violence associated with struggles for land here and elsewhere demonstrates that it is contrary to the evidence to dismiss the territorial and home orientation of diasporas; this orientation is not merely symbolic but addresses the real, concrete territory of home: even today, not America, but Israel is the promised land.

Appadurai furthermore sees minorities within the framework of homogenized "diasporic public spheres" (Appadurai, 1996: 161) where the various diasporas, aided by modern means of communication and "increasingly mobile populations of refugees, tourists, guest workers, transnational intellectuals, scientists and illegal aliens"—Sikhs, for example, in Vancouver, London or 'Khalistan'—all are part of the same transcultural community, "unrestrained by ideas of spatial boundary and territorial sovereignty" (ibid.). Again, the case of German Jewry suggests differently. Post-War German Jewry occupied a very specific position among Jewish diaspora communities. Considered traitors for living in the land of the murderers, Jews in Germany were treated as pariahs and were largely ostracized by the rest of world Jewry; they were very much a diaspora independent of other diasporas. Even today, when much of the opprobrium has disappeared, Jews in Germany—as do Jewish communities elsewhere—have their very own issues to contend with. The majority of German Jews today, all their affection for Israel and American Jewish culture notwithstanding, are very much rooted, albeit antagonistically—within their own environment and locality. A Jewish parent in Munich, Berlin or Frankfurt might be visiting every few months their children and relatives in Tel Aviv, New York or Los Angeles and still be so deeply rooted within their network of friends back home that they would find it inconceivable ever to be moving away from Frankfurt or Munich.[7]

It has become a commonplace, moreover, to state that the Jewish diasporas and the state of Israel have become mutually estranged; notwithstanding international tourism, migration, and Jewish cultural exchange due to the new forms of communication, the realities of all of these different communities are no less diverse from one another today as they have been in the past. Recently, for example, and not for the first time, an Israeli minister suggested the dismantling of the Jewish diaspora organization per excellence—the Jewish Agency, obviously because of the diminished financial aid arriving from abroad and the ever increasing mutual incomprehension

---

[7] The commonplace story in this respect is of young German and Austrian Jews who emigrate to Israel from Germany or Austria with great aplomb and yet are quietly back a year later, to their familiar surroundings. See, for example, the fine short story by Vertlib (1999).

between the diaspora and Israel, but especially mutual incomprehension of American Jewish and Israeli mentalities (Jessen, 2000). Numerous political pronouncements, moreover, indicate how the languages of the diasporas are at odds with those of the 'homelands'. President Ezer Weizmann's disparaging comments about German Jews are being criticized as sharply by the German Jewish community as, on the other hand, American Jewish meddling in Israeli political affairs is being criticized by Israelis: the new media may have brought everyone closer together, but their political and social realities remain as far apart as ever, and each ethnic diaspora is conjugated by the realities of their own social and political environment.

Still, the role of the new media and the far greater mobility and travel opportunities today that are being addressed by Appadurai and to some extent Beck should by no means be dismissed. What the new media have indeed accomplished is a continuous infusion of new ethno-national cultural influences from abroad: re-ethnicization, yes, but not de-ethnicization. If we take the case of the Indo-Trinidadians for example, we can see how with the arrival of television and VCRs, cultural productions, mostly films produced in Bombay, have had a notable impact on the re-Indianization, and re-Hinduization of Indo-Trinidadians. Yet unquestionably, the revival of Indian ethno-national consciousness is taking place under local conditions, there is nothing like an Indian diasporic public sphere: most Indo-Trinidadians do not understand Hindi, the language of the films they are watching, and their re-Indianization is taking place in the context of, and against the hegemonic Creole-African environment and the powerful calypso and carnival culture of the island.[8]

German Jewry is a further eloquent example for this re-ethnicization due to the new mobility and the new media. From the end of the war to the beginning of the 1970s, the cultural reservoir of Jews in Germany was, of course, the legacy of pre-war German Jewry; Heinrich Heine, Albert Einstein, Sigmund Freud, Curt Weill, Max Liebermann and many others provided a legacy that also buttressed the status of the new Jewish community. Yet that legacy, at best, musealized the Jewish community, and increasingly, Israeli and North American Jewish cultural influences took hold of the community: Hebrew teachers, scholars and rabbis were recruited from abroad, youth were sent to Israeli summer camps, and Jewish cultural festivals brought in musicians and dance troupes from New York and Jerusalem.

Yet here as well, the consumption of these cultural productions have been taking place locally, and under local conditions, largely against the wider

---

[8] For a splendid account of this, see Verma (2000).

German environment, yet often with German financial support, clearly an effort by German Jews to be part of an imagined larger Jewish world community. Today, the only globalization of a diasporic consciousness in this regard could perhaps be seen in the confines of Europe: as European integration proceeds at a wide range of institutional levels, German Jewry— with considerable caveats—may also be evolving into a larger European Jewish community;[9] a feat that has not been accomplished so far by most European cultural institutions where barriers of culture, language and national egotisms still seem to predominate. Here is the only possible avenue for this ethnic community to transcend the nation state; it could only do so, however, against the background of the political, economic and possibly cultural structures of a European federation. Such a transcendence within the confines of Europe, however, is a far cry from a global diasporic public sphere.

---

[9] This case is being made most forcefully perhaps by Pinto (1999) who conceives of a European Jewry as a third balancing block between Israel and North America.

THE DECLINING ACCOUNTABILITY OF THE STATE

INTRODUCTION

Pierre Birnbaum's chapter opens Section Four by analyzing recent developments among France's '*Juifs d'Etat*'. He points out that, in the nineteenth
century, Jews became full members of the society on the basis of assimila-
tionist Jacobinism. For decades, Jews felt fully Jewish only in the closed
space of their consciousness, but in return, they gained access to the liberal
professions and public administration. For some time, however, new trends
in France's Jewry have been discernible. The major phenomenon here is
that Jews seem to illustrate a process of rebuilding communities. This is
explained by the author as expressing the Jews' experience during the Vichy
regime, the Holocaust, and the creation of Israel. Many State Jews make
now a point of being involved in Jewish affairs, while their relation with
the state has lost much of its ideological aura. In fact, their cohorts are getting fewer and fewer, and this reflects a general slackening and outmoding
of the state's image as the embodiment of republican universalism.

Ilana Silber considers similar questions from the angle of philanthropic
giving. Philanthropy tends to emerge as a sort of informal, relational process
that is apt to reflect, but also helps to mediate, the tension between social
identity and social solidarity. Philanthropic giving has long remained a marginal feature of modern societies, and only recently has there been new
interest in giving. It may be argued that this development is principally due
to the decline of the state and its impaired capacity for maintaining its commitment to welfarism. *Eva Etzioni-Halevy* turns, at this point, to the operation
of political elites. Focusing on the case of Israel, she draws attention to the
circular flow of resources among politicians, businessmen and high-ranking
officials, a state of affairs that do not accord with the exigencies of the theory
of modern democracy. Such developments, which are probably not unique
to the case of Israel—though illustrated here with particular saliency—are
indicative of the problematic character of political accountability in contemporary democratic regimes. *Denise Ferreira da Silva* unveils the shortcomings of
the modern nation-building project when applied to a heterogeneous society
like Brazil. The intensity of miscegenation in the Brazilian population made
it possible to refute the argument that whiteness is essential for achieving
modernity. It was, however, argued in response that the 'spirit' of the
Brazilian people is European, rejecting non-whites to the status of 'others
of modernity'. However, open speech about race and class has recently
enabled the black Brazilian movement to construct blackness as a global
(political) and separate signifier, undermining Brazil's pervasive national text.

23. BECOMING STATE JEWS:
FROM VISIBILITY TO DISCRETION

Pierre Birnbaum

In the nineteenth century, Jews became full fledged members of French society. As a result of the revolutionary manner of their emancipation, which was based on the Jacobin denial of collective identities, they attained the status of citizens and, as did all other citizens, gained admission to the public space without any restrictions. This entrance into modernity is unique; it occurred in no other society—neither the Anglo-Saxon democracies nor the authoritarian regimes of continental Europe. In the authoritarian countries, the Jews, kept isolated and firmly under control, retained their community organizations, traditions, and collective identity, and the rabbis their roles. On an individual level, the break from the milieu of their community of origin inspired some Jews to join in international or national forms of collective action, such as Socialism or Zionism, in the process largely turning their backs on traditional Judaism, at least at the time. In contrast, in the open society of the liberal democracies, the Jews found themselves confronting a process of assimilation, which nevertheless left them free to preserve the collective structures which could assure the transmission of their cultural and religious identity. Leaving the fold led only to assimilation and loss of identity, not to one or another form of revolution.

In France, things proceeded differently. The prevailing unitarian idea of society imposed a form of homogenization in the public space, which denied all religions, which, therefore, found themselves relegated exclusively to the private space. From that point on, the cost of revolutionary emancipation was clear, as all the great Jewish historians (Dubnow, Graetz, Baron, etc.) would observe. In a society whose public space nevertheless remained largely imbued by Catholicism, notwithstanding its more or less extreme forms of secularization, the only thing Judaism could do was to decline—adapting itself to society as a whole and shrinking into the innermost parts of individuals—who became modern Marranos, fully Jewish only in the closed space of their consciousness. Many rabbis, aware of this state of affairs, tried to draw their co-religionists' attention to the attendant dangers and to moderate their revolutionary zeal. Taking the process to its logical conclusion, Napoleon convened the Great Sanhedrin. Its debates were conducted under the leadership of his own representatives, who proved extremely firm in

their demands. They simply expected the eventual end of Judaism: the calling into question of Jewish identity, private as well as public; its submission
to general norms and laws; its assimilation, by means of exogamic marriage,
which would be imposed or, at the very least, strongly advised; and its complete mergence into the nation-state. Even if there were probably unforeseen consequences which proved advantageous to the Jewish world, the
'consistoralization' of Judaism—the establishment of the *consistoires*—at that
time was intended as a means of enabling the placement of Judaism under
state control and its eventual control by the State within society as a whole
(Anchel, 1928; Hadas-Lebel and Oliel-Grausz, 1992).

Inconspicuousness of Judaism, visibility of the Jews

From the beginning of the nineteenth century to the First World War, the
assimilation of the Jews continued apace. First the Jews of Bordeaux and
the Comtat Venaissin, then those of Alsace and Lorraine, as well as those
who had taken refuge in Paris or in the provinces following the 1870 defeat,
each group in turn entered the public space and moved away from their
former collective identity, becoming more and more discreet. In their sermons the rabbis preached respect for the law of the country (Chouraqui,
1990). Moving from Metz to Paris, the famous rabbinical seminary became
a mere shadow of its former self. Synagogues began to resemble temples or
even churches in some respects, losing their visibility. Buildings, inscriptions
and even services were inaugurated with a prayer for the Republic (or the
King), choirs with organ music were incorporated, and so on, further symbolizing the assimilation so desired by the public authorities. Things went
so far that some Jewish figures, for example, Salomon Reinach, even suggested shifting Shabbat to Sunday. The Jews, transformed into Israelites or
Hebrews, often turned their backs on their former vocations and, thanks to
the Republican meritocracy, gained access, through the *grandes écoles* (the
equivalent of the Ivy League) and the universities, to the liberal professions
and public administration. As much of the former Catholic ruling elite left
the service of the State in their rejection of the triumphant Third Republic,
the State Jews (Birnbaum, 1994), along with the Protestants, were allowed
to reach the highest pinnacles of the administration. Thousands of Jews
became captains or colonels, and some even became generals; while others
served on the Conseil d'Etat or the Cour de Cassation, or became prefects
or sub-prefects; and still others, in even greater numbers, became university professors and, in some cases, even members of the prestigious Collège
de France. Jews became members of the municipal councils, mayors, and

elected members of the lower or upper houses of parliament, sometimes even joining the government. Not only did these State Jews never convert; but most of them maintained their Jewish identity, often marrying Jewish wives, sometimes going to synagogue, taking part in the community institutions, and being buried in the presence of a rabbi.

True, they refrained from intervening as Jews in the public space. It is also true that as the end of the nineteenth century approached, their awareness of their identity seemed to fade: their religious knowledge shrank; they less often gave their children first names charged with religious symbolism; and more and more of them married Catholic or Protestant wives. Yet though profoundly assimilated in their behavior and lifestyles, they nevertheless managed to preserve a loyalty to Judaism, though it was probably less and less grounded solely in religious conviction. Thus, however remote the positivist sociologist Durkheim was from Jewish institutions, even he set out every year, in all his finery, on a lengthy journey to Epinal to take part in the Passover festivities, which were doubtless celebrated in due religious form. Furthermore, during the Dreyfus Affair, when antisemitism reared its head, large numbers of these Jews supported the pro-Dreyfus camp. Just as the peasants did not simply turn into Frenchmen, just as forms of regional awareness and multiple cultural identities continued to exist—despite the energetic actions of the 'Black Hussars' (who, we now know, were frequently tolerant of patois)—so too, even the most extreme republican assimilation did not obliterate the loyalty and memory through which religion, in one form or another, sometimes emerges (Cohen, 1992).

Captain Dreyfus can be seen as the epitome of the State Jews. A graduate of the prestigious Ecole Polytechnique, Dreyfus was appointed to the General Staff of the French Army; he was a 'devotee of the Republic' and the nation, an armed defender of the homeland. Despite the calumny he suffered, he was careful never to appear in the public arena as a Jew but simply as a citizen, a French officer. Yet he mixed socially in Jewish circles, and—something most people do not know—he even married in a religious ceremony in synagogue. Though religion no longer shaped his life, and though he had hardly any familiarity with the traditional texts and even less with Hebrew, there was a loyalty which would drive Captain Dreyfus, late in life, to join charitable Jewish institutions and, much like Durkheim, to come to the defense during World War I of immigrant Russian Jews who were being treated unfairly.

Visibility of the 'community' and inconspicuousness of State Jews

Moving in a single leap to the present day, we see that a century later things have changed considerably. Like their fellow citizens, contemporary Jews are sensitive to the process of secularization which is affecting all of society: like them, they are less apt to go to synagogue other than on major holy days; like them, too, they have been affected by revivalism—the return to a warmer, more emotional form of religion; and, like them, they do not hesitate to give public expression to their religious faith (e.g., Yom Ha Torah, etc.). The return to religion in a less institutional form, hence outside the consistoires, is striking: the desire to go back to ritual is daily more pronounced; more and more study circles are springing up; religious schools are attracting thousands of young students; entire sections of Paris and Strasbourg are taking on an indisputably Jewish religious hue, all making this return to religion highly visible (Lubavitch, etc.) (Cohen, 1993). Perhaps more than others, Jews are in the process of constructing communities, both from 'bottom up' and 'top down', furthered by the reifying eye of the public authorities and by the desire of some of their own leaders to reassert, in this new and more favorable context, their own authority over a milieu which had increasingly eluded them (Birnbaum, 1995; Becker and Wieviorka, 1998).

The return to religion, the rise of community, the assertion of Judaism in the public space, and Jews' greater visibility, which may be grounded on open dialogue with the State, which is making efforts to publicly obtain the opinion of the major faiths—all these run counter to the processes of secularization and assimilation which evolved from the French Revolution. It is undoubtedly true that some of these processes are just as prevalent in other religions, which, having been reinvented and endowed with new rituals and more user-friendly forms, even outside their traditional structures, are undergoing an increasingly striking renewal (Champion and Hervieu-Léger, 1990). This, however, does not make the Jewish break with the nineteenth century model any less impressive. Indeed, the roots of the break may lie elsewhere, and not in these social changes.

The following few pages will focus on the disintegration of the nineteenth century model of the State Jew, with an attempt to outline the causes and to consider the consequences of the disintegration.

Undoubtedly, the recent history of French Jewry weighs heavily on its future. The Vichy episode marks a turning point in the Jews' return to civil society. This episode has not effected other religions in a similar way. These religions are undergoing changes linked solely to the questionings of a society deprived of its former ideological certainties. As noted above, French Jewry has certainly been affected by the general return to religion in all forms, but Vichy, the Holocaust, and the birth of Israel confer a further dimension to the common search for a strong identity which is capable of confronting the silences and feelings of helplessness. The State's betrayal was a shock which France's State Jews found utterly unimaginable, and their unexpected abandonment was totally beyond comprehension. With the enactment of the two statutes which organized the systematic exclusion of the Jews from public life, all the Jewish government officials, who had been devoted body and soul to the State, suddenly found themselves firmly outside the public space which had constituted their entire world. The many letters which they wrote to Pétain, the head of the Vichy State, testify to their deep sense of having been let down. Through the incredible collaboration between the State and Nazi Germany, they felt, the Dreyfus Affair had been taken all the way. Excluded, pursued, deported, many State Jews suffered a tragic destiny, probably even worse than that of the other French Jews.

In the absence of research, the impact of these events on how the State Jews, both those who returned from the camps or who had managed to hide and those embarking on a public-service career for the first time, went on to fulfill their role within the State is not known. At work they mixed with their colleagues, both former and new, who had remained peacefully at their jobs, many of them compromised by having collaborated with the occupiers, at least on an administrative level, in a way which inevitably facilitated the Nazis' tasks. Nothing has emerged about these 'reunions'. Nor, unfortunately, has there been any published research on the activities of the State Jews between 1945 and the present. Hence only a few general observations will be offered here, based on an overly rapid examination of *Who's Who* (1998) and of the *Annuaire des anciens élèves de l'ENA* (1995), to which will be added some unsystematic comments about the composition of the top echelons of the contemporary Jewish community.

An initial observation can be readily offered. Whereas in the second half of the nineteenth century large numbers of State Jews made a point of regular involvement in religious or secular Jewish organizations, their modern day descendants have generally kept aloof. A century ago, there would always have been several State Jews, especially generals, conseillers d'Etat, judges, and university professors, who were regular and outspoken members in the decision making bodies of both the Consistoire and the Central Committee of the Alliance Israélite Universelle. After World War II, very few State Jews, other than René Cassin at the Alliance, made their administrative skills available to these organizations, which are responsible for managing the sometimes dramatic problems facing French Jewry. In recent times, the involvement of State Jews in these bodies has become extremely rare. In the last twenty or thirty years, the number of State Jews who have assumed decision making roles can be counted almost on the fingers of two hands. At the end of the 1960s, Robert Badinter, a university professor and lawyer, not yet part of the political echelon, and Jacques and Bernard Attali, both graduates of the prestigious ENA School of Administration and working in the senior branches of the civil service, played active roles in the leadership of the FSJU, the Fonds Social Juif Unifié, a crucial body in the running of French Jewry's social affairs, covering education and assistance to the elderly and poor. Some others, such as Conseiller d'Etat François Bernard and Prefect Kalfon, were members of the political committee of the CRIF (Conseil représentatif des Juifs de France), a body which has failed to acquire any genuine influence; but the number of such Jews is very few. Today, State Jews appear to have disappeared both from the Consistoire and the FSJU.

The State Jews who are still active are more visible in liberal institutions outside the Consistoire. It is as if the growing communitarization of the Consistoires and their increasingly pronounced Orthodoxy—which are distancing them from the Consistoire of the nineteenth century—have driven them away. This is an interesting hypothesis which remains to be examined, yet it is somewhat supported by the fact that the same State Jews who avoid the institutions of Consistoires are involved in the Central Committee of the Alliance Israélite Universelle, an organization whose roots lie in the nineteenth century and which is still firmly attached to modernity and emancipation. On this committee, David Kessler, François Bernard, Raphael Hadas-Lebel, and senior officials of the Conseil d'Etat sit alongside Robert Badinter, Simon Veil and David Goldet, the latter a member of the Cour des Comptes (France's equivalent of the Government Accounting Office), reinforcing a liberal tendency in Judaism, which sees itself as maintaining a discreet, Republican bent, not much influenced by communitarist Orthodoxy. A tiny number of these Jews also play a discreet role in specific structures which are not central to Jewish life. Examples include conseiller d'Etat Jean-François Guthman, who is in charge of the children's charity Oeuvre de secours des enfants (OSE); Joel Rochard, the chief inspector of finances, who is actively involved in the Cercle Bernard Lazare and in ASH, an organization which manages welfare housing projects; David Kessler, a Conseiller d'Etat who has headed the Mouvement Juif Libéral de France and is a member of the committee which organizes symposiums of French-speaking Jewish intellectuals; Rémy Schwartz, another Conseiller d'Etat who heads a liberal religious association in the 18th arrondissement of Paris and also organizes symposiums; and François Bernard, also a member of the Conseil d'Etat, who is on the MJLF board of directors. With the exception of Lionel Stoléro, a Polytechnique graduate and a government minister who chairs the France-Israel Chamber of Commerce and who, when he agreed to work with Valéry Giscard d'Estaing, specified that he could not come in on Saturday (Szafran, 1990: 216), and Simone Veil, who only chairs two boards devoted to the Holocaust, the presence of State Jews on Jewish bodies, whether religious or secular, is infinitesimal. Moreover, the extent to which they speak up on Jewish matters is limited, to put it mildly. Rare examples include statements by Dominique Strauss-Kahn, who did not hide her Jewish commitment in her race for parliament in Sarcelles in 1990, and Pierre Lellouche's 1994 request to Charles Pasqua, then Minister of the Interior, to change the date of the second round of cantonal elections, which had been scheduled for the first day of Passover. Leadership of Jewish organizations has shifted to professionals, physicians, lawyers, members of the liberal professions, and Polytechnique graduates who have often moved to the private sector. This change testifies to a transformation in the relationship with the State. While the State paradoxically pushes for more and more communitarization, it does so from the outside, since its quasi-institutional connections with the Jews via the ruling elites, with their multiple roles, have all but disappeared. With the end of this relative symbiosis, the Jews' relations with the State have probably been transformed, apparently strengthening a form of instrumentalization of politics, an American-style way of negotiating advantages in the name of a specific group.

This distancing is taking place at a time when the State is in considerable retreat. The State has relinquished its claim to manage social life and to be the only body to nourish and sustain the public space, and it can no longer derive its support directly from the citizens. The State's actions are becoming more modest, more complex, grounded more in incremental negotiations than in its erstwhile view of itself as an authority that relies on reason. No longer is the State the image of Republican universalism. Its borders are becoming less clear as the public and the private become inextricably intertwined; its boundaries are becoming blurred as its values come ever closer to those which drive the market. The Republic itself has lost part of its glory to civil society and to the proliferation of diverse groups. Multicultural demands also limit the State's universal claims, exacerbating the identity-based demands of the diverse groups which are seriously disputing the State's legitimacy as guarantor of the general interest—a notion which seems to be increasingly outmoded. The tearing apart of the State (Birnbaum, 1998) cannot fail to impact on the future of the State Jews, who have always associated their fate with its preeminence. In the past, they had served a State which was the symbol of the emancipatory Republic, focused on progress and reason, and responsible for bringing enlightenment to civil society to further its emancipation. Their passion for the State service arose from a social vision able to mobilize the energy of the citizens, a liberating secularism, the more or less planned management of the economy, and so on. The retreat of this State has particularly severe consequences for the State Jews, insofar as it calls into question an alliance which sprang out of the beginnings of the Third Republic, and may perhaps encourage those modern Jews who are graduating from France's *grandes écoles* to enter the world of business, communications, the liberal professions, and so on, more than they had in the past. It is true that this change is affecting all of France's elites, which appear to be less enthusiastic about making their talents available to the State. Nevertheless, the retreat of the state has special consequences for the State Jews who have for so long embodied the meeting between the State and the Jews.

Here too, unfortunately, no scientific study is available, so a few quick findings will have to suffice. An examination of the *Annuaire des anciens élèves de l'ENA* and of *Who's Who* made it possible to identify a total of some 76 former students out of around 6,000 ENA alumni—i.e., a little over 1%, corresponding roughly to the proportion of Jews in French society—with some connection to Judaism.[1] Allowance must of course be made for errors in this figure because of the name-based approach, whether of the person in question or of his or her mother or spouse. With the exception of Fabrice Reinach, who is now retired, these alumni did not include a single representative of the great, long-established dynasties of State Jews—the Hendlés, the Reinachs, and so forth. Looking through the *Who's Who*, one can similarly see that the other names—Bédarridès, Lisbonne, Valabrègue, Weiller, Berr, Lion, Mossé, Caen, Sée, Millaud, and so on—have also disappeared from public life. The State Jews who contributed so much to the functioning of the State's structures from the start of the Third Republic up to World War II are no longer present in the public space.

Is the number of these former ENA graduates, to which should be added several judges and army officers not discussed here, smaller than that of the State Jews during a more or less comparable period in the past? Their number should be far greater, given the growth in governmental structures and the expansion of government bodies during the State's years of splendor. They should also be greater in consequence of the general meritocratization of appointment to the State service. And yet this does not appear to be the case. It looks as if there are factors that have been encouraging

---

[1] In his recent thesis, Jean-Michel Eymeri (1999, Volume 3, Appendices, p. 27) found four Jews—two practicing and two non-practicing—in his sample of 74 high-ranking civil servants currently acting as aides to ministers.

the Jews of France to focus more on the liberal professions and the business world, as well as on the *grandes écoles*, such as the Polytechnique, which is now geared to the world of economics and many of whose former students, as has been noted, are apparently well represented in community organizations.

These 76 ENA alumni also appear to pay less attention to maintaining strong identity-based links. While the State Jews of the past had a highly marked endogamous tendency, their present-day counterparts are, in contrast, greatly attracted by exogamy. Unfortunately, marital information is available for only 34 of the alumni. Of these, 21 married a non-Jewish wife or husband, while only thirteen married someone with ties to Judaism. Admittedly, endogamy does not necessarily entail greater loyalty to tradition. In some cases, exogamous marriages may even, by way of compensation, trigger a marked and definite affiliation with Jewish identity. Yet, although the meaning of such indicators is tenuous, they have their uses in measuring a form of loyalty and concern about transmitting identity. These proportions show a massive reversal of trends. Under the Third Republic close to 90% of State Jews were endogamous. Not only did they regularly serve on community bodies, but they almost always chose to marry a Jewish wife. In contrast, today's State Jews are almost totally absent from community bodies and, moreover, most of them choose non-Jewish partners. On the whole, the State Jews who emigrated from North Africa following the major wave of decolonization seem to be more prone to marry out than those with an Ashkenazi Jewish background. Despite the small number of individuals in our study, it may be observed that while ten Ashkenazim married endogamously and thirteen exogamously, among the Sepharadim three married endogamously and eight exogamously. As an underlying hypothesis, can it be cautiously suggested that the Sepharadim are taking the process of assimilation further and entering the larger society, and that their rapid rise through the power structure is accompanied by a marked degree of social assimilation? Such a state of affairs would refute the oft-advanced idea that the Sepharadim constitute the bulk of those advocating returning to the religious fold and communitarization.

In contrast, those Jews who were not high-ranking government officials but belonged to the political echelons (in total, there seem to have been only sixteen ministers or members of the upper or lower Houses during the Fourth and Fifth Republics, in comparison to higher figures under the Third Republic) were more inclined to practice endogamy. Of the ten individuals for whom information is available, seven married a partner who had ties with the Jewish world, while only three made an exogamous choice. In the nineteenth century, things were different, since it was among political figures

that exogamy was most common. It is as if today, the creeping communitarization of society and the underlying ethnicization of politics (on this subject see Geisser, 1997) somewhat encourage the involvement in politics of
individuals with a stronger ethnic identity, especially since on the regional
level several Jews can be found among those political echelons which have
solid local roots.

It may also be noted that a very large number of Jewish senior government officials rapidly move on to the private sector. In this, they are acting much like all other top officials. Nevertheless, the Jews' departure from
the State nevertheless holds special meaning, because, once again, it points
to a break with—or at least a certain indifference to—the Republican State
that was for so long idealized. It may also be pointed out that while the
careers of a large number of these State Jews, like those of many of their
colleagues, at some stage involve serving as ministerial advisers, today they
gravitate to socialist ministers, while in the nineteenth century, they could
be found working only for liberal ministers, of a Gambettist or Clemenceaust
persuasion. The attraction of the Socialist Party probably derives from its
greater inclusion of its members in party life, which, by its very nature,
differs from the exclusive logic of the State.

And to conclude, it may be emphasized that it is precisely those very
rare State Jews who are concerned with the future of French Jewry who
take positions which run counter to those of their nineteenth century predecessors. In the nineteenth century, many State Jews played a not insignificant
role in establishing an exacting form of secularism to further the triumph
of the Republic's universalist values. In contrast, the rare State Jews of today
are devoting their talents, for example, as Conseil d'Etat jurists in the veils
controversy, to defending an open secularism, more tolerant of religion in
all areas, including in the public space (Birnbaum, 1998: 310 ff.). This shows
the extent to which the meaning of the meeting between the State and the
Jews has changed today, even though a State Jew like Robert Badinter is
still battling in the French Senate against the bill introducing parity between
men and women in political offices. Badinter has remained faithful to the
values of the State Jews of yesteryear, who were fiercely opposed to any
form of particularism in the public space. In this he still has as his frame
of reference the universalism of a single and indivisible Republic (*Le Monde*,
January 28, 1999).

24. THE GIFT-RELATIONSHIP IN AN ERA OF 'LOOSE' SOLIDARITIES

Ilana F. Silber

On voit comment on peut étudier, dans certains cas, le comportement humain total, la vie sociale tout entière; et on voit aussi comment cette étude concrète peut mener non seulement à une science des moeurs, à une science sociale partielle mais même à des conclusions de morale ou plutôt—pour reprendre le vieux mot—de civilité, de civisme, comme on dit maintenant.

Marcel Mauss, *Essai sur le don*, 1950: 279

Introduction

The last decade has witnessed a remarkable growth of practical and academic interest in the study of philanthropy.[1] Naturally enough, much of this body of work has focused on the United States, where so-called 'modern' philanthropy (as contrasted with more traditional and mainly religious forms of charity) has thrived into a characteristic feature of the 'American way of life' for now over a century (Bremner, 1988). Spreading now much beyond the United States, this surge of interest appears to be closely related to the impressive expansion of the so-called 'third' or 'nonprofit sector', a term commonly used to subsume the whole spectrum of nonprofit or non-governmental organizations and associations (including philanthropic foundations) usually dependent, if to varying extents, upon philanthropic donations (see McCarthy et al., 1992; Wuthnow, 1992; Salamon, 1994; Salamon and Anheier, 1996; James, 1997).[2] As such, it is also seen to correspond, like the growth of the nonprofit sector more generally, to a widespread disappointment with the welfare state (in either its liberal or socialist versions),

---

[1] The focus here is on financial philanthropy, defined as the voluntary contribution of private wealth for public purposes. Looser usages of the word also include all forms of benevolent, (non-remunerated) voluntary action for 'altruistic' or public purposes.

[2] Private giving was assessed in Salamon, Anheier et al. (1998) as averaging around 11% of all sources of nonprofit financial support in 19 countries in 1995 (and previously, 10% in seven countries in 1990), ranging from 1% (Japan) to 20% (Hungary). Such figures do not refer to the more informal forms of private giving, unmediated by any form of organization.

and to the search for new forms of relation between state and society, often centering on the notion of 'civil society'.[3]

Loaded with positive moral connotations, this notion of 'civil society' is often invoked as a sort of all-redeeming panacea, capable of healing modern societies of their many illnesses, enabling entire populations to emancipate themselves from totalitarian regimes or at least mitigate the negative, corrosive effects of large-scale state bureaucracy and market capitalism. Crucial to such a beneficient leverage, in this account, are such key features as the multiplication of non-governmental social organizations (mainly voluntary associations and social movements) and a well-developed public sphere allowing for a high level of expression, confrontation and tolerance of diverse interests and opinions.[4] Societies bearing a strong configuration of such features, it is regularly implied, will be better able to maintain democracy and combine industrial growth with social welfare, while tolerating and even encouraging cultural diversity and pluralism within a commonly acknowledged macrosocietal, legal and political framework.

The relation between philanthropy and civil society, in that perspective, may appear to be one of rather unproblematic, mutual reinforcement. Defined as the voluntary giving of private money for public causes and institutions,[5] philanthropy is commonly considered as one of the components of a healthy and vibrant civil society: the more robust the civil society, the more pronounced its citizens' practice of philanthropic giving, and vice-versa.

However, much depends on how civil society and philanthropic giving are conceived. Or more precisely, which kind or aspect of philanthropy, and which dimension or mode of civil society we have in mind. Rather than working with one general, blanket definition of each of the terms entailed, there is need to introduce sub-categories, nuances and distinctions as well as a dose of historical and cultural variability—tasks already well undertaken in the field of civil society (e.g. Taylor, 1990; Chandhoke, 1995;

---

[3] While this increase in philanthropic giving is often related to the growth of the nonprofit sector, it is not to be taken automatically as identical to it. Relatedly, neither is the study of trends in the field of philanthropy, more generally, to be equated with that of voluntarism or associationalism, under which philanthropy has tended to be overly subsumed.

[4] Some approaches also stress these as basically dependent upon a high level of individual commitment and participation, or add a well-developed market economy. These two features are more characteristic of early, eighteenth century approaches to civil society if meant positively, as 'civilizing' and benevolent forces. The inclusion of the market however is more distinctive of Marxian approaches that hold a critical, rather than positive view of civil society. See however Perez Diaz (1998b) for a non-Marxian, maximalist conception also including economic markets.

[5] As already indicated in fn. 1, I shall only focus here on the philanthropic provision of *financial* support.

Dunn and Dunn, 1996; Alexander, 1998; Hefner, 1998a), but much less so in research on philanthropy.

Philanthropy and civil society: a self-understood kinship?

To begin with, much of our current understanding of philanthropy and its importance for Western models of civil society is influenced by the example of the United States, where philanthropic giving is perceived as integral to a distinctive form of liberal, weak-state democracy. Advocates, and even more detached scholars of philanthropy have thus seen it as the embodiment of such all-American values as individualism, self-help and communal localism, endowing individuals with the right and even duty to shape the public sphere according to their specific needs and preferences, and as unhampered as possible by state interference (Payton, 1988a; 1988b). Implied in this view of American philanthropy, moreover, is the rejection of any kind of state bureaucracy imposing a standardized vision of social priorities from above and the promotion, instead, of a highly diversified and pluralistic society, where a multiplicity of public interests, institutions and social movements may coexist, as long as they find the necessary individuals or associations to sponsor it. This is a conception not limited to right-wing conservatives, but shared, significantly, by people on many different points of the political spectrum, including those closer to an American variant of 'socialism' (see Magat, 1994).[6]

In the European model, by contrast,[7] civil society has developed to a large extent in distinction from and even against a relatively 'strong' state. Within that context, and even when other aspects of civil society (such as social and political movements) were otherwise thriving strongly, philanthropic giving (be it by individuals, institutions or corporations) has long remained a relatively weak and marginal feature (Clough, 1960). Only recently, has there been a novel interest and a recognizable quantitative growth in giving, both private and corporate, at times even actively encouraged by the state. This is the case for instance in France where the state, since the 1980s, has been actively involved in legalizing and encouraging corporate sponsorship and private foundations—after having practically

---

[6] Moreover, even the relatively 'weak' American state has been shown to have played, and to still play a favorable, rather than antagonistic role in the development and sponsoring of voluntary organizations (Salamon, 1987; Skocpol, 1997).
[7] There are of course important variations among European countries, which I cannot delve into here. Increasing attention to heterogeneity even applies to the United States (Wolpert, 1995; Schneider, 1996).

outlawed the latter since the 18th century (Archambault, Boumendil and Tsyboula, 1999). France also offers the opportunity to observe what in American terms looks like a rather bizarre and paradoxical type of philanthropic giving: voluntary donations to, and incorporation of non-autonomous foundations under the umbrella of, large state-approved 'public foundations' (fondations reconnues d'utilité publiques) or public institutions, partly subsidized, as well as often partly managed and supervised by the state (Archambault, Boumendil, Tsyboula, 1999).

If only from this very rough and quick comparison of the American and European context, it should be clear that not only are there very different patterns or modes of civil society, but also that the role played by philanthropy in such diverse contexts can very much vary. Moreover, it is crucial to remember that philanthropic giving is not limited to modern liberal democracies but can also be found, and even thrive, in authoritarian regimes, such as Tsarist Russia, colonial and post-colonial Latin America or China, that is, in contexts where civil society is considered to be relatively weak or quasi-absent.

Compounding the complexity, philanthropy itself is a highly differentiated and diversified phenomenon. There are thus many important distinctions to be made between the philanthropic giving of individuals, foundations or corporations; and within each of these categories, between many further sub-categories,[8] resulting in a broad and expanding range of motivations and modes of operation. It is thus not too surprising that two studies that recently tried to assess the political impact of foundations in the United States, have specifically converged on the conclusion that the world of foundations is far from homogeneous, and in fact displays a wide range of moral and political orientations (Nagai, Lerner and Rothman, 1994; Sealander, 1997).

Such differentiated conclusions lead us far beyond simply distinguishing, as often done hitherto, between 'traditional' charity and 'modern' philanthropy or between liberal vs. non-liberal philanthropy (Riley, 1992). Because much more nuanced, they also tend to undermine the standard Marxian critique of foundations, in particular, that virulently attacks them for defending the interests, and contributing to the political hegemony, of American big business and capitalism (e.g. Arnove, 1980; Fisher, 1983). Similarly, it also mitigates other types of critiques, not necessarily all of Marxian or 'leftist' inspiration, that oppose what is seen as philanthropy's tendencies to elitism and lack of accountability. Surfacing time and again to this very day, such attacks often tend to focus on foundations (actually responsible for only

---

[8] E.g. donations while alive; bequests; planned giving; self-initiated or sollicited; family, community or corporate foundations; demand-oriented vs. donor-oriented etc.

about 5%–6% of all philanthropic giving in the United States),[9] and to promote an overly simplified perception of the very institutions they criticize.[10] Yet they do clearly contribute to defeating the idea of a simply positive, all beneficent philanthropy and of a 'natural', mutually supportive relation between it and such other positively loaded notions as democracy and civil society.

Civil society itself, however, is increasingly recognized as entailing internal tensions, dilemmas and paradoxes of its own. One of the most obvious problems it confronts is that of over-fragmentation, even explosion into a chaotic magma of divisive interest groups, cultural particularisms or newer transnational 'cosmopolitan' forms of networks and associations, leading to the loss of all unitary, local or 'national' solidary frameworks. Philanthropy itself is certainly not immune to such trends, already spawning discussions of the entailed dilemmas and implications in widely diverse political regimes and cultural constellations (e.g. London, 1991; Dinello, 1998; Juergensmeyer and McMahon, 1998). The point is, for now, that the precise way in which philanthropy intertwines with the internal tensions and contradictions of civil society at large—at times counteracting, at times feeding or even amplifying them—may greatly vary. This opens a wide field of comparative investigation, which I cannot enter into here.[11] The question that I wish to raise here, rather, is whether it is possible to identify any generic features of philanthropic giving that may help better understand, precisely, both its expanding scope and its protean expression in the context of late-twentieth century, turn of the millenium civil societies.

Philanthropy and civility

Notwithstanding the diversity that has just been suggested above, there have been signs of a significant growth in philanthropic giving, and increased interest in the practical implications of such growth, in many countries. One common way of accounting for that growth is simply that philanthropy,

---

[9] Even though this figure seems to have now slightly risen due to the multiplicity of foundations and the recent establishment of a few mega-foundations, it does not go beyond 8%.

[10] This was already suggested in the 1984 Fisher-Bulmer debate and again in Karl and Katz (1987). One major issue in this regard was that of the weight to be given to the founding donors' motivations vs. a more differentiated account of the various actors involved in the foundations' operation—as a key to the latter's policy and broader political implications.

[11] Although there has been a welcome increase of interest in the comparative, cross-cultural analysis of the nonprofit sector (James, 1989; McCarthy et al., 1992; Wuthnow, 1992), it has not much discussed philanthropy more specifically. See however, focusing on foundations, Anheier and Toepler, 1999.

together with the whole range of non-profit or non-governmental associations it contributes to finance, helps to fulfill certain needs that neither market nor state can or should fully provide for.[12]

One problem with such a conception, also often suggested to explain the growth of the nonprofit sector at large, is that there is much evidence of increasing interpenetration and blurring of boundaries, and of both competition and cooperation, between the three sectors—market, state, and nonprofit and philanthropic institutions—in the delivery of services or so-called 'provision of social needs' (Gidron, Kramer and Salamon, 1992; Billis 1993; Salamon, 1993).[13] The active part often played by the state in the development, sponsoring and even operation of voluntary organizations more generally has already been amply shown, in the American context at least (Salamon, 1987; Skocpol 1997). Moreover, there is much evidence of mutual borrowing of methods and criteria of efficiency between the three sectors, threatening their distinctive 'logic' in general. For better or for worse (and here the opinions vary),[14] there is thus no clear basis to expect a zero-sum relation between needs or functions filled by either market or state on the one hand, and philanthropic processes and institutions on the other.

Another problem with this emphasis on the alternative provision for social needs is that it often combines with an overly organizational conception of civil society, as rooted in organizations and institutions displaying significant autonomy from the state while engaged in activities of public interest. This organizational-institutional bias is true even of approaches that bring into relief the often forgotten, spontaneous and fragile aspects of what seem to be highly bureaucratized institutions (Ahrne, 1998). And it also applies to more macro-institutional approaches that see civil society as a distinctive systemic configuration encompassing not only voluntary organizations but also economic markets, as well as legal and state institutions, even when also giving a part to such ideological dimensions as people's feeling of commitment to a specific community—in this macro-institutional configuration (Perez Diaz, 1998b).

---

[12] As such, it is well-equipped to help in the key political task awaiting civil society.

[13] Another problem worth mentioning is the functionalist overtones of a focus on social needs (as already known and defined) that will, somehow, find a solution in case the state refuses or is unable to solve them. Also, it is not at all self-evident that philanthropic giving is best understood as a form of 'mutual support and exchange'.

[14] Promoting the idea of synergy, i.e. cooperation and mutual reinforcement of NPOs and the state, see Evans, 1997. Opposing the penetration of commercial criteria and discourse into the world of philanthropy, see Godbout, 1997. Developing a general theoretical rationale for a positive rather than oppositionary or reactive relation between civil society and the state, see Chandhoke, 1995; Barber, 1999.

While the organizational and institutional dimension is important, it tends to overshadow the part of such less formalized forces as social relationships and processes of interaction, as well as the agency of individuals. Greater sensitivity to relational processes and individual agency, however, is now called for in the wake of approaches stressing not organizations, but the public sphere as the litmus test of civil society and the arena of distinctive symbolic and discursive dynamics (e.g. Habermas, 1989; Alexander, 1998).[15] Most relevant for our own purposes, in this regard, is the more systematic elaboration of a relational mode of analysis now taking place in the context of approaches addressing the public sphere as the arena, more specifically, for the symbolic constitution, negotiation and contention of personal and collective identities (see especially Somers, 1994; 1999; Calhoun, 1995a: 193–230; Donati, 1995).

Focusing on philanthropy, I submit, has the important advantage of shifting the focus of attention, precisely, to such more individualized and symbolic-relational aspects of civil society—of which it also becomes a distinctive, if as yet underexplored and undertheorized, symptom. Civil society indeed, or preferably phrased in a less reifying fashion, the nature and degree of 'civility' of any extant society at a specific point in time, is not only a matter of organizations, institutions, or even associations. As has been already well suggested in discussions of the closely related idea of 'democratic civility', organizations and associations may as well favor or hamper 'civility', depending on which values and modes of participation they happen to identify with and promote; and even when themselves 'civilly-oriented', they can very well remain a segmentary phenomenon that does not automatically scale up into a broader 'civil' political culture at the macrosocietal level (Hefner, 1998a). The precise position of the state, moreover, should be seen as an empirical and variable, rather than definitional or principled, matter. New attention has been paid in fact to manifold patterns of mutual cooperation and synergetic reinforcement, rather than only tension and opposition, between NPOs or any voluntary civic initiatives and the state (Putnam et al., 1993; Evans, 1997) as well as to the positive role of the state as possibly integral, rather than external, to civil society (Chandhoke, 1995; Barber, 1999).

This is also why, at any rate, civility can never be reduced to the so-called 'third' or 'nonprofit sector'. Rather, 'civility' is helpful in connoting

---

[15] This could be shown across widely differing approaches to the public sphere, be it as the privileged arena of rational communication (à la Habermas) for some; or of a distinctive form of symbolic categories and discourse in a neo-Durkheimian fashion for others also crucial (in yet another—neo-functionalist—variant), to the differentiation and boundary-work of civil society as a sphere vis-à-vis other social spheres (Alexander, 1998).

a certain type of relation or interaction between individual citizens and other individual citizens or groups, in and *via* the 'public sphere': a type of relation that is voluntary, or at least uncoerced, while mindful of not only one's own private, personal or particularistic interests but also of those of others *and* even more distinctively, of the collective at large.

Who are the 'others', or in other words, how large is the 'collective at large' may vary according to whether one adopts a weaker or stronger, or more conflictual vs. more solidary view of civil society. Entailed in such relations, in any case, is neither the need to sacrifice oneself, nor just the idea or ideal of being 'nice', 'decent' or at least 'civilized' to each other (although it is also that). A voluntary interaction between two or more individuals or groups meant to benefit only themselves in particular—as may be the case in many instances of 'clientelism', but is also true of many so-called 'self-help', voluntary associations—would thus not be sufficient in itself to satisfy the requirements of stronger conceptions of 'civility' as just defined even if it is commonly taken as an important dimension of 'civil society'. And of course even less, were this interaction consciously designed as utterly oblivious of or even harmful to the collective at large.

Necessary to civility, in the 'stronger' view, is rather an ingredient of uncoerced participation in the creation, sustaining or transformation of public goods, or any aspect of a broader public sphere, potentially open to more—and ideally, all—citizens beyond those actively involved in that mutually beneficial voluntary interaction. This also means that limiting oneself to an active form of self-help by promoting one's own interests or the interests of the immediate, 'primordial' or 'elective' group one belongs, or has chosen to identify with, is not 'civil' enough, even were it to entail a high level of participation in the public sphere and of care not to harm any one else's interests in the process.

Quintessential to the ideal of a 'civility', therefore, is a form of social relationship displaying a combination of private and public interests such that it may enable participants to both stay within and yet also reach out beyond their own immediate and particular 'community of participation', however concretely defined.[16] Like the ideal of civil society (or even democratic civility) itself, at any rate, the notion of civility as outlined above is of course more of an ideal blueprint than the description of actual, observable patterns of interaction. Yet as such, it can also be used typologically and analytically as a way of further assessing the nature and role of philanthropic giving in the context of concretely diverse and 'imperfect' civil societies.

---

[16] See Shils (1991) for a closely related conception of the 'virtue' of civil society.

Modern philanthropy: a symbolic-relational perspective

It is precisely from the point of view of these symbolic-relational aspects of 'civility', that I wish now to approach modern philanthropy. In so doing, and in more ways than I can convey here for reasons of space, I extend an avenue of analysis that was already inaugurated more than twenty years ago by the French historian Paul Veyne in his monumental historical sociological study of 'evergetic' giving in the context of the Greek cities of Late Antiquity (Veyne, 1976).

Not unlike Greek 'evergetic giving' (pace Veyne's own vigorous denial of any possible revival of a similar pattern in modern societies),[17] modern philanthropic giving is perhaps best understood as rooted in the urge for the expression of one's personal identity, at the same time as it is also a deeply relational practice, having to do with the imagined interaction between oneself and an often abstract group of others in and through the public sphere.

Obviously enough, however, there are major historical and 'contextual' differences, which would deserve a much more detailed and systematic discussion. But perhaps above all, the current field of possible personal and collective identities and combinations thereof, and of their mode of expression in the public sphere, is a much more complex and fluid one than that of the Greek city-state. Relatedly, philanthropy is much less clearly geared than Greek 'evergetism' was to a unified and consensual definition of the civic, public good. In other words, it is much less 'civic', but perhaps (at least potentially, if not always de facto) more 'civil', in the sense developed above. This also means that it is not primarily characterized, as it was indeed in the Greek model, by the direct, relatively spontaneous or at least self-initiated contributions of private wealth by individuals to the 'city as a whole', to the collective, societal public good.

Rather, philanthropy in the current context is to be seen as part and parcel of what Craig Calhoun sees as the workings of large-scale integration under conditions of increasing proliferation of indirect relationships—i.e. relationships mediated by information technology, bureaucratic organizations,

---

[17] Veyne indeed ridicules the utopian desire of some (including Mauss) to revive 'evergetism' in modern society. In his view, modern societies could make room for philanthropic donations in the framework of sub-groups and 'clubs' type of associations (associationalism, incidentally, which he stresses as also a thriving feature of the Graeco-Roman world of Late Antiquity), but not in the public sphere itself (as in the Greek case), where modern societies give preference to the state, and do not tolerate the penetration of private interests and preferences. Veyne's stance, however, seems to stem from his deeper knowledge of the European, and especially French, than American context, and his limited cognizance of American philanthropy, partly due, no doubt, to the quasi-absence of academic literature on the topic at the time he wrote *Bread and Circus*.

and more or less self-regulating systems such as markets—and of imagined communities, i.e. communities that are the result of people's capacity to conceive of themselves as members of very large collectivities linked primarily by common identities but minimally by networks of directly interpersonal relationships. (Calhoun, 1991).

In such a context, philanthropy may range from operating in the mode of secondary relationships (as when contributing to a local nonprofit organization) still entailing partly face-to-face relationships, but more functionally specialized than primary relationships; or tertiary relationships (as in the case of contributing to a cause through the mediation of a distant organization) that entail less accessible, relatively formal and abstract relationships, but still maintain the possibility in principle to bring the parties to more direct interaction; or perhaps even quaternary relationships, as when one of the parties (for example the recipients of aid through foundations hiding their original sources of funding) is kept systematically unaware of the existence of the relationship.

Significantly enough, philanthropy in this highly indirect and mediated context does not necessarily follow the model of the bureaucratized, anonymous gift to strangers which Richard Tittmus famously derived from his study of blood donations (Tittmus, 1970). Though, it is this model that Tittmus propounded as paradigmatic of the type of giving increasingly needed and expected to spread in modern societies where one finds so many 'communities of strangers'—a point I have already discussed more fully somewhere else (Silber, 1999).[18] Neither does it fulfill the expectations of Rudolf Stichweh, who saw a state of 'benign indifference' as increasingly constitutive of our everyday experience of other persons as neither friends nor strangers, but rather something in between (Stichweh, 1997).

Beyond the undeniably and increasingly impersonal, anonymous and bureaucratized nature of modern giving, and despite it, philanthropy actually often retains very significant aspects of personalization, and even a lasting interpenetration of gifts and personal identities. To begin with, the amount of philanthropic giving and choice of a recipient are very much matters of personal commitment, taste and identification. Modern giving is characterized by a much stronger element of individual choice, and by a much greater range of options as to what to give and to whom, than could

---

[18] Our stress here is on the symbolic constitution of donor's identity through gift-relationships, however it is not utterly alien to Pitirim Sorokin's idea of 'creative altruism', which Tittmus adopts, and according to which individuals reach a better fulfillment and definition of themselves through others (Tittmus, 1970).

possibly be contained by Tittmus' highly mediated, anonymous giving to strangers. This also means that a much heightened importance is given to personal taste, commitment, and involvement with the choice and management of one's giving. Thus far from becoming detached from the gift, the identity of the donor does seem to leave its imprint and remain attached to the gift, which often becomes a vehicle for that identity and a mechanism for its self-definition and expression.[19]

In fact, a major feature of current philanthropy is precisely the contempt for anonymous, impersonal giving, and the search of many actual or potential philanthropists for enhanced personal involvement or as it is often called, 'partnership' with the cause and the organization sponsored. Unlike the previous and accepted tendency to give 'with no strings attached', new formulas are now trying to allow for ongoing communication and greater symmetry between donors and recipients, while also avoiding total donor control over the recipient organization's goals and activities.

All this, however, does not necessarily mean that philanthropic donations are only oriented to the self in the sense of solely giving expression to the donor's emotional and expressive needs (or so-called 'structure of preferences'), and are not at all other- or public oriented. Rather, philanthropic giving in current context is better seen as very much in tune with a new form of reflexive, self-referential individualism which far from automatically leading to atomized utilitarian selves, may paradoxically facilitate personality ideals that also contain the perception of an emotional commitment towards significant others and essential moral orientations towards generalization and collective responsibility (Berking, 1999: 151 esp.).

The generalizing or collective orientation entailed, however, may greatly vary. Like all non-selfish behavior perhaps, its object may be either an individual, a group, or a moral or abstract ideal. Systematic monitoring of philanthropic giving across countries is still too much in its infancy to provide us with rich evidence, statistical or else, on that score. With regard to the 'civility' of the gift-relationship entailed, more specifically, the important point would seem to be the nature of the group involved; be it a sub-group of which the donor is a member; another sub-group or sub-sector (e.g. ethnic, religious, professional) within a broader collective; or as in the ancient Greek pattern briefly alluded to above, that broader collective itself; or a group, or groups, outside it; or even more universally, mankind at large.

---

[19] Money does allow the recipient, however, a much greater range of potential freedom in adapting the gift to his own, rather than the donor's, personal needs, or passing money on to someone else. See Zelizer, 1994.

Significantly in this regard, there is by now increasing evidence that individual giving is not only shaped by totally idiosyncratic tastes and preferences, but also by the religious, ethnic or even economic and professional group to which they belong or (the distinction is important) with whom they choose to identify, thus providing individuals with basic frameworks of participation and sources of identity (Schervish, 1997). Some of it is simply due to the realities of fund-raising, often operating through informal if very effective networks of personal relationships: wealthy individuals often give in answer to the personal petition of close professional peers, business partners, or even friends (Galaskiewicz, 1985). Further defeating the idea of a fully impersonal and anonymous giving, is that fact that much giving is done within very localized, communal frameworks where donors and recipients know each other quite well, or can easily, if they want to, get to know and meet face to face. In fact, trends show a decrease in trans-local giving and increased giving to local, communal goals and institutions (Wolpert, 1995), reinforcing the probability and weight of such informal and personalized networks of interaction.

Finally, one has to recall that all the great first American foundations were after all, family foundations, bearing the name and otherwise perpetuating a certain family tradition and identity. Far from disappearing, family foundations (of all sizes) have since thrived and multiplied. Even when not through the vehicle of such family foundations, innumerable donations are made with the double intent not only to contribute to a specific cause or organization, but also somehow to perpetuate the memory of a (usually deceased) close relative.

These strong 'primordial' and identity-related aspects of philanthropic giving should not be taken to mean that it simply operates as a direct outcome of extant, given identity. Rather, it appears to be a way of forging, consolidating or changing one's identity, of expressing or resolving tension between collective identities, or even opting out from identities in a world where identities are not fixed, but ever-evolving, fluid and contested. In all such ways, we are very far from the Tittmus-like picture of a wholly impersonal and anonymous modern philanthropic giving. And we are definitely closer to Veyne's analysis of the 'evergetic' gift as the symbolic-relational vector of one's civic persona and participation in the public sphere. Reformulated to suit the present, much more variegated and contested context, philanthropic giving emerges as one of the most significant and flexible vehicles for the symbolic expression, constitution and communication of otherwise unstable and volatile personal and collective identities.

Admittedly, it is only in a very minor part of the whole spectrum of possible, protean gift-combinations that we may still find the type of profoundly localized and hierarchical symbolic relation between wealthy donors and their audience *via* one common and unitary 'public sphere', that was nurtured by the ideological and institutional structures of the Greek polis of Late Antiquity. More typically, and raising once again the issue of 'civility', the symbolic dynamics of philanthropic giving tend now rather to proceed through its contribution to the ongoing constitution of a highly dispersed and localized sphere of 'public', or more often and more precisely, 'semi-public' goods and institutions.

'Semi-public' refers here to the fact that donors often give to institutions they themselves enjoy the use of, or that they intend a specific group of citizens, rather than all citizens, to use. Donations, in the process, become commonly addressed to specific groups, sectors or even professions. This is evident, for example, in those forms of grant-making where the recipient is selected, as a rule, as member or representative of a certain social group or category, carefully assessed in terms of whatever criteria (socio-economic, ethnic, intellectual, religious, artistic, etc.) are deemed important by the individual donor or donating organization. This categorial-collective orientation should not be taken for granted; it goes against the grain, for example, of Andrew Carnegie's early 'heroic' philosophy of giving, which sought instead to identify and sponsor individuals, rather than groups, of outstanding potential. The categories entailed, moreover, are not primarily economic. It is significant in this respect that donations to institutions serving the 'poor' are an only minor aspect of modern philanthropy, amounting at the very most to 25% of all philanthropic giving in the United States, a fact that nourishes many of its staunchest critics (e.g. Odendahl, 1990). More significant it would seem are professional and sectorial (e.g. welfare, medical, academic, artistic) and cultural (e.g. ethnic; regional) social categories. Much of modern philanthropic giving, in fact, may be seen as giving across professional groups or sectors, as when citizens made wealthy by profession (such as businessmen, lawyers, doctors) financially sponsor other professions (e.g. artists, doctors, scholars, scientists etc.).

One implication of the symbolic-relational perspective developed here is that, far from an exclusive focus on donors, there is therefore need to further explore the relation between donor and recipient, and even the entire chain of interaction between solicitor, donor, and recipient. Significantly, a number of studies in the field of fund-raising and philanthropic giving have started to direct the attention precisely to such more comprehensive social-relational aspects (e.g. Ostrander and Schervish, 1990). Both scholars and practitioners thus now recognize that an overly exclusive focus on donors tends to ignore the ways in which recipients actively take part in defining what goes on in the world of philanthropy, ways in which recipients are agents in creating philantropic institutions and relations (Ostrander and Schervish, 1990: 670).

This does not mean that the relation is or has to be fully symmetric and equal, and some scholars of philanthropy are now in fact systematically developing the idea of philanthropy as an asymmetric, essentially donor-led relation. More generally, however, combining attention both to donors and recipients and to the various agents and organizations mediating the relation on each side has generated a rich typology of possible philanthropic and fund-raising strategies, varying in number of parameters, such as the involvement, contact and communication between the two parties or sides, the kind of specific knowledge each has or tries to obtain about the other, or the relative priority given by the two parties to what donors want in comparison to what recipients need.[20] Increasing usage of the Internet at all steps of the philanthropic process appears to further increase, rather than diminish, the range of possible strategies, by cutting across national boundaries world-wide, and thus quickly multiplying the range of possible elective international connections between individuals, groups, causes and identities *via* philanthropic gift-relationships.

One important feature common to those multiple forms of philanthropic giving, at any rate, is that it does not necessarily require donors to love, sacrifice themselves to, or totally identify with those people, groups, organizations or abstract causes which they choose to sponsor. Moreover, the gift never needs be governed by only one set of motivations. On the contrary, the same practical act of giving may correspond to any one or a combination, however paradoxical, of precise motivations. This was, to my mind, already a central insight of Marcel Mauss' classic essay on the gift (Mauss, 1950), and was deployed again and again by Veyne as a leading theme in his treatment of Greek 'evergetism'. Putting this idea to work in the context we are discussing here, gifts do not need to be utterly 'disinterested' in order to be philanthropically 'civil'. But neither does this mean that disinterestedness is beyond the pale. Following T. Vandevelde's useful distinctions, there is no reason why not to expect philanthropic gifts, like gifts more generally, to range from mainly strategic to purely altruistic, expressive of an already existing identity or social relation, symbolic in establishing or constituting novel identities and relations, or agonistic, i.e. challenging

---

[20] There are also important distinctions to be brought into both the donor's and recipient's philanthropic 'strategies' (see Schervish, 1997).

entailed identities and relations. Or in other words, to richly vary in the precise nature and degree of their 'civility'.

Conclusion

Philanthropy emerges thus as a sort of informal, relational process that is apt to reflect, but also helps to mediate, the tension between social identity and social solidarity in the new so-called 'culture of difference', typically triggering new links between identities and solidarities, new forms of societal (vs. state) citizenship (Donati, 1995). Philanthropy fits well indeed with the idea of newer modes of citizenship, not only capable of "reconciling collective goals and self-management practices, solidarity and identity issues," but also intermingling "particular and universal symbolics, individual and collective identities, private and public interests in a relational rather than an oppositional way . . . as the poles of continuous trade-off and interaction" (Donati, 1995: 305 ff.).

As such, philanthropic giving refreshingly corrects both theories that focus on the capacity of the state or intermediary institutional frameworks to provide for solidarity, and those that grant that role to shared norms and values. In that sense, Marshall Sahlins' interpretation of Mauss' *Essai sur le Don* as a counter-Hobbesian answer to the problem of social conflict through the gift touched on an important nerve : "If friends make gifts, gifts make friends. Thus do primitive people transcend the Hobbesian chaos" (Sahlins, 1972: 142). But of course, one needs now to allow, as perhaps 'primitive people' already did to some extent, for many degrees and modes of 'friendship'. Further consideration of philanthropy's symbolic and relational dynamics, moreover, may help us move away from an overly 'hot' and effervescent Durkheimian model of solidarity, and find ways of conceptualizing solidarity that bear better affinity to the workings of modern civil societies. After all, we are reminded,

> civility . . . is a cool concept. It does not require us to like those whom we deal with civilly, and as such it contrasts strongly with the warmth of communal, religious and national enthusiasms (Bryant, 1993: 399).

It is this same relative and of course variable 'coolness' that makes philanthropy able to play a growing part in the making and unmaking of 'connective' (rather than either merely 'communicative'—à la Habermas—or utterly 'solidary') processes in late-twentieth liberal democracies. Contributing perhaps to the search for new ways of theorizing current forms of sociality, this notion of 'connective' process may be a way of pointing to weaker, or looser notions of solidarity than traditionally extant. Talking of connective processes, in this perspective, means still making allowance for the capacity, even the urge, of individuals to forge some form of meaningful, dialogical connection with 'others'—be these only mildly significant 'others'—while being neither merely selfish and interested, nor altogether altruistic. It is only in such terms that gift-analysis may lead us again, as Mauss already intimated long ago in the closing sentences of his famous essay, to not only "a partial social science but even to conclusions of morality, or rather, to adopt once more the old word, of 'civility' . . ." (Mauss, 1990: 83).[21]

---

[21] Indicative of interesting swings in semantics, Mauss then adds: ". . . or 'civics' as it is called nowadays." I have slightly modified the translation, replacing here "moral conclusions" by "conclusions of morality".

25. THE ELITE CONNECTION IN ISRAEL

Eva Etzioni-Halevy

Israel is distinguished from other Western-style democracies by an especially close 'elite connection'. This finds expression in a circular or reciprocal flow of resources between them, including money and other material resources, appointments and promotions, irregular types of influence, as well as political support and legitimation. This connection is especially prominent with respect to the political elite on the one hand, and the business, administrative and military elites, on the other hand. Over the years there have been various changes and developments, but there has been no fundamental transformation of this system, which has prevailed since the establishment of the state (and even before), until the present. Throughout this period, it has had adverse effects on the quality of Israeli democracy, which still persist today.

The elite connection and the quality of democracy

This thesis is elaborated in the framework of a democratic-elite theoretical perspective, presented in the wake of the theories of Max Weber;[1] Gaetano Mosca;[2] Joseph Schumpeter;[3] and Raymond Aron,[4] by this author.[5] An elite is defined as a relatively small group of people that wields inordinate power and influence. In contemporary society, we can identify several elites, including the political elite (the government, members of parliament and various high-ranking politicians within political parties); the business elite (the owners and managers of large-scale economic enterprises); the administrative elite (holders of top positions in the state administration)[6] and the military elite (the holders of top positions in the military and security forces). Since the armed and security forces are part of the state apparatus, the military elite may be considered as a special branch of the administrative elite.

---

[1] Weber, 1947; 1968a.
[2] Mosca, 1939.
[3] Schumpeter, 1994.
[4] Aron, 1968b.
[5] Etzioni-Halevy, 1985; 1993b; 1997a.
[6] Etzioni-Halevy, 1993a; 1997b.

The most central tenet of democratic elite theory is that democracy requires a certain distancing, or relative autonomy, of elites, and that, conversely, a close elite connection forms a threat if not to the essence, at least to the quality of democracy. Democracy includes, at the very least, free competitive elections by universal suffrage and basic civil liberties. These are the basic criteria that distinguish a democratic—from a non-democratic regime. Beyond this, however, there are qualitative differences between democracies. According to some observers such as Buckhart and Lewis-Beck,[7] this quality may be assessed by the degree to which elections are meaningful, as well as fair. Elections are meaningful when those elected hold the power to govern not only formally, but also in actual practice. That is to say, when the real power is in fact vested in those who are elected, rather than in others, who are not. And elections are fair when they are based on fair electoral campaigns. That is, they cannot be manipulated, for instance, by government politicians' handing out state resources and benefits to individuals, in return for political/electoral support. In the democratic state as it has actually taken shape, only the government, as holder of political power, is elected. By contrast, other elites hold power without being elected. A high quality of democracy thus requires that the power of non-elected elites be under the control of the elected government. Any elite power which is exempt from government control thus detracts from the quality of democracy.

A high quality of democracy also requires, however, that elections be fair, and not subject to manipulation by the government. Yet, this is precisely what happens when the other elites are closely connected, or even subordinated, to the government. For in this case, government politicians may use the resources of those other elites to enhance their own power and, in particular, they may use those other elites' resources as an instrument of electoral manipulation so as to gain re-election and perpetuate their power. Such manipulation may take place, for instance, when government politicians gain material resources from the business elite, which they use in their electoral campaigns. And in return, they provide those business magnates with various benefits for their corporations and businesses, or accord them undue influence in the shaping of policy. Electoral manipulation may also take place when the members of the government use the administrative elite as a channel for handing out irregular benefits to people, with the aim of gaining their electoral support. And in return for their collaboration in this electoral manipulation, they provide the obliging administrators with appointments and promotions in the state bureaucracy. Finally, manipulation may

---

[7] Buckhart and Lewis-Beck, 1994.

occur when the government uses the military elite as a source of legitimation for its policies, so as to gain political support from the public, as over the opposition. And in return, they reward the high-ranking officers with appointments and promotions, or accord them undue influence in the policy process.

A close connection of the political elite with the business, administrative and military elites thus makes inroads into the fairness of elections, and thereby detracts from the quality of democracy. In short, what is optimal for the quality of democracy is a balance, which includes a degree of subordination of the three other elites to the elected political/government elite, while also preserving a distance between them. The optimum for the quality of democracy thus is, *that these elites be separate but unequal.* This, however, is not what has happened in Israel over the years, where these elites have been anything but separate.

The political-business elite connection in Israel

One facet of the elite connection is that between the political and the business elites. Business magnates provide politicians with money for their campaigns, and government politicians award the captains of business state-controlled benefits for their enterprises, and/or behind-the-scenes access in the shaping of policy. Such an exchange is not uncommon in Western-style democracies. In the United States, business contributions to political parties and candidates, with the expectation that such favors will be reciprocated, are a matter of daily routine, and this is the case in many other democracies as well. But in Israel the connection between the political and the business elites has been especially close because of the pervasive control which the government has had over the economy. Hence, in this country the connection has developed its own patterns, which in some respects resemble, and in some respects differ from, those in other democracies. The patterns have changed over the years, but the exchange system itself has been maintained.

The roots of the system

The origins of the system are to be found in the pre-state Yishuv era. Almost from the beginning, the budding Jewish community in Palestine developed a powerful public-sector economy, mainly under the auspices of the Histadrut. Although established as a federation of labor, the Histadrut was much more than that. In view of the harsh conditions prevailing at the time, it assumed the task of providing employment opportunities for workers, by setting up its own economic enterprises. Eventually, these became some of the largest and most powerful economic corporations in the country. The Histadrut was also a party-connected body, in which the Ahdut Ha'avoda (Unity of Labor) Party, which later became Mapai (the Israel Labor Party), dominated. Consequently, the people appointed to top positions in the Histadrut corporations were this party's faithful, and they saw to it that most positions in their enterprises were allocated to party members and supporters. Once appointed, all these people had an interest in perpetuating this party's power, in order to ensure their own positions and promotions. Hence they and their families could be relied on to vote for the party in Histadrut elections. They also tended to support the Labor party in the elections to the authority of self-government, established by the Jewish community under British Mandatory rule. And the same pattern was retained in the elections after the establishment of the state in 1948. For many years, then, the chiefs of the Histadrut enterprises acted as what came to be known as the party's 'vote contractors'. The pre-state era also saw the development of a private sector economy, whose size exceeded that of the public one. Although there were some large private entrepreneurs, they frequently required loans and other economic aid from the authority of self-government. This authority was in charge of large-scale economic resources, accruing mostly from contributions of Jews in the diaspora, and by stipulating conditions for such aid, they gained considerable control over the private sector economy as well, a pattern that was perpetuated after statehood.

The beginning of the state era

With the establishment of the state, the government assumed the task of planning the economy and intervening in all its aspects. This was done, in the first place, through the swelling public sector economy. Apart from the Histadrut conglomerates, this sector now included corporations attached to the Jewish Agency, as well as government corporations, including those engaged in arms production. Overall, the share of this sector in the economy encompassed over 40 percent of the GNP. Relatively speaking, it became one of the largest in the world; particularly, its size exceeded that in other democratic countries. The public sector formed an especially favorable site for the link between political and economic leaders. The heads of public sector corporations were appointed by political leaders. Hence they were the politicians' party faithful and committed to furthering their interests, which in many respects coincided with their own. They furthered those, by seeing to it that jobs and positions in their enterprises went first and foremost to party members and sympathizers, who then had an additional motivation to support the party at the ballot box.

The government also gained greater control over the private sector economy than is customary in other Western-style democracies. As far back as the 1950s, the government began using its resources to encourage private investment. It did so, while giving preferential treatment to some areas of economic activity over others. It also gave preferential treatment to investors who had personal-political ties to the government. Thus, the private sector economic elite was not only smaller, but also more dependent on the government than is customary in most Western democracies.

The perpetuation of the system

Up until 1977 the Labor Party was the chief party in power and had most of the appointments in the public sector economy at its disposal. After the 1977 change of government, the Histadrut enterprises (which still accounted for some 30 percent of the GNP) remained under the control of the Labor Party. But appointments in the other public sector corporations became the patronage of the Likud and, later on, of whatever government was in office at the time. In this manner, both major parties, Labor and the Likud, utilized appointments to economic elite positions—and the elite connection growing out of these—in their favor. Research on this topic by Mash[8] demonstrates, that not only the chairpersons and managers, but also the members of those corporations' directorial boards were frequently political appointees. Consequently, politicians used the heads and senior appointees in these corporations as their representatives. These representatives no longer allocated virtually all jobs in their corporations to the party faithful. Still, the above research showed that they could be relied upon to procure such jobs whenever the ministers who had appointed them required openings for their protégés. These were usually party activists, who in one way or another had assisted, or could be expected to assist, the ministers and their factions and parties in their electoral campaigns.

In 1979 the Likud government announced its adoption of a privatization policy. In practice, however, privatization proceeded at a sluggish pace. The size of the government sector (some ten percent of the GNP) was not extraordinarily large. The picture was different, however, when taking the entire public sector into account. In 1991 this sector still employed more than half of the country's workforce, and encompassed more than half of its business activity.

In addition, the Likud government perpetuated its connection with the elite of private business as well, by maintaining its control over the private sector economy. In accordance with its ideology, it initiated some steps of

---

[8] Mash, 1999.

liberalization, and towards the end of the 1980s it withdrew its direct control
of the financial market. However, government control of the economy was
perpetuated through a combination of general encumbrances (high taxes,
tight regulations and restrictions), interlaced with particular and selective
favors (grants, tax and other exemptions and subsidies). In this manner, government politicians (in conjunction with senior bureaucrats) had a major
impact on the fate of private sector enterprises. This made it profitable for
entrepreneurs to maintain close links with government politicians. During
the years in which the Likud was in government, business people who required favors from government ministries, were expected to, and did, recipro-
cate by making large scale monetary contributions to the Likud. The State
Comptroller's Report of 1990[9] states that from many large scale contributions to the Likud there emanated a heavy smell of suspicion that they were
nothing but investments. These assisted the Likud in financing its organizational and electoral activities, with the aid of which it could then enlarge
its support among the public.

According to research on the Likud Party by Moshkovitch, before the
1988 election, some prominent business people made contributions in particular to the election campaign fund of a candidate expected to become
the Minister of Housing. They did so in the hope that, in the event of his
actually gaining this portfolio, they would be favored in the award of contracts for housing projects. Their aim was to gain such contracts, without
having to participate in tenders, and without having to meet the restrictive
criteria normally set out by the ministry in such tenders. And, indeed, according to the State Comptroller's Report of 1991,[10] under the subsequent Likud
government, the Housing Ministry granted large numbers of contracts for
housing projects without tenders, and without regard to pertinent criteria
and standards. Moreover, many of the people who obtained such contracts
had some affinity to the Likud, and some were special confidants of the
Minister for Housing.

We may learn something on the dimensions of the system during those
years—with respect to both the Likud and Labor—from a research project
on this topic by Brill[11] based on interviews with knowledgeable informants
among members of the Knesset. By the testimony of one such informant,
the mutual dependence between politicians and business was to the extent
of "an osmosis that impairs the entire tissue of public-political life in Israel."

---

[9] State Comptroller's Report no. 40, Jerusalem: 1990.
[10] State Comptroller's Report no. 41, Jerusalem: 1991.
[11] This was a research project carried out by a student, Siomi Brill, under my supervision, in the framework of a seminar paper at Bar-Ilan University, in the early 1990s.

Another Knesset member clarified that politicians "assist business people, and those offer politicians [a variety of] enticements. This pattern has been perfected in recent years. They are quite attached to each other."

Recent developments

In recent years the Histadrut sector economy has remained connected to the Labor Party and thus, during 1992–6, when Labor was in power, to the government. But the Histadrut was weakened, and sold off many of its enterprises. In fact, in recent years, it has been nothing but a shadow of its former self. Also, recently, the trend toward privatization gained more momentum. The previously mentioned research by Mash shows that, once an enterprise has been privatized, political appointments in it cease. In private sector enterprises though, the political-business elite connection still persists, via the previously mentioned system of mutual favors.

The recent labor years

After Labor (under Prime Minister Yitzhak Rabin) came to power, private-sector business magnates still made contributions to politicians' campaign funds, in the hope of gaining advantages for their businesses in return. Thus, an erstwhile senior official in the Rabin administration was recently charged in court with having handed out special favors to business people who had made large scale contributions to a senior politician's election campaign. In return for such contributions, he allegedly convinced the planning commission for housing to enable those contractors to build a project in the center of Jerusalem, under extraordinarily favorable conditions, far in excess of what is usually permitted. Thus, he allegedly ensured irregular profits for them, to the tune of hundreds of millions of dollars. So far, the erstwhile senior official has not denied the charges, but has merely claimed that all was done with the Prime Minister's knowledge and consent.

The recent likud years

The situation did not change during 1996–9, when the Likud once more returned to power. The previously mentioned research on the Likud by Moshkovitch shows, that at that time, too, business people tended to extend financial support to the electoral funds of those candidates who stood a good chance of obtaining ministerial positions in the event of the party's gaining office. Especially prominent in this respect was the Likud politician who had previously been the Housing Minister, who during those years became the Minister for Infrastructure. In the framework of this position, he had considerable influence on state-owned land allocation, and accord-

ing to press reports, he saw to it that special benefits in this respect went
to his personal and political allies. During those years, although the Labor
Party was out of office, it nonetheless gained a large amount of financial
support from the business elite. The Labor candidate for the position of
Prime Minister, Ehud Barak, and his political allies set up an entire voluntary network of educational projects for children and adults in poorer
neighborhoods and localities. They did so with the aim of gaining widespread electoral support—for both the candidate and his party—in those
areas. These projects were financed largely by business magnates. Although
there is no precise information on what these contributors hoped to gain
by means of their contributions, it stands to reason that they expected to
gain something. A large proportion of business people in Israel are Labor
supporters, and it is possible that their aim was simply to oust the Likud
and bring Labor to power, on the assumption that it would invigorate the
peace process, and that this is generally good for business. But it is not
inconceivable that some of them, at least, hoped to gain more tangible
benefits as well.

Our businessmen abroad

An interesting variation of the political-business elite connection has become
especially prominent in recent years. This takes the form of top-ranking
politicians gaining large-scale financial support from highly affluent Jewish
business people abroad. These people generally have little to gain from such
contributions for their own businesses. But their aim is to gain a foothold
in the Israeli policy process, and to exert an influence on it in line with
their ideological preferences. A few such phenomenally rich right-wing business people from abroad extended large-scale aid to Binyamin Netanyahu's
election campaign. In return, they gained some influence on Israel's settlement policy, particularly in East Jerusalem, where two new Jewish neighborhoods are now in the process of being settled. In the previously mentioned
research project by Moshkovitch, Likud leaders interviewed by the researcher
testified, that the 1996 opening of a tunnel in East Jerusalem, which led to
widespread Arab unrest in which fifteen Israelis were killed, was carried out
in response to pressure from a billionaire living abroad, who served as one
of Netanyahu's financiers in his election campaign. The previous Labor
Party candidate, Shimon Peres, also had some overseas Jewish business people who were his staunch political and financial supporters, and so does the
present Labor Party leader, Ehud Barak. It remains to be seen what, if anything, these business people will gain in policy-access, in return for their
contributions.

The political-business elite connection: the bottom line

This link has been based on an exchange between the two elites, whereby each provides the other with precisely those resources which it has in abundance, and the other lacks. In previous years, when the public sector economy was especially large and prominent, it took place in particular in this sector. In recent years, as the public sector has been weakened through the enfeeblement of the Histadrut and through privatization, the center of gravity of this elite connection has moved to the private sector. Importantly, the system itself has been maintained, and in recent years has acquired a markedly anti-democratic manifestation: it has led to the interference of Jewish business magnates from abroad, in the shaping of Israeli policies.

The political-administrative elite connection in Israel

Another instance of the elite connection in Israel is that between the government and administrative elites, based on political appointments and promotions in the administration. This leads to the connivance of the administrators in the allocation of benefits to the public, with the purpose of gaining political support for those politicians and parties who are responsible for their appointments. For mandarins, who owe their appointments and promotions to government political leaders, besides being their political supporters to begin with, are also under an obligation to them. Moreover, once appointed, they are still dependent on these politicians for maintaining their positions, and also for their subsequent promotions. Hence they may be relied upon to serve their patrons' interests, by collaborating in their political manipulations for electoral purposes. Mostly, such manipulation involves no outright electoral bribery. Rather, the system is one of "cast thy bread upon the waters, for in the next election thou shall find it."

Unlike in the United States, where political appointments at the top of the civil service are the official practice, in Israel, appointments and promotions, even at the top of the bureaucracy, are (with a very few exceptions), formally non-partisan, and dependent solely on merit. Hence they are to be effected following advertisement of the positions. In fact, however, this formally meritocratic procedure is frequently circumvented.

Unlike in the United States, where political appointees in the bureaucracy leave their positions when their political sponsors are voted out of office, bureaucrats in Israel have tenure and cannot be dismissed. When their political patrons lose an election, though, they are frequently displaced from their key positions, and pushed to the margins. While they retain their salaries, they are deprived of their power, which reinforces their motivation to do their utmost for the re-election of the government party that sponsored them, even if this entails illicit distribution of funds or the equivalent, as has frequently been the case.

The roots of the system

The roots of the system are to be found in the pre-state era. Specifically, they originate in the authority of self-government set up by the budding Jewish community, under British Mandatory rule. This authority's bureaucracy had no entry by merit, and appointments in it were made by the party-key: all parties that cooperated with it were allocated positions according to their electoral size. Since this bureaucracy was party-political, it was also involved in the allocation of large-scale funds (most of which came from Jews in the Diaspora) to parties and party-connected bodies. This created the 'pillarization' of parties, that sought to bind supporters to themselves by impressive networks of banks, housing construction companies, loan societies, economic concerns, employment and health services and the like. And the people who relied on the parties as supporting pillars throughout their life cycles, also bestowed on them their allegiance and their votes. The largest party was the Labor Party—Mapai—which held hegemony in the authority, and obtained the largest chunk of administrative positions. Hence it was able to secure the largest funds for itself and the bodies connected with it, including the Histadrut. But other parties benefited as well. These included the other labor parties, the religious parties, and the right wing liberal parties. Only one party, the Revisionist Party, did not participate in the arrangement.

The beginning of the state era

With the establishment of the state in 1948, the newly created state administration largely perpetuated the patterns it inherited from its predecessor. In 1959 a new law was enacted, and subsequently new civil service regulations came into effect, which were designed to mould the new bureaucracy according to the British blueprint. Henceforward, positions were to be advertised, and candidates were to be selected solely by merit. Nonetheless, senior appointments, and a large part of the more junior ones, remained party-political. In the 1960s, almost one third of the senior appointments were made without prior advertising of the positions. Also, advertisements for vacancies were frequently 'tailor-made'[12] so as to fit the qualifications of

---

[12] Werner, 1999.

candidates who had been pre-selected on the basis of their political affiliations. This made it possible for the pillarization of parties to continue, and for patronage to serve as an enticement for political backing. The first years of statehood saw a mass immigration in which the country's population was tripled within a few years. The new immigrants were absorbed by various Histadrut and party-linked institutions: housing corporations, labor exchanges, banks and the like. This enabled the parties to tie the new immigrants to themselves, through the provision of jobs and other economic aid. The horn of plenty was, once again, mainly in the hands of Mapai, and to a lesser extent in the hands of its allied labor parties. Since it was the chief party in power, it had under its control a major part of the state administration, and of the state administration-controlled economic resources. But when the religious parties participated in the government coalition, they also obtained their share. The ultra-orthodox party Agudat Israel left the coalition in the early 1950s, but the National Religious Party (NRP) (previously the Mizrahi and Hapoel Hamizrahi parties) was Mapai's almost constant coalition partner. It had several ministries under its control, and used them—and the resources under their charge—to channel funds to various institutions connected to it, and to hand out jobs and financial aid to actual and potential supporters. Thus, party-linked but state-financed institutions still provided people's necessities, in return for their support.

The perpetuation of the system

In the 1970s the politicization of the state bureaucracy was curbed to some extent, but in 1977, when the right-wing Likud Party came to power, this led once more to the connection of the administration to politics. While they were in opposition, the Likud leaders had vociferously criticized the practice. Indeed, at the beginning of the Likud era, party-political appointments in the state administration declined. Gradually, however, the practice was reinstated. The religious parties were especially successful in this respect. While the Labor Alignment Party (previously Mapai) and the Likud had changed places in government, the religious parties were the coalition partners of both sides. The NRP remained in the coalition, Agudat Israel rejoined it, and newly created religious parties, in particular the ultra-orthodox Shomrei Torah Sfaradim (Shas), followed suit. A tradition developed, whereby certain ministries (such as those of the Interior and of Religious Affairs) remained almost permanently in the religious parties' domain, and appointments in these ministries gave preference to those parties' supporters, as a matter of course. In this manner, the system was perpetuated into the 1980s, and into the beginning of the 1990s. According to the State

Comptroller's Reports for the years 1989 and 1990,[13] at that time political appointments were still widespread in all parts and all ranks of the state administration. Sometimes appointments were made without advertisement of the positions. At other times, formally correct procedures were observed, but candidates were in fact selected on the basis of their political connections. Furthermore, promotions of political appointees proceeded at a faster pace than those of other appointees.

All this was reflected in the manner in which state resources were distributed to the public. In the 1970s, when political appointments in the civil service declined to some extent, and the administrative elite gained a degree of autonomy from politics, the handing out of benefits by political criteria abated as well. These years were characterized by a process in which political parties were depillarized. Various spheres of activity, which had previously been in the hands of parties and the Histadrut, were transferred to government departments which, by then, were less politicized than they had been in the past. Thus various goods and services (such as benefits for housing) were now meted out to the public by criteria of need and entitlement, rather than by partisan considerations. Under Likud rule, however, the renewed subjugation of the administrative elite to politics was reflected in a new pattern of partisan allocation of funds, which came to be known as 'special' funding. By this pattern, institutions linked mainly to the religious parties were the chief beneficiaries.

The flow of 'special' funds

Part of these 'special' funds were channeled from the Ministry of the Interior to local authorities, and therefrom to party-connected institutions and associations. During the years in which the ministry was in the hands of the NRP, funds were channeled to institutions connected to that party. In more recent years, when this ministry was under the aegis of Shas, the bodies linked to that party became the main beneficiaries. By the testimony of the State Comptroller's Report of 1991[14] such political funding reached unprecedented dimensions at that time. The allocation of another part of such 'special' funds was anchored in coalition agreements. These were agreements whereby the religious parties joined the government coalition, in return for 'special' allocations to their institutions and associations. In this, they were similar to funds that went through local authorities, except that in this case, other ministries were involved, particularly those of Education, and Religious

---

[13] State Comptroller's Reports no. 39 and 40, Jerusalem: 1989 and 1990.
[14] State Comptroller's Report no. 41, Jerusalem: 1991.

Affairs. In both cases, the funds were allocated, first and foremost, to religious educational institutions and other religious associations. The organizations that benefited were chiefly those connected to the ultra-orthodox parties Agudat Israel, which later became Yahadut Hatorah (Torah Jewry), and Shas. They included kindergartens, primary and secondary schools and colleges of higher religious education, as well as ritual baths, synagogues and more.

We may learn something about the dimensions of such funding from the testimony of Uzi Bar-Am who for a short time was Minister for Religious Affairs in the Labor Government, elected in 1992. According to his testimony,[15] on assuming office he found that out of the ministry's budget of 800 million shekels, 500 million had gone to party-linked religious bodies. To this must be added the funds that accrued to party-connected religious educational institutions through the Ministry of Education. All in all, in 1992, some 600 million shekels in 'special' funds went to religious party-allied organizations and associations. As far back as 1982, the Director-General of the Interior Ministry published rules and guidelines whereby the distribution of funds through local authorities by political criteria was to be curbed. Also, in 1983, the Knesset passed a resolution, whereby 'special' funds were to be allocated solely by objective criteria. Accordingly, the Ministry of Religious Affairs drew up regulations whereby, to qualify for 'special' funding, an educational institution must have at least 25 registered students, and the absence of more than a quarter of these at the time of an inspection would lead to the cessation of payments. This, however, is not what happened in practice. According to the State Comptrollers' Reports for 1984 and 1985,[16] the Ministries continued to disregard even the most elementary rules of fund allocation. Some of the students of the funded institutions were registered simultaneously in different institutions. Checks on the number of students who actually attended the institutions were rare; when they took place, in some cases, as many as 60 percent of the registered students were absent. In spite of this, no steps were taken to penalize such institutions.

The allocations were designed to entice the many beneficiaries of these institutions and associations—directors, teachers, administrators, other employees, religious functionaries, students and their families, clients and parishioners—to support the party, from whose generosity they benefited. This is evident from the fact that children in politically funded educational institutions enjoyed better conditions than pupils in other institutions. Children in

[15] Reported in *Ha'aretz*, 28 December 1992.
[16] State Comptroller's Report nos. 34 and 35, Jerusalem: 1984 and 1985.

the Shas-sponsored educational system (unlike children in regular schools) received hot meals, and were kept in school for longer hours. Students in religious colleges (unlike university students) paid no tuition, unmarried ones obtained free boarding, and married ones drew monthly allowances.

Since the various beneficiaries of the party-linked bodies could continue to gain those benefits only if the party's electoral power enabled it to take charge of the ministry once more after the election, it was in their interest to increase this party's electoral success. The overall number of students in the 'special' educational institutions numbered tens of thousands of students, who all had parents and any number of siblings and other family members. Hence, the electoral support the parties sponsoring such institutions could hope for, was not inconsiderable. A major explanation for the willingness of civil servants to serve as an intermediary for the flow of political funds may be found in the party-politicization of the bureaucracy. Had this not been the case, senior administrators would have been likely to follow the clear-cut rules that prohibited the practice. Only the political allegiance of these administrators to the ministers and their parties explains their willingness to act according to their instructions, even when these contravened the rules laid down by their own ministries.

Moreover, had the funds indeed been allocated according to the rules which called for objective criteria of need and entitlement, they would have lost their 'special' status. Thus they would have continued to flow even without the parties' patronage. Therefore, they could no longer have served to tie supporters to the parties. Indeed, it is precisely the *absence* of proper criteria that made 'special' funding contingent on the sponsoring party's electoral success, and consequent political clout. So, only the irregularity of funding could motivate the beneficiaries to extend their electoral support to the party, in order to ensure the continuation of the funding. And it is precisely such irregularity, which an independent bureaucratic elite, acting according to objective, rather than political, criteria could have prevented.

Recent developments

From 1994 to 1996, when Labor was in office, some attempts were made to reform the civil service, but to no avail. A special committee set up by the then Civil Service Commissioner recommended that political appointments be confined to national policy positions and to the level of director-general only. Ministers would appoint small staffs of aides, but these would come and go with their ministers. However, these recommendations were not implemented. Especially with the subsequent changeover of government in 1996, the depoliticization of the civil service was halted, and the goal of redefining the relationship between the political and the administrative elites was frustrated.[17] Subsequently, the Civil Service Commissioner was replaced, and the Civil Service Commission was transferred from the Ministry of Finance to the Prime Minister's Office. This was a step toward the further subordination of the administrative- to the political elite. More recently, top administrative appointments have remained political. Senior officials have remained loyal not only to their party, but also to the factions and ministers responsible for their appointments. Thus, the state administration has remained highly responsive to the politicians in charge.[18] Moreover, political appointments have not been confined to this level. According to the testimony of a senior aide to the late Prime Minister Yitzhak Rabin[19] even recently political appointments have encompassed thousands of jobs at all levels. This has been most clearly evident in the ministries allocated to the religious parties, but it has by no means been confined to them. In the Ministry of Communications, which from 1996 to 1999 was in the hands of the Likud, dozens of Likud activists were appointed. In addition, the Minister for Communications was in charge of various statutory bodies, such as the post office, and the telephone company. Here, too, political appointments abounded. And this will probably continue.

From 'special' funding to 'special' criteria

In view of this, it is not surprising that the bureaucracy is still being used for the flow of patronage. In 1992 the Knesset passed a law that officially abolished 'special' funding. The law provided that, henceforward, state allocation of funds through the various ministries would not be made to individual bodies, but would be executed in accordance with objective, equitable criteria, to be set up by these ministries. It soon became apparent that this attempt to transform the system failed as well. The law's provision to set up criteria for fund allocations was upheld, but the criteria were manipulated to suit the convenience of politicians. Indeed, institutions and associations that were previously politically funded now drew even larger funds.[20] Thus, 'special' funding, has been replaced by 'special' criteria, which serve the same purpose. The situation did not remain static over the years. During 1992–6, when Labor was in office, the NRP did not join the coalition. Thus it lost the Ministries of Education and Religious Affairs—that had frequently

---

[17] Galnoor et al., 1998.
[18] Galnoor et al., 1998.
[19] Haber, 1998.
[20] De-Hartuch, 1998.

been in its domain—and the flow of funds appertaining thereto. The ultra-orthodox parties Yahadut Hatorah and Shas did not join the government coalition either, but they demanded—and obtained—additional funds for their institutions whenever an important issue came up for a vote in the Knesset, for which the government required their support.

With the advent of the Likud government in 1996, the religious parties once more joined the government, and the flow of funds to their institutions flourished. As before, the channeling of funds was effected through the ministries of which the religious parties were in charge, chiefly the Ministries of Education, Religious Affairs, and Labor & Welfare. And, as before, this was done with the connivance of the politically appointed civil servants. The system has not only been partisan, but frequently has verged on corruption or beyond. The State Comptroller's Report of 1995[21] again revealed that the institutions and associations which obtained political funding were not held accountable on how they spent the funds. Several of them existed on paper only, and could not be located at their registered addresses. Some of them obtained funds from more than one ministry at one and the same time. The State Comptroller's Report further revealed that the same practice that had been previously followed under the Likud government was also being followed under the Labor Government. Towards the end of Labor's term of office some reforms were initiated,[22] but in 1996 when the Likud once more came to power, the previous trends again gained momentum; some 181,000 students (and their families) benefited from them.

The machinations of the system

How does the system work? Usually it is the minister who issues the instructions for the allocations. The allocations are made by committees composed of the ministry's auditor general, legal adviser and senior officials, almost all of whom are the minister's appointees and political allies. There are no independent bodies that effectively oversee the allocations. Formally, the Registrar of Associations is in charge of doing so. In fact, he is incapable of carrying out the task, because of understaffing and lack of powers of enforcement. The State Comptroller's Office, because of its small staff, can do no more than examine a few of the thousands of bodies that obtain political funding each year. In practice, the only authority that can hold the funded organizations accountable for the manner in which they operate (or fail to operate), and for the manner in which they spend the funds

---

[21] State Comptroller's Report no. 45, Jerusalem: 1995.
[22] Werner, 1999: 142.

allocated to them, is the same ministry whose senior civil servants made the allocations in the first place.

The political-administrative elite connection: the bottom line

Administrative power in Israel has worked in the service of politics from the very beginning, and until today. Nevertheless, there have been some changes. During the pre-state era and at the beginning of statehood, this system benefited first and foremost the main party that was in power, Mapai. And only in the second place did it work in the interest of the other labor parties and the religious parties. At that time, it certainly contributed to the situation whereby Mapai, later the Labor Party, remained in office from the early 1930s (in the pre-state National Institutions) and up until the late 1970s. Since the 1970s, when the right-wing Likud first came to power— and subsequently the Likud and Labor periodically replaced each other in office—the main beneficiaries of the system have been the religious parties, and in particular the ultra-orthodox parties Yahadut Hatorah (previously Agudat Israel) and Shas.

Whenever they have been in office, the Likud and the Labor Party, too, have been able to stack parts of the state administration with their supporters. Unlike the religious parties, however, they have not had substantial success in utilizing their footholds in the administration for the purpose of handing out material benefits to large numbers of their potential supporters. Thus, unlike Mapai of previous years, and unlike the religious parties in later years, these two parties have not been successful recently in translating the political-administrative connection into a major electoral asset. By contrast, the religious parties have been much more successful in this respect. This is so especially for the two ultra-orthodox parties, a large part of whose voters obtain party-channeled benefits. These voters stand to incur major material losses if their parties lose much of their electoral power and cease to be attractive coalition partners to whichever party happens to be in office. Hence, such administration-channeled material benefits serve as a major factor in motivating the voters of the ultra-orthodox parties to extend their allegiance to them. This is particularly so in the case of Shas, for while Yahadut Hatorah voters are generally ultra-orthodox themselves, and probably would have supported this party in any case, this is not so for Shas. This party has also been able to marshal support among many people who are not orthodox, but merely 'traditional'. These are generally people whose origin is from Middle Eastern countries, who are of relatively lower socioeconomic background, and stand in need of the benefits that Shas has been able to provide for them and their children. Many of these tend to vote for Shas chiefly for the sake of these administration-channeled benefits. Indeed, this may be a major explanation for Shas' phenomenal success in the 1999 election, in which it gained 17 seats in the Knesset.

The political-military elite connection in Israel

Another aspect of the multifaceted elite connection in Israel is that between the political and the military elites. Israel, which regards itself as an out-post of Western democracy, has nevertheless developed especially close political-military relations that differ in several respects from those of other democratic countries. These have taken the form of political appointments at the top of the military, frequent transitions from the military to the polit-ical elite, military participation in the forging of policy and the military elite lending legitimation to one part of the political elite, as over the other, in the eyes of the public. Thus, top military officers have been endowing this part of the political elite with an unfair (though not necessarily decisive) advantage in elections.

The formative years

The roots of the system are to be found in the pre-state era, when the Jewish underground military forces were attached to political movements and parties: the main underground military organization, the Haganah, was attached to the labor movement headed by the Labor Party, Mapai, and the smaller IZL was aligned with the Revisionist Party. After the establish-ment of the state, the underground forces evolved into the Israel Defense Force (IDF). But in line with the tradition handed down from the pre-state era, the leadership of the Labor Party, which became the leadership of the government, continued to forge close relations with the military elite. In the 1950s and 1960s the ruling Labor leadership made intensive efforts to induce army officers to identify with the party, to induct them into its ranks, and to convince them to join the party's political elite upon their retirement from active duty. In addition, the party/government leadership, headed by David Ben-Gurion, effected a host of party-political appointments and pro-motions within the army. Those who owed their appointments to the party's leadership, were indebted to it. They were also aware of the fact that their allegiance to the party would net them further promotions, and open up a political career for them after retirement from the military. In all these ways the party/government leadership caused the top ranks of the military to be stacked with its supporters, thereby ensuring its control over the military. Later on, partisan considerations in appointments and promotions became less blatant. But subsequent Labor/government leaders, too, preferred to promote their own party supporters whenever possible.

The Likud's failure in perpetuating the system[23]

When the Likud came to power in 1977, its leadership was not as successful as its predecessor had been in stacking top army positions with its supporters, and in inducting top military officers into its ranks. By this time, partisan promotions within the army, together with the fact that several top military officers had reached the age of retirement from active duty (which in Israel is exceptionally early), helped create a channel of mobility which is not common in Western democracies: from the top of the military pyramid, to the top of the political pyramid. Thus, since 1977, some ten percent of all members of parliament have been retired senior officers (from the rank of colonel and above), who retained their military ranks as reserve officers. In this, however, the Likud suffered a distinct disadvantage compared to Labor. For although the Likud was now in office, it was markedly less successful than the Labor Party in mobilizing retired military officers into its leadership. Some prominent army officers did join the Likud and other right wing parties (e.g. Ariel Sharon and Rafael Eitan). But more than twice as many of the officers who went into politics were absorbed into left-wing labor parties (chief among them the Labor Party)—40 percent—than were absorbed into the parties that later formed the Likud and into the Likud itself: 17 percent only. The Likud's lesser success in this respect was due, first and foremost, to the political appointments previously carried out by Labor. These ensured that when the Likud came to power, it inherited a high command whose political leanings were far removed from its own. Beyond this, and even later on, the views of the top army brass were more closely akin to those of the more 'dovish' Labor Party, than they were to those of the more 'hawkish' Likud. Thus, when they retired from active duty, they more frequently joined the opposition Labor Party, rather than the Likud. In any case, the Likud leadership inadvertently presided over a situation in which the ties between the government and the military leadership were looser than they had been before.

---

[23] The analysis in this part of the paper is based on several sources. These include, first, my own research on Israel's political elite: its members of parliament and government, including all retired military officers who became members of parliament and of government since the establishment of the state and up to the twelfth Knesset, whose term ran until 1992. This research is based on parliamentary publications and archive material. This part of the paper is also based on content analysis of statements made by high-ranking military officers, as testified to in various press reports, most prominently: Harel, 1993; Ben, 1993; Ben Yishai, 1994; Barnea, 1994; Rabin, 1994 (all in Hebrew).

Recent developments: the renewed Labor-military elite connection

The elite connection between the party in government and the military command gained renewed strength when Labor came to office again in 1992. The Labor government did not renew the erstwhile blatant party-political appointments within the army, but people with pronounced religious or right-wing orientations were considered 'controversial', and had difficulty in gaining promotion to top army ranks. Moreover, the military command was generally akin in its views to those of Labor. This strengthened its connection to the Labor government, which found expression in several ways.

Military involvement in policy formation

One of these was that of high-ranking military officers becoming directly involved in the shaping of government foreign and defense policy. They did so at the instigation of Prime Minister Yitzhak Rabin, by taking part in negotiations between the government, and representatives of foreign powers. This was not an unprecedented phenomenon. As far back as 1956, Moshe Dayan, then chief of the general staff, had participated in negotiations with the French leadership in preparation for the Sinai campaign, which took place shortly afterwards. But in more recent years this was not a common practice, until Labor came to power in 1992. After that, the then chief of the general staff, Ehud Barak, and other high ranking officers frequently participated in negotiations between the government and American representatives on the issue of Israel's withdrawal from the territories occupied in 1967. Also, military officers were put in charge of one branch of the negotiations with PLO representatives. Although not involved in working out the first Oslo agreement, such officers (headed by the then Maj. Gen. Amnon Lipkin-Shahak and Maj. Gen. Uzi Dayan) were put in charge of negotiations with PLO representatives over the practical agreement for relinquishing Gaza and Jericho. Such negotiations entailed first and foremost the implementation of policy decided on by the government, but negotiators had a certain leeway, and thus also participated in policy formation. This became evident, for instance, from a lecture delivered by one of the participants in the negotiations, then Maj. Gen. Danny Rothschild, shortly after their conclusion, at the Tel-Aviv University. Rothschild initially maintained that he had acted merely as a 'civil servant', conducting the negotiations strictly according to government guidelines. However, when questioned more closely by members of the audience, he admitted that through the feedback about the negotiations, which he conveyed to Prime Minister Rabin, he also had an input into their outcome.

Military statements in favor of party/government policy

During this time-span military commanders frequently advocated government defense and foreign policy in public, even when such policy was controversial and contested by the opposition. The then chief of the general staff and other officers several times made public statements to the effect that Israel could manage without the Golan Heights, in the event of a peace agreement with Syria. This conception was in line with that of the Labor government, and contrary to that of the opposition. Senior officers also made public statements in praise of government policy with respect to the agreement with the PLO on withdrawal from Gaza and Jericho. Thus, in 1993, then Maj. Gen. Uzi Dayan, made a public statement in which he congratulated Israel's political leaders for having brought about the agreement. Further, in the spring of 1994, in an interview with a journalist, Dayan said: "The agreement largely satisfies our security needs . . . The negotiations [with the PLO] were a task with which I identified." And then Maj. Gen. Matan Vilnai, in a similar interview stated: "It is totally clear to me, also emotionally, that we must get out [of Gaza], and I am glad that I am doing it." In another interview he added: "It seems to me that this is the right step. I think most of the people of Israel understand that this is what needs to be done." These statements, once again, were in line with the Labor government's policy, to which the opposition objected.

The Likud-military elite disconnection: a crisis of confidence[24]

The Likud's return to power in 1996 brought about a drastic change: unprecedented tension and a crisis of confidence developed between the government and the military command. Thereafter, the military was no longer called upon to participate in negotiations, although it continued to prepare documents for them. Also, there was a rupture of communication between the political and the military echelon. The previous Prime Minister held frequent meetings with the chief of the general staff. By contrast, Prime Minister Binyamin Netanyahu virtually discontinued the practice. In addition, and in stark contrast to what had happened under the previous government, the government and the military elite frequently vilified each other, and saw to it that their mutual accusations were brought to public attention. On the one hand, military officers voiced repeated criticisms of government policy, of the prime minister's decision-making procedures, and of

---

[24] This part of the paper is based on: Peri, 1998 (Hebrew), and on press reports, including: Schiff, 1997 and Kadmon, 1998 (all in Hebrew).

his handling of the peace process. Thus, in April 1998, the then chief of
the general staff, Amnon Lipkin-Shahak, in a press interview on this topic
stated: "I feel that the result today, as I see it, is not good enough." On
the other hand, there were recurrent criticisms of the military command by
the Likud government. In December 1997, a government spokesperson
strongly criticized certain military officers with respect to a local security
agreement they had reached with the Palestinian Authority. Also, several
Likud leaders, including Uzi Landau, made no secret of their mistrust of
the military command, and accused it of being 'in bondage' to the previous government, an accusation which the officers strongly rejected.

Before and after the 1999 election

The strong ties between the military elite and the elite of the Labor Party
once more came to light in the run-up to the 1999 election. By that time,
several of the high ranking officers who had been closely connected with
the previous (1992–6) Labor government when they were still in uniform,
had retired from active duty. And virtually all of the most senior among
them joined the leadership of the Labor Party, or of the Center Party, both
of which in fact were left of center, and intent on ousting the Likud government: both these parties are now coalition partners in Barak's government. Thus, apart from the erstwhile chief of the general staff Ehud Barak
himself, there were some ten senior reserve officers (from the rank of colonel
and above) who were active in Barak's election campaign, publicly supported his election, or were themselves Labor Party candidates to the Knesset.
A similarly large number of senior reserve officers (most prominently former Chief of General Staff Amnon Lipkin-Shahak), were active at the top
of the pyramid of the Center Party. The major part of the military elite,
which—while still on active duty—had been closely linked to the previous
Labor government, and in some respects had acted as a *latent* opposition to
the subsequent Likud government, had now become a reserve military elite.
As such, it acted as a *manifest* opposition to the Likud government, and its
major aim was to bring about the Likud's downfall, in which it in fact succeeded. It thus engaged in what Yoram Peri of the Hebrew University
termed a 'democratic coup d'état'.

The political-military elite connection: the bottom line

Over the years, there have been changes in the political-military elite connection. The practice of partisan appointments within the army has been
attenuated, but officers with Labor-akin left of center views, still have a better chance of promotion to top positions than officers with blatant religious

and right-wing affinities. Partly for that reason, and also because senior officers generally tend to have left of center views, in recent years there has been a close connection between the government and the military elite, whenever Labor has been in power. In the framework of this connection the military elite has lent legitimation to Labor policies by participating in their formation, by making public statements in their favor and by joining the Labor- and Center Parties' political elite upon retirement from active duty. By contrast, there has been a blatant disconnection between the government- and the military elite when the Likud was in power, and the military elite has lent *de*legitimation to Likud policies. All this has injected an element of military expertise and military glory into the party-political arena. Legitimation of Labor policies and delegitimation of Likud policies—coming from the most high-ranking experts in the field, who also enjoy a high esteem and charisma as military leaders—cannot but fulfill a certain role in increasing support for Labor, and decreasing support for the Likud among the public. Certainly this is not the only, and not even the decisive factor: in 1992, and despite the staunch support it had from the military elite, Labor was ousted from office in favor of the Likud. However, there can be no doubt that Israeli voters accord some weight to the expertise and charisma of prominent military commanders in shaping their electoral decisions, and that this gives Labor a distinct electoral advantage over its rival.

Conclusion

The political-business elite connection has been one in which financial resources aimed at increasing political support for government politicians were exchanged for irregular benefits and influence, for the—non-elected—business elite (some of whose members are not even citizens of Israel). To put it differently, government politicians have meted out large scale favors to business people, who injected large-scale fluid assets into the government parties' veins, and these assisted in augmenting their power. The political-administrative elite connection has involved the exchange of appointments and promotions for the appointees' connivance in the handing out of irregular benefits to parts of the public, with the similar aim of increasing support for government parties and politicians. Unlike these instances of the elite connection, the political-military elite connection did not always involve an immediate tit-for-tat, or a direct exchange of resources. Still, there has been a certain causal relationship between the appointments within the top ranks of the military, and the legitimation which the top ranking appointees have lent to one part of the political elite. There has also been a causal link between such legitimation to one part of the political elite, and the legitimators' subsequent induction into that same part of the political elite.

All this has worked in the service of electoral manipulation of several parties. The business elite connection has worked in favor of both major parties, Labor and Likud, whenever they have been in power. The administrative elite connection has recently worked in favor of the religious—especially the two ultra-orthodox parties, and chiefly in favor of Shas, while the military elite connection has worked chiefly in favor of the Labor Party. This has created a certain balance, which has given various parties a range of electoral advantages. But other parties have been virtually excluded from the exchange system, and so the electoral chances this system has provided have never been equal or fair. Overall, the multi-faceted elite connection has never been the sole determinant of the outcome of elections. The parties' ideologies, and the personalities of their leaders have also been of great importance in influencing people's votes, as have been the voters' religious versus secular allegiances. Political battles among the parties have always been of major importance, and are still vigorously fought. Nevertheless, the electoral manipulation brought about by the elite connection has been a not inconsiderable factor in determining electoral outcomes. Hence this connection has not destroyed Israeli democracy: competitive multi-party elections continue, and changes of government occur in their wake. However, the situation thus created contravenes if not the letter, at least the spirit, of democracy and hence it has greatly detracted from its quality. Certainly it has done nothing to promote its health. In addition, those links between the military elite and one part of the political elite without any mechanisms for counterbalancing this link, lead to a unitary conception in the shaping of security policy. Once (during the 1973 Yom Kippur War) this homogeneity in outlook has led to disaster. It can only be hoped that some ways of diversifying this conception will be worked out, but so far this seems unlikely.

Prospects

By now, at the time of the writing, it is impossible to tell how things will work out under future governments. In theory, it is possible that all the previously entrenched arrangements will be abolished under new rulers. But in view of past records, this also seems unlikely. With respect to the political-military elite connection, knowledgeable commentators voice expectations that generals who have been staunch supporters of the policies of previous governments will continue to be appointed by heads of governments as

Chiefs-of-General Staff or senior members of the General Staff. It is also expected that heads of governments will put the most prominent members of the reserve military elite in charge of renewed negotiations with the Palestinian Authority and with Syria. Thus, in general, it is more than likely that there will be a semblance of change, but no transformation in the core of the system.

26. VOICING 'RESISTANCE': RACE & NATION IN THE GLOBAL SPACE

Denise Ferreira da Silva

During 'first contact' between the Europeans and 'natives', Religion was the privileged strategy of power. For centuries, *religious conversion* remained the primary means for transforming 'innocent creatures' into 'knowledgeable' (proper) subjects of a Catholic or Protestant Empire. Among other things, the Portuguese sailor Pero Vaz de Caminha observed, it required teaching the 'natives' not to "reveal their *vergonhas* [sexual body parts] with the same innocence they show their faces" (Caminha, 1894: 188). With the emergence of modernity in the nineteenth century, Science displaced Religion, and 'knowledge' would then flow in the opposite direction. As power required the manipulation, classification, and identification of bodies, a whole new field of science emerged, within which (American, Asian, and African) 'empty souls' were transformed into 'racial bodies'. At the closing of what Hobsbawm has named the long nineteenth century, the new demands of the imperial project required a re-signification of the distinction between Europe and its 'Others'. With the anthropological notion of culture, yesterday's natives were placed within the field of history, as knowledge devoted itself to investigating the contents of their souls (Boas, 1911; Stocking, 1968).

Most accounts of global cultural conditions ignore these constructions of the 'Others of modernity'. The global scene is recurrently described as the state in which 'natives' and 'sailors', 'particulars' and 'universals', 'locals' and 'cosmopolitans' meet for the first time in the global market of cheap labor and exotic goods. Whether describing the global cultural process as a heterogenizing, homogenizing, or hybridizing trend, such definitions ignore the epistemological conditions of possibility of the subjects populating the global political scene. That is, they ignore now that today's global subaltern subjects deploy modern categories of knowledge and being, in the attempt to circumscribe their particular place of articulation. Because I believe with Foucault that, in modernity, knowledge has been a most productive site of material activity, I also believe that social theorizing of 'global change' should not only be attentive to the various ways in which globalization is talked about, rejected and claimed (Robertson and Khondker, 1998). It should also address the very conditions of possibility of these discourses.

Latin America constitutes a most strategic site for interrogating constructions of global cultural conditions that ignore the political effects of
knowledge. Since the late nineteenth century, these former Catholic colonies
have recurrently been written as borderlands, places where modern European
material and cultural forms coexist with lingering traditions.[1] Precisely the
centrality of hybridity (miscegenation and creolization) in the constitution of
Latin American nations requires that any discussion of nationalism and ethnicity in this region be preceded by an examination of the relations between
race and the nation. Many have argued that the centrality of miscegenation for the hegemonic constructions of the Brazilian nation has constituted
the most central obstacle to the mobilization of aggrieved Brazilians of color
(Hasenbalg, 1979; Monteiro, 1991; Andrews, 1992; Hanchard, 1994; Winant,
1994). While there has been increasing ethnic and racial emancipatory discourses in Latin America in the last thirty years or so—of which the black
Brazilian movement is an early example and the Guatemalan Pan Mayan
movement a more recent one (Nelson, 1999; Grandin, 2000)—it seems to
me that it would be at best a simplification and at worse a mis-represen-
tation to suggest that these emancipatory narratives totally depart from the
conditions producing the subaltern subject they re-present. Racial and ethnic
emancipatory narratives are formulated *within* the constraints of hegemonic
national and global discourses.

Rethinking the race/nation divide

Many cultural analysts have addressed the proliferation of political claims
grounded upon racial, ethnic, and gender identity, either in terms of a fragmentation of the nation into smaller 'cultural' entities, or as the constitution of larger cultural entities whose boundaries cut across national borders
(Robertson, 1992b; Vattimo, 1992; Hall, 1996a; Hannerz, 1996). In these
perspectives on global cultural politics, 'time' remains the privileged frame
for interpreting contemporary conditions. They assume that the 'new' political collectivities are 'newcomers' to the domain of History ('transcendental'
or 'materialistic' history). And they construct contemporary conditions as
another manifestation of the processes that followed the 'first contact' and
as another episode of engulfment and resistance. All this as if neither the
ever-expanding modernity nor the never-changing 'Others of modernity'

---

[1] Not surprisingly, Latin America has been useful for writing globalization and postmodernity as hybridizing processes. See, for instance, Canclini, 1989.

were affected by the historical and epistemological shifts that followed the 'first encounter'. Precisely because these culture/identity-based collectivities deploy modern categories to produce themselves as political subjects, the scene of global cultural politics cannot be written as the locus of yet another 'first contact'.

Perhaps the best point of departure for understanding the global scene is to examine the categories deployed in the writing of the 'particular'. How do narratives that share the same basic feature—tales of unfolding, self-actualization, and self-realization—produce modern subjects in their specificity? How is the articulation of difference possible within a general text in which being presupposes the continuous sublation of an 'Other' by the transcendental 'Same'? It is true that modern subjectivities emerge out of the deployment of small teleologies, which emulate Hegel's (1900) account, within which modernity emerges as the final stage of the unfolding of a transcendental subjectivity, coming into self-consciousness as the substance and essence of the world. But it is also true that the text of universal history does not constitute the sole domain of production of modern categories of being. It seems to me that modern subjectivities emerge in a quite complex universe of signification, which is constituted by categories produced in two modern domains of inquiry into the genesis of cultural differences among human groups: history and science. The concepts of nation and race, respectively, constitute the privileged categories produced in these modern signifying contexts.

Both emerged in the nineteenth century as privileged categories of collective being: and even as they were sometimes used to identify the same collectivity, they did so in rather different ways. Written from within the text of universal history, the nation is a category of being which describes collectivities whose cultures are but the embodiment of modernity's cultural principles. What it constructs is the culture of a people, which, in Hegel's formulation, is nothing other than the concrete activities of the transcendental subject which, entailing the union of the State (its abstract form) and human subjectivity, provides the means for its own actualization. The notion of race, on the other hand, emerged from an inquiry into the natural laws informing human cultural diversity. What it indicates is that culture, a people's peculiar mental and intellectual abilities, is but the result of the organic features of their members, more particularly the conformation of their brains. Moreover, as the category produces the body as a signifier of place (continent) of 'origin' and form of consciousness, race writes 'being' primarily in relation to the spiritual and material projects of modernity. Nineteenth-century self-proclaimed scientists of *Man* were not merely prejudiced deviants; their project was to provide scientific grounds for the narrative of the 'being' of modernity. In that endeavor, they constructed race as a signifier of cultural difference, which presupposed that modern cultural specificity derives from nature, not history.[2]

One may object that race only appears as a privileged signifier in postcolonial national narratives and that, in the metropolitan regions, the nation has been written as a continuous being, whose temporality needs no signifier of territoriality. While there is not enough space to address this particular question here, it seems that to capture the material (political) effects of the deployment of race, one should examine precisely those regions of the global space where the descendants of Europeans and of their 'Others' attempted to construct a modern nation state during the initial moment of the historical nation's deployment. Along these lines, what emerges from a reading of early statements on the Brazilian nation is a particular appropriation of the products of the knowledge of race, to write the specificity of the Brazilian national subject.

The Brazilian national text

> The mestiço is the psychological product, ethnic and historic, of Brazil; it is the new form of our national difference. Our popular psychology is a product of this initial stage. This does not mean that we will constitute a nation of mulattos; since the white form is prevailing, and will continue to prevail; it means only that the European here allied with other races, and from this union the genuine Brazilian emerged, the one which does not confound with the Portuguese and upon which our future rests (Romero, 1888: 91).

> Raimundo wandered the streets, with his hopeless heart. The narrowness of the situation tormented him more than the brutal obsession of that family, which preferred to let their daughter be disgraced than to have her married to a mulatto. It was to take too far the purity of blood . . . In his disturbed stream of ideas, suicide mingled, as a false coin that stained the others (Azevedo, 1881/1973: 285).

Written under historical and epistemological conditions in which *miscegenation* was deployed to indicate danger, degeneracy, and destruction, Azevedo's naturalist novel, *O Mulato*, could not help but capture a central dimension of the 'histories' of *modern subjects* that emerged out of colonialism and slavery. In 1880s Brazil, suicide, madness, or assassination seemed the only possible closures for subjects who either rejected their 'partial' blackness or who,

---

[2] Unlike Foucault, I believe that race is a central concept in the discourse of modernity, where it emerges as the signifier of cultural difference, which enables the articulation of difference in the very process of constituting modern subjectivities.

like Raimundo, had been unaware of their 'mixed origins'. As in other accounts of the 'tragic mulatto', Raimundo's impossibility derived not from his partial blackness but from his foes' rejection of the ambiguity signified by the hybrid body. Similarly, contemporaneous political statements on the Brazilian nation predicted an eschatological closure which seemed the only possible fate for those beings whom the text of Science of Man defined as degenerate, undesirable, and un-productive—the dangerously ambiguous off-spring of the power/desire which produced slavery and colonialism. If the hybrid/miscegenated/*mestiço* condition signifies the 'trace' where modernity emerged in its difference from other cultural conditions, out of the dangerous proximity required by the strategies of power/desire that produced modern material conditions, Latin America provides a unique point of departure for interrogating prevailing constructions of global conditions.

Miscegenation is an ever-present signifier in the Brazilian text. Not only can one easily identify the statements where it is deployed to write the Brazilian subject, but it does not require much interpretive acrobatics to realize that this product of the Science of Man was re-signified in the Brazilian text as a historical signifier. However, the writing of the Brazilian text, the attempt to constitute the Brazilian people as a modern subject, was complicated by the prevailing argument that *miscegenation* produced an unstable, degenerate, and inferior 'racial type'. The nineteenth-century literary critic Sylvio Romero has been identified as the first formulator of the 'whitening thesis' as well as the first intellectual to attempt to write Brazil as a historical nation (Silva, 1989; Schwarcz, 1993; Skidmore, 1993). Lost in most interpretations of Romero's statements, however, is the placing of race and nation in the same context of signification which aimed to produce the *temporality* of the Brazilian subject. What I am suggesting is that, since the initial use of the historical nation, the mestiço emerged as the only condition of possibility for writing Brazilian 'being' in its difference. Written in the 1880s, Romero's statements were the products of epistemological conditions where the strategies of intervention of the Science of Man constituted the privileged elements of signification for writing the *territory* of modernity. Since the specific material conditions of the European space were constructed as the result of its unique historical processes, the possibility of fulfilling the material and political projects of modernity was also seen as a privilege of those whose bodies communicated an origin in the European space, and those regions of the globe with a climate similar to Europe's.

A quintessential nationalist, Romero's project was to explain the cause of political and economic backwardness while defending miscegenation as a necessary process for the building of a modern tropical civilization. Early Republican intellectuals and politicians, Romero believed, failed to understand that radical structural and cultural transformations were necessary to actually re-organize Brazil as a modern social space. Such concerns were expressed in Romero's (1894) mapping of the Brazilian political/ideological field in the early years of the Republic. Marking a transitional moment in the intellectual scene, this book is a philosophical essay in which he compares the principles of positivism and evolutionism. Its political significance, however, is explicit in its critique of the pervasive influence of positivism in the political life of the country, to which Romero attributed the country's poor economic and social conditions. According to Romero, the crucial problem with the country resided in its political institutions. "The political constructions which are not organized by popular work, which do not represent the fruits of what the nation's ideals are the flower" he claimed, "cannot be stable" (Romero, 1894: 266). In Romero's assessment, Brazil was far from being a stable political entity. That such was the case, Romero argued, resulted from the influence of positivist intellectuals and politicians in the conceptualization and administration of the newborn Republic. According to Romero, such a model was totally in contradiction with the form and principles of the modern nation-state. Romero attributed this influence to the country's inability to constitute itself as a modern democratic nation-state. Such poor political organization was reflected in the country's weak economic development, as compared with the United States and Europe. Romero's description of the country's social and economic organization as a whole accentuated the impossibility of characterizing it as a modern social space. The proletariat, he noticed, was virtually absent:

> Economically, we are an embryonic nation, whose important industry is still a rudimentary agriculture, extensive, with two million national workers and some tens of thousands of European colonists . . . National capitalism is scanty, almost stingy (Romero, 1894: 274).

But his was not a negative evaluation of the Brazilian people. Romero's criticisms of the national elites was intended as a call for the elimination of the economic, intellectual, and political distances between them and the Brazilian people. Thus, while in this text, the political and economic organization of the Brazilian space is described as lagging behind that of other capitalist societies, particularly the United States and Europe, the 'Spirit' of the Brazilian people was characterized as inherently democratic and modern:

> Brazil is an unavoidably democratic country. Son of modern culture, born in the era of great navigation and discoveries . . . it is, besides, the result of the mixture of distinct races, where evidently the tropical blood predominates. Well, the two greatest factors in the equalizing of men are democracy and miscegenation (Romero, 1894: 267).

Accordingly, as in Europe and elsewhere, Brazil had always moved towards democratization, the realization of freedom and equality, and the privileged signifier of this historical process was *miscegenation*. According to Romero, democratization operated at two levels, natural and social, biological and historical. Hence, he argued that Brazil had yet to become a modern nation-state, not so much because of its people, but because of the elites' misunderstanding of the people's role in modern nations' cultural and political life. Blinded by the positivist perspective, according to Romero, they had not learned a fundamental principle of modern culture. What was necessary in Brazil was the total reorganization of its political institutions according to the model of modern democratic nation-states.

In another text published later, Romero (1906) made explicit that his concerns with the country's future were fed by the recognition of its place in the global space. Here Romero articulated his critique of Brazilian elites through a distinction between *traditional* and *modern* social spaces or as he posed it, 'communal' and 'particularistic' societies. Romero responds to the anthropologist and journalist Euclydes da Cunha's observations that the *mestiço* people of Northeast Brazil were in such a state of abandonment and alienation that the future of the people was at risk. "Either we progress or we are going to disappear", Cunha predicted in this speech at the Brazilian Academy of Letters. In response to this alert, Romero prepared a text in which his criticism of the elites focused mainly on the need for economic reform. For Romero, the dire circumstances Cunha had witnessed in his trip to the inland did not derive from degeneration brought about by miscegenation. Rather than providing a defense of the people and reiterating his belief that it was destined to constitute a 'modern civilization', Romero proceeded by diagnosing the problem as one affecting non-modern societies.

> It should suffice to say that our suffering people present the general symptoms of the nations, to which group it belongs, this great number of people of disposition and communal formation, especially the Latin-Americans, which have to withstand the competition of nations of particularistic formation, placed today in the front of the industrial civilization of our time: the English, German, North American, Australian, Dutch, northern French, peoples who keep in their hands the capital which moves our modern world (Romero, 1906: 8).

While such symptoms were common among 'communal nations', Romero observed that in Brazil they were colored by the specificity of Brazilian history and ethnicity. Such conditions, he argued, resulted from Brazilian history: since the colonizers relied on the work of enslaved Indians and blacks, a society was built with a huge gap between the very rich and the very poor on the one side, and between the intellectual and prejudiced elite and

the illiterate population on the other, ensuring that it would not be organized as a class society. Not only did Brazil lack an organized "rural proletariat accustomed to regular and continuous work" and "a numerous and
widespread class of small and medium landowners". The country also lacked
an "urban proletariat, organized across the country, a petite bourgeoisie,
fast and right, even less a great bourgeoisie comparable to the strong particularistic nations, powerful, and progressive" (Romero, 1906: 13–14). Brazil's
problem, he noted, was that it was organized neither as a patriarchal social
space, like the Orient, nor as a 'particularistic' one. However, unlike Cunha,
Romero did not believe that Brazil would disappear. Quite the opposite.
"Brazil will progress for sure", Romero wrote, "because it will have to be
dragged by the enormous reserve of force, power, and wealth which is in
the hands of three or four great nations which are today at the front of
modern imperialism" (Romero, 1906: 31).

Such was for Romero the country's destiny: like other Latin American
nations at the beginning of the century, Brazil was destined to occupy a
second place in that new phase of capitalist development. Why did Romero's
diagnosis of the problems affecting the nation change during this short period
of years? It seems to me that his assessment of the country's position was
related to the fact that in 1894, imperialism had not shown its entire face,
at least not regarding the place countries like Brazil would occupy in the
new configuration of the global capitalist economy. While Romero's view
of the responsibility of the elite in the country's economic and political backwardness had not changed, he acknowledged that such conditions depended
not so much on the constitution of the nation according to the modern
model, but also on the country's position in relation to 'particularistic societies'. What this privileging of 'cultural factors' suggests is the epistemological transformation under which historical culture was introduced as the new
category for mapping the modern global space. Unquestionably, the centrality of *miscegenation* in the Brazilian national text was anything but a complete rupture with the nineteenth century's arguments that *whiteness* was the
'essential quality' of the people able to fulfill the material and cultural projects of modernity. It was precisely for this reason that the 'whitening thesis'
constituted a strategy of re-signification of *miscegenation*, where its eschatological results were not the degeneration of the European, but the elimination of the Indian and the African, from Brazilian bodies, and minds. Not
only was the *mestiço*, the embodiment of Portuguese desire, the privileged
agent of Brazilian history. By the end of the nineteenth century, the number
of 'mixed-race' individuals in the Brazilian population could support the
argument that Brazil was ahead on the road to complete *whiteness*.

Why was *whiteness* a necessary condition for the constitution of the Brazilian
nation? Under the pervasiveness of the argument of the text of the Science

of Man, *whiteness* signified the cultural and material conditions of modern Europe. With the appropriation of *miscegenation* as a historical signifier, Romero and others concerned with the re-organization of the Brazilian space as a modern space would write the nation's future as the fulfillment of a European desire. Indeed, like the United States, the Brazilian was produced as a raced subject but whose 'Spirit' was European, while the body, given the particularity of the South American space, had retained traits of inferior and subaltern peoples 'originating' in the tropical regions of the global space. I have argued elsewhere (Silva, 1998) that the re-signification of *miscegenation* to write Brazilian subjectivity has resulted in that neither blackness nor Africanness would become available for demarcating the space of emergence of a black Brazilian subject. I have also contended that it also constituted class as the privileged category for characterizing the Brazilian subaltern subject. In the following, I will show how through the appropriation of race and class to delineate the space of subalternity, the black Brazilian movement was able to produce a text in which blackness could be re-appropriated from the national text while it was simultaneously constructed as a global (political) signifier.

Re-writing Zumbi: the black hero of the global oppressed

So-called modernity is the suppression of the future for the black population. The new forms of production and consumption, the celebration of the market, the radical exclusion of the populations situated at the margins of the system compose the scenery where the black population is found in Brazil and in the world. Unemployment reaches record levels. It is a structural unemployment precisely because it is a fruit of the combination of increasing industrial productivity with the elitization of the consumer market. It has hardened the competition among workers, intensifying the racist criterion for hiring ... Excluded from the labor market, the black population is excluded from the consumer market ... The situation is the following: from the Neoliberal point of view everything is market, everything is organized according to the logic of the market, including citizenship rights. To be a citizen is to be a consumer. Not to be a consumer means not to be a citizen. FOR THAT REASON, THE EXCLUSION OF THE LABOR MARKET MEANS NOT ONLY THE EXCLUSION OF THE SYSTEM OF CONSUMPTION, BUT ALSO AND MAINLY, THE EXCLUSION OF CITIZENSHIP RIGHTS. School, health, social security, habitation are no more rights, but expensive commodities inaccessible to the black population [UNEGRO manifest distributed in the March of Brasilia, emphasis in the original].

Zumbi dos Palmares was the last leader of the longest-lived community of runaway slaves in Brazil, the *Quilombo dos Palmares*. Over the past twenty years, the black movement has chosen Zumbi as the symbol of a separate identity and has declared November 20th (the supposed date of his death) as the national day of black consciousness. In 1995, however, Zumbi was

under the risk of being appropriated back into the prevailing racial discourse, as a national hero, as *Palmares* was reconstructed by academics and
politicians as the first experience of racial democracy in Brazil. Throughout
the year, city, state, and federal administrations promoted several events to
celebrate the third centennial of Zumbi's death while resisting Portuguese
troops. Black movement organizations, on the other hand, seized the opportunity to (once again) denounce 'racial democracy' as a myth. For the
Brazilian subaltern, the threat is not as much exclusion and segregation as
it is incorporation into the text of racial democracy as a subaltern collab-
orator and/or instrument. But 1995 would not be just another year in the
history of the tropical racial wonderland. The President, Fernando Henrique
Cardoso, a scholar whose early work challenged the hegemonic constructions of the Brazilian national text, fully recognized the black movement's
demands and also promised measures to eliminate racial inequalities from
the Brazilian social space.

The most significant political event in 1995 was the *Marcha Zumbi dos
Palmares*, the March of Brasilia where black political and cultural institutions, unions, the various communist parties, the workers party, and other
progressive cultural and political organizations joined to denounce race
inequality and the elimination of Brazilian people's already limited social
rights. When Cardoso, the sociologist, threatened to write another version
of the hegemonic text, the March of Brasilia took hold of the official rhetoric
of the celebration and deployed an emancipatory text where citizenship was
written against race and class subjection and in which the erasure of the
line between race and class prevented the loss of Zumbi to the hall of
national heroes.

In the course of the March, documents and speeches emphasized that
which is usually absent from the discourse on globalization, what the structural adjustment policies entail in those regions of the global space (Latin
America, Asia, and Africa), race has placed in the outskirts of modernity:
increased poverty, unemployment, and elimination of social rights. The
March discourse erased the line that the black movement has been attempting to draw in the last thirty years, separating the black subject from the
Brazilian people without, however, writing another version of the national
text.

In the March's text, race and class were not held apart as names that
identified totally distinct social groups; they were simultaneously articulated
to circumscribe a social region inhabited by those most affected by the policies of the global economy, a region which reaches beyond the frontiers of
the Brazilian space. In statements that refused to reduce this region of
subalternity to a single sociological category, the March produced Zumbi

as the hero of the oppressed. But Zumbi could only be constructed as the
hero of the oppressed because he had first been constructed as a black hero.
Expectedly, the *Quilombo dos Palmares* was also appropriated to indicate that
social space which embodies the desire of a global oppressed subject. In the
official document of the March one reads:

> The realization of the *Marcha Zumbi dos Palmares* emerges as a real cry of the
> oppressed against the loss of the right to life, because the *Quilombo dos Palmares*
> was and continues to be the historical expression of the desire for change that
> pulses in the hearts of everyone who struggles, truly, for a society with social
> justice.

In re-writing Brazilian history as a history of racial oppression, the March
discourse combined the oppressive global economic conjuncture with the
historical resistance of the *Quilombo dos Palmares* to create Zumbi as the hero
of the oppressed peoples of the globe. In this movement, Palmares emerged
as a space of subalternity that could now be re-claimed as a transracial,
transnational, radically egalitarian social space. It appropriated blackness—
Zumbi's blackness—as a global signifier that signifies not immediate bio-
logical/cultural/material distance from the cultural, political, and material
projects of modernity, as it has been written in sociological texts, but that
region of subalternity, that race and class produce/capture in modern social
spaces. The March of Brasilia deployed an emancipatory text which did not
only undermine Brazil's pervasive national text but, more importantly perhaps, revealed that race and class do simultaneously produce and capture
the regions of subalternity that blacks and other peoples of color inhabit in
the national and global spaces.

Voicing

Of the many 'manifestations' of the foundational dichotomy, universalism/
particularism seems to be the one which opens more easily to critical interventions. Much of what is called postmodern in social and cultural analysis can be said to be constructs that make use of 'traditional', 'particular'
elements to counter, challenge, and transform otherwise 'universal' constructs.[3]
I would like to propose an alternative. We should finally move away from
this dichotomy and recognize that the universal and the particular are but
products of the same universe of signification within which the 'Others

---

[3] Yet, as Wallerstein (1991b) suggests, to merely pose the 'particular' against the 'universal' is to remain within the same logic that has produced 'the African' as somewhat less
than 'the European'.

of Europe' have been written as modern subaltern subjects. I suggest an interpretive strategy which constructs modern subjects as effects of modern strategies of power/knowledge, constituting instances of what Butler (1993) calls 'spaces of inhabitability'. The subaltern regions they inhabit are but the product of the intersection of various texts written with the deployment of multiple modern categories such as gender, the nation, class, the West. Nevertheless, these subjects are basically the products of the two privileged modern categories of being: the nation and race. What this means is that because emancipatory texts write modern subjects according to the hegemonic principle of *transcendentality*, i.e., they envision material and political freedom as manifest in a consciousness undetermined from without (what remains of Hegel in Marx), they write emancipation as a movement towards self-presence. In this movement, the 'being of the Other'—when conceived from within what Derrida (1976) named 'metaphysics of presence'—always expresses that *distance* which was written in the texts of Science to produce its difference from modernity. That is, subaltern subjects write their position to mark a condition which is a product of the textual and material deployment of European power/desire.

What I am suggesting is that political (cultural) texts, narratives of cultural specificity, as well as critical interventions, that attempt to introduce the perspective of the 'Others of modernity' are all written according to the rules of the field of history. By this I mean that to construct the 'Other' as subject demands a gesture which is a trap: to recuperate the 'Other's difference' which is given in its immanence, and to present that difference as the basis for political and knowledge strategies. To escape this trap, one should consider *spatiality*, which is implicit in the notion of *voicing*, and recognize this as a necessary moment in strategies of emancipation. If one accepts the hegemonic rule of the text of history, and privileges *temporality* as a moment of interpretation, when comparing the always-already self-present modern subject the 'Others of modernity' remain trapped in their immanence (Chow, 1993). Any writing, interpretation of emancipatory statements being deployed in the scene of global politics should read beyond their claim for a *voice*, and its discursive construction as *speech* and instead privilege *voicing* (utterance, enunciation) and the textual moments rendering it possible: *articulation, displacement, and citation*. In *voicing*, what is said cannot be separated from *context* and *purpose*, the web of political (material, textual, discursive) relations within which it takes place. Because *cultural specificity* belongs to the discourse of modernity, in articulating their 'being', the 'Others of modernity' produce an alteration in the confines of that universe of signification, through the articulation of modern signifiers. Accordingly, to account for claims of cultural specificity without relying on dichotomies such as *tradi-*

tional and *modern*, 'authentic' and 'inauthentic' and so on, one should notice that these claims are not deployed in an empty space. *Voicing* presupposes an audience; whether it is *heard* or not, what is said must be comprehensible. Because race and the nation have produced the region of subalternity they inhabit and therefore also constitute the general (con)text in which their statements are deployed, these emancipatory statements deploy both signifiers of cultural difference to write the specificity of subaltern subjects. In other words, it implies that these signifiers are necessary strategies of intervention which produce the boundaries of these subaltern subjects, and in doing so they enable the differentiation among collectivities inhabiting the same temporal, spatial, political, and textual space.

The configuration of the global space in the last decades of the twentieth century results from the play of modern categories of being 'in time', as they were appropriated in political statements that have produced the surface of the global and the human body as embodiments, as the materialization of the power of history. Modernity, then, has come to be defined not solely as the culture of Western peoples, but fundamentally as a discourse within which the 'cultures' and (subsequent) 'histories' of the peoples of the world can be interpreted. Knowledge, as Levinas (1996) suggests, produces not only authoritative representations but also entails a social relation. "These two relations are intertwined. In other words, the comprehension of the other is inseparable from his invocation" (Levinas, 1996: 6). Although this invocation has precluded the articulation of other 'beings' and 'meanings' outside the discourse of modernity, the ruling principle of *transcendentality*, it has also—along with the material subject—constituted the 'Other' as such, as modern subaltern subjects.

I would like to suggest voicing as a metaphor for capturing contemporary global scene privileges, *voicing* rather than *speech*. Emancipatory statements, national or otherwise, produced from within the discourse of modernity as *voicing*, deploy signifiers produced in the domain of science and in the domain of history to convey a *specificity* which, while named *cultural*, aims at the recognition of a collectivity as a political subject. Culture, in this approach, is primarily *difference* as it is represented in the discourse of modernity and, as such, conveys the 'meanings' indicated in both categories that were produced to write the *territory* of modernity, race and historical culture. It refers to re-signification—*articulation, displacement,* and *citation*—of different signifiers in the effort to construct the 'being' of a (*national, ethnic, racial, religious,* and so on) modern collectivity. In this configuration of the global scene, these statements re-write not national spaces but the global space as the privileged political (con)text for the understanding of voicing, and the production of *modern subjects*. Yet, the *voicing* of cultural specificity does not produce the global space as homogeneous context. Instead, episodes of voicing write the globe as a space of *entwinement*: yesterday's and today's collective political subjects have been weaving a *kente cloth*,[4] which acquires its colorful and complex pattern from the juxtaposition of several pieces, of different shapes and textures, woven with threads of different colors.

---

[4] "Kente is an Asante ceremonial cloth hand-woven on an horizontal treadle loom. Strips measuring about four inches wide are sown together into larger pieces of cloth. In a total cultural context, kente is more important than just a cloth. It is a visual representation of history, philosophy, ethics, oral literature, moral values, social code of conduct, religious beliefs, political thought and aesthetic principles". Retrieved from Kente Internet site, 1995.

SECTION FIVE

POSTMODERNITY

INTRODUCTION

In Section Five, *Craig Calhoun* focuses on fragmentation processes. He discusses collective identities as produced by the confrontation of cultural groups with each other and with the state. Similarly, it is within the global transnational reality, he contends, that national identities are forged. Elaborating on the loyalties and obligations of individuals to nations, he outlines an intellectual agenda which focuses on the formulation of identity and agency in ways that would not tacitly equate society with nation, or presume that one identity is automatically a trump card against others. For *Zygmunt Bauman*, the spectacular rise of the 'identity discourse' discloses primarily the present-day state of human society. We experience a globalized reality where 'individualization' transforms human identity from a 'given' into a 'task'. In this reality, it is not only the individual's place in society, but also the actual places that individuals can access, which are rapidly dissolving and can hardly serve as targets for life projects. This fragility of goals affects unskilled and skilled, uneducated and educated, work-shy and hard-working individuals alike. 'Disembeddedment' is now an experience which is likely to occur many times in the course of life. In a world where nothing is permanent, people look for groups to belong to. *Mike Featherstone* also describes a social reality where steady references are rare, thus leading many to search for tradition, ethnicity, kinship and other identity markers. A part of this reality, he says, consists of the new global managerial class and cultural intermediaries, who develop cosmopolitan dispositions and syncretism, and staff the countless international bodies. Another part of this reality consists of 'reactionary' fundamentalisms, nationalism, independence movements and localisms. In a similar vein, for *Bryan Turner*, the notions of irony, distance and detachment in postmodern cultures can be redeployed as components of a cosmopolitan ethic. Homelessness is the intellectual condition of today's cosmopolitanism and there can be no return to non-hybrid, homogeneous, and unified cultures. This, moreover, does not preclude local wars based on ethnic identity, to gainsay optimistic perspectives.

Confronted with research data, such theses about postmodernity require subtle and mitigated conclusions. *Masamishi Sasaki* indicates that Japanese individuals tend, in many areas of their life experience, to depart from traditional attitudes and to favor conjunctively both modern and postmodern attitudes. On the other hand, it also transpires that the Japanese may differ in more than a few respects from Westerners, by their enduring attachment to some aspects of Japan's particular social and cultural legacy.

Craig Calhoun

Nationalism is a vexed subject, and modernism scarcely less so. It is not enough that we are unsure of their historical significance, whether they are basic or mere epiphenomena. We do not agree about what the words mean, or to what time period they refer, or how precisely the 'ism' form relates to the root term. In this chapter, I do not propose to fix these problems with some single theory of nationalism or simple location of modernism. Rather, I want to suggest that the very complexities of each derive from the constitutive role they play in our entire, but contradictory epoch. We have little choice but to call this epoch modernity, because even to say 'the capitalist era', though it adds something, also narrows the scope of reference too much. But modernity is not a simple set of constants nor even of linear trends. If it is a single epoch, it is one characterized by widely diverse but equally modern projects.

Pursuing uniformity and producing difference in unprecedented ways, defined equally by the slave trade and the post-Reformation ideal of tolerance, modernity has been an epoch of crossed purposes from its outset. To imagine modernity as simply one side of struggles over subjectivity, solidarity, power/knowledge, or contextualization/decontextualization is to misunderstand the era deeply. Modernity is an era shaped by contradictions.

Nowhere are the contradictions of modernity more apparent than in the proliferation of claims to nationhood and the attendant transformations of both collective and individual identities. The idea of national identity has been a crucial part of the democratic project in the struggles of 'peoples' against kings. It has been equally basic to fiercely anti-democratic campaigns of irredentism, secession, and the imposition of uniform ideas of what sort of behavior is acceptable among the members of a nation. Nationalist projects have helped draw disparate principalities and quasi-autonomous cities together into larger and more effectively centralized polities. They have also challenged political integration with secessionist movements and seeming

[1] An earlier version of this paper was presented to the Sawyer Seminar on Modernism, Cities, and the Problem of National Identity, International Center for Advanced Studies, New York University, 12 November, 1998. I am grateful for comments from the audience.

fragmentation. Nationalism is thus not one side to a contradiction within modernity, but rather one of the basic dimensions of contradiction constitutive of modernity.

Nationalism and modernism figure in our era as 'discursive formations', in Foucault's sense.[2] That is, they are ways of talking that inescapably exceed the bounds of any single usage, that endlessly generate more talk, and that embody tensions and contradictions. Nationalism and modernism are not simply settled positions about our epoch, but clusters of rhetoric and reference that enable people to articulate positions which are not settled and to take stands in opposition to each other on basic issues in society and culture. In the present chapter, I cannot even remotely approach a general account of either, let alone an analysis of their relationship. What I would like to do is to suggest some of the ways in which nationalist rhetoric provides the modern era with a constitutive framework for the identification of collective subjects, both the protagonists of historical struggles and those who experience history and by whose experience it can be judged good or bad, progress or regress or stagnation. In this, nationalism most resembles another great discursive formation, also constitutive for modernity, individualism. Indeed, I shall argue that they are closely related.

Modernism is related to this aspect of nationalism in several ways. First, modernism in a relatively general way is a rhetoric that helps to constitute the idea of history for the modern era, particularly in relation to notions of progress and novelty. Second, modernism in a somewhat narrower sense, in the late 19th and early 20th centuries, refers to a movement of artists, writers, and indeed social theorists. These explored the way in which the wholes of modernity—individuals and nations, biographies and histories— were put together, and how they could be deconstructed and reconstructed. Third, the sense of modernism as a project opens the idea of multiple modernist projects, a diverse range of potential modernities. This way of speaking suggests that the modern is not simply one direction through the present epoch, but a multiplicity of potentials built into the age and its social formations.[3] Though these multiple modernities may differ, they are not disconnected; part of what makes them modern is precisely their interconnection. Just as the idea of nation posits a self-subsistent being that moves through history—but in fact only makes sense when related to a multiplicity of nations—so multiple modernities may claim radical originality but in fact reflect sharing of culture as much as separate pasts or choices.

---

[2] Foucault, 1969b; 1980.
[3] For various related notions of multiple modernities, see *Public Culture* 11(1). Also Göle, 2000b.

I

A first important point is that national identities are neither simply inherited from a premodern past nor arbitrarily created by elites struggling for power and seeking to enlist followers in their projects. Both of these are possible dimensions of nationalism in particular settings, but neither explains it. Moreover, much writing on nationalism and modernism (or modernity) tends to assume uncritically that the last five centuries of history reveal a unilateral decline in human diversity. The whole modern era has been shaped by globalization, to be sure, but I will argue against assuming that differences among human groups are simply inherited from the past. Implicitly, this continues an argument I have started elsewhere against an *a priori* realism of groups. Too commonly, analysts assume that nations exist, and then ask why some or all of their members become nationalists. It is much better, I contend, to keep in mind that human groupings may be constructed in a variety of different ways and ask what is distinctive about the nationalist way, and why it dominates group construction and representation in the modern era.

It is surprising, at least to me, how readily social scientists accept the proposition that nearly all of the important differences among human beings originated in the relatively distant past, and are thus *found* by rather than created in modernity. Here is Ernest Gellner:

> Cultural nuances in the agrarian world are legion: they are like raindrops in a storm, there is no counting of them. But when they all fall on the ground . . . [during modernization] they aggregate into a number of distinct, large, often mutually hostile puddles. The aggregation, the elimination of plurality and nuance anticipated by the internationalists, does indeed take place, but it leaves behind not one large universal culture-puddle, but a whole set of them.[4]

Gellner is disagreeing here with liberal internationalists who imagined that nations would give way to a single world-culture, but he accepts the notion that in the main diversity was produced in the past, and is now being erased (or at least consolidated) by "the tidal wave of industrialization or modernization".

It is as though analysts imagine that there was great cultural creativity in tribal and agrarian societies, but that moderns wield only the capacity to homogenize, or manipulate, but not to create—and create differences. This view, I think, is one that early moderns helped to produce by the way

---

[4] Calhoun, 1997: 34.

they revered the classics and the way they understood historical time, reason, and the struggle against prejudice. But it is false. And in fact, I don't
think most social scientists believe it—that is, they don't really believe that
peasant societies are more culturally fertile—they only write about nationalism as though they believed this. What they seem actually to believe is
that the sort of 'culture' that counts for the construction of deeply felt ethnicity is necessarily ancient, even if obviously created at some point. Oddly,
even those who seek to demonstrate the novel and invented character of
national culture tend to accept the same assumption. They argue that
'invented traditions', in the phrase of Hobsbawm and Ranger, are not as
real as those which grow by gradual accretion over the centuries.[5] It is taken
as obvious that the spread of CNN and McDonald's franchises, following
the spread of English and global trade, simply betoken growing uniformity
of culture and that modernists (by contrast to postmodernists) endorse this
because they are universalists. This representation of one historical trend
leaves out others, including not only resistance to this sort of modernism
but the production of competing modernisms.

Some of the most striking misunderstandings come from the burgeon-
ing (but often not very intellectually serious) literature on globalization. In
the first place, globalization needs to be seen as a basic feature of the entire modern era, not something distinctive to the 20th century, or to the last
ten years. Secondly, it is a serious mistake to see globalization simply as the
spread of capitalism and Western culture. Thirdly, the error is compounded
when such globalization is equated with modernization and all resistances
understood as antimodernisms. The weakness of such understanding is evident, for example, in Benjamin Barber's well-intentioned and surprisingly
well-reviewed best-seller, *Jihad vs. McWorld*. I propose to make an example
of this, not because it is the worst case in the literature on globalization,
but because it is representative and the product of a political theorist who
ought to have known better.

Barber is among those who have recently popularized the idea of an end
to the nation-state. He writes of 'Jihad' as a shorthand for all the reactionary anti-modernisms and fundamentalisms of the world, and 'McWorld'
as global economic integration (which he understands mainly in terms of
the spread of Western consumer culture):

> Jihad and McWorld operate with equal strength in opposite directions, the one
> driven by parochial hatreds, the other by universalizing markets, the one re-
> creating ancient subnational and ethnic borders from within, the other making

---

[5] Hobsbawm and Ranger, 1983.

war on national borders from without. Yet Jihad and McWorld have this in common: they both make war on the sovereign nation-state and thus undermine the nation-state's democratic institutions.[6]

This is not so clear. In many respects, minor aid for Sudan aside, Iran has pursued a policy of 'Islam in One Country' not unlike Stalin's 'socialism in one country'. Both declared more internationalism than they practiced. Most Islamic militants in power have been builders and defenders of their nation-states, if not of democratic institutions. Barber greatly overestimates, moreover, the extent to which fundamentalisms and reactionary ethnic nationalisms are rooted in ancient identities which are clear to all those involved. He fails to consider, for example, that the spread of Islam and so-called Islamic fundamentalism or Islamism may be less a resistance to modernity than an alternative modernism. He imagines Islam simply surviving from the past, embedded in traditional communities, rather than focusing on the extent to which Islam spread as a universalistic religion, itself challenging and transforming traditional life in many settings. Islam thus was before modernity and remains within modernity a globalizing force. Part of what is going on in Islamism today is a struggle over the definition of Islam, not simply a reaction of Muslims to modernization. Religious leaders like some followers of the Ayatolla Khomeini are fighting against not only secularists and foreign influences such as global capitalism, they are fighting against Muslims who would modernize in other ways. They are attacking intellectuals who claim the right to make their own interpretations of the Koran, advocates of women's rights who point to the fact that the Koran at least arguably gives women a number of rights that male-dominated Islamic courts and families deny them. They are trying to enshrine one definition of the faith as the only acceptable one—and theirs may in many ways be as new as some of those they attack.[7] Among those they have attacked, advocates of mass literacy and critical reinterpretation of sacred texts loom very large (and this helps to explain why they were so eager to mobilize non-readers against Salman Rushdie's novel, *The Satanic Verses*). By the same token apparent symbols of conservatism and allegiance to the premodern past may take on very different meanings, as when wearing the veil provides security for women to enter the public sphere and mixed gender occupations (even while obviously reproducing certain aspects of gender inequality).[8] Afghanistan's Taliban may in this sense look more like Barber's model for Jihad, but neither Khomeini's Iran nor Turabi's Sudan fit.

---

[6] Barber, 1995: 6.
[7] See Fischer and Abedi, 1990; and for an Indonesian case study of the processes of modernization within Islam, see Bowen, 1993.
[8] See, e.g., Göle, 1996.

Bizarrely, Barber assumes that what he terms 'Jihad' is a reaction of small and relatively homogenous entities. But Islam—his primary example—is neither small nor homogenous. Islam's billion adherents are citizens of dozens of countries; many are fiercely patriotic at a national level while others profess loyalty only to the whole community of faith, the Umma Islam. The largest Islamic country, after all, is Indonesia. It is not immune to fundamentalist currents, but it is also extraordinarily different from Iran or Iraq—as they are from Algeria and Afghanistan. In each case, Islam is interwoven with local and national cultural traditions, histories, disputes, and patriotisms. And each of the countries I just mentioned has a different dominant language from the others; only one is Arabic-speaking (to tweak a popular stereotype and confusion). Islam, like Christendom and Communism at different times, is the ideological glue of a world-system of its own—on a scale more comparable to global capitalism than to narrow nationalisms.

Despite the fact that they find it far easier to spread messages by means of modern communication technology, Muslims today are arguably less unified than, say, Christians in the era of the Crusades (who were not so very unified, as Western European Catholics learned when they were disappointed to find Eastern and Greek Orthodox Christians relatively indifferent to their fundamentalist adventure). In the case of Islamic fundamentalism, as of all religious fundamentalisms, there are people who think that there is one simple truth and that everyone ought to follow precisely the same understanding of that single truth that they have. In other words, there are people who would like Islam to be homogenous. But they do not agree amongst themselves about the definition of the single truth which everyone ought to believe. There are Sunni and Shi'a and divisions within each; there are debates as to whether Ismaili are really Muslims. What Barber fails to realize, is that while in the modern world many people find ideologies that *claim* homogeneity very appealing, this does not mean that in fact those people *are* homogenous with each other.

On the side of what he calls 'McWorld', Barber tells one-sidedly the story of global homogenization—without considering the ways in which global capitalism itself creates the settings for new forms of cultural creativity and the production of new differences. Were people really more free and more heterogeneous in their cultural tastes when nearly all of them were peasants? The spread of capitalism into China, for example, does bring new commonalties between Chinese buyers of Kentucky Fried Chicken and those in Budapest and Boston. But it also allows for the development of a variety of taste cultures within China. It allows for some teenagers to prefer to listen to rock music—admittedly a Western import at first, but now produced by a wide range of Chinese artists, some of whom like Cui Jian articulate a vision of China at odds not just with many of their elders but with the communist party.[9] If McWorld eliminates the difference between Szechuan and Cantonese cooking, that will be a loss. But markets are at least as likely to encourage the stylization of each—both within China and for global consumption—and to give chefs the chance to innovate. Similarly, while Hollywood cinema may look like McWorld, world cinema does not.

Differences among human groups, then, are not simply inherited from premodern cultural formations. It is true that much 'ethnocultural' difference is of relatively old provenance, both in the sense of differences in ways of life and differences in the content of historical memories. But even this is often transformed and redistributed. Serbian identity has ancient roots, but was transformed during the 19th and early 20th centuries by the rise of both literary and political nationalism, an effort to define sharper cultural distinctions from Croats and an effort to gain both autonomy from the Hapsburgs and dominion over a 'greater Serbia'. Talk of rights, and especially of the rights of free-born Englishmen, is of relatively old provenance but has changed its significance through time. Among the changes are not just new meanings for Englishmen (and women), but resonance among English-speakers outside England—in the American Revolution, of course, but on through to the present day.

This, one may suggest, is a matter of ideas rather than ethnicity, and ethnicity is more enduring, more premodern. I think there is more than a hint of ethnicity in the language of rights, but I also want to suggest that ethnic identities are not simply premodern. Ethnicity as we understand it today is not the same as kinship. It is not simply an inheritance from primordial times, whether in the imagery of Wagnerian mists or African jungles. Rather, ethnicity is a product of confrontation among peoples of different group identities and cultural backgrounds. It is a mode of identity forged largely in cities, not in the countryside. Migrants to cities developed ethnicity by accenting commonalities with people to whom they would not necessarily have been close in the countryside, people from the 'wrong' clan or a distant village. In the context of a city, these could appear as speakers of the same language, practitioners of the same religion, people with whom one could feel at home. But common ethnicity was not primarily a

---

[9] Without giving any serious evidence, Barber dismisses the much more persuasive arguments of Orlando Patterson that 'world musical homogenization' is simply not occuring. Barber actually does not consider the production of music or systematic studies of audiences, but rather notes anecdotally that MTV content is disproprotionally American even in non-English-speaking countries. Barber, 1995: 105; see Patterson, 1994. See also Gilroy (1993) for a critique of the illusions of the idea of 'authentic culture', including in music, and an account of how musicians of African descent creatively mixed different influences in different settings in Europe and America.

matter of specific relationships of marriage and descent, like those of kin-based societies, nor of place. Though ethnics might marry within their ethnic group, and even try to keep alive more specific norms about proper matches, the ethnic group was in fact a category rather than a network. That is, it was constructed out of cultural similarities salient in the urban context rather than the specific webs of relationships that constituted alliances and rivalries in the countryside. It might contain more or less of those webs of relationships, but it was not defined by them. Ethnic groups were and are defined by their juxtaposition to other ethnic groups and to the state. In the eyes of each other and under the gaze of the state, each tends to be a category, a set within which members are largely equivalent.[10] Ethnicity in this sense certainly existed in the premodern world, with religion often dominant in the ascriptive constructions, as in the Ottoman millet system. But ethnicity also flourished and was constructed anew in the modern rise of cities. In this sense, the construction of ethnicity out of kinship continues. New identities are formed. Many, like Asian-American, have no analog 'at home' and cannot be understood simply as an amalgamation of prior local identities.

In addition to transforming older identities and helping to produce new identities such as ethnicities, modern life occasions increasing juxtapositions among identities. It brings a new 'dynamic density' of intergroup contacts (to borrow Durkheim's under-remarked phrase). Markets, media, migration, state-building, and the growth of cities all bring together people of different cultural and social-organizational backgrounds. This is not radically new; trading cities and the capitals of empires always produced contact across cultural lines. The point here is simply that even without the production of new identities, modernity helps to produce in each person a greater awareness of diversity of identities. The world of others is represented to each person in terms of a welter of different groups. As in the past, and perhaps more often, many individuals experience belonging to more than one of these at the same time.

It is also true that new differences are created, and suppressed differences are given new public voice. Science, for example, may be universalistic as in the stereotype of modernism, but it produces change and multiplication and diversities of knowledges. The very expansion of what is known—far beyond the capacity of any single human knower—makes it inevitable that

---

[10] I have elaborated on this theme, and on the language of category and network at more length in Calhoun (1997), esp. ch. 3. My usage is indebted to the anthropological distinction of clan and lineage, and to the specific formulation in Nadel (1957).

the common knowledge of different groups will partake differentially of the ever-expanding whole. Beyond science, literary and artistic activity produce novel culture all the time, and at least as much now as ever before. They also are appreciated in different communities of reception and help thus to contribute to cultural differentiations among groups (as in the way Asian-American novels may help to make, not just reflect, Asian-Americans). There is also an expansion of occupations and economic niches in the modern world. A quick glance at the Dictionary of Occupational Titles produced by the US government should give pause to anyone who thinks diversity is being erased, even if most of these exist in capitalist labor markets that commodify labor and establish class differences. So should the inverse thought: wasn't the way of life of traditional peasants impressively uniform, at least within broad ecological and material-cultural zones?

Indeed, local communities vary a great deal today, and at least in the world's richer countries afford the relatively novel luxury of choice of 'lifestyles'. The differences from one peasant village to another in Vietnam or Burkina Faso are hard to describe in terms of this kind of diversity, but despite widespread condemnation of the homogeneity of suburbs by comparison to cities, there is this sort of diversity—at least up to a point—between one suburb and another in Westchester County. But lifestyle communities are not generally coincident with local government boundaries. Look at the emergence of more strongly self-identified and publicly recognized communities based on sexual orientation. Homosexuality may have existed through history (though there are tendentious issues of definition here that I do not want to try to engage at the moment). But opportunities to form differentiated social groups based on gay lifestyles—or indeed other lifestyles 'alternative' to conventional heterosexual family formation—have certainly proliferated. This is an achievement unevenly distributed both among and within 'modern' countries, but it is also modernist, not post or pre-modern.

This may seem to take us rather far from nationalism, and I certainly don't mean to suggest that I see gay nationalisms as the next step in global history (though something like this, if short of a request for a UN seat, may not be totally inconceivable). The connection lies, rather, in the fact that new cultural diversity is produced in the modern era. The very multiplicity of possible bases for the structuring of group identities should focus our attention on the questions of how some of them are constructed (or reconstructed) as nations, why only some of them are, and what the implications of this are.

II

Nationalist rhetoric is commonly employed to produce the image of a pre-politically unified population. It allows those who employ it to judge contemporary politics—and culture and economics—by the standard of a people understood as always already there, constituted in a kind of primal innocence outside the realm of ordinary politics. The people may be understood simply as given, on ethnic or other cultural grounds, or as the creation of martyrs, heroes and law-givers acting outside or above the normal politics of individual and sectional interests. Both images may be evoked at the same time. The important thing is the implication that the nation is established in advance of, separately from, the more quotidian developments which may then be judged as serving or failing to serve its interests.

This is, of course, an illusion insofar as processes of collective identification (as of cultural transformation) are never altogether without politics. Saying so does not make the illusion any less powerful, either in its grips on individual imaginations and emotions or in its capacity to constitute a cultural order. People who have read Hobsawm are still moved by national anthems, enlist in armies, and understand themselves to have 'home' countries when they migrate.

Nationalism offers distinctively modern ways of reasoning about identities: their 'natural' origins, their 'categorical' distinctions, their integrity. These had an older provenance, especially in Europe, but in the course of the 19th and early 20th centuries they helped to constitute a global discourse about national identity, sovereignty, and legitimacy. This discourse shapes not only the way in which we try to understand movements for self-determination, but the creation of such movements and the contests over recognition. Self-determination presumes a self.

At the individual level, debates about what constitutes such a self inform and were informed by the emergence of modern ideas of legal personality, a growing emphasis on the autonomy of moral subjects, and psychological concerns for the integration and integrity of the person. Understanding of collective selves grew in close tandem with that of individual persons. At its most influential, collective self-determination demanded a self composed not of a dynasty or a state, nor of a disconnnected, unintegrated population, but of *a* people, an organized, meaningfully integrated collectivity. This the idea of nation supplied.

An ancient concept at one level, 'nation' was as much transformed in the modern era as the idea of person. In their transformed and never quite fixed meanings, each term was also constitutive of modernity. Though represented sometimes as opposites, the two ideas were intimate partners. They were joined among other things by the claim to refer to integral, indivisible wholes—individuals. Likewise, their objects were presented as simultaneously natural, always already there, and in need of energetic making, of *bildung* (Herder and Fichte offer classic versions of such accounts).

The discourse of nationalism helped shape identities and movements not only in Europe but throughout the world. At the same time, it informed the very way in which society came to be conceptualized as the basic unit of analysis in the social sciences. Bounded, discrete, internally integrated societies (and cultures) were understood on the model of nation-states, reflecting nationalist rhetoric as well as institution-building in both Europe and colonies. In social science and politics alike, nations also provided the idea of progress with one of its primary subjects. Along with classes and individuals, nations figured as both the agents and the beneficiaries of progress. Progress was assessed by measuring the strength, freedom, or material well-being of nations. Yet, though the idea of nation was implicitly basic to the social science that gained institutionalization during the 1890s, it was seldom the object of explicit or sustained attention. The shaping of social science during the last *fin de siècle* thus contributed to the surprise of social scientists at the resurgence of nationalism during the current *fin de siècle*.

Modernity itself was one of the crucial projects taken on in the name of nations. Modernization meant variously strength, freedom, intellectual advancement; it always meant progress. For many intellectuals in Western Europe's advanced capitalist societies, the *fin de siècle* marked the moment at which faith in modernization lost its innocence. In a curious contradiction, this is part of 'high modernism'. Deconstruction of the putative wholes of individual and nation was one of its central motifs, whether in cubist painting or Musil's simultaneous examination of the man without qualities and mockery of Austrian nationalism. Simmel asked how both individual and society were possible, implicitly challenging their naturalness. Freud argued, in a sense, that they were not possible, or at least, that they represented ideas towards which actual persons and nations might strive but never completely reach.

When Durkheim argued that organic solidarity was stronger than mechanical, or that moral education and the empowerment of occupational associations could overcome anomie and social disintegration, he also addressed modernity as progress that includes growing purposiveness. Weber, in the same vein, sounded a good deal like Marx and more than a little like Hobbes, when he wrote of the state as definitive of modern society, rendering it a cohesive and rational-purposive whole:

> The modern state is an enterprise [*Betrieb*] just like a factory. This exactly is its historical peculiarity. Here as there authority relations have the same roots . . . The hierarchical dependence of the wage worker, the administrative

and technical employee, the assistant in the academic institute as well as that
of the civil servant and the soldier is due to the fact that in their case the
means indispensible for the enterprise and for making a living are in the hands
of the entrepreneur or the political ruler.[11]

The state allows the ruler to exert purpose, but likewise, enables the ruler
to act—and ideally achieve progress—on behalf of the nation. Recall that
despite his own protestations to the contrary, Weber the politician was not
so far distant from Weber the social theorist, and he was committed to what
he saw as "the historical tasks of the German nation."[12]

But while the turn of the century sociologists continued to understand
modernity through narrations and ideas of progress and purpose, they had
become ambivalent about the capacity of social actors to guide progress
through their purposive action. In common with others in the generation
of the 1890s, they developed deep worries that progress might end or become
perverted.[13] The idea of progress had already received radical challenge
from Nietzsche and was increasingly out of fashion with the esthetes who
gave the *fin de siècle* its name and fame. In *The Man Without Qualities*, Musil
mocked the facile celebration of progress in much the way that Voltaire in
Candide mocked the complacent belief that this was the best of all possible
worlds. The confident expectation of continuous improvement was under
critical re-evaluation, but even more basically, the notion of a common set
of criteria for judging such improvement was losing adherents. An increasing chorus of intellectuals granted modernity its material progress but worried about its philistinism. The idea of 'the good', argued many, was being
lost in more quotidian notions of 'goods' or the surplus of benefits over
costs.[14] Most ideas of progress privileged the latter; intermittent attempts to
reclaim the former would punctuate the next century and are current today
in communitarianism, parts of conservative thought, and the post-postmod-
ernist turn to ethics.

For the Enlightenment thinkers, emphasis lay on people's self-conscious
efforts to make a better world. Many 19th century social scientists carried
forward this faith in purposive action. Some others, however, took evolutionary thought as a cue to treat progress as much less dependent on purpose. This was also a dimension of the thought of Durkheim, Weber and

---

[11] Weber, 1968a: 1394.

[12] Weber, 1968a: 1391. The influence of Nietzsche is evident in Weber's efforts to think
through problems of leadership and the progress of nations. More generally, see Mommsen,
1984; and Beetham, 1985.

[13] Hughes (1961) is a classic source on the generational experience of the early institu-
tionalizers of social science.

[14] This is the theme of Arendt (1968).

other *fin de siècle* theorists of modernity. Modernization was not always achieved by conscious struggles, but was also something that happened to people as an unintended consequence of their purposive actions. This is, for example, the basic message of Max Weber's *The Protestant Ethic and the Spirit of Capitalism*, and of a good deal of the rest of his work on rationalization and its consequences. Much the same is true for Durkheim, Tönnies and others who prominently brought forward characterizations of the transformations that wrought modernity: mechanical to organic solidarity, *gemeinschaft* to *gesellschaft*, etc. Marx was quintessentially ambivalent on this very point, both ascribing responsibility for progress to the laws of history and demanding voluntary revolutionary action in its behalf. In the 1890s, Marxists were divided precisely over the extent to which an 'evolutionary' path to socialism might adequately substitute for revolution. Evolutionary socialism embodied a faith in progress, reminding us that this had not vanished from Europe at the turn of the century.

The First World War produced a deeper rupture. Though some of the intellectual struggles continued, Maurice Mandelbaum is quite right to suggest that

> if there has been any one factor which, more than others, has led to a revolutionary shift in twentieth-century thought and which has involved a break with those nineteenth-century movements which still dominated the earlier years of this century, it has been the loss of belief in Progress.[15]

And as Mandelbaum notes, this was not just a change in academic fashions, but one rooted in basic social experiences.

> One must take cognizance of the experience of the first World War, especially in Germany, and of the widespread social and political upheaval that began in the 1930s and have continued unabated ever since. Such experiences have left little room for the earlier forms of optimism which, on the whole, dominated Western thought since the Enlightenment.[16]

Social science was institutionalized, thus, not with a simple faith in progress, but at the point of high modernist doubts about the capacity of ordinary people to be the agents of their own progress. This is one reason why it is misleading to counterpose the idea of modernity to putative postmodernity.

---

[15] Mandelbaum, 1971: 369.
[16] Mandelbaum, 1971: 370. We might note the heroic attempts of some mid-20th century thinkers like Talcott Parsons to recover the stance of naive optimism about progress in the midst of an epoch of devastating conflicts and widespread disillusionment. That Parsons reflects important aspects of his context in postwar America does not fundamentally challenge Mandelbaum's generalization.

On the one hand, the ideology of universal progress that is commonly taken as basic to modernity had much more to do with the late 18th century than the late 19th; on the other hand, the late 19th and early 20th centuries are precisely the era of *modernism* as style and ideological position. Postmodernists, who often refuse to take seriously any goal of historicall specificity, thus define their account of the late 20th century unstably against two very different modernities.

III

In the 1890s, the thinkers for whom modernity most conveyed a singular sense of purpose were not the world-weary sophisticates of *fin de siècle* Europe. They were those for whom modernity remained to be appropriated, to whom modernity could still appear as enlightenment bundled together with a host of other forms of progress, and at the same time as occasion for Romantic exaltation of individual action. These thinkers were for the most part outside the centers of European thought. Being a little bit outside was one of the sources of the naive enthusiasm many Europeans both disparaged and envied when looking at Americans. But we grasp the stance better if we try to look at early 20th century modernity from still further outside the metropoles of West Europe.

Though the modern has been identified as the Western, the most active appropriators of the idea of modernity, those who most clearly constitute modernity as a project to pursue, have been intellectuals and political activists in the colonial and post colonial world, in East Asia, and indeed, in Europe's own East and other fringes. From China's self-strengthening movement and revolutionaries to Attatürk and even Zionists in Central and Eastern Europe and Spain's generation of 1898 in the West, the pursuit of modernity was a powerful agenda on the periphery of modernity's apparent capital. Here too, a key issue was the question of the subject—the agent—of progress and of modernizing action. If progress demanded agency, there seemed to thinkers of the late 19th century to be three main choices: setting individuals free, empowering the working class, and pursuing the collective good of the nation.[17]

---

[17] Though there were hints of pan-Asian thinking, and foreshadowings of negitrude, race did not inform the positive construction of the would-be agents of progress nearly so much as it did the negative arguments as to why some outside Europe and countries of European settlement failed to attain so much progress. At least before national socialism, European usage of race was mainly about 'them', while nation referred to 'us' (though in very early writings the terms 'race' and 'nation' were often used in closely overlapping senses). See

Both class and nation were constructed for the most part as categories of individuals, and indeed often as 'superindividuals', bearers of the same sort of unitary identities in the metabiographical space of history as individuals bore in their more immediate and smaller scale contexts.[18] As Benedict Anderson has noted, regardless of the analytic merits of each conception, it has been nation that has commanded the stronger allegiance, especially measured by the willingness of individuals to die for the collectivity.[19] Sometimes the two came together, as the working class was presented as the historical actor that would save or advance the nation. There was a version of individualism, to be sure, that emphasized competition among individuals to the exclusion of any emphasis on larger units (suggesting, sometimes, the biological distinction between individual and group selection). But for the most part, social Darwinists were greatly interested in the links between the 'fitness' of individuals and that of the collectivities they made up. Even most anti-collectivist thought tended to accept the salience of nations, while challenging that of classes. And as World War I drove home, when the chips were down, the idea of the nation became the most basic, operating as a trump card against class and nearly all other collective identities. Nations thus came to be understood, almost everywhere, as both the potential agents of progress and the units for which values or goods could be measured and progress assessed. The discourse of nation gave definition and boundaries to the idea of society, but nations came to be tacitly accepted—even naturalized—to such a degree that the implicit presumption of national identity was accepted even where nationalism was criticized. Nationalism was separated as an ideology from the alleged simple reality of national identity, and seen not as modern but as a carryover from traditional social organization and identities.[20]

This could happen partly because the cosmopolitan nationalism of the 18th and early 19th centuries, including the 'Springtime of Nations', gave way to a more reactionary and xenophobic discourse.[21] This was employed in movements many moderns found it easy to dismiss as backward-looking inheritances from a pre-modern era. Even theorists deeply influenced by nationalist ideas often failed to see nations and nationalisms as fundamental

---

Arendt's classic account of the transformation of racist thought in Nazi ideology (Arendt, 1951). More generally, see Hannaford, 1996. In the early 19th century, race and civilization were presented more commonly as candidates for the 'subject' of modernity.

[18] Outside marxism, attempts to construct classes as 'superindividual' agents were limited, and more collective, less emergent notions of class dominated in sociology.

[19] Anderson, 1991.

[20] I have reviewed much of the debate on this issue in Calhoun, 1993.

[21] See Meinecke, 1970; Ishay, 1996.

categories of modernity as a historically specific era. The idea of nation was
reduced to a hidden influence or assumption in much social science, thus,
rather than made a major object of theoretical attention. The canonical
story of the origins of sociology, for example, rooted the discipline in intellectual responses to domestic changes in European countries—as though
those countries were always already there, and as though cross-cultural comparisons had not played a crucial part in the invention of sociology.[22]

The *fin de siècle* was not just an era of world-weary sophisticates, but a
period when the contradictions of modernity began to become widely manifest. High modernist artists responded with both pursuit of radical formal
clarity and celebration of ambiguity; Malevich and Joyce are equally typical. Max Weber argued that the advancement of rationality could entrap
moderns in an iron cage; Emile Durkheim linked freedom to anomie;
Sigmund Freud discovered the sexual unconscious in the midst of some of
the most elaborate schemes of cultural repression the world has known.

The late 19th century was not a heroic age for European nationalism,
but a sort of interregnum; a calm between the enthusiasms of the mid-19th
century and the cataclysms of the 20th. Europe was busy with imperial
acquisitions and related conflicts, but for the most part there was peace on
the continent (which helped to foster the 'progressive' view that nationalism was a problem to be solved by modernization). Nationalism was mobilized, indeed, as much against domestic 'fifth columns' of radical workers as
against outsiders. But the late 19th and early 20th centuries were crucial
years for the building and deepening of the nationalist consciousnesses that
would spill over in World War I, the rise of the Navy League in Prussia,
the Dreyfus affair in France. The world-weary sophisticates of the *fin de siècle*
were not immune; within two decades, all too many were able to find in
nationalism the inspiration to shoot each other, or praise those who did so.

The 1890s were halcyon years for the deployment of nationalism as a
rhetoric of identity outside Western Europe. On Europe's Eastern fringe,
nationalists sought to shape countries from the decrepit Austro-Hungarian
empire. Russians sought to make the empire of the Czar into a modern
nation. Turks fashioned Turkey from the center of the old Ottoman Empire,
and Egyptians and others pursued similar projects on its periphery. In Spain,
the "generation of '98" (though not directly very political) sought to achieve
both the Enlightenment and the national identity that more 'modern'
Europeans had found a century earlier. In East Asia, this was the era in

---

[22] See Calhoun, 1995a; Connell, 1997; and Randall Collins' critique of Connell (Collins,
1997).

which the Japanese, and only slightly later the Chinese and Koreans, began to use the Western rhetoric of national identity to claim their distinctive, non-Western place in the world. And this was true not just far afield but as close to home as possible. These were the crucial years in the creation of black nationalism.

One of the central paradoxes of modernity is that an international rhetoric of national identity should become the preferred, early universal, mode of claiming autonomous and distinct local cultural identity. As Wilson Moses has remarked,

> In its secular form, black chauvinism derives, ironically enough from European racial theory. Like the concept of civilization, racial chauvinism can be traced back to the writings of Hegel, Guizot, Gobineau and other continental racial theorists of the nineteenth century. Indeed it was the German, Herder, who in the eighteenth century, developed theories of organic collectivism upon which Blyden and Crummel later built their own brand of ethnic chauvinism.[23]

These roots are of course commonly obscured by claims to complete intellectual autonomy, or the naturalness of the nation. To see that the discourse of nationalism was always international does not mean that all discourses of Third World or subaltern nationalism were merely derivative discourses; they were not.[24] But it does mean that the world was already integrated on a global scale, and that it was within that transnational reality that national identities were forged, and it does mean that this was done often in large part by reproducing or appropriating—albeit sometimes with considerable transformations—the European discourses of enlightenment, romantic individualism, and national identity.

There was a deeper contradiction in the spread of this discourse and many kindred discourses of modernity. This was the attempt to constitute identities in sharp, categorical terms, to render boundaries clear and identities integral even while the processes of capitalist expansion, slave trade (integrally modern though recently abolished in moves Western thinkers could assure themselves were modernizing), colonization, war, and the globalization of culture all ensured the production of ever more multiplicities and overlaps of identities. The phenomenon of 'double consciousness' that W.E.B. DuBois analyzed in the situation of those who were both Negro and American was a resistance to this dominant pattern in the construction of identities.[25] But it was in more than one sense a minority voice.

---

[23] Moses, 1988: 25.
[24] See Chatterjee's argument against this view (Chatterjee, 1986).
[25] DuBois, 1989.

However common, even ubiquitous, double consciousness really was, the prevailing rhetoric of identity and agency sought singular, integral subjects. Thus lines were drawn on maps and populations understood—at least ideally—to fit as unambiguously as possible within them. Moreover, the loyalties and obligations of individuals to nations were commonly described as unmediated and direct. Unlike traditional kinship systems with their reckoning of identity in a series of nested groups from families outward to larger lineages and clans, and often cross-cut by age-sets and other groupings, modern thought understood individuals to be immediately members of a nation, as though nationality were inscribed in their very bodies. Nationalism launched a war on traditional intermediate associations. And ways of constituting local identities throughout the world, from China to India to Turkey to Spain were all influenced by this discourse of individuals and nations. Even in the manifestly international culture of 'the Black Atlantic', produced by the slave trade and maintained by later migrations of people and cultural products, there was a tendency to construct Black identities in essentialist terms. In Paul Gilroy's words,

> . . . original, folk, or local expressions of black culture have been identified as authentic and positively evaluated . . . while subsequent hemispheric or global manifestations of the same cultural forms have been dismissed as inauthentic and therefore lacking in cultural or aesthetic value precisely because of their distance (supposed or actual) from a readily identifiable point of origin.[26]

In a wide range of other contexts and for other identities, similar processes were at work, constituting certain versions of collective culture as authentic, claiming certain historical precursors as definitive. The issue is not just the invention of new traditions, in the sense analyzed by Hobsbawm and Ranger, but also the fixing of previously more flexible and continually renewed traditions and the institutionalization both of biases and of powerful agents of cultural regulation.[27] Thus, for example, the creation of modern Turkish identity drew on precursors that could be understood as 'always already' Turkish—a mixture of Anatolian culture, Ottoman imperial heritage, and Islam—but it also constituted something new, something distinctively related to a non-imperial state and to the idea of nation as well as (more famously) to Western-influenced secularism. It is precisely because a nation was being forged on a model that seemed to require internal homogeneity and authenticity that Turkish nation-building was accompanied by the genocide of Armenians.

---

[26] Gilroy, 1993: 96.
[27] Hobsbawm and Ranger, 1983.

In the late 19th century, ironically, precisely as the globalization of political and economic organization and the world wide flows of culture were reaching unprecedented levels, the urge to organize social life in terms of sharp boundaries, national identities, and essentialist cultural categories likewise reached a peak. In Europe, it was in this period that nationalists began effectively to urge immigration controls; in this period they created the standing citizen armies that fought World War I; in this period they opposed socialism in part precisely because it was internationalist.[28] It was in this period that modern anti-Semitism took shape. And it was in this period that nationalism became most conclusively identified, in the European context, with movements for secession rather than amalgamation of existing states.[29] No era placed greater emphasis on the autonomy of the nation state or the capacity of the idea of nation to define large-scale collective identities. But it did so precisely when and partly because the world was becoming pronouncedly international. In this there may lie some lesson for the present era when the acceleration of global processes of capital accumulation, the rapid global transfer of technology, the almost instantaneous spread of cultural products, and huge waves of migration lead many to imagine the nation state is likely to vanish quickly into the shadows of history.

IV

To use the international rhetoric of nationalism to claim local self-determination was not only to commit oneself to representing local distinctiveness in internationally recognizable terms. It was also to make the local nation a token of a global type, to construct it as equivalent to other nations. In this we see the ways in which multiple modernist projects were linked, and the modern as such constituted in multiplicities.

Before the end of the 19th century, for example, China had never been constructed by either rulers or ordinary citizens as simply one country among many. Whether understood grandly as civilization, or as the middle kingdom, or simply as the terrain on which competing dynasties fought for power, it was not conceptualized as an exemplar of a type. Other countries—Korea, say, or Japan—were understood more in this way, as subordinate polities on the frontier of China, ideally at least fitting into the class of tribute payers. Early attempts were made to fit European countries into this model. But at least from the self-strengthening movement on, and especially as

---

[28] Hobsbawm, 1990: 123.
[29] See E.H. Carr's emphasis on this point (Carr, 1945: 24–25).

Chinese recognition of the transformation in Japan deepened after 1895, thinkers and officials began more often to think of China as one nation among many. Whether it was sick and weak or the only truly civilized nation were in a sense secondary questions to this deeper transformation of the basic conceptualization of the unit.

The transformation of collective identity was accompanied by, and perhaps entailed, a transformation of personal identity. Projects of reform sought to remake the person—just as they had a generation or two earlier in Germany, the country from which China (like Japan) perhaps borrowed most on this score. Schemes for popular education, an end to foot-binding, emancipation of sons (as well as daughters) from tyrannical fathers, and even reform of the language all signalled the change. The person was being freed from certain constraints, the rhetoric of the time suggested, but also made into the sort of person who could be an effective contributor to the cause of the nation. Aesthetic modernism spread along the same vectors, as with the poet Xu Zhimo who exemplified its more Romantic side, or Lu Xin, more of a rationalist.

Similarly in a host of other settings, the emancipation of the nation from empire and dynasty went hand in hand with the emancipation of the person from subjection to patriarchy, religion, and village custom. Subjects were rethought from the vantage point of the nation.

Nationalism was not the whole, but only the most important part of the tacit consensus forged in the late 19th century as to what would count as politically appropriate identities. It played a central role in the development of 'essentialist' thinking that was also basic to the way race, gender, sexual orientation and other modalities of collective identities came to be constituted. In all cases, the assumption has been widespread both in social theory and in more popular discourses that these cultural categories address really existing and discretely identifiable collections of people—and more surprisingly that it is possible to understand each category by focusing on its primary identifier rather than on the way it overlaps with, contests and/or reinforces others.

Put another way, it has been the tacit assumption of modern social and cultural thought that people are normally members of one and only one nation, that they are members of one and only one race, one gender, and one sexual orientation, and that each of these memberships describes neatly and concretely some aspect of their being. It has been assumed that people naturally live in one world at a time, that they inhabit one way of life, that they speak one language, and that they themselves, as individuals, are singular, integral beings. All these assumptions came clearly into focus in the late 19th century, and all seem problematic.

The underlying issues are hard to get at because social and cultural theory did not consistently study the constitution of nations, races, genders or
other categories. Rather, a variety of putatively neutral terms—society, culture, subculture—were introduced. Their seeming neutrality obscured the
extent to which they reflected the presumptions about categorical distinctiveness that were forged especially with sex, race, and nation in mind.
Social scientists came to a remarkable extent to take for granted the objects
of their study—notably societies—without reflecting on the extent to which
their view of what societies were had been produced largely on the foundation of 19th century nationalist reasoning.

The unraveling of this tacit equation of nation and society has been a
key theme of the late 20th century. The problematic nature of these assumptions has been raised most prominently by postmodernism, but also by discussion of globalism and the 'clash of civilizations'.[30] One problem with the
term 'postmodern' is that it suggests that these assumptions may once have
held, but that something has changed in the world to render identity newly
problematic and to render the old fixity of categories obsolete. When the
change should be located and whether it happened equally throughout the
world is at best only fuzzily suggested.[31] The power of the category of nation
was always embedded in modernizing projects, never simply a stable condition of modernity; particular nationalist claims were always subject to
contestation.

Whether it solves any specific problems or not, postmodernism rightly
encourages us at the end of the 20th century to revisit the question of the
'purpose' of modernity as it figured in the late 19th century. If the last *fin
de siècle* saw the purpose of modernity as progress, at least a large postmodernist current in the present one sees the purpose of modernity as repression.[32] This is by no means so familiar an opposition as to be uninteresting.
Postmodernist discourse extends certain of the late 19th and early 20th century themes of high modernism—like the instability of the subject, as interesting to Musil as to Kundera. At the same time, it focuses attention on
themes that were either neglected a hundred years ago or pushed to the
margin of social and cultural theory as they were consolidated in that period.
Simmel, paradigmatic high modernist among social theorists, thus anticipated themes of postmodernism.[33] But while the high modernism of Joyce,
Baudelaire and the Bauhaus was enormously influential in aesthetic domains,

---

[30] Robertson, 1992b; Barber, 1995; Huntington, 1996.
[31] See Calhoun, 1995b.
[32] See, paradigmatically, Lyotard, 1984.
[33] Compare Frisby (1985) and Weinstein and Weinstein (1993).

social theory proved more resistant. For all the ubiquity of the contrast of countryside to city in modern social theory, one reason may be that theorists' deepest commitments were to nation-states as the primary units of analysis. Artists and writers might inhabit cities more than countries, and become suspect to nationalists on this account. Most social scientists compared countries, and indeed helped to reproduce the very dominance of a division of the world into states made legitimate by representing nations.

Modernism was, however, also a critical response to much of what we call modernity. That this doesn't figure much in the historical self-reflections of the social science disciplines is due largely to the success of efforts at canonization and discipline formation that worked systematically to extract the thought of the late 19th and early 20th centuries from its historical context, to cut Durkheim off from Sorel, to insulate Weber from Mann and Lukacs, to minimize Marx. Talcott Parsons thought he could distill the essence of the social thought of the generation that matured in the 1890s into a theory of voluntary but highly structured social action and a general picture of gradual social evolution. But this may tell us more about him and about mid-twentieth century America than about thinkers who came of age at the end of the last century in Europe. And in any case, the era when his optimism (both about the world and about the unity of theory) seemed justified proved brief. It is worth recalling that to a much greater extent, the theorists we associate with the *fin de siècle* were pessimists or at least committed to an idea of disillusioned realism and opposed to Romanticism even when they drew substantively on its intellectual currents. The great thinkers of the late 19th century, like Darwin and Spencer may have been believers in a simpler and more Providential progress (though it is worth recalling that their age was also Nietzsche's). Freud and Weber and Simmel certainly were not, and even Durkheim hedged his bets on progress well before World War One. Yet surprisingly, especially but not exclusively in America, the social sciences were established as autonomous academic disciplines in such a fashion that reflection on the basic anxieties of twentieth-century life—including the instability of nations and other organizing collective identities—would seem foreign to each, an unscientific interpolation.

Especially under the influence of nationalist ideas, social scientists developed notions of societies as singular, bounded, and internally integrated, and as realms in which people were more or less the same. On this basis, a great deal of modern social theory came to incorporate prereflectively the notion that human beings naturally inhabit only a single social world or culture at a time. People on borders, children of mixed marriages, those rising through social mobility and those migrating from one society to another were all constituted for social theory as people with problems by contrast to the presumed ideal of people who inhabited a single social world and could therefore unambiguously place themselves in their social environments. The implicit phenomenological presumption was that human life would be easier if individuals did not have to manage a heterogeneity of social worlds or modes of cultural understanding. An ideal of clarity and consistency prevailed. This ideal of course reflected broadly rationalist thinking, but it should not be interpreted as limited to rationalistic (or Enlightenment) views. Much of the jargon of authenticity in Romantic and later anti-rationalist thought shares the same idealization of the notion of inhabiting a single self-consistent life world.[34] This notion of the external world mirrored a pre-Freudian (not to mention pre-Bakhtinian) notion of the potential self-consistent internal life of the individual—one represented in the very term 'individual' with its implication that the person cannot be internally divided.

This notion of inhabiting singular social or lifeworlds as integral beings reflected both assumptions about how actual social life was organized and ideals about how social life ought to be organized. It invoked, in other words, an idea of normality. But the early theorists did not for the most part see their contemporary world as unproblematic on this dimension. Rather, they recognized that people around them faced challenges in trying to come to terms with differences, border crossings and interstitial positions. This led to an understanding of the past as one in which singular social worlds more completely enveloped people; in which society was less differentiated and less complicated. Societies differed, but internally each was unified. This was for some a golden age, but most social scientists emphasized that for better or worse modernity meant parting with such visions.

We should also be careful not to follow the many classical social theorists whose examination of 'other cultures' was conducted in a way that hypostatized both the otherness and the integral unity of cultures. People have long inhabited multiple social worlds at the same time. Multilinguality is as 'natural' as monolinguality. Trade has established linkages across political and cultural frontiers. The great religions have spread across divergent local cultures and maintained connections among them. Even in the relatively small scale, low technology societies that most informed Durkheim's notion of mechanical solidarity, people inhabited multiple horizons of experience, for example as members simultaneously of local lineages and far-flung clans. In great civilizations like India that were not organized as singular political units, this was all the more true.

---

[34] See Adorno, 1973.

V

The 20th century arguable reached its *fin de siècle* in the early 1990s. I would date it not from the great events which inspired so much hope in 1989, but from the bafflement and disappointment that spread as it became clear to what extent the collapse of communism renewed old problems rather than ushering in the end of history. The resurgence of nationalism in the former communist countries helped to draw attention to the fact that nationalism was not simply a fading inheritance of the premodern era. Indeed, nationalism flourished well beyond the range of former communist countries, suggesting that however prominent it was as a 'successor ideology' in some, it was not to be explained by the peculiarities of post-communist transitions.

Nationalism turned bloody quite quickly in the 1990s. From the first fighting in Nagorno-Karabakh and other previously obscure regions of the former USSR to the protracted struggles in what was once Yugoslavia, the nationalist fighting was a direct challenge to Western intellectuals, policymakers and citizens. It challenged faith in progress, of course, which had briefly been revitalized by the fall of communist rule. It also challenged postmodernists, though, despite their rejection of the metanarrative of progress. Not only did the manifest horrors undermine the happy relativism of some, they revealed the continuing power of a very modern form of collective identity, politics and—for many—evil. This led some postmodernists fruitfully to clarify their arguments away from claims that an epoch had ended to calls for an end to certain ways of thinking and theorizing deeply implicated in clearly continuing problems.[35]

The resurgence of nationalism around the world also offered a counterpoint to the celebratory politics of identity that had been flourishing, especially since the 1960s. There had been an innocent pleasure to the proliferation of such calls for recognition, and to many of the refigurations of self that ensured. Noticing that a politics of identity could be horrific put the more peaceful and benign movements of the Western democracies under a new light. Rather than easily assuming the possibility of a 'springtime of identities' not unlike the mid-19th century Springtime of Nations, many thinkers

---

[35] Bauman (1989a) addressed some of these continuing problems in an earlier historical case, developing postmodernist challenges to some core ideas of modernism without getting caught in an illusory claim that the epoch had ended. Resurgent nationalism was of course not the only factor pressing postmodernists to rethink certain themes; many, including Bauman, explicitly eschewed earlier relativisms while pursuing forms of ethnical engagement not tied to modernist universalism.

have begun to treat identity-politics as a more complex phenomenon, potentially liberatory perhaps, but also fraught with dangers. It became clearer that success for one identity movement often infringed on the claims and hopes of others—as with nationalism.

A gloomy *fin de siècle* attitude has informed some recent attempts to put the genie of identity politics back in its bottle, lest it produce nothing but endless fragmentation. In *The Twilight of Common Dreams*, for example, Todd Gitlin evokes a classical image of 'progressive' politics and argues that identity movements are increasingly undermining it.[36] Such views are widespread. Yet in a sense they fail to do justice to the difficulty of both the intellectual and political situation. In this current *fin de siècle*, it is no longer possible to take for granted the 'national' subject of modern progress. The identity politics movements flourish partly for this reason. Global integration challenges the tacit assumption of the self of self-determination, not just with trade and production organization across borders, but with global information flows and media corporations, and with global flows of people as migrants especially, but also as travelers. In this context, there is no escape from identity politics. To attempt to unify people at the level of existing states, for class politics or communitarianism or conventional party programs, also requires attempts to convince people that certain understandings of their individual and collective identities should have priority over others. No subject for progress can be taken for granted, and this is one of the most basic reasons why progress—or more profoundly, the good itself—is so hard to assess.

A key intellectual agenda at the beginning of the 21st century, thus, is to find a way to speak of identity, and agency in ways that do not tacitly equate society with nation, or presume that one identity is automatically a trump card against others. Likewise, it is crucial to be able to speak of multiple modernities—in the sense of different projects and potentials, and of the multiplicities inherent in the modern epoch. It is not obvious that today's social scientists will move much farther than their predecessors of the 1890s. One way to do so, however, would be to develop a way of addressing the challenges of cultural and historical difference, that does not render observed differences the bases for hypostatizing 'whole' societies or cultures as though they were internally integral.[37] We need to see not only that empirical

---

[36] Gitlin, 1995.

[37] In something of the same spirit, Sorokin (1957) generations ago criticized those who studied cultures with the presumption that these were necessarily cognitively or logically integrated units, rather than seeing such integration as an empirical variable. His criticism had regrettably little effect on developments in sociology.

variable, however, but the practical activity by which ordinary people manage cultural complexity and the interfaces among social worlds.[38] The issue is not just to avoid 'essentialist' invocations of integral identity, but to see that just pointing to 'social construction' offers little if any analytic purchase. It is not just that collective identities and ways of life are created, but that they are internally contested, that their boundaries are porous and overlapping, and that people live in more than one at the same time.

The prominence of postmodernism generally and a range of more particular challenges to the idea of clearly demarcated and internally coherent identities has not kept contemporary thinkers from imagining the world in those terms. When Samuel Huntington argued that the crucial conflicts of the future would be those between civilizations, thus, he saw civilizations in the same manner as the dominant 19th century discourse saw nations: discrete, internally self-consistent, and perduring tokens of a common type.[39] He wrote of a world minimally marked by multiplicities of identities, though maximally by conflicts over territories. Accounts of the horrors of Bosnia, Somalia, Rwanda and other national and/or ethnic conflicts evoke premodern imagery of 'tribal warfare'. These are all the results, political leaders assure us on the basis of respectable academic sources, of ancient ethnic conflicts. Because the clashes are primordial we can do nothing about them except to try to reduce the scale of the bloodletting by sending in the Red Cross or embargoing weapons.

Such accounts are, of course, a way of getting ourselves off the hook because they justify inaction. At the same time, though, they point to a deeper sense in which we seek to exculpate ourselves, perhaps unconsciously. This is our effort to disengage such horrors from our image of modernity. It is as though we seek to salvage the remaining vestiges of a tattered idea of progress by relegating the most pressing and substantial conflicts and challenges of contemporary world affairs to the category of 'the traditional', against which the late 19th century thinkers identified the modern. Above all, perhaps, with such rhetoric and views we abandon the possibility of recovering any sense of the extent to which modernity did not just happen to us, but was produced and then exported from Europe (and later America) as a project. It is not a project from which we can disengage at will.

---

[38] See Hannerz (1992) for a suggestion concerning this issue. Also, Hannerz, 1988.
[39] Huntington, 1996. Ajami's response (Ajami, 1993) to Huntington's early article on this theme makes a similar point about how "Huntington has found his civilizations whole and intact, watertight under an eternal sky."

28. IDENTITY IN THE GLOBALIZING WORLD

Zygmunt Bauman

"There has been a veritable discursive explosion in recent years around the concept of 'identity'"[1]—observed Stuart Hall in the introduction to a volume of studies published in 1996. A few years passed since that observation was made, during which the explosion triggered an avalanche. No other aspect of contemporary life, it seems, attracts these days a similar attention of philosophers, social scientists and psychologists. Not just the 'identity studies' are fast becoming a thriving industry in their own right: more than that is happening—one may say that 'identity' has become by now a prism through which other topical aspects of contemporary life are spotted, grasped and examined. Established issues of social analysis are being rehashed and refurbished to fit the discourse now rotating around the 'identity' axis. For instance, the discussion of justice and equality tends to be conducted in terms of 'recognition', culture is debated in terms of individual, group or categorial difference, creolization and hybridity, while the political process is ever more often theorized around the issues of human rights (that is, the right to a separate identity) and of 'life politics' (that is, identity construction, negotiation and assertion).

I suggest that the spectacular rise of the 'identity discourse' can tell us more about the present-day state of human society than its conceptual and analytical results have told us thus far. And so, rather than composing another 'career report' of contentions and controversies which combine into that discourse, I intend to focus on the tracing of experiential grounds, and through them the structural roots, of that remarkable shift in intellectual concerns of which the new centrality of the 'identity discourse' is a most salient symptom.

We know from Hegel that the Owl of Minerva, the goddess of wisdom, spreads its wings, prudently, at dusk; knowledge, or whatever passes under that name, arrives by the end of the day when the Sun has set and things are no more brightly lit and easily found and handled (long before Hegel coined the tarrying-Owl metaphor, Sophocles made the clarity of sight into the monopoly of blind Teiresias). Martin Heidegger gave a new twist to

---

[1] Hall, 1996b: 1.

Hegel's aphorism in his discussion of the priority of *Zuhandenheit* to *Vorhandenheit* and of the 'catastrophic' origin of the second: good lighting is the true blindness, one does not see what is all-too-visible, one does not note what is 'always there', things are noticed when they disappear or go bust, they must fall first out from the routinely 'given' for the search after their essences to start and the questions about their origin, whereabouts, use or value to be asked. In Arland Usher's succinct summary, "The world as world is only revealed to me when things go wrong".[2] Or, in Vincent Vycinas' rendition,[3] whatever my world consists of is brought to my attention only when it goes missing, or when it suddenly stops behaving as, monotonously, it did before, loses its usefulness or shows itself to be 'unready' for my attempts to use it. It is the awkward and unwieldy, unreliable, resistant and otherwise *frustrating* things that force themselves into our vision, attention and thought.

Let us note that the discovery that things do not keep their shape once for all and may be different from what they are is an ambiguous experience. Unpredictability breeds anxiety and fear: the world is full of accidents and surprises, one must never let vigilance to lapse and should never lay down the arms. But the unsteadiness, softness and pliability of things may also trigger ambition and resolve: one can make things better than they are, and needs not settle for what there is since no verdict of nature is final, no resistance of reality is unbreakable. One can now dream of a different life—more decent, bearable or enjoyable. And if in addition one has confidence in one's power of thought and in the strength of one's muscles, one can also act on those dreams and perhaps even force them to become true . . . Alain Peyrefitte[4] has suggested that the remarkable, unprecedented and unique dynamism of our modern capitalist society, all the spectacular advances made by the 'Western civilization' over the last two or three centuries, would be unthinkable without such confidence: the triple trust in oneself, in others, and in the jointly built, durable institutions in which one can confidently inscribe one's long-term plans and actions.

Anxiety and audacity, fear and courage, despair and hope are born together. But the proportion in which they are mixed depends on the resources in one's possession. Owners of foolproof vessels and skilled navigators view the sea as the site of exciting adventure; those condemned to unsound and hazardous dingies would rather hide behind wave-breakers and think of sailing with trepidation. Fears and joys that emanate from instability of things are distributed highly unequally.

---

[2] Usher, 1995: 80.
[3] See Vycinas, 1969: 36–7.
[4] See Peyrefitte, 1998: 514–516.

Modernity, we may say, specialized in making *zuhanden* things into *vorhanden*. By 'setting the world in motion', it exposed the fragility and unsteadiness of things and threw open the possibility (and the need) of re-shaping them. Marx and Engels praised the capitalists, the bourgeois revolutionaries, for 'melting the solids and profaning the sacreds' which for long centuries cramped human creative powers. Alexis de Tocqueville thought rather that the solids picked for melting in the heat of modernization had been already in the state of advanced decomposition and so beyond salvation well before the modern overhaul of nature and society has started. Whatever was the case, human nature, once seen as a lasting and non-negligible legacy of one-off Divine creation, has been thrown, together with the rest of Divine creation, into a melting pot. No more was it seen, no more could it be seen, as 'given'. Instead, it has turned into a *task*, and a task which every man and woman had no choice but to face up to and perform to the best of their ability. 'Predestination' was replaced with 'life project', fate with vocation—and a 'human nature' into which one was born with 'identity' which one needs to saw up and make fit.

Philosophers of Renaissance celebrated the new breathtaking vistas that the 'unfinishness' of human nature opened before the resourceful and the bold. 'Men can do all things if they will', declared proudly Leon Battista Alberti; 'We can become what we will', announced, with joy and relish, Pico della Mirandola. Ovid's Proteus, who could turn at will from a young man into a lion, a wild boar or a snake, a stone or a tree, and the chameleon, that grandmaster of instant reincarnation, became the paragons of the newly discovered human virtue of self-constitution and self-assertion.[5] A few decades later Jean-Jacques Rousseau would name *perfectibility* as the sole no-choice attribute with which nature endowed the human race: he would insist that the capacity of self-transformation is the only 'human essence' and the only trait common to us all.[6] Humans are free to self-create. What they are, is not a no-appeal-allowed verdict of Providence, not the matter of predestination.

Which did not mean necessarily that humans are doomed to float and drift: Proteus may be a symbol of the potency of self-creation, but protean existence is not necessarily the first choice of free human beings. Solids may be melted, but they are melted in order to mould new solids better shaped and better fit for human happiness than the old ones—but also more solid and so more 'certain' than the old solids managed to be. Melting the solids

---

[5] See Davies, 1978: 62 ff.
[6] See Rousseau, 1986: 148 ff.

was to be but the preliminary, site-clearing stage of the modern undertaking to make the world more suitable for human habitation. Designing a new—tough, durable, reliable and trustworthy setting for human life was to be the second stage, a stage that truly counted since it was to give meaning to the whole enterprise. One order needed to be dismantled so that it could be replaced with another, purpose-built and up to the standards of reason and logic.

As Immanuel Kant insisted, we all—each one of us—are endowed with the faculty of reason, that powerful tool which allows us to compare the options on offer and make our individual choices; but if we use that tool properly, we will all arrive to similar conclusions and will all accept one code of cohabitation which reason tells us to be the best. Not all thinkers would be equally sanguine as Kant was: not all were sure that each one of us would follow the guidance of reason on one's own accord. Perhaps people need to be forced to be free, as Rousseau suspected? Perhaps the newly acquired freedom needs to be used *for* the people rather than *by* people? Perhaps we still need the despots, though 'enlightened' ones and so less erratic, more resolute and effective than the despots of yore, to design and fix reason-dictated patterns which would guarantee that people make right and proper uses of their freedom? Both suppositions sounded plausible and both had its enthusiasts, prophets and preachers. As it were, the idea of human self-construction and self-assertion carried the seeds of democracy mixed with the spores of totalitarianism. The new era of flexible realities and freedom of choice was to be pregnant with unlikely twins: with human rights—but also with what Hannah Arendt called 'totalitarian temptation'.

These comments are on the face of it unrelated to our theme; if I made them here, I did it with the intention to show that the ostensible unrelatedness is but an illusion, if not a grave mistake. 'Incompleteness' of identity, and particularly the individual responsibility for its completion, are in fact intimately related to all other aspects of modern condition. However it has been posited in our times and however it presents itself in our reflections, 'identity' is not a 'private matter' and a 'private worry'. That our individuality is socially produced, is by now a trivial truth; but the obverse of that truth needs yet to be repeated more often: the shape of our sociality, and so of the society we share, depends in its turn on the way in which the task of 'individualization' is framed up and responded to.

What the idea of 'individualization' informs of, is the emancipation of the individual from his or her ascribed, inherited and inborn determination of social character: a departure rightly seen as a most conspicuos and seminal feature of modern condition. To put it in a nutshell, 'individualization' consists in transforming human 'identity' from a 'given' into a 'task'—and charging the actors with the responsibility for performing that task and for the consequences (also the side effects) of their performance; in other words, it consists in establishing a 'de jure' autonomy (though not necessarily the *de facto* one). One's place in society, one's 'social definition', has ceased to be 'zuhanden' and become 'vorhanden' instead. No more one's place in society comes as a (wanted or unwanted) gift. (As Jean-Paul Sartre famously put it: it is not enough to be born a bourgeois—one must live one's life as a bourgeois. The same did not need, nor could not be said about princes, knights, serfs, or townsmen of the pre-modern era.) Needing to *become* what one *is* is the feature of modern living (not of 'modern individualization'—that expression being evidently pleonastic: to speak of individualization and of modernity is to speak of the same social condition). Modernity replaces the *determination* of social standing with a compulsive and obligatory *self*-determination.

This, let me repeat, holds for the whole of the modern era: for all periods and for all sectors of society. If so—then why 'the veritable explosion' of concerns with identity has occurred in recent years only? What if anything new happened to the problem as old as modernity itself?

Yes, there is something new in the old problem—and this explains the current alarm about the tasks which past generations seemed to handle routinely in a 'matter-of-factly' way. Within the shared predicament of identity-builders there are significant variations, which set apart successive periods of modern history. The 'self-identification' task put before men and women once the stiff frames of estates had been broken in the early modern era boiled down to the challenge of living 'true to kind' (as the Americans say, 'up to the Joneses'): of actively conforming to the established social types and models of conduct, of imitating, following the pattern, 'acculturating', not falling out of step, not deviating from the norm. The falling apart of 'estates' did not set individuals drifting. 'Estates' came to be replaced by 'classes'.

While the estates were the matter of ascription, class membership entailed a large measure of achievement; classes, unlike the estates, had to be 'joined', and the membership had to be continuously renewed, re-confirmed and documented in day-by-day conduct. In other words, the 'disembedded' individuals were prompted and prodded to deploy their new powers and new right to self-determination in the frantic search of 're-embeddenment'. And there was no shortage of 'beds' waiting and ready to accommodate them. Class allocation, though formed and negotiable rather than inherited or simply 'born into' as the *estates*, *Stände* or *états* used to be, tended to become as solid, unalterable and resistant to individual manipulation as the pre-modern assignment to the estate. Class and gender hung heavily over the individual range of choices; to escape their constraint was not much easier than to challenge one's place in the 'Divine chain of beings'. If not in theory, then at least for *practical* intents and purposes, class and gender looked uncannily like 'facts of nature' and the task left to most self-assertive individuals was to 'fit in' into the allocated niche through behaving as its established residents did.

This is, precisely, what distinguished the 'individualization' of yore from the form it has taken now, in our own times of 'liquid' modernity, when not just the individual *placements* in society, but the *places* to which the individuals may gain access and in which they may wish to settle are melting fast and can hardly serve as targets for 'life projects'. This new restlessness and fragility of goals affects us all, unskilled and skilled, uneducated and educated, work-shy and hard-working alike. There is little or nothing we can do to 'bind the future' through following diligently the current standards.

As Daniel Cohen pointed out,

> Qui débute sa carrière chex Microsoft n'a aucune idée de là ou il la terminera. La commencer chez Ford ou Renault s'était au contraire la quasi-certitude de la finir au meme endroit.[7]

Not just the individuals are on the move but also the finishing lines of the tracks they run and the running tracks themselves. 'Disembeddenment' is now an experience which is likely to be repeated an unknown number of times in the course of individual life since few if any 'beds' for 'reembedding' look solid enough to augur the stability of long occupation. The 'beds' in view look rather like 'musical chairs' of various sizes and styles as well as of changing numbers and mobile positions, forcing men and women to be constantly on the running and promising no rest and no satisfaction of 'arriving', no comfort of reaching the destination where one can disarm, relax and stop worrying. There is no prospect of 'final reembeddenment' at the end of the road; being on the road has become the permanent way of life of the disembedded (now chronically) individuals.

Writing at the beginning of the 20th century, Max Weber suggested that 'instrumental rationality' is the main factor regulating human behaviour in the era of modernity—perhaps the only one likely to emerge unscathed from the battle of motivational forces. The matter of ends seemed then to have been settled, and the remaining task of modern men and women was to select the best means to the ends. One could say that uncertainty as to the relative efficiency of means and their availability would be, as long as Weber's

---

[7] Cohen, 1997: 84.

proposition held true, the main source of insecurity and anxiety characteristic of modern life. I suggest, though, that whether or not Weber's view
was correct at the start of the 20th century, its truth has gradually yet relentlessly evaporated as the century drew to its close. Nowadays, not the *means*
are the prime source of insecurity and anxiety.

The 20th century excelled in the over-production of means; means have
been produced on a constantly accelerating speed and in excess of the
known, let alone acutely felt, needs. Abundant means came to seek the ends
which they could serve; it was the turn of the solutions to search desper-
ately for not-yet-articulated problems which they could resolve. On the other
hand, though, the ends have become ever more diffuse, scattered and uncertain: the most profuse source of anxiety, the great unknown of men's and
women's life. If you look for a short, sharp yet apt and poignant expression of that new predicament in which people tend to find themselves these
days, you could do worse than remembering a small add published recently
in the 'jobs sought' rubric of an English daily: "Have car, can travel; awaiting propositions".

And so the 'problem of identity', haunting men and women since the
advent of modern times, has changed its shape and content. It used to be
the kind of problem which pilgrims confront and struggle to resolve: a problem 'how to get there?'. It is now more like a problem with which the
vagabonds, people without fixed addresses and *sans papiers*, struggle daily:
'where could I, or should I, go? And where this road I've taken will bring
me?' The task is no more to muster enough strength and determination to
proceed, through trials and errors, triumphs and defeats, along the beaten
track stretching ahead. The task is to pick the least risky turn at the nearest crossroads, to change direction before the road ahead gets impassable
or before the road-scheme has been re-designed, or before the coveted destination moved elsewhere or has lost its past glitter. In other words, the
quandary tormenting men and women at the turn of the century is not so
much how to obtain the identities of their choice and how to have them
recognized by people around—but *which* identity to choose and how to keep
alert and vigilant so that *another* choice could be made in case the previously chosen identity has been withdrawn from the market or stripped of
its seductive powers. The main, the most nerve-breaking worry is not how to
find a place inside a solid frame of social class or category, and—having
found it—how to guard it and avoid eviction; what makes one worry is the
suspicion that the hard won frame will be soon torn apart or melted.

In his by now classic, about forty years old statement Erik H. Erikson
diagnosed the confusion suffered by the adolescents of that time as 'identity crisis' (a term first coined during the war to describe the condition of

some mental patients who 'lost a sense of personal sameness and historical continuity'). 'Identity crisis' in adults, as Erikson put it, is a pathological condition which requires medical intervention; it is also a common yet passing stage in 'normal' personal development, which in all probability will come to its natural end as the adolescents mature. To the question what the healthy state of a person should be, 'what identity feels like when you become aware of the fact that you do undoubtedly have one', Erikson answered: it feels "as a *subjective sense* of an *invigorating sameness* and *continuity*".[8]

Either Erikson's opinion has aged, as opinions usually do, or the 'identity crisis' has become today more than a rare condition of mental patients or a passing condition of adolescence: the 'sameness' and 'continuity' are feelings seldom nowadays experienced by the young and the adults alike. Furthermore, they are no more coveted—and if desired, the dream is as a rule contaminated with sinister premonitions and fear. As the two prominent cultural analysts, Zbyszko Melosik and Tomasz Szkudlarek, pointed out,[9] it is a curse of all identity construction that 'I lose my freedom, when I reach the goal; I am not myself, when I become somebody'. And in a kaleidoscopic world of reshuffled values, of mobile tracks and melting frames, freedom of manoeuver rises to the rank of the topmost value—indeed, the *meta*-value, condition of access to all other values: past, present and above all those yet to come. Rational conduct in such a world demands that the options, as many as possible, are kept open, and gaining an identity which fits too tightly, an identity that once for all offers 'sameness' and 'continuity' results in the closing of options or forfeiting them in advance. As Christopher Lasch famously observed, the 'identities' sought these days are such as "can be adopted and discarded like a change of costume"; if they are 'freely chosen', the choice "no longer implies commitments and consequences"—and so "the freedom to choose amounts in practice to an abstention from choice",[10] at least, let me add, from a *binding* choice.

In Grenoble in December 1997, Pierre Bourdieu spoke of 'précarité', which "est aujourd' hui partout" and "hante les consciences *et* les inconscients". The fragility of all conceivable point of reference and endemic uncertainty about the future affect profoundly those who have been already hit and all the rest of us who cannot be certain that the future blows will pass us by. "En rendant tout l'avenir incertain", says Bourdieu, 'la précarité' interdit toute anticipation rationalle et, en particulier, ce minimum de croyance et d'espérance en l'avenir qu'il faut avoir pour se révolter, sur tout

---

[8] Erikson, 1974: 17–19.
[9] Melosik and Szkudlarek, 1998: 89.
[10] Lasch, 1984: 38.

collectivement, contre le présent, meme le plus intolérable . . . Pour concevoir un projet révolutionnaire, c'est-à-dire une ambition raisonnée de transformer le présent par référence à un avenir projeté, il faut avoir un minimum de prise sur le présent"[11]—and the grip on the present, the confidence of being in control of one's destiny, is what men and women in our type of society most conspicuously lack. Less and less we hope that by joining forces and standing arm to arm we may force a change on the rules of the game; perhaps the risks which make us afraid and the catastrophies which make us suffer have collective, social origins—but they seem to fall upon each one of us at random, as individual problems, of the kind that could be only individually confronted and repaired, if at all, by individual efforts.

There seems to be little point in designing the alternative modes of togetherness, in stretching imagination to visualize a society better serving the cause of freedom and security, in drawing blueprints of socially administered justice, if a collective agency capable of making the words flesh is nowhere in sight. Our dependencies are now truly global, our actions however are, as before, local. The powers which shape the condition under which we confront our problems are beyond the reach of all agencies which modern democracy invented in the two centuries of its history; as Manuel Castells put it—real power, the exterritorial global power, flows, but politics, confined now as in the past to the framework of nation-states, stays as before tied to the ground.

A vicious circle, indeed. The fast globalization of the power network seems to conspire and collaborate with the privatized life politics; they stimulate, sustain and reinforce each other. If globalization saps the estabilshed political institutions' capacity to act effectively, the massive retreat from 'body politics' to the narrow concerns of life-politics prevents crystallization of alternative modes of collective action on a par with the globality of the network of dependencies. Everything seems to be in place to make *both* the globalization of life conditions *and* the 'morcellement', the atomization and privatization of life-struggles, self-propelling and self-perpetuating. It is against this background that the logic and the endemic illogicality of contemporary 'identity concerns' and the actions they trigger need to be scrutinized and understood.

As Ulrich Beck pointed out, there are no biographical solutions to systemic contradiction—though it is such solutions which we are pressed or cajoled to discover or invent. There can be no rational response to the rising *précarité* of human conditions as long as such response is to be confined to the individual's action; the irrationality of possible responses is inescapable,

---

[11] Bourdieu, 1998: 96–97.

given that the scope of life-politics and of the network of forces which determine its conditions are, purely and simply, incomparable and widely disproportionate.

If you cannot, or don't believe you can, do what truly matters, you turn to things which matter less or perhaps not at all, but which you can do or believe you can; and by turning your attention and energy to such things, you may even make them matter—for a time at least . . .

"Having no hope", says Christopher Lasch,

> of improving their lives in any of the ways that matter, people have convinced themselves that what matters is psychic self-improvement; getting in touch with their feelings, eating health food, taking lessons in ballet or belly-dancing, immersing themselves in the wisdom of the East, jogging, learning how to 'relate', overcoming the 'fear of pleasure.' Harmless in themselves, these pursuits, elevated to a programme and wrapped in the rhetoric of authenticity and awareness, signify a retreat from politics . . .[12]

There is a wide and widening spectrum of 'substitute pastimes' symptomatic of the shift from things that matter but can be done nothing about to things that matter less or do not matter but can be dealt with and handled. Compulsive shopping figures prominently among them. Mikhail Bakhtin's 'carnivals' used to be celebrated inside the home territory where 'routine life' was at other times conducted, and so allowed to lay bare the normally hidden alternatives which daily life contained. Unlike them, the trips to the shopping malls are expeditions to *another world* starkly different from the rest of daily life, to that 'elsewhere' where one can experience briefly that self-confidence and 'authenticity' which one is seeking in vain in routine daily pursuits. Shopping expeditions fill the void left by travels to alternative, more secure, humane and just societies, no more undertaken by the imagination.

The time-and-effort-consuming activity of putting together, dismantling and re-arranging self-identity is another of the 'substitute pastimes'. That activity is, as we have already seen, conducted under conditions of acute insecurity: the targets of action are as precarious as its effects are uncertain. Efforts lead to frustration often enough for the fear of ultimate failure to poison the joy of temporary triumphs. No wonder that dissolving personal fears in the 'might of numbers', trying to make them inaudible in the hubbub of boisterous crowd, is a constant temptation which many a lonely 'identity builder' finds difficult to resist. Even stronger is the temptation to pretend that it is the similarity of individual fears that 'makes a community' and so one can make a company out of solitude.

---

[12] Lasch, 1979: 29–30.

As Eric Hobsbawm recently observed, "never was the word 'community' used more indiscriminately and emptily than in the decades when communities in the sociological sense became hard to find in real life";[13] "Men and women look for groups to which they can belong, certainly and forever, in a world in which all else is moving and shifting, in which nothing else is certain".[14] Jock Young supplies a succint and poignant gloss: "Just as community collapses, identity is invented".[15] 'Identity' owes the attention it attracts and the passions it begets to being a *surrogate of community*: of that allegedly 'natural home' which is no more available in the rapidly privatized and individualized, fast globalizing world, and for that reason can be safely imagined as a cosy shelter of security and confidence and as such hotly desired. The paradox, though, is that in order to offer even a modicum of security and so to perform its healing role, identity must belie its origin, must deny being just a surrogate, and best of all needs to conjure up a phantom of the self-same community which it has come to replace. Identity sprouts on the graveyard of communities, but flourishes thanks to its promise to resurrect the dead.

The 'era of identity' is full of sound and fury. The search of identity divides and separates; yet precariousness of the solitary identity-building prompts the identity-builders to seek pegs on which they could hang together their individually experienced fears and anxieties and perform the exorcism rites in the company of others, similarly afraid and anxious individuals. Whether such 'peg communities' provide what they are hoped to offer—a collective insurance against individually confronted risks—is a moot question; but mounting a barricade in the company of others does supply a momentary respite from loneliness. Effective or not, something has been done, and one can at least console oneself that the blows are not being taken hands down. As Jonathan Friedman put it, in our globalizing world "one thing that is not happening is that boundaries are disappearing. Rather, they seem to be erected on every new street corner of every declining neighbourhood of our world."[16]

Boundaries are not drawn to fence off and protect already existing identities. As the great Norwegian anthropologist Frederick Barth explained—it is exactly the other way round: the ostensibly shared, 'communal' identities are by-products of feverish boundary-drawing. It is only after the border-posts have been dug in that the myths of their antiquity are spun and the

---

[13] Hobsbawm, 1994: 428.
[14] Hobsbawm, 1996: 40.
[15] Young, 1999: 164.
[16] Friedman, 1999: 241.

fresh, cultural/political origins of identity are carefully covered up by the genesis stories. This stratagem attempts to belie the fact that (to quote Stuart Hall again)[17] what the idea of identity does *not* signal is a 'stable core of the self, unfolding from the beginning to end through all the vicissitudes of history without change'.

Perhaps instead of talking about identities, inherited or acquired, it would be more in keeping with the realities of the globalizing world to speak of *identification*, a never-ending, always incomplete, unfinished and open-ended activity in which we all, by necessity or by choice, are engaged. There is little chance that the tensions, confrontations and conflicts which that activity generates would subside. The frantic search of identity is not a residue of the pre-globalization times not-yet-fully-extirpated but bound to become extinct as the globalization progresses; it is, on the contrary, the side-effect and by-product of the combination of globalizing and individualizing pressures and the tensions that spawn. The identification wars are neither contrary nor stand in the way of the globalizing tendency: they are a legitimate offspring and natural companion of globalization and far from arresting it, lubricate its wheels.

---

[17] Hall, 1996b: 3.

29. POSTNATIONAL FLOWS, IDENTITY FORMATION AND CULTURAL SPACE

Mike Featherstone

> Human affairs are not so far divided by empires and coun-
> tries, but that in many cases they still preserve a connec-
> tion: whence it is proper enough to view, as in one picture,
> the fates of an age.
>
> Francis Bacon, 1900: 57, cited in Mazlish, 1993: 121–122

Introduction: Global modernities

How are we to make sense of the process of globalization? The term is
used in a variety of imprecise ways by academics and critics to suggest both
an actualized state of affairs and a gradual process. The fact that we live
in conditions of rapid circulation of ideas between academic life and the
media, means that academic concepts like fashion apparel, have shorter and
shorter lives. Hence some academics have already asked us to move beyond
the term globalization in search of new variants, preferring terms such as
globality (Robertson, 1995a), 'the global age' (Albrow, 1996). While the use
of such terminology represents a hardening and extension of the concept of
globalization into a more extensive condition or epoch, presumably the ultimate one for humanity, there are yet others who deny the relevance of the
term altogether and preferring to see what is designated as globalization as
merely a superficial symptom of the cyclical phase of hegemonic decline in
the evolution of global systems (Friedman, 1994; 1999).

On one level the debates about globalization seem to have picked up
some of its momentum in academic life from the debates surrounding the
modern and postmodern. This is particularly the case for those who seek
to link postmodernism not to artistic modernism, but seek to subsume its
implications under a wider epochal notion of postmodernity, itself a derivative and transformation of modernity. For those who have invested in the
concept modernity, the term postmodernity is preferable to postmodernism
as it channels debates on to familiar territory: behind them lies tradition,
ahead is the alleged postmodernity. One can then focus on whether society has made, or ever can make, the transition or not. This formulation is
constructed at a high level of abstract generality and assumes a generic form

common to all societies. The terminology betrays survivals of evolutionary thinking which many claim to have surpassed. Especially when one finds further differentiations such as high and late modernity (Giddens, 1991), or postmodernism recuperated into the cultural dominant of the third (and last?) stage of capitalism, as we find in Jameson's (1984) influential writings which work off Mandel's (1975) formula. Yet we should raise here Martin Jay's (1998) question: why should modernity or capitalism have only three stages and not twenty-three?

The problems become intensified when we find globalization recovered into modernity, as in Giddens' (1991) assumption that globalization is an extension of modernity. Here we have the master sociological logic at work with a universal process unfolding itself not only through time, the usual dimension for conceiving modernity, but also extending itself though space to the limits of the globe. Hence modern social and cultural forms become extended across the globe to create common institutional forms, modes of experience and identity problems. The assumption is of a singular globalization process which relentlessly empties out cultural differences as it integrates the world.[1]

When a society calls itself modern, it marks its newness through a time line in which the old is relegated into the past. The modern becomes a praise-word and the not-modern becomes reduced to the blame-word tradition. Hence the modern, with its concern for the new, becomes identified with the temporal dimension. For Luhmann (1998b: 3) its construction of identity is through constant allusions to its own past. Its mode of identity construction is through disidentification through difference. It assumes that the characteristics of today's modernity are different from yesterday's and those of tomorrow. This constant search for and commitment to the new engages modernity in a form of non-identification with its past, and a process of creation and distancing from otherness. This focus on history as the new progress and overcoming, which many commentators see as central to modernity, is seen as reaching its limit by Vattimo (1988). For Vattimo postmodernity is the experience of 'the end of history', the end of the notion of progress and not a new stage of history, an epoch somehow beyond modernity. Postmodernity, for Vattimo, then, is within modernity and coexists in the same historical space.[2] It points to the crisis of the notion of

---

[1] For critiques of Giddens' neglect of culture see Robertson, 1992a; Tomlinson, 1999. For a critique of Giddens' theory of globalization and his capacity to make lists without discussing social mechanism and processes see Friedman, 1994.

[2] This, is of course, a confusing use of postmodernity. For a discussion of the various meanings of the derivatives of modern and postmodern see Featherstone, 1991.

progress, the loss of a sense of end point, of the teleological notion which was inherited from the Christian tradition.

The secularization of progress means a crisis for the traditional Western notion of history, as the expectation of something totally new becomes diluted and dissipated into the constant supply of new goods within consumer culture. There is a loss of the sense of history, which gives rise to the feeling of 'post-history', or 'the end of history'. The conception of a unitary history becomes increasingly contested; this has a number of aspects. Firstly, there is the focus upon the discovery of the lesser traditions of history, the suppressed histories of outsider groups such as women, slaves, ethnic minorities, the various 'step-children' of the Enlightenment, whose significance was ignored in narratives held together by the sense of the unified onward drive of progress.

Secondly, there was the historical reflexivity through the focus upon the procedures of its own narrative construction. Here we think of the work of Foucault (1970) and Hayden White (1973, 1987) who emphasize the narrative structuring of history and the various tropes, or rhetorical devices, which we unavoidably use when we write histories. Hence we can speak of history as an endless process of writing strategies which circle around the material, but never capture history 'out there'. Rather, the metaphor becomes one in which the historian, or the formal literary conventions of the age, structure the writing in such a way as to reflect back one's own preoccupations and formal conventions and narrative structures: one's writings provide a mirror which one cannot go beyond. This focus upon writing history was paralleled by a shift within anthropology on the part of theorists influenced by White. Hence Clifford and Marcus (1986) emphasized 'writing culture', whereby the anthropologists' rhetorical strategies and quest for a convincing unified narrative also lead to a form of projection or mirroring in which the other culture cannot be captured. Said's (1978) writings on orientalism also influenced by Foucault's work, have a similar focus upon the construction of the other as a form of projection of a set of fantasies and desires.

The corollary of this is that the other starts to speak back, that we have contested histories and stories. Not only do we have local, and microhistories seeking to assert themselves against a unified history within the nation-state, but postcolonial histories start to be written which effectively 'speak back to the West'. It is not least because their advocates have themselves become part of the West through the intensified global migrations of the last 30–40 years. In this context it is interesting to note that postmodern thought was not only stimulated by the writing of migrants from former colonies who moved to the West—in particular we think of those from India, such as Homi Bhabha, Giatri Spivak and Salman Rushdie. Perhaps the first impetus in this direction came from those who lived in France in the aftermath of the Algerian independence struggle, who were either born, or lived or had visited Algeria. Here we think of Helen Cixous, Jacques Derrida, Jean-François Lyotard and others (see Mazlish, 1993: 115).

The task of establishing history in the context of contested global histories, becomes exceedingly demanding. Who for example could write the history of the Balkans, or Palestine-Israel, or Korea? Such problems beset the efforts of UNESCO in seeking to write a history of the world. The hundreds of historians they brought together from the various nations of the world to write the definitive history of the world could not agree, or even agree how to proceed (see Burke, 1989; Featherstone, 1995: ch. 6). This massive problem of scope and integration, was anticipated by Ernst Troeltsch who long ago dismissed the idea of groups of scholars working together as a 'book binder's synthesis' (Kossok, 1993: 93). We will return to this crucial problem of modes of synthesis below: the question of whether and how one can transform inchoate heaps of data through various modes of theoretical integration into models or systems, which go beyond the practice of making lists or collages.

In one sense a universal history is the history of everything that has happened in the world. To this extent it is inclusive and has global scope, but this is not to imply that the various component histories necessarily have interacted or influenced each other. The second sense of universal history, is somewhat narrower and refers to the history of the world as it becomes integrated into a world system of reciprocal communication (see Kossok, 1993: 97). The growing integration and interdependence of the world through a world economy with world-wide communications systems in many ways ensures that humanity has a common fate. Yet the direction of the fate and the types of integration are something which we are only just beginning to contemplate through the lens of a pluralized global public sphere: a space in which different traditions, cultures, ideologies and views of the world start to clash. It may well have been easier to construct a world, or universal history, a century ago at the height of the power of European and Western nation-states. At this time the sense of Western identity and confidence in progress, evolution and the hierarchical ordering of cultures, with a trickle down modernization to those outside the West, was assumed with greater confidence.

It was, therefore, easier to construct a universal history, as we find for example in the writings of Max Weber if one assumes that what happened in the West lay in a line of development which had universal significance (see discussion in Mazlish, 1993). What developed over time in the West was assumed to spread out elsewhere over space. Universal history is hence closely connected with modernization—as is Giddens' theory of modernity, with its Weberian derivations and assumptions of globalizing force. Yet there are many possible ways of conceiving a universal history which does not limit it to the history of the West writ large. For example, rather than assume Western modernity became dominant through the superiority of its rationality, which derived from the Judaic-Christian tradition, and became transformed into the capitalist spirit of discipline and enterprise and the scientific spirit of deduction and empirical inquiry, it is possible to argue that the globalization of Western modernity involved a considerable amount of contingency. Certainly, this would seem to be the case if one considers the origins of Western trade and colonial expansion by examining the tentative efforts of Portuguese trading companies to move down the coast of Africa, round the Cape and head out to India and East Asia, and compare this to the superiority of the Chinese at that time in science, military techniques, shipping. The Chinese had in fact reached the East Coast of Africa somewhat earlier, but political machinations at the Chinese court in the fifteenth century, meant that they abandoned exploration and conquest by sea and turned to the land with the triumph of the army party (Inkster, 1997; Levathes, 1996). A more radical critique of this 'Eurocentric' perspective has been developed by Gunder Frank (1998) who advocates a 'globological perspective' to argue that the world economic system did not begin in Europe and that up until the start of the 19th century Europe was a relatively minor part of the Afro-Eurasian global system. An analysis which simultaneously criticizes European exceptionalism and highlights the centrality of East Asia, particularly China, before the process of rewriting world history from the European perspective developed with a vengeance in the 19th and 20th centuries.

The problems mount if one assumes that the current phase of increasingly globally interdependence is accompanied by shifts in the balance of power between the East and West. This relative decline in the power of the West means a challenge to the Western control over the flows of goods, resources and information and from the West to the rest. These reversals do not just mean that the rest talks back to the West, but should eventually lead to broader disputes over the West's authority and modes of classification. To move in this direction we have to investigate the possibility of multiple modernities, formed in different ways. Of course the realpolitik of global history has been the economic and political dominance of the West in recent centuries through the power potential of industrial, commercial and military superiority. This was accompanied by a taken-for-granted superiority in science, art, law, philosophy and other cultural forms. It was to be expected that Western theories, their self-understanding of the process of modernization, would be assumed to be universal, and that various modes of patronage and clientalism would be used to draw in non-Westerners in to hierarchical relationships where they participate and are associated to the dominant centres with their modernizing and progressive impulses, while genuine outsiders who sought to retain their own cultural identity and traditions would be excluded, or discredited and denied the means of access to the arenas of legitimate culture and thought.[3]

But what happens with a shift in the balance of power, such as has been noticeable over the last thirty years with the rise of East Asia? Should we not only contemplate global modernit*ies*, with the emphasis on the plural, but different globalizations: Japanese globalization, Chinese globalization etc. (Befu, 1998). At the very least it suggests that history once thought to be unified and linear now has to be re-thought as spatial and relative (see Sakai, 1989; Featherstone, 1995: ch. 8). Certainly, the potential of people to think and articulate such theories, has to be in some way related to the rise in the power potential of their nation-states, and depends upon their capacity to cast a critical eye over the modernization theories exported by the West which have become dominant strands of their own intellectual life, coupled with a capacity to reinterpret their own historical development and immanent modernizing tendencies in different ways. In short, it also depends upon the power struggles for recognition and independent self-identity within intellectual and academic groups in the various non-western nation-states which are starting to realize their power-potential. Hence the shifts in the global balance of power holds out the prospect of the theorization of multiple modernities (Venn, 1999).

How are we to proceed to develop a greater understanding of globalization if we admit to multiple perspectives and differential modernization projects? It is clear we need to move from the 'book-binders', view of global history and the global present to identify the social, economic and cultural processes and mechanisms which give rise to the various forms of global integration and the 'global condition'. We need in effect to move beyond lists to the construction of models. But this is by no means an easy task and as yet the social sciences and humanities are in a very rudimentary stage for considering globalization. We should also bear in mind that some commentators on the global condition, dispute that we can create models using categories and modes of classification based upon social and economic

---

[3] The dynamic is clearly more complex than can be discussed at this point. Artistic modernism and bohemianism always managed to develop identifications with outsiders (the gypsy, the peasant, the South Sea Islander, the nomad). Hence there was always a sub-current which sought to confront the dominant culture with its other.

theories largely developed within the confines of nation-states. Hence for those fascinated with global mobility and fluid identities, chaos theory and postmodernism are seen as holding out considerable promise. To move beyond a book-binders synthesis we need to be aware of the importance of integrative holistic perspectives. While it may well be useful to dwell on the differential modernities as a correction to the notion that there was only one modernity originating in Western Europe, we need also to be aware that the world out of which various regional modernities developed were already connected into a global system, a Eurasian system which was linked together through interdependencies long before the Portuguese navigators set out on their voyages in the 15th century.

We also have to be aware of the politics and sociology of knowledge with respect to globalization. However much its advocates seek to stress the need to construct a new frame of reference beyond nation-state societies, their attempt to revolutionize disciplinary foci encounters all the sorts of problems Thomas Kuhn spoke about when he referred to the resistance of normal science to new ideas. Professionalized disciplines guard their boundaries jealously, and discipline their members in terms of what is permissible as suitable topics of study. Hence one might assume a considerable tension will continue to exist between sociological and cultural studies approaches to globalization. Finally, we should add that there is the need to investigate the possibilities of global praxis, of various modes of cosmopolitanism, global public spheres and global citizenship being developed, which would suggest new forms of global integration and political intervention (Falk, 1999).

In what follows, we will first examine briefly some of the assumptions about global social and economic processes. Then we will, secondly, focus upon the contrasting perspectives on global culture and identity formation of Arjun Appadurai and Jonathan Friedman with respect to the possibility of developing explanatory models. Thirdly, we will address the questions of the scope of globalization and the difficulties of developing common modes of investigation, and conceptual development. Finally, we will focus on the potential for global intervention and public sphere formation.

Globalization processes

Although the term global, can be traced back in the English language for over 400 years, according to the *Oxford English Dictionary* the term globalization, along with the related terms globalize and globalizing, seems to have first come into use in the 1960s, largely in economic contexts (Waters, 1995: 2). In economics and management literature the first use seems to have been Levitt's paper on the globalization of markets published in 1983 (Dicken, 1998: 15). In sociology Roland Robertson (1992b) was one of the first to use the term in articles published in 1985. In media and cultural studies Marshall McLuhan was probably the significant influence, with his use of the term 'global village' in his book *Understanding Media*, published in 1960. In the 1990s the term has rapidly become part of the everyday vocabulary not only of academics, but also business people, and has been taken up and circulated widely in the media.

The term globalization possesses a sense of immediate intelligibility for wider publics, which terms such as postmodernity have never been able to attain. In drawing on the root 'global' it seems self-evident that it points to the spatial integration of the world through increased communication and trade. In the popular imagination then, globalization has become associated with a global economic integration process, something which on the level of the nation-state is held to inevitably cause social, cultural and political deregulation and disintegration. While globalization is associated with marketization, this need not necessarily be seen as limited to the furthering of economistic perspectives which are hostile to cultural particularity. Marketization is associated with the general goal of the 'emptying out of culture', in the short run at least it can lead to an upsurge of interest in culture, (which is evident, for example, in business and management courses) through the need to be aware of the particularities of different regional and local markets across the globe. Hence many transnational firms adopt the Japanese strategy of *dochakuka*, a farming term which refers to the capacity to grow what is best suited on the land in question, which became adopted by business. Something which is the basis of the more familiar academic terms 'glocalism' and 'glocalization' (Robertson, 1995a).

One dominant meaning of globalization, then, is built around marketization and economic deregulation to permit the freer flow of money, raw materials, information and commodities across national borders. A perspective which is often accompanied by an implicit or explicit evolutionism: that the social dislocations which result from the spread of the market are the inevitable price of progress, changes which in the long term will necessarily be beneficial for humanity. When combined with technological optimism marketization is often presented as a panacea for the world. In an extensive article entitled 'The Long Boom', which appeared in the influential Internet magazine *Wired*, Schwartz and Leyden (1997) remark

> We are watching the beginnings of a global economic boom on a scale never experienced before. We have entered a period of sustained growth that could eventually double the world's economy every dozen years and bring increasing prosperity for—quite literally—billions of people on the planet. We are

riding the early waves of a 25-year run of a greatly expanding economy that will do much to solve seemingly intractable problems like poverty and to ease tensions throughout the world. And we'll do it without blowing the lid off the environment.

If this holds true, historians will look back to our era as an extraordinary moment. They will chronicle the 40-year period from 1980 to 2020 as the key years of a remarkable transformation. In the developed countries of the West, new technology will lead to big productivity increases that will cause high economic growth—actually, waves of technology will continue to roll out through the early part of the 21st century. And then the relentless process of globalization, the opening up of national economies and the integration of markets, will drive the growth through much of the rest of the world. An unprecedented alignment of an ascending Asia, a revitalized America, and a reintegrated Russia—together will create an economic juggernaut that pulls along most other regions of the planet. These two metatrends—fundamental technological change and a new ethos of openness—will transform our world into the beginnings of a global civilization, a new civilization of civilization, that will blossom through the coming century.

This is a clear example of the Western-centric mode of thinking which links together progress for the world as a whole, to the modernization and positive regeneration of almost every aspect of social life and nature, something which results from the twin motors of technology and marketization which drive globalization. What is good for the United States is by corollary assumed to be good for the rest of the world. Globalization depends upon the speed, mobility and flexibility of the networked society, which as it erodes tradition social, cultural and political restrictions will allow us to harness untold benefits. Such perspectives that present the market as a panacea, can be regarded as "an attempt to impose chaos on order", (Marcuse, 1995: 241, cited in Scott, 1997: 13), something which clashes with the other major force behind modernization: the Foucaultian project of the modernist state to impose order on chaos.

From the very beginning of the discipline of economics in the eighteenth century, the market was always something of a project, something which people used with rhetorical power to seek to convince others of its social benefits (in the first instance the sovereign, then wider publics) and translate a potentiality into an actuality, thereby rendering possible the social conditions which would permit scientificity (see Elias, 1984). As Karl Polanyi (1957) reminds us markets did not come into being spontaneously, especially since the 19th century they came into being through the active intervention of the state (see discussion in Scott, 1997: 8 ff.; Boyer and Drache, 1996a: 8 ff.). The nation-state was the key instrument in bringing about marketization and economic deregulation, as the example of the free trade and Utilitarian movements along with Liberal governments in 19th century England exemplify. The late 20th century revival of marketization in the form of neo-liberalism, provided a similar set of arguments about the superior efficiency and lasting benefits of opening up competition along with the deregulation of markets. The project, which was an essentially globalizing one then in the 19th century, (yet of limited effect in an era in which the competitors of England sought to protect their domestic markets to foster industrialization, and the figuration of European nation-states were drawn into the tighter figuration of interdependencies and power balances which led to the First World War), became globalized in the 1980s through the efforts of particular sets of politicians, businessmen and academics, who were able to steer their monetarist project through to first dominate political parties and then the governments, of first the United States and Britain, and then other countries.[4]

It has been argued that the role of the United States has been crucial in this process, that decisions which were taken in the Nixon presidency in the 1970s emphasized the importance of globalization as marketization as the key strategy to maintain the global dominance of the United States (Gowan, 1999). In contrast to many accounts of globalization, which present it as driven by economic and technological forces and present nation-states as increasingly powerless survivals of a previous age, Gowan emphasizes the way in which the US government and business elites actively devised a global strategy. In addition, predictions of the death of the nation-state in terms of a global logic, or logic of globalizing modernity, frequently operate with an over-simple zero-sum model, which assumes if markets are winning states must be losing (Huntington cited in Gowan, 1999: 5).

Polanyi (1957) also emphasized the rationalizing role of markets, how the penetration of monetary exchange and market relations destroyed traditional social relations. For many of the critics of globalization, from both the left and the radical right this becomes a rallying cry against markets, who see the destruction of communities, traditional patterns of employment and cultures. In England, from the left we see the writings of Will Hutton (1996) and in Germany, Martin and Schumann (1997) and from the radical right in England (see Gray, 1993) and in France people such as de Benoist (Dahl,

---

[4] There are still those such as Hirst and Thompson (1996) who argue against globalization, by pointing out that the volume of world trade was higher in 1914 than today. Yet this was largely trade in raw materials. There was little integration of financial markets or foreign direct investment, with transnational corporations spatially differentiating their production through a global division of labour. Globalization represents a process which is advancing not always with the consent of nation-states—hence above the international level.

1999a; 1999b). If marketization is seen as destroying trust, solidarity and community and therefore catastrophic in social terms, then globalization is regarded as a further intensification of the process leading to greater social fragmentation.

A similar perspective can be found in the writings of Castells (1996a, 1996b, 1998) in his analysis of the globalizing effects of the network society, in which business increasingly uses electronic networks not only for the global currency and stock markets, but for foreign direct investment in which the production activities which are horizontally differentiated around the world are coordinated through intranets. While Castells (1996a: ch. 5) acknowledges the potential of the emergence of a new culture through the new media (multimedia, the Internet), his general position is to see the network society as creating an increasing distance between globalization and self identity (Castells, 1996a: 23; 1996b). Here culture is defined as the support for identity with traditional forms of collective identity construction under siege, or driven into fundamentalisms. In the long term there is the assumption that identity will give way, and that reconstituted localisms or the impermanent identities of the type Maffesoli (1995) refers to, are inadequate substitutes. Likewise cultures are seen as fragile things which must be preserved and protected: there is little sense that community entails authoritarian patriarchal domination. This again has tinges of the romanticism which seeks to protect original cultures and works off a strong dichotomy between rationality and emotion, technology and culture, without seeking to investigate the ways in which they interpenetrate.

Generally, it is the deregulation of social and cultural life which is emphasized in discussions of marketization. But the extension of the global market necessarily gives rise to re-regulation in a number of ways. Firstly, as Polanyi (1957) argues, we should not underestimate the power of states to re-regulate markets. Indeed, while the increasing integration of the global financial markets, financial deregulation and lowering of tariffs through agreements such as GATT, create the parameters within which nation-state governments have to act, they have considerable scope to act differently to modify the effects of these processes. Clearly France, Germany and Sweden have different views on the benefits of marketization and the need for state regulation than, for example, the United States and Britain (Boyer and Drache, 1996a: 5). Japan, also still retains its long-term sense of a national project and seeks to channel and control the effects of globalization and marketization. Hence we should treat with caution accounts which predict the end of nation-states as significant actors on the global stage (see Reich, 1992; Horsman and Marshall, 1994). The economic integration of the

European Union also is creating a bloc in which social, cultural and polit-ical affairs cannot be assumed to follow the dictates of the market; indeed the move towards monetary union has been referred to by one commenta-tor as 'post-globalization' (Helleiner, 1996). Hence, one possible future sce-nario for the world is a struggle between large blocs each of which has its own social and cultural agenda within a protected tariff area, along with its own semi-periphery. Something which could conceivably not only lead to trade-wars, but limited military clashes in the semi-periphery areas—something George Orwell predicted in his novel *1984*.

Secondly, the extension of global electronic networks, the inter- and intranets which coordinate the global financial markets, the foreign direct investment and the spatially diversified corporate production sites around the world, not only result in fragmentation, but point to the need for greater centralized command coordination and planning from stock markets, cor-porate headquarters and the specialist services which are drawn together in global cities (Sassen, 1991, 1994, 1999a). Hence new transnational institu-tions and modes of association, interaction, sociability and means of orien-tation start to develop out of the intensification of deregulation. They seek to construct well-worn channels through which regular activities will take place in order to reduce uncertainty and complexity, as well as aiming to establish legal and other procedures to resolve disputes and conflicts. Hence there is a whole set of underpinning social and cultural practices which become necessary to sustain the spread of marketization. In this context it is interesting to note that cosmpolitanism need not be linked to the high-minded efforts of intellectuals and social movements to establish a global ecumene, the impetus may come from the business sector itself and we should remember that cosmopolitanism always had an economic side (Rob-bins, 1998).

Hence the Trilateral Commission: World Shadow Government, which was established in 1973 by the international financier, David Rockefeller, the chairman of the Rockefeller family-controlled Chase Manhattan Bank and director of his family's global corporate empire, aimed to follow the ideas developed by Zbigniew Brzezinski in his book *Between Two Ages* (1970). Brzezinski argued that the United States government needed to accommo-date itself to the new international context to protect its interests. The Trilateral Commission, grew out of the work of the Bilderberg Group, founded in 1954 and also funded and influenced by the Rockefeller cor-porate empire. The Bilderberg Group is composed of international financiers, industrialists, media magnates, union bosses, academics and political figures, with its membership restricted to the United States, Canada, Western Europe and Japan. Hence if the calls for re-regulation of the global economy, which have become more vociferous in the wake of the East Asian, Russian and Brazilian financial crises of 1998–99, lead to some forms of institutional structures and even global taxation, such as the Tobin tax, it is to be expected that those members of global elites, who have long seen the need for some forms of global governance to protect their economic and business interests, will be in at the start of the formation process. Even the most optimistic advocate of global governance has to admit that relatively little can be achieved without the development of monopolies of violence and taxation on the part of some form of global superstate.

One thing seems certain, that whatever re-regulation emerges on a global level, it will not replicate the processes which were germane to the formation of the nation-state. The prospective struggle between different interest groups, each with their own globalization project and particular vision of the end-state of globalization is much more complex, if nothing else through the sheer number of different agents involved. Hence it is not just a question of global deregulation versus a reregulation process leading to a global state: there are strongly divergent views as to the policy goals, values and intervention capacities such a global superstate should have.

At the same time, while the processes which come from marketization and economic deregulation provide some form of synthesis, the same forms of electronic networks and other technologies of communication which move goods, information, images and people around the world also can be used for and give rise to many types of social relationships whose purpose is anything but in line with the market. Not only does McWorld lead to defensive Jihad or fundamentalist and other localistic reactions which play out their struggles on the world stage as Barber (1995) argues, the electronic communicative networks and other forms of communication heighten connectedness and integration and threaten to add new levels of social, cultural and political complexity.

If we seek to understand globalization processes sociologically one common reference point central to assumptions of global integration is the suggestion that the world has become compressed into a single social space (Robertson, 1992b). Here the simple image is that we increasingly find ourselves in each other's backyard: that the networks of interdependencies along with constraints and power balances we operate in through our everyday social institutions have increased in scope. While much of everyday life is lived orientated to people we encounter face-to-face in specific well-known locales, the ease in terms of speed and cheapness with which we can move out of these locales and contact others by telephone, or the Internet has not only increased the informational resources we have to hand, but potentially can take us out of the rigidities and confines of existing established clientalist networks to form new alliances and interdependencies. In an increasingly competitive global economy, the capacity to find cheaper suppliers, sources of capital and new markets, necessarily drives firms to innovate and establish wider contacts.

At the same time there are also constantly efforts on the part of businesses and other institutions which operate within a global environment to control and monopolize information, to install fire-walled exclusive intranets and protect their corporate information from competitors (Sassen, 1999a). This applies not only for business corporations, but for public sector institutions such as universities, research institutes, NGOs and governments. The scope of their activities and density of interdependencies have globalized. Not only are we able to *disintermediate*, to contact directly those further fields to supply our work and consumption needs: a form of activity made simple by the Internet, where for example we buy our books through the Web from Amazon Books and not our local bookseller. At the same time, the sheer volume of information we are becoming accustomed to have close to hand through electronic modes of communication, and the opening up of new ranges of choices and possibilities, also means we still need *intermediation*: the services of cultural intermediaries who can advise us on how to deal with the problems and anxieties of selectivity. The advance of digitalization with its Moore's law of the doubling of computer power and halving of cost every 18 months also dramatically increases the capacity for innovation and mobility of modes of association (Mulgan, 1998: 31).

It is, then, not just the ways in which the market is globalizing under its own dynamic, or we should say permitted to globalize through the activities of powerful alliances of businessmen, industrialists, politicians, academics and cultural intermediaries who have made it their project, rather globalization builds a storey underneath global economic integration by encouraging the development of patterns of sociality, cultural expectations, and means of orientation which recursively form and are formed by the enlarged network of interdependencies. In a similar way that one can speak of the development of a market culture in the 18th century, in which people sought to give a positive import to a particular image of social relationships based on the market as superior and beneficial for all, something which eventually became in varying degrees sedimented into everyday life and treated as a commonsense actuality through its capacity to reform people's habitus and practices, in the late 20th century we can also speak of a global market culture. Yet then as now, the capacity to discipline and reform habitus had its limits and necessarily gave rise to counter claims through the incapacity of the market culture to deliver what it promised. Likewise today, the global financial crises, unemployment and underemployment and growth of social inequalities in many parts of the world, are perceived as proof that the market has its limits. At the same time today, the density of global communications networks, the ease, speed and cheapness suggests that many non-business organizations and outsider groups formerly denied the means of communication, now are able to experience a degree of democratization of access. It is the density, regularity and habitual nature of the practice of communicating beyond the boundaries of one's locality, which is creating another facet of social life, a dimension of everyday existence made possible through the electronic communication networks which span the world to create shared spaces of virtual interactivity.

If we were confronted with the question: 'where is the global'?, the implication being that the global is somehow an emergent level of social life orientated beyond the confines of nation-state societies, then, perhaps the easiest response would be to say the global exists within global cities. There is of course a number of dimensions to global cities such as London, New York, Tokyo, Singapore and São Paulo, which gain their prominence as key nodes within the global information networks. The global cities house the corporate headquarters which coordinate the transnational corporations' dispersed productive activities. They are financial and foreign direct investment centres. They also act as centres for specialist management and business services (financial, regional business activities, marketing, design, culture intermediation). They house business and entertainment districts with the bars, cafés, restaurants, clubs, galleries and theatres which create the suitable ambience for the face-to-face trust to be established on which deals depend, or the chance encounter which could be the spark for a new opportunity (see Sassen, 1994; Castells, 1996a; Featherstone, 2000c).

Hence the city of bits, the virtual data-city which is being constructed through the Internet and intranets is one level of global culture. But such digital cities are insufficient in themselves. Strangers and associates need to meet and look into each other's eyes, the establishment of trust is crucial if they are to enter into contract and longer term association. Global cities supply these spaces and therefore have become centres for the new global managerial class, the creative groups of symbol analyists (Reich, 1992), new cultural intermediaries and those sectors of the new middle classes who work in service and cultural occupations. These are the groups which develop cosmopolitan dispositions and have weaker attachment to localities. They value mobility, creativity, syncretism, change and innovation. They easily identify with the other: with other places and other cultures (Santos, 1999; Tomlinson, 1999).

At the same time many of this group face an uncertain future, as marketization, financial deregulation, outsourcing and downsizing begin to bite for them too. The loyalty and commitment associated with the lifelong career gives way to the job, or short term contract and the anxieties of flexible capitalism (Sennett, 1998; 1999). Above them are the global elites who show little long term commitments to either employees, collectivities or place. Indeed, it has been argued that the new global elites have little concern with civic culture and selfishly prize their own flexibility and mobility, to the extent that the key problem of political culture of the current time is not the apathy or revolt of the masses, but 'the revolt of the elites' (Lasch, 1996), the elites' lack of the capacity for recognition, empathy, identification and responsibility for the other.

Global cities have been characterized as divided or dual cities, with bifurcated class structures in which the elites and new middle classes often live in segregated gated-neighbourhoods with surveillance and private policing to keep out the excluded. Los Angeles is often seen as the exemplar of this type of divided global city (Davis, 1990; Dear, Schockman and Hise, 1996; Dear and Flusty, 1999) with its teleintegrated, 'netted up' middle classes and enclaves of the excluded poor, unemployed and criminals who exist in varying degrees of informational poverty. Increasingly the excluded lower orders are confined to locality, whereas the middle and upper classes possess high potential physical and virtual mobility. Global marketization drives down wage levels, especially at the bottom end and according to Will Hutton (1996) is seen as producing the 30/30/40 society: the bottom 30% are unemployed and inactive, the middle 30% are in work, but their employment is insecure and they are constantly in danger of falling into the exclude bottom layer, the top 40% have tenured jobs (see Hoogvelt, 1997: 147). More recent predictions for the next decade present even more dramatic downsizing and resultant unemployment with the middle classes exposed to many of the job insecurities of the working classes. Martin and Schumann (1997) argue that as we cross the millennium, we are on the edge of the 20/80 society, in which 20% participate in full employment (the group necessary to keep the global economy working, the so-called 'creatives', and Robert Reich's, 1982, 'symbolic anylists'), with the remaining 80% unemployed or under-employed, either with no work or confined to part-time or insecure telecommuting work, or government and local state 'workfare' pseudo jobs.

If the sharpest contrasts of the globalization processes effects on social life can be found in global cities through their integration into the global economy in which they experience the effects of marketization in its most immediate forms, this should not be taken to suggest that other processes are not taking place which seek to globalize forms of economic regulation or formulate and disseminate new global political and cultural agendas. Economic processes can be seen as giving rise to '3rd cultures', in which specific groups, such as those working in the 24-hour trading in the financial sectors of global cities, are orientated to processes outside their own nation-state and whose work routine may be geared to those of other global cities. To this extent, these and other groups in the new middle classes may develop dispositions and habituses which are less orientated to their own society, but become to some degree transnationalized. The extent to which this broader group develops a positive cosmopolitanism, in the sense of broader identifications with others, a form of the 'cultural goodwill' Bourdieu (1984) speaks of, which could make them potential carriers, committed to the project of developing a new global culture, or they remain confined to a narrower selfish cosmopolitanism, with little sense of responsibility for the other, remains to be seen.

It is clear, however, that one of the sites which such positive cosmopolitan orientations might be expected to develop would be those 3rd cultures which are non-business, the NGOs (non-governmental organizations) which have increasingly developed their own global networks, interdependencies, identifications and power potential in recent years. The numbers of NGOs from the various quasi-political bodies such as the United Nations, UNESCO, WHO, international courts, bodies regulating international standards, along with foundations, the arts, health, sporting bodies, trade unions, human rights organizations such as Amnesty International, charities such as Oxfam and ecological organizations such as Friends of the Earth and Greenpeace who see their remit as global, has dramatically increased over the last 30 years.[5] They do not all operate contiguously in the same global space, but the density of such organizations within certain global cities such as New York, Paris and Tokyo and various ancillary sites such as Geneva, and their awareness of the growth of global public opinion suggests that nascent global public spheres are in the process of formation. The Internet is certainly helping this process and we can envisage cross sector flexible alliances developing between foundations, academics, business, trade unions, NGOs which link up with the excluded and develop various experimental programs in the politics of global citizenship.

Such global public spheres could well provide some of the discussions about the need to regulate global marketization, through schemes such as

---

[5] It is estimated that the number of global NGOs has grown from less than 200 in 1909 to more than 2000 by the early 1970s (Appadurai, 1996: 168).

the Tobin tax proposals to regulate the estimated \$1–3 billion a day flows of hot money which has had such a destabilizing effect upon not only world trade, but the potential governability of nation-states such as Russia, Brazil, Indonesia and others in recent years (Henderson, 1996; Featherstone, 2000c; Patomäki, 2000). It is advisable at this stage to speak of the global public sphere in the plural, indeed, it has been argued contra Habermas that there never can be a public sphere in the singular. The global public spheres are also inhabited by various fundamentalisms, nationalism, independence movements (Tamil Tigers, Zapatistas) and localisms which advocate de-globalized reactions and balkanization solutions to the world's problems (Mestrovic, 1994). Yet they too function in a full awareness of the import of global public opinion and how to use the Internet and other modes of communication to broaden the base of their support (see Castells, 1996b, for an interesting discussion of the Zapatistas movement in Mexico).

Global regulation then is a historical possibility, as various stepping stones are cast in to the spaces between nation-states which may become pathways for constructing various fora, or levels of social life, which operate with procedures and sets of priorities which are no longer the property of nation-states. This is a different kind of threat to the integrity of the nation-state than the de-regulation of global marketization. It is the identification of the latter with globalization per se which has led some to call for post-globalization (Helleiner, 1996). Yet while we cannot rule out the possibility of a new de-globalizing phase, a retreat back to strong nation-states which seek to re-establish strongly centred competitive identities vis-à-vis others in their reference group and hence suppress internal regionalisms and balkanization, this is not the only alternative. The other option is global regulation through the active creation of global public spheres, NGOs and other spaces for political, social and cultural association. Hence we should not throw out the word globalization because it has been identified with marketization and the instabilities of economic integration, rather we should be aware of the possibility of multiple globalizations, of different agendas which seek to inscribe their visions of the world into the global space.

Consequently, theories of globalization which just see the world through the lens of global flows need some qualification. There are many who seek to erect barriers and walls to stem flows, and yet others who are seeking to establish flexible alliances, public movements and institutions to form new levels of social life which operate beyond the confines and value nexus of both nation-states and business marketization. Such entities need not be seen as advocating a socially destructive forced superstatism, the corollary of the painful episodes to remould traditions, discipline work-forces and construct citizens as part of the state formation and nation-building projects which were evident in the 19th and 20th centuries. Rather, it could be argued that it is only through some form of global regulation, that the destructive processes taking places within nation-states can be checked. In this sense the long term process of marketization has locked nation-states and regions in a competitive figuration of states, regions and cities, which acts as a double-bind process, through forcing them to compete in providing the lowest local cost advantages to transnational corporations, and thereby taking a 'beggar thy neighbour' stance which trades off short term employment advantages for longer term instabilities.

Postnational flows, identities and global system processes: Appadurai versus Friedman

One of the vogue words of contemporary accounts of globalization is the term 'flow'. It points to the way in which the movement of material goods, bodies, electronic and digitalized textual information and images around the world has emerged as a social and cultural force. The term flow suggests that these movements have a distinctive tempo, rhythm and direction. As Rob Shields (1997: 3) remarks: "flows signal pure movement, without the suggesting point of origin or a destination, only a certain character of move-ment, fluidity and direction." Deleuze and Guattari (1987) are the inspira-tion here with their influential notions of deterritorialization, fluidity and nomadology which have been absorbed into the cultural studies vocabulary. For Shields (1997: 2) flow is associated with a paradigm shift within cul-tural studies from the study of objects to processes along with the break-down of fixed boundaries. It points to the ambiguities of borderline conditions, in-between-ness and edge-states. Also influential has been the writings of Arrighi (1994: 23) who contrasts the 'spaces of place', the disciplinary enclo-sures, with the 'spaces of flows', which are between and beyond them (O'Connor, 1997). The spaces of place seek to regulate the places of flows, but as is the case with the surveillance regimes evident at national immi-gration points, it is only possible to channel, capture and record part of the flow of bodies. Arrighi's writings have been used by Castells (1989) in his book on the informational city and subsequently been widely used by other writers on globalization, such as Lash and Urry (1994).

The concept of flow points to movement, mobility, to the speed, volume and intensity of interchanges in a globalizing world. The implication for social and cultural life is that the intensity of global flows helps to estab-lish new connections and patterns of association and social relationships, along with new modes of identification. There is also the assumption that the speed, volume and variability of connections and routes of flows have somehow take us beyond stable system models of explanation. Instead, it is argued that we need to call on chaos and complexity theory to make sense of this new phase of global connectedness (see Appadurai, 1996). If this is indeed the case, then the argument for a new conceptual armoury and a reconfiguration of academic disciplinary boundaries could well be justified. Alternatively, there are those who argue that processes of identity formation can still be mapped and related to shifts in hegemony within the world system, that our use of notions such as cultural hybridity and in-betweenness is based upon a fundamental conceptual misunderstanding (Friedman, 1994). We can now turn to these contrasting arguments via an examination of the writings of Arjun Appadurai and Jonathan Friedman.

Arjun Appadurai (1990, 1996: 32 ff.) argues that we have moved into a new global cultural economy in which existing models, such as the centre-periphery ones favoured by Wallerstein (1974, 1980) and others are no longer adequate to explain the current phase of disorganized capitalism which is characterized by fundamental disjunctures between economy, culture and politics. He points to the way in which flows of people, machinery, money, images and ideas now increasingly follow nonisomorphic paths. Noticeable here is the assumption that the sheer speed, scale and volume of each of the flows is now so great that the disjunctures are central to understanding the politics of global culture. For example, the Japanese welcome inflows of ideas, but export machinery and other goods, while they are steadfastly closed to immigration. While the Swiss and Saudis are closed to immigration unlike the Japanese they accept guest-workers. For Appadurai there are five dimensions of the global flows which he categorizes as: a) ethnoscapes, b) mediascapes, c) technoscapes, d) financescapes and e) ideoscapes, which afford different perspectival landscapes, which are the building blocks of the imagined worlds, the multiple worlds that are constituted by the various groups of people located around the world. The fact that people live in these imagined worlds means that they are able to contest and even subvert the imagined worlds of state officialdom and the market economy. Each of these landscapes is subject to its own particular set of constraints and incentives which are disjunctive and unpredictable, yet act as parameters for the other sets of flows.

Appadurai's book focuses upon two sets of flows: people and images which constitute the ethnoscapes and mediascapes. He argues that we need to conceptualize a break or rupture in the process of globalization and the production of locality, because since the 1970s the electronic media and mass migration have become 'massively globalized', (Appadurai, 1996: 9). Intensified migration results in the deterritorialization of the imagination and the potential to construct diasporic public spheres. Classical modernization theory was firmly attached to the nation-state, but globalization has shrunk the distance between elites and through migration it has broken many of the links between work and family life and redefined the relationship between imaginary national attachment and one's temporary locale. As the mass media become dominated by the electronic media and depend less and less on the capacity to read and write and link people across national boundaries, audiences are able to develop diasporic public spheres, which are the key vehicles of a postnational political order through their capacity to link together workers, students, activists and refugees along with various social movements, NGOs.

Diasporic public spheres form the basis for postnational imagined communities. Here Appadurai (1996: 28, 161) builds on the work of Benedict Anderson (1991) who pointed out the importance of the construction of an imagined community through the mass media in the formation of nationalism. If Anderson emphasized the importance of 'print capitalism', Appadurai stresses 'electronic capitalism' and points to the role of the film, television, video and the Internet with their post-symbolic imagistic communicative forms. Hence postnational imagined communities are deterritorialized, yet permit people to communicate over distance. The Sikh taxi-driver in Chicago can listen to a temple speech from India on cassette while driving, the Pakistani worker in Los Angeles can watch videos of religious movements in Pakistan.

Appadurai argues that the ethnic conflict that developed around the destruction of the Babri Masjid mosque in Ayodha, Northern India in December 1992 by Hindu militants, was fuelled by the efforts of Hindu activists in various parts of the world. This potential to sustain imagined communities means that localities are influenced by events distant in space and time. Distant people see themselves as having a stake in each other's lives, as we find in the case of Bosnian Muslims who were under pressure from Islamic forces in Saudi, Sudan, and Egypt who felt they had a legitimate stake to reconstitute Bosnian Islamic identity more in line with their own perspectives. Appadurai (1996: 167–168) emphasizes the novelty of the new level of emergent socio-cultural forms when he remarks

> . . . what we are looking at are not just international slogans, or interest groups, or image transfers. We are looking at the birth of a variety of complex, post-national social formations. These formations are now organized around principles of finance, recruitment, coordination, communication and reproduction that are fundamentally postnational and not just multinational or international . . . The new organizational forms are more diverse, more fluid, more ad hoc, more provisional, less coherent, less organized, and simply less implicated in the comparative advantages of the nation-state.

As more people possess double identities we need more forms of dual or multiple citizenship to cope with the hyphenated identities such as Italian-Americans, Asian-Americans, where loyalties are often to a delocalized non-territorial transnation (see also Santos, 1999 on multiple citizenship). Appadurai argues that as states fragment and splinter and populations become deterritorialized and less committed to the nation-state, it is the transnations which become the most important sites in which the idea of homeland is played out. The vision of the world is one of flows of people, people constantly in motion sustained by their imaginary postnational communities. At one point Appadurai (1996: 4) remarks that

> few persons in the world today do not have a friend, relative, or co-worker who is not on the road to somewhere else or already coming back home, bearing stories and possibilities.

Yet perhaps Appadurai and others who speak of global flows overestimate the degree of mobility (see Tomlinson, 1999: ch. 1). It is salutary to note that only 1.5% of the global labour force works outside its own country, and that over half of this total is in the Middle East and sub-Sahara Africa (Mulgan, 1998: 55). Perhaps academics who enjoy high levels of global mobility, who enjoy the rhetoric of intellectual and artistic modernism about the benefits of travel and movement, are disposed to see mobility in a very positive light. Yet we have also to consider the down side of mobility, the ecological and social costs, and not least respect the vast majority of the world's population who have low mobility prospects, or are busy trying to find a place to settle or dwell (see Featherstone, 1998b).

There are two further implications of Appadurai's work which need to be drawn out. The first concerns his view of the relationship between cultural flux and habitus which he argues throws into doubt the work of social reproduction. The cultural flux associated with the postnational communication of globalization processes means that the search for steady points of reference becomes difficult, making the search for stable tradition, ethnicity, kinship and other identity markers problematic. Appadurai (1996: 44) adds

> As group pasts become increasingly part of museums, exhibits, and collections, both in national and transnational spectacles, culture becomes less of what Pierre Bourdieu would have called habitus (a tacit realm of reproducible practices and dispositions) and more as an arena for conscious, choice, justification, and representation, the latter often to multiple and spatially dislocated audiences.

At another point he argues

> There has been a general change in the global conditions of life-worlds, put simply, where once improvisation was snatched out of the glacial undertow of

habitus, habitus now has to be painstakingly reinforced in the face of life-worlds that are frequently in flux (Appadurai, 1996: 56).

For Appadurai we live in a world in which more and more people who are on the move around the world are able to pull their lives together and engage in the fabrication of their own characters. Even the most localized of worlds, in societies like India, he adds, have been afflicted by "cosmopolitan scripts that drive the politics of families, the frustrations of laborers, the dreams of local headmen" (Appadurai, 1996: 63). It is no longer possible to find a bedrock of reproductive cultural practices untouched by the world at large.

Here Appadurai's approach shares some common features with modernization theory, such as the notion that the old cultures and identities can be emptied out and replaced as culture is no longer a resistant bedrock to change. The emphasis upon flows, albeit disjunctive: summons up the connectedness of the world and the development of new levels of social life beyond the nation-state. Indeed his book title *Modernity at Large* points to the globalization of modernity. Yet unlike many modernization theorists he gives much greater importance to the independent role of culture in the process, which through the speed and volume of transmission of the electronic media can become a massive set of resources from which people select to construct their identities. Indeed, in many ways this would seem to be a postmodern view of cultures as inherently unstable and fluid. He sees mobile people and migrants as less under the surveillance of local neighbourhood power structures and interdependencies, and hence they are given a greater capacity to use their imagination, construct imaginary worlds and realize the dreams stimulated by the electronic media. Yet whether this alleged syncretism in producing new global cosmopolitanisms through selecting and combining elements and experiences drawn from a range of forms which include: the cinema, video, restaurants, spectator sports and tourism, drawn from a variety of different national and postnational origins, means that we have moved to a new stage beyond the reproduction of habitus and stable identities is open to dispute, as we shall see when we shortly examine Jonathan Friedman's theory.

The second area is the question of the theoretical models adopted to make sense of these processes. Appadurai (1996: 46–47) is attracted to elements of postmodernism along with chaos theory, which goes beyond what he sees as the mechanical metaphors of systems theory. This fits in with his anti-objectivist view of culture; rather than conceptualized as a static thing, Appadurai sees global cultural forms as fundamentally fractal, possessing no boundaries, structures of regularities, they overlap and flow. For Appadurai

the need to move beyond older images of order, stability and systematic-
ness, to focus on questions of how we understand a volatile world of disjunctive global flows, takes us down to particularity and context and away
from the possibility of higher level generalities.

    This is in marked contrast to the approach of Jonathan Friedman (1994)
in his book *Cultural Identity and Global Process*, for one of Friedman's main
targets is theories of cultural globalization and hybridization, which he sees
as less based upon a plausible explanation of the current situation, but better understood in terms of the politics of identification of groups of intellectuals who give a one-sided emphasis upon hybridization and underclass
creativity. Such perspectives are too preoccupied with notions such as 'the
invention of culture', with its assumption that modern traditionalisms are
inauthentic inventions along with terminology such as hybridization and creolization. The problem is that these notions are based upon a baseline
definition of aboriginality, real traditions and pure cultures (Friedman, 1994:
12). Rather than emphasize a break with the past through globalization,
which creates an artificially homogenized past against which the present can
be counted as fragmented and decentred, Friedman asks us to see cultural
fragmentation, hybridization, narcissistic identities, postmodernism and localization strategies, as part of cyclical phases of the world system. Such phenomena existed at certain points in past cycles, they could well do so again
in the future. At the very least this involves a relativization of the assumption
that the current phase of globalization with its alleged fluidity and fragmentation is some kind of postmodern end point—i.e. ushering in a permanent
state of cultural mixing. The opposite stage could equally be envisaged as
a historical possibility which could return: that is strong centred identities,
the homogenization of culture and strict cultural hierarchies are not to be
seen as confined to the distant past, but themselves have to be seen as cyclical factors.

    Friedman's position then is that globalization does not occur because it
is possible: the development of information technology, electronic banking,
jet travel etc. Rather, globalization and cultural fragmentation are to be
understood as part of the de-hegemonic of global system processes. Global,
or world systems, are not to be regarded as new—they can be traced back
to at least 5,000 years in the Old World (Friedman, 1994: 18). Contra views
of this early phase as comprising of isolated social groupings each with their
intrinsic and distinctive modes of social organization and cultural identity,
Friedman emphasizes the connections among the Old World's populations
which were organized into various prestige goods systems with various modes
of exchange. Even in the New World, we should be aware of holding onto
an image of isolated tribal communities: for example, evidence suggests that

the Inca system extended deep into the Amazon basin. Such regional systems and the subsequent commercial civilizations are all characterized by the accumulation of capital, something which can take a number of forms and is a concept closer to Weber's notion of abstract wealth. They go through cyclical phases of centralization and accumulation and then decentralization which are manifest in shifting centre periphery relations (Friedman, 1994: 22). It is argued that there is a strong relationship between changes in the flow and accumulation of capital and changes in identity construction and cultural production.

Two major phases of global systems can be identified (Friedman, 1994: 168). The first is a stable hegemonic phase characterized by strongly hierarchical relationships between centers and peripheries, with the latter acting as supply zones of raw materials and labour for the center which is the focal point for industrial manufacturing. This is a phase of the strengthening of a homogenous cultural identity and ethnicity, with the various populations identifying though hierarchized relations with the elite in the center. Clearly, this is a process we see extending throughout the global system with the rise of Western modernity.

The second phase in an unstable phase of de-hegemonization. This entails a process of decentralization of capital accumulation as the centers become rich and expensive, leading them to export large quantities of capital to the peripheries. New smaller centres emerge on the peripheries which outcompete the old center, leading to the decline of industry and re-investment of some of the surplus capital in services, financial capital, stock markets, real estate and the luxury and arts sectors. Hence in the centers we have the characteristics elsewhere characterized as 'dual cities' (Mollenkopf and Castells, 1991): the combination of deindustrialization and gentrification with the simultaneous appearance of slummification and yuppification. Friedman (1994: 169) tells us that what critics refer to as 'post-industrial society', is the product of deindustrialization, a consequence of the switched investment patterns in the de-hegemonizing phase of the global system.

It is in this phase that culture emerges as a central visible feature of social life and a central topic for intellectuals; this is because culture loses its taken for granted homogeneity, value hierarchical ordering and association with strong stable identities. Hence in this phase we have the emergence of narcissism and postmodernism in the West, the references to decentred, fragmented and multiple identities. We have the identification with nature and 4th World movement. In the phase of Western hegemony and the emergence of strong identities with a hierarchical ordered global system meant there was a strong 3rd World identification with the center, which was seen as the source of power and wealth and hence the desire for development to move up the ladder to the Western level. In the phase of decline of Western hegemony, on the other hand, many groups and cultural movements in the West who have postmodernist allegiencies, have a strong disposition to protect local identities (including nature) across the world; they, therefore, identify and ally themselves with the 4th World, the world of the excluded and tribal peoples, which seek to reject modernity (Friedman, 1994: 192). In the phase of de-hegemonization of the West, in addition, the relative decline of the West and export of capital and manufacturing has seen the rise of East Asia as another potential centre, which is developing new forms of modernism and centred identities (around neo-Confusion ethics).

For Friedman globalization and localization must be understood as related to phases in global systems processes. Whereas globalization is most likely to be associated with the decline of Western hegemony, as we will see below, the position is more complicated in that a 'strong' globalization can also occur in the first phase of the establishment of a stable hegemony. In this phase, the phase of the development of Western modernity, elites in local cultures on the periphery tend to identify with the centre. A version of this is found in the late 20th century in what Friedman (1994: 191) refers to as the '3rd World strategy', which is a phase of orientation to the centre as a source of wealth; it is a dependence, pro-development strategy, entailing the consumption of the prestige symbols of modernity through cliental chains and the imposition of sumptuary laws. The case of *La sape, the sapeurs (flâneurs*, or elegant dressers) of the People's Republic of the Congo, is discussed at length by Friedman (1994: 105–108, 158–166) as an example of subversive prestige accumulation by outsiders operating in this type of 3rd world context. Localization, is associated with the alternative 4th World strategy and is practised by people on the margins of their own culture, or those who have lost their cultural identity. This strategy can be contrasted to the usual acceptance of their marginal status and existence on the peripheries of the social structure. It often takes the form of cultural movements who seek to reject modernity and exit from the system through re-establishing their former identity and unified way of life which have been repressed. Friedman (1994: 109–113, 123 ff., 173 ff.) discusses at length two cases. Firstly, the Ainu of Hokkaido who were integrated into the Japanese state after the Meiji Restoration and use heritage tourism as a strategy to rebuild their former villages, language and way of life. Secondly, the Hawaiian cultural movement, which is strongly anti-tourist, rejects Americanization in favour of the reformation of their identities in the search for authentic roots—a process which has seen a massive increase in the people, who although only partly Hawaiian, came to identify themselves as totally Hawaiian.

Globalization, then, for Friedman cannot be understood as an independent process with its own dynamic, either driven by modernity, technology or the market; it is not an inevitable outcome of modernization. Rather, it should be seen as related to a phase of global systems. As he puts it

> Globalization refers in this context to the formation of global institutional structures, that is, structures that organize the already existing global field, and global cultural forms, that is, forms that are either produced or transformed into globally accessible objects and representations. The fact that Western intellectuals interpret the world as a single place is not in itself a fact of globalization unless it becomes a prevailing interpretation for the rest of the world system. (Friedman, 1994: 201)

For Friedman, then, globalization is a subset of global systemic processes. It can take two forms: strong globalization and weak globalization. Weak globalization refers to the existence of a global field of reference, in which different parts of the world have access to the same set of cultural expressions and representations, which depends upon global connectivity, the fact that global media and means of transportation of goods and materials exist. It does not imply similarity of reception, for the emphasis here is on the differential ways in which the local assimilates the global into its own sphere of meaning. Strong globalization, on the other hand, implies that "the mechanisms of appropriation of the global have themselves become globalized, that we understand in the same way the objects and representations that circulate in the larger arena" (Friedman, 1994: 203). This depends upon the creation of subjects around the world who all interpret the world in similar ways; it entails some homogenization of local contexts.

Friedman (1994: 204) raises the question whether there can be transnational or transcultural identities or cultures and argues that this can only occur when the identification process is transcultural, that is mixed, or occurs on a level above the nation-state and not between them. This is typically the position of the cosmopolitan, who peruses and participates in many worlds, without ever becoming part of them. He adds "It is the position and identity of an intellectual self situated outside of the local arenas among which s/he moves" (Friedman, 1994: 204). It is a typically modern stance in its dependence upon distance. Formerly cosmopolitan anthropologists were 'masters of otherness', able to move through and pronounce judgement on the discrete cultures which made up 'the classic mosaic of relativism'. But with the move to a phase of de-hegemony in the West, for reasons outlined above the separateness of cultural boundaries has dissolved. The survival strategy for the anthropologist is to focus on global objects, to become an expert on global culture and "join the ranks of global art curators, and art and literary critics, once monopolists of otherness, now recuperating their monopoly by redefining the object as creolized, mixed-up otherness" (Friedman, 1994: 205).

With regard to what we have referred to as 3rd cultures, the level of emerging global institutions, Friedman reminds us that they are not new and disputes whether they produce a cultural globalization process, as this depends upon global awareness, and such an awareness can only be found in the international elite of top diplomats, heads of state, aid officials and representatives of NGOs who enjoy common forms of sociability and association. This group overlaps with an international cultural elite of art dealers, publishers and media representatives. These are the people who make the news and communicate a particular vision of reality. Friedman (1994: 106) argues that this elite is a kind of cultural cohort which has shared properties and common positions and is the source of much of the globalization discourse. As is the case with anthropologists and other academics, this group often operates with a view of culture as specificity and the assumption that where we have different populations we have different cultures: something which is distinctly modern too and which generates an essentialization of the world. It is the gap between the texts and representations of culture of the elites and the way that culture is constituted out of practice which is the problem for Friedman (1994: 207), for the danger is that it "confuses our identification with theirs and trivializes other peoples' experience by reducing it to our cognitive categories."

Friedman illustrates his position here by taking the example of creolization, which he argues is a concept predicated on the notion of culture as text or substance; a hypostatization of culture which mistakenly presents cultures as substances, like matter or fluids which can be mixed and blended. One of his targets here is Ulf Hannerz (1992: 96) who presents cultural mixing and creolization as something intrinsically impure. In linguistics the term creole has been heavily debated. It refers to colonial situations where a secondary rudimentary language (e.g. pidgin) used to communicate between groups becomes assimilated to first language status by a new generation of speakers. Yet more recently the category has been under attack, as it is argued that all languages are creole given the absence of adequate linguistic criteria for distinguishing between creole and 'natural languages'. When the concept of creole was used in the context of essentialist notions of culture, it suggests the mixing of two formerly pure cultures. Yet this classification arose from the dominant elites, who used it to refer to the mixing of plantation labour, in this context it was a stable mechanism of identification based on an essentialized view of culture. Hence Friedman (1994: 209) argues that "the establishment and maintenance of a creole identity was a social act rather than a cultural fact." He adds

If the world is to be understood as largely creolized today this expresses the identity of the classifier who experiences the transgression of cultural, that is, ethnic, national, boundaries as a global phenomenon. The problem is not that we have suddenly been confronted with cultural flows on a world scale compared to what occurred in a more restricted way in the plantation sector of the Caribbean or Southeast Asia. The problem is that conditions of identification of both self and other have changed. Cultures don't flow together and mix with each other. Rather, certain actors, often strategically positioned actors, identify the world in such terms as part of their own self-identification. Cultural mixture is the effect of the practice of mixed origins (Friedman, 1994: 210).

Likewise Friedman (1994: 110) is critical of Appadurai's notions of disjunctive global flows, which seems to suggest the introduction of turmoil and disorder into a formerly more systemic world. Yet what appears as disorder may be none the less systemic. Rather for Friedman disorder must be seen as a result of both the processes of the fragmentation of the global system which has permitted the space for multiple localization strategies to develop. It is also seen as the result of the globalization of class associations and means of representation. Hence for Friedman the identification of mixing is only a problem for cultural experts who operate with a notion of culture as substance and "whose identification of origins is disturbed by the global processes of changing identities, a disturbance that is consequently translated into a disauthentification of other people's 'actually existing' cultures."

In a more recent paper entitled "The Hybridization of Roots and the Abhorrence of the Bush" Friedman (1999) sharpens his critique of the intellectuals' misunderstanding of global cultural processes. Friedman again raises the question whether there is actually more mixing today than in the past when we had blues, jazz, pasta etc. If today there is a greater consciousness of mixing, this may have more to do with the formation of a particular type of gaze on the part of upper class and middle class Westerners who are consumers of cultural objects and images. Hybridization and creolization can be seen as the ideology of the intellectuals drawn from these groups. Something which is a particular reading of the world, a reading of the more sophisticated cosmopolitans. But for Friedman this cosmopolitan celebration of rootlessness and their anti-ethnic orientation, should be seen as part of the logic of modern experience. Unlike previous groups of cultural specialists, the cosmopolitans do not have a civilizing mission or high culture, rather they engage in the accumulation of differences.

According to Friedman there is a clear connection between intellectual decline and hegemonic decline. This is manifest in the decline of the public sphere. As the public sphere becomes weakened, the principle of rational argumentation along with notions of falsification and an ethical code suffers and other modes take over. We get the formation of various groupings and clientalisms whose aim is to colonize the public sphere, and do so by what

one might term 'outsider' strategies. For these groups intellectual life becomes
subordinated to the logic of accumulating social power and status: they are
new groups striving to become cultural elites who take it on themselves to
become self-appointed representatives of the non-white poor of the world.
The postcolonial critics engage in a rhetoric of the flowing and mixing of
cultures, something which is only surprising if one expected to find a prior
ordered and highly classified world.

The problem is that cultural products may well seem mixed to outsiders,
but if one looks closely there may be little evidence of cultural hybridization in the activities and discourses of actual groups of people. If we say
all cultures are hybrid and mixed, this is merely a truism, which denies any
operational significance to the term hybridization. Rather, according to
Friedman, we need to focus on how cultures are actually experienced.
Hybridity may well be a form of identity which is on the increase, but
largely among certain groups such as cultural specialists and intermediaries.
Cultures may well travel and move around the world, but ethnicity is still
about the maintenance of social boundaries, something which remains a
powerful force in the current phase of globalization. What appears as a new
stage of mixing and flows should be understood in terms of the decline of
Western hegemony. The fragmentation of nation-states and multiculturalism in the West are expressions of this process. In the global circuits of
intellectual and high culture, along with the media and diplomatic elites
who inhabit the global cities, a cosmopolitan identity of a multicultural world
has developed, giving rise to perspectives from which localisms and local
identities seem backward.

Inhabiting global cultural space

The approaches of Appadurai and Friedman clearly offer very different conceptions of the world. Appadurai's emphasis upon fluidity and cultural flows
which are seen as producing postnational communities which no longer
reproduce identities in predictable stable ways, amounts to a position which
challenges the capacity of global systems to continue to function in a structured way. On the other hand Appadurai's perspective is relativized by
Friedman who argues that fluidity and cultural mixing has less to do with
significant shifts in the actual practices of particular groups in the world,
but more to do with the gaze of small groups of cultural specialists who
identify these processes. The views these groups have about postnationality,
translocality, flexible habitus, hybridization, then, are seen as derivations
from a particular view of the world. A perspective which clearly bears the

stamp of outsider fractions of the intellectuals, academics and other members of the middle and upper classes, the nascent global elite, who have adopted a cosmopolitan cultural outlook.

One characteristic of this perspective is 'the tourist gaze', of the new middle classes, in particular the new cultural intermediaries and specialists, who are at home handling and playing with images and experiences of culture garnered on the move (Urry, 1990; Featherstone, 1991, 1998b; Rojek and Urry, 1997). The perception of this group is a transient mobile gaze, which situates, attempts a preliminary contextualization, locating the experience or images within some wider loose archival classificatory schema, and then quickly moves on. The question is how far are these changes found in wider groups of people?

At the same time, Appadurai would seem to overestimate the extent to which everyone is mobile, travelling, or associating and dreaming of travel. It has to be considered that some 3rd and 4th world people dream of dwelling. Certainly the enforced internal migrations of groups such as the *Movimento cem Terra*, the landless in Brazil, are one group which wants to settle down, to dwell in one place. Others are seeking to establish a permanent homeland. There is a complex pattern of group identifications at play here, with de-globalizing reactions one alternative strategy, even if it means as is the case with certain Amazonian tribes, the global stage is used as a space for protest and bargaining to defend themselves from the negative effects of economic globalization which threatens to destroy their habitat.

Cultural specialists and intermediaries

If Friedman is arguing that, the mixing and hybridization is largely a projection of the cosmopolitan rootlessness of new middle class groups, academics and intellectuals, then this is a similar argument to one I made some years ago with respect to postmodernism. I argued contra those who celebrated a move into a new fluid postmodern epoch which has taken us beyond the social, that it was important to try to locate the 'where', and the 'who' of postmodernism to specify the sites and groups which might act as carriers of postmodern dispositions (Featherstone, 1991). Friedman likewise identifies the carriers of hybridization as cosmopolitan elites who identify with rootlessness and outsiderism. In fact, there is a similar genealogy at work to that of postmodernism here for he sees this disposition as developing in the climate of the decline of modernism, which saw the replacement of universalistic values and anti-ethnic particularity with a rediscovery of the fragmented national and regional identities. For Friedman (1999) then we have the equation: cosmopolitanism minus modernism equals hybridization. Such identifications are to be expected in periods of intellectual de-monopolization and the decline of the public sphere, which favours the entry of outsiders who seek to establish new criteria of legitimation. At the same time Friedman's loose sociology of knowledge approach[6] contains considerable 'bite': he clearly does not like the new group, or their strategies and sees it as a weakening of intellectual life. Yet it is possible to see the de-monopolization of intellectual symbolic hierarchies and older patronage structures which were maintained from the Western centres, as containing many positive democratizing features, not least for the outsiders within the West and the excluded on the global peripheries.

A further problem, is in the hard distinction Friedman draws between the wilful projection of a hybridized view of the world by the intellectuals on various groups around the world, and their actual everyday practices. Here we have the authority of the everyday practice of ordinary groups of people contrasted to the misguided 'textualized' reading from above by the intellectuals, who discover complexities and mixing unnoticed by the actual practitioners in daily life. Yet perhaps this sharp distinction has become blurred to a greater extent since the 1960s with the expansion of higher education, consumer culture and the globalization of the media. Middle class migrants are more likely to have been through higher education and be in touch with others who are able to articulate the construction of post-national communities as a project. Their undermining of the authority of the intellectuals and academics and older more tightly regulated public sphere provides opportunities for the diffusion of intellectual knowledge and the blending of it with consumer culture and electronic media forms. There are more new cultural intermediaries around in the middle classes who adopt a learning approach to life and who can recycle and package cultural goods and develop pedagogies. Hence presenting culture as an object and textualization, or the consciousness that culture can become the subject of distanced contemplation and aestheticization, or that culture can be a project or projection, is by no means confined to tightly integrated elite groups.

---

[6] Although he doesn't name his sources, Bourdieu and to a lesser degree Mannheim would seem to be influences here. With regard to the targets, often they seem to be ill-founded and poorly documented. In one chapter he tells us he is going to contrast two very different approaches to global process: Birmingham-inspired cultural sociology and the global systems approach (Friedman, 1994: 195), yet he makes no further reference to the former approach. Also referring to bell hooks as 'the self-proclaimed queen of postcolonialism' (Friedman, 1999) without adding a more detailed analysis of the group processes involved, only provides an opportunity for his opponents to not take him seriously.

The interplay between culture as an articulation of imaginary longings and desires, and the awareness of the arbitrariness of it as a construction, need not be confined to lifestyle constructing groups such as one finds in gay city districts, but has become a more general phenomenon constantly replayed on the media. It would seem that the new middle classes are the groups more attracted to this form of experimentation and habitus reconstruction, yet it is diffused to other groups through both a variety of electronic and print media, and through the weakening of patriarchal authority structures within families, and the greater mobility both spatial and virtual, which presents life as a wider field of realizable opportunities to larger publics. This increased mobility is often accompanied by the use of guidebooks and handbooks, both of the tourist and the etiquette type. Indeed this process of habitus formation, interest in other people's habituses and ways of cultural production and artefacts, can be traced back a long way— Norbert Elias in *The Civilizing Process*, for example, argues that the fact that manners books such as Erasmus's *De civilitate morum puerilium*, first published in 1530, went through many editions suggests they were of use to people concerned about how to change their behaviour in the appropriate way. Hence in everyday practices there is a tendency to use objective accounts of culture, with a circulation today of anthropological notions and vignettes along with those of travellers, novelists, artists which are re-packaged for electronic and print media sources. Consumer culture encourages a mood of experimentation and 'what if . . .' imaginary identifications and while these may rarely surface into a lifestyle or full life project, these minor identifications co-exist alongside more routine ascribed identities linked to work, place and ethnicity. For some it may be the identification with the powerful, as in the 3rd World, where prestige may be gained through smoking Marlboro, drinking Coca-Cola or Budweiser and wearing a Chicago Bulls singlet. At the same time there are many other possible alternative and temporary identifications through music, fashion and sport with a variety of sources, not all of them coming out of dominant centres and a singular hierarchy of taste.

Then we have the associated question about how the intellectuals' depiction of culture relates to everyday practices. From Friedman's perspective the alleged creolization, hybridization and mixing is a projection which is a privileged reading from above which does not capture everyday practices. Yet despite referring to three contemporary studies (the Hawaiian Cultural Movement, the Ainu of Hokkaido and the Sapeurs of the People's Republic of Congo) we are given little sense of the cultural practices of groups of people around the world. The examples given are those of 4th World cultural movements and an outsider group from the 3rd World. We need more evidence of other groups, especially in those locations where transnational identifications are allegedly taking place, not just the mobile global elites and new middle classes, but the migrants working as cleaners, along with the dwellers in favelas and shanty-towns. In short if we are to talk about practices, and one of the inspirations here is Pierre Bourdieu (1977), we need a sense of the broader field of cultural identifications and social groups within which they take place, as we find exemplified in Bourdieu's field analysis. This raises the related question about the structural parameters of fields of culture and symbolic power under conditions of globalization, along with the associated issues of habitus transmission and reproduction.

The strength of approaches such as Friedman's is to situate particular identities and identitification processes as part of longer wave movements in the global system. Friedman's approach is schematic, he paints with a broad brush and covers great swathes of history and social life with ease. His is a relational model in which the shifting hegemony and power balances between the various entities of the global system affects the sense of prestige and status of its members. Hence, with the rise to global hegemony of the West we expect a strong sense of identity to emerge based upon feelings of superiority. As we find in Wallerstein's (1974, 1980) world-system theory, the assumption is that the accumulation of economic capital and power at the center in periods of hegemony, such as the rise of Western modernity, will be accompanied by identities constructed around notions of development, change and expansion. In periods of hegemonic decline, such as are being experienced in the West today, there will be the export of capital and production from the center to the peripheries and a concomitant fragmentation of identities (narcissistic, postmodern, return to ethnicity etc).

Such models are sketched at a high level of generality, with little sensitivity to the possibilities that nation-state particularity, or internal social processes, could be crucial to mediating identity formation. The novelty is that Friedman goes outside the usual focus on the internal dynamics of particular nation-state societies to focus on the relationship between societies and blocs. Yet higher level concepts such as the West, the 3rd and 4th World, tend to be blunt conceptual instruments. For example, sometimes Japan is co-opted to the West—sharing their success and then de-hegemonizing postmodern decline, sometimes, it is seen as part of the ascending East Asian capitalism which is the rising bloc which is experiencing hegemony and the ascendant modernity which has migrated from the West, along with the development of centered modern identities. To speak of identity formation within such blocs is to work at a very high level of generality, especially when the significance of internal processes is played down.

Intra and inter-societal processes

Here, we could usefully examine Norbert Elias' (1978,1982) remarks on globalization in the Synopsis at the very end of *The Civilizing Process*. While Elias is known for drawing attention to the relationship between state formation and the development of personality and habitus controls, his model had always taken him beyond the confines of the nation-state to focus upon the figuration of competing and independent states, within which the nascent state was a part. Hence the power balances and interdependencies between European states such as France, England and Spain have to be seen as relevant to the internal changes within their societies.

As Haferkamp (1987) argues there is a move in his work from a focus on intra-state to inter-state civilizing processes. Certainly the networks of independencies have been extended to pull together more local places not just on a national level, but on a global level too. One way to see this would be to see alongside state integration and Western expansion, not only the adoption of modes of conduct of increasing self-restraint on the part of the lower stratum who follow the upper stratum, but for both the upper and lower stratum of Western societies as becoming a kind of upper stratum to networks of independencies spreading across the world, drawing in more outsider groups and regions (Elias, 1982: 250). While on the one hand the Western nations seek to strictly regulate their own institutions and build a wall between themselves and the groups they colonize, they cannot at the same time help spreading their own style of conduct and institutions to these places, which leads to a reduction of differences and diminishing of contrasts. Yet the process is not a singular one and Elias sees it as better conceived as entailing 'spurts' or 'waves', with the oscillations depending upon the shifting struggles between established and outsider groups.

Two phases are distinguishable. The first, is a phase of colonization and assimilation in which the lower and larger outsider class senses its own inferiority and has its pattern of conduct permeated by that of the upper group. The second is a phase of repulsion, differentiation and emancipation which the rising groups gain in power and confidence and the upper group is forced to withdraw into greater isolation and restraint—hence the contrast and tensions in society increase (Elias, 1982: 311). In the first phase of distinction, outsider groups seek to assimilate and mould their conduct to that of the established group, but the efforts to follow their conduct are purchased only with great effort and often result in more severe, less balanced patterns of imitation, with consequent oscillations between feelings of shame and embarrassment. In the second phase, the phase of equalization, de-monopolization processes set in and outsider groups gain in relative power and oppose their own codes and manners more confidently to those of the established. Patterns of conduct migrate from those below to those above and there is a more general interpenetration of standards of conduct of different groups and classes (Elias, 1982: 325). There is greater uncertainty about conduct and people start to scrutinize and question conduct which was formerly taken for granted by their parents. In addition, Elias emphasizes that as a result of increased mobility and encounters between people from different parts of the world, people learn to relativize: they see themselves from a greater distance and raise questions about why their own modes of conduct differ from that of others.

One could well make a link between this form of reflexivity and consumer culture through the ways in which advertising and the electronic and print media seek to publicize and introduce new tastes, lifestyles and habits from around the world, to educate and stimulate the consumer gaze. Hence Elias' approach is one which moves easily between intra- and inter-societal processes, being able to focus on the detail of the actual conditions of specific groups as well as the wider inter-state and emergent global relations.

Habitus and embodiment

The term habitus has been widely used by Pierre Bourdieu (1977, 1984) and Norbert Elias (1978, 1982) to refer to the set of shared flexible dispositions, modes of classifying the world which are not just cognitive, but are sedimented and written into bodies and evident in body styles of sitting, movement, talking, demeanour etc. Hence the habitus is the habitual state of approaching others and the world and is the source of our particular embodied tastes in food, consumer goods or art. The habitus has a reflexive 'see and be seen', or 'classify the classifier' quality to it, because in social life we constantly are required to make judgements about others on the basis of our habitus which structures the way we see the world. Others, of course, are at the same time engaged in making judgements about us by observing our bodies and speech, judgements which are made from the perspective of their habituses and therefore they are able to locate our position in the social space. Much of this classificatory work happens below the level of consciousness and is taken for granted and habitual. It rarely surfaces into speech. Yet the smallest gesture of a hand, or the way a person looks away or glances aside, unconsciously pass onto us much information about the nature of their habitus. Elias (1982: 330) emphasizes the body at one point where he discusses the ways in which parents' fears are transmitted to the child as much by gestures as by words.[7] Hence within the social space of the field of consumption and lifestyle it is possible, as Bourdieu (1984) does in *Distinction*, to map tastes for consumption goods and lifestyles onto the matrix of occupational groups and class fractions which are often structured through the binary logic of oppositions.

The social field of tastes, however, is generally conceived by Bourdieu in state-societal terms. Indeed, he has been criticized to the extent to which his scheme fits best the status games of French society and may have far less relevance elsewhere (see discussion in Featherstone, 1995: ch. 2). When we move to the global or transnational level, we have people dealing with goods or persons whose significance and habitus may be difficult to classify. The mobility of the flows of goods and people may place us in situations where there are greater dangers of misreading. Familiar goods, images and lifestyle practices, then have to be understood within the specific national context in which they occur, as the social field they operate in cannot be assumed to work on identical principles to our own. Objects, then, become recontextualized as they circulate across different social spheres and groups.

In addition, the level of ambiguity and cohesion of fields may vary a great deal, especially outside of the West. Cultural and economic capital are forms of capital which operate much more clearly in modern societies. In other parts of the world the fields of social power and consumption may be far less precise and readable (Palumbo-Liu, 1997: 11). The introduction of heterogeneous ranges of goods and people from different parts of the world, complicates greatly the capacity to generate an ordered field. Especially in countries like Brazil, where although the state aspires to strong integration, the level of state formation has been relatively low with states enjoying a good deal of local autonomy. In addition in Brazil over 50% of the economy operates in the informal sector, that is it does not pay taxes or appear in the official statistics. Consequently, to construct the field of consumption, tastes and lifestyles in Brazil would be an almost impossible task.

Hence Palumbo-Liu (1997: 13) argues

> In short, we have not yet been able to come up with a model that might predict the outcome of the transposition of cultural objects across an increasing disjunctive world wherein the particular habitus of social agents is shot through

---

[7] Gestures which may be copied by the child without ever being articulated. Something which provides the grounds for those types of therapy such as Shiatsu, Reiki and Alexander Technique, which seek to alter the mind by working on the body, seeing the experiences of life as unconsciously written into the body, something which only works on the body can correct.

with new information and new objects from around a globe to which we have yet to become habituated, nor have we arrived peacefully at a sense of how the differentials of class, race, gender, ethnicity, sexual orientation, and so forth, might be accommodated in any modelling system.

The problem is also one of the range of different political and economic contexts within which habitus is asked to operate, and the unpredictability of the rules of play of the games which operate (Palumbo-Liu, 1997: 19). It is possible to find different parties reading the same game through different sets of rules. Aihwa Ong (1997, cited in Palumbo-Liu, 1997: 20) discusses how wealthy ex-Hong Kong Chinese capitalists who moved to California, subsequently sought to acquire cultural capital to attempt to reproduce their high status overseas. They assumed that their patronage of high culture institutions, would help transcend the old racial categories, by giving them higher symbolic value. But they discovered that they were not allowed to make this transition by the Anglo social elite, who operated various modes of exclusion.

Of course, a closer reading of Bourdieu would show that the possibilities and rates of translation of cultural, symbolic, educational, body, social and economic capital into each other are by no means clear. A reading of *Distinction* would show that lower middle class outsider audotdicacts who had invested a good deal of time learning about opera, are not easily admitted into established upper class circles where opera serves a range of ancillary functions. The key category Palumbo-Liu misses to discuss is social capital, or connections. Social capital is more than network connections, but less than clientalism. Rather, it is a place in a network of people who are somewhere between friends and associates. In the distinction battles between the new rich and the old rich, the latter have always possessed something which the former were never allowed to purchase. In effect social capital relates to habitus, and is visible in manners and bodily dispositions, but it also relates to how one's family is known and one's reputation functions in a wider order of things.[8]

At the same time, the exclusion of the Chinese may also be a form of racism. The Chinese would not be able to pass as white Anglo Californians. An alternative strategy would be to dispute or relativize this particular prestige hierarchy. We see this in Jonathan Friedman's example of the Hawaiian movement, where mixed ethnicity Hawaiians who may formerly have attempted to 'pass' (in the Goffman, 1971, sense) as ordinary Americans,

---

[8] See the discussion of 'patina', the possession of family valuables such as silver, or a collection of model ships, which are never normally allowed to enter the marketplace and whose 'pricelessness' is itself a sign of distinction (McCracken, 1988).

now cultivate their Hawaiian separate identity. This may involve a good deal of body work, in terms of modifying the shape of the body, type of food one eats, demeanour, hairstyle, expression, way of speaking, style of dress etc. To re-work habitus takes considerable investment and is not an easy set of changes to contemplate and actualize. But it may be one of the effects of globalization that distinctive styles migrate rapidly around the world and become appropriated by particular groups who seek to opt out of existing prestige hierarchies and conventional modes of accumulating cultural, social, economic and body capital.

To be black and reject the possibility of passing as white or cultivating a body which approximates to the respectable consumer culture ideal, and adopt a Rastafarian style with long dreadlocks and appropriate insignia and apparel, is to embrace what conventional society denies and stigmatizes. It is the outsider group's attempt to turn a negative into a positive a sign, by closing off the possibility of rejection by the established group and developing alternative prestige hierarchies. Likewise the young person who sports a pierced face full of studs and rings, is wearing what conventional modes of body capital would define as an extreme stigmata, in a gesture which courts rejection and outsiderism, which will have a range of consequences for capital accumulation (for a discussion of body modification see Featherstone, 1999). In this context too we should mention the ways in which gays, increasingly refuse to pass as 'straight', but more openly adopt body styles: demeanour, hairstyle, body shape, adornment and clothing which are more openly associated with gayness and its various parodies. The aestheticization and sexualization of inner city areas as 'gay cities', turned into a saleable aspect of the city image by marketers, creates sites in which such reformed people who wish to display their habitus and associate with other lifestyle experimenters, can associate, live and work (Bech, 1998; Weeks, 1998).

The body habitus, then, can become reconstituted and made to function within alternative symbolic hierarchies. Yet there are limits to the body as a project, to the re-sexualization, re-gendering, or production of queer or gay bodies. It is also clear that such bodies function best within certain sites and collectivities. The fatefulness of removing such bodies and placing them in what has been referred to as the 'trucking parts of America', or middle America, has been a well-rehearsed plot in movies and television soaps, which delight in playing with these lifestyle experimenter stereotypes and their impact on local awareness contexts. To successfully achieve the re- or de-racialization of the body, or re- or de-ageing of the body habitus are also challenging to say the least. Clearly the body has limits, its boundaries are not totally flexible, however much the advertising and consumer culture rhetoric proclaims the ease of shape-overs and make-overs: bodies break-down, gender-change operations and plastic surgery go wrong, bodies get old and die.

At the same time we have a practical interest in bodies as we move around through everyday spaces in urban worlds of strangers. Bodies are seen and seeing: others look at us and seek to classify us, we do the same. Particularly in dangerous urban spaces at night, the reading of bodies is not a playful activity, but can be a survival skill. The potential violence of certain types of bodies can lead to unfair stereotypes which result in racial discrimination. The police and private security agencies train their personnel to recognize certain types of bodies, demeanour and movements, as potentially dangerous and threatening. Hence there is a good deal of body work, surreptitious looking, surveillance and forms of recognition and misrecognition taking place as people move through public spaces. When we think of the strategies of recognition and information checking necessary in global cities with large influxes of migrants and temporary visitors from various parts of the world, the mapping of this data onto a social field, or universe of class, ethnic, aged, gendered and sexualized bodies is very complex. Yet it is worth stating that if Bourdieu's field analysis means anything, it is an abstraction and reconstruction of a practical reason, a practical sense which people employ unconsciously in everyday life guided by the classifications and dispositions embedded in their habitus. This means that Bourdieu's field is a systematic reconstruction of the everyday partial perspectives manifest in the practical knowledge of particular sets of people.[9]

Hence if we seek to follow Appadurai and refer to the instabilities, mixing and flux of the postnational global lifeworlds, then what he calls 'the painful reconstruction of habitus', captures some of the difficulties to be encountered. The constant round of misrecognitions through global mixing demand harder work on habitus recognition and classification, yet as such work has important practical value for those who live, work, play, or pass through the spaces of greatest mixing. Such work will have to be undertaken, both to create a feeling of security, a sense of ease of inhabitation, and to minimize potential risks.

---

[9] There are similarities here with Elias' (1983) discussion of 'court rationality', a term he uses to refer to the fine distinctions people employ to judge the changing fortunes of courtiers—who is in, who is out, who is up and who is down—something equivalent to a set of daily stock exchange quotations. A practical rationality people carry in their heads and constantly update and reconstruct, but which is of course not modelled or abstractly represented, as we find with the actual stock market indices.

Global identifications

The greater mobility and mixing which we find through globalization, can therefore lead to a more flexible and mobile habitus which is periodically reconstituted (although as we have emphasized there are limits to this process). Of course, for the participants of the Hawaiian cultural movement, or other ethnic movements, the potential postnational communities they participate in and the identities they form, may well seem to be permanent, and not something which is selected from a range of alternatives. Yet such postnational communities will vary a great deal in the extent to which they incorporate members and seek to tighten the circle of identification. In some, the affiliation may be loose, with participants free to move on, in others once one has joined and is 'in', the chances of getting out may be remote. In short, some of the organizations may function as mafias, and employ strong sets of controls to ensure the complicity of members. The shift in the balance of power of local ethnic groups, in for example Bosnia, where armed paramilitary mafia style groups were able to gain control and act as spokespersons for communities, suggests that the social dynamics of the face-to-face world, with its chains of interdependencies, obligations and power balances, and potential violence to bodies, should not be ignored. Indeed mafias have been very successful in globalizing in the current phase (Castells, 1998).

There are, nevertheless, the prospects of other forms of identification processes. According to Norbert Elias (1991: 207) on the one hand we can detect a process of individualization of identities, in which people escape from the strict family obligations imposed in the past. What he refers to as the 'I-we balance', therefore, shifts towards the 'we-less-I', in which autonomous action of the allegedly isolated individual who is able to construct identities, is stressed. On the other hand, Elias emphasizes that nation-states are born for wars and in wars, which helps to explain the power and emotional charge the state level of integration, the 'I-less-we', carries for many groups. The contradiction between the two perspectives is usually managed by strict compartmentalization. At the same time the we-identity of the nation, helps to create a distinctive national habitus, or national character, within which individualization processes take place.

The intensification of the globalization process brings about a number of further possibilities. One, is that of mixed or ambiguous identifications, the postnational identities Appadurai refers to which we have discussed at length, the 'double consciousness' of the blacks who move across the Atlantic and are inside and outside the West which Gilroy (1993) discusses, the irreconcilable 'betwixt and between' border identities of mobile minorities which Bhabha (1994) speaks of.

A second possibility, is the identification with humanity. Elias (1991: 165) argues that we are currently involved in the early stages of an immense process of integration, a process whose direction is towards the total integration of humankind. He remarks that "The early forms of a new, world-wide ethos, and especially the widening of identification between person and person, are already clearly discernible" (Elias, 1991: 168). Signs of this process are to be found in the new sense of global responsibility of people from different parts of the world share for those in distress, the victims and refugees from wars, natural and man-made disasters. Movements such as Amnesty International, Greenpeace, Oxfam, can also be cited as further evidence of a growing sense of responsibility for a generalized other as well as specific others around the world. Feelings which are premised on the assumption that we are all interdependent human beings who share many common characteristics. Elias sees the mobility of people, the great increase in the mass movement of tourists and migrants beyond the borders of their nation-states in the 20th century as sharply contrasting to the preceding century. The lengthening and tightening of the chains of interdependencies and the integration of nation-states into a more closely knit worldwide network, hence holds out the potential of greater possibilities for individualization.

The current identification of the 'revolt of the elites', and the accusation that mobile upper class groups lack any sense of responsibility, needs to be balanced against these more cosmopolitan impulses of identification with the other which have been developing in the middle classes and other groups. It has also been suggested that there is more giving today than ever before, that people support charities and empathize and identify with the other to a much greater extent (Berking, 1999). Yet we know relatively little about the habitus, values and identifications of the new emerging global elites and their middle class counterparts, or for that matter the lower class 3rd World migrants. We need not only to study these groups in global cities such as New York, Paris and London, but look at them in various sites such as the Cayman Islands and other tax-havens, the specialist resorts and gathering places such as Davos in Switzerland, Punto de l'Este in Uruguay, Monte Carlo etc. If as Elias (1982) argues, there has been a shift from the tightly integrated court centers, the archetype being Louis XIV's Versailles, which produced strong aristocratic social codes and habituses, to economic centers such as New York, London and Tokyo, where the new upper classes do not have to participate in 'society' and 'the season' to anything like the same extent. The mobility and diffusion of establishments in the upper classes has been a neglected topic by sociologists and cultural studies specialists, who always find it easier, and more worthy, to study the poor and outsiders.

But the dynamic of the established and the outsiders in upper class groups, the forms of association, networks and identifications, but for a few exceptions (e.g. Sklair, 1998) is as yet a closed topic.

Elias pointed to the compartmentalization between national identity and self-identity, likewise we can add postnational imagined and other lifestyle identifications. Formerly, the contexts in which one used a particular identification were clear-cut, they involved particular sites and institutional arrangements and interdependencies with groups of people. Bounded sites meant for a clearer sense of hierarchy, structures of relevance and codes of appropriate behaviour. If the urban worlds and crowds of people in the big cities introduced a more complex set of potential affiliations and offered a new life as a range of possibilities for certain groups, then, the mobility of modern transportation and the electronic media offer further extensive sets. The speed and mobility of vehicles of transportation and the static virtual transportation vehicles of the electronic media (television, the Internet) offer greater possibilities to escape contexts (Featherstone, 1998b, 2000b; Armitage, 1999; Virilio, 1999). To escape the domination and obligation structures which operate in the more tightly organized face-to-face groups in family, work, leisure and associational milieu. As discussions of the cinematic gaze suggest, outsider groups are able to identify with a range of others and cross conventional racial and gender lines through the new media (Hansen, 1991, Friedberg, 1994; Featherstone, 1998a).

This mobility is also evident in the new electronic communicative forms such as the Internet. Not only does this increase the ease, speed and flexibility of communication, it helps to widen networks beyond usual patterns of association. While the World Wide Web has many exclusive spaces and no-go areas, such as the intranets of transnational corporations and governments, at the same time the capacity to make new contacts and reach people formerly, beyond one's circle, can have a de-monopolizing and democratizing effect on communication. The use of hypertext links and the development of post-symbolic modes of communication not only through an increased use of images and icons, but through the configuration of data in three dimensional forms, so that one moves from inhabiting texts, to inhabiting worlds, would also seem to be significant and far-reaching in their implications for modes of perception and classification. Something which entails a struggle for control and access to databases and archives which is just beginning (Featherstone, 2000a).

The questions of habitus formation in a more mobile world with greater flexibility of communicative sources which enable greater individualization and allow people to escape the surveillance of former authority structures, and how this relates to patterns of association and the reading of bodies in face-to-face contexts, is a complex question. People have to learn new generative structures which permit them to switch contexts more rapidly. They also learn to do many things simultaneously, walk or drive and talk on a mobile telephone, watch television in a pc window while on the Internet while listening to music from the hi-fi, to work on a pc notebook while watching the in-flight movie.[10] The learning process of inhabiting a technological culture should not be divorced from globalization processes. The flexibility of identifications with abstract humanity or nature, or a distant tribe or endangered species such as the whale, are facilitated by the new electronic technologies. Yet as a species we still have much to learn about the broader implications of inhabitation on the move, of learning to live while in passage.

---

[10] Cyberpunk novels by Sterling (1989), William Gibson (1984) and Stephenson (1992) are instructive on this. All three authors seem to envisage a future scenario in which we will be able to wear virtual reality sunglasses which can take us into the immersive VR cyberspace world to communicate with others, or summon up data on the lens in front of our eyes. In such scenarios it is possible to turn down the brightness or 'immersion' control and hence see both the projected virtual world and the everyday world through the same lenses at the same time.

30. POSTMODERNITY, COSMOPOLITANISM AND IDENTITY

Bryan S. Turner

Introduction

This discussion is intended to be a critical but paradoxical reading of post-modernism as a theory of cultural diversity and fragmentation. Throughout this analysis, I attempt to preserve a distinction between postmodernism as a theory of society and postmodernity as a social condition that primarily results from social diversity (Turner, 1990: 2). I both criticize the comfortable relativism of postmodern theory and argue that the notions of irony, distance and detachment in postmodern cultures can be re-deployed as components of a cosmopolitan ethic. Although the postmodernization of cultures is an important aspect of social change, we cannot remain overly optimistic about the consequences of postmodernism, especially for political and moral debate. The notion that postmodern relativism means that moral permissiveness makes us deeply happy with the world was effectively dismissed by Nietzsche (1933: 9) as "the most contemptible of all things", namely the contentment of 'the Last Man' in *Thus Spake Zarathustra*. If relativism means that everything is permitted, then nothing is valued. My argument is that, precisely because the moral world is fragmented and identities are increasingly negotiable, we need an ethic that can speak to questions of justice and human rights across cultural divisions. It is important to remain critical of any assumption that we can derive comfort from the cultural relativism that flows from multiculturalism and globalism. The importance of Heidegger for contemporary analysis of technology and modernity is that *The Question Concerning Technology* points to the discomfort of being, namely the homelessness of human beings in a modern technological society (Heidegger, 1977). I am interested in the ambiguity of homelessness as a social condition and as an ethical platform from which we can construct moral sympathy. In terms of McLuhan's theory of communication (McLuhan, 1964), the coolness of social relations in postmodernity makes possible an ethic of cosmopolitanism.

Postmodernity has rendered traditional claims about the universality of knowledge and culture distinctly unfashionable among anthropologists and sociologists. The current scepticism for 'grand narratives' dates from the publication of Lyotard's *Postmodern Condition* (1984), but cultural relativism clearly has a longer historical presence in the western imagination. The assumption that there might be Truth to which our beliefs about society could be authoritatively measured has been criticized from a variety of positions.

For example, the legacy of American pragmatism is profoundly relativistic in that for pragmatist philosophers we should ask, not whether a belief system is true, but does it serve some useful social purpose? Any notion that modern societies can effectively share moral systems has become an increasingly obsolete assumption (Rorty, 1999).

I treat the postmodern debate as a contemporary version of the problem of cultural relativism, and suggest further that postmodern relativism is an effect of multiculturalism, post-war labour migration, and globalization. I further argue that we can grasp these cultural changes as a version of a well established problem, namely how we can understand other cultures. In the western world, this problem of Otherness has been closely connected with imperialism, especially with respect to western contact, from the sixteenth century, with literate and urban cultures in Asia, especially Buddhism and Islam. We should therefore attempt to avoid any artificial disconnection between postmodernism as an aspect of popular culture, globalization and Orientalism (Turner, 1994).

While cultural relativism probably dates from the fabulous travels of Herodotus, an important alliance has evolved in the last two decades between anthropological relativism and postmodern critiques of the universalistic assumptions of conventional moral discourse. Of course, anthropology, given its commitment to ethnographic detail, has probably been relativistic through most of the twentieth century, but it has in recent years found additional support from both postmodernists and the literature of decolonization. Enlightenment ideals of reason and justice have become the targets of philosophical criticism that suggest we need to entertain very different ideals of difference and recognition, because these principles are more consistent with the social and political needs of multiculturalism. In a similar fashion, the cosmopolitan ideals and aspirations for a perpetual peace of Kant appear to be remote from contemporary intellectual debates.

Although cultural and moral relativism are generally shared views of intellectuals, it is also the case that globalization is widely recognized as the dominant trend of modernization. Of course, the fact that the modern world is shaped profoundly by global pressures in economics, politics and culture does not necessarily suggest that there is any corresponding set of assumptions that the social world is becoming more uniform. Globalization does not automatically produce cultural McDonaldization, because there can be equally powerful social and political pressures towards both localism and hybridity. Nevertheless, there is a widespread view in sociology that the modern world creates an experience of the global village. The rise of global tourism, world sport, global information and communication networks, global agencies such as ILO and UNESCO, the global experience of common health crises in AIDS and HIV, and the threat of new plagues are features of globalism that result in a common experience of social change. Globalization brings cultures together in a single place and demands that we give answers as to how any community might be possible in a postmodern environment. The notion of an electronic global community may not provide an entirely satisfactory answer to the pressing question: how shall we live?

Cultural relativism has a much longer history obviously than nineteeth-century anthropology. In this discussion, I want to approach the question of cosmopolitanism and cultural relativism from the point of view of western Orientalism from the end of the sixteenth century when Europe was divided by religious wars and Islam (in the shape of the Ottoman Empire) was a powerful and real threat to European political autonomy. The point of this exercise is to note simply that there is a certain historical naivety and intellectual arrogance in the postmodern assumption that 'modernity' is a modern phenomenon and that hybridity is a contemporary effect of global change. Postmodernism has typically embraced both the tragic vision of *posthistoire* and the implicit assumption that history is depthless; history is merely the methods by which the present is socially produced. Postmodern cultural analysis, for example, discounts the fact that the Baroque confronted and to some extent celebrated difference, diversity and complexity in the seventeenth century, or that the 'world religions' confronted the problem of Otherness for thousands of years before the arrival of globalization.

In order to give this discussion some general shape, I want to examine the issue of difference and otherness through a preliminary discussion of Orientalism and postmosdernism. We can argue that the debate about Orientalism provides us with a paradigmatic case of cultural (mis)understanding in a context of changing power structures and competing moral systems. In order to give this analysis a specific focus, I shall concentrate initially on the contributions of Edward Said to the debate over Orientalism (Said, 1978). A discussion of Said's analysis of Oriental identities provides the framework for presenting the possibility of a cosmopolitan ethics of tolerance.

Through his account of the emergence of Orientalism, Said has systematically addressed what social scientists have otherwise blandly called the problem of 'understanding other cultures' through an application of Michel Foucault's analysis of power-knowledge to Islam and the Orient. Although Said appears to be a relativist, he is not in any meaningful sense 'postmodern' and indeed the Foucaultian perspective turns out to be somewhat accidental to Said's central concerns. Said's work can be read as a reflection

on the problem of the homelessness of the modern intellectual, and by extension the homelessness and discomfort of modern cultures.

Oriental otherness

The controversy about 'other cultures' in western thought can be traced
back historically to the ancient encounter between the Abrahamic religions.
The fundamental problem is that Islam, Christianity and Judaism can be
appropriately conceived as variations of a generic religion of the descendants of Abraham, but they have become differentiated through centuries
of inter-civilizational conflict in order for the West to be categorically distinguished from the East. In historical and cultural terms, the Abrahamic
faiths cannot of course be neatly and definitely assigned to specific geographical locations and destinations, but for political reasons such a designation has to take place. These Abrahamic religions share the traditions of
a high god, a sacred text, a religious teleology, and a lineage of charismatic
prophets. While the modern equation of Christendom and Europe may
be for practical purposes unproblematic, Christianity is a religion whose
theological foundations lie in the prophetic tradition of Jewish radical mono-
theism and whose geographical origins are Near Eastern. In this respect,
Orientalism is more like a family feud than a conflict between distant cultures.
  These religious conflicts have a long history beginning with the foundation of Islam as a 'household of faith' in the seventh century. These inter-
civilizational relationships are complex and diverse rather than simple and
narrow, and the religious connection between Islam and Christianity is overshadowed by inter-regional conflicts over economic and political resources.
It is instructive to think of the nature of religious ecumenicalism as a model
for secular cosmopolitanism and the opportunities for secular co-operation
and understanding (Watt, 1991). In this respect, I am less interested in the
political economy of inter-religious conflict and co-operation, and more concerned to understand the texts that shaped Orientalist discourse itself.
  The Orient is, in Said's perspective, conceptualized overtly through the
Foucaultian analysis of the necessary combination of power/knowledge, and
the lineage of Oriental concepts is mapped out by the historical formation
of power between Occident and Orient, namely through the history of imperialism and colonial expansion. For Foucault, the conventional separation
of power and knowledge in liberal theory obscures the fact that the Orient
is an effect of imperial powers, and cannot be known independently of that
knowledge/power combination. The Foucaultian argument is that discursive
formations are constructed around both positive and negative contrasts or

dichotomies. These polarities constitute knowledge of an object; for example, we understand Islam through a series of contrasts. As a result, Orientalism produces a balance sheet or an audit of negativities between West and East in which the Orient is defined by a series of lacunae: the absence of revolutionary social change, the missing bourgeoisie, the erosion or denial of active citizenship, the failure of participatory democracy, the absence of autonomous cities, the lack of ascetic disciplines and the limitations of instrumental rationality as the critical culture of natural science, industrial capitalism and rational government. The sociological analysis of the cultural system of industrial capitalism (possessive individualism, the Protestant ethic, rational norms of bureaucratic process, and personal asceticism) was developed through a complementary understanding of the defective ethos of Oriental societies (Turner, 1978).

In the cultural geography of the modern imagination, the Orient is that part of the intellectual map by which the West has historically and negatively oriented itself. The 'Orient' maps out a geographical arena by which we can orient our passage through cultural reality. Orientalism constructs a political and psychological audit that fabricates social identities in a condition of political antagonism. As a textual practice, Orientalism divided the world into friends and enemies whose endless struggles have defined 'the political'. The Orient has been the negative Other that defines the boundaries of the civilized world, and thus regulated the transgressive possibilities of culture. The Orient was a necessary part of the emotional and moral cartography of the West. These cultural borders celebrated the puritan consciousness in terms of a set of principles about moral responsibility and probity. These spatial constructions of culture were in turn crucial for the creation of identity, and underline the fact that individual identity is always a synthesis between national and individual biography. There has always been a strong connection between personal identity, gender and national culture (Nelson, 1998). Hence, the construction of a powerful set of masculine identities cannot be easily separated from the production of Otherness in the imperialist version of Oriental culture.

It is this geographic Otherness that at the same time defines our subjective inwardness; our being is articulated in a terrain of negativities that are oppositional and, according to Said, permanent and inescapable. In *Culture and Imperialism* Said (1993) claims that the modern identity of the West has been defined by its colonies, but these colonies are not merely physical places in a political geography; they also organize the emotional boundaries of our consciousness by defining our attitudes towards, for example, sexuality and race. Within the paradigm of the Protestant ethic, the aboriginal is produced as somebody who is, not only poor and traditional, but licentious and lazy. Colonial policy and ideology generated a complex range of national types based on the myth of the lazy native. Exploration and colonization laid the foundations for western capitalism and reinforced the psychological assumptions behind hard work and asceticism.

The plays of Shakespeare, in the evolution of Orientalism, present an acute insight into the characterology of such Oriental figures, and specifically the themes of Otherness in Shakespeare indicate the interconnectedness between sexual identity, power and racism in the formation of western imperialism. Caliban, who was based on early encounters with the indigenous peoples of the West Indies and North America, is treacherous and dangerous, appearing in *The Tempest* as a negative mirror image of Miranda, who is perfect, naive and beautiful. Caliban's sexual lust for Miranda forms part of the moral struggle of the play under the careful scrutiny of the island's patriarch. Prospero's rational interventions master both storms and characters. In this respect, it is the foundation of the literary analysis of modern colonialism. The magical island offered an ideal context for the literary representation of the struggles between European reason and its colonial subjects as a confrontation between magic and anarchy on the one hand and reason and state craft on the other. It was Prospero's neglect of statesmanship that resulted in his original downfall and his careful management of the sexuality of his island subjects that eventually restores peace and good order to the land. While Prospero's original neglect of his sovereign responsibilities resulted in political despotism, his island kingdom offers a model of patriarchal control and formed the basis for subsequent utopian discussions of the politics of state craft.

Said's analysis of modern Orientalism has been primarily a history of French Orientalism and his approach was dependent on Schwab's monumental *La Renaissance Orientale* (Schwab, 1950). French Orientalism dominated European perspectives on the Orient, mainly as a consequence of the influence of Silvestre de Sacy (1755–1838). Students of Sacy filled the chairs of oriental languages in universities throughout Europe and guaranteed the continuity of French Orientalist studies. Sacy and his students prepared the way for the New Philology that dominated intellectual developments in nineteenth-century Europe. While philological studies laid the basis for humanities research in France with Renan, in Denmark with Rask (1787–1832) and in Germany with Bopp (1791–1867), in England philology was marginalized. With the exception of Edward William Lane's *The Manners and Customs of the Modern Egyptians* of 1836, the Orient surfaced principally in English fictional writing rather than in mainstream scientific publications. By contrast, French Orientalism, especially in the figures of Ernest Renan and Louis Massignon (1883–1962), was central to French culture as such, precisely because the French elite, unlike the British, assumed both a mission and a responsibility for Islamic culture (Said, 1983: 268–289).

Said (1983: 10–16) has discussed these changes in intellectual climate through an analysis of Matthew Arnold's *Culture and Anarchy* (1969). Writing of culture as the best that can be thought in a society, Arnold was able to assume the moral authority of English high culture and the role of intellectual as its defender. Arnold could also assume that a strong national culture required a powerful state to impose its hegemonic force at home and abroad. The fragmentation of modern cultures and the growing hybridity of national traditions have reinforced the feeling among public intellectuals, not only that there are no final vocabularies, but that multiculturalism imposes a certain detachment from one's own culture. The intellectual context of Orientalism has changed radically since the publication of *Culture and Anarchy* in 1869 because the certainty by which the western elite is attached to the local nation state has been challenged by the cultural globalization and the erosion of the authority of the western canon.

The study of Orientalism must also include an analysis of anti-Semitism. In the West, the negative view of Islam is part of a larger hostility towards Semitic cultures. If Caliban represents one formative figure in the evolution of European notions of Otherness, Shylock in *The Merchant of Venice* presents another. There has been a general anti-Semitism in Europe, in which antagonism to Jews has often accompanied hostility to Muslims. Generally speaking, the critique of Orientalism has not taken notice of the ironic connection between these two forms of racism, namely against Arabs and against Jews. In his Introduction to *Orientalism*, Said writes that

> in addition, and by an almost inescapable logic, I have found myself writing the history of a strange, secret sharer of Western anti-Semitism. That anti-Semitism and, as I have discussed it in its Islamic branch, Orientalism resemble each other very closely is a historical, cultural and political truth that needs only be mentioned to an Arab Palestinian for its irony to be perfectly understood (Said, 1978: 27–28).

In a reply to his critics, Said also noted the parallels between what he calls 'Islamophobia' and anti-Semitism. There are in fact two discourses of Orientalism for Semites, one relating to Islam and the other to Judaism. Within Orientalism, there are two related discourses for Semites, namely the doctrine of Islamic failure and decline, and the theory of Jewish ritualism (Turner, 1991: 29). While Islam had been defined by the absences of rationality, cities, asceticism and the middle class, Judaism had been defined by the contradictory nature of its religious injunctions, where its dietary laws transferred the quest for personal salvation into a set of ritualistic prescriptions that inhibited the full expression of its monotheistic rationalism (Weber, 1952). The West oriented its collective identity between two negative poles—the lazy, sensual, violent Arab and the untrustworthy, greedy Jew. While Weber criticized the Islamic paradise as merely an erotic reward for warriors, he controversially described Jewish communities as a 'pariah status group', because their social and geographical migrations were seen to be politically dangerous. Throughout the medieval and modern periods, Jews disturbed the consciousness of the Christian West. Identities in this Weberian paradigm emerge from the endless processes of social closure whereby dominant social groups exert their power through exclusionary or monopolistic practices.

The experience of Diaspora and ethnic hatred meant that displaced Jews were seen to be cosmopolitan and strange; the notion of the 'wandering Jew' pinpoints the idea that their commitment to the national polity could not be taken for granted. While Jews were strange, they were also guilty in New Testament theology of a betrayal of the Son of God. These anti-Semitic stereotypes have been crucial from a cultural point of view, because Christianity, as the foundation of western values, has traditionally attempted to maintain its difference from other Abrahamic faiths through its theology and exclusionary ritualistic practices, despite its apparently dominant commitment to universalism and forgiveness. Precisely because Judaism and Islam shared so much in common, they had to be separated culturally by a discourse of ethnic and moral difference from the Christian tradition.

Cosmopolitanism versus Orientalism

Although the history of Orientalism has been in large measure the melancholy history of inter-civilizational misunderstanding, antagonism and racial bigotry, Said has also been concerned to identify a number of scholars whose work attempted to transcend the narrow limitations of the Orientalist tradition of which they were members. In this respect his observations on Louis Massignon and Raymond Schwab are instructive, because they provide us with a model of what we might call cosmopolitan charity through their humanistic scholarship. Massignon's principal work was on the ecstatic religious experiences of al-Hallaj, who became a martyr for peace in Baghdad in 922. For Massignon, al-Hallaj was a religious figure through whom one can apprehend the mystical truths of both Christianity and Islam. It is through suffering that one can learn compassion, and through compassion a scholar might sympathetically approach and value other cultures. Massignon was, following a shattering religious experience in Iraq, converted to Christianity through the witness of Islam. Many of his colleagues regarded him as a

Muslim, although in his later life he also practised as a Melkite priest. A withdrawn scholar, Massignon became publicly involved in the protests against the Algerian War and in 1961 struggled with friends to drag the bodies of murdered Algerians from the Seine. In Massignon's theology of mysticism, the religious experiences of the divine presence in different traditions provides a common experience of alienation (or homelessness) and humanity's need for reconciliation. Schwab plays an equally important role in Said's vision of intellectual responsibility towards other cultures. While Schwab's intellectual world was quite remote from the Catholicism of Massignon, Schwab's task was to understand the impact of the Orient on the West in the period 1770–1850, roughly that is from the French Revolution to the high tide of western imperialism in the Middle East. In this period, Orientalism became a great adventure of human consciousness in which the polarities between East and West generated a new range of humanistic possibilities, namely a renaissance. While the first Renaissance asserted the integration of European cultures, the second Renaissance constructed a culture of differences through its comparative philology, historical studies and sociology. Orientalism expressed the European need to assimilate and absorb the Other through a set of linguistic strategies, but Schwab's own position was driven by an implicit notion of 'integral humanism', of the need for a dynamic humanism which could transcend these differences.

In *The World, the Text and the Critic* (Said, 1983) we see a different dimension to this cosmopolitan debate. In this work, part of which formed an introductory essay to Schwab's *Oriental Renaissance* we see a different perspective on Orientalism. Schwab's work sought to comprehend the modern approach to the Orient as the legacy of a 'second Renaissance'. While the classical Renaissance immersed Europeans within the confines of a self-sufficient Greco-Latin culture, this later Renaissance deposited the whole world before them. The humanistic vision of modern philology took the world as its province and asserted that there was a common rationality behind the diversity of human cultures.

Cosmopolitan irony is generally incompatible with nostalgia and is specifically a product of globalization and modernity. It follows directly from Said's vision of Orientalism as laid out in *The World, the Text and the Critic*. On closer inspection, his approach to the subject of Oriental knowledge in fact owes little to Foucault and is based directly on his reading of Schwab's *La Renaissance Orientale* and Auerbach's *Mimesis* (1953). Schwab's study was grounded in the assumption, in the 'Domaine Orientale', that western culture is but a particular version of the transcendental generality of human culture as a totality. Auerbach's study of the problem of representation in western culture articulated the conviction that the study of world literature and philology pointed to a common humanity. Because the themes of home-lessness, nostalgia and Orientalism have been dominant aspects of his liter-ary studies, it is not surprising that in *The World, the Text and the Critic* Said quotes with approval Auerbach's moral observation—"our philological home is the earth; it can no longer be the nation". Those who have discovered their true home have merely started a journey that leads to a commitment to a common place for humanity. Said quotes Auerbach's quotation from Hugo of St. Victor's *Didascalion* with approval in which Hugo asserts *perfec-tus vero cui mundus totus exilium est* (he is perfect to whom the entire world is foreign). Of course, the saintly Hugo meant that we must be able to dis-connect ourselves from the pleasures of our place in this world in order to journey in a spiritual world. Both Auerbach and Said convert this Christian argument into a contemporary ethic of a journey into homelessness. This journey is the cosmopolitan ideal.

Said's analysis of these writers prepares the groundwork for a defence of cosmopolitanism as the ethical world view of scholars in a global context, where cultural hybridity and multiculturalism are beginning to re-write the traditional Orientalist agenda. Cosmopolitanism can be defended morally, because exclusive national loyalties and ethnic solidarities are more likely to be points of misunderstanding, conflict and violence in culturally diverse societies. We need to develop a concept of membership, therefore, that will celebrate the uncertainty of belonging, where our 'final vocabularies' can never achieve finality. One can initially suggest that the components of cos-mopolitan virtue in an age of multicultural diversity are as follows: home-lessness both as a factual condition and as a set of moral assumptions about the transformative nature of exile; irony both as a sympathetic method of understanding and as a mentality that questions its own vocabularies; emo-tional distance from place and national identity; critical self-reflexivity with respect to our own cultural values and moral systems; systematic uncertainty about and doubt over the authority of any grand narratives; transcultural sympathies and interests; care for other cultures arising from an awareness of the precarious condition of all cultures in a global age, and therefore acceptance of cultural hybridization; support for positive programs of mul-ticulturalism that do not deny local cultures; and an ecumenical apprecia-tion of other religions and cultures.

Homelessness and otherness

It has been difficult to uncover much about Said the person from the schol-arly studies of Orientalism, literature and politics (Sprinker, 1992). What is clear from his academic work and from his autobiography (Said, 1999), however, is the persistence of the themes of homelessness and nostalgia, not descriptively as factual states of affairs, but as moral or even aesthetic conditions of a writer. We can derive an important principle from Said's autobiography which is that, broadly speaking, anybody who takes the vocation of the intellectual life seriously cannot be wholly comfortable or content at home. Thus the theme of the homeless intellectual played an important part in his analysis of intellectual integrity in his *Representations of the Intellectual* (Said, 1994).

It is equally clear that this moral principle of exile is not peculiar to Said; indeed it is at the centre of the moral vision of the western world. The notion of the exclusion and isolation of the poet or artist has been fundamental to western notions of creativity. The image of home and exile is on further inspection central to the idea of revelation in religious systems. In the Abrahamic religions, religious truth as revealed through a violent experience of rejection or exclusion was the foundation of prophetic disclosures, and thus the sequence—catastrophe, exile, loss, return and recovery—has been inescapable as a theme of modern cultures. The prodigal son becomes a narrative structure of all forms of redemption. Loss of home and exclusion from the everyday comforts of familiar places were also themes about the experience of wisdom in Buddhism. We can conclude from this comment that the theme of exodus is a primordial experience, because the sacred presupposes 'spatial nonhomogeneity', namely human movement between the sacred and the profane (Eliade, 1959). Given his interest in the moral and political significance of the spatial division between East and West, it is not wholly surprising, that Said should be compelled by the force of his own research to address the question of place in relation to ethical commitment.

Said's interest and involvement in the ethics of displacement are explicit in *The World, the Text and the Critic*, where, as we have seen, he approves of Auerbach's analysis of philology and world literature (Auerbach, 1953), namely that only through exile and homelessness can we come ultimately to a true understanding of humanity. The existential condition of being out of place is an ethical status through which one can achieve the necessary Stoical detachment to embrace humanity. Auerbach's notions of representation were critical in Said's development of a critique of Orientalism, but Auerbach's personal experience of exile was also formative in Said's ethical outlook. In Auerbach's case , it was as a Jewish refugee from Nazi Germany that he came to write *Mimesis* in Istanbul. In Said's case, we can detect the consequences of a threefold exile—national, familial and personal.

Firstly, the nationalistic exile is the most explicit and obvious. Said inherited American citizenship from his father Wadie Said, who gained his US passport from service in the American Expeditionary Force under General Pershing in 1917, but his ethnic identity and social roots remained in Arab culture. His childhood experiences were formed by the evolution of this sense of exile from the culture of English preparatory schools, remoteness from American youth culture and alienation from the resilient nationalism of American universities. Secondly, there was a familial exile from the dominating masculinity and self-confidence of his father, whose commercial acumen, material success and asceticism represented a permanent challenge to Said's emerging identity. The sympathetic and intellectual figure of his mother offered some compensation for the dominant character of the father. The personal exile is constituted by the contradiction between his cultural roots and his educational experiences. These contradictions are explored in *Out of Place* as a series of tensions between 'Edward' and 'Said'. 'Edward' was the creation of his parents who were themselves self-creations. They were two Palestinians, with significantly different backgrounds and temperaments, living in colonial Cairo as members of a Christian minority in a society of minorities, without any precedent for what they were doing except an odd combination of pre-war Palestinian habit. They picked up American lore in books and magazines.

As I have already observed, Said throughout his painstaking unpicking of Orientalism has always been aware of the paradoxical relationships between western hostility to 'Arabs' and anti-Semitic notions of the 'Jews'. Both the Moor in *Othello* and Shylock in *The Merchant of Venice* expressed the anti-Semitism of Elizabethan England, but they continue to stand for the ambivalence of sentiment towards Semitic outsiders in modern cultures. Because Said's work has been sensitive to the exile of both religious communities in his academic work on colonialism and literature, the irony of the Palestinian Diaspora dominates his overtly political writing.

It is instructive to compare Walter Benjamin's 'A Berlin Chronicle' (Benjamin, 1978) and *Out of Place*. Benjamin's *Berliner Chronik*, published in Germany in 1970, was sketched out in his first stay in 1932 in Ibiza, Spain, and explored the Berlin of his childhood and youth. It presents a haunting image of Berlin before national socialism, but the real topic is in fact the act of memory itself, of the necessary techniques for remembering. Whereas Said's act of memory is crowded out with people (mother and father, aunts and uncles, school children, English teachers, girl friends, doctors and officials), Benjamin's memory is essentially topographical, an architectural audit of gardens, cafes, city-scapes and grand streets. The two memories nevertheless come together as works of generic melancholy. We know that Benjamin, recalling in 1932 the comforts of his middle-class background and his excursions to the Zoo and Tiergarten with nursemaids, was to face death at the hands of fascists. We know that Said, remembering the comforting intimacy of the relationship with his mother and the caring relationship with Auntie Mela, will face the evolving tragedy of Palestine against the background of his illness and isolation. But this is merely to say that all acts of memory are melancholic practices, and that most of the time we are, if not out of place, than at least out of joint. We cannot fashion the history of our times to satisfy the needs of our own biographies. Hence the tendency of human life to exhibit the debris of an exilic experience. As Nietzsche (see Nietzsche, 1980) had noted in *On the Advantage and Disadvantage of History for Life*, men are driven to melancholy by their reflections on their own passage through time. A healthy life requires men eventually to overcome their historical melancholy by a sense of critical history if they are to survive at all.

Irony, stewardship and cosmopolitan virtue

Intercultural sensitivities and the need to interact constantly with strangers promote irony as the most prized norm of wit and principle of taste. For Said (1983: 29), irony is a useful word to use alongside 'oppositional' and 'critical'. Cosmopolitanism within this globalized world can be justified morally, because hot loyalties and thick solidarities are more likely to be points of conflict and violence in postmodern, ethnically diverse labour markets. Indifference and distance may be useful personal strategies in a risk society where ambiguity and uncertainty reign. In a more fluid world, the ironic citizen needs to learn how to move on, how to adjust and to adapt to a world of cultural contingency. Because historically we have learned to respect the virtues of loyalty and duty, we find it difficult to embrace the suggestion that in the twenty-first century we will not be able to afford strong nationalist commitment in a global community, where hybridity and diversity have all but obscured the stable world of nineteenth-century nationalism. It was the political environment of loyalty to the state and trust in the leadership which, at least, contributed to twentieth-century authoritarianism on both the left and the right. The ironic citizen of the global city may hopefully be less likely to give her undivided support to whatever government happens to be in power.

Given the complexity and the hybridization of modern society, there is no convenient place for real or hot emotions. Irony is sensitive to the simulation which is necessary for interaction in multicultural societies (Rorty, 1999). In such a world, ironic distance is functionally compatible with global cultural hybridity, because we are forced into the role of strangers in the cosmopolitan city. Hot emotions and thick solidarities are dysfunctional to social intercourse, which has to take place in a superficial and artificial plane. Although there has been much criticism of the emotional stagnation and barrenness of the metropolitan city, postemotionalism (Mestrovic, 1997) may be functionally necessary for modern society to exist, at least in public spaces. The art of disinterestedness and role distance may be important as a precondition of successful interaction.

Although homelessness is a general condition of modern cosmopolitanism, we must be suspicious of romantic nostalgia, because we have to recognize that there is, so to speak, no way back. There is no simple route of return into homogeneous and unified cultures, because we are all influenced by a cultural hybridity. By rejecting nostalgia, one can accept the present world of multiculturalism and religious diversity. If one retains any significant religious attachments, these commitments must lead to a quest for ecumenical dialogue. The cosmopolitan ironist cannot be in any simple sense a cultural or religious fundamentalist. As a world tourist in the metaphorical sense, we know that the global city is a meeting place of cultures brought into proximity by migration, global labour markets, the displacement of peoples by war and famine, and a market place of religions and cults. We could imagine the Third Renaissance as a period where cosmopolitan virtue rather than relativism or global optimism might be relevant. The Third Renaissance has revealed not only the historic diversity of Europe, not only the complexity of the world outside Europe, but the presence of otherness within, of internal differences.

Conclusion: Montaigne, humanism and postmodernism

In this context of cultural diversity, perhaps Montaigne's humanistic notion of Stoical scepticism is more appropriate than postmodern irony. Perhaps irony is too closely associated with the attitude of complacent and rootless intellectuals and salesmen to serve as a moral platform for respect for other cultures (Rorty, 1998). Scepticism has a dual nature. It both signifies that nothing is true (and nothing is false), and it opens up an experience of the totality of the truth, where contradiction is an important aspect of our experience (O'Neill, 1982: 14). While Montaigne asserted that barbarism is simply what other people do, his *Essays* actually challenge that argument because he recognized that questions of justice cannot be easily discussed if relativism is accepted naively. Said too appears to accept a Foucaultian view of Orientalism as an ideological construction of the Orient, but develops a political position which is not dependent on a deconstructionist epistemology.

My argument is that we can learn much that is valuable from Montaigne's scepticism. His humanism is politically useful as a criticism of optimistic versions of globalization theory that may lull us into a false vision of the world as culturally integrated. Cultural relativism precludes any serious debate about justice. Montaigne presents an argument which gives priority to *humanité* as the basis for mercy and sympathy. Humanité moderates vengeance and resentment. Montaigne was shocked by the cruelty and violence of his own times. Men have become like beasts of the field; they delight in the torture of others. How can this be regarded as truly noble? Hunting as the principal past-time of the nobility prepares them for a warrior calling in which they will inflict terrible violence on human beings. He drew a parallel between aggressive French noblemen, intransigent religious zealots, Roman gladiators and Brazilian cannibals. In many respects they all exhibit the virtues of Stoicism which Montaigne argues have negative consequences. The unyielding behaviour of the Stoic warrior rules out compromise and co-operation. Montaigne embraces the softer (feminine) values of mercy, compassion and tenderness.

Montaigne's ethics—yielding, forgiveness, clemency, talking it out rather than fighting it through, adopting feminine virtues rather than masculine Stoicism—can make men behave more humanely to one another, perhaps lead his country men out of their civil war and restore conditions of justice. Montaigne's ethical position ends in a tension between sympathy and understanding towards the other and the quest for justice. Montaigne's general purpose was to problematize the comfortable assumption that the division between barbarism and civilization is as simple and natural as the division between culture and nature. Montaigne was able to relativize civilization and barabarism in order to jeopardize the distinction between Christianity and paganism and also to question the rationalist distinction between the natural and the artificial. Although the nature is not identical with goodness, it was Montaigne's view that natural evils are less barbarous than the artificial evil of Christian colonialism. Montaigne refers the cannibals to achieve the same rhetorical end as Tacitus in his discussion of the German tribes in order to expose the military vices of Roman civilization (O'Neill, 1982: 205–206).

We live in a violent age of global confrontations. The power of ethnic loyalties and racial identities should make us sceptical about all claims that postmodernity is an age in which the driving force of ideology has been eroded. Globalization has constrained the political sovereignty of nation states, but local wars based on ethnic identity continue to bring into question the optimism that followed the collapse of communism. In many respects, we may be in the process of re-inventing the imperial cultures of Greek and Roman imperialism. I am conscious of the irony of advocating postmodern cosmopiltanism as an ethic of a multicultural civilization as a re-invention of the cosmopolitanism of the Roman Stoics. Cosmopolitan Stoics saw their obligations as series of concentric circles from the general to the local (Hill, 2000). Because they optimistically saw the foundations of good citizenship in reason and service to the state, they did not seriously entertain the problem of conflicting loyalties. The success of their cosmopolitan virtue rested in the last analysis on the security of Roman law through its imperial dominion. Cicero came to regard the power of Rome as a protectorate rather than a dominion, because it secured the cultures and societies of its subjects under the regulation of Roman law. Postnational cosmopolitanism faces the dilemma that either its moral authority depends on the acceptance of the prior authority of the world powers, or that its moral authority has no force because there is no secular institution that could impose its humane intentions.

Contemporary cosmopolitanism does however exist under circumstances that are very different from the Roman cosmopolitanism of the Stoics. Firstly, the processes of globalization do in fact extend to the whole world, and thus it is increasingly difficult to differentiate between core and periphery. Secondly, humane standards of conduct are imposed by the global norms of human rights legislation. Of course, the Middle Stoa developed a notion of universal law applied equally to all its subjects within the empire, but contemporary human rights laws apply to all humans qua humans. My argument is that in a period of globalization there has been much talk of cosmopolitan democracy as social scientists have attempted to understand the implications for democratic governance of globalization and the decline of national sovereignty, but there has been little attention given to the obligations that correspond to human rights, or to the civic cultures that might blossom in a global society (Turner, 2000). Stoic cosmopolitanism and Christian ecumenicalism might be treated as precursors of such a development, but the task today is to develop a perspective on virtue that does not carry such powerful grand narratives of empire or righteousness. In a paradoxical fashion, postmodernism may provide a more appropriate response to contemporary multiculturalism and diversity by remaining sceptical about grand narratives, recognizing the coolness or thinness of social relations, and celebrating irony as a form of reflexivity that precludes too much arrogance about our local wisdom.

31. MODERNITY AND POSTMODERNITY IN JAPANESE ATTITUDES

Masamichi Sasaki

Before discussing how changes in social attitudes in Japan may relate to modernity and postmodernity in Japan, in this era of globalization, we need to lay some groundwork by reviewing current thought on modernity. By so anchoring our discussion, we can then begin to talk about the implications of observed changes in Japanese social attitudes for modernity/postmodernity.

Introduction and literature review

Of course, the literature on modernization is vast (see, e.g., Smelser, 1959; Hagen, 1962; Lerner, 1964; Levy, 1966; Parsons, 1966; Apter, 1968; and Eisenstadt, 1973 on the theory of modernization). By way of sweeping introduction, we cannot say it better than Sztompka (1993: 129), who describes modernity as

> . . . a rich complex of social, political, economic, cultural, and mental transformations occurring in the west from the sixteenth century onward, and reaching its apogee in the nineteenth and twentieth centuries. It involves processes of industrialization, urbanization, rationalization, bureaucratization, democratization, the ascendancy of capitalism, the spread of individualism and achievement motivation, the affirmation of reason and science, and many other processes . . . "Modernization" in this sense means attaining modernity, coming closer to that specific, historically located institutional, organizational and attitudinal syndrome: "the process, through which a traditional or pre-technological society passes as it is transformed into a society characterized by machine technology, rational and secular attitudes, and highly differentiated social structures" (O'Connell, 1976: 13). In this sense, most classical work in sociology is about modernization: Comte and Spencer, Marx and Weber, Durkheim and Tönnies produce accounts of this process crucial for the history of Europe and the US in their time.

Sztompka's summation is superb and, in light of what we see around us in this globalizing era, it would seem reasonable to accept most of these observations as fact, or at least to adopt them as working assumptions about the process of modernization. (We will shortly explore more fully some of the non-Western elements of the process). Logically, it might be appropriate to move directly into a discussion of postmodernity; however, we first need to

take a closer look at how to view modernity, as there are numerous variations on this particular theme. Of necessity, we will focus here on just one
such view. The economics of modernization are relatively cut and dried and
while the politics of modernization are perhaps less well defined, they are
beyond our present scope. Where real differences emerge is when we begin
to talk about the cultural components of modernization, including norms,
values, attitudes and the like. Alex Inkeles (1976: 321), for instance, has said
that "The effective functioning of modern society requires that citizens have
certain qualities, attitudes, values, habits, and dispositions." The so-called
'modern personality' points to a psychological approach—or at least perspective—to modernization, where a society's populace must adopt this
modern personality as one of the essential prerequisites for making the
modernization process work. Specifically, the modern personality is defined
by its traits: (1) independence of traditional authorities, anti-dogmatism in
thinking; (2) concern with public matters, (3) openness to new experience,
(4) belief in science and reason, (5) planning, anticipation, orientation towards
the future, ability to defer gratification, (6) high aspirations: educational, cultural and professional (Inkeles and Smith, 1974; Inkeles, 1976).

As we will see shortly, the notion of modernization from an individual
perspective, i.e., the modern personality or individual modernity, has significant implications for the notion of 'postmodernity'. When it comes to postmodernity, there are no broad sweeping statements like that of Sztompka
above. Rather, controversy is rampant. What is postmodernity? Is it a new
era altogether? Or is it merely a new perspective on modernization, on
modernity? Indeed, today's theorists of postmodernity (see, e.g., Lyotard,
1984; Habermas, 1987; Bauman, 1989b; Giddens, 1990) are still trying to
work through the question of its existence, nature and character. The ultimate goal of this study is to contribute, at least partially, to the evidence
about postmodernity's existence, nature and character. To do that, however,
we first need to look more closely at postmodernity theories. For our purposes, the literature on postmodernity would seem to distill to the question
of whether postmodernity is in fact an entirely new era into which some
modernized societies have already passed, or whether postmodernity is in
fact only a changed perspective of modernity. On the one hand, Inglehart
(1997: 8) sees postmodernity as a new era: ". . . social change is not linear.
In the past few decades, advanced industrial societies have reached an
inflection point and begun moving on a new trajectory that might be called
'Postmodernization.'" He goes on to say that

> A new worldview is gradually replacing the outlook that has dominated indus-
> trializing societies since the Industrial Revolution. It reflects a shift in what
> people want out of life. It is transforming basic norms governing politics, work,
> religion, family, and sexual behavior. Thus, the process of economic develop-

ment leads to two successive trajectories, Modernization and Postmodernization. Both of them are strongly linked with economic development, but Postmodernization represents a later stage of development that is linked with very different beliefs from those that characterize Modernization. These belief systems are not mere consequences of economic or social changes but shape socioeconomic conditions and are shaped by them, in reciprocal fashion (Inglehart, 1997: 8).

Kumar (1995) also explores the era versus perspective controversy and notes that Charles Jencks and Ihab Hassan envision an emergent new culture distinct from and transcending modernity.

These observations proclaiming postmodernity as an entirely new era are compelling, but we cannot stop here because there is a substantial converse which sees the world remaining within the era of modernity but now looking at that era very differently. Giddens (1990: 51) puts it this way: "We have not moved beyond modernity but are living precisely through a phase of its radicalisation." He continues:

> . . . this is not a simple continuity of earlier trends. Rather, qualitatively new phenomena appear, which basically reshape the contemporary world and 'move us into a new and disturbing universe of experience' (Giddens, 1990: 53).

Beck, Giddens and Lash (1994) see the dominant characteristic of this radicalized modernity as reflexivity; that modernity has entered into a stage where it must now (and now has the capability to) look back on itself. Modernity, at this stage, can look back upon itself and see that, along with its benefits, came many costs—hence its radicalization. Bauman's (1992: 187) view differs in that he sees 'postmodernity' as modernity at full development, knowing the consequences of its own history and therefore "conscious of its true nature." Lyotard (1984) characterized the 'ambiguity of modernity', while Lyon (1994) adopted the label 'the ambivalence of modernity'. Regardless of the conceptualization chosen, the fact remains that things are happening which transcend modernity, some of which reflect upon and reverse many of the qualities with which we traditionally characterized modernity. Indeed, Lyon's phrase 'the ambivalence of modernity' (1994: 28) is right on target, a description which Dunn (1998: 82) reflects upon and concludes that no matter how one chooses to view postmodernity, modernity is consistently accepted as being

> divided against itself, existing in perpetual tension among contending social and discursive frameworks . . . modernity has unleashed a torrent of energies and forces, taking many forms and directions, both illuminating and dark, progressive and destructive, insinuating both freedom and order, liberation and oppression . . .

Dunn further points to other scholars' conceptualizations in which the theoretical or epistemological elements of postmodernism are starkly contrasted to and distinguished from postmodern culture as it relates to 'structural and technological change'. Clearly, whether we view postmodernity as fact or perspective is among today's key questions. We spoke above about 'modern man' and the 'modern personality'. Whichever approach to postmodernity we might choose, the question then arises, is there a 'postmodern man'? This question is valid for either conceptualization of modernity/postmodernity, so we could rephrase the question as: is there a radicalized, reflective modern personality? Albrow (1996: 194) discusses this issue in some detail, with specific reference to Inkeles:

> The main exponent of research into individual modernity, Alex Inkeles, insisted on defining modernity in such a way as to be able to test empirically just how far people could be judged modern . . . But it was no part of his research to suggest that everyone, or even a majority of people, was becoming modern worldwide . . . In the words of Inkeles, the individual modernity of today might become a "historical anachronism no longer appropriate to the structural features of some as yet unimagined future society" (Inkeles, 1983: 321). In fact, even on Inkeles' account, a "postmodern man" was emerging, although on terms which suggested the continuing hold of modern concepts.

Key to this discussion, for our present purposes, is the notion of testing empirically 'how far people could be judged modern' (or 'postmodern' or 'radically and reflectively modern'). Most famous of all empirical work is Inglehart's research on materialism and postmaterialism through the Eurobarometer and World Values Surveys. Inglehart observed people's values shifting from materialistic to postmaterialistic orientations in consistently and ever-increasing numbers. Indeed, Inglehart (1990:105) cites ratios of 4:1 materialists: postmaterialists in 1970 and 4:3 in 1988, among six European nations. In his study of the 'affluence effect' (another means of describing the impact of economic growth, development and modernization at individual and societal levels), Yankelovich (1994: 17) describes several areas where the affluence effect has brought about changes in values, including

> greater tolerance and acceptance of pluralism; sweeping changes in family related values; the changing meaning of success; a new relationship between work and leisure; changes in social morality; and new values in relation to health and physical well-being.

Integrating the concepts of a modern or postmodern personality and the empirical work previously carried out in the area of modernization, it would seem reasonable to propose the use of general social attitudes as indices of (or at least pointers to) modernization. This proposal comes about in part from observing national, longitudinal and cross-national studies of general social attitudes and realizing that these studies and their findings seem to reflect upon many of the issues forming the substance of the process of modernization. Thus, our intent here is at least partially to contribute to the evidence about the existence, nature and character of postmodernity in its various conceptualizations. Toward a realization of this considered contribution to the evidence about modernity—through an exploration of Japanese general social attitudes—we seek to identify, in the context of the processes of modernity/postmodernity, what has changed, what has not changed and what has remained the same in those attitudes over the past 45 years.

Before proceeding any further, though, the caveats of Howard Schuman et al. (1997: 6–7) should be explicitly acknowledged; that is,

> Attitudes frequently provide useful clues to behavior, even though they are not always direct and powerful determinants of behavior . . . attitudes are only one type of evidence about a society, and . . . must be weighted and evaluated rather than taken at face value.

Thus, revealing a nation's postmodern bent, through its citizens' general social attitudes, certainly does not prove the existence of so-called postmodernism or postmodern behavior, though it may certainly signal a potential onset or, at the least, alert us to paying further heed to emerging possibilities. Throughout the ensuing discussion, several issues deserve particularly close attention. These include:

1. the impacts of fluctuations in economic development and stability as they may relate to the all-important issue of security, personal and otherwise, which we view as one of the quintessential elements of modernism/postmodernism;

2. the roles of culture, cultural filters and religion, controversial and occasionally overlooked components;

3. the positioning of tradition within the processes of modernization, a positioning which has been somewhat elusive;

4. as an outgrowth of this elusive positioning of tradition emerges a prevalent hypothesis intrinsic to many thoughts about postmodernity; that is, the 'revalorization of tradition', an area where Japan, we believe, may be able to contribute particularly well;

5. so often thought of as integral to modernity, perhaps Westernization is merely coincidental and thus deserving of removal from the picture;

6. verification that core values, or at least certain core values, remain unchanged in the 'postmodern' world;

7. intergenerational shifts in attitudes over time, their presence and/or absence being validated by cohort analysis of attitudinal data; and finally,

8. implications for global change using the Japanese experience as precursor to predict outcomes in the now rapidly modernizing East.

Security

From individual, social and cultural standpoints, the security afforded by
the onset and continuation of modernization is extraordinarily significant.

> Modernization is widely attractive because it enables a society to move from
> being poor, to being rich. Accordingly, the core process of Modernization is
> industrialization; economic growth becomes the dominant societal goal, and
> achievement motivation becomes the dominant individual-level goal. The tran-
> sition from preindustrial society to industrial society is characterized by "the
> pervasive rationalization of all spheres of society" (as Weber put it), bringing
> a shift from Traditional, usually religious values, to Rational-Legal values in
> economic, political, and social life (Inglehart, 1997: 5).

From being (relatively) poor, to being (relatively) rich, industrialization has
indeed engendered a sense of security; economic security to be sure, and
perhaps as its logical extension, existential security, fostered by urbanization,
mass education, occupational specialization, bureaucratization, and communications development. All these elements have proved 'functionally advantageous' to creating and perpetuating economic and likely existential security.
That something is functionally advantageous implies optimality and, on the
whole, we all seek to optimize our opportunities, indeed our very existence.
Economic security, as Japan well knows recently, does fluctuate. The logical
extension is that existential security, as its logical outgrowth, fluctuates as
well. Despite the ebb and flow, which may also manifest itself in shifting
social attitudes, the long-term economic trends are now fairly clear, along
with their long-term implications for the 'postmodernity' phenomenon.

Culture

The next issue is culture. "One could argue that cultural changes are caused
by societal changes, or that cultural changes are contributing to societal
changes, or that the influences are reciprocal" (Inglehart, 1997: 4). Inglehart
goes on to discuss 'cultural filters' which serve to filter one's perception of
reality, and he asserts that the role of these cultural filters takes on increasing importance in the postmodern world. Under conditions of relative economic security, individual choice expands and operationalizes the cultural
filters to a greater extent than would be the case for individuals concerned
with everyday survival. Rather than getting mired down in the issues of
economic or cultural determinism, our purposes are better served by agreeing with Inglehart that the causes and effects are an empirical question.
And we hope to contribute useful knowledge to these issues through our

examination of the Japanese data, in much the same way that the World
Values Survey seeks to describe the causal role of culture. Indeed, Inglehart
(1997) places great stress on culture and cultural change, citing new values
and lifestyles as one indicator of a new culture emerging. Lyon (1994: 28)
also makes the case for culture when he states:

> As we examine the ambivalence of modernity the cultural dimensions return
> to the foreground again and again, to be interwoven with the social, political
> and economic. So while [Giddens'] fourfold scheme of industrialism, capital-
> ism, surveillance and the military is very useful for encapsulating modernity,
> it also needs to be dovetailed with the dimensions of ethnicity and gender and
> of culture and religion.

Once again, whether we view postmodernity as fact or merely as perspective is among today's key questions. Kumar (1995: 4) begs the question of
culture's role by stating that "Postmodernism includes in its generous embrace
all forms of change, cultural, political and economic. None is seen as the
privileged 'carrier' of the movement to post-modernity." At the risk of getting bogged down in this particular controversy, there is justification for
Kumar's position as the types of cultural changes we see certainly could not
have occurred in the absence of the economic changes. The role of political change, on the other hand, is perhaps still open to discussion and certainly has not yet played itself out in this globalizing era. Before moving
on to the issue of tradition, let us first say a few words about religion, as
it is so closely entwined with the issue of culture. While some, like Berger
(Lyon, 1994: 20) would accept the intertwining as axiomatic, my previous
studies on secularization depict something different. Whereas Western thought
envisions a waning of the Protestant ethic, considered by some to be a core
element of modernization, my previous studies with Suzuki (1987: 1055)
indicate that ". . . secularization cannot be viewed as a 'global phenomenon'
of modern societies." Those studies found that the secularization thesis is

> . . . fully supported over generations and periods for Holland in the seven-
> decade study, is partially supported for recent generations in the United States,
> but is not supported for historical periods or generations in Japan. These find-
> ings imply that generational difference factors, such as religious socialization
> as well as peer-group socialization and idiosyncratic experiences that people
> have during their sensitive childhood years and youth, have had significant
> effects on secularization for people in the United States and Holland in later
> life. Such is not the case for Japan . . .

> [T]he available short-term data used here do not validate the general claim
> of the secularization thesis—which is rooted in the assumption that scientific,
> rational, technological man cannot really accept the mythological and the

sacred—that secularization is simply part of a worldwide trend toward industrialization, modernity, rationalization, and urbanization (Sasaki and Suzuki,
1987: 1074).

These results then, it could be argued, point to certain, probably minor,
fallacies in the assumptions underlying the role of culture in modernization,
which in turn have implications for how we might view the process of postmodernization.

Tradition

Conversely, if we subsume religion under the rubric of tradition we are perhaps on more secure footing, simply because the positioning of tradition in
the grand design is and has been, most scholars would probably agree,
somewhat elusive. This elusiveness probably stems from the battering tradition takes during modernization, where the modern perspective often sees
tradition as signifying outright opposition to progress. The habitual status
quo became repugnant to modern man and was summarily attacked as
being utterly counterproductive to the inertia of the modernization process.
The traditional foundations lending legitimacy to authority became unacceptable. But postmodern man or the postmodern perspective, in reassessing the costs of progress, questions the outright destruction of tradition.
Postmodernity, acknowledging that traditions have both costs and benefits,
recognizes the 'functional ambivalence' of tradition (Giddens, 1991) and
seeks to revive, reinvent or revalorize tradition according to "a balance sheet
of functions and dysfunctions" (Giddens, 1991: 68). Turning to 'quality of
life' issues, postmodernity reaches back into tradition and provides "persuasive symbols of collective identity" (Giddens 1991: 65) to resurrect personal and social bonds (cf. Yankelovich's, 1994 'affluence effect'). In Dunn's
words,

> In contemporary cultural politics, we find evidence not only of rigid and auto-
> cratic reassertions of traditional values but also a revalorization of the personal
> and social sustenance that cultural tradition can offer (Dunn, 1998: 168).

Dunn further refers to postmodern culture as calling for the "construction
of a new set of understandings about the meanings and uses of tradition"
(p. 168). Finally, Sztompka, in his critique of modernization, offers some
important insights:

> The anti-traditionalist bias of early theory is corrected by pointing out that
> indigenous traditions may hide important pro-modernization themes. Instead
> of rejecting tradition, which may be counterproductive by provoking strong

resistance, it is rather proposed to exploit tradition, by discovering 'traditions of modernization', and treating them as the legitimation for current modernizing efforts (1993: 139).

Sztompka's argument is a compelling one, even though some might argue that it is premature. Confounded with culture, tradition indeed persists in its elusiveness and it may be many decades before we can look back and say with certainty what role tradition played in the processes of modernization or postmodernization.

Revalorization of tradition

Inglehart sees the revalorization of tradition as constituting one of three broad schools of postmodern thought: "Postmodernism is the revalorization of tradition. Since Modernization drastically devalued tradition, its demise opens the way for this revalorization" (1997: 23). Thus it would appear that the hypothesized revalorization of tradition will take a front-row position in studies of modernization. Kumar (1995), for example, describes Jencks' position: that postmodernism embraces at least a part of the traditions which modernism had swept aside, that postmodernism embraces a 'striking synthesis of traditions'. As stated earlier, the positioning of tradition remains elusive, but certainly we can attempt to relate some of our survey data to issues indicative of tradition in an effort to pin down that position, and in so doing validate or invalidate the revalorization hypothesis. Our Japanese data are particularly cogent as Japan began to modernize from a point at which tradition was extraordinarily important.

Westernization

Having discussed culture, religion and tradition with some reference to the Japanese experience, it is now time to talk about Westernization. Japan's experience with modernization clearly demonstrates the fallacy of equating modernization with Westernization, a fallacy which will undoubtedly show up even more sharply as we all watch the unfolding of the modernization process in the remainder of the East. Durkheim (1964: 88, note 10) knew this: "Japan may in the future borrow our arts, our industry, even our political organization; it will not cease to belong to a different social species from France and Germany." Sztompka (1993: 139) has yet another perspective. In addition to doubt about the Western modernization model's applicability to Japan and the rest of the Pacific Rim, Sztompka suggests that the model also may not apply to post-communist societies. We certainly don't want to dwell on this issue as it would seem that most scholars today have rejected the ethnocentricity of the 'Western' model. Kumar (1995: 199) provides perhaps the best closing remarks for the issue of Westernization:

> Modernization, as the example of Japan best shows, is now a global process which will find its own forms, suitable to the time and place in which it is promoted—just as world religions such as Christianity and Islam have adapted themselves to the particular culture circumstances of their local environments.

Core values

With regard to core values and their hypothesized persistence over time, there is still insufficient empirical data to conclude that core values have persisted in the shadow of otherwise sweeping social, economic, political, indeed cultural, changes. Our intent here is to contribute, as directly as possible, to this question's resolution. There is evidence that, for the most part, core values are persisting despite the presence of so many other changes consequent to modernization. Yankelovich (1994: 17), for example, hypothesizes that "the affluence effect is a powerful driver of changing cultural values" and notes that "Despite the transformations in America's life-styles . . . core values have endured. Virtually all Americans share them; completely, they make American culture distinctive" (p. 24). Yankelovich devotes a good deal of space to discussion of the persistence of core values:

> Despite the affluence effect and other agents of change, many of America's most important traditional values have remained firm and constant . . . while many traditional values are in upheaval, a small number continue to win the allegiance of most Americans (1994: 23; also cf. Dahrendorf, 1979, and Bellah et al., 1985 for a case study approach).

If we take religious belief as a core value, then our studies of Japan, the United States and Holland depict mixed findings; that is, the persistence of religious belief in Japan and to a somewhat lesser extent in the United States. The data from Holland, however, support the secularization thesis and therefore suggest that at least one core value has not persisted in that country. Interestingly, Popenoe (1994: 88; also cf. Schooler, 1998) has some pertinent remarks about Japan:

> The advanced society today that has shifted least in the direction of radical individualism and postnuclear familism is Japan. Of the advanced societies, Japan ranks highest on "doing one's duty" collectivism and lowest on "self-fulfillment" individualism; in turn, Japan has the highest degree of internal social order and Japanese citizens have the lowest degree of personal autonomy. This cultural situation can be attributed mainly to Japan's tremendous cultural

homogeneity and very recent affluence, and because Asian cultures have traditionally been much more collectivist than Western cultures.

Notably, Popenoe (1994: 88) does hedge by concluding: "Nevertheless, by all indications Japan is moving in the individualistic, postnuclear direction, showing signs of both growing personal autonomy and increased social disorder, including family breakup." In search of a basis for his findings on core values, Yankelovich (1994: 20) notes that:

> Dahrendorf sees all historic shifts in Western culture as efforts to balance choices and bonds. Choices enhance individualism and personal freedom; bonds strengthen social cohesiveness and stability. In societies where the bonds that link people to one another and to institutions are rigid, the individual's freedom of choice is limited. As people struggle to enlarge their sphere of choice, the bonds that bind them together slacken.

Dahrendorf's perspective is not dissimilar to the oft-cited dichotomous ambivalence identified in Japanese society as traditional versus modern, or Japanese versus non-Japanese. We will revisit the topic of core values in our discussion of the general social attitude data on Japan.

Intergenerational shifts

Moving on to the issue of intergenerational shifts in attitudes, this gets at a basic purpose of the present study, and in particular our observations of Japanese general social attitudes generated through cohort and correspondence analyses of our data. But first, let's talk about the World Values Survey, where Inglehart (1997) has focused much attention on intergenerational shifts:

> ... a process of intergenerational value change ... is gradually transforming the politics and cultural norms of advanced industrial societies. The best documented aspect of this process is the shift from giving top priority to economic and physical security, to giving top priority to self-expression and the quality of life (p. 32).

The phenomenon of intergenerational attitude shift is present in many places and in much survey data, and thus its salience to our pursuits must not be de-emphasized. For example, our secularization studies identified strong intergenerational shifts in Holland and some such shifts in the United States, but not in Japan.

In summary, we propose awarding careful attention to a pluralistic approach as the basis for continuing and new theoretical constructs to describe modernity and postmodernity (cf. McLennan, 1995). We view all this as multiple modernities driven by a 'plurality of cultures and discourses'. At the empirical level, we would propose asking whether the expression of modernism/postmodernism in Japan is unique or not. Before moving on to a discussion of our method, data and findings, it seems appropriate to enumerate the obvious differences between Japan and, in most cases, the rest of the modern/postmodern world. Let us first talk about some fairly obvious differences. Unlike the United States and Europe taken as a whole, Japan is not multicultural. This homogeneity contrasts sharply with the cultural, or at least ethnic, character of most of the rest of the Western world upon which early models of modernization were based. With regard to religion, Japan's religious orientation and religious beliefs contrast markedly with those in the West, a fact which has strong implications for the role of the Protestant ethic in modernization. Thus Weber's shift of the Protestant ethic to the Rational-Legal is not relevant to Japan. Here again we see modernization in the absence of what was once considered one of its major elements. Religious concepts in Japan simply do not speak to issues affecting modernization. Japan (as well as Germany) modernized without massive Cold War spending. The implications of this fact may not be entirely clear, but nonetheless it is another sharply contrasting element. Japan's (as well as Germany's) political structure was forced upon it following World War II. Here again, while the implications for modernization may not be entirely clear, this certainly contrasts sharply with the case for most of the West during the modernization phase.

To briefly mention some similarities, we first should note the distinct similarities in economic growth and development, industrialization, urbanization, mass education, occupational specialization, bureaucratization and communications development. We also see an expansion of the welfare state; lower birth rates; higher life expectancies; a move away from the earlier lifetime employment system toward 'meaningful' employment and quality of life issues with a consequent displacement of the achievement motivation; a rise of self-expression, autonomy, diversity and pursuit of 'aesthetic satisfaction'. Similar patterns can be observed with regard to the family, equal rights movements and gender roles. Finally, anecdotally, I have observed a significant rise in volunteerism in both Japan and the United States in recent years.

Based on these few observations alone, clearly not all of Japan's modernizing can be considered "purposeful imitation of western societies" (Sztompka, 1993: 131), nor can all of Japan's modernizing be considered "a process of emulation, of the transplantation of patterns and products from the achievements of other countries to one's own" (Chodak, 1973: 257, quoted in Sztompka, 1993: 131).

Data and method

The Japanese National Character Surveys (JNCS), conducted by the Institute of Statistical Mathematics in Tokyo at five-year intervals between 1953 and 1998, were used for the present study. These nationwide surveys of general social attitudes are the only ones in the world to have asked the same questions for nearly half a century. In the surveys, not all questions were asked in all years, thus some questions do involve shorter intervals, though this discussion is limited to those of at least 35 years duration. The present study utilizes frequency, cohort and correspondence analyses. Cohort analysis and correspondence analysis can reveal insightful trends about what has changed and not changed in general social attitudes, trends which may speak to issues of modernity/postmodernity. For a more detailed discussion of cohort analysis, which is a method designed to separate cohort, age, and historical period effects, the reader is referred to Sasaki and Suzuki (1987), Hobcraft, Menken, and Preston (1982), and Glenn (1977). With regard to the identification problem—related to the logical confounding of these three effects—described by many cohort analysts, see Mason et al., 1973; Glenn, 1977; Fienberg and Mason, 1978; and Mason and Fienberg, 1985. The present study relies on the work of Nakamura (1982; 1986), who introduced a Bayesian cohort model by adopting Akaike's (1980; 1985) ABIC (A Bayesian Information Criterion), to overcome the identification problem. Correspondence analysis is particularly useful for analyzing cross-tabular frequency data and yields graphs of Euclidean space which facilitate data interpretation (see, e.g., Greenacre, 1984; 1993).

Findings and discussion

Religion

The JNCS asks questions about religious faith. One is simply "Do you have any religious faith?" Whether an individual in Japan has religious faith has consistently split at about one-third yes and two-thirds no throughout the period 1958 through 1998. In my work with Suzuki (Sasaki and Suzuki, 1987), these data were studied extensively to explore hypotheses about religiosity and secularization, neither of which phenomenon was identified for Japan. There have been no appreciable changes in these data since 1983, the ending date adopted for that work. Cohort analysis revealed some minor period and cohort effects and did reveal strong age effects, indicating that the aging process tends to influence the Japanese people to become progressively more religious, with the younger Japanese being potential religious believers.

The older one becomes, the more religious one becomes. Despite the early importance of religion in the Western models of modernization, it is apparent that these data underscore the irrelevance of the issue for the Japanese. Clearly, modernization can occur entirely absent of the drivers ascribed to the Protestant ethic. This, as we noted earlier, invalidates at least a portion of the Westernization component of modernization. The other principal implication of these findings is that, if we reasonably accept religion as a core cultural value, here then is an example of an unchanging core value. We mean that modernization in Japan has not influenced the Japanese to become less religious or more secular than they were before the onset of modernization.

Nepotism

From 1963 through 1998, the JNCS have asked: "Suppose that you are the president of a company. The company decides to employ one person, and then carries out an employment examination. The supervisor in charge reports to you saying, 'Your relative who took the examination got the second highest grade. But I believe that either your relative or the candidate who got the highest grade would be satisfactory. What shall we do?' In such a case, which person would you employ?" Responses: 1. One with the highest grade; and 2. Your relative.

The results show that there has been very little change over time with regard to this question.[1] The Japanese consistently favor employing the individual with the highest grade rather than being nepotistic. Looking at Parsons' pattern variables, modern societies tend to be universalistic in their recruitment practices, while traditional societies exhibit particularism, where the personal traits of potential candidates are not necessarily relevant (cf. Sztompka, 1993: 74). These consistent results over the long term demonstrate a persisting modern attitude.

Paternalistic supervisor preference

The question asked is: "Suppose you are working in a company. Which one of the following department heads would you prefer to work under? 1. A person who always sticks to the work rules and never demands any unreasonable work, but who, on the other hand, never does anything for

---

[1] About 70% favoring the individual with the highest grade and about 20% favoring the relative.

you personally in matters not connected to work; or 2. A person who sometimes demands extra work in spite of rules against it, but who, on the other hand, looks after you personally in matters not connected to work."

The results show that there has been no change over 45 years.[2] The Japanese always prefer paternalistic supervisors. It is generally believed that the Japanese consider the workplace to be governed by the rules of primary group relations under a family-like atmosphere. In fact, the Japanese often refer to the workplace as 'uchi', meaning 'my family' or 'household' (cf. Hayashi and Kuroda, 1997). (Interestingly, about half of Americans prefer paternalistic supervisors, putting them closer to the Japanese than a number of other countries in this respect.) These results run counter to the depersonalized rationalization and bureaucratization characteristics often cited as central to modernity. On the other hand, the results are clearly indicative of a radicalized modernity, or of postmodernity. Taken as a core value, or a pointer to a core value, then, the Japanese maintained this 'paternalistic' attitude and resisted the temptation to succumb to its usurpation during modernization.

Adoption

"If you never had children yourself, would you think it desirable to adopt a child in order to continue the family line, even if there is no blood relationship, or do you not think this is important? 1. Desirable; 2. Undesirable; 3. Maybe/Depends." The results from the adoption question show drastic change with regard to Japanese attitudes about adoption as a means of continuing one's family line.[3] These results support the prevalent notion that the Japanese concept of family has changed dramatically in recent decades. Another notable observation from these data is that the cross-over from adoption as desirable to undesirable occurred about 1970. Indeed, a number of the JNCS results reflect noticeable shifts in attitudes around 1970. The dramatic nature of these results begs for interpretation. Hayashi and Kuroda (1997) hypothesized that among other factors, the abolition of the primogeniture system after World War II and the imposition of stiff progressive inheritance taxes might explain the nearly complete reversal in attitudes about adoption as a means of continuing one's family line. It was

---

[2] About 80% preferring paternalistic supervisors.
[3] At the beginning of the period less than 20% answered that it is not desirable whereas at the end of the period almost 60% answered that it is not desirable. The respective figures for the desirable answer were about 75% at the beginning and just above 20% at the end of the period.

traditionally thought that continuing one's family line was quite important to the Japanese. Certainly the mechanisms cited by Hayashi and Kuroda would have a pragmatic impact.

Yet other variables may be coming into play here. In a sense, this is a two-part question in that it targets the issues of adoption and one's family line. Perhaps the salience of one or the other of these elements has shifted over time in the minds of respondents. Alternatively, today there are many more biotechnologically-driven alternatives to adopting a child than there were in 1953. Perhaps the Japanese still value continuing their family lines but would look to medicine's latest options for solutions, as opposed to adoption, which would have been the only infertility solution during the early years of the survey. Because of the numerous possible explanations for these interesting findings, their relevance to modernity/postmodernity remains obscure.

Gender preference

"If you could be born again, would you rather be a man or a woman? 1. Which gender do you think has more pleasure in life? 2. Which gender do you think has a harder life?" For the first part of the question, the results reveal a near convergence on 50 percent in 1998, from significantly different starting points in 1958.[4] Not surprisingly, women have changed their minds about wanting to be born again as men, with the cross-over interestingly occurring around 1970.[5] These findings are certainly indicative of the processes of modernization. To determine whether the dramatic change in preferred gender for rebirth stemmed from period, age or cohort effects, cohort analysis was applied (Sakamoto, 1995). The results indicate that there is a significant period effect for women. Therefore, the trend for women preferring to be reborn as women stems from a period effect rather than an age effect or an intergenerational shift.

With regard to which gender has more pleasure in life, we see significant change, again toward a convergence for men and women, from significantly higher and lower percentages in the earlier years.[6] With regard to which gender has the harder life, there is some change, though it is not as dramatic as that seen for the issue of pleasure. Overall, the results indicate the

---

[4] In 1958 more than 75% answered man and less than 20% answered woman.

[5] The men, during the relevant period, showed consistency in preference to be reborn as men (about 90%); whereas the figures for women changed from less than 30% to almost 60% preferring to be reborn as women.

[6] At the beginning of the period almost 70% answered men and less than 10% answered women.

expected change in values regarding gender roles assumed to accompany postmodernity.

Attitudes toward life

"There are all sorts of attitudes toward life. Which one of the approaches on this list come closest to how you would like to live your life? 1. Work hard and get rich; 2. Study hard and then make a name for yourself; 3. Not think about money or fame, just live the kind of life that suits your own taste; 4. Live each day as it comes, cheerfully and without worrying; 5. Resist all evils in the world and live a pure and just life; or 6. Never think about yourself, but work to serve the community and society." Notably, "living a life that suits one's own tastes" and "living each day as it comes" (carpe diem) both increased markedly, while "pure and just life resisting all evils" decreased markedly. The results (from Sakamoto, 1995) of a cohort analysis of the "living a life that suits one's own taste" response indicate that for both males and females there are significant cohort effects, meaning there is intergenerational shift in this item. We believe the increased popularity of this and the carpe diem response support Inglehart's and others' thoughts on postmodernity and postmaterialism. However, taking this approach, the 'work hard and get rich' response should exhibit a downward trend, but it does not; it is consistently flat throughout the 45-year period.

Man and nature

"Here are three opinions about man and nature. Which one of these do you think is closest to the truth? 1. In order to be happy, man must follow nature; 2. In order to be happy, man must make use of nature; 3. In order to be happy, man must conquer nature." 'Conquer nature', which some would correlate with modernity, shows an interesting pattern. After rising steadily for 15 years,[7] in 1973 it suddenly dropped quite dramatically and has been on a downward trend ever since,[8] indicative of a more postmodern attitude toward nature. Recall that the postmodern man sees that some of the elements of progress have had high costs, such as environmental pollution. Apparently, the Japanese began identifying at least some of those costs in the early 1970s, coinciding with the major energy crisis of 1973.

---

[7] From almost 25% to almost 35%.
[8] About 5% at the end of the period.

To further validate these assertions, the notably upward trend in 'follow nature' and the relatively flat line for 'making use of nature' would be consistent with the postmodern perspective.

Follow custom?

"If you think something is right, do you think you should go ahead and do it even if it is contrary to usual custom, or do you think you are less apt to make a mistake if you follow custom? 1. Go ahead even if contrary; 2. Follow custom; 3. Undecided/it depends." The results of this question are difficult to interpret. While there are slight shifts in the two main responses, in which we see a cross-over from not following custom to following custom, perhaps the most notable aspect of these results is the comparatively dramatic rise in undecided responses. Perhaps the question is making less sense to respondents as time goes on. There is a temptation to speculate about the implications of these results because custom (tradition) was once a powerful behavioral determinant in Japan and thus might be regarded as a core value. Future trends in the responses to this question may enable greater insight.

Life principles

"Which two of the principles of living on this list are most important to you personally? 1. Respecting your parents; 2. Repaying your obligations to people who have done the most for you; 3. Respecting the legal rights of others; 4. Respecting the freedom of the individual to do whatever he or she wants." There is very little change in the results over the 45-year period. Thus, if we were to attach any of these principles to core values, their persistence over time would be validated by these results.

Obligation

"a) Imagine this situation: John was orphaned at an early age and was brought up by Mr. Smith, a kind neighbor. The Smiths gave him a good education, sent him to college, and now John has become the president of a company. One day John gets a message saying that Mr. Smith is seriously ill and will probably die and asking him to come at once. This message arrives just at the moment John is going to an extremely important meeting which will decide whether his firm will go bankrupt or will survive. What should John do? 1. Leave everything and rush to Mr. Smith's side; 2. However worried he might be about his adopted father, he should go to his business meeting." There has been very little change in the responses to this question over the 45-year period, with respondents about evenly split between the two options.

"b) Now suppose the situation is similar to the one in the last question, but in this case it's John's real father who is dying. What should John do in this case? 1. Leave everything and rush to his father's side; 2. However worried he might be about his father, he should go to the business meeting." There is effectively no change here as well and the respondents are as evenly split on the options as they were with the benefactor. The absence of any change here might be ascribed to the persistence of the Japanese core value related to obligation (giri-ninjo).

Separation of state and religion

The Ise Shinto shrine is considered to be Japan's national shrine. The question asked was: "Some Prime Ministers, when they take office, pay a visit to the Imperial Shrine at Ise. What do you think about this practice? 1. Should go; 2. Better to go; 3. Can please himself; 4. Better not to go; or 5. Should not go." Notably 'please himself' shows a dramatic rise over time,[9] while 'better to go' shows a comparatively sharp drop over time.[10] According to Hayashi and Kuroda (1997: 57), 'better to go' reflects the traditional view because Shinto was considered the state religion during the war. Separation of the state from religion was made explicit following the war. Our position is that the results here show a marked trend away from tradition as well as a marked trend toward a more individualistic stance, i.e., that the prime minister should do as he pleases, both phenomena therefore indicative of modern, but not necessarily postmodern, attitudes.

Mechanization and human feeling

"Some people say that no matter how mechanized the world gets, nothing can reduce the richness of human feelings. Do you agree with this opinion, or do you disagree? 1. Agree; 2. Disagree; 3. Undecided." The results would seem to indicate that the Japanese people's attitudes about mechanization reducing the richness of human feeling are trending toward belief that mechanization does in fact reduce the richness of human feeling. This supports the postmodern contention that the mechanization brought on by industrialization isn't all it was originally held up to be; that numerous costs have accompanied the benefits.

---

[9] From just over 20% to just over 60%.
[10] From 50% to just over 15%.

Science and technology and human feeling

"Some people say that with the development of science and technology, life becomes more convenient, but at the same time a lot of human feeling is lost. Do you agree with this opinion or do you disagree? 1. Agree; 2. Disagree; 3. Undecided." The Japanese attitudes on this issue reflect exactly that seen for the previous question on the issue of mechanization and loss of human feeling.

Importance of money

"In bringing up children of elementary school age some people think that they should be taught as early as possible that money is one of the most important things in life. Do you agree with this or not? 1. Agree; 2. Disagree; 3. Undecided." The results for this question clearly describe a postmodern attitude about money, consistent with Inglehart's postmaterialism. Once again, note that the cross-over from respondents agreeing that the importance of money should be taught to children, to disagreeing, occurred around 1970.[11]

Tell the truth

"Suppose that a child comes home and says that he has heard a rumor that his teacher had done something to get himself into trouble, and suppose that the parent knows this to be true. Do you think it is better for the parent to tell the child the truth, or to deny it? 1. Tell the truth; 2. Deny it; 3. Other." The results show that from a nearly even split on this issue in 1953, the percentage of respondents who favor telling the truth has risen to over 60, while those favoring denial has dropped to 20. This is a significant reversal and might suggest that Japanese society is becoming more rationalistic.

Most important thing in life

"What is the single most important thing in life for you? 1. Health, myself; 2. Children (child); 3. Family; 4. Ancestor, household; 5. Money, treasure; 6. Love, spirit; 7. Work, trust; 8. Nation, society; 9. Others." Postmodern values are reflected significantly for most of the results for this question.

---

[11] At the beginning of the period about 65% agreed whereas at the end of the period about 30% agreed. The respective figures for disagreeing are about 25% at the beginning and about 50% at the end of the period.

Increased frequencies are seen for 'health, myself' and 'love, spirit'. 'Family' shows a comparatively dramatic increase. 'Money', on the other hand, falls rather dramatically, as does 'nation, society'. In combination, these results demonstrate postmodern attitudes. Explaining the comparatively dramatic rise for 'family' is a bit puzzling in that strong family values were traditionally associated with Japan, but the 'ancestor, household' response was virtually never selected throughout the 45-year period. 'Health, myself' would seem to indicate a simultaneous rise in individual values.

Tradition vs. Modernity

Reasonably assuming the presence of a Japanese traditional-modern continuum as specifically manifested by the responses to a set of six of the JCNS questions, Hayashi and Kuroda (1997) applied correspondence analysis to identify changes in attitudinal response patterns. The results tend to validate the hypothesized traditional-modern continuum with notably sharp divisions between the two ends of the continuum. Beginning in 1973 and continuing through 1988, this relatively fixed pattern slowly but steadily decays for two of the six 'modern' responses. What this means is that "... some younger Japanese started to hold more traditional views than older Japanese" (Hayashi and Kuroda, 1997: 69). This is indicative of a breakdown in the Japanese traditional-modern way of thinking. Not surprisingly, the 'conquer/follow nature' responses contribute to these results. Hayashi and Kuroda (1997: 69) also see "... limited signs of growing individualism," but they are quick to point out that these results are not without contradiction, as seen in the 'follow custom' responses. Thus, while there is evidence of postmodern leanings in the Japanese way of thinking, some traditions conversely continue to prevail.

Conclusion

What can we discern from all these results? Several of the findings would appear to validate a postmodern phenomenon, whether it is an outright new era or a new perspective. Clearly indicative of postmodern phenomena are the results for several questions, including the gender rebirth question, which indicates changing attitudes among Japanese women about their roles in society, the many dimensions of which are expressions of postmodern thought. The life attitudes question also provides clear parallels with postmodern thought in that the Japanese are changing their attitudes about

life to ones more individualistically oriented to their own personal quality
of life. The man and nature results support the postmodern backlash against
the ideas of environmental exploitation inherent to modernization. The richness of human feeling results also suggest emerging postmodern attitudes
among the Japanese, again as a sort of backlash against the mechanization
and technologization characteristic of industrial development and modernization. Finally, the paternalistic supervisor results exhibit postmodern inclinations; however, on this question it must be kept in mind that the Japanese
have always taken this attitude about supervision at work. Despite these
rather copious observations consistent with postmodern concepts, there is
evidence for a persistence of at least certain core values in Japan. Most
notable among the results attributable to core values are those for the religious faith question. In the half century under study, the Japanese have not
wavered in their religious faith. Keep in mind, however, that the results for
Holland (Sasaki and Suzuki, 1987), and to a lesser extent for the United
States, suggest that modernization does influence religious faith.

The paternalistic supervisor question can be extended to the core value
level in that the Japanese consider the workplace as an extension of family
life. In this sense, then, this core value has persisted through Japan's entire
recent modernization phase, indicating that modernity did not usurp this
core value. In all fairness, however, there are other results (gender preference, for example) which suggest that changes have occurred in the Japanese core value loosely associated with the family. The death bed/obligation
(giri-ninjo) questions clearly show a persistence of a core Japanese value
loosely related to obligation in that there has been very little shift in the
results over the past 45 years. As well, the life principles question, which
exhibits very little change over time, gets at core issues of obligation, respect,
rights, and individual freedom. A possibly expected shift away from these
values in modernity and a shift back toward them in postmodernity is not
observed.

Other results, however, which might well reflect core value issues, do not
show persistence, including the gender preference questions and the most
important thing in life question. Still other results would appear to express
attitudinal ambivalence on the part of the Japanese; e.g., the question on
how to live one's life (where carpe diem type responses are way up and
purity and justice are way down, and where 'get rich' remains flat throughout the survey period). Also expressive of ambivalence about issues related
to core values is the man and nature question, where harmony with nature
does not persist but is reemerging as the preferred attitude. Three questions
in particular yield results which would appear to underscore some uniquely
Japanese attitudinal characteristics. These include the results of the questions

on religious faith, nepotism and paternalistic supervisor. A topic to which we have given some considerable attention is tradition. Recall that the onset of modernization in Japan occurred in a context in which tradition was extraordinarily important to the society. Six questions in particular have special relevance to the issue of tradition. The results from the six questions, however, do not consistently indicate the persistence of tradition. While the religious faith question, the supervisor preference question and the 'family' response to the most important thing in life question show persisting Japanese traditions, the gender preference question exhibits clear evidence of the usurpation of the traditional Japanese female role. The traditionally diminutive and silent Japanese woman is no longer that person.

The other two questions related to tradition are the nepotism and follow custom questions. The Japanese have been traditionally and persistently anti-nepotistic. Most of the rest of the world has not held this as traditional. Following custom was another strong Japanese tradition. We said previously, however, that the results for this question were obscure in that they appear to be somewhat backward of expectation. Nonetheless, the key might be the marked rise in undecided responses, suggesting growing ambivalence about the tradition of following custom. There also is some suggestion in these results of support for the revalorization of tradition hypothesis.

This discussion of tradition leads us to some brief remarks on intergenerational shifts. The follow custom question, in particular, was identified by Hayashi and Kuroda (1997) as one of the six questions in their correspondence analysis which suggested a revalorization of tradition amongst some younger Japanese. Recall also that age effects were identified in the cohort analysis of the religious faith data. Further work with cohort and correspondence analysis is needed to uncover more about the dynamics of intergenerational shifts in attitudes consistent with or contrary to the whole concept of postmodernism.

Finally, there are a number of questions of which the results remain obscure and difficult to evaluate, although we have occasionally referred to some of their specific findings in special contexts. These include the death bed/obligation questions, the adoption and following custom questions.

Taking a more far-reaching, global view of these results, the Japanese, very much a part of the globalizing post-industrial era, would seem to be changing in the directions predicted by the postmodernity phenomenon, in particular with respect to (radicalized) individuality and self-expression, the waning importance of some, but not all, traditions along with a concomitant rise in the importance of some other traditions, and the persistence of at least some core values (family, ancestry). But clearly all is not succinctly indicative of a stark shift to postmodernity. Thus, while cultural change is obvious, its specific nature and character is far from obvious. Inherent in these results is a recurring theme of ambivalence. *Certain* core values persist, *certain* traditions persist, while others do not.

If we adopt the notion of functional advantage as the overarching principle operating in global modernization, and construct a balance sheet of modernity's assets and liabilities, perhaps we can make more sense out of the apparent ambiguities and ambivalence. By seeking to maintain balance, we seek to identify that which is functionally advantageous to that endeavor. That is, we seek optimality, at the individual, group, societal, national, cultural and global levels. If certain core values and traditions are functional in this optimizing behavior, then so be it. Conversely, those core values or traditions which are no longer functionally advantageous should be discarded. In a sense, this optimizing, then, is an exploitative behavior: exploit the functional traditions, discard the dysfunctional ones.

Taking this approach to modernity/postmodernity, it is not at all surprising to find ambivalence and ambiguities present in large numbers. Modernization is a process, and in that process, as one functionally advantageous element shifts toward dysfunctionality, there will be an interim period during which we will experience ambivalence, as the position of the element on the balance sheet becomes ambiguous. The search for balance, the search for optimality will occur at all levels, from the very micro to the very macro.

During modernization, the achievement motive, to take just one example, proved functionally advantageous for economic growth, but at some point it exceeded its utility and the balance sheet went awry, as quality of life was seen to deteriorate. As a backlash, quality of life has come to take on greater and greater functional advantage.

So, while the Japanese expression of modernity/postmodernity is not like others' expressions of it, at the same time it is not necessarily a unique expression of it either. This fact clearly proves the case for multiple modernities and implies that we can expect yet similar but differing expressions to emerge throughout the Pacific Rim, Latin America, parts of Asia and Africa in the next century. Modernity does indeed find its own form and seeks its own optimal balance in each and every context in which it occurs. Japan, for instance, has modernized, but its culture is still very much Japanese, a fact which will no doubt persist indefinitely.

It is important to realize that the overarching principle and these optimizing processes operate all the way down to the individual level. There is indeed a postmodern individual, a postmodern personality who seeks, just as assiduously, optimality in the face of global modernization.

This brings us full circle and recalls again the phrase 'multiple modernities'. Japan is expressing its modernity and its reactions to modernity in multiple and diverse ways. No single hypothesis or theory about postmodern evolution is yet functional, as observations and findings continue to manifest evidence of a sense of functional ambivalence toward the future. Indeed, it may be many decades before we can look back and say with certainty what drove the processes of modernization and postmodernization and where the era took us.

IN CONCLUSION: TOWARD A NEW AGENDA

INTRODUCTION

Michel Wieviorka, who opens this concluding section of the book, deduces from his analysis of today's society that sociology faces the dual threat of domination by one prevailing and exclusionist perspective, and of the discipline's fragmentation into multiple sociologies, unable or unwilling to communicate with each other. The major challenge now facing sociologists is to keep sociology both universal and capable of analyzing specific realities. Widening the discussion to social knowledge as a whole, *Erwin Scheuch* sees no 'salvation' for it outside sociology—despite the disarray resulting from growing divisions among sociologists. In the present time, sociology alone may transcend its disciplinary splits and regain its role as the encompassing arena for discourse on social reality as a whole. *Karin Knorr Cetina* widens the discussion still further by considering knowledge itself. Knowledge, she contends, has become a productive force. A number of scientific fields do not simply reflect the world 'out there' but rather create the phenomena they investigate. Knowledge is not only the goal and target of professional work, but also a relational object that includes our concept of sociality, and increasingly mediates human relationships. This, we may assume, also applies to sociological analysis itself.

32. SOME COMING DUTIES OF SOCIOLOGY

Michel Wieviorka

From the end of the 1960s, in Western societies (though does the term 'Western' still mean anything?) there was an increasing awareness that very profound transformations were taking place. At the time, some researchers stressed the idea that there was a move from one type of society to another, with Alain Touraine and Daniel Bell, in particular, speaking of a post-industrial society.[1] Others drew attention to the themes of doubt and crisis, particularly in the mid-1970s after the impact of the first oil crisis, which in turn followed the Yom Kippur War. In this historical context, economists, political scientists and sociologists began to consider the crisis of the state and the institutions. For example, James O'Connor[2] was concerned with the crisis in the welfare state and the fiscal crisis of the State. He and many others have given further thought to the decline in the capacity, and perhaps also in the will, of western countries to ensure the principles of solidarity, equality, welfare and assistance which, in these Western societies, began to find concrete expression in the 19th century. The institutions set up to implement these principles were often at their height in the 1950s and 1960s of our century in various forms: social-democratic, Labor, Republican, etc.

In the same mid-1970s period, others preferred to speak in terms of a global ecological crisis; their ideas were part of, or generated, doubts as to our most fundamental values. The end result was a challenge to the idea of progress. We only have to recall the origin of the ecologist movement, the warnings of the Club of Rome and its well-known report, *The Limits to Growth*; or Ivan Illich's utopian proposals which were also widely discussed at this time.[3]

As from the end of the 1970s, there was another range of explanations of change, mainly in terms of the breakdown in social life. In the last resort, the idea of society itself was challenged. At that point discussion focused on the social vacuum, the loss of meaning, cover-ups and widespread individualism; we also witnessed the predominance of schools of thought many of which were described as post-modern. New themes began to emerge, while new insights informed or developed public discussion.

---

[1] Bell (1973) and Touraine (1971) have both published a book under this title.
[2] O'Connor, 1973.
[3] Illich, 1971; 1976.

On the one hand, the end of the 1970s and particularly the 1980s was the era of neo-liberalism, of Ronald Reagan, Margaret Thatcher and the Chicago School. Neo-liberalism as an ideology and a practice in political economy reached its peak at the end of the 1980s, when the Soviet Empire collapsed and policies based on liberalism were implemented in several countries: while at the same time there was a return of the Hegelian theme of the end of history with Fukuyama's well-known book.[4] On the other hand, in those same years the theme of globalization was forcefully asserted and with it the image of the establishment of a global economic order, dominated by the capitalists whose sphere of intervention was no longer that of the Nation-State and whose concerns or interests were much more with finance or commerce, than with production. At the same time, anxiety concerning the crisis in state institutions gained ground: according to various critical schools of thought the difficulties inherent to States and to the institutions of which these states are the guarantors, stem at least in part from the predominance of participants in economic globalization and from their indifference to the problems and constraints of the State. Finally, the question of cultural identities, whether it be that of the nation or other sorts of particularisms—such as ethnic, religious, regional or other—became an obsession. These had begun to take shape in the 1960s and 1970s with themes like those of 'Roots' or of 'ethnic revival' and gained momentum for various reasons, some of which seem to be linked to economic globalization: does the latter not have the effect of producing, at one and the same time, cultural homogeneity at global level, a sort of 'Macdonaldization' of the world, to use a phrase of the times, and the fragmentation and exacerbation of cultural, national or other identities? This being the case, culture becomes a cause for concern, discussion and anxiety that refers to numerous spheres, from the most global, the planet, to the most local—the neighborhood, the housing estate, the town and the region, for example. Some people think in terms of big blocks of civilizations—for example, Samuel Huntington and his well-known hypotheses on the 'clash' of civilizations, while others become interested in diasporas, and transnational phenomena. Some people turn their attention to the national question, while others research into the rise in specific cultural identities within national entities; there are discussions in political philosophy, in particular, which explore extensively the themes of recognition and multiculturalism.

These superficial and partial observations can obviously in no way take the place of a general framework of a history of ideas which would itself be constructed on a history or sociology of the major recent changes. They

[4] Fukuyama, 1992.

are simply a reminder of how, in some thirty years, we have had to consider far-reaching changes which challenge our societies both at home and abroad and the interrelationship between their internal functioning and inter-societal relations.

This reminder, superficial as it may be, also confronts us as sociologists, at the outset, with a major theoretical question which calls for a response validated by concrete, empirical knowledge: should we think of the major contemporary processes in terms of crisis, or of change, or transformation? And if, as we think, we should adopt the hypothesis of change, can we develop an argument which includes in one and the same approach, the changes internal to such or such country, and changes at global level, in their economic (globalization), cultural (internationalization of culture under North American hegemony, cultural fragmentation, the hypothesis of the 'clash' of civilizations),[5] institutional (transformation of the institutions) and geopolitical (end of the Cold war) dimensions?

I am going to restrict myself to exploring the idea of a societal transformation and, to that end, to considering the changes which are internal to the major countries in the Western world. I am aware of the risk of ethnocentrism of my point of view, but it is not possible or serious, I think, to speak of too many issues. The changes I am talking about concern the three main spheres that Daniel Bell considers as defining modernity:[6] social relationships in the strict sense of the term, the political and institutional systems, and culture. Each of these spheres has been subject to continual change since the end of the 1960s. Moreover, there has been a considerable evolution in their mode of integration, for the most part in the direction of dislocation.

The end of industrial society

The societies I am talking about are no longer industrial, by which I mean societies structured by a fundamental social conflict between the working class movement and employers. Until the mid-1970s, the majority of the countries in the Western world experienced a period of growth and full employment and were at the same time organized on the basis of being industrialized. The peak of this period was characterized by the short-lived triumph of 'scientific' modes of organization of labor, in which workers were deprived of control over their production, and denied their subjectivity as

[5] Huntington, 1996.
[6] Bell, 1979.

the result of the appropriation by others of the fruits of their labor. In the division of labor no thought was given to the workers, since thinking had to be concentrated in the time and motion offices and other areas where the directors exercised their powers. Work was none the less a central, inescapable value, and the most important social relationships had to be understood in terms of domination and exploitation.

Contrary to the far too superficial evolutionist arguments, we did not move from an industrial society to a service society in which the so-called 'tertiary' activities took the place of the 'secondary'—in other words, industrial—activities, along lines similar to the replacement of agriculture by the latter. The end of industrial society did in fact mean much more than a shift in the most fundamental activities: it brought about a break with Taylorism and other forms of scientific organization of labor, and stressed the question of the centrality of work in the human experience. It also put an end to a principle of structuring through conflict which could take the form of a grand narrative or an epic, with its heroes, its great moments in history, its strikes, its myths, its demands and its hopes which gave form to all collective life. The conflict between the working class movement and the employers did indeed determine political life to a large extent, and was more or less deeply the basis of the division between right and left. It was also the driving force in intellectual life, associations, the conflicts even in spheres very remote from industry, in rural areas or the universities for example. Today, the main area of conflict has shifted to issues which are more cultural than social properly speaking—I'll come back to this point.

The end of industrial society meant the breakup of big working-class communities, for instance in England, where there were very impressive examples with their own cultures. It did not necessarily mean the end of workers who still account for between 20% and 25% of the active population in most European countries. But the worker—a social character so often extolled to the point of sometimes being described as the salt of the earth, has disappeared from our representations of the social scene and in particular from the media. At the same time, the very idea of a social structure inclusive of the whole population on the basis of a conflictual social relationship has given way to other images. Some authors such as Robert Castel[7] spoke of disaffiliation of those whom waged labor previously integrated. In numerous countries, there has been a discovery or recognition of the extent of the importance of themes of non-contractual, unofficial labor—illegal or clandestine—on which a considerable proportion of our economies is based. In numerous countries also, there has been, or still is, talk of social exclu-

---

[7] Castel, 1995.

sion to account for both a process and a situation characteristic of a part of the population which has been left behind by change and is now not so much dominated and exploited as segregated and propelled out of society. We have also seen the controversial category of underclass emerge in numerous studies, to designate the social categories that are victims of exclusion. In fact, there is no reason for us to argue that the end of industrial society and exclusion or disaffiliation are in some way linked. It is true that in Western Europe where the rate of unemployment is frequently as high as 10% or 12% of the active population, the end frequently takes place in this mode. And if one considers post-Communist countries, this is also true, and frequently much more. But, in the past, throughout the age of industry, periods of high rates of unemployment have alternated with periods of full employment. From the point of view of the type of society, the issue today is primarily one of structural transformation in the organization of the activities of production or exchange. In the 1980s these far-reaching changes have had the effect of encouraging an enterprise culture which was particularly strong at that time when the virtues of participant management and internal and external flexibility were extolled. Then the novelty wore off and criticism of the new forms of organization of work began to develop. In particular they were accused of leading to renewed forms of inequality and especially to a rise in job insecurity for wage-earners. These criticisms met with widespread agreement, and were sometimes connected with issues such as the disorienting personal effects of 'flexible capitalism', as Richard Sennett showed in a recent book.[8] From this point on, in the social sciences and elsewhere, interest turned to the transformation in labor relations and their economic and social implications, while agreeing that the most decisive conflicts in social life no longer necessarily originate in the sphere of labor.

Crisis in the institutions

Modern societies have set up a framework of institutions ensuring the main functions of integration, sometimes concomitant with their entry into the age of industry, and then spurred on by the working-class movement, but sometimes also well before, or without this impetus, or even in opposition to it. The school socializes children, enabling them, as Durkheim believed, to construct themselves as individuals; the police and justice ensure law and order; the public services and various administrations ensure equality and

---

[8] Sennett, 1998.

cohesion in a framework which may be the state regulations and the law, or equal representation of both sides. But, since the 1970s, in Western countries at least, and also elsewhere, for instance, in the former Soviet empire, a widespread phenomenon of deinstitutionalization has challenged their capacity to perform their tasks. Moreover, the important private institution of the family has also been subject to considerable transformation.

This phenomenon can be analyzed in several ways. One can stress the growing incapacity of institutions to keep their promises, to adequately fulfill their traditional vocation, to ensure law and order, socialization or the subjectivation of the individual. What have become mere shells of institutions then appear to be staffed by personnel who are unable to identify fully and appropriately with their functions, as if they were the locus of organizational tensions in which new modes of working and new conceptions of their mission have become confused with old rules, and who are no longer even sure or clear about the ultimate aims. In other words, the institutions are in crisis. But this initial diagnosis is too one-dimensional. Not only are the institutions in crisis to varying degrees, they are also changing and, whether they like it or not, they are part of general processes of change. The staff in public institutions often think of themselves as agents identified with principles or an abstract mission; but, increasingly, they observe, admit and sometimes want to participate more actively in numerous relations in which they have to take into account the subjectivity of those for whom they are responsible—pupils in school, clients in administrations, etc. The institution is no longer the embodiment of abstract principles, values and norms transcending individuals. It has become a place where individuals can be recognized and dealt with as such, and themselves participate actively in their transformation, their socialization and their subjectivation. From this point of view, the institutions are not only under threat from the crisis, which may mean their disappearance as such; in my country, for instance, this has happened with the army which is no longer an institution and is becoming a professional army of experts; and in several countries the privatization of public organizations which were formerly public service institutions means that they are now commercial firms. They are also likely to be described in terms of transformation and change, at least if they are not in the grip of increasingly inappropriate modes of functioning. The characteristic of countries with a strong state, in this respect, is that institutions are constantly taking harder positions to avoid change, and many political actors would rather defend the classical conception of the institutions than envisage change.

Theses remarks can be extended to the family. A recurrent theme, both in the literature and in the social sciences, is the claim that the family is threatened with destructuring, especially in the working class and even more so in poverty. It is common to amalgamate poverty, the breakup of the family—for example the trend to one-parent families—and juvenile delinquency. This comes down to stressing the fact that the present-day family is in crisis, because it is losing the capacity to fulfill its traditional role. But the family is also becoming disinstitutionalized because it is becoming democratic, relational in the words of the French sociologist François de Singly, liberal, a sphere of relationships in which each individual, adult or child, can assert his or her subjectivity. It cannot then be reduced uniquely to the image of crisis; it is also undergoing change.

The national question

Since the end of the 1960s there has also been a considerable reorientation of the national question. As the economy was changing, through the processes of globalization on one hand and the move to a post-industrial society with scarcely any further need for a high proportion of industrial wage-earners on the other, in some countries at least the nation no longer appeared to offer an adequate framework for economic life in the outside world and powerless, or fraught with economic difficulties, at home. Globalization does indeed mean that in any given country, some parts of the economy are vulnerable and are doomed, even if the country does succeed in finding its footing in the world economy. It is well known that the establishment and relocating of financial capital is determined by the pursuit of its own interests, with no consideration for national aims. Sectors of the economy which are poor competitors at the international level are either bound to decline or be highly dependent on the State and protectionist measures. The idea of globalization fundamentally undermining nations has impacted Western societies in varying ways. France has perhaps been the scene of the most active and virulent criticism; the 'Economic Horror' (*L'Horreur économique*[9] is the title of a highly successful book by the journalist Viviane Forrester) has been exposed, the Juppé government's policy of reform was rejected because, it was argued, public service in France was an exceptional situation, and the construction of Europe is seen as a Trojan horse of liberalism and globalization. In actual fact, the most serious analyses of the phenomena do relativize it and insist on their ideological character, in a critical perspective: globalization of the economy is not as widespread or as new as some people say and, for example, from the European point of view, it has less influence

---

[9] Forrester, 1996.

on the national economies than might be thought. Elie Cohen's work,[10] is one example which demonstrates that for France international trade still takes place mainly within the European sphere and is not crushed out of existence by the all-powerful multinationals. But, in the words of Benedict Anderson, the nation is an imagined community and the idea of the nation is nurtured by symbols, representations, perceptions, which may be mythical and ideological in nature without necessarily being correctly informed by reality.

The idea of nation has often become a fixation in a context fraught with anxiety about globalization and exacerbated by the rise in unemployment and the worsening of social inequalities. In some countries, and particularly in Belgium, Germany, Austria, etc., this fixation has found expression in racist and xenophobic nationalism which aims to curb economic difficulties by sealing off the nation and by expelling or excluding those elements considered to be culturally impure, beginning with the immigrants. In other cases, nationalism, while presenting considerable racist and xenophobic dimensions, has instead aimed at separating one part of the country, which tends to be economically prosperous, from other parts which are viewed as parasitical or useless: this is particularly true of Italy with the Northern League, which would like the so-called 'Padania' to become an autonomous region in the country to improve its integration into modern Europe, or again in Belgium, with the Vlaams Blok which advocates the separation of Flanders, a rather well-to-do region, from Wallonia which is in the grip of deindustrialization.

The waning of the idea of the nation reveals that the concept has difficulty in embodying modernity, progress, development, and democracy; ideologies of hatred that appeal to withdrawal into oneself are gaining the upper hand. This is not uniquely an economic phenomenon but is also sustained by more directly cultural concerns. On one hand this is one of the dimensions, or one of the extensions, of the fears and anxieties associated with economic globalization: the financial and commercial internationalization of the economy does also mean the domination of cultural industries operating at global level, for example in information and communication. It therefore goes along with the internationalization of culture which is taking place under American hegemony. Some countries willingly accept this hegemony, particularly when they in fact participate very directly in this culture; others maintain a more complex and more ambivalent relationship to it. France, once again, is an extreme case of a more ideological than practical rejection of the international culture of the masses—the 'French exception'. The fact remains that

---

[10] Elie Cohen, 1996.

anxiety for the cultural entity represented by the nation culminates in the rise of nationalism everywhere.

In Europe, however, could it be that we have now got over the main thrust of nationalism? Some signs give us food for thought. The construction of Europe which has just successfully negotiated the hurdle of the Amsterdam agreements and the birth of the single European currency, the Euro, is in fact taking place in a climate where references to liberalism do appear to be outdated. Throughout Europe, but also elsewhere in the major international organizations, like the IMF or the World Bank, it is recognized that states have a decisive role to play, through their institutions, their concept of public policies including social policies which could weaken the most nationalist positions and discourses in favor of closing the borders. Europe appears as a bulwark, fragile it is true, in the face of the financial tornadoes which have recently swept South East Asia, Russia and Brazil. The threat of pure liberalism retreats, new options take shape, like, for example, appeals to a 'third way'.[11] Here we have to tread carefully to avoid the over-hasty positing of a decline in nationalism in Europe: while the *Front National* in France has split into two opposing and declining factions, which would tend to confirm such a hypothesis, in Austria the success of Jorg Haider in the regional elections in Carinthia (March 7th 1999) and, later, at the national level, tends instead to the opposite view.

Do contemporary trends mean the decline of the very idea of nation, which is one of the theses defended in particular by the historian Eric Hobsbawm?[12] Should we consider that somewhere along the line between the waning of nationalism and its pure and simple decline, the nation might become an obsolete category? Here also we have to be very careful. The fact is that nothing stops us from thinking that the phase of the emergence of the downside of the nation could be followed by a return to confidence in its brighter side; this can be observed in European countries with people on both the left and the right asserting the compatibility between belonging to the nation and European identity, or demanding an end to the quasi-monopoly of the nation by the extreme and radical right. The issue at stake for the countries in Europe is in fact to steer clear of any opposition between their nation and Europe; on the contrary, they should endeavor to articulate their belonging to Europe with their national and social integration. This is an important issue: is it or will it be possible in the future to reconcile national and social integration, and belongings with other transnational or intranational identities; and if so, under which conditions?

---

[11] Giddens, 1999.
[12] Hobsbawm, 1990.

The emergence of specific cultural characteristics

Since the end of the 1960s Western societies have experienced an intense mobilization of new or reinvigorated actors who, even if they emerge in very different spheres, are characterized by their pleas for cultural changes that concern them intimately. In this instance, culture is linked with specific identities—in some countries, but not all, there is talk of minorities—and this phenomenon poses important questions for both sociology and political philosophy.

Sociologically, the most pressing issue is the acceptance of the idea of a process in which culture is not only reproduced but is also, and primarily, produced. Admittedly, the present-day emergence of identities does provide a visibility, even a legitimacy, to cultural forms which are endowed with considerable historical depth and which at first sight seem to originate more in reproduction. Thus in modern societies we can stress the importance of identities which have resisted the erosion of modernity, including in its most destructive forms, colonialism, for example. The Indians from the north to the south of the three Americas, and the Australian aborigines, are illustrations of this observation. Similarly, the 'ethnic revival' which Anthony Smith[13] discusses does seem to correspond to regional identities which have successfully resisted destruction by money and the modern economy or dissolution in political entities which function in an assimilation mode. Yet again, emigration, in the first instance, seems to signify the displacement in space of groups or individuals transporting with them their culture of origin and possibly finding the means of ensuring its reproduction.

But in these three situations, we should beware of stereotypes or superficial ideas and of believing that everything is a question of reproduction and maintenance of traditional identities. The latter are never reproduced in absolute purity and strict respect of origins, they are *bricolées*, 'cobbled together' in Lévi-Strauss' well-known words, they are produced and not only reproduced, in a process of mixing or hybridization which makes of them an invention and never a mere heritage. The Indians and the Aborigines no longer live as their ancestors did before the colonization which almost destroyed them, even if they invoke their traditions. As Serge Gruzinski[14] has just discerningly demonstrated, the mixing of cultures is not new: since the arrival of Europeans in the New World, a hybridity of thought characterized the artistic production and the imaginative world of the native peoples. Similarly, immigrants construct their cultural, religious, ethnic or national

---

[13] Anthony Smith, 1981.
[14] Gruzinski, 1999.

references, even if it means dipping into their reservoir of traditional identities; for example, as Farhad Khosrokhavar has demonstrated, the Islam of young people in Europe is different from that of their parents.[15]

What is true of groups classically thought of as being solely concerned with reproduction is truer still if other cultural identities are taken into consideration; they may be very different from one another, but they share in demanding recognition in the public sphere. Thus, in the past thirty years, many societies have witnessed claims associated with gender (in particular the movements of homosexuals), with illness or disability (the action of deaf people, or the victims of AIDS), as well as various forms of ethnicization which owe little to reasons of reproduction and a great deal to reasons of production.

The nature of the production of cultural identities depends on whether it is directly associated with a social dimension, or only indirectly so. In the first instance, assertions of identity may correspond to processes in which, for example, a group is socially excluded, this being to some extent in terms of its nature with its rejection involving racial discrimination: the group is thus driven to think of itself as being different, possibly despite a desire for integration, or even assimilation. Thus, in some European countries, young people of immigrant origin, contrary to their fathers, are socially excluded (whereas their fathers came to work) and culturally integrated (whereas their fathers intended to return home and made no great effort to integrate in the host country). But a combination of racial discrimination and social segregation gave them to understand or to feel that they were culturally and even naturally different. In a classical operation of interiorization and reversal of the stigma, this encouraged them to assert their differences, in particular national (for example, Arab) or religious (especially Muslim) aspects.

The social production of identities is not confined to working-class, even poor, actors, but also occurs amongst socially diversified, even well-to-do, categories. For example, one frequently observes identities of origin being asserted and reasserted by people or groups who come from successful immigrations and for whom a certain amount of ethnicity is a source of pride and gives meaning to their lives. Similarly, communitarianism often provides groups stemming from certain diasporas with economic and social resources. Or yet again, national, religious or ethnic identity may be advanced to justify the tendency or appeals to disassociation of part of the population, those who are comfortably-off and well established in economic modernity

---

[15] Khosrokhavar, 1997.

and who want to differentiate themselves from the poorer part, or those who suffer most from economic difficulties such as the Northern League in Italy to which we have already referred.

An apparent paradox

It is only superficially paradoxical to say that the contemporary production of cultural particularisms has two-fold links with modern individualism. In the post-war years, and until the 1960s and 1970s, cultural change was mainly linked to the consumer society and the spread of mass culture. Change did not involve processes of cultural fragmentation, but the spread of modernity and individualism through cinema, television, advertising and mass cultural production; in the United States, David Riesman or Vance Packard—with huge differences of course—could illustrate this point. In France, Edgar Morin was one of the first to understand the phenomena and to discuss it, and in a way, Roland Barthes also understood how to deal with it. There was a link between cultural change and individualism.

Today, the logic of the 1960s and 1970s has not disappeared but other orientations, which also involve both individualism and culture, have come up. To grasp their significance, we have to begin by stressing the two dimensions of modern individualism. The latter implies a variety of consequences. On the one hand, people want to participate in modern life, to accede to consumerism, money, work, health or education. This takes us back to the most spontaneous conceptions of the individual which define it by interests, calculations and, in the last and more extreme resort, by consumerism, selfishness and hedonism. On the other hand, it also refers us to the theme of the subject, to the fact that people are increasingly defined by their personal capacity, possibly frustrated or denied, to construct themselves, to produce their own existence, to control their experience, to guide their ambition, to make choices which are not entirely conditioned by the norms and values of the group or society to which they belong.

The individualism of participation is not necessarily an alternative to the affirmation of specific cultures. On the contrary, it frequently contributes thereto: when one part of the population is to some extent excluded from consumerism and money, from jobs or from citizenship—for example as a result of racism—, it may find in references to its identity the answer to its frustrations and difficulties and a resource, as well, that might help it to achieve these objectives, with a heightened moral strength. This is one of the sources of the spread of Islam in Western Europe. When downward social mobility and the destructuring of social cohesion ejects people from the modernity to which they belonged until then, the latter can give a new meaning to their existence, once again, by referring to a collective identity such as the nation—in numerous situations national-populism owes part of its success to this type of process.

The subject's individualism explains what is precisely the main characteristic—the most decisive or the most significant element—in the emergence of specific identities within contemporary societies: the fact that they are a matter of production and not only of reproduction. Today if an individual claims to belong to a particular group, it is more and more frequently the outcome of a choice, a personal decision, possibly after having given the matter long consideration. It tends to be the outcome of work on himself or herself and not because he or she has to assume a heritage imposed on him or her by the group to which he or she belongs without it being necessarily a very conscious decision. Culture develops and changes in the process in which individual subjects assert and construct themselves in collective definitions which bear the mark of their subjectivity and which are the ways in which their subjectivization is implemented. This is true in many situations, including religious ones: the religious revival is to a large extent the outcome of individual decisions in which persons assert themselves. For example, in the research I directed on young Muslims working, temporarily, for a big public company in the Parisian region, I noted that it was through Islam, which some discovered or re-discovered at the time of this job, that they asserted themselves. In Islam they found the spiritual strength to construct themselves in a closed and hostile environment, to keep going and to retain their dignity, to cope with the ordeals of a difficult job (they had to ensure the security in buses driving through deprived urban areas). To sum up briefly, let's say that the actors who define themselves in terms of one (or several) collective identities in fact constantly move within a triangle bounded by three poles: collective identity, the concern to participate as an individual in the life of the city, and the desire to constitute themselves and to behave as subjects of their action thus controlling their experience—a desire which comes up against many limits, constraints and, sometimes, impossibilities.

We should not deduce from this emphasis on the theme of the subject and modern individualism that the construction of cultural identities is reduced to the work of actors on themselves. The fact is that the construction of cultural identities also owes a great deal to the work of the society under consideration on itself, and in particular to the way in which it sees the individuals and groups which it contributes to producing as cultural (possibly natural) images of otherness. As far back as the end of World War Two, Jean Paul Sartre explained in his famous *Reflections on the Jewish*

Question that the Jew is the creation of the anti-Semite: closer to us in time, the sociology of stigma and discrediting has taught us to give serious consideration to the processes whereby the internalization and then the reversal of the stigma can contribute to shaping not only individual personalities, but also collective identities. Besides, the very words we use invite us to take the idea of the social production of specific differences seriously: for example, in France we use the term 'Maghrebin' to describe populations who previously would never spontaneously refer to themselves as such, even if they do use this term fairly widely. Similarly, we constantly hear references to Asians for people who do not consider themselves as such, at least at the time of their arrival in France, when they were Chinese, Vietnamese, Cambodian, etc., or even from particular areas in China or Vietnam, etc. Or in the 1980s, in England, there was a debate, due to the fact that people from Asian origin no longer agreed to being called 'Black', which was often the case previously. We should add that other lines of argument, which are separate but complementary, may go in the direction of these observations, in particular by insisting on the importance of interpersonal and intercultural communication. Thus James Clifford[16] explains that

> . . . because in all systems of global power, discourse is worked out face to face, the idea of difference and particularism can never be located in the continuity of a culture or a tradition. Identity is linked to a context and is not innate.

This approach differs from ours but supports our idea of the production of difference. We might even consider, as does this author, that we should refute the theses of Lévi-Strauss, not when he observes the destruction of genuine cultures as a result of modernity, but when he sees this as a victory for the 'garbage' which the expansionist West has imposed throughout the world—because this 'garbage' does not prevent the invention and transformation of differences, but quite the contrary.

From sociological analysis to political action

Politically and philosophically, the rise of cultural specificities within contemporary societies means they are confronted with fundamental problems that they do not always know how to handle satisfactorily. When cultural differences are internal to our societies, and not only between one society and another, and, moreover, when they are subject to change because they are being produced and not only reproduced, with the result that they often

---

[16] Clifford, 1988: 19.

prove to be unstable, to be the outcome of processes of decomposition and recomposition, and, finally, when they are related to individual subjectivity, there has to be a new approach to considering how to deal with them politically.

This consideration involves the articulation of a huge range of registers which it is important not to conflate. The cultural question is indeed autonomous, but is also closely linked to the social question and that of the institutions. Socially, culture is linked to the question of exclusion and inequality; it may be an expression of exclusion and inequality or it may shape them to the benefit of dominant actors or in support of dominated or excluded actors, or again function to amalgamate them for example by combining heterogeneous arguments and interests in populism. Institutionally, it refers to the crisis in states and in institutions, but also to their changes. In cases where the political and administrative culture is traditionally receptive to cultural difference, demands for public recognition of the latter do not appear as a threat or a challenge to the institutions or, at least they do not appear to fundamentally challenge the core values and the concepts of social cohesion. In other countries like France, which is an extreme case again, on the contrary, it is difficult to deal with cultural difference politically because of the resonance of a universalist conception of the nation-state which is hostile to any recognition of cultural specificity. To illustrate this remark we have only to recall the words of the Count de Clermont-Tonnerre during the Revolution, explaining that the Jews should be granted everything as individuals and nothing as a nation. In the French context, the sudden emergence of cultural difference is often experienced as very dangerous, as a radical challenge to the Republic, and the sign of a tendency towards communitarianism. This makes the search for a democratic way of tackling cultural demands and expectations difficult and gives rise to extremely hard-line positions on the part of intellectuals and political actors for whom the idea of democracy is subservient to that of the Republic.

These questions are now well known. In their Anglo-Saxon variants, the discussions have been dominated by the opposition between 'communitarians' and 'liberals'. In other debates, in France or in Turkey, those in favor of a purist conception of the Republic, possibly going as far as advocating assimilation of differences raise the spectre of communitarianism, which in fact no democrat defends, making it even more difficult for any dialogue between those who uphold a tolerant conception of the public sphere and those who question what the possibilities are for a democracy receptive to cultural difference. Today, the cultural question has to be formulated by taking into consideration the social and institutional dimensions and not only the cultural aspects, and by taking on the theme of the individual. Moreover, some thought must be given to the fact that cultural specificities function in all sorts of spheres, some of which are local and small scale, and others at global level, some being totally confined within a national context, and others extending beyond it, for example in diaspora mode. We might as well admit that highly simplified or one-dimensional suggestions are inappropriate.

Conclusion

If we recognize that we have to deal altogether with this kind of issues— what is creativity when work is perhaps not so central? Which institutions could develop where there are such vast processes of deinstitutionalization? How to deal with cultural processes of decomposition and recomposition of identities? How to give a central place to this concept of the subject? If we do not forget that these issues are certainly different in our own countries, then we shall be able to talk and meet together. If not, I am afraid that globalization leads sociology to a double problem: on the one hand, a domination which could lead to exclusion, when Anglo-Saxon sociology would be more and more dominant, and on the other hand, sociological fragmentation, where the idea of multiple modernities leads to the idea of multiple sociologies unable to converse. Let me put it differently: sociology should be able to be at the same time, universal and specific.

33. SOCIOLOGY AS THE HEIR OF THE SOCIAL SCIENCE

Erwin K. Scheuch

I

For a short moment, some 40 to 50 years ago, it was at last possible to imagine that the quest for the identity of sociology was settled. At that time, structural-functionalism as developed by Talcott Parsons had reached the peak of its world-wide influence, even though the publication of the basic text "The Structure of Social Action" preceded this focusing of attention by some 15 years.[1] The 14th World Congress of the International Sociological Association in Montreal from July 26 to August 1, 1998 demonstrated, however, that this dominance of one approach was merely an episode.[2] The Montreal congress showed both the appearance of a sociology fragmented into fields of attention and theoretical denominations, on the one hand, and attempts to propagate a sense of identity, on the other. Fifty Research Committees, five Working Groups, four Thematic Groups, and seventeen Ad Hoc Groups, most of them holding several meetings spread over more than one day, meant that most of the 5,000 people attending the gigantic market-place experienced different congresses. Even more significant was the splintering into different denominations such as 'postmodern sociology', 'systems theory', 'sociotechnics', or 'rational choice'. Research Committee 45 'Rational Choice' is an extreme example of a new sociological sect, akin to the older sectarianism of 'critical theory'.[3] The parting president of the ISA, Immanuel Wallerstein, claimed instead a basic cohesiveness of sociology, a common 'culture of sociology'. This common culture meant to Wallerstein a sharing of elementary premises. He reminded the audience that only about 100 years earlier, the social science had still a common paradigm; he probably meant the belief in progress and the perspective of evolution. Then a fragmentation took place along three cleavage lines in looking at social reality:

(a) The emphasis on the past instead of the present separated history from the other (later) social science disciplines.

---

[1] Parsons, 1937.
[2] Eisenstadt with Curelaru, 1976, especially chapters 7 & 8.
[3] 'Sectarianism' is indicated as a designation for groupings that pay attention largely only to each other. For a diagnosis of such developments, see Merton, 1972.

(b) Accentuating the difference between Western ('civilized') societies and non-Western populations split off ethnology/cultural anthropology from other social science fields.

(c) Distinguishing markets—states—civil society lead to the separation of economics, political science, and sociology from each other.

Within this spectrum of the social sciences (plural) the special field of sociology has as its boundaries the already mentioned 'shared premises'. There is, according to Wallerstein, a continuing influence of the 'formative thinkers': Emile Durkheim, Karl Marx, and Max Weber. To each of these founding fathers Wallerstein assigns an axiom that presumably is central both to his own thinking and to the 'culture of sociology':

Axiom 1: There exist social groups that have explicable, rational structures (Emile Durkheim);

Axiom 2: All social groups include subgroups that are ranked in hierarchy, and are in conflict with each other (Karl Marx);

Axiom 3: To the extent that groups/states contain their conflicts, it is in large part because lower ranked subgroups accord legitimacy to the authority structure of the group, on the grounds that this permits the group to survive, and the subgroups see a long-term advantage in the group's survival (Max Weber).

Wallerstein summarizes what he sees as the core of the common culture:

> What I have been trying to argue is that the culture of sociology, which we all share, but which was strongest in the period 1945–1970, contains three simple propositions—the reality of social facts, the perennity of social conflict, and the existence of mechanisms of legitimation to contain the conflict . . .[4]

Unfortunately, this is an arbitrary claim for underlying communalities between authors who were either in conflict with each other (as Weber with Marx) or who studiously ignored each other (as Durkheim and Weber). It would be surprising if this imposition of hidden communalities were to be more successful than Parsons' grouping of Pareto, Durkheim and Weber around 'social action'. Citing classical authors in identifying cohesion as a core of shared knowledge is an approach that is not uncommon in sociology. Earlier, Anthony Giddens had maintained that Durkheim, Marx and Weber had "established the principal frames of reference of modern sociology".[5] Prior to that, Talcott Parsons based his notion of a core of the social sciences on

---

[4] Wallerstein, 1998: 17.
[5] Giddens, 1971: vii.

a trio of classics: Vilfredo Pareto, Emile Durkheim, and Max Weber.[6] A parallel effort in delineating the core of sociology through a larger listing of classical authors is the anthology by Dirk Käsler.[7] Obviously, such lists mirror the preferences of their compilers. Whether there is a widespread consensus is then open to question. To establish a more reliable base for such a definition of a 'common culture of classical authors', the ISA Program Committee in 1997 took a poll among ISA members who were asked to list five books published in the twentieth century that were most influential in their work. These were the ten most frequently cited publications by the 16% who responded (455 out of 2,785):[8]

ISA – Books of the XX Century. Top Ten

	Author	Title	% votes
1	Weber, Max	Economy and Society	20.9
2	Mills, Charles Wright	The Sociological Imagination	13.0
3	Merton, Robert K.	Social Theory and Social Structure	11.4
4	Weber, Max	The Protestant Ethic and the Spirit of Capitalism	10.3
5	Berger, P.L. and Luckmann, T.	The Social Construction of Reality	9.9
6	Bourdieu, Pierre	Distinction: A Social Critique of the Judgment of Taste	9.5
7	Elias, Norbert	The Civilizing Process: Power and Civility	6.6
8	Habermas, Jürgen	The Theory of Communicative Action	6.4
9	Parsons, Talcott	The Structure of Social Action	6.2
10	Goffman, Erving	The Presentation of Self in Everyday Life	5.5

There are many peculiar aspects to this list. First of all, it mirrors the college bookstores of American universities, as in the high marks for C.W. Mills. The top place for the posthumously published Economy and Society by Max Weber—to us the least readable and most opaque of his major publications—is probably due to the fascination of Talcott Parsons with part of the tome.[9] It is difficult to understand the presence of both Merton and

---

[6] In his later publication, Parsons had the ambition to resurrect a social science (singular): Parsons and Shils, 1954.

[7] Käsler, 1976–1978.

[8] Books of the XX Century. In: International Sociological Association. Bulletin 77, p. 17, 1998.

[9] Max Weber left the completed chapters of the total volumes envisaged without a definite order of content. The version of Economy and Society that is available in print was heavily edited by Marianne Weber, his surviving wife.

Habermas on the same list, or the absence of both Tönnies and Simmel. The most striking aspect of this shopping list of 'classics' is the absence of all the earlier star authors from the United States such as Ross, Ward, Cooley, Small, Sumner, Ogburn, or all of the Chicago School (Park & Burgess), as well as the rapid decline of Parsons. Conclusion: should there be a 'common culture of sociology', then this list does not support the claim. 'Common culture' could here only mean a shared eclecticism, defined by the marketing effectiveness of textbook publishers.

II

Fractionization does exist not only in sociology, but in most fields of scholarship, and especially in those that are empirical.[10] Economics as one of the older specializations within the social science (singular) is today divided into such specialties as economic policy, economic theory, econometrics—which in turn is subdivided into macro-economics—and the booming field of micro-economics. Political science knows such subdivisions as government, international relations, political parties, electoral behavior—to name but a few. And cohesion between these areas is not more pronounced than in the subfields of sociology. It is not the specialization as such that is worrisome but a lack of transfer of knowledge from one specialty into another. Insofar as disciplines under the broad umbrella of the social sciences are held together at all, it is not thanks to a core of 'classics', or a common culture, but rather to two elements: common concepts from a variety of unrelated theoretical orientations, and a common knowledge in methodology. The latter is currently in doubt with the ascent of mathematical models of individual choice on the one hand, and qualitative approaches on the other. Still, if one compares curricula in Western systems of tertiary education, concepts and methodology are shared knowledge even where they are not shared practice. Looking back to the decades of the 1960s and 1970s, politization appeared to be a means for forging a common identity in the social sciences, not the least in sociology. Remnants of this surface today, as occasionally happens in sociological meetings. However, when during the last congress of the ISA Maria Mies from a college in Cologne attributes the male use of force against females to the persistence of patriarchal capitalism, it is now no longer provocative but merely funny in an archaic way.

A lack of cohesion has frequently been diagnosed, and then used as an argument that the discipline as a whole was in serious trouble. Pitirim A.

---

[10] On the crisis in fields that are neighbors to sociology, see Olsen and Clague, 1971; Scholte, 1971; Graham and Carey, 1972; Hudson, 1973.

Sorokin criticized already in the 1920s: "At the present moment the field of sociology is overcrowded by a multitude of various and contradictory systems".[11] This is, of course, not the same argument as the lament over the fragmentation into dozens of specialities. Sorokin rather deplores what we now call—in accordance with Kuhn's revolutions in science[12]—the lack of a common paradigm. In the literature by sociologists criticizing fragmentation in sociology, these two perspectives are frequently confounded, although possible remedial actions would be quite different; and intellectually multiple paradigms have little to do with fragmentation of the domains of explanation.

Sorokin was much of an isolated prophet of impending doom, and the ascent of structural-functionalism rendered his warnings implausible. So pervasive was the influence of the network of Parsonians at the peak of their dominance that the much better informed and well argued criticism of the dominant paradigm by Sorokin, "Fads and Foibles", had no impact when published in the 1950s.[13] A main criticism of Sorokin unfortunately has not been adequately considered up until now, namely, that both structural functionalism and the micro-sociology of small group research mainly studied what we now call research artifacts. The criticism by C. Wright Mills that followed the same line of arguments, and supported it by analyzing a variety of empirical studies, fared much better.[14] In comparing the classics with contemporary research, he coined the concept 'abstracted empiricism' to characterize the presumed tendency to so delimit a subject area to be studied in order to fit the researchers concepts and tools. Probably this criticism received a wide resonance because it was phrased in the language of the cultural left—the favorable response to the small volume foreshadowing the later rise of the New Left. This was also a major factor in the success of Alvin W. Gouldner who attacked all 'mainstream approaches' of sociology in their claims to be objective.[15] The central concern of sociology should not be the explanation of existing conditions, but a kind of knowledge that empowers social change. Obviously, this is not a mere critique of the primacy of one dominant approach—for Gouldner, too this is structural-functionalism—but of all scholarship that pursues objectivity.

Multiple paradigms are quite common in fields of science, as e.g. in medicine, history, or even physics. Thus, Wallerstein's plea that all social scientists

---

[11] Sorokin, 1928: XVI. Critical assessments have accompanied sociology all along. See e.g. the influential Lynd, 1939.
[12] Kuhn, 1962.
[13] Sorokin, 1956.
[14] Mills, 1959.
[15] Gouldner, 1970.

should understand themselves as disciples of the same founding fathers is not only utopian but also unnecessary for the cohesion of sociology. By way of contrast, the claims of all versions of neo-Marxism and Critical Theory are indeed divisive, as they postulate entirely different criteria for the acceptance or rejection of propositions.[16] Given the influence of these approaches that require a commitment-before-the-facts, Busino and also Coleman are pessimistic about the chances of sociology to meet the standards for a respectable field of scholarship.[17] In his influential portrayal of the 'Classics' Wolf Lepenies shows them to be quite remote from the ideal of a detached scholar, and indeed Emile Durkheim and Max Weber were passionately involved in the controversies in their time.[18] However, this is of course not an argument against the validity of such work unless one were to confuse the genesis of an argument with its validity.

The explosion of specializations as well as the coexistence of partly incompatible paradigms do imperil the cohesion of any discipline, but by itself this is not yet destructive.[19] A standard central to any empirical discipline is cumulativeness. However winding, deviating, and wavering the development of a discipline might be, as time goes by positive knowledge has to increase—otherwise a field of scholarship is a failure, is at best some kind of literature. It is precisely the lack of cumulativeness that Turner and Turner diagnose even for sociology as practiced in the USA.[20] Every once in a while most sociologists read the same book by a sociologist. It is hard to imagine that those who learned the profession in the 1960s did not read at least some contributions by Talcott Parsons, and certainly also something by Robert K. Merton, Paul Lazarsfeld, and George Homans. If one had been enrolled in a French University, one could not have bypassed Raymond Aron, or as a student in Germany Ralf Dahrendorf's Homo Sociologicus. This short list is meant to be instructive in two ways: the publication dates end in the 1960s, and many of the concepts in these publications have indeed become part of our collective heritage. Examples are 'pattern variable', 'latent function', or in methodology the notion that a variable is an 'indicator'.

---

[16] This could also apply to some versions of a feminist sociology, or a Black Sociology in so far as they maintain that only females or blacks are capable of pertinent insights, by virtue of their ascribed properties.

[17] Busino, 1993; Coleman, 1990.

[18] Lepenies, 1985.

[19] The several meanings of crisis in sociology are analyzed in Eisenstadt with Curelaru, 1976: especially chapter 12 with copious footnotes on the subject matter.

[20] Turner and Turner, 1990.

It is more difficult to identify more recent publications that have had a similar impact. Two examples for the German speaking area are 'postmodern personality'[21] and 'postmodern society',[22] and the success of both concepts owes more to the 'Zeitgeist' than to scholarly evidence.[23] This is also true for a concept that was and is influential among the cultural intelligentsia, Schulze's 'Erlebnisgesellschaft'.[24] The one series of books that was similarly prominent in the majority of the social science audience and the cultural intelligentsia alike, are the debates between Jürgen Habermas and Niklas Luhmann on the centrality of communicative processes for the construction of reality, extending over a period of more than two decades.[25] It is of great significance that this concentration of attention occurred on the margin between social philosophy and cultural criticism. The lack of cumulativeness that Turner and Turner identify is not as complete as maintained, although this refers mainly to the demarcation lines between sociology as a scholarly field and various cultural concerns. We shall later try to identify the limits of cumulation in concept and theory—which will have to remain tentative. Before that we will be on firmer ground when we shortly examine the state of fragmentation due to specialization.

III

It was in the United States that specialization was first debated as a problem in the social sciences, for the obvious reason that only in the USA had the social sciences been institutionalized as a major area of scholarship already

---

[21] Inglehart, 1977. Since the publication of this report which became a cult-text with some of the younger sociologists, Inglehart was able to recruit a larger number of sociologists to participate in his 'World Values Survey'.

[22] Beck, 1986. A newer statement of his position emphasizing the conflictual nature of the new type of society is found in Beck and Sopp, 1997. Beck is close to Anthony Giddens in his later publications: Giddens, 1995.

[23] Inglehart, Beck and Giddens all share the distrust of 'instrumental rationality' and its presumed consequences as it was already argued in the Frankfurt variety of neo-Marxism. According to Adorno and subsequently Habermas, the dominance of instrumental rationality is not only a rationality in the sense of the enlightenment truncated into half, but a cage preventing human self-actualization. 'True' modernity is breaking these chains. The success of Inglehart, Beck, and Giddens with the cultural intelligentsia is due to this message of cultural criticism and not their more sociological arguments.

[24] A fairly literal translation would be society of experiences. What Schulze wants to convey is rather 'life as a continuous happening'. Schulze, 1992.

[25] Habermas, 1981; Luhmann, 1980–1989. This, by the way, is not the magnum opus of Luhmann but Luhmann, 1992; 1997; 1998a; 1999—all published with Suhrkamp in Frankfurt. Luhmann (1984) may be viewed as a sort of introduction to this theory of differentiated social systems.

in the 1920s. This social science was very much oriented towards social problems, with the perspective of application.[26] Such an action orientation greatly encouraged fractionation into unrelated specialities. Examples are social work, juvenile delinquency, urban sociology, migration. In some of these special fields, the disciplinary bond to general sociology was quite weak, and the label 'special field of social science' would have been more appropriate, even though the official institutional anchoring in sociology remained.[27]

To counter the tendency to unrelated specialization, and to keep alive the tradition of a family-likeness of all social sciences, the Social Science Research Council was organized in 1923. Seven professional associations affiliated themselves with the SSRC:

American Anthropological Association
American Economic Association
American Historical Association
American Political Science Association
American Psychological Association
American Sociological Association
American Statistical Association

The SSRC greatly encouraged the development of research methods as an element of cohesion between the various fields of the social sciences. Its emphasis on interdisciplinarity lead to a series of stock-taking studies, such as the analysis of the reasons for the erroneous pre-election polls of 1948,[28] or the re-examination of such major empirical studies as the Authoritarian Personality, or the American Soldier through groups of scholars selected by official professional committees.[29] Specialization by itself is not at odds with the cohesion of a field; it is rather the lack of cross-fertilization from one specialty to another. A case where such cross-fertilization did occur were investigations by teams around Robert K. Merton. The notion of 'anomie' fashioned by this team to explain aspects of juvenile delinquency was carried over into other contexts, and the same is true for such concepts as latent function, functional equivalence, or serendipity (for a discovery by

---

[26] This was very much encouraged by the influential Russell Sage foundation whose purpose was remedial work on social problems.
[27] Young, 1949: especially chapters II and III.
[28] Mosteller et al., 1948.
[29] The title of the series is "Continuities in Social Research", and suggests that more re-examinations of important monographs were envisaged than were actually published. The two important publications in the series were Stouffer (1950) and Christie and Jahoda (1954).

chance) by the same author.[30] Other concepts that traveled from one field of explanation to others were reference group or anticipatory socialization, or earlier informal organization. However, we have the impression that such cross-fertilization is declining, and that this is especially true for the last two decades of the 20th century.

Disciplines with heterogeneous fields of explanation—and that is certainly the case for sociology—can nevertheless maintain cohesion through several mechanisms. The most important one is an 'invisible college', a network of scholars who pay attention to each other, regardless of mutual dissent or agreement.[31] Sub-fields of sociology, organized in Research Committees (as in the International Sociological Association) or Sektionen (Deutsche Gesellschaft für Soziologie) or Groupes de travail are by now so often large that they constitute associations of their own. Such fields as voting research, family sociology, or social stratification can count world-wide on between 500 and 1,000 practitioners—a world of their own.

Another vehicle for cohesion can be periodicals, and in most languages they do function as a bond for sociologists—but no longer for international discourse in English. Publishers such as Sage have shown considerable ingenuity in inventing ever more specialties in the social sciences.[32] Nowhere is this crumbling of invisible colleges more evident than in the large congresses of the professional associations. In the 1950s, plenary meetings dominated; in the 1960s research committees for special areas were officially recognized; by now the largest part of a world congress of the ISA is organized by the Research Committees, and the audience for the former plenary sessions has been broken up into six and more parallel meetings, no longer deserving the label 'plenary'. There are many means for preserving or forging a new invisible college for sociology in general. Most sociologists subscribe to journals still central to the discipline, such as the American Sociological Review, and the American Journal of Sociology, or in Germany the Kölner Zeitschrift für Soziologie und Sozialphilosophie, or the Soziologische Revue, or the Zeitschrift für Soziologie. As it was common in the USA to publish the same research project several times over, in variations, one could be confident not

---

[30] Merton, 1957.
[31] Kuhn, 1962.
[32] An example for new periodicals as vehicles for fragmentation is the new periodical "Rationality and Society" as the house journal for the rather sectarian network 'rational choice'. Another example, since 1997, is the new periodical "Soziale Systeme", Leverkusen: Leske + Budrich. It is dedicated to just one approach in sociology, namely systems theory as practiced by the late Niklas Luhmann. It is safe to predict that this will advance the evolution of Luhmannisten into a sect insulating itself from other approaches by furthering a private language.

to miss any major research project by following only a limited number of journals. With the proliferation of journals, this is no longer as true as it was some decades ago.

Major attempts to hold the social sciences together were publications involving a representative assembly of scholars. An early example is the anthology by Gurvitch and Moore, but already at the time of publication a single volume had to be unsatisfactory.[33] The latest attempt to summarize the field in one publication was undertaken by Edgar and Marie Borgatta; it can be read as a demonstration that, without a selective perspective, the field has grown in such a way that today the broadest reference works are of only limited usefulness.[34]

The most useful overview in English is now the Annual Review of Sociology, published since 1975. Parallel to the Annual Review, a yearbook on comparative Social Research that is topically non-specialized, is also being published.[35] There were, of course, parallel efforts in other languages, of which we single out the Handbuch der empirischen Sozialforschung as possibly the most successful effort in any language.[36] Intellectually more stimulating were attempts to emphasize the relatedness of the social sciences (Plural). A path-breaking work was the Encyclopedia edited by David Sills.[37] It is currently being updated and broadened under the new editorship of Neil J. Smelser.[38] Similar monumental reference works exist in German and in Italian.[39]

Parallel to these encyclopedic endeavors were attempts to summarize findings for all behaviorally-oriented social scientists. Two most ambitious works should be singled out for attention: Hadley Cantril's compilation of survey results from 16 countries for the period 1935 through 1946;[40] and the attempted inventory of all scientific findings on human behavior.[41] The very fact that such ideas could be entertained and even put into practice should surprise a current reader: obviously, knowledge could not have been

---

[33] Gurvitch and Moore, 1945.

[34] Borgatta and Borgatta, 1992.

[35] The series began in 1978 and is published by JAI Press in Greenwich/Connecticut. The editors are sociologists from the University of Oslo/Norway.

[36] König, 1967. This is not a source on methods, but aims at representing sociology insofar as it is empirically grounded.

[37] Sills, 1968.

[38] Smelser, 1999; 2 supplements 2001. The encyclopedia is already completed and was originally to be distributed by Pergamon Press. The change of publisher caused a delay.

[39] *Handwörterbuch der Sozialwissenschaften*, 1965. This is the new edition of the classic *Handwörterbuch der Staatswissenschaften*.

[40] Cantril, 1951.

[41] Berelson and Steiner, 1964.

as dispersed then as we take for granted now. As it became unlikely that books, however monumental, could serve the purpose of integration within the social sciences, holding the field together via institutions appeared to many as an alternative. On the initiative of the late Stein Rokkan from Norway, the 'International Social Science Council' invited a number of young researchers from several countries to La Napoule.[42] The meeting was to outline a program for international comparative research, and parts of such a program were later implemented. More important, however, was the development of a network of scholars crossing national and disciplinary boundaries. In 1964 Szandor Szalai from Hungary joined the group and became the second anchor person. In 1964 the group met in New Haven (Yale University) to critically examine two major interdisciplinary and international projects: the 'Yale Political Data Program' and the 'Human Relations Area File'. In a critical discussion new methodological concepts were developed, such as the 'individualistic fallacy' (as the reverse of the 'ecological fallacy').[43]

The emphasis of the development shifts back to Europe. With funds from various foundations in addition to those of the ISSC, the Standing Committee for Comparative Research was founded in 1967. The main official purpose was training, during the course of which the 'Data Confrontation Seminar' was developed as a tool.[44] In parallel to this, five comparative projects were carried out, with the newly founded 'Vienna Center' of the ISSC as the institutional anchor. In 1972 the new 'invisible college' met in Budapest to analyze both the methodology and the substantive gains of the following international projects: the Time Budget Project, Juvenile Delinquency and Development, Images of the World in the Year 2000, the Jacobs and Jacobs study on values, and the Verba and Nie project on political participation.[45] Subsequently, Petrella, Rokkan, Scheuch and Szalai with the help of the ISSC and the Vienna Center organized seven international workshops and three European summer-schools. Some of the intellectual yields were the

---

[42] The ISSC was founded with the SSRC of the USA as a reference by UNESCO as a so called NGO, i.e. an advisory body that could take over functions that the ISSC were to allocate. At the time of the founding and well into the 1970s, the ISSC general assembly was a kind of parliament of the disciplinary associations in the broadly understood meaning of the social sciences. Later the ISSC was taken over by the national representations to UNESCO, and subsequently could no longer serve the functions reported below.

[43] This is not the place to elaborate on the content of the meetings and the projects. They are referred to here in order to illustrate the growth of an invisible college.

[44] Meant as a training device for advanced researchers, the Seminar analysed a major social science text—e.g. Lazarsfeld's "The Academic Mind", or Lipset's "Union Democracy"— and compared this with a secondary analysis of the original data from the respective studies.

[45] The publication on the Budapest conference, and at the same time the bridge to the various projects listed here, is Szalai and Petrella, 1977.

re-discovery of 'Galton's Problem' which led to important insights about the nation-state as a sampling frame.[46]

With the crumbling of the organizational frames in which these social scientists (from several disciplines and a number of countries) operated, personal trust had been established and remained as a basis for further cooperation. The growth of this group as sketched here was neither the first nor the last of such networks of personal trust; it is described here at some length only because this is the group with which the author is most familiar. Earlier networks developed immediately after the war, and partly through common experiences in the war: in either case, the emphasis was on the USA. One such group clustered around Samuel Stouffer as the organizer of social research for the American Army. Another such network committed to international comparisons included such names as Ruth Benedict, Daniel Lerner, Alex Inkeles, Hadley Cantril, Maurice L. Farber, Natalie Rogoff, Frederick W. Frey, Kurt W. Back and Mayone Stycos.[47] The network disintegrated for political and structural reasons. The political reason was McCarthyism: the publication which served as an intellectual center, the "International Journal of Opinion and Attitude Research" had as its editor Laszlo Radvanyi who somehow became the victim of a McCarthy hunt. Hadley Cantril grew too old, others were scattered around the US as a consequence of their professorial career which at this juncture in their biographies took preference over time-consuming research. Above all, they had not created significant international support, conducting their research in a manner that was later called 'safari research'.

The very lack of an institutional structure means that such networks need scholars who serve as referent figures. After the early deaths of Stein Rokkan and Szandor Szalai, and the transformation of the ISSC into an instrument of national UNESCO councils, other networks than theirs took the lead in interdisciplinary and international research. Ronald Inglehart's contention of a 'silent revolution' touched off a series of investigations into the stability of value orientations today. This culminated in a network of scholars in by now 43 countries, the 'World Value Survey'. Since 1981, the WVS has carried out an international survey every decade.[48] While the belief in the

---

[46] The then famous statistician Galton pointed to diffusion as calling into question the treating of individual cultures as context units. Whether the nation-state is the appropriate frame in explaining internal and external variations depends on the degree to which the nation-state as a political organization penetrated domains of life.

[47] Even earlier, international comparative work was not rare. Stuart C. Dodd and Jiri Nehnevasja identified for the period 1925 to 1955 1,100 comparative studies of some sort or other.

[48] The most recent publication of this group is Inglehart, 1997.

reality of an international value change is the bond of the group, it is remarkable for accommodating opposing interpretations within one network. Ronald Inglehart is basically still part of the 1968 cultural revolution mentality, while scholars clustering around the University of Louvain evaluate the results as indicating societal decay.

'BiG' is the abbreviation for the working group 'Beliefs in Government' including 15 scholars from 12 European countries. Sponsored by the European Science Foundation, the Group carried out the most voluminous secondary analysis so far, using the resources of Europe's oldest data archive, the Zentralarchiv at the University of Cologne. The guiding spirits of this group, whose substantive focus was the transformation of state's role in the second half of the twentieth century, were Max Kaase and Kenneth Newton.[49]

Of several other interdisciplinary and international networks that are currently active, we merely mention the following: a group around the Japanese scholars Chikio Hayashi, Masamichi Sasaki and Tatsuzo Suzuki investigating value changes over time, primarily between the USA and Japan.[50] A network analyzing national election over time in the major Western Democracies.[51] A group around Jay G. Blumler and Elihu Katz on mass communication research, all sharing the perspective of the 'uses and gratifications approach';[52] the 'International Social Survey Programme' begun in 1985 as a joint undertaking of general social surveys in the USA, Great Britain, Australia and (then) Western Germany. The ISSP conducts a survey every year in by now 25 countries, repeats question modules every five years, and offers internationally integrated data sets to the social science community at large.[53] Disciplinary boundaries do not matter in all of the cases mentioned above where scholars cluster around some charismatic persons, or some shared perspective in analyzing data and above all around a shared substantive concern. This clustering occurs side-by-side to processes of fractionization in fields of scholarship.

Disciplinary boundaries are primarily not of intellectual relevance but indispensable for examinations and subsequent certifications. By way of contrast, most research problems insofar as they refer to the real world we live in, call for a social science perspective, and at the same time for some substantive specialization. The often lamented specialization is heinous only

---

[49] Klingemann and Fuchs, 1995 (Vol. 1); Niedermayer and Sinnott, 1995 (Vol. 2); Borre and Scarbrough, 1995 (Vol. 3); van Deth and Scarbrough, 1995 (Vol. 4); Kaase and Newton, 1995 (Vol. 5).

[50] Hayashi, 1996.

[51] Mochmann et al., 1998.

[52] Rosengren et al., 1985.

[53] Becker et al., 1990; Jowell et al., 1993.

insofar as it leads to neglecting research on other subject matters and/or a perspective different from one's own. However, the multitude and effectiveness of networks such as the ones we presented here demonstrates that the decay of the social science is not as total as is often maintained. It was with this in mind that efforts are underway in several countries to develop an infrastructure for the social sciences in general. In the case of Germany, this began with the founding of the Zentralarchiv as a data bank primarily for the machine readable data from survey research in 1965. Later, two further units were added: the Informationszentrum as a unit providing online information on research in progress, and annotated bibliographical information along the line of the 'Sociological Abstracts' but without their disciplinary limitations; and ZUMA as a public service institute advising scholars in planning and conducting empirical research, plus fielding surveys of their own along the lines of NORC in the USA. In the meantime, these units in Cologne, Bonn and Mannheim are joined in a federation GESIS,[54] and GESIS in turn establishes links with corresponding institutions in other countries. The goal is the development of an international infrastructure for the social sciences in general, in order to provide an institutional base that makes research and publishing more cumulative than it is now.

IV

The particular character of both social science (singular) and the social sciences (plural) is due to the changing character of their object of explanation. That was not the perspective of those, however, who had the ambition to develop the social science (singular) as an analogy to the natural science (singular)—most successful at the time in what we now see as distinctive fields of their own, namely astronomy and theoretical physics. At the time of the Scottish Moral Philosophers, the world was understood by the scientists as a gigantic mechanism, and the task of science was to find out in which way the movement of the parts were interdependent.[55] The foremost ambition was the discovery of 'laws' that are valid without limiting time-space coordinates and preferably of a counter-intuitive kind. Claims of three of such 'laws' shall be singled out here.

---

[54] Mochmann and Scheuch, 1987; Mohler and Zapf, 1995.
[55] The identification of the Scottish Moral Philosophers as the founding fathers of the modern social sciences is controversial. We emphasize the scientific character of the social sciences in a narrow understanding of science, excluding social philosophy and all versions of 'Geisteswissenschaften'. With this orientation, the identification of the origins of the social science with the Moral Philosophers is not so controversial.

Adam Smith, with his analysis of the division of labor, meant to demonstrate such a mechanism that in the conventional wisdom of his time was counter-intuitive. Rephrased from a contemporary perspective, the pin-example was to prove that low skilled workers could outstrip in quantity and quality the work of skilled craftsmen. It was not the skill of the individual worker that caused the superior result but the intelligence of the organization of production. Thus, a social organization is superior to individual skills. In our context here, it is irrelevant that we now know that a division of labor[56] does not always have a superior effect; what matters here is the perspective of the author.

Central to the moral philosophy of Christian churches is the appeal to motives: good intentions are presumed to be the basis for good outcomes. Bernard de Mandeville argued against this idealism that in his times was associated with Shaftesbury, in a widely distributed essay, which was phrased as a satire but was meant seriously: Fable of the Bees or Private Vices made Public Benefits.[57] It is the self-interest of man, the very egoism, the quest for luxurious living, that stimulate social progress and in this way improve living conditions. Again, this is obviously not always the case but it is definitely accurate that motives that we depreciate in our private world may be beneficial in public affairs. Karl Marx later reaffirms as a general proposition that individual motivations do not determine social consequences.

Intuitively we know that countries should concentrate their production for exports on those fields where they are better than the importing countries. Wrong, argues David Ricardo: it is not the relative cost of production that governs trade between countries but rather differences in price structure internal to one country. For his 'Law of Comparative Advantage' Ricardo uses an example with a very high level of abstraction: assume that there were only two countries trading with each other—Portugal and England—and only two commodities for such a trade, namely wine and cloth. If production costs were lower for both commodities in one country, international trade would still be beneficial for the two; provided production costs for wine were very much lower in Portugal, while the edge in producing cloth was much smaller. In this case it would be advantageous for both countries to just concentrate on producing the commodity where they were doing better relative to the other commodity. Basically this is the same mechanism that is behind the current philosophy of 'lean production'. It is obvious that this works only if one abstracts from a variety of factors

---

[56] In this case, of the variety called in the German Historical School of economics 'Arbeitszerlegung'.

[57] First published in 1705 under the title *The Grumbling Hive*.

other than the relative cost differentials in production within one country, at this age of globalization especially from the mobility of capital.

The appropriate level of abstraction is a precondition for a successful application of laws in natural science. Predicting the fall of an apple by means of Newton's law of gravitation should be quite successful; predicting the falling of a leaf certainly not. The factors excluded by 'ceteris paribus' are in either case of differing weight—which is irrelevant for the validity of the law but quite relevant for its applicability. In the social sciences, the search for laws such as Newton's gravitational force has not been successful. To our mind, the notion of marginal utility comes closer to this ideal than the law of comparative advantage. The latter characterizes what we would like to call a 'universal tendency'.[58] The same applies to the tale of the bees—an early statement of what we now call 'latent functions'. Another such universal tendency in economics, incorrectly called law, are the Statements by Heinrich Gossen about satiation effects in demand.[59]

In sociology, Simmel's observation about the relations between the size of a group and group processes is also a universal tendency. It is not possible to express this function in exact numbers, and in view of the importance of such factors that would have to be excluded by a ceteris paribus statement, such an attempt would be of little use. Yet even though such universal tendencies lack the precision of many—although by no means all!—laws in the natural sciences, they are knowledge that is worth seeking. However, the search for universal tendencies were not and are not the glue that keeps the social sciences (plural) together. For quite a while, social change was a common experience, translated into a shared concern that provided some unity—even though it was later the development of different perspectives in dealing with the same concern that encouraged the drifting apart of the social sciences. The common experience of social change called for an answer to the question: will there be an end to change and what will social existence then be? Unlike the objects of explanation in the natural sciences, societies in the West were changing not as a temporary deviation from a state of equilibrium, or as a return to a 'golden age', but were

---

[58] 'Universal tendencies' we would like to call such 'laws' that on the one hand are not limited to specific situations defined by narrow time-space coordinates, but on the other hand are not strong enough in their effect to allow, in general, the neglect of time-space coordinates. Examples: the fragility of triads; if formal organizations, then there exists informal organizations—and the more detailed the formal organization the stronger the informal organization; the sharper the distinction between ingroup and outgroup, the stronger the group cohesion.

[59] 'Gesetz der Bedürfnissättigung', 'Gesetz des Genußausgleichs', 'Gesetz der Wertabnahme'. Gossen, 1854.

moving towards a new kind of human existence. Finding laws that govern this change, or at least developing concepts that aid a better understanding of change, remained a central concern until the beginning of the 20th century, the advent of what was then thought to be 'modern times'. Since then this common focus has largely gone, replaced by the attention for changes in particular areas—such as the family, the workplace, and urban structures. In recent decades, the foci of attention became even more narrow: instead of the family it became feminism, instead of the workplace self-actualization, instead of urban structure gentrification. A process is repeating itself that characterized American social sciences in the 1920s, when social problems instead of social structures became the objects of studies.

Economics as political economy could still be seen as part of social science, at least from Adam Smith to Karl Marx. This is also true for the Historical School of Economics in German-speaking areas, and of the Institutional Economics in the United States. Around 1870, however, a major shift in dealing with economic topics occurred when, instead of the classical accent on production, attention focused on demand and processes towards equilibrium. This coincided with the use of mathematics as a language in dealing with economic processes. Beside Lèon Walras, it was Carl Menger as the founder of the marginal utility school who advocated the concentration on market mechanisms in abstracto. Economists such as Schumpeter, in England John Maynard Keynes, or Paul Samuelson in the United States today, argued on a lower level of abstraction where e.g. personalities, time, and institutions mattered. By way of contrast, the current neoliberal approach ignores the fact that economic processes are embedded in social structures.[60] It is the high level of abstraction that greatly facilitated the development of theory. Having prices as the chief dependent variable in economics, and profit-taking as a dominant motive, makes sociology in comparison an undertaking where nearly everything is blurred.

Around the turn of the century, adherents of the Historical School of Economics such as Gustav Schmoller, and proponents of the Marginal Utility School such as Carl Menger engaged in the then named 'Methodenstreit'. The issue was phrased as 'Power or Economic Law'—can political interventions into economic processes be successful, or are the 'economic forces' of such strength that they will render interventions as useless.[61] Like most

---

[60] An example is the implication in analyses of international capital flows that the ideal state would be one of identical mobility of capital and labor. Critical of this abstraction is Scheuch, 1999.

[61] Schneider and Watrin (1973) look back at this controversy. This is only the second of the two methodological controversies in the German social sciences, the first one having as the issue value judgements in the social sciences.

fundamental cleavages in the social sciences, the issue was never settled, but the current heir to the Marginal Utility School, the Chicago brand of neoliberalism, quite self-consciously refuses to understand itself as part of the social sciences. Economic laws as expressed in the formal models are not only valid—which is self-evident as they are tautological—but are relevant regardless of social context. This is currently the dominant self-understanding in academic economics. In other social sciences that broke away from the social science (singular), the character of the process of emancipation from the formerly undifferentiated discipline is different: sometime between the last quarter of the 19th century and the end of the 1920s of the following century, the scope of explanation did narrow. At the same time, the level of abstraction in formulating findings was reduced, which later facilitated the application.

Emile Durkheim used ethnographic material in a sociological manner, and was in this way a social scientist (singular), even though he is treated as one of the founding fathers of sociology.[62] Subsequently, however, ethnology became the social science of pre-literate cultures, specializing on institutions central to cultures at this stage of development—such as kinship, religion, and localities. In spite of this narrowing, few if any general laws could be found,[63] but quite a number of generalizations with limited time-space coordinates were indeed identified.[64] The overlap between sociology and political science is greater in that part using quantitative research (such as voting behavior), but 'classical' political science emphasizes the institutional structure of large contemporary political systems. Changes in systems is a frequent, and system change a recurring, topic, but this usually has to be treated in a descriptive manner. The few attempts at stating general laws have not withstood the test of time. An example is the claim of Ferdinand Hermens about the effect of different electoral systems. Presumably proportional representation would result in political instability, while majority representation would ensure stability. If indeed there was a correlation between electoral systems and system stability, then this would hold only within time-space coordinates: for India the effects would be opposite to those for Italy.

---

[62] This is undoubtedly more due to his own insistence rather than his work, as he was not comfortable with contemporary modernizing societies.

[63] The search for these laws concentrated on kinship, e.g. whether double descent was related to status rules in the nuclear family, or post partem sex taboo to the regularity of food supply.

[64] For an attempt at finding general laws see Banks and Textor, 1963. We consider this attempt to be a failure, if judged by its own goals.

Since the second half of the twentieth century the speed of fragmentation in all the social sciences, and specifically within sociology, has increased. In 1988 an anthology surveyed the growth of specializations within the sub-fields of sociology.[65] In none of the sub-fields did the various authors detect a tendency towards convergence. To a degree this is a necessary response to the real processes of differentiation in modern societies.[66] However, there is at the same time a countervailing tendency, of modes of thought, in the social sciences in general. While agreeing that further specializations will occur, Neil Smelser sees this fragmentation being cross cut by approaches affecting several sub-fields, in this way creating a lattice structure in the social sciences.[67] The two dimensions of the lattice structure would be sub-divisions by domains, and then by approaches. One such perspective permeating a variety of specialties is the version of microeconomics called rational choice. For decades, economists from Chicago have tried to extend economic explanations to other fields such as politics (Anthony Downs) and sociology (Gary Becker).[68] The axiom is the stability of preferences within an individual; given the character of a situation such as costs and rewards insofar as the actor perceives this (bounded rationality), the analyst then predicts choices. The approach has been applied in a variety of fields such as family sociology, demography, juvenile delinquency, and even the sociology of religion. Rational choice is especially popular in Germany among sociologists in their middle fifties.[69]

An earlier but still active approach overarching fields of specialization is ethnomethodology.[70] Central to this approach is the search for certainties for the actors which are then revealed—often by shock tactics—to be cultural constructs. This approach, too is limited to micro-sociological projects. With the 1968 cultural revolution, versions of Marxism became ubiquitous. Already in the 1920s, left-wing and right-wing Hegelians dominated social science disputes.[71] Smelser is right in emphasizing these mechanisms of dedifferentiation that are effective parallel to the dominant elements of fragmentation. To the general public, or rather the intellectual minority paying attention to publications ranging from the New York Review of Books to Time Magazine, the social sciences are not a highly fragmented intellectual spectrum. Every so often a book claiming to define the character of

---

[65] Borgatta and Cook, 1988.
[66] Gerstein et al., 1988.
[67] Smelser, 2000: 46 ff.
[68] Becker, 1976.
[69] Critical of this perspective is Etzioni, 1988.
[70] Garfinkel, 1967.
[71] König, 1987: 230 ff.

our society and its direction of change gains a wide circulation. Herbert Spencer's "Principles of Sociology" (1876–1882) was such a publication, as was Edward Ross with "Social Control" (1901), Gustave le Bon with "Psychologie des foules" (1895–1899), Oswald Spengler with "Der Untergang des Abendlandes" (1918–1922), Ortega y Gasset with "La rebelion de las masas" (1929), David Riesman with "The Lonely Crowd" (1950). Viewed from a scholarly perspective this is a wild mixture of more or less respectable works together with highly speculative and unreliable contributions. More recently two bestsellers shaped the views of opinion leaders about the impact of television on our civilization: Marshall McLuhan's "Global Village" and Neill Postman with the catchy title "Amusing ourselves to Death" (which we obviously do not do). The success of such books is probably a combination of a sense of disorientation on the part of the readers plus a high degree of plausibility. Insofar as social sciences are motivated to influence the orientation of a general public, they have to accept that they can do so only by painting with a broad brush. Consequently, some tolerance is indicated if standards of academic pedantry are not always followed. However, if such 'broad brush' social science contributes to the disorientation of the general public and does this with the claim to be social science, the disciplines are called upon to correct this. A case in point are variations of the claim that in so called postmodern societies, social structures have melted away setting individuals free to fashion their life course.

A somewhat moderate variety of these postmodern imaginations is Giddens: "Structures should not be conceptualized as simply placing constraints upon human agency, but as enabling".[72] With such a general statement it is hard to take issue. Indeed, who treats structures merely as constraints? But issue needs to be taken with Giddens' rule 'A One': "Sociology is not concerned with a pre-given universe of objects, but with one which is constituted or produced by the active doing of subjects".[73] This suggests a society that is created every day anew "as a skilled performance on the part of its members".[74] Which means explicitly that society as a reality in which individuals have to find their way would have disappeared.[75] Exit sociology.

In Germany the most successful 'broad brush' publication by a sociologist during the last 15 years is "Risikogesellschaft" by Ulrich Beck.[76] As the

---

[72] Giddens, 1976: 161.
[73] Giddens, 1976: 160.
[74] Giddens, 1976: 160.
[75] Giddens combines his message of liberation from social structure with a projection of impending doom. Modernity (old fashioned) crushes familiar living conditions as a 'juggernaut', as an irresistable force. Thus we have no choice but to become postmodern.
[76] Beck, 1986.

title indicates it is in part a message of doom, as with Giddens, namely that our life is at risk due to conditions beyond our control. As in the case of Giddens, this is combined with a message of hope: we are liberated from structural constraints. It is due to conventional sociology emphasizing e.g. the importance of the nuclear family, that we do not use the opportunity to live a life of self actualization. Abolish sociology! In Germany the success of Beck's risk society with the cultural intelligentsia is indicating the distance of the cultural tradition of that country from social thought. As Ralf Dahrendorf points out, Beck's assertion that the new postmodern condition of society cannot be analyzed by sociology as we know it means that this sociology was relevant only for a short moment in time, nothing but an epiphenomenon; thus it never existed as a branch of science.[77]

This is a curious state of affairs. Diagnoses of the state of society formulated by social scientists in the 'broad brush' manner were influential in keeping alive the hope of the founding generation, namely that the social sciences provide a sense of direction. However, for the postmodern 'reflexive' social scientists this hope exists only if we no longer understand ourselves as social beings. More confusing still is the incessant production of new labels to denote a new type of society. A recent overview of diagnoses of our time offered, between the two covers of just one book, the following labels: postmodern; multicultural society; shameless society; multi-options society; disciplinizing society; individualized society; world society; post-industrial society; civil society; society at risk; market society; sensate society; information society.[78] It is not overspecialization, sectarianism or punctilious scholarship that endangers the ability of the social sciences to provide interpretation and directions for a general public; rather it is the eagerness of social scientists to be at the service of breathless media even if there is really nothing to report but safe neologisms.

If we step back from this media image of the social sciences and orient ourselves towards events designed to be representative of our discipline—presidential addresses, major symposia, laudations—we can realize that most of what was reported here after our sketching the process of fragmentation is intellectually quite marginal. In addition we need to understand that the accent on fragmentation is one-sided. Among the social sciences it is sociology where issues are debated again and again that are of concern to several—if not all—of the social sciences. Among the social sciences, it is only sociology where the scope of explanation is not pared down to facilitate

---

[77] Dahrendorf, 1989: 6.
[78] Kneer et al., 1997.

generalizations. This is both the drawback and the advantage of the discipline. There are first the issues in methodology such as the controversy about the place of value judgments, or the place of historical arguments, or application as a source of information. While the proper use and the character of formal models was the subject of controversies in several social sciences, the proper language of design and propositions was mainly the concern of sociologists. Last but not least, concepts central to the social sciences are developed foremost in sociology. This is obvious in the context of the structural functional approach (functional prerequisite, functional substitute, functional differentiation, multifunctionality). Whether this arena for topics cross-cutting disciplinary demarcations is called sociology is of secondary importance. Whatever label, we can agree with Dahrendorf: "Let me confess that since quite some time I call myself a social scientist singular".[79] Certainly not all the time, but recurringly, conditions appear that become the shared concern of several social sciences. On these occasions sociology tends to be the arena for discourses that transcend disciplinary divisions. 'How was national socialism possible in a developed society?' was such a topic in the 1940s. In view of processes of differentiation: 'what are the elements of cohesion', is a recurring issue.

And these days the processes of internationalization and globalization are a concern that is shared across disciplinary demarcations. Wallerstein's notion of world system was an important correction for the tendency to treat the nation-state as a unit of analysis. In tackling such large issues we realize that at these moments sociology is the heir to the social science (singular).

---

[79] Dahrendrof, 1989: 5.

34. TRANSITIONS IN POST-SOCIAL KNOWLEDGE SOCIETIES

Karin Knorr Cetina

Introduction: five transitions

This paper is an effort to identify significant 'structural' (underlying, hidden) features and transitions in a knowledge regime which I think should be included in any framework of analysis for what I call postsocial knowledge societies (Knorr Cetina, 1997). These features are 'structural' in the sense that they underlie a variety of surface phenomena. They also extend, and to some degree reverse, previous descriptions of knowledge in society. At the same time, many earlier assessments continue to be valid, and arguments for a complete break with the past would be difficult to make. Hence what I have to say will not generally discredit previous understandings but will suggest a more differentiated picture. In some cases, my proposals will challenge beliefs that lie at the core of the sociological imagination. The main point of the paper is one that has been blithely ignored, or one-sidedly interpreted (Lyotard, 1984: meta-narratives/anti-essentialism), in the recent literature on social and cultural transitions as it tries to come to grips with the end of industrial society. One important dimension of the transitions we are currently experiencing is the rise of knowledge as a determining feature in post-industrial and post-traditional societies. What the literature ignores are the changes in knowledge regimes that are part of these developments and shape their outcomes. Much of the literature is concerned with the economic and organizational consequences of the new importance of professional knowledge in society. It is less concerned with our models of knowledge with the features of knowledge processes per se, or with the forms of sociality entailed by knowledge structures. Transformation theorists discuss science, technology and knowledge as though these are ahistorical forces that are as stable and sociologically indefinable as a geological formation. Much of the literature also considers the economy as the primary destination of knowledge processes—a sort of obligatory landing-site (like Coney Island) through which knowledge has to pass and which determines its effect upon society.

In the following, I will discuss five points of departure from ruling ideas. The first brings up the institutional structure of knowledge and confronts the differentiation theory model with one that emphasizes the dehiscence

and integration of knowledge processes into social spheres. My second point
relates to the Baconian or instrumental view of knowledge as a general
model, which I suggest should be replaced by a constructive model of knowledge and science. The third point of departure shifts the kaleidoscope again
and extends the second. It concerns the shift from a model of technology
as an important factor in the simplification of work and in inducing the
alienation of the worker to a model that emphasizes work complexification
and identification. My fourth point extends the second further by proposing a notion of knowledge entities as indefinite and relational objects and
by demanding the inclusion of these objects into conceptions of the social.
I will conclude by discussing a cultural dimension of current transitions,
which is the concern with transparency. It reflects, I will argue, a wider
shift from an exclusionary regime of knowledge to a more inclusionary one,
that can be witnessed in many social areas.

First transition: from institutional differentiation to dehiscence

Ideas about linkages between knowledge and society are not new in sociology. In the past, they have been bound up primarily with transformation
theories and their views on modernization and industrialization. A number
of seminal commentators have discussed how modernity depends on knowledge. One only needs to recall Marx's conception of technology as a productive force, or the relationship Weber saw between modernization and
rationalization, which he also specified in terms of the professionalization of
technical competence and in terms of knowledge-based organizational structures (Weber, 1976: 128 ff., 565). In the phase of sociological theorizing that
followed, the themes of rationalization and technology did not disappear
from work that unfolded under the Marxian and modernization theory
rubric. At the same time, though, differentiation theory forcefully brought
another picture of knowledge in society into theorizing, which henceforth
became central to the field. As Alexander has shown, the modern notion
of social change as differentiation may be traced back to Durkheim and his
ideas that societies that were once mechanically organized gradually moved
toward a greater specialization of functions and their institutional separation. It was Parsons who then turned these ideas into a sweeping theoretical argument according to which differentiation is the "division of a unit
or structure in a social system into two or more units or structures that
differ in their characteristics and functional significance for the system"
(Parsons, 1971: 26). Accordingly, the undifferentiated state is the 'primitive'
condition, while in the course of evolution, differentiation takes place not

only between roles and specialized functions but also within specialized functions, between levels of action and organization of action around differentiated objects of orientation—as when early modern science emerged, as Luhmann has it, from the splitting-off of procedures for establishing scientific truth from the conventions for producing matters-that-are-the-case within civil conversation (this account is wrong; see Shapin, 1994: 120, for a genuinely historical account). Luhmann has gone furthest among differentiation theorists in emphasizing the auto-poetic and regulative autonomy of functional subsystems that have become historically 'liberated' from the meddlesome interference of other systems, particularly religion. Science, of course, is one of these liberated systems (Luhmann, 1990).

Differentiation theory presents a sophisticated picture of the evolution of modern society. It is also fair to say that differentiation theorists, from Parsons onward, have paid some attention to integrative process as illustrated by the concept of interpenetration (Münch, 1990: 455; an example is the penetration of family ties by positive law), structural coupling (Stichweh, 1994) or dedifferentiation (e.g. Lechner, 1990). Yet at the same time, these notions somehow bypass the very real postmodernist concerns with fragmentation, the pluralization of life-worlds, and with ambiguity. The pluralization of life worlds is not a question of functional differentiation, but of the reduplication of holistically conceived centers of activity. Ambiguity erases sharp distinctions between differentiated media and spheres, and the notion of fragmentation lacks the connotations of evolutionary adaptiveness and advantage that lend glamour to differentiation as a functionalist idea. Even the very plausible idea of increased specialization appears under attack from notions of 'functional flexibility' in the workforce, decreased standardization, and requirements on behavior that are not coded in terms of task-specific performance but in terms of properties of culture and the human body, such as gender (Lash and Urry, 1994: 201). While these ideas clearly lack the coherence of the integrated theoretical framework that differentiation theory presents, they are at the same time suggestive of the weaknesses of that framework.

One of these weaknesses concerns knowledge and can perhaps be summarized as follows. Differentiation views suggest that throughout history, each sphere of society gradually becomes more independent of all others. This also implies that the power of each sphere over others is markedly diminished; no sphere dominates others; each constitutes itself through its own organizational choices. The picture suggests that all spheres co-exist in parallel, on equal terms. This view challenges sweeping distinctions like that between an infrastructural economic base of society and a (cultural) superstructure that stands in some general and obscure relationship of dependence to the infrastructure. But it also ignores the pervasive everyday phenomenon of coalitions and conjunctions between spheres that are institutionally separated; and historically specific processes of interlocation and super ordering on a larger scale that can be analyzed concretely in phase-specific studies of social change. The implication of much of the current thinking on societal transitions outside differentiation theory is, in my view, that we experience such a phase in regard to knowledge. Consider the widespread argument that knowledge transforms the economy from the inside out, turning an industrial economy into one that is knowledge-based. In a nutshell, the argument here is that knowledge has become a productive force that to some degree replaces capital and labor (Bell, 1973; 1987; Drucker, 1993). The immediate impact of this are shifts in the division of labor, the development of specialized occupations, the emergence of new enterprises, shifts in economic sectors (from a production economy to a service economy) and sustained growth. Similar changes have been diagnosed with regard to individual life. For Giddens, knowledge provided by expert systems acts as a medium of interpretation and reflection in what he calls post-traditional societies. Though Giddens allows that institutions also become reflexive, his most developed account so far concerns individuals and their needs for ontological security—for how we can cope with the psychological and social hazards of contemporary life (see also Lash, 1994: 117). In contemporary life, the answer is that we maintain reasonable levels of stability in our personalities and in society through the mediation of expert systems. Hence, a world of intensified reflexivity is a "world of clever people" (Giddens, 1994a: 7), of individuals who engage with the wider world (and with themselves) through information produced by specialists which they routinely interpret and act on in the course of everyday action.

The infusion of expert systems into daily life and the increased dependence of production systems on expert systems can be described on a more general level as the dehiscence of knowledge processes into society. The latter suggests the unboundedness of the process and the uncertainty of its outcomes. Sociology so far has not come to terms with the structures and significance of this discharge; it continues to treat questions of knowledge in society in terms of the premises set by Bell, for whom social patterns seem to have been incidences of economic organization. Sociological investigations of knowledge in society have also been hampered by a second problem. The weakness of differentiation-based models of knowledge has been that they sustained a picture of knowledge as functionally confined to one institution—science—and as specialized to the degree of being inaccessible to sociological investigation. These views have played into the hands of (and been informed by) philosophical conceptions of science as demarcated from the rest of social life through the logic of scientific procedure and the progress of science. It was, curiously enough, a model that the specialty devoted to the study of knowledge—the sociology of science—also bought and let itself be confined by (e.g. the Mertonian paradigm of science). The confinement has been overcome in recent years in regard to the empirical investigation of science, but not in regard to its treatment as differentiated from, rather than integrated with, social life. We have opened up knowledge processes to empirical investigation and described their multiple rationalities and interdependencies with social factors inside science. But we have not opened up societal processes in regard to how knowledge structures operate within them, nor made a serious sociological attempt to come to terms with the significance of these structures. It seems plain that these processes comprise many sets of elements that are not of one kind (Giddens points out one set of elements), and that must first be distinguished and identified before anything like a theory of knowledge societies becomes plausible. With respect to differentiation ideas, what seems plain is the historical outdatedness of a model that separates knowledge and science epistemically, institutionally, and functionally from other social spheres and that ignores the (new) defining impact of professional knowledge structures on social structures and relationships. Dehiscence includes the insertion of expert systems in most areas of social life, the transformation of some systems into expert systems (an example are production systems; Lash and Urry, 1994: 108), and the replacement and overlaying of some social structures (e.g. social authority structures) by knowledge and information structures.

Second transition—from Baconian science to constructive science and knowledge

Let us now consider a second transition, which spells out the model of science and technology which I think fits well with, and perhaps enhances, the discharge of knowledge into societies. The model that informed Berger et al. (1974) and which still informs discussions today, if only because we lack an articulated alternative, can be traced back to Francis Bacon. Bacon is thought to have been the first who, at the turn of the 17th century, identified the aims of science as the control and domination of nature. He provided a forceful vision of the scientific impulse that was both provocative in rejecting all major traditions which preceded him and aggressive in promoting his own view. His view appears to have been that science was power, and the moral responsibility of men was to assume and exercise this power. His metaphors of the 'command of nature in action' were interlaced with sexual images of penetrating, subduing and mastering nature as 'she', which have been subtly analyzed by Fox Keller (1985: 33 ff.). What concerns us here is less this imagery than his notion that man needed to make nature sub-serve his purposes (Fox Keller, 1985: 54). More than a century later, Robert Boyle endorsed this vision with his plea against 'the veneration men commonly have for what they call nature', a nature which he saw as material and composed of 'inferior creatures' over whom men ought to rule (Shapin and Schaffer, 1985). As many observers of science have argued, the subsequent history of science bears out these values. The most recent attempt to theorize the Baconian model of science in a contemporary idiom is Habermas' (1971) notion that natural science is not characterized by distantiated, disinterested, objective reflection but rather by the active interest in a kind of knowledge that is technically usable. What Habermas sees as institutionalized in science and technology is a particular form of action, which he calls instrumental, and which he distinguishes from communicative action. The latter is informed by unique individual experience and oriented toward sustaining inter-subjectivity through the usage of hermeneutic procedures. The former involves replicable experience, means-end rationality, the separation between theory and data, and language disengaged from interaction and used monologically in the description of objects.

I do not wish to provide a detailed refutation of such claims which seem irrelevant to understanding science in practice, as 20 years of sociological research on contemporary science have now taught us (e.g. Latour and Woolgar, 1979; Knorr Cetina, 1981; Collins, 1985). Nor do I wish to deny that science and technology can be used to control and exploit our natural environment. I rather want to draw on the research just mentioned to point out a different understanding of the knowledge areas that have been investigated. This is the view of knowledge as constructive rather than merely descriptive of nature. In other words, nature is not the only and perhaps no longer the main referent of science. Constructivism has been the dominant approach in the investigation of science in the last decades. I want to maintain that ideas about the constructed character of scientific reality are rooted not only in sociological thinking but in existence, in the phenomenon that science has become more constructive. A number of scientific fields such as economics or artificial intelligence, but also natural sciences such as high energy physics and molecular biology, do not simply reflect, or even aim to reflect, the world 'out there'. Rather, they quite literally create the phenomena they investigate. High energy physics spends much of its time on creating and exploring particles which simulate situations at early stages of the universe, but are not now found anywhere in nature. In this area, we can distinguish at least three levels of 'reality' which are all alternate with respect to the concurrent reality of nature Bacon must have had in mind: that of the machine generated particles, which is an endogenous laboratory reality, that of technical simulation, and the intended, supposed and internally regenerated reality which resides somewhere in the early stages of the universe and hardly left any archeological traces. You will notice that Bacon's reality does not figure at all in this picture. It is also interesting that measurements in this area are curious hybrids which include yet another different province of meaning—theory: they are intersections of traditional empirical data (on created objects) with simulations of the measurement instrument and with theoretical predictions. The modified new life forms that molecular biologists create are, on the one hand, technological inventions, and simultaneously research instruments and study objects within an empiricist program. In these cases, traditional empirical attempts at representing the world have become inter-articulated with procedures of making or simulating 'nature' in striking ways. Constructivity implies this specialization and differentiation of realities in science, when whole areas of alternate provinces of meaning, of alternate realities are created and inhabited by research. It also implies the constructive clearing, knowledge-extending 'application' of knowledge in the work place and other fields.

Third transition: from mechanization & alienation to
complexification & identification

Consider now a third transition. The view I am going to argue against is conveniently summarized in a book by Berger et al. (1974) which seeks to uncover a core dilemma of modernity, the 'homelessness', or, in a more recent idiom, the 'disembeddedness' of modern human beings. Berger et al. conceive of modernization in terms of the growth and diffusion of a set of institutions "rooted in the transformation of the economy by means of technology" (Berger et al., 1974: 9). Following Weber and many others, the authors see the institutions of technological production and bureaucracy as the primary carriers of modernization. They also identify secondary carriers, such as urbanization and the socio-cultural mobility and pluralism that comes with it. With these arguments, the book situates itself firmly within a tradition of works that attempt to identify the common characteristics of (advanced) industrial societies. Where Berger et al. break new ground is in relating these characteristics to people's reality definitions and to what they call structures of consciousness that reflect the institutions they describe. The causal mechanism at work is the abstractness of technological production which carries over into everyday life. "Everyday life in just about every one of its sectors is ongoingly bombarded," the authors say, "not only with material objects and processes derived from technological production but with clusters of consciousness originating within the latter" (Berger et al., 1974: 24, 39). What Berger et al. have in mind are such features of technological production as its machine-like functionality, so that the action of the worker becomes an intrinsic part of a machine process, its lack of uniqueness or broad reproducibility by anyone having comparable training, its measurability, the dividability of the work into components that seem freely exchangeable, and the separation of means from ends, such that the work is abstract and divorced from the product. The suggestion is that the logic of the production process also dictates the technological management of social relations and causes the identity of others at the workplace and of oneself to become divided and anonymized. The overall consequence of this overhaul of the self and the carried-over effects of technological production into private life is not only exploitation, but alienation. In a society in which the work of a vast number of people is structured around technological production, a vast number of people may suffer from no longer recognizing themselves in their work, in the anonymity of their personal relations, and in their own divided and alternating self.

The alienation of the worker, and his or her commodification and exploitation, have often been associated with industrial society that centers around technological production. Berger et al. wrote in the 1970s, and their account presumably still captures something of the spirit of factory work even today, when workers salaries are high in some countries and workers benefits have reduced exploitation. But is the work of a vast number of people still structured around technological production? As we know, no more than 18% of the work force are today employed in the production sector in most countries, and the percentage is less in advanced capitalist economies. The change from a production economy to a post-industrial, third sector economy may not have been evident 30 years ago but it is now, and the rise of knowledge-based industries further changes the picture. The question we must ask is whether the model Berger et al. use to describe technological production can be transferred to knowledge-based work.

My answer to both questions is that we must change these models if we are adequately to grasp current knowledge regimes. Consider work. The process of technological production that Berger et al. point out, has also been described by Weber and his followers, as a process of rationalization as understood in terms of efficiency, which involves the reflexive consideration of existing processes with a view to how they can be reorganized such as to make them more purposeful and time and cost-effective with respect to their goals. Mechanization is a dimension of this process; machines can often perform repetitive tasks much faster and more effectively than human beings. Job-simplification entailing the de-skilling of workers (Braverman, 1974) is another aspect; breaking up work into smaller components can achieve higher volumes of production, and Ford's assembly line, as documented by Chandler (1977) and others, is the classic example. Hage and Powers (1992: 48 ff.) have emphasized that rationalization is not defined by the addition of new knowledge but by better ways of organizing what is known. Seen in this way, rationalization contrasts sharply with what they call complexification: the countervailing process that is driven by the accumulation of additional knowledge and the adding in of more demanding activities. While it is doubtful that Weber and others meant rationalization to exclude new knowledge, the distinction Hage and Powers make is nonetheless important in understanding work related transition in knowledge regimes. For Hage and Powers, complexification is the prevailing pattern of social change in post-industrial societies. The pattern is associated with the replacement of simple machines by sophisticated instruments in the work process, with performance criteria that relate not so much to speed, quantity and large volume but to quality, innovation and personalized service, with fewer specific rules and more room for human agency, and with an emphasis on information search and the proliferation of specialization in the sense of an upgrading of skill levels for most roles and the addition of new roles that reflect the growth of knowledge (Hage and Powers, 1992: 50 ff.). Hage and Powers also extend these ideas to the self, arguing that as role-sets become more complicated, they require and sustain more complex selves that can simultaneously entertain different identities with equal salience and have the ability to handle change in the definition of roles.

Let us recall that Berger et al. were also concerned with the self, but took it to be negatively marked by the role divisions and alternations technological production brought with it. Hage and Powers offer a fresh perspective linked to the different potential requirements of knowledge and technology in a post-industrial workplace. What lends support to these ideas are empirical studies of company employees which suggest that for many work is no negative experience, but rather the place where they not only spend most of their time but also feel emotionally more at home than in their actual home life (Hochschild, 1997). We need not accept all of the assessments and predictions in these studies to appreciate the attempt to address different work requirements and attitudes. It is plain that the idea of complexification in Hage and Power's study is too much of a simple reversal of earlier models of routinization and simplification; and any assumption of a linear increase of complexity is clearly implausible. On the other hand, if we read these notions as an indicator of divisions in work attitudes associated with changes in the role knowledge and technology plays in professional, service and factory work, then these claims take on a different meaning. They signal a subtle but significant transformation in dominant sociological (and everyday) conceptions of the relation between work and technology/knowledge and between work and how it relates to the self. One can relate this transformation to the shift from a model of instrumental action to one that is constructive. I have argued that this shift is also visible in science, where the Baconian model of understanding science needs to be replaced by a constructive model.

Fourth transition: from social relations to object relations

I would now like to relocate these themes in a more general relational framework, moving away from the sociology of work. It will be recalled that Berger et al. made a serious attempt to understand the technological production in terms of its cognitive style. They included the technological object of work in their treatment, however inadequate we might think this treatment has been. In this section, I also want to address certain qualities of knowledge objects which I think are relevant to an understanding of knowledge regimes and knowledge societies. My argument is that knowledge objects ought to be considered not only as the goal and target of professional work but as relational objects, which is what they are in the areas they come from, science. As relational objects, they must be included in our concept of sociality. As more and more objects in work and everyday life take on features of epistemic objects, they make relational demands and offer relational opportunities to those who deal with them. In an earlier paper (Knorr Cetina, 1997), I argued against concepts of individualization and disembedding which focus exclusively on human relations, as practically all of these concepts do. I said that these concepts ignore the degree to which the disembedding of the modern self has been accompanied by the expansion of object-centered environments which situate and stabilize selves, define individual identity just as much as communities or families used to do, and which promote forms of sociality that feed on and supplement the human forms of sociality studied by social scientists. Objects may also be the risk winners of the relationship risks which many authors find inherent in contemporary human relations (e.g. Coleman, 1993). To press the point, one might argue that human beings compete with objects as relationship partners and embedding environments, and that this is increasingly so as objects become information products and take on particular qualities. We might also argue, following suggestions by Calhoun (1992) and Wise (1993), that objects increasingly mediate human relationships, making the latter dependent on the former.

What qualities turn the bleak and black-boxed mechanical technologies Berger et al. saw in the workplace into knowledge objects? The first point to note is that objects of investigation in science are characteristically open, question-generating, and complex. They are processes and projections rather than definitive things (Rheinberger, 1992). Observation and inquiry reveals them by increasing rather than reducing their complexity: think of a picture of the cell approximately 50 years ago and compare this with a picture of it now, which summarizes the increase in complexity. In other words, objects of knowledge seem to have the capacity to unfold indefinitely. In this sense they lie at the opposite end from the tools and commercial goods which are ready-to-hand or to be traded further. These tools and instruments have the character of closed boxes. Objects of knowledge, on the other hand, are more like open drawers filled with folders extending indefinitely into the depth of a dark closet. Since objects of knowledge are always in the process of being materially defined, they continually acquire new properties and change the ones they have. But this also means that objects of knowledge can, as a rule, not be fully attained, that they are, if you wish, never quite themselves. What we encounter in the research process are representations or stand-ins for a more basic lack of object.

I want to emphasize that what I just said about objects of knowledge in research also holds true for technological objects, which should not be equated with tools like the hammer Heidegger (1962) used as an example. Many of today's technologies are simultaneously things-to-be-used and things-in-a-process-of-transformation: they undergo continual processes of development and investigation. Computers and computer programs are typical examples; they appear on the market in continually changing updates (progressively debugged issues of the same product) and versions (items marked for their difference to earlier varieties). These objects are both present (ready-to-be-used) and absent (subject-to-further-research), the same and not the same.

Within science, objectual relationships—engagements with objects of the kind just described—define knowledge processes. These engagements are emotional, even libidinal, and I have elsewhere attempted to show how the open, unfolding character of knowledge objects uniquely matches the 'structures of wanting' by which one can characterize selves. The basic idea is that objects provide for the continuation of a chain of wantings through the signs they give off of what they still lack; and subjects (experts) provide for the possibility of the continuation of objects which only exist as sequences of absences, or as an unfolding structure. What we have here is a basic mutuality, and at times solidarity and reciprocity, that can fill in sociological frames for conceptualizing sociality. I maintain that the binding components of experts' object ties make it plausible to construe these relationships as forms of sociality rather than only as work or instrumental action. The wider relevance of the shift in interpretation I proposed lies with the assessment that object relationships of the sort exemplified in knowledge culture are on the increase in contemporary society. As objects in everyday life become high technology devices, some of the properties these objects have in expert contexts may carry over into daily life, turning an instrument or a commodity into an epistemic everyday thing.

One needs to stress that the concept of an object-centered sociality needs to be construed broadly, also bringing into view aggregate levels of sociality that are object-centered. One can start with the notion of integration, which in the social sciences is almost universally understood in terms of human bonds forced through normative consensus and shared values. This form of integration has become highly problematic, given the increased cultural and ethnic consciousness and diversity of nation state populations. As common values are no longer the outgrowth of shared traditions and cannot be imposed by some authority, integration via norms and values appears less and less effective. Peters (1993) has argued that integration may also ensue from other factors, for example from the joint prosperity which binds large segments of the population into society. Joint prosperity significantly involves objects, whose role in bringing about integration may need to be spelled out. In a global context, basic webs of relationship that link people together include global objects to which participants are oriented and which have to be included in any account of social integration. One object of this sort familiar to all investors are global financial markets; they are thoroughly suffused with knowledge and in fact representational; they are never the same; and they constantly demand attention and engagement and the readiness to find out more about them. A second object along these lines is the world wide web; a third in more specialized contexts are massive technological instruments around which groups form (e.g. a high energy physics accelerator and detector).

It is not insignificant that the objects just mentioned all display qualities of epistemic things, of things that bind through their indefiniteness, incompleteness and the informational opportunities they offer and the knowledge demands they make. A market needs to be continuously observed by those who want to succeed with it. It is the continuity of knowledge and of moving in the know that makes a market-maker and reciprocally constitutes the market. I do not deny the phenomenon that certain forms of relatedness with and through objects have always been with us; what I maintain is that

these forms are on the rise in societies in which the spread of expert contexts and knowledge cultures throughout society is significant. A serious
attempt to come to terms with the meaning of the discharge of these cultures into society must also consider the relationship level, or what knowledge societies imply with regard to the very concept of sociality.

Fifth transition: from exclusionary regimes of truth to transparency regimes

I now want to turn to a public aspect of current transitions, one that concerns the 'epistementality' of beliefs and attitudes about the correct distribution of knowledge and the 'naturalness' of access to it, and which also
takes form within more or less institutionalized structures. What I have in
mind refers not only to a preoccupation but also to a whole set of occupations, of roles and organizational arrangements which attempt to implement a particular epistemic attitude but which also give rise to it, enhance
it, reinforce it. The attitude I mean is best circumscribed by a native term,
that of transparency. What we can observe on several levels and in several
areas of public life at the turn of the millennium, is a discourse on transparency and the striving to implement it. I will argue that this interest in
transparency must be seen in the wider context of the displacement of exclusionary regimes of truth by inclusionary frameworks.

Consider first the exclusionary framework. By an exclusionary framework
I mean any setting or system in which boundaries count and are socially
accentuated in regard to the distribution of knowledge. Industrial settings
in which knowledge is not published, but restricted to being used within
the firm or patented, constitute an example. But on another level, academic science also offers examples of such boundaries. There, specialized journals and the esoteric language of specialized disciplines usually prevents
'outsiders' from participating in scientific communication. On a more general level, exclusionary regimes of knowledge seem to wish to derive power
effects by limiting access to the special knowledge they produce or acquire.
Quite obviously, much of the information policy in complex organizations
is, and used to be, based on limiting access to knowledge and on allowing
certain categories of participants to acquire information, which others then
can obtain only through privileged contacts, information leaks, gossip and
so on. As a consequence, many conflicts and struggles in organizations center
around information exclusions; these are familiar problems in all organizational life. It should also be noted that where social order is territorialized—
where social organization involves the expansion and proliferation of social
spaces for purposes of task fulfillment and communication—knowledge will

have an embedded affinity to place; it not only originates in a particular place, but to some degree will be shaped by the occurrences and facilities of the place. In these cases, the transfer and distribution of knowledge beyond the place involves conscious effort, for example strategies of summarizing and representing information. Territorialization and the existence of boundaries are thus two conditions which imply and facilitate exclusionary regimes. But systems differ in the degree to which they attempt to counteract such exclusions, and in the degree to which social organization is spatial organization.

Exclusionary systems can be compared today with more inclusionary frameworks. These frameworks are, in a Foucaultian idiom, regimes of truth in the same sense in which exclusionary systems fit the category: both derive power effects and seek power from knowledge. Foucault saw 'truth' as a 'system of ordered procedures for the production, regulation, distribution, circulation and operation of statements' and he held this system to be linked to power. His notion of a 'regime' of truth was meant to capture the phenomenon that 'systems of power' produce and sustain systems of truth, and effects of power induce and extend it. In my analysis, inclusionary systems gain power from laying open the information they gain. In the area of 'private life', the (post)modern individual may derive trust and other benefits from permitting others to see and understand his or her personal predicaments. The Goffmanian distinction between front stage and backstage then no longer holds, the backstage is drained from the meaning content it once had as the sphere of intensely private activity and experience. Switching from an exclusionary to an inclusionary information policy in organizations can mean actively employing strategies of information disclosure instead of relying on position and authority in directing members and in extracting conformity with what one proposes. In a university, making student evaluations of courses publicly available is an unpleasant but effective way of sanctioning those whose marks are not excellent. On trading floors of investment banks, disclosing the earnings of every trader for the bank at the end of the day is an equally effective (though not generally used) information tool. Organizations may also become more inclusionary by simply reducing the number of internal environments or social spaces they generate. This is exactly what has happened with the flatter, leaner, network-organization which is the outgrowth of recent industrial restructurings. The shift toward inclusionary knowledge is not, however, a uni-linear development in which there are no reversals or which is all-encompassing. What we do witness today is a struggle between the two knowledge policies and regimes. The notion of transparency, and the call for greater transparency epitomizes this struggle. It is not, one must emphasize, the force behind, or the reason for, a trend towards a more inclusionary regime of truth in some areas. It is, however, closely bound up with it, pressing and expressing a tendency that has independent roots.

There are two domains upon which the demand for more transparency is very apparent and perhaps most striking. One concerns national economies in relation to an international financial system and the effective functioning of global capital markets. The other concerns companies and their management in relation to their financial performance. In both cases, transparency demands are made by outside groups and agencies upon the economies and companies. And in both cases. these demands are sustained and carried forward by the advent and institutionalization of what might be called 'third roles' in dyadic relationships, the roles of (interested and professional) observers. On the level of national economies, international financial institutions like the IMF and the World Bank or the Institute of International Finance as well as credit rating agencies and 'working groups' play these roles. On the level of companies, analysts located at financial institutions, but also independent analysts and research firms, as well as accounting firms, are observers. On another level, though, shareholders are observers of the organizations whose shares they hold, though they also look to analysts for the information they require. Producer services take on the respective roles, but they are clearly not the only relevant agencies. Let me try to summarize some features that I consider relevant here. The transparency regime of truth I briefly sketched implies the following features:

1. It implies the institution of a set of 'third roles' and agencies centered on the observation of certain national and international actors and their performance and dyadic relationships (similar to Simmel's 'stranger' who has a permanent presence but is also a permanent outsider in a social context; Simmel, 1908).

2. These roles and agencies take on various 'corporate' forms, which range from legally established institutions taking on observational activities to short-term task forces and working groups spelling out the rules of transparency and relatively informal groups of professionals acting as 'watchers' (native term) in a particular arrangement. Recent examples include the Working Group on Transparency in Emerging Finance Markets of the International Institute of Finance in Washington (Report March 1999), a similar Working Group on Transparency and Accountability of Finance Ministers and Central Bank Governors of the group of 22 industrial and major borrowing countries (Report October 1998), and a task force by the world's 12 largest banks and securities firms formed in January 1999, which issued its report in June 1999.

3. The arrangement involves multiple and reciprocal levels of observers and observation, also paraphrased, in native terminology, as 'transparency

about transparency'. This includes sequential orders of watching, as when analysts watch companies, and shareholders watch analysts. It includes the monitoring of transparency by mechanisms and groups that watch compliance with it. And it includes the phenomenon that observational agencies are themselves being observed, and the demand for more transparency is not only launched by them but also demanded of them. An example is the demand for more transparency that is made of the IMF or the ECB (European Central Bank), agencies who have the role of watching national governments and economies. Transparency-demanding institutions also direct this demand against themselves. Thus observation includes self-observation and self-interrogation.

4. A whole further set of issues concerns the meaning of the notion of transparency, and the negotiations of this meaning. I cannot in this paper say much about it other than to note that transparency tends to be defined in relation to an opposite which is taken to be (intentional) non-disclosure. In other words, transparency tends to be defined in relation to secrecy and reasons for this secrecy. In relation to this alleged secrecy, what is sought is a transition from a low transparency regime to a high transparency regime.

5. Another set of issues concerns the construal of the relationship between observer and observed. It should be noted that observation is not as a rule directed against individuals, but rather involves social spaces which may be as large as nation states, or as small as management floors in companies. What this suggests is that transparency is bound up with the territorial forms of organization that characterize modernity. Modernity can be associated with a proliferation of such social spaces and of internal environments.

6. This connects with the phenomenon that the discourse on transparency appears to be a global discourse, and the demand for transparency has global extension and reach. By global extension, I mean that demands for more transparency circle the globe and are not limited to western societies, but rather are actively brought forward against developing countries. By penetration (or reach), I mean that demands for more transparency are reported nearly every day not only in 'global' papers like the Herald Tribune (or the Financial Times, the Wall Street Journal etc.), but can also be found in local and very local papers, such as daily business papers in national languages (like the German Handelsblatt) and non-specialized 'dailies' of particular cities like the Berlin Tagesspiegel. In addition, the discourse is, as far as I can see, not 'glocalized'. It may refer to national or regional institutions (as when it refers to the European Central Bank in Europe), but there appears to be no progressive inner diversification or adaptation of the discourse as one goes from the global to the local plane.

I consider the quest for transparency as a cultural dimension of current developments that is bound up with the dehiscence of knowledge processes into society, but that is also bound up with a capitalist dynamic that has not only not stopped but has shifted into new gear by switching from production and consumption to colonizing trade. In a sense, a transparency regime is a regime of truth like the confessional regime (truth through confession) that has dominated notions of truth and evidence in the legal system and the area of sexuality at some points in history. But the root metaphor here, the model upon which it is built and which stimulates and sustains it, is no longer religion but science/knowledge.

Conclusion

The dehiscence model suggests that contemporary knowledge processes take root in large areas of social life in ways that drain older models of knowledge and technology in society of the power and of the meaning content they once had. If the argument I presented is correct, the sphere of these older models (for example, of knowledge processes that are safely tucked away in a subsystem which is extraneous to society, or the sphere of technological production as alienated work) has weakened and is shrinking in Western societies. One implication of this is that we need to pay more attention, as sociologists, to the 'alien elements' of knowledge structures and objectual relationships in social processes, and of cultural dimensions and contexts that are defined in terms of knowledge. When I used the term post-social in the title of this chapter, what I had in mind was the interlaying (the interlocation) of social processes with their alternate knowledge variants—which are not non-social but do contain elements not traditionally foregrounded in older social analysis. These elements require:

1. An awareness of the limits of defining the social (society) solely in human terms, for example, in terms of interpersonal relationships and social integration. Post-social societies are characterized by object-relations, where the term object includes non-human entities.

2. It will also mean an awareness of the phenomenon that knowledge structures replace social structures in some areas, as when whole links in an interaction chain are replaced by information structures, or when knowledge authority structures replace social authority structures (one example being transparency mechanisms in organizations; Knorr Cetina, 1999: ch. 7).

3. It will mean, finally, an awareness of the rise and relevance of cultural dimensions and contexts that are related to knowledge—as is, for example, the discourse on transparency and the heightened relevance of the social-cultural role of the institutional, occupational and lay observer in relation

to actors and their performance. The media also play such roles. The discourses they put before us transmit their observations and provide us with the running commentary of outsiders on the inhabitants of social life. If one wanted to formulate this development within a dramaturgical idiom, one would say that a shift of focus has occurred which matches performers with watchers, and twins every action with an observation—as it should be on stage.

EPILOGUE

Wieviorka, we have seen, speaks of the present difficulties of sociology as a discipline; Scheuch has followed suit by elaborating on sociology as *the* social science; Knorr Cetina proposes new premises regarding scientific knowledge as a whole. In spite of the common tendency to formulate general views, none of these three has been willing to suggest an encompassing theory of contemporary social reality. At the same time, all three share a common rejection of a fragmentation and splits of sociology into narrowly delimited and unconnected sub-fields, a-theoretically oriented. These approaches thus justify seeing the sociological debate about today's social and global reality as primarily outlining and delineating what may be called a 'space of discourse'. This space consists of reflexions—nurtured by research, of course—about major interacting areas which are of concern to sociologists who aspire to 'understand' the newness of our time.

This space, as we have attempted to show, can be substantiated by the basic contentions which we formulated in Chapter 1, and which refer to the five facets—that structure this book—debated by sociologists as the most salient ones of the present-day social experience. These contentions, we think, are quite representative of the common denominator that links to each other the various competing outlooks that partake the litterature of the field. By the same token, these contentions are meant to designate not only the—more or less—shared convictions that emerge from the sociologists' disputes, but beyond this aspect, also to demarcate this universe of sociological discourse about the 'newness of our time'. A universe of discourse signaled, marked and evinced by the concepts of multiple modernities, globalization, multiculturalism and transnational diasporas, the declining accountability of the state, and postmodernity.

Each of these basic contentions, we have seen, 'says something' about the newness of our time and when considered together, they somehow 'summarize'—in very broad terms—, how sociologists view their world and contribute to its conceptual construction. The links that this book has evinced among those five phases (see Figure 1) adds a sense of coherence and consistence to this universe of discourse about a world that is constantly reaching unknown shores and revealing new horizons.

Figure 1. Five interconnected foci of the discourse about the newness of our time

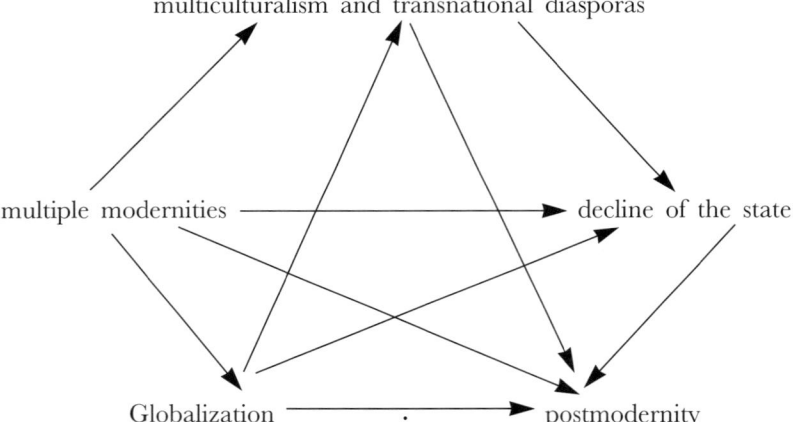

BIBLIOGRAPHY

Abu-Lughod, J. 1991. "Going Beyond Global Babble", pp. 131–137 in King, A.D. (ed.), *Culture, Globalization and the World System*. London: Macmillan.
Ackerman, B. 1991. *We The People*. Cambridge: Harvard University Press.
Adelkhah, Fariba. 1998. *Etre Moderne en Iran*. Paris: Karthala.
Adorno, Theodore. 1973. *The Jargon of Authenticity*. Evanston: Northwestern University Press.
Ager, Dennis. 1996. *Language Policy in Britain and France: The Processes of Policy*. Edited by Fawcett, Robin F., *Open Linguistics Series*. London and New York: Cassell.
Ager, Dennis. 1999. *Identity, Insecurity and Image: France and Language*. Clevedon, Philadelphia & Adelaide: Multilingual Matters Ltd.
Ahrne, Goran. 1998. "Civil Society and Uncivil Organizations", pp. 84–95 in Alexander, J.C. (ed.), *Real Civil Societies: Dilemmas of Institutionalization*. London: Sage.
Ajami, Fouad. 1993. "The Summoning", *Foreign Affairs* 72(4): 2–9.
Akaike, H. 1980. "Likelihood and the Bayes Procedure", pp. 143–166 in Bernardo, J.H., DeGroot M.H., Lindley, D.V. and Smith, A.F.M. (eds.), *Bayesian Statistics*. Valencia: University Press.
——— 1985. "Prediction and Entropy", pp. 1–24 in Atkinson, A.C. (ed.), *A Celebration of Statistics*. New York: Springer-Verlag.
Al-Haj, Majid. 1993. "The Changing Strategies of Mobilization Among the Arabs in Israel", pp. 67–87 in Ben-Zadok, E. (ed.), *Local Communities and the Israeli Polity*. New York: SUNY.
al-Tahtawi, Ahmad. 1987. *Ahwal al-qubur wa-ma ba'd al-mawt*. Cairo: Dar al-Bashir.
al-Turabi, Hasan. 1983. "The Islamic State", in Esposito, John L. (ed.), *Voices of Resurgent Islam*. New York: Oxford University Press.
Albrow, M. 1996. *The Global Age. State and Society Beyond Modernity*. Cambridge: Polity Press.
Alexander, J.C. 1982–1983. *Theoretical Logic in Sociology*. Berkeley: University of California Press.
——— 1988. *Action and Its Environments: Towards a New Synthesis*. New York: Columbia University Press.
——— 1989. *Structure and Meaning: Rethinking Classical Sociology*. New York: Columbia University Press.
——— 1992. *Post-Modernization Theory*, (mimeo). Uppsala: SCASSS.
——— 1995. "Modern, Anti, Post, and Neo: How Intellectuals Have Coded, Narrated, and Explained the 'New World of Our Time'", pp. 6–64 in Alexander, J.C., *Fin de Siecle Social Theory*. London: Verso.
——— 1998. "Introduction. Civil Society I, II, III: Constructing an Empirical Concept from Normative Controversies and Historical Transformations", in Alexander, J.C. (ed.), *Real Civil Societies: Dilemmas of Institutionalization*. London: Sage.
Amin, S. 1997. *Capitalism in the Age of Globalization*. London and New York: Zed Books.
Ammon, Ulrich. 1992. "The Federal Republic of Germany's Policy of Spreading German", *International Journal of the Sociology of Language* 95: 33–50.
Anchel, Robert. 1928. *Napoléon et les juifs*. Paris: Presses Universitaires de France.
Anderson, B. 1991. *Imagined Communities: Reflections on the Origin and Spread of Nationalism*. Revised edition. London: Verso.
Anderson, P. 1984. "Modernity and Revolution", *New Left Review* 144(2): 96–113.
Andrews, G. Reid. 1992. *Blacks and Whites in São Paulo*. Madison: University of Wisconsin Press.
Anheier, H. and Toepler, Stefan (eds.). 1999. *Private Funds, Public Purpose: Philanthropic Foundations in International Perspective*. New York: Plenum/Kluwer.
Annuaire des anciens élèves de l'ENA, 1995.
Appadurai, Arjun. 1990. "Disjuncture and Difference in the Global Cultural Economy", in Featherstone, Mike (ed.), *Global Culture: Nationalism, Globalization and Modernity*. London: Sage.

———— 1996. *Modernity at Large. Cultural Dimensions of Globalization.* Minneapolis: University of Minnesota Press.

Appiah, Kwame A. 1992. *In my Father's House; Africa in the Philosophy of Culture.* New York: Oxford University Press.

Apter, David. 1968. *Some Conceptual Approaches to the Study of Modernization.* Englewood Cliffs, NJ: Prentice Hall.

Aras, Bulent. 1998. "Turkish Islam's Moderate Face", *Middle East Quarterly* 5(3): 23–30.

Archambault, E. with Boumendil, J. 1994. *Les Dons et le Bénévolat en France.* Paris: Paris I-Sorbonne University, Laboratoire d'Economie Sociale.

Archambault, E., Boumendil, Judith and Tsyboula, Sylvie. 1999. "Foundations in France", pp. 185–197 in Anheier, H.K. and Toepler, S. (eds.), *Private Funds, Public Purpose.* New York: Kluwer Academic/Plenum Publishers.

Ardener, E. 1989. *The Voice of Prophecy.* Oxford: Blackwell.

Arendt, Hannah. 1951. *The Origins of Totalitarianism.* 2nd edition. New York: Harcourt Brace.

———— 1968. "Tradition and the Modern Age", in Arendt, H., *Between Past and Future.* New York: Viking Penguin.

Arieli, Y. 1992. "American Civilization as an Archetype of Modern Civilization", pp. 278–299 in Arieli, Y., *History and Politics.* Tel Aviv: Am Oved. (Hebrew)

Armitage, J. 1999. "From Modernism to Hypermodernism and Beyond: An Interview with Paul Virilio", *Theory, Culture & Society* (special issue on Paul Virilio) 16(5–6): 25–55.

Arnason, J.P. 1988. "Social Theory and the Concept of Civilization", *Thesis Eleven* 20: 87–105.

———— 1993. *The Future that Failed.* London: Routledge.

———— 2000. "Communism and Modernity", *Daedalus* 129(1): 61–90.

Arnold, M. 1969. *Culture and Anarchy.* Cambridge: Cambridge University Press.

Arnove, Robert F. 1980. *Philanthropy and Cultural Imperialism: The Foundations at Home and Abroad.* Boston: G.K. Hall and Co.

Aron, R. 1968a. *18 Lectures on Industrial Society.* London: Weidenfeld and Nicolson.

———— 1968b. *Progress and Disillusion.* London: Pall Mall.

Arrighi, G. 1994. *The Long Twentieth Century: Money, Power and the Origin of Our Times.* London: Verso.

Ashford, Douglas E. (ed.). 1992. *History and Context in Comparative Public Policy.* Pittsburgh: University of Pittsburgh Press.

Auerbach, E. 1953. *Mimesis. The Representation of Reality in Western Literature.* Princeton: Princeton University Press.

Avineri, S. 1968. *The Social and Political Thought of Karl Marx.* Cambridge: Cambridge University Press.

Azaria, V. and Chazan, N. 1987. "Disengagement from the State in Africa—Ghana and Guinea", *Comparative Studies in Society and History* 19: 106–131.

Azevedo, Aluizio. (1881) 1973. *O Mulato.* São Paulo: Martins.

Bacon, F. 1900. *The Advancement of Learning and Novum Organum.* New York: Colonial Press.

Bagby, P. 1958. *Culture and History: Prolegomena to the Comparative Study of Civilizations.* London: Longmans, Green and Co.

Baker, Keith Michael. 1994. "Enlightenment and the Institution of Society: Notes for a Conceptual History", in Melching, Willem and Wyger, Velema (eds.), *Main Trends in Cultural History: Ten Essays.* Amsterdam: Rodopi.

Banks, Arthur S. and Textor, Robert B. 1963. *The Cross Polity Survey.* Cambridge, MA: The MIT Press.

Barandan, A. 1998. personal communication.

Barber, B. 1995. *Jihad vs. McWorld.* New York: Times Books.

Barber, B.R. 1999. "Civil Society: Getting beyond the Rhetoric: A Framework for Political Understanding", pp. 115–143 in Jasnning, J., Kupchan, C. and Rumberg, D. (eds.), *Civic Engagement in the Atlantic Community.* Gütersloh: B. Ertelsmann.

Barbero, J. Martin. 1998. *De los Medios a las Mediaciones.* Bogota: Ed. Andrès Bello.

Barkan, J. and Gordon, D. 1998. "Democracy in Africa—No Time to Forsake", *Foreign Affairs* 77(4): 107–111.

Barnea, Nahum. 1994. "The Palestinians and Us", *Yediot Aharonot* (Holiday Supplement), May 15. (Hebrew)

Barnes, Dayle. 1982. "Nationalism and the Mandarin Movement: The First Half-Century", in Cooper, Robert L. (ed.), *Language Spread: Studies in Diffusion and Social Change*. Bloomington: Indiana University Press.

Bartelson, Jens. 2000. "Three Concepts of Globalization", *International Sociology* 15(2): 180–196.

Barth, Fredrick. 1969. *Ethnic Groups and Boundaries. The Social Organisation of Culture Difference*. Boston: Little, Brown & Co.

Bartlett, R. 1993. *The Making of Europe*. Princeton: Princeton University Press.

Bartolini, Stefano. 1993. "On Time and Comparative Research", *Journal of Theoretical Politics* 5(2): 131–167.

Baubock, R. 1994. *Transnational Citizenship*. Aldershot, UK: Edward Elgar

———— 1998. "The Crossing and Blurring of Boundaries in International Migration: Challenges for Social and Political Theory", pp. 17–52 in Baubock, R. and Rundell, J.F. (eds.), *Blurred Boundaries: Migration, Ethnicity, Citzenship*. Aldershot, UK: Ashgate.

Bauman, Z. 1989a. *Modernity and the Holocaust*. Ithaca: Cornell University Press.

———— 1989b. "Sociological Responses to Postmodernity", pp. 127–152 in Mongardini, C. and Maniscalco, M.L. (eds.), *Moderno e Postmoderno*. Rome: Bulzoni.

———— 1992. *Intimations of Postmodernity*. London: Routledge.

———— 1998. *Globalization: The Human Consequences*. Cambridge: Polity.

———— 2000. "A Sociological Theory of Postmodernity", pp. 27–42 in Nash, K. (ed.), *Readings in Contemporary Political Sociology*. Oxford: Blackwell.

Baykan, A. 1999. *In Istanbul Music is the Opium of the Masses: Reflections on the Displaced of a World City*. Paper presented at the Columbia University, Center for Comparative Literature and Society, Middle East and African Languages and Cultures, East Asia Languages and Cultures, April 7.

———— 2000. "The Place of Minority Literature as Testimonial Narratives: The Challenge to Historiography and Literature", pp. 489–492 in *Crossroads of History: Experience, Memory, Orality*. Vol. 2. Istanbul: International Oral History Association in Collaboration with the Department of History at Bogazici University.

Baykan, A. and Barlas, D. 1999. *Turkish-Italian Relations Between WW I and WW II: Searching for the Impact on Turkish Culture and Politics*. Unpublished report submitted to Fiat and Agnelli Foundation. Istanbul: Koc University.

Bazagran, A. 1998. *From Self-Evaluation to Accreditation for Quality Improvements in Higher Education: Recent Trends in Iran and Outlines of a Model*. Paper presented at the UNESCO Regional Seminar on Higher Education in the Coming Century, Tehran (February 16–18).

Bech, H. 1998. "Citysex: Representing Lust in Public", *Theory, Culture & Society* (special issue on Love & Eroticism) 15(3–4): 215–241.

Beck, U. 1986. *Risikogesellschaft—Auf dem Weg in eine andere Moderne*. Frankfurt/M.: Suhrkamp.

———— 1992. *Risk Society: Towards a New Modernity*. London: Sage.

———— 1996. "Risk Society and the Provident State", pp. 27–43 in Lash, S., Szerszynski, B. and Wynne, B. (eds.), *Risk, Environment and Modernity: Towards a New Ecology*. London: Sage.

———— 2000a. "The Cosmopolitan Perspective: Sociology of the Second Age of Modernity", *British Journal of Sociology* 51(1): 79–105.

———— 2000b. *What is Globalization?* Cambridge: Polity Press.

Beck, U., Giddens, A. and Lash, S. 1994. *Reflexive Modernization*. Stanford: Stanford University Press.

Beck, U. and Sopp, Peter M. (eds.). 1997. *Individualisierung und Integration*. Opladen: Leske + Budrich.

Beck-Gernsheim, Elisabeth. 1999. *Juden, Deutsche und andere Erinnerungslandschaften. Im Dschungel der Ethnischen Kategorien*. Frankfurt/M.: Suhrkamp.

Becker, Gary S. 1976. *The Economic Approach to Human Behavior*. Chicago: University of Chicago Press.

Becker, Jean-Jacques and Wieviorka, Annette (eds.). 1998. *Les Juifs de France de la Révolution française à nos jours*. Paris: Liana Levi.

Becker, J.W. et al. (eds.). 1990. *Attitudes to Inequality and the Role of Government*. Rijswijk, NL: Sociaal en Cultureel Planbureau.

Beebe, L.M. and Giles, H. 1984. "Speech-Accommodation Theories: A Discussion in Terms of Second-Language Acquisition", *International Journal of the Sociology of Language* 46: 5–32.

Beetham, David. 1985. *Max Weber and the Theory of Modern Politics*. Revised edition. Cambridge: Polity.

Befu, H. 1998. *Japanese Globalization*. (mimeo). Kyoto Bunkyo University.

Bell, A. 1984. "Language Style as Audience Design", *Language in Society* 13: 145–204.

Bell, D. 1973. *The Coming of Post-Industrial Society: A Venture in Social Forecasting*. New York: Basic Books.

——— 1976. *The Cultural Contradictions of Capitalism*. New York: Basic Books.

——— 1979. *Les Contradictions Culturelles du Capitalisme*. Paris: PUF.

——— 1987. "The World and the United States in 2013", *Daedalus* 116(3): 1–30.

Bell, R.T. 1983. *Sociolinguistics—Goals, Approaches and Problems*. London: B.T. Batsford.

Bellah, Robert N. 1967. "Civil Religion in America", *Daedalus* 96: 1–21.

Bellah, Robert N. et al. 1985. *Habits of the Heart*. Berkeley: University of California Press.

Beloff, M. 1954. *The Age of Absolutism: 1660–1815*. London: Hutchinson & Co.

Ben, Aluf. 1993. "Barak Looks Through the Window of Opportunities", *Ha'aretz*, December 24, p. B2. (Hebrew)

Ben-Rafael, E. 1994. *Language, Identity and Social Division: The Case of Israel*. Oxford: Oxford University Press/Clarendon.

——— 1996. "Multiculturalism in Sociological Perspective", pp. 133–154 in Baubock, R., Heller, A. and Zolberg, A. (eds.), *The Challenge of Diversity—Integration and Pluralism in Societies of Immigration*. Aldershot, UK: Gower/Avebury and European Centre Vienna.

——— 1998. *Contemporary Multiculturalism*. Paper delivered at the 14th ISA World Congress of Sociology, Montreal (July 26–August 1).

Ben-Rafael, E. and Brosh, H. 1995. "Jews and Arabs in Israel: The Cultural Convergence of Divergent Identities", pp. 18–34 in Nettler, R. (ed.), *Medieval and Modern Perspectives on Muslim-Jewish Relations*. London: Harwood Academic Pubs.

Ben-Rafael, E., Olshtain, E. and Geijst, I. 1997. 'The socio-linguistic insertion of Russian Jews in Israel', in Lewin-Epstein, N. et al. (eds.), *Russian Jews on Three Continents*. London: Frank Cass.

Ben Yishai, Ron. 1994. "Matan Vilnai Takes Leave of Gaza", *Yediot Aharonot* (Weekend Supplement), May 13, pp. 6–7. (Hebrew)

Benavot, A., Cha, Y.K., Kamens, D., Meyer, J.W. and Wong, Suk-Ying. 1991. "Knowledge for the Masses: World Models and National Curricula, 1920–1986", *American Sociological Review* 56(1): 85–100.

Bendaoud, L. 1999. "Langue Arabe/La 'Bataille Politique' de Hadjar", *El Watan*, March 22, p. 5.

Bendix, Reinhard. 1967. 'Tradition and Modernity Reconsidered', *Comparative Studies in Society and History* 9: 292–346.

Benjamin, W. 1978. *Reflections*. New York: Schocken Books.

Berelson, Bernard and Steiner, Gary A. (eds.). 1964. *Human Behavior*. New York: Harcourt, Brace & World.

Berger, P., Berger, B. and Kellner, H. 1974. *The Homeless Mind. Modernization and Consciousness*. New York: Vintage Books.

Bergier, J. 1974. *Naissance et Croissance de la Suisse Industrielle*. Bern: Francke Verlag.

Berking, H. 1999. *Sociology of Giving*. Translated by P. Camiller. London: Sage.

——— 2000. "Homes away from Home": Zum Spannungsverhältnis von Diaspora und Nationalstaat. *Berliner Journal für Soziologie* 1: 49–60.

Berman, E.H. 1983. *The Influence of Carnegie, Ford and Rockefeller Foundations on American Foreign Policy: The Ideology of Philanthropy*. Albany: State University of New York Press.

Berman, M. 1983. *All that is Solid Melts into Air: The Experience of Modernity*. London: Verso.

Bessis, S. 1994–1995. "Entretien avec Mohammed Arkoun", *Les Cahiers de l'Orient* 36/37 (4th term 1994 and 1st term 1995): 231–243.

Bevir, Mark. 1992. "The Errors of Linguistic Contextualism", *History and Theory* 31(3): 276–298.
———— 1996. "Mind and Method in the History of Ideas", *History and Theory* 35(2): 167–189.
Beyer, Peter. 1998. "Globalizing Systems, Global Cultural Models and Religion(s)", *International Sociology* 13(1): 79–94.
Bhabha, H. 1994. *The Location of Culture*. London: Routledge.
Bhagwati, Jagdish. 1988. *Protectionism*. Cambridge, MA: MIT Press.
Bhaskar, Roy. 1989. *Reclaiming Reality: A Critical Introduction to Contemporary Philosophy*. London: Verso.
———— 1991. *Philosophy and the Idea of Freedom*. Oxford: Blackwell.
Biagioli, Mario. 1993. *Galileo, Courtier: The Practice of Science in the Culture of Absolutism*. Chicago: University of Chicago Press.
Billis, D. 1993. "Sector Blurring and Nonprofit Centers: The Case of the United Kingdom", *Nonprofit and Voluntary Sector Quarterly* 22(3): 241–257.
Biltereyst, Daniël. 1992. "Language and Culture as Ultimate Barriers? An Analysis of the Circulation, Consumption and Popularity of Fiction in Small European Countries", *European Journal of Communication* 7: 517–540.
Birnbaum, Pierre. 1994. *Les Fous de la République*. Paris: Le Seuil, Points.
———— 1995. *Destins Juifs*. Paris: Calmann-Lévy.
———— 1998. *La France Imaginée*. Paris: Fayard.
Blaas, P.B.M. 1980. "Begripsgeschiedenis en Historische Semantiek", *Theoretische Geschiedenis* 7: 161–174.
Black, C.E. (ed.). 1976. *Comparative Modernization: A Reader*. New York: The Free Press.
Blank, Jonah. (in press). *Mullah on the Mainframe. Islam and Modernity among the Daudi Bohras*.
Blankart, Charles B. and Knieps, Günter. 1991. *Path Dependence, Network Externalities and Standardization*. Groningen: Memorandum nr. 439, Institute of Economic Research, University of Groningen.
Boas, Franz. 1911. *The Mind of Primitive Man*. New York: Macmillan.
Bodemann, Y. Michal. 1986. "Staat und Ethnizität. Der Wiederaufbau der jüdischen Gemeinden im Kalten Krieg", in Brumlik, Micha et al., *Jüdisches Leben in Deutschland nach 1945*. Frankfurt: Athenäum.
———— 1990. "The State in the Construction of Ethnicity, and Ideological Labour: The Case of German Jewry", *Critical Sociology* 17(3): 35–46.
———— 1996a. *Gedächtnistheater. Die jüdische Gemeinschaft und ihre deutsche Erfindung*. Hamburg: Rotbuch Verlag.
———— (ed.). 1996b. *Jews, Germans, Memory. Reconstructions of Jewish Life in Germany*. Ann Arbor: University of Michigan Press.
Bogdanov, A. 1949. *The Theory of Political Economy*. Second edition. Hakibbutz Hameuchad. (Hebrew)
Boli, John. 1987. "World Polity Sources of Expanding State Authority and Organization, 1870–1970", in Thomas, George M. et al. (eds.), *Institutional Structure: Constituting State, Society and the Individual*. Beverly Hills: Sage.
Bonacich, Edna. 1980. "Class Approaches to Ethnicity and Race", *Insurgent Sociologist* 10(2).
Borgatta, Edgar F. and Borgatta, Marie L. (eds.). 1992. *Encyclopedia of Sociology*. 4 Vols. New York: Macmillan.
Borgatta, Edgar F. and Cook, Karen S. (eds.). 1988. *The Future of Sociology*. Newbury Park: Sage.
Borkenau, Franz. 1981. *End and Beginning*. New York: Columbia University Press.
Borre, Ole and Scarbrough, Elinor (eds.). 1995. *The Scope of Government*. Oxford: Oxford University Press.
Bosi, Alfredo. 1970. *História Concisa da Literatura Brasileira*. São Paulo: Cultrix.
Boudon, Raymond. 1979. *Effets Pervers et Order Social*. Paris: PUF.
———— 2000. *L'Acteur et ses Raisons*. Paris: PUF.
Boumelha, P. 1998. "Arts: Revival of the Fittest", *Higher Educational Supplements (No. 948), The Australian* (September 2): 37–43.
Bourdieu, P. 1977. *Outline of a Theory of Practice*. Cambridge: Cambridge University Press.
———— 1979. *La Distinction; Critique Sociale du Jugement*. Paris: Éditions de Minuit.

———— 1984. *Distinction*. London: Routledge.
———— 1985. "The Social Space and the Genesis of Groups", *Theory and Society* 14: 723–744.
———— 1987. "What Makes a Social Class? On the Theory and Practical Existence of Groups", *Berkeley Journal of Sociology* 32: 1–17.
———— 1998. *Contre-Feux*. Paris: Liber.
Bourricaud, F. 1987. "Modernity, 'Universal Reference' and the Process of Modernization", pp. 12–21 in Eisenstadt, S.N. (ed.), *Patterns of Modernity. Vol. I: The West*. New York: New York University Press.
Bowen, John R. 1993. *Modernizing Muslims Through Discourse*. Princeton: Princeton University Press.
———— 1999. "Legal Reasoning and Public Discourse in Indonesian Islam", pp. 80–105 in Eickelman, Dale F. and Anderson, Jon (eds.), *New Media in the Muslim World: The Emerging Public Sphere*. Bloomington and Indianapolis: Indiana University Press.
Bowles, S., Gintis, H. and Gustafsson, B. (eds.). 1993. *Markets and Democracy*. Cambridge: Cambridge University Press.
Boyer, R. and Drache, D. 1996a. "Introduction", in Boyars, R. and Drache, D. (eds.), *States Against Markets: the Limits of Globalization*. London: Routledge.
———— 1996b. *States Against Markets: The Limits of Globalization*. London: Routledge.
Bozdogan, S. 1994. "Architecture, Modernism and Nation-Building in Kemalist Turkey", *New Perspectives on Turkey* 10: 37–55.
Bratton, M. 1994. "Civil Society and Political Transitions in Africa", pp. 51–81 in Harbeson, J.W., Rothschild, D and Chazan, N. (eds.), *Civil Society and the State in Africa*. Boulder: Lynne Rienner.
Bratton, M. and Van de Walle, N. 1997. *Democratic Experiments in Africa*. Cambridge: Cambridge University Press.
Braudel, F. 1980. *On History*. Chicago: University of Chicago Press.
———— 1994. *A History of Civilizations*. London: Penguin Books.
Braverman, H. 1974, *Labor and Monopoly Capital*. New York: Monthly Review Press.
Bremner, Robert H. 1988. *American Philanthropy*. Chicago: University of Chicago Press.
Brenner, Michael. 1997. *After the Holocaust. Rebuilding Jewish Lives in Postwar Germany*. Princeton: Princeton University Press.
Brian, Eric. 1994. *La Mesure de l'Etat. Administrateurs et Geiomitres au XVIIIe Siecle*. Paris: Albin Michel.
———— 1998. "Mathematics, Administrative Reform and Social Sciences in France at the end of the Eighteenth Century", in Heilbron, J., Magnusson, L. and Wittrock, B. (eds.), *The Rise of the Social Sciences and the Formation of Modernity: Conceptual Change in Context, 1750–1850*. Dordrecht: Kluwer.
Briggs, Asa. 1961. *History of Broadcasting in the United Kingdom. Vol. I: The Birth of Broadcasting*. London: Oxford University Press.
Briggs, Susan. 1981. *Those Radio Times*. London: Weidenfeld and Nicolson.
Broder, Henryk and Lang, Michel (eds.). 1979. *Fremd im Eignen Land. Juden in der Bundesrepublik* (Stranger in One's Own land. Jews in the Federal Republic). Frankfurt: Fischer.
Bryant, C.G.A. 1993. "Social Self-Organization, Civility and Sociology: A Comment on Kumar's 'Civil Society'", *British Journal of Sociology* 44: 397–401.
Bryce, James. 1891. *The American Commonwealth*. New York: MacMillan.
Brzezinski, Zbigniew. 1970. *Between Two Ages; America's Role in the Technocratic Era*. New York: Viking Press.
Buber, Martin. 1961. *Between Man and Man*. London: Collins.
Buckhart, Ross E. and Lewis-Beck, Michael S. 1994. "Comparative Democracy: The Economic Development Thesis", *American Political Science Review* 16: 903–910.
Bulmer, M. 1984. "Philanthropic Foundations and the Development of the Social Sciences in the Early Twentieth Century: A Reply to Donald Fisher", *Sociology* 18: 573–587.
Burgauer, Erica. 1993. *Zwischen Erinnerung und Verdrängung—Juden in Deutschland nach 1945*. Reinbek bei Hamburg: Rowohlt Verlag.
Burke, P. 1989. "New Reflections on World History", *Culture and History 5*.

—— 1997. "Review of Two Books by M. Richter", *History of European Ideas* 23(1): 55–58.

Busino, G. 1993. *Critique du savoir sociologique*. Paris: Presses Universitaire de France.

Butler, Judith. 1993. *Bodies That Matter*. London: Routledge.

Calhoun, C. 1991. "Indirect Relationships and Imagined Communities: Large-Scale Social Integration and the Transformation of Everyday Life", pp. 95–120 in Coleman, J. and Bourdieu, P. (eds.), *Social Theory in a Changing Society*. Boulder: Westview Press.

—— 1992. "The Infrastructure of Modernity. Indirect Social Relationships, Information Technology, and Social Integration", pp. 205–236 in Haferkamp, H. and Smelser, N.J. (eds.), *Social Change and Modernity*. Berkeley and Los Angeles: University of California Press.

—— 1993. "Nationalism and Ethnicity", *Annual Review of Sociology* 19: 211–239.

—— 1995a. *Critical Social Theory: Culture, History, and the Challenge of Difference*. Cambridge, MA: Blackwell.

—— 1995b. "Postmodernism as Pseudohistory", in Calhoun, C., *Critical Social Theory: Culture, History, and the Challenge of Difference*. Cambridge, MA: Blackwell.

—— 1997. *Nationalism*. New York: New York University Press.

Caminha, Pero Vaz de. (1500) 1894. "Carta de Pero Vaz de Caminha a El-Rei Dom Manuel, dando-lhe noticia do descobrimento da terra de Vera Cruz, hoje Brazil, pela Armada de Pedro Alvares Cabral", in *Revista Trimestral do Instituto Geographico e Historico da Bahia*. Anno I, vol. I.

Canclini, N. Garcia. 1989. *Culturas Hibridas*. Ciudad de Mexico: Grijaldo.

—— (ed.). 1994. *Los Nuevos Espectadores: Cine, Televisión y Video en Mexico*. Ciudad de Mexico: Consejo Nacional de la Cultura y Artes.

Candau, J. 1998. *Mémoire et Identité*. Paris: PUF.

Cantril, Hadley (ed.). 1951. *Public Opinion 1935–1946*. Princeton: Princeton University Press.

Caplow, Theodore. 1998. "Trends and Contexts: The Principle of Singularity", *International Journal of Comparative Sociology* 39(1): 4–15.

Cardiff, David and Scannell, Paddy. 1987. "Broadcasting and National Unity", in Curran, J., Smith, A. and Wingate, P. (eds.), *Impact and Influences: Essays on Media Power in the Twentieth Century*. London: Methuen.

Carey, James. 1967. "Harold Adams Innis and Marshall McLuhan", *Antioch Review* 27(1): 5–39.

Carnoy, Martin. 1993. "Whither the Nation-state?", in Carnoy, Martin et al. (eds.), *The New Global Economy in the Information Age; Reflections on Our Changing World*. University Park: Pennsylvania State University Press.

Carr, E.H. 1945. *Nationalism and After*. London: MacMillan.

Castel, Robert. 1995. *Les Métamorphoses de la Question Sociale*. Paris: Fayard.

Castells, M. 1989. *The Informational City*. Oxford: Blackwell.

—— 1996a. *The Information Age, Volume 1: The Rise of the Network Society*. Oxford: Blackwell.

—— 1996b. *The Information Age, Volume 2: The Power of Identity*. Oxford: Blackwell.

—— 1998. *The Information Age, Volume 3: The End of the Millennium*. Oxford: Blackwell.

—— 1999. *Le Pouvoir de l'identité, Vol. 2: L'ère de l'information*. Paris: Fayard.

Castoriadis, C. 1997a. "The Retreat from Autonomy: Postmodernism as Generalized Conformism", pp. 32–43 in Castoriadis, C., *World in Fragments: Writings in Politics, Society, Psychoanalysis and the Imagination*. Stanford: Stanford University Press.

—— 1997b. *World in Fragments: Writings in Politics, Society, Psychoanalysis and the Imagination*. Stanford: Stanford University Press.

Ceyhan, K. 1996. *Seferberlik Turkuleriyle Buyudum*. Istanbul: Aras Yayincilik.

Chabal, P. 1998. "A few Considerations on Democracy in Africa", *International Affairs* 74(2): 289–303.

Chabal, P and Daloz, J.P. 1999. *Africa Works—Disorder as Political Instrument*. Bloomington: Indiana University Press.

Champion, Françoise et Hervieu-Léger, Danièle (eds.). 1990. *De l'émotion en Religion. Renouveaux et Traditions*. Paris: Centurion.

Chandhoke, Neera. 1995. *State and Civil Society: Explorations in Political Theory*. London: Sage.

Chandler, A. 1977. *The Visible Hand*. Cambridge, MA: Harvard University Press.
Chatterjee, P. 1986. *Nationalist Thought and the Colonial World*. London: Zed Books.
Chazan, N. 1992. "Africa's Democratic Challenge," *World Policy Journal* (Spring): 279–307.
Chehabi, H.E. and Linz, J. (eds.). 1998. *Sultanistic Regimes*. The Johns Hopkins University Press.
Chodak, Szymon. 1973. *Societal Development*. New York: Oxford University Press.
Chouraqui, Jean-Marc. 1990. "De l'émancipation des Juifs á l'émancipation du judaisme. Le regard des rabbins français au XIXᵉ siècle", in Birnbaum, Pierre (ed.), *Histoire politique des juifs en France*. Paris: Presses de la FNSP.
Chow, Rey. 1993. *Writing Diaspora: Tactics of Intervention in Contemporary Cultural Studies*. Bloomington: University of Indiana Press.
Christie, John (ed.). 1993. "Origins of the Human Sciences". Special issue of *History of the Human Sciences* 6(1).
Christie, Richard and Jahoda, Marie (eds.). 1954. *Studies in the Scope and Methods of "The Authoritarian Personality"*. Glencoe: Free Press.
Church, Jeffrey and King, Ian. 1993. "Bilingualism and Network Externalities", *Canadian Journal of Economics* 26(2): 337–345.
Clapham, C. 1993. "Democratization in Africa: Obstacles and Prospects", *Third World Quarterly* 14(3): 423–439.
Clark, I. 1997. "The Challenges of Political Reform in Sub-Saharan Africa: A Theoretical Overview", pp. 23–39 in Clark, J.F. and Gardinier, D.E. (eds.), *Political Reform in Francophone Africa*. Boulder: Westview Press.
Clifford, J. 1988. *The Predicament of Culture: Twentieth-Century Ethnography, Literature, and Art*. Cambridge, MA: Harvard University Press.
——— 1997. *Routes: Travel and Translation in the Late Twentieth Century*. Cambridge, MA: Harvard University Press.
Clifford, J. and Marcus, G. (eds.). 1986. *Writing Culture*. Berkeley: University of California Press.
Clough, S.B. 1960. "Philanthropy and the Welfare State in Europe", *Political Science Quarterly* 75: 87–93.
Cohen, Bernard. I. (ed.). 1994. *The Natural Sciences and the Social Sciences: Some Critical and Historical Perspectives*. Dordrecht: Kluwer.
Cohen, Daniel. 1997. *Richesse du Monde, Pauvretes de Nations*. Paris: Flammarion.
Cohen, Elie. 1996. *La Tentation Hexagonale*. Paris: Fayard.
Cohen, Martine. 1993. "Les Juifs de France. Affirmations identitaires et évolution du modèle d'intégration", *Le Débat*, May–August.
Cohen, Phyllis Albert. 1992. "Israelite and Jew: How did [the] Nineteenth-Century French Understand Assimilation?", in Frankel, Jonathan and Zipperstein, Steven J. (eds.), *Assimilation and Community. The Jews in Nineteenth-Century Europe*. New York: Cambridge University Press.
Cohen, R. (ed.). 1996. *The Sociology of Migration*. Cheltenham, UK: E. Elgar
Cohen, R., Layton-Henry, Z. (ed.). 1997. *The Politics of Migration*. Cheltenham, UK: E. Elgar.
Colas, Dominique. 1997. *Civil Society and Fanaticism: Conjoined Histories*. Translated by Amy Jacobs. Stanford: Stanford University Press.
Coleman, J. 1990. *The Foundations of Social Analysis*. Cambridge, UK: The Belknap Press.
——— 1993. "The Rational Reconstruction of Society: 1992 Presidential Address", *American Sociological Review* 58: 1–15.
Collini, S. et al. 1983. *That Noble Science of Politics. A Study in 19th Century Intellectual History*. Cambridge: Cambridge University Press.
Collins, H.M. 1985. *Changing Order: Replication and Induction in Scientific Practice*. London: Sage.
Collins, Randall. 1987. "A Micro-Macro Theory of Intellectual Creativity: The Case of German Idealist Philosophy", *Sociological Theory* 5(1): 47–69.
——— 1997. "A Sociological Guilt Trip", *American Journal of Sociology* 102(6): 1558–1564.
——— 1998. "The Transformation of Philosophy", in Heilbron, J., Magnusson, L. and Wittrock, B. (eds.), *The Rise of the Social Sciences and the Formation of Modernity: Conceptual Change in Context, 1750–1850*. Dordrecht: Kluwer.

Congressional Commission on Education. 1991. *Making Education Work*. Manila and Quezon City: Congress of the Republic of the Philippines.

Connell, Robert. 1997. "Why Is Classical Theory Classical?", *American Journal of Sociology* 102(6): 1511–1557.

Connolly, Cyril. 1961. *Enemies of Promise*. Harmondsworth: Penguin.

Cooper, Robert L. 1989. *Language Planning and Social Change*. Cambridge: Cambridge University Press.

Copeaux, E. 1998. *Turk Tarih Tezinden Turk-Islam Sentezine*. Istanbul: Tarih Vakfi Yurt Yayynlari.

Costa, H de la. 1961. *The Jesuits of the Philippines, 1581–1768*. Cambridge: Harvard University Press.

Coulmas, Florian. 1992. *Die Wirtschaft mit der Sprache: Eine sprachsoziologische Studie*. Frankfurt/M.: Suhrkamp.

Cowan, G. 1992. "Zambia Tests Democracy," *CSIS Africa Notes* 141 (October).

Creevey, L. 1997. "Senegal: The Evolution of a Quasi-Democracy", pp. 204–222 in Clark, J.F. and Gardinier, D.E. (eds.), *Political Reform in Francophone Africa*. Boulder: Westview Press.

Crystal, David. 1987. *The Cambridge Encyclopedia of Languages*. Cambridge: Cambridge University Press.

Cunningham, Andrew and Jardine, Nicholas (eds.). 1990. *Romanticism and the Sciences*. Cambridge: Cambridge University Press.

Curran, James. 1998. "Crisis of Public Communication: A Reappraisal", in Liebes, T. and Curran, J. (eds.), *Media, Ritual, Identity*. London: Routledge.

Daalder, H. 1971. "On Building Consociational Nations: The Case of the Netherlands and Switzerland", *International Social Science Journal* 23: 355–370.

Daedalus. 1998. Issue on "Early Modernities", 127(3).

Dahl, G. 1999a. *Radical Conservatism and the Future of Politics*. London: Sage.

———— 1999b. "The Anti-Reflexivist Revolution. On the Affirmationism of the New Right", in Featherstone, M. and Lash, S. (eds.), *Spaces of Culture: City/Nation/World*. London: Sage.

Dahrendorf, R. 1959. *Class and Class Conflict in Industrial Society*. London: Routledge.

———— 1979. *Life Chances*. Chicago: University of Chicago Press.

———— 1988. *The Modern Social Conflict: An Essay on the Politics of Liberty*. London: Weidenfeld & Nicolson.

———— 1989. "Einführung in die Soziologie", *Soziale Welt* 40.

Daston, Lorraine. 1988. *Classical Probability in the Enlightenment*. Princeton: Princeton University Press.

———— 1991. "Marvelous Facts and Miraculous Evidence in Early Modern Europe", *Critical Inquiry* 18: 93–124.

———— 1992. "Objectivity and the Escape from Perspective", *Social Studies of Science* 22: 597–618.

Davies, N. 1996. *Europe—A History*. Oxford: Oxford University Press.

Davies, S. 1978. *Renaissance View of Man*. Manchester: Manchester University Press.

Davis, M. 1990. *City of Quartz*. London: Verso.

De Francis, John. 1984. *The Chinese Language: Fact and Fantasy*. Honolulu: University of Hawaii Press.

De-Hartuch, Amnon. 1998. "State Support for Public Institutions: The Blooming of Special Funding", *Mishpatim* 29: 109–137. (Hebrew)

De Swaan, Abram. 1988. *In Care of the State: Health, Education and Welfare in Europe and the USA in the Modern Era*. Cambridge/New York: Polity Press/Oxford University Press.

———— 1991a. "Kwaliteit is Klasse; De Sociale Wording en Werking van het Cultureel Smaakverschil", pp. 59–92 in *Perron Nederland*. Amsterdam: Meulenhoff.

———— 1991b. "Language Politics in India and Europe: A Comparison Based on a Model of Conflict of Language Interests", *Journal of Education and Social Change* 5(3): 13–34.

———— 1993a. "Introduction", *International Political Science Review* [Special Issue on The Emergent World Language System] 14(3): 219–226.

———— 1993b. "The Evolving European Language System: A Theory of Communication Potential and Language Competition", *International Political Science Review* [Special Issue on The Emergent World Language System] 14(3): 241–256.

——— 1995. "Die Soziologische Untersuchung der Transnationalen Gesellschaft", *Journal für Sozialforschung* 35(2): 107–120.

——— 1998a. "A Political Sociology of the World Language System (1): The Dynamics of Language Spread", *Language Problems and Language Planning* 22(1): 63–78.

——— 1998b. "A Political Sociology of the World Language System (2): The Unequal Exchange of Texts", *Language Problems and Language Planning* 22(2): 109–128.

Der Spiegel. 1997. Issue 16, April 14.

Der Standard. 1996. January 27–28.

Decalo, S. 1992. "The Process, Prospects and Constraints of Democratization", *African Affairs* 93: 7–35.

——— 1997. "Benin: First of the New Democracies", pp. 43–61 in Clark, J.F. and Gardinier, D.E. (eds.), *Political Reform in Francophone Africa*. Boulder: Westview Press.

Dear, M. and Flusty, S. 1999. "Postmodern Urbanism and the Spatial Logic of Global Capitalism", in Featherstone, M and Lash, S. (eds.), *Spaces of Culture*. London: Sage.

Dear, M.J., Schockman, E.H. and Hise, G. 1996. *Rethinking Los Angeles*. London: Sage.

Dear, Peter (ed.). 1991. *The Literary Structure of Scientific Argument: Historical Studies*. Philadelphia: University of Pennsylvania Press.

Degler, Carl. (1971) 1986. *Neither Black Nor White; Slavery and Race in Brazil and the United States*. Madison: University of Wisconsin Press.

Delanty, Gerard. 2000. *Modernity and Postmodernity*. London: Sage.

Deleuze, G. and Guattari, F. 1987. *A Thousand Plateaus: Capitalism and Schizophrenia*. Minneapolis: University of Minnesota Press.

Denzin, N.K. 1991. *Images of Postmodern Society: Social Theory and Contemporary Cinema*. London: Sage.

Department of Employment, Education and Training, Higher Education Division. 1993. *National Report on Australia's Higher Education Sector*. Canberra: Australian Government Publishing Service.

Derrida, Jacques. 1976. *Of Grammatology*. Baltimore: John Hopkins University Press.

Desosieres, Alain. 1993. *La Politique des Grands Nombres. Histoire de la Raison Statistique*. Paris: Editions La Decouverte.

Diamond, L. 1987. "Class Formation in a Swollen African State", *Journal of Modern African Studies* 25(4): 567–596.

——— 1996. "Is the Third Wave Over?", *Journal of Democracy* (July): 20–37.

Dicken, P. 1998. *Global Shift: Transforming the Global Economy*. 3rd Edition. London: Chapman.

Dinello, Natalia 1998. "Elites and Philanthropy in Russia", *International Journal of Politics, Culture and Society* 12(1): 109–133.

Diongue, Marietou. 1980. *Francophonie et Langues Africaines en Sénégal*. Dakar: École Nomale Supérieure des Bibliothèques.

Donati, Pierpaolo. 1995. "Identity and Solidarity in the Complex of Citizenship: The Relational Approach", *International Sociology* 10(3): 299–314.

Donnely, Michael. 1998. "From Political Arithmetic to Social Statistics: How Some Nineteenth-Century Roots of the Social Sciences were Implanted", in Heilbron, J., Magnusson, L. and Wittrock, B. (eds.), *The Rise of the Social Sciences and the Formation of Modernity: Conceptual Change in Context, 1750–1850*. Dordrecht: Kluwer.

Dorian, Nancy. 1981. *Language Death; The Life Cycle of a Scottish Gaelic Dialect*. Philadelphia: University of Pennsylvania Press.

Dorian, Nancy (ed.). 1989. *Investigating Obsolescence: Studies in Language Contraction and Death*. Cambridge: Cambridge University Press.

——— 1998. "Western Language Ideologies and Small-Language Prospects", pp. 3–21 in Grenoble, Lenore A. and Whaley, Lindsay J. (eds.), *Endangered Languages: Current Issues and Future Prospects*. Cambridge: Cambridge University Press.

Douglas, Mary. 1986. *How Institutions Think*. Syracuse, NY: Syracuse University Press.

Drucker, P.F. 1993. *Post-Capitalist Society*. New York: Harper Collins.

Dua, Hans R. 1994. *Hegemony of English; Future of Developing Languages in the Third World*. Mysore: Yashoda Publications.

Duara, P. 1996. "Historicizing National Identity, or Who Imagines What and When", in Eley, G. and Suny, R.G. (eds.), *Becoming National*. New York: Oxford University Press.

Dubnow, S. 1916. *History of the Jews in Russia and Poland*. Philadelphia: Jewish Publication Society of America.

DuBois, W.E.B. (1903) 1989. *The Souls of Black Folk*. New York: Dover.

Dunn, Chris and Dunn, Elizabeth (eds.). 1996. *Civil Society: Challenging Western Models*. London: Routledge.

Dunn, John (ed.). 1994. Special issue of *Political Studies* 42.

Dunn, Robert G. 1998. *Identity Crisis: A Social Critique of Postmodernity*. Minneapolis: University of Minnesota Press.

Durkheim, E. 1964. *The Rules of Sociological Method*. New York: The Free Press.

———— 1973. *On Morality and Society. Selected Writings*. Chicago: University of Chicago Press.

Durkheim, E. and Mauss, M. (1913) 1971. "Note on the Notion of Civilization", *Social Research* 38(1): 808–813.

Eco, Umberto. 1993. *La Ricerca della Lingua Perfetta*. Roma/Bari: Laterza.

Edwards, J. 1988. *Language, Society and Identity*. Oxford: Blackwell.

Eickelman, Dale F. 1997. "Muslim Politics: The Prospects for Democracy in North Africa and the Middle East", in Entelis, John (ed.), *Islam, Democracy and the State in North Africa*. Bloomington and Indianapolis: Indiana University Press.

———— 1998. "Inside the Islamic Reformation", *Wilson Quarterly* 22(1): 80–89.

Eickelman, Dale F. and Anderson, Jon. 1997. "Print, Islam, and the Prospects for Civic Pluralism: New Religious Writings and Their Audiences", *Journal of Islamic Studies* 8(1).

Eickelman, Dale F. and Piscatori, James. 1996. *Muslim Politics*. Princeton: Princeton University Press.

Eisenstadt, S.N. 1963. *The Political Systems of Empires*. New York: The Free Press.

———— 1964. "Institutionalization and Social Change", *American Sociological Review* 29: 235–247.

———— 1966. *Modernization: Protest and Change*. Englewood Cliffs: Prentice Hall.

———— (ed.). 1970. *Readings in Social Evolution and Development*. Oxford: Pergamon Press.

———— 1973. *Tradition, Change and Modernity*. New York: John Wiley and Sons.

———— 1978. "European Expansion and the Civilization of Modernity", pp. 167–186 in Wesseling, H.L. (ed.), *Expansion and Reaction*. Leiden: Leiden University Press.

———— 1982. "The Axial Age: The Emergence of Transcendental Visions and the Rise of Clerics," *European Journal of Sociology* 23(2): 294–314.

———— (ed.). 1986. *The Origins and Diversity of Axial-Age Civilizations*. Albany, NY: SUNY Press.

———— (ed.). 1987. *Patterns of Modernity (Volume I: The West)*. New York: New York University Press.

———— 1992. *Jewish Civilization: The Jewish Historical Experience in a Comparative Perspective*. Albany: SUNY Press.

———— 1994. *Japan and the Multiplicity of Cultural Programmes of Modernity*. Occasional Paper 15, Truman Institute, The Hebrew University of Jerusalem.

———— 1995. *Power, Trust, and Meaning: Essays in Sociological Theory and Analysis*. Chicago: University of Chicago Press.

———— 1996a. *Japanese Civilization*. Chicago: University of Chicago Press.

———— 1996b. "The Jacobin Component of Fundamentalist Movements", *Contention* 5(3): 156–165.

———— 1997a. *Introductory Address*. Delivered to the World Congress of the International Institute of Sociology, Cologne (July).

———— 1997b. *Modernita, Modernizzazione e Oltre*. Roma: Armando Editore.

———— 1998. "The Construction of Collective Identities. Some Analytical and Comparative Indications," *European Journal of Social Theory* 1(2): 229–254.

———— 1999a. *Fundamentalism, Sectarianism and Revolution: The Jacobin Dimension of Modernity*. Cambridge: Cambridge University Press.

———— 1999b. *Paradoxes of Democracy: Fragility, Continuity and Change*. Baltimore, Maryland: The Woodrow Wilson Center Press and the Johns Hopkins University Press.

———— 2000. "Multiple Modernities", *Daedalus* 129(1): 1–29.

Eisenstadt, S.N. and Azmon, Y. 1975. *Socialism and Tradition*. Atlantic Highlands, NJ: Humanities Press.

Eisenstadt, S.N. with Curelaru, M. 1976. *The Form of Sociology—Paradigms and Crises*. New York: John Wiley.

Eisenstadt, S.N. and Giesen, B. 1995. "The Construction of Collective Identity", *European Journal of Sociology* 36(1): 72–102.

Eisenstadt, S.N. and Schluchter, Wolfgang. 1998. "Introduction: Paths to Early Modernities— A Comparative View", *Daedalus* 127(3): 1–18.

Eisenstein, Elizabeth L. 1979. *The Printing Press as an Agent of Change*. Cambridge: Cambridge University Press.

Eliade, M. 1959. *The Sacred and the Profane. The Nature of Religion*. New York: Harcourt & Brace.

Elias, N. 1978. *The Civilizing Process Volume 1*. Oxford: Blackwell.

———— 1982. *The Civilizing Process Volume 2*. Oxford: Blackwell.

———— 1983. *The Court Society*. Oxford: Blackwell.

———— 1984. "The Sociogenesis of Sociology", *Sociologish Tijdschrift* 11(1).

———— 1987. "The Retreat of Sociologists into the Present", *Theory, Culture & Society* 4: 223–247.

———— 1991. *The Society of Individuals*. Oxford: Blackwell.

———— (1939) 1994. *The Civilizing Process*. Oxford: Blackwell.

———— 1998. "Civilization, Culture and Identity", pp. 225–240 in Rundell, John and Mennell, Stephen (eds.), *Classical Readings in Culture and Civilization*. London: Routledge and Kegan Paul.

Elias, N. and Scotson, J. 1994. *The Established and the Outsiders*. London: Sage.

Entelis, J.P. 1981. "Elite Political Culture and Socialization in Algeria: Tensions and Discontinuities", *Middlle East Journal* 25: 191–208.

Erikson, Erik H. 1974. *Identity: Youth and Crisis*. London: Faber & Faber.

Etzioni, Amitai. 1988. *The Moral Dimension*. New York: Basic Books.

Etzioni-Halevy, Eva. 1985. *Bureaucracy and Democracy: A Political Dilemma*. 2nd edition. London: Routledge & Kegan Paul.

———— 1993a. *Kesher Ha'elitot Vehademocratia Beyisrael (The Elite Connection and Democracy in Israel)*. Tel-Aviv: Sifriat Poalim. (Hebrew)

———— 1993b. *The Elite Connection: Problems and Potential of Western Democracy*. Cambridge: Polity Press.

———— (ed.). 1997a. *Classes and Elites in Democracy and Democratization*. New York: Garland Publishing.

———— 1997b. *Makom Batzameret: Elitot Ve'elitism Beyisrael (A Place at the Top: Elites and Elitism in Israel)*. Tel-Aviv: Tcherikover Publishers. (Hebrew)

Eurobarometer, 34, 1991. "The Young Europeans", May, (prepared by the Task Force for Human Resources of the European Communities). Brussels: European Coordination Office.

Eurobarometer, 44, 1996. "Languages in the European Union", April. Brussels: European Coordination Office.

Evans, P. (ed.). 1997. *State-Society Synergy: Government and Social Capital in Development*. Berkeley: University of California Press.

Evans, Peter B., Rueschemeyer, Dietrich, and Skocpol, Theda (eds.). 1985. *Bringing the State Back In*. Cambridge: Cambridge University Press.

Eymeri, Jean-Michael. 1999. *Les gardiens de l'état. Une sociologie des énarques de ministère*. Ph.D. thesis in political sciences, Université de Paris I.

Faidutti-Rudolph, A.M. 1964. *L'Immigration italienne dans le Sud-Est de la France*. Paris: Gap, Edition Ophrys.

Falk, R. 1999. *Predatory Globalization: A Critique*. Cambridge: Polity.

Farjadi, G.A. 1998. "Identifying the Origins of the Educated Unemployment and Increasing Demands for Higher Education in Iran", paper presented at the UNESCO Regional Seminar on Higher Education in the Coming Century, Tehran (February 16–18).

Fasold, R. 1987. *The Sociolinguistics of Society*. Oxford: Blackwell.

Faubion, James D. 1993. *Modern Greek Lessons: A Primer in Historical Constructivism*. Princeton: Princeton University Press.

Featherstone, M. (ed.). 1990. *Global Culture: Nationalism, Globalization and Modernity*. London: Sage.

———— 1991. *Consumer Culture and Postmodernism*. London: Sage.

—— 1995. *Undoing Culture: Globalization, Postmodernism and Identity*. London: Sage.

—— 1998a. "The *Flâneur*, the City and Virtual Public Life", *Urban Studies* 35(5–6): 909–925.

—— 1998b. *The Globalization of Mobility: Experience, Sociability and Speed in Technological Cultures*. Paper presented to the 5th World Leisure and Recreational Association Congress, São Paulo.

—— 1999. "Body Modification: An Introduction", *Body & Society* (special issue on Body Modification) 4(2–3).

—— 2000a. "Archiving Cultures", *British Journal of Sociology* 51(1).

—— 2000b. "Technologies of Post-Human Development and the Potential for Global Citizenship", in Nederveen Pieterse, J. (ed.), *Global Futures*. London: Zed Books.

—— 2000c. "The Global City, Information Technology and Public Life", in Davis, C. (ed.), *Identity and Social Change*. Boston: Transaction Books.

Featherstone, M., Lash, S. and Robertson, R. (eds.). 1995. *Global Modernities*. London: Sage.

Featherstone, M. and Lash, S. 1995. "Globalization, Modernity and the Spatialization of Social Theory: An Introduction", pp. 1–24 in Featherstone, M., Lash, S. and Robertson, R. (eds.), *Global Modernities*. London: Sage.

Febvre, L. 1973. "Civilisation: Evolution of a Word and a Group of Ideas", pp. 219–257 in Febvre, L., *A New Kind of History and other Essays*. New York: Harper & Row.

Ferguson, Charles A. 1959. "Diglossia", *Word* 15.

—— 1977. "Sociolinguistic Settings of Language Planning", pp. 9–29 in Rubin, Joan, Jernudd, Björn H., Das Gupta, J., Fishman, Joshua A. and Ferguson, Charles A. (eds.), *Language Planning Processes*. Hague: Mouton Publishers.

Fieldhouse, D.K. 1967. *The Theory of Capitalist Imperialism*. London: Longmans.

Fienberg, S.E. and Mason, W.M. 1978. "Identification and Estimation of Age-Period-Cohort Models in the Analysis of Discrete Archival Data", pp. 1–67 in Schuessler, K.F. (ed.), *Sociological Methodology*. San Francisco: Jossey-Bass.

Fischer, D.H. 1989. *Albion's Seed: Four British Folkways in America*. New York: Oxford University Press.

Fischer, Michael M.J. and Abedi, Mehdi. 1990. *Debating Muslims: Cultural Dialogues in Postmodernity and Tradition*. Madison: University of Wisconsin Press.

Fisher, D. 1983. "The Role of Philanthropic Foundations in the Reproduction and Production of Hegemony", *Sociology* 17: 206–233.

Fishman, J.A. 1967. "Bilingualism With and Without Diglossia: Diglossia With and Without Bilingualism", *Journal of Social Issues* 23: 29–38.

—— 1969. "National Languages and Languages of Wider Communication in the Developing Nations", *Anthropological Linguistics* 11: 111–135.

—— 1972. "Domains and the Relationship Between Micro- and Macrosociolinguistics", pp. 435–453 in Gumperz, John J. and Hymes, Dell (eds.), *Directions in Sociolinguistics*. New York: Holt Rinehart and Winston.

—— 1973. "Language Modernization and Planning in Comparison with other Types of National Modernization and Planning", *Language in Society* 2(1): 23–43.

—— 1989. *Language and Ethnicity in Minority Sociolinguistic Perspective*. Clevedon, Philadelphia: Multilingual Matters.

Fishman, J.A., Cooper, Robert L. and Ma, Roxana. 1971. *Bilingualism in the Barrio*. Bloomington: Research Center for the Language Sciences, Indiana University.

Fishman, J.A., Ferguson, Charles A. and Das Gupta, J. 1968. *Language Problems of Developing Nations*. New York: Wiley.

Flaitz, Jeffra. 1988. *The Ideology of English: French Perceptions of English as a World Language* [Contributions to the Sociology of Language 49]. Berlin: Mouton De Gruyter.

Fleischmann, Lea. 1982. *Dies ist nicht mein Land. Eine Jüdin verläßt die Bundesrepublik*. Hamburg: Hoffmann und Campe.

Ford, A. 1985. *Medios de Comunicación y Cultura Popular*. Buenos Aires: Ed. Legasa.

Forrest, Alan. 1994. "A New Start for Cultural Action in the European Community: Genesis and Implications of Article 128 of the Treaty on Europan Union", *European Jounal of Cultural Policy* 1(1): 11–20.

Forrester, Viviane. 1996. *L'horreur économique*. Paris: Fayard.

Foucault, Michel. 1965. *Madness and Civilization: A History of Insanity in the Age of Reason*. New York: Pantheon Books.
——— 1966. *Les Mots et les Choses*. Paris: Gallimard.
——— 1969a. *L'archeiologie du Savoir*. Paris: Gallimard.
——— 1969b. *The Archaeology of Knowledge*. New York: Pantheon.
——— 1970. *The Order of Things: An Archeology of the Human Sciences*. London: Tavistock.
——— 1973. *The Birth of the Clinic: An Archaeology of Medical Perception*. New York: Vintage Books.
——— 1975. *Surveiller et Punir: Naissance de la Prison*. Paris: Gallimard.
——— 1978. *The History of Sexuality. An Introduction*. New York: Vintage Books.
——— 1980. *Power/Knowledge: Selected Interviews and Other Writings, 1972–1977*. New York: Pantheon Books.
——— 1988. *Technologies of the Self: A Seminar with Michel Foucault*. Amherst: University of Massachusetts Press.
Fowler, A. 1993. "Non-Governmental Organizations as Agents of Democratization: An African Perspective", *Journal of International Development* 5(3): 325–339.
Fox, Christopher, Porter, Roy and Wokler, Robert (eds.). 1995. *Inventing Human Science: Eighteenth Century Domains*. Berkeley: University of California Press.
Fox Keller, E. 1985. *Reflections on Gender and Science*. New Haven: Yale University Press.
Frank, A.G. 1998. *Re-ORIENT*. Berkeley: University of California Press.
Freidson, Eliot. 1953. "The Relation of the Situation of Contact to the Media in Mass Communication", *Public Opinion Quarterly* 17: 230–238.
Freud, S. 1961. *Civilization and Its Discontents*. New York and London: W.W. Norton & Company.
Friedberg, A. 1994. *Window Shopping: Cinema and the Postmodern*. Berkeley: University of California Press.
Friedman, J. 1994. *Cultural Identity and Global Process*. London: Sage.
——— 1995. "Global System, Globalization and the Parameters of Modernity", pp. 45–68 in Featherstone, M., Lash, S. and Robertson, R. (eds.), *Global Modernities*. London: Sage.
——— 1999. "The Hybridization of Roots and the Abhorrence of the Bush", in Featherstone, M. and Lash, S. (eds.), *Spaces of Culture*. London: Sage.
Frisby, David. 1985. *Fragments of Modernity*. Cambridge, MA: Blackwell.
Fröbel, Folker, Heinrichs, Jürgen and Kreye, Otto. 2000. "The New International Division of Labor in the World Economy", pp. 257–273 in Timmons Roberts, J. and Hite, A. (eds.), *From Modernization to Globalization: Perspectives on Development and Social Change*. Oxford: Blackwell.
Fromm, E. 1962. *Beyond the Chains of Illusion*. New York: Simon and Schuster.
——— (ed.). 1965. *Socialist Humanism*. New York: Doubleday.
Frye, R.N. 1975. *The Golden Age of Persia*. London: Weidenfeld.
Fukuyama, F. 1992. *The End of History and the Last Man*. New York: The Free Press.
Furet, F. 1981. *Interpreting the French Revolution*. London: Cambridge University Press.
——— 1995. *Le passé d'une illusion: Essai sur l'idée communiste au XXe siècle*. Paris: Clamann-Levy.
Gadamer, Hans-Georg. 1987. "Historik und Sprache—eine Antwort", in Koselleck, Reinhart and Gadamer, Hans-Georg, *Hermeneutik und Historik*. Sitzungsberichte der Heidelberger Akademie der Wissenschaften. Heidelberg: Carl Winter Universitatsverlag.
Galaskiewicz, J. 1985. *Social Organizations of an Urban Grants Economy*. Orlando: Academic Press.
Galnoor, Yitzhak, Rosenbloom, David and Yaroni, Allon. 1998. "Creating New Public Management Reforms: Lessons from Israel", *Administration and Society* 30: 393–420.
Garfinkel, Harold. 1967. *Studies in Ethnomethodology*. Englewood Cliffs, NJ: Prentice Hall.
Garmadi, J. 1981. *La Sociolinguistique*. Paris: Presses Universitaires de France.
Gebhardt, Jürgen. 1990. "Amerikanismus—Politische Kultur und Zivilreligion in den USA", *Politik und Zeitgeschichte* 49: 3–18.
Geisser, Vincent. 1997. *Ethnicité républicaine. Les élites d'origine maghrébine dans le système politique français*. Paris: Presses de Sciences Po.

Gellner, E. 1973. "Introduction", pp. 11–21 in Gellner, E and Micaud, C. (eds.), *Arabs and Berbers. From Tribe to Nation in North Africa*. London: Duckworth.
———— 1983. *Nations and Nationalism*. Ithaca: Cornell University Press.
———— 1994a. *Conditions of Liberty: Civil Society and Its Rivals*. London: Hamish Hamilton.
———— 1994b. *Encounters with Nationalism*. Oxford: Blackwell.
George, Asha M. 1995. *Sovereignty Starts in the State of Mind not in the State of Hawai'i*. Honolulu: University of Hawai'i, Department of Political Science.
George, H. Jr. 1984. *American Race Relations Theory: A Review of Four Models*. Lanham: University Press of America.
Germani, G. 1981. *The Sociology of Modernization*. New Brunswick, NJ: Transaction Books.
Gerstein, Dean R. et al. (eds.). 1988. *The Behavioral and Social Sciences. Achievements and Opportunities*. Washington, DC: National Academy Press.
Gervais, M. 1997. "Niger: Regime Change, Economic Crisis and Perpetuation of Privilege", pp. 86–108 in Clark, J.F. and Gardinier, D.E. (eds.), *Political Reform in Francophone Africa*. Boulder: Westview Press.
Geyl, P. 1958. *The Revolt of the Netherlands*. New York: Barnes & Noble.
Gibson, W. 1984. *Neuromancer*. London: Harper Collins.
Giddens, A. 1971. *Capitalism and Modern Social Theory*. Cambridge: Cambridge University Press.
———— 1976. *New Rules of Sociological Method*. London: Hutchinson.
———— 1985. *The Nation-State and Violence*. Berkeley and Los Angeles: University of California Press.
———— 1990. *The Consequences of Modernity*. Stanford: Stanford University Press.
———— 1991. *Modernity and Self-Identity*. Cambridge: Polity Press.
———— 1994a. *Beyond Left and Right. The Future of Radical Politics*. Stanford: Stanford University Press.
———— 1994b. "Living in a Post-Traditional Society", pp. 56–109 in Beck, U., Giddens, A. and Lash, S., *Reflexive Modernization*. Stanford: Stanford University Press.
———— 1995. *Soziologie*. Graz: Hausner und Hausner.
———— 1999. *The Third Way. The Renewal of Social Democracy*. Malden, MA: Polity Press.
———— 2000. "The Social Revolutions of Our Time", pp. 83–99 in Nash, Kate (ed.), *Readings in Contemporary Political Sociology*. Oxford: Blackwell.
Gidron, B., Kramer, R. and Salamon, L. (eds.). 1992. *Government and the Third Sector: Emerging Relationships in Welfare States*. San Francisco: Jossey-Bass.
Gigerenzer, Gerd (ed.). 1989. *The Empire of Chance. How Probability Changed Science and Everyday Life*. Cambridge: Cambridge University Press.
Giles, H., Bourhis, R.Y. and Taylor, D.M. 1977. "Towards a Theory of Language in Ethnic Group Relations", pp. 307–348 in Giles, H. (ed.), *Language, Ethnicity and Intergroup Relations*. London: Academic Press.
Gilroy, Paul. 1993. *The Black Atlantic: Modernity and Double Consciousness*. Cambridge, MA: Harvard University Press.
Gitlin, Todd. 1995. *The Twilight of Common Dreams*. New York: Holt.
———— 1998. "Public Sphere or Public Sphrecules", in Liebes, Tamar and Curran, James (eds.), *Media, Ritual, Identity*. London: Routledge.
Glenn, N.D. 1977. *Cohort Analysis*. Beverly Hills: Sage.
Godbout, Jacques T. 1997. "Consommateurs de don et producteurs de causes: la philanthropie et le marché", *Revue Internationale de Psychosociologie* 3(8): 119–126.
Goffman, E. 1971. *The Presentation of Self in Everyday Life*. Harmondsworth: Penguin Books.
———— 1972. "The Neglected Situation", pp. 61–66 in Gioglioli, P.P. (ed.), *Language and Social Context*. Harmondsworth: Penguin Books.
———— 1973. *La mise en scene de la vie quotidienne*. 1&2. Paris: Editions de Minuit.
Goldthorpe, J.H. 1971. "Theories of Industrial Society", *Archives Europeennes de Sociologie* 12(2): 263–288.
Göle, N. 1996. *The Forbidden Modern: Civilization and Veiling*. Ann Arbor: University of Michigan Press.
———— 2000a. "Snapshots of Islamic Modernities", *Daedalus* 129(1): 91–117.

——— 2000b. *Studying Islam as a Contemporary Social Movement*. Unpublished manuscript, presented to the conference on The Sociology of Islamic Social Movements, NYU, Feb. 19–20.

Gong, G.W. 1984. *The Standard of 'Civilization' in International Society*. Oxford: Clarendon Press.

Gonzalez-Quijano, Yves. 1998. *Les gens du livre. Edition et champ intellectuel dans l'Egypte republicaine* [People of the Book: Publishing and Intellectual Field in Republican Egypt] Paris: CNRS Editions.

Goodman, Dena. 1992. "Public Sphere and Private Life", *History and Theory* 31: 1–20.

Gordon, D. 1997. "On Promoting Democracy in Africa: The International Dimension", pp. 153–163 in Ottaway, M. (ed.), *Democracy in Africa—The Hard Road Ahead*. Boulder: Lynne Rienner.

Gorny, Y. 1986. *The Arab Question and the Jewish Problem*. Tel-Aviv: Am Oved. (Hebrew)

Gossen, Heinrich. 1854. *Entwicklung der Gesetze des menschlichen Verhaltens und der daraus fließenden Regeln für menschliches Handeln*. Braunschweig: Vieweg.

Gouldner, Alvin W. 1970. *The Coming Crisis of Western Sociology*. New York: Basic Books.

Gowan, P. 1999. *The Global Gamble. Washington's Faustian Bid for World Dominance*. London: Verso.

Graham, G.J. and Carey, G.W. (eds.). 1972. *The Post-Behavioral Era*. New York: McKay.

Grandguillaume, G. 1983. *Arabization et politique linguistique au Maghreb*. Paris: Maisonneuve & Larose.

——— 1995. "L'islam en Algérie", *Esprit* 208 (Janauary): 9–11.

Grandin, Greg. 2000. *The Blood of Guatemala: A History of Race and Nation*. Durham: Duke University Press.

Graubard. S.R. (ed.). 1986. *Norden: The Passion for Equality*. Oslo: Norwegian University Press.

Gray, J. 1993. *Beyond the New Right: Markets, Government and the Common Environment*. London: Routledge.

Greenacre, Michael J. 1984. *Theory and Application of Correspondence Analysis*. London: Academic Press.

——— 1993. *Correspondence Analysis in Practice*. London: Academic Press.

Grillo, R.D. 1989. *Dominant Languages: Language and Hierarchy in Britain and in France*. Cambridge, UK: Cambridge University Press.

Grosjean, F. 1982. *Life with Two Languages—An Introduction to Bilingualism*. Cambridge, MA: Harvard University Press.

Gruzinski, Serge. 1999. *La pensée métisse*. Paris: Fayard.

Guarnizo, L.E. and Smith, M.G. 1998. "The Locations of Transnationalism", pp. 3–34 in Smith, M.P. and Guarnizo, L.E. (eds.), *Transnationalism from Below*. New Brunswick: Transaction.

Gumperz, J.J. 1967. "Linguistic Markers of Bilingual Communication", *Journal of Social Issues* 23: 137–153.

——— 1968. "The Speech Community", pp. 381–386 in Sills, David L. (ed.), *International Encyclopedia of the Social Sciences*. New York: The Macmillan Company.

——— 1971. *Language in Social Groups*. Edited by Anwar Dil. Stanford: Stanford University Press.

——— 1987. "The Speech Community", pp. 219–231 in Giglioli, P.P. (ed.), *Language and Social Context*. Harmondsworth: Penguin Books.

Gunes-Ayata, A. 1994. "Roots and Trends of Clientalism in Turkey", in Roniger, L. and Gunes-Ayata, A. (eds.), *Clientalism and Civil Society*. Boulder: L. Rienner Publishers.

Gupta, A. and Ferguson, J. (eds). 1997. *Culture, Power, Place: Explorations in Critical Anthropology*. Durham and London: Duke University Press.

Gurvitch, G. and Moore, Wilbert E. (eds.). 1945. *Twentieth Century Sociology*. New York: The Philosophical Library.

Guvenc, B. 1994. *Turk Kimligi: Kultur Tarihinin Kaynaklari*. Ankara: T.C. Kultur Bakanlygy.

Haber, Ethan. 1998. "Hollander's Finger in the Hole of the Dam", *Yediot Aharonot*, November 8, p. 5. (Hebrew)

Habermas, J. 1970. "Technology and Science as 'Ideology'", pp. 81–127 in Habermas, J., *Toward a Rational Society*. Boston: Beacon Press.

—— 1971. *Erkenntnis und Interesse.* Frankfurt/M.: Suhrkamp.
—— 1981a. "Modernity versus Postmodernity". *New German Critique* 22 (Winter): 3–14.
—— 1981b. *Theorie des kommunikativen Handelns.* 2 vols. Frankfurt/M.: Suhrkamp.
—— 1985. *Le discours philosophique de la modernité.* Paris: Gallimard.
—— 1987. *The Philosophical Discourse of Modernity.* Cambridge, MA: MIT Press.
—— (1962) 1989. *The Structural Transformation of the Public Sphere: An Inquiry into a Category of Bourgeois Society* (T. Burger, trans.). Cambridge, MA: MIT Press.
—— 1998. *Après l'Etat-Nation.* Paris: Fayard.
Hacking, Ian. 1990. *The Taming of Chance.* Cambridge: Cambridge University Press.
Hadas-Lebel, Mireille and Oliel-Grausz, Evelyne. 1992. *Les juifs et la Révolution française.* Louvain: E. Peeters.
Haferkamp, H. 1987. "From the Intra-State to the Inter-State Civilizing Process?", *Theory, Culture & Society* (Special Issue on Norbert Elias and Figurational Sociology) 4(2–3): 545–557.
Hage, J. and Powers, Ch. H. 1992. *Post-Industrial Lives. Roles and Relationships in the 21st Century.* London: Sage.
Hagège, Claude. 1987. *Le français et les Siècles.* Paris: Odile Jacob.
Hagen, Everett. 1962. *On the Theory of Social Change.* Homewood, IL: Dorsey Press.
Halecki, O. 1966. *Sacrum Poloniae Millenium (A Thousand Years of Catholic Poland).* Rome: The Gregorian University.
Hall, P. 1987. "Abandoning the Rhetoric of Independence: Reflections on the Non-Profit Sector in the Post-Liberal Era", pp. 11–28 in Ostrander S., Langton, S. and Van Til, J. (eds.), *The Shifting Debate: Public/Private Sector Relations in the Modern Welfare State.* New Brunswick, NJ: Transaction Books.
Hall, Stuart. 1990. "Cultural Identity and Diaspora", in Rutherford, Jonathan (ed.), *Identity: Community, Culture, Difference.* London: Lawrence & Wishart.
—— 1996a. "New Ethnicities", in Morley, David and Chen, Kuan-Hsing (eds)., *Stuart Hall: Critical Dialogues in Cultural Studies.* London: Routledge.
—— 1996b. "Who Needs 'Identity'?", in Hall, Stuart and du Gay, Paul (eds.), *Questions of Cultural Identity.* London: Sage.
—— 2000. "The Question of Cultural Identity", pp. 115–122 in Nash, Kate (ed.), *Readings in Contemporary Political Sociology.* Oxford: Blackwell.
Hallaq, Wael B. 1997. *A History of Islamic Legal Theories.* Cambridge: Cambridge University Press.
Halpern, Manfred. 1963. *The Politics of Social Change in the Middle East and North Africa.* Princeton: Princeton University Press.
Hamilton, Alexander. (1787) 1961. "Federalist" No. 1, (October 27, 1787) in Cooke, Jacob E. (ed.), *The Federalist.* Middletown, Conn.: Wesleyan University Press.
Hanchard, Michael. 1994. *Orpheus and Power.* Princeton: Princeton University Press.
Handelman, Don and Katz, Elihu. 1990. "State Ceremonies of Israel", pp. 191–233 in Handelman, Don, *Models and Mirrors: Towards an Anthropology of Public Events.* New York: Cambridge University Press.
Handwörterbuch der Sozialwissenschaften. 1965. A new edition of the classic *Handwörterbuch der Staatswissenschaften.* 12 Vols. Stuttgart: Gustav Fischer.
Hannaford, Ivan. 1996. *Race: The History of an Idea in the West.* Baltimore: Johns Hopkins University Press and the Woodrow Wilson Center Press.
Hannerz, U. 1988. "The World in Creolisation", *Africa* 57: 546–559.
—— 1992. *Cultural Complexity.* New York: Columbia University Press.
—— 1996. *Transnational Connections. Culture, People, Places.* London: Routledge.
Hansen, M. 1991. *Babel and Babylon: Spectatorship in American Silent Film.* Cambridge, MA.: Harvard University Press.
Harbeson, J.W. 1994. "Civil Society and Political Renaissance in Africa", pp. 1–29 in Harbeson, J.W., Rothschild, D. and Chazan, N. (eds.), *Civil Society and the State in Africa.* Boulder: Lynne Rienner.
Harbi, M. 1994. *L'Algérie et son Destin. Croyants ou Citoyens.* Algiers: Médias Associés.

Harel, Israel. 1993. "Flatterers and Gentlemen", *Ha'aretz*, November 7, p. B1. (Hebrew)
Hartz, L. 1964. *The Founding of New Societies: Studies in the History of the United States, Latin America, South Africa, Canada, and Australia.* New York: Harcourt, Brace & World, Inc.
Harvey, David. 1989. *The Condition of Postmodernity.* Oxford: Blackwell.
——— 2000. "Capitalism: The Factory of Fragmentation", pp. 292–297 in Timmons Roberts, J. and Hite, A. (eds.), *From Modernization to Globalization: Perspectives on Development and Social Change.* Oxford: Blackwell.
Hasenbalg, Carlos. 1979. *Discriminação e Desigualdades Raciais no Brasil.* Rio de Janeiro: Graal.
Havel, Vaclav. 1999. "Kosovo and the End of the Nation-State", *New York Review of Books* (June 10).
Hawthorn, G. 1993. "Sub-Saharan Africa", pp. 330–354 in Held, D. (ed.), *Prospects for Democracy.* Stanford: Stanford University Press.
——— 1976. *Enlightenment and Despair: A History of Sociology.* Cambridge: Cambridge University Press.
Hayashi, Chikio. 1996. "Cultural Link Analysis (CLA) for Comparative Quantitative Social Research and its Applications", pp. 209–229 in Hayashi, Chikio and Scheuch, Erwin K. (eds.), *Quantitative Social Research in Germany and Japan.* Opladen: Leske + Budrich.
——— 1998. "The Quantitative Study of National Character; Interchronological and International Perspectives", pp. 91–114 in Sasaki, Masamichi (ed.), *Values and Attitudes Across Nations and Time.* Leiden: Brill.
Hayashi, Chikio and Kuroda, Yasumasa. 1997. *Japanese Culture in Comparative Perspective.* New York: Praeger.
Hayashi, Chikio, Suzuki, Tatsuzo and Sasaki, Masamichi. 1992. *Data Analysis for Comparative Social Research: International Perspectives.* Amsterdam: Elsevier.
Hayes, C.J.H. 1956. "The American Frontier—Frontier of What?", pp. 66–75 in Taylor, G.R. (ed.), *The Turner Thesis: Concerning the Role of the Frontier in American History.* Boston: D.C. Heath and Company.
Head, Brian. 1982. "The Origins of 'la science sociale' in France, 1770–1800", *Australian Journal of French Studies* 19: 115–132.
Healy, G. 1998. *The Australian Higher Education Supplement, The Australian,* (August 19): 35.
Hechter, M. 1975. *Internal Colonialism: The Celtic Fringe in British National Development, 1536–1966.* Berkeley: University of California Press.
——— 1978. "Group Formation and the Cultural Division of Labor", *American Journal of Sociology* 84(2): 293–318.
Hefner, Robert W. (ed.). 1998a. *Democratic Civility: The History and Cross-Cultural Possibility of a Modern Political Ideal.* New Brunswick: Transaction Books.
——— 1998b. "Multiple Modernities: Christianity, Islam, and Hinduism in a Globalizing Age", *Annual Review of Anthropology* 27: 83–104.
Hegel, G.W.F. 1900. *The Philosophy of History.* New York: Willey Book Co.
——— (1807) 1977. *Phenomenology of Spirit.* Oxford: Oxford University Press.
Heidegger, M. (1927) 1962. *Being and Time.* New York: Harper & Row.
——— 1977. *The Question Concerning Technology and Other Essays.* Translated and with an introduction by William Lovitt. New York: Harper & Row.
Heideking, Jürgen. 1988. *Die Verfassung vor dem Richterstuhl: Vorgeschichte und Ratifizierung der amerikanischen Verfassung, 1787–1791.* Berlin/New York: W. de Gruyter.
——— 1994. "The Federal Processions of 1788 and the Origins of American Civil Religion", *Soundings* 77: 367–387.
Heilbron, Johan. 1995a. "Nederlandse Vertalingen Wereldwijd; Kleine Landen en Culturele Mondialisering", in Heilbron, J., de Nooy, W. and Tichelaar, W. (eds.), *Waarin een Klein Land . . . Nederlande Cultuur in Internationaal Verband.* Amsterdam: Prometheus.
——— 1995b. *The Rise of Social Theory.* Cambridge: Polity Press.
——— 1998. "French Moralists and the Anthropology of the Modern Era: On the Genesis of the Notions of 'Interest' and 'Commercial Society'", in Heilbron, J., Magnusson, L. and Wittrock, B. (eds.), *The Rise of the Social Sciences and the Formation of Modernity: Conceptual Change in Context, 1750–1850.* Dordrecht: Kluwer.
Heilbron, J., Magnusson, L. and Wittrock, B. (eds.). 1998. *The Rise of the Social Sciences and the Formation of Modernity: Conceptual Change in Context, 1750–1850.* Dordrecht: Kluwer.

Heilbrunn, J. 1997. "Togo: The National Conference and Stalled Reform", pp. 225–245 in Clark, J.F. and Gardinier, D.E. (eds.), *Political Reform in Francophone Africa*. Boulder: Westview Press.

Held, David. 2000. "Regulating Globalization? The Reinvention of Politics", *International Sociology* 15(2): 394–408.

——— et al. 1999. *Global Transformations*. Cambridge: Polity Press.

Helleiner, E. 1996. "Post-Globalization: Is the Financial Liberalization Trend Likely to be Reversed?", in Boyer, R. and Drache, D. (eds.), *States Against Markets: The Limits of Globalization*. London: Routledge.

Heller, A. 1982. *A Theory of History*. London: Routledge & Kegan Paul.

——— 1992. "Modernity's Pendulum", *Thesis Eleven* 31: 1–13.

Heller, M. 1988. 'Introduction', pp. 1–24 in Heller, M. (ed.), *Codeswitching—Anthropological and Sociolinguistic Perspectives*. Berlin: Walter de Gruyter.

Henderson, H. 1996. *Building a Win-Win World*. San Francisco: Berrett-Koehler.

Herb, G.H. and Kaplan D.H. (eds.). 1999. *Nested Identities: Nationalism, Territory, and Scale*. Lanham: Rowman & Littlefield Publishers, Inc.

Hetherington, K. 1997. *The Badlands of Modernity: Heterotopia and Social Ordering*. London: Routledge.

Hill, L. 2000. "The Two *Republicae* of the Roman Stoics. Can a Cosmopolite be a Patriot?", *Citizenship Studies* 4(1): 65–79.

Hindley, Reg. 1990. *The Death of the Irish Language*. London: Routledge.

Hirst, P and Thompson, G. 1996. *Globalization in Question*. Cambridge: Polity.

Hobcraft, J., Menken, J. and Preston, S. 1982. "Age, Period and Cohort Effects in Demography: A Review", *Population Index* 48: 4–43.

Hobsbawn, E.J. 1987. *The Age of Empire 1875–1914*. New York: Pantheon Books.

——— 1990. *Nations and Nationalism Since 1780. Programme, Myth, Reality*. Cambridge: Cambridge University Press.

——— 1994. *The Age of Extremes*. London: Michael Joseph.

——— 1996. "The Cult of Identity Politics", *New Left Review* 217: 38–47.

Hobsbawm, E.J. and Ranger, T. (eds.). 1983. *The Invention of Tradition*. Cambridge: Cambridge University Press.

Hochschild, A.R. 1997. *The Time Bind*. New York: Henry Holt and Company.

Hofstadter, R. 1968. "Introduction" pp. 3–8 in Hofstadter, R. and Lipset, S.M. (eds.), *Turner and the Sociology of the Frontier*. New York: Basic Books.

Hollinger, R. 1994. *Postmodernism and the Social Sciences*. London: Sage.

Hollingsworth, Rogers J., Schmitter, Philippe C. and Streeck, Wolfgang (eds.). 1994. *Governing Capitalist Economies*. New York: Oxford University Press.

Holmes, Janet and Meyerhoff, Miriam. 1999. "The Community of Practice: Theories and Methodologies in Language and Gender Research", *Language in Society* 28(2): 173–183.

Hont, I. and Ignatief, M. (eds.). 1983. *Wealth and Virtue. The Shaping of Political Economy in the Scottish Enlightenment*. Cambridge: Cambridge University Press.

Hoogvelt, A. 1997. *Globalisation and the Postcolonial World*. London: Macmillan.

Hooks, Bell. 1989. *Talking Back. Thinking Feminist. Thinking Black*. Boston, MA: South End Press.

Horkheimer, Max and Adorno, Theodore. 1972. *Dialectic of Enlightenment*. New York: Continuum.

Horsman, M. and Marshall, A. 1994. *After the Nation-State*. London: Harper Collins.

Hoskins, Colin and Mirus, Rolf. 1988. "Reasons for the US Dominance of the Intenational Trade in Television Programmes", *Media, Culture and Society* 10: 499–515.

Hudson, L. 1973. *The Cult of the Fact*. New York: Harper.

Hughes, H. Stuart. 1961. *Consciousness and Society*. New York: Random House.

Hugo, G. 1998. "The Demographic Underpinning of Current and Future International Migration in Asia", *Asian and Pacific Migration Journal* 7(1): 1–26.

Huizinga, J. 1955. *Homo Ludens. A Study of the Play Element in Culture*. Boston: The Beacon Press.

——— 1972. *America. A Dutch Historian's Vision, From Afar and Near*. New York: Harper & Row.

Huntington, S.P. 1991. *The Third Wave: Democratization in the Late Twentieth Century*. Norman: University of Oklahoma Press.

——— 1993. "The Clash of Civilizations?", *Foreign Affairs* 72 (Summer): 23–49.

—— 1996. *The Clash of Civilizations and the Remaking of World Order*. New York: Simon & Schuster.

Huq, Maimuna. 1999. "From Piety to Romance: Islam-Oriented Texts in Bangladesh", pp. 133–161 in Eickelman, Dale F. and Anderson, Jon (eds.), *New Media in the Muslim World: The Emerging Public Sphere*. Bloomington and Indianapolis: Indiana University Press.

Hutchinson, William R. and Lehmann, Hartmut (eds.). 1994. *Many are Chosen: Divine Election and Western Nationalism*. Minneapolis: Fortress Press.

Hutton, W. 1996. *The State We're In*. London: Vintage.

Hymes, Dell. 1967. "Models of the Interaction of Language and Social Setting", *Journal of Social Issues* 23(2): 8–38.

—— 1974. *Foundations in Sociolinguistics: An Ethnographic Approach*. Philadelphia: University of Pennsylvania Press.

Ianni, O. 1975. *A formacão do Estado Populista na América Latina*. Rio de Janeiro: Civilização Brasileira.

—— 1993. *O Labirinto Latinoamericano*. Petrópolis: Vozes.

Ihonvbere, J. 1993. "Threats to Democratization in Sub-Saharan Africa: The Case of Zambia", *Journal of Asian and African Studies* 27(3): 217–240.

—— 1996a. "Are Things Falling Apart? The Military and the Crisis of Democratization in Nigeria", *Journal of Modern African Studies* 34(2): 193–225.

—— 1996b. "On the Threshold of Another False Start?", *Journal of Asian and African Studies* 31(1–2): 125–142.

Illich, Ivan. 1971. *Deschooling Society*. New York: Harper & Row.

—— 1976. *Medical Nemesis: The Expropriation of Health*. New York: Pantheon Books.

Inglehart, Ronald. 1977. *The Silent Revolution—Changing Values and Political Styles Among Western Publics*. Princeton: Princeton University Press.

—— 1990. *Cultural Shift in Advanced Industrial Society*. Princeton: Princeton University Press.

—— 1997. *Modernization and Postmodernization*. Princeton: Princeton University Press.

Inkeles, A. 1976. "A Model of the Modern Man: Theoretical and Methodological Issues", pp. 320–348 in Black, C.E. (ed.), *Comparative Modernization: A Reader*. New York: The Free Press.

—— 1983. *Exploring Individual Modernity*. New York: Columbia University Press.

—— 1997. *National Character. A Psycho-Social Perspective*. New Brunswick and London: Transaction Publishers.

—— 1998. *One World Emerging? Convergence and Divergence in Industrial Societies*. Boulder: Westview Press.

Inkeles, A. and Smith, David H. 1974. *Becoming Modern: Individual Change in Six Developing Countries*. Cambridge: Harvard University Press.

Inkeles, A. and Usui, Chikako. 1989. "Retirement Patterns in Cross-National Perspective", in Kertzer, David K. and Warner Schaie, K. (eds.), *Age Structuring in Comparative Perspective*. Hillsdale, NJ: Lawrence Erlbaum Associates.

Inkster, I. 1997. Inaugural professorial lecture, Nottingham Trent University.

Innis, Harold. 1950. *Empire and Communication*. Toronto: University of Toronto.

International Herald Tribune, August 31, 1995.

International Herald Tribune, October 10, 1995.

Institute for Research and Planning in Higher Education (IRPHE). 1996. *Directory of State Universities in Iran*. Tehran: IRPHE.

—— 1997. *Statistics of Higher Education in Iran*. Tehran: IRPHE.

Ishay, Micheline. 1996. *The Betrayal of Internationalism*. Minneapolis: University of Minnesota Press.

Ishitsuka, S. 1998. "A Thematisation of the Post-Modern Situation—a Sociological Theory", paper delivered at the ISA World Congress of Sociology, Montreal (July 25–August 1).

James, E. (ed.). 1989. *The Nonprofit Sector in International Perspective: Studies in Comparative Culture and Policy*. New York: Oxford University Press.

—— 1997. "Whither the Third Sector? Yesterday, Today and Tomorrow", *Voluntas* 8(1): 1–10.

Jameson, F. 1984. "Postmodernism, or the Cultural Logic of Late Capitalism", *New Left Review* 146: 53–92.

——— 1991. *Postmodernism, or, the Cultural Logic of Late Capitalism.* Durham: Duke University Press.

Jameson, F. and Miyoshi, M. (eds.). 1998. *The Cultures of Globalization.* Durham and London: Duke University Press.

Jaspers, Karl. 1953. *The Origin and Goal of History.* New Haven: Yale University Press.

Jay, M. 1998. *Cultural Semiotics.* London: Athlone.

Jencks, C. (ed.). 1992. *The Post-Modern Reader.* London: Academic Editions.

——— 1996. *What is Post-Modernism?.* London: Academic Editions.

Jessen, Norbert. 2000. "Das Ende einer Symbiose. Jom Haazmaut: Ein Halbes Jahrhundert Nach Seiner Gründung löst sich Israel von der Diaspora", *Allgemeine Jüdische Wochenzeitung,* 11 May.

Joas, H. 1996. "Die Modernität des Krieges," *Leviathan* 24: 13–27.

——— 1999a. "For Fear of New Horrors: A Reply to Edward Tiryakian and Ian Roxborough", symposium on War and Modernization Theory, *International Sociology* 14(4): 501–504.

——— 1999b. "The Modernity of War: Modernization Theory and the Problem of Violence", symposium on War and Modernization Theory, *International Sociology* 14(4): 457–472.

Johnson, Chalmers. 2000. *Blowback: The Costs and Consequences of American Empire.* New York: Holt.

Jones, Mari C. 1998. *Language Obsolescence and Revitalization: Linguistic Change in Two Sociolinguistically Contrasting Welsh Communities.* Oxford: Clarendon Press.

Joseph, R. 1997. "Democratization in Africa After 1989—Comparative and Theoretical Perspectives", *Comparative Politics* 25(3): 363–382.

Josephson, E. and Josephson, M. (eds.). 1962. *Man Alone: Alienation in Modern Society.* New York: Dell.

Jowell, Roger et al. (eds.). 1993. *International Social Attitudes—the 10th BSA Report.* Aldershot: Gower.

Juergensmeyer, Mark and McMahon, Darrin M. 1998. "Hindu Philanthropy and Civil Society", in Ilchman, Warren F., Katz, Stanley N. and Queen II, Edward L. (eds.), *Philanthropy in the World's Traditions.* Bloomington: Indiana University Press.

Kaase, Max and Newton, Kenneth (eds.). 1995. *Beliefs in Government.* Oxford: Oxford University Press.

Kachru, Braj B. 1986. *The Alchemy of English; The Spread, Functions and Models of Non-Native Englishes.* Delhi: Oxford University Press.

Kadmon, Sima. 1998. "The Chief of the General Staff Amnon Lipkin-Shahak: A Special Interview", *Ma'ariv* (Independence Day Supplement), April 24, pp. 2–5. (Hebrew)

Kamenka, E. (ed.). 1983. *The Portable Karl Marx.* New York: Viking Press.

Kanté, B. 1994. "Senegal's Empty Election", *Journal of Democracy* 5(1): 96–108.

Karl, B.D. and Katz, S.N. 1981. "The American Private Philanthropic Foundation and the Public Sphere, 1890–1930", *Minerva* 19: 236–270.

——— 1987. "Foundations and Ruling Class Elites", *Daedalus* (Winter): 1–40.

Käsler, Dirk (ed.). 1976–1978. *Klassiker der Soziologie.* 2 Vols. München: C.H. Beck.

Katz, Elihu. 1988. "Disintermediation: Cutting Out the Middle Man", *Intermedia* 16: 30–31.

——— 1992. "Individualisation, Segmentation, Mondialisation: la technologie de la television et l'État-Nation", pp. 133–144 in Caron, A. and Juneau, P. (eds.), *Le Defi des Televisions Nationales a l'Ère de la Mondialisation.* Montreal: Presses de l'Universite de Montreal.

——— 1996. "And Deliver Us from Segmentation", *Annals of the American Academy of Political and Social Science* 546: 22–33.

——— 1998. "Mass Media and Participatory Democracy", in Inoguchi, T. et al. (eds.), *The Changing Nature of Democracy.* Tokyo: UN University Press.

Katz, Elihu, and Adoni, Hanna. 1973. "Functions of the Book for Society and Self", *Diogenes* 81.

Katz, Elihu, Dokter, Sharon, Gusek, Jodi, Metzger, Miriam, O'Connell, Jacqueline and Stollon, Jane. 1998. "Press–Conversation–Opinion–Action: Gabriel Tarde's Public Sphere", in Lautman, J and Lecuyer, B. (eds.), *Paul Lazarsfeld (1901–1976): La Sociologie de Vienne a New York.* Paris: L'Harmattan.

Katz, Michael L. and Shapiro, Carl. 1986. "Technology Adoption in the Presence of Network Externalities", *Journal of Political Economy* 94(4): 822–841.

Katz, Ruth and Katz, Elihu. 1998. "McLuhan: Where Did He Come From, Where Did He Disappear?", *Canadian Journal of Communication* 23(3): 307–319.

Keane, John. 1999. "The Limits of Secularism", *Times Literary Supplement*. January 9.

Kepel, Gilles. 1994. *The Revenge of God: The Resurgence of Islam, Christianity and Judaism in the Modern World*, trans. Alan Braley. University Park: Pennsylvania State University Press.

Kerr, C. et al. 1962. *Industrialism and Industrial Man*. London: Heinemann.

Keyder, Ç. 1999. *Istanbul: Between the Global and the Local*. Lanham: Rowman & Littlefield.

Khosrokhavar, Ferhad. 1997. *L'Islam des jeunes*. Paris: Flammarion.

Kilminster, R. 1997. "Globalization as an Emergent Concept", in Scott, A. (ed.), *The Limits of Globalization*. London: Routledge.

Kincheloe, Joe L. and Steinberg, Shirley R. 1997. *Changing Multiculturalism*. Buckingham and Philadelphia: Open University Press.

Kindleberger, Charles P. 1983. "Standards as Public, Collective and Private goods", *Kyklos* 36(3): 377–396.

King, A.D. (ed.). 1991. *Culture, Globalization and the World System*. London: Macmillan.

Klein, M. 1992. "Back to Democracy", *African Studies Review* 35(3): 1–12.

Kleineidam, Hartmut. 1992. "Politique de diffusion linguistique et francophonie: l'action linguistique menée par la France", *International Journal of the Sociology of Language* 95: 11–31.

Klemperer, Victor. 1998. *I Will Bear Witness: A Diary of the Nazi Years, 1933–1941*. Vol. I. (trans. Martin Chalmers). New York: Random House.

Klingemann, Hans Dieter and Fuchs, Dieter (eds.). 1995. *Citizens and the State*. Oxford: Oxford University Press.

Kneer, Georg, Nassehi, Armin and Schroer, Markus (eds.). 1997. *Soziologische Gesellschaftsbegriffe*. München: Wilhelm Fink.

Knorr Cetina, K. 1981. *The Manufacture of Knowledge: An Essay on the Constructivist and Contextual Nature of Science*. Oxford: Pergamon Press.

——— 1997. "Sociality with Objects: Social Relations in Postsocial Knowledge Societies", *Theory, Culture and Society* 14(4): 1–30.

——— 1999. *Epistemic Cultures. How the Sciences Make Knowledge*. Cambridge: Harvard University Press.

Kolakowski, L. 1990. *Modernity on Endless Trial*. Chicago and London: University of Chicago Press.

Kolchin, Peter. 1993. *American Slavery 1619–1877*. New York: Hill and Wang.

König, René (ed.). 1967. *Handbuch der empirischen Sozialforschung*. 2 Vols. Stuttgart: Ferdinand Enke Verlag. (Revised edition, 14 Vols., 1979)

——— 1987. *Soziologie in Deutschland*. München: Hauser Verlag.

Kornhauser, William. 1959. *The Politics of Mass Society*. Glencoe: Free Press.

Koselleck, R. 1959, *Kritik und Krise. Ein Beitrag zur Pathogenese der bürgerlichen Welt*. Freiburg/Munich: Verlag Karl Alber.

——— 1967a. *Preussen zwischen Reform und Revolution*. Stuttgart: Ernst Klett Verlag.

——— 1967b. "Richtlinien für das Lexicon politisch-sozialer Begriffe der Neuzeit", *Archiv für Begriffsgeschichte* 11: 81–99.

——— (ed.). 1979a. *Historische Semantik und Begriffsgeschichte*. Stuttgart: Klett-Cotta.

——— 1979b. *Vergangene Zukunft. Zur Semantik geschichtlicher Zeiten*. Frankfurt/M.: Suhrkamp.

——— 1985. *Futures Past. On the Semantics of Historical Time*. Cambridge, MA: The MIT Press.

——— 1987a. "Das achtzehnte Jahrhundert als Beginn der Neuzeit", in Herzog, R. and Koselleck, R. (eds.), *Epochenschwelle und Epochenbewusstsein*. Munich: W. Fink Verlag.

——— 1987b. "Historik und Hermeneutik", in Koselleck, R. and Gadamer, Hans-Georg, *Hermeneutik und Historik*. Sitzungsberichte der Heidelberger Akademie der Wissenschaften. Heidelberg: Carl Winter Universitatsverlag.

——— 1988. *Critique and Crisis. Enlightenment and the Pathogenesis of Modern Society*. Cambridge, MA: The MIT Press.

——— 1994. "Some Reflections on the Temporal Structure of Conceptual Change", in Melching, Willem and Wyger, Velema (eds.), *Main Trends in Cultural History*. Amsterdam: Rodopi.

Koselleck, R., Brunner, Otto and Conze, Werner (eds.). 1972–1997. *Geschichtliche Grundbegriffe. Historisches Lexicon zur politisch-sozialen Sprache in Deutschland.* Vols. 1–8. Stuttgart: Klett-Cotta.

Koselleck, R. and Gadamer, Hans-Georg. 1987. *Hermeneutik und Historik.* Sitzungsberichte der Heidelberger Akademie der Wissenschaften. Heidelberg: Carl Winter Universitatsverlag.

Kossok, M. 1993. "From Universal History to Global History", in Mazlish, B. and Buultjens, R. (eds.), *Conceptualizing Global History.* Boulder: Westview Press.

Krakau, Knud (ed.). 1997. *The American Nation, National Identity, Nationalism.* Münster: LIT.

Kraus, Sidney. 1962. *The Great Debate: Background, Perspective, Effects.* Bloomington: Indiana University Press.

Kreindler, Isabelle T. 1993. "A Second Missed Opportunity: Russian in Retreat as a Global Language", *International Political Science Review* [special issue on The Emergent World Language System] 14(3): 257–274.

Kroeber, A.L. 1963a. *An Anthropologist Looks at History.* Berkeley: University of California Press.

——— 1963b. *Style and Civilizations.* Berkeley: University of California Press.

Kroeber, A.L. and Kluckhohn, C. 1952. *Culture: A Critical Review of Concepts and Definitions.* New York: Vintage Books.

Krohn, W., Küppers, G. and Nowotny, H. (eds.). 1990. *Selforganization: Portrait of a Scientific Revolution.* Sociology of the Sciences Yearbook. Dordrecht: Kluwer.

Kuhn, Thomas S. 1962. *The Structure of Scientific Revolutions.* Chicago: University of Chicago Press.

Kuhnle, Stein. 1975. *Patterns of Social and Political Mobilizations. A Historical Analysis of the Nordic Countries.* Beverly Hills: Sage.

Kumar, K. 1995. *From Post-Industrial to Post-Modern Society. New Theories of the Contemporary World.* Oxford: Blackwell.

Kunz, F. 1991. "Liberalization in Africa—Some Preliminary Reflections", *African Affairs* 90: 223–235.

Kymlicka, Will. 1995. *Multicultural Citizenship. A Liberal Theory of Minority Rights.* Oxford: Clarendon Press.

La Vopa, Anthony J. 1992. "Conceiving a Public: Ideas and Society in Eighteenth Century Europe", *Journal of Modern History* 64: 79–116.

Laitin, David D. 1987. "Linguistic Conflict in Catalonia", *Language Problems and Language Planning* 11(2): 129–146.

——— 1989a. "Language Policy and Political Strategy in India", *Policy Sciences* 22: 415–436.

——— 1989b. "Linguistic Revival: Politics and Culture in Catalonia", *Comparative Studies in Society and History* 31(3): 297–317.

——— 1992. *Language Repertoires and State Construction in Africa.* Cambridge: Cambridge University Press.

——— 1993. "The Game Theory of Language Regimes", *International Political Science Review* [special issue on The Emergent World Language System] 14(3): 227–240.

——— 1994. "The Tower of Babel as a Coordination Game; Political Linguistics in Ghana", *American Political Science Review* 88: 622–634.

Lal, B.B. 1983. "Perspectives on Ethnicity: Old Wine in New Bottles", *Ethnic and Racial Studies* 6: 154–173.

Lambert, Richard D. 1995. *Language Policy: An Overview.* Paper read at the International Symposium on Language Policy, December 20 at Bar-Ilan University, Israel.

Lancaster, C. 1993. "Democratization in Sub-Saharan Africa", *Survival* 35(3): 38–50.

Landau, J.M. 1969. *The Arabs in Israel: A Political Study.* London: Oxford University Press.

Langlois, Simon et al. (eds.). 1994. *Convergence or Divergence: Comparing Recent Social Trends in Industrial Societies.* Frankfurt/M.: Campus Verlag, and Montreal: McGill-Queens University Press.

Language 68(1) [March 1992]: 1–42.

Laponce, Jean. 1984. *Langue et Territoire.* Québec: Presses de l'Université de Laval.

Larrain, J. 1989. *Theories of Development.* Cambridge: Polity Press.

Larrain Ibánez, J. 1996. *Modernidad, Razon e Identidad en America Latina.* Santiago de Chile: Ed. Andrès Bello.

Lasch, C. 1979. *The Culture of Narcissism*. New York: Warner Books.
———— 1984. *The Minimal Self: Psychic Survival in Troubled Times*. London: PAN Books.
———— 1996. *The Revolt of the Elites*. New York: Norton.
Lash, S. 1994. "Reflexivity in its Doubles: Structure, Aesthetics, Community", in Beck, U., Giddens, A. and Lash, S., *Reflexive Modernization*. Stanford: Stanford University Press.
Lash, S. and Urry, J. 1994. *Economies of Signs and Space*. London: Sage.
Latour, B. and Woolgar, S. 1979. *Laboratory Life: The Social Construction of Scientific Facts*. Beverly Hills: Sage.
Lazarsfeld, P.F. and Merton, Robert K. 1948. "Mass Communication, Popular Taste and Organized Social Action", in Bryson, L. (ed.), *The Communication of Ideas*. New York: Harper.
Lechner, F.J. 1990. "Fundamentalism and Sociocultural Revitalization: On the Logic of Differentiation", in Alexander, J. and Colomy, P. (eds.), *Differentiation Theory and Social Change*. New York: Columbia University Press.
Lefebvre, H. (1962) 1995. *Introduction to Modernity*. London: Verso.
Lehmbruch, G. 1967. *Proporzdemokratie: Politisches System und politische Kultur in der Schweiz und in Österreich*. Tübingen: Mohr.
Lemieux, V. and Hudon, R. 1975. *Patronage et Politique au Québec*. Québec: Boréal Express.
Leon, Abram. (1944) 1970. *The Jewish Question. A Marxist Interpretation*. New York: Pathfinder Press.
Lepenies, Wolf. 1978. *Das Ende der Naturgeschichte. Wandel kultureller Selbstverstdndlichkeiten in den Wissenschaften des 18. und 19. Jahrhunderts*. Frankfurt/M.: Suhrkamp.
———— 1985. *Die drei Kulturen—Soziologie zwischen Literatur und Wissenschaft*. München: Hanser.
———— 1988. *Between Literature and Science: The Rise of Sociology*. Cambridge: Cambridge University Press.
Lerner, Daniel. (1958) 1964. *The Passing of Traditional Society: Modernizing the Middle East*. New York: Free Press.
Lerner, M. 1993. *New Entrepreneurs and Entrepreneurial Aspirations among Immigrants from the former USSR in Israel (research report)*. Tel-Aviv: Tel-Aviv University, Faculty of Management, The Israel Institute of Business Research, Working Paper no. 25.
Levathes, R. 1996. *When China Ruled the Seas: The Treasure Fleet of the Dragon Throne, 1405–1433*. Oxford: Oxford University Press.
Levinas, Emmanuel. 1976. *Difficile Liberté*. Paris: Albin Michel.
———— 1996. *Basic Philosophical Writings*. Edited by Peperzak, A.T., Critchley, S. and Bernasconi, R. Bloomington: Indiana University Press.
Levine, Daniel H. and Stoll, David. 1997. "Bridging the Gap Between Empowerment and Power in Latin America", in Hoeber Rudolph, Susanne and Piscatori, James (eds.), *Transnational Religion and Fading States*. Boulder: Westview.
Levitt, T. 1983. "The Globalization of Markets", *Harvard Business Review* 61(3): 92–102.
Levy, Marion J. 1966. *Modernization and the Structure of Societies*. Princeton: Princeton University Press.
Lewis, M.W. and Wigen, K.E. (eds.). 1997. *The Myth of Continents: A Critique of Metageography*. Berkeley: University of California Press.
Lijphart, A. 1977. *Democracy in Plural Societies*. New Haven: Yale University Press.
Lipset, S.M. 1990. "Government, Welfare, Philanthropy", in Lipset, S.M., *Continental Divide: The Values and Institutions of the United States and Canada*. New York: Routledge.
———— 1996. *American Exceptionalism*. New York: W.W. Norton & Company.
London, N.R. 1991. *Japanese Corporate Philanthropy*. New York: Oxford University Press.
Lorwin, V. 1971. "Segmented Pluralism, Ideological Cleavage and Political Behavior in the Smaller European Democracies", *Comparative Politics* 3: 141–175.
Luhmann, N. 1980–1989. *Gesellschaftsstruktur und Semantik*. 3 Vols. Frankfurt/M.: Suhrkamp.
———— 1984. *Soziale Systeme*. Frankfurt/M.: Suhrkamp.
———— 1990. "The Paradox of System Differentiation and the Evolution of Society", in Alexander, J. and Colomy, P. (eds.), *Differentiation Theory and Social Change*. New York: Columbia University Press.
———— 1992. *Die Wissenschaft der Gesellschaft*. Frankfurt/M.: Suhrkamp.
———— 1997. *Die Gesellschaft der Gesellschaft*. 2 Vols. Frankfurt/M.: Suhrkamp.

—— 1998a. *Das Recht der Gesellschaft*. Frankfurt/M.: Suhrkamp.
—— 1998b. *Observations on Modernity*. Stanford: Stanford University Press.
—— 1999. *Die Wirtschaft der Gesellschaft*. Frankfurt/M.: Suhrkamp.
Lynd, Robert. 1939. *Knowledge for What?*. Princeton: Princeton University Press.
Lyon, D. 1994. *Postmodernity*. Minneapolis: University of Minnesota Press.
Lyotard, J.-F. 1984. *The Postmodern Condition: A Report on Knowledge*. Minneapolis: University of Minnesota Press.
MacKenzie, P.A. 1995. "Australia", in Postlethwaite, T. Neville (ed.), *International Encyclopaedia of National Systems of Education*. London: Pergamon Press.
Madan, T.N. 1987. "Secularism in Its Place", *Journal of Asian Studies* 6: 747–759.
Madison, James. 1961. "Publius", essay No. 39 in Cooke, Jacob E. (ed.), *The Federalist*. Middletown, Conn.: Wesleyan University Press.
—— (1788) 1990. Speech in the Virginia Ratifying Convention, June 7, 1788, in Kaminski, John P., Leffler, Richard and Saladino, Gaspare J. (eds.), *Documentary History of the Ratification of the Constitution*. Vol. IX. Madison, WI. (1976–): State Historical Society of Wisconsin.
Maffesoli, Michel. 1995. *The Time of the Tribes*. London: Sage.
Magat, R. 1994. *Unlikely Partners: Philanthropic Foundations and the Labor Movement*. Ithaca: Cornell University Press.
Malia, M. 1994. *The Soviet Tragedy*. New York: Free Press.
Mandel, E. 1975. *Late Capitalism*. London: New Left Books.
Mandelbaum, M. 1971. *History, Man, and Reason: A Study in Nineteenth-Century Thought*. Baltimore: Johns Hopkins University Press.
Manent, Pierre. 1994a. *An Intellectual History of Liberalism*. Princeton: Princeton University Press.
—— 1994b. *La cite de l'homme*. Paris: Fayard.
—— 1994c. "The Contest for Comment", in Lilla, Mark (ed.), *New French Thought: Political Philosophy*. Princeton: Princeton University Press.
—— 1994d. "The Modern State", in Lilla, Mark (ed.), *New French Thought: Political Philosophy*. Princeton: Princeton University Press.
Manicas, Peter T. and Rosenberg, Alan. 1985. "Naturalism, Epistemological Individualism and 'The Strong Programme' in the Sociology of Knowledge", *Journal for the Theory of Social Behaviour* 15(1): 76–101.
—— 1988. "The Sociology of Scientific Knowledge: Can We Ever Get It Straight?", *Journal for the Theory of Social Behaviour* 18(1): 51–76.
Mann, M. 1987. *The Sources of Social Power*. Vol. I. Cambridge: Cambridge University Press.
—— 1993. *The Sources of Social Power*. Vol. II. Cambridge: Cambridge University Press.
Mansouri, R. 1998. *The Role of Higher Education in Iran and the Society's Needs*. Paper presented at the Regional Seminar on Higher Education in the Coming Century, National Commission of UNESCO, Tehran (March 18–20).
March, James C. and Olsen, Johan P. 1989. *Rediscovering Institutions*. New York: The Free Press.
—— 1995. *Democratic Governance*. New York: The Free Press.
Marcus, G. (ed.). 1993. *Perilous States. Conversations on Culture, Politics, and Nation*. Chicago: University of Chicago Press.
Marcus, George and Fisher, Michael. 1986. *Anthropology as Cultural Critique*. Chicago: University of Chicago Press.
Marcuse, H. 1968. *One Dimensional Man*. London: Sphere Books.
Marcuse, P. 1995. "Not Chaos, But Walls: Postmodernity and the Partitioned City", in Watson, S. and Gibson, K. (eds.), *Postmodern Cities and Space*. Oxford: Blackwell.
Margosyan, M. 1995. *Gavur Mahallesi*. Istanbul: Aras Yayincilik.
—— 1996. *Soyle Margos Nerelisen?*. Istanbul: Aras Yayincilik.
Marias, J. 1970. *Generations: A Historical Method*. University, Ala.: University of Alabama Press.
Martin, H.-P. and Schumann, H. 1997. *The Global Trap*. London: Zed Books.
Martin, Julian. 1992. *Francis Bacon, the State, and the Reform of Natural Philosophy*. Cambridge: Cambridge University Press.
Marty, Martin E. and Appleby, R. Scott (eds.). 1991. *Fundamentalism Observed*. Chicago: University of Chicago Press.

————— 1993a. *Fundamentalism and the State. Remaking Polities, Economies, and Militance*. Chicago: University of Chicago Press.

————— 1993b. *Fundamentalisms and Society. Reclaiming the Sciences, the Family and Education*. Chicago: University of Chicago Press.

————— 1994. *Accounting for Fundamentalism. The Dynamic Character of Movements*. Chicago: University of Chicago Press.

————— 1995. *Fundamentalism Comprehended*. Chicago: University of Chicago Press.

Marx, Anthony W. 1998. *Making Race and Nation*. Cambridge: Cambridge University Press.

Marx, K. (1875) 1941. *Critique of the Gotha Programme*. Southampton: Lawrence & Wishart.

Marx, K. and Engels, F. 1959. *Basic Writings on Politics and Philosophy*. Edited by Lewis S. Feuer. New York: Anchor Books.

Mash, Roni. 1999. *Organizational Behaviour of Privatized Enterprises*. PhD Thesis written under Eva Etzioni-Halevy's supervision at Bar-Ilan University.

Mason, K.O., Mason, W.M., Winsborough, H.H. and Poole, W.K. 1973. "Some Methodological Issues in the Cohort Analysis of Archival Data", *American Sociological Review* 38: 242–258.

Mason, W.M. and Fienberg, S.E. (eds.). 1985. *Cohort Analysis in Social Research*. New York: Springer.

Matlosa, K. 1999. "Military Rule and the Withdrawal from Power: The Case of Lesotho", pp. 471–502 in Hutchful, E. and Bathily, A. (eds.), *The Military and Militarism in Africa*. Dakar: CODESRIA.

Mauss, M. (1924) 1950. "Essai sur le don: formes et raisons de l'échange dans les sociétés archaiques", in Mauss, M., *Sociologie et Anthropologie*. Paris: Presses Universitaires de France.

————— 1990. *The Gift: The Form and Reason for Exchange in Archaic Societies*. Translated by W.D. Halls. London: Routledge.

Mazlish, B. 1993. "Global History in a Postmodern Era", in Mazlish, B. and Buultjens, R. (eds.), *Conceptualizing Global History*. Boulder: Westview Press.

Mazlish, B. and Buultjens, R. (eds.). 1993. *Conceptualizing Global History*. Boulder: Westview Press.

McCarthy, K.D. et al. 1992. *The Nonprofit Sector in the Global Economy: Voices from Many Nations*. San Francisco: Jossey-Bass.

McCracken, G. 1988. *Culture and Consumption*. Bloomington: Indiana University Press.

McLennan, Gregor. 1995. *Pluralism*. Minneapolis: University of Minnesota Press.

McLuhan, M. 1964. *Understanding Media: The Extensions of Man*. New York: McGraw-Hill.

McMichael, Philip. 2000. "Globalization: Myths and Realities", pp. 274–291 in Timmons Roberts, J. and Hite, A. (eds.), *From Modernization to Globalization: Perspectives on Development and Social Change*. Oxford: Blackwell.

Meinecke, Friedrich. 1970. *Cosmopolitanism and the National State*. Princeton: Princeton University Press.

Melko, M. 1969. *The Nature of Civilizations*. Boston: Porter Sargent Publisher.

Melko, M. and Scott, L.R. (eds.). 1987. *The Boundaries of Civilizations in Space and Time*. Lanham, MD: University Press of America.

Melosik, Z. and Szkudlarek, Tomasz. 1998. *Kultura, Tozsamosc i Edukacja*. Krakow: Impuls.

Merton, Robert K. 1957. *Social Theory and Social Structure*. 2nd edition. Glencoe: Free Press.

————— 1972. "Insiders and Outsiders: A Chapter in the Sociology of Knowledge", *American Journal of Sociology* 78: 9–47.

Mestrovic, S.G. 1994. *The Balkanization of the West*. London: Routledge.

————— 1997. *Postemotional Society*. London: Sage.

Metaoui, F. 1999. "Cheb Mami á Riadh El Feth/Bladi El Djazajr", in *El Watan*, 6 July, pp. 1 & 24.

Metzger, Thomas. 1988. "Will China Democratize? Sources of Resistance", *Journal of Democracy* (January): 18–26.

————— 1991. "The Chinese Reconciliation of Moral-Sacred Values with Modern Pluralism: Political Discourse in the ROC 1949–1989", in Myers, Ramon H. (ed.), *Two Societies in Opposition*. Stanford: Hoover Institution Press.

————— (in press). "The Western Concept of the Civil Society in the Context of Chinese History", in Kaviraj, Sudipta and Khilnani, Sunil (eds.), *Civil Society: History and Possibilities*. Cambridge: Cambridge University Press.

Meyer, H.D. 2000. "Taste Formation in Pluralistic Societies: The Role of Rhetorics and Institutions", *International Sociology* 15(1): 33–56.

Meyer, John W. 2000. "Globalization: Sources and Effects on National States and Societies", *International Sociology* 15(2): 233–248.

Meyer, John W. and Hannan, Michael T. (eds.). 1979. *National Development and the World System: Educational, Economic, and Political Change, 1950–1970*. Chicago: University of Chicago Press.

Meyer, John W., Boli, J., Thomas, G. and Raminez, F. 1997. "World Society and the Nation-State", *American Journal of Sociology* 103: 144–181.

Meyer, John W., Ramirez, Francisco O. and Soysal, Yasemin. 1992. "World Expansion of Mass Education, 1870–1980", *Sociology of Education* 65(2): 128–149.

Mills, C. Wright. 1959. *The Sociological Imagination*. New York: Oxford University Press.

Milroy, L. 1989. *Language and Social Networks*. Oxford: Basil Blackwell.

Mintz, Sidney and Price, Richard. 1992. *The Birth of African-American Culture: An Anthropological Perspective*. Boston: Beacon Press.

Miyoshi, Masao and Harootunian, H.D. (eds.). 1989. *Postmodernism and Japan*. Durham: Duke University Press.

Mochmann, Ekkehard and Scheuch, Erwin K. (eds.). 1987. *Infrastruktur für die Sozialforschung*. Köln: Zentralarchiv für empirische Sozialforschung.

Mochmann, Ekkehard et al. (eds.). 1998. *Inventory of National Election Studies in Europe 1945–1995*. Bergisch Gladbach: Erwin Ferger.

Mohler, Peter and Zapf, Wolfgang. 1995. "GESIS—Gesellschaft Sozialwissenschaftlicher Infrastruktureinrichtungen", in Schäfers, Bernhard (ed.), *Soziologie in Deutschland*. Opladen: Leske + Budrich.

Mollenkopf, J.H. and Castells, M. (eds.). 1991. *Dual City; Restructuring New York*. New York: Russell Sage Foundation.

Mommsen, Wolfgang. 1984. *Max Weber and German Politics, 1890–1920*. Revised edition. Chicago: University of Chicago Press.

Monga, C. 1995. "Civil Society and Democratization in Francophone Africa", *Journal of Modern African Studies* 33(3): 359–379.

Montagu, Ashley. 1964. *Man's Most Dangerous Myth: The Fallacy of Race*. Cleveland: World Publishing Company.

Monteiro, Helene. 1991. *O Resurgimento do Movimento Negro na Década de 70*. (unpublished M.A. Thesis). Rio de Janeiro: Universidade Federal do Rio de Janeiro.

Moore, R.I. 1997. "Western Europe as a Eurasian Phenomenon", *Modern Asian Studies* 3(3): 583–601.

Moore, Wilbert. 1966. "Global Sociology: The World as a Singular System", *American Journal of Sociology* 71(5): 475–482.

Mosca, Gaetano. 1939. *The Ruling Class*. Translated by H.D. Kahn. New York: McGraw Hill.

Moses, Wilson. 1988. *The Golden Age of Black Nationalism, 1850–1925*. New York and Oxford: Oxford University Press.

Moshkovitch, Jafa. (in progress). *Changes in the Likud Party*. Ph.D. Thesis written under Eva Etzioni-Halevy's supervision at Bar-Ilan University.

Moss, T.J. 1995. "U.S. Policy and Democratization in Africa: The Limits of Universal Liberalism", *Journal of Modern African Studies* 33(2): 189–209.

Mosteller, Frederick et al. 1948. *The Pre-election Polls of 1948*. New York: Social Science Research Council.

Mulgan, G. 1998. *Connexity: How to Live in a Connected World*. Boston: Harvard Business School Press.

Münch, R. 1990. "Differentiation, Rationalization, Interpenetration: The Emergence of Modern Society", in Alexander, J. and Colomy, P. (eds.), *Differentiation Theory and Social Change*. New York: Columbia University Press.

Mundt, R.J. 1997. "Cote d'Ivoire: Continuity and Change in a Semi-Democracy", pp. 182–203 in Clark, J.F. and Gardinier, D.E. (eds.), *Political Reform in Francophone Africa*. Boulder: Westview Press.

Murakami, Y. 1987. "Modernization in Terms of Integration: The Case of Japan", pp. 65–88 in Eisenstadt, S.N. (ed.), *Patterns of Modernity*. Vol. 2. London: Frances Pinter.

Muth, Richard F. 1968. "Rent", pp. 458–459 in Sills, David L. (ed.), *International Encyclopedia of the Social Sciences*. Vol. 13. New York/London: MacMillan/Free Press.

Myers Scotton, C. 1980. 'Explaining Linguistic Choices as Identity Negotiations', in Giles, H., Robinson, W.P. and Smith, P.M. (eds.), *Language: Social Psychological Perspectives*. Oxford: Pergamon.

———— 1983. 'The Negotiation of Identities in Conversation: A Theory of Markedness and Code Choice', *International Journal of the Sociology of Language* 44: 115–136

———— 1993. "Elite Closure as a Powerful Language Strategy: The African Case", *International Journal of the Sociology of Language* 103: 149–163.

Nadel, S.F. 1957. *The Theory of Social Structure*. London: Cohen and West.

Nagai, A.K., Lerner, R. and Rothman, S. 1994. *Giving for Social Change: Foundations, Public Policy and the American Political Agenda*. Westport, Connecticut and London: Praeger.

Nakamura, T. 1982. "A Bayesian Cohort Model for Standard Cohort Table Analysis", *Proceedings of the Institute of Statistical Mathematics* 29: 77–97. (Japanese)

———— 1986. "Bayesian Cohort Models for General Cohort Table Analyses", *Annals of the Institute of Statistical Mathematics* 38 (part B): 353–370.

Nakhleh K. 1975. "Cultural Determinants of Collective Identity—The Case of the Arabs in Israel", *New Outlook* 18(7): 31–40.

Nalbantoglu, G.B. 1997. "Silent Interruptions: Urban Encounters with Rural Turkey", in Bozdogan, S. and Kasaba, R. (eds.), *Rethinking Modernity and National Identiy in Turkey*. Seattle and London: Univertsity of Washington Press.

National Office of Overseas Skills Recognition. 1995a. *Country Education Profiles: The Philippines*. Second edition. Canberra: Department of Employment, Education and Training.

———— 1995b. *Country Education Profiles: Australia*. Second edition. Canberra: Department of Employment, Education and Training.

———— 1992–1996. *Country Education Profiles*. Canberra: Australian Government Publishing Service:
Set I *Europe*, 24 volumes, December 1992;
Set II *Asian Subcontinent and Middle East*, 17 volumes, May 1992;
Set III *Africa*, 9 volumes, August 1993;
Set IV *Australia and its Immediate Neighbours: South East and North East Asia and the Pacific*, 20 volumes, second edition, 1996;
Set V *The Americas*, 16 volumes, June 1993.

Ndue, P.N. 1994. "Africa's Turn Toward Pluralism", *Journal of Democracy* 5(1): 45–54.

Nederveen Pieterse, J. 1995. "Globalization as Hybridization", pp. 45–68 in Featherstone, M., Lash, S. and Robertson, R. (eds.). *Global Modernities*. London: Sage.

———— 1996. "Melange Modernities in the East: Modernization and Globalization", *The Annals of the International Institute of Sociology* 5: 91–106.

Nelson, B. 1981. *On the Roads to Modernity: Conscience, Science and Civilizations*. Totowa, NJ: Rowman and Littlefield.

Nelson, D.D. 1998. *National Manhood. Capitalist Citizenship and the Imagined Fraternity of White Men*. Durham and London: Duke University Press.

Nelson, Diane. 1999. *A Finger in the Wound: Body Politics in Quincentennial Guatemala*. Berkeley: University of California Press.

Neuberger, B. 1971. "Classless Society and One-Party State Ideology", *African Studies Review* 14(2): 287–292.

———— 1974. "One-Party State Ideology in Africa—Contrasts and Contradictions", *Hamizrah Hahadash (The New East-Quarterly of the Israeli Oriental Society)* 24(4): 280–292. (Hebrew)

———— 1986. *National Self-Determination in Postcolonial Africa*. Boulder: Lynne Rienner.

———— 1999. "Ethnic Groups and the State in Africa", in Ben-Ami, S., Peled, Y. and Spektorowsky, A. (eds.), *Ethnic Challenges to the Modern Nation State*. Houndmills: Macmillan.

Neuberger, B. and Keren, A. 1997. *Anti-Colonial Nationalism—The Ideological Dimension*. Tel Aviv: The Open University of Israel. (Hebrew)

Ngugi wa Thiongo. 1986. *Decolonising the African Mind: The Politics of Language in African Literature*. London: J. Currey.

Niedermayer, Oskar and Sinnott, Richard (eds.). 1995. *Public Opinion and Internationalized Governance*. Oxford: Oxford University Press.

Nietzsche, F. 1933. *Thus Spake Zarathustra*. London: J.M. Dent.

——— 1980. *On the Advantage and Disadvantage of History for Life*. Indianapolis: Hackett Pub. Co.

Noyes, D. and Abrahams, Roger D. 1999. "From Calendar Custom to National Memory: European Commonplaces", pp. 77–98 in Ben-Amos, D. and Weissberg, L. (eds.), *Cultural Memory and The Construction of Identity*. Detroit: Wayne State University Press.

Nyerere, J. 1998. "Africa: The Current Situation", *Africa Philosophy* 11(1): 7–12.

O'Connell, James. 1976. "The Concept of Modernization", pp. 13–24 in Black, Cyril E. (ed.), *Comparative Modernization*. New York: Free Press.

O'Connor, D. 1997. "Lines of (F)light: The Visual Apparatus in Foucault and Deleuze", *Space and Culture* 1: 49–67.

O'Connor, James. 1973. *The Fiscal Crisis of the State*. New York: St. Martin's Press.

Odendahl, Teresa. 1990. *Charity Begins at Home: Generosity and Self-Interest among the Philanthropic Elite*. New York: Basic Books.

Offenberg, Ulrike. 1998. "Seid vorsichtig gegen die Machthaber", *Die jüdischen Gemeinden in der SBZ und der DDR, 1945–1990*. Berlin: Aufbau Verlag.

Ollman, B. 1971. *Alienation. Marx's Conception of Man in Capitalist Society*. London: Cambridge University Press.

Olsen, Morton and Clague, C.K. 1971. "Dissent in Economics: The Convergence in Extremes", *Social Research* 38: 751–776.

Olson, Mancur. 1965. *The Logic of Collective Action: Public Goods and the Theory of Groups*. Cambridge, MA: Harvard University Press.

Olson, Richard. 1993. *The Emergence of the Social Sciences, 1642–1792*. New York: Twayne Publishers.

Omotoso, Kole. 1994. *Season of Migration to the South; Africa's Crises Reconsidered*. Cape Town: Tafelberg.

O'Neill, J. 1982. *Essaying Montaigne. A Study of the Renaissance Institution of Writing and Reading*. London: Routledge & Kegan Paul.

Ong, A. 1997. "Chinese Migrants", in Palumbo-Liu, D. and Gumbrecht, H. (eds.), *Streams of Cultural Capital*. Stanford: Stanford University Press.

Ortiz, R. 1985. *Cultura Brasileira e Identidade Nacional*. S. Paulo: Brasiliense.

——— 1988. *A Moderna Tradição Brasileira*. S. Paulo: Brasiliense.

——— 1997. *Mundialización y Cultura*. Buenos Aires: Alianza Editorial.

——— 2000. "From Incomplete Modernity to World Modernity". *Daedalus* 129(1): 249–260.

Osborne, P. 1992. "Modernity is a Qualitative, Not a Chronological Category", *New Left Review* 192(2): 65–84.

Ostrander, Susan and Schervish, Paul G. 1990. "Giving and Getting: Philanthropy as a Social Relation", in Van Til, John (ed.), *Critical Issues in American Philanthropy: Strengthening Theory and Practice*. San Francisco: Jossey-Bass.

Ostrower, Francie. 1995. *Why the Wealthy Give: The Culture of Elite Philanthropy*. Princeton: Princeton University Press.

O'Toole, T. 1997. "The Central African Republic: Political Reform and Social Malaise", pp. 109–124 in Clark, J.F. and Gardinier, D.E. (eds.), *Political Reform in Francophone Africa*. Boulder: Westview Press.

Ottaway, M. 1997. "From Political Opening to Democratization", pp. 1–14 in Ottaway, M. (ed.), *Democracy in Africa—The Hard Road Ahead*. Boulder: Lynne Rienner.

Outhwaite, W. 1988. *New Philosophies of Science: Realism, Hermeneutics and Critical Theory*. London: Macmillan.

Owusu, M. 1997. "Domesticating Democracy: Culture, Civil Society and Constitutionalism in Africa", *Comparative Studies of Society and History*: 120–152.

Ozbudun, E. 1987. "Constituonal Law", in Ansay, T. and Wallace, D. (eds.), *Introduction to Turkish Law*. Boston: Kluwer Law and Taxation Publishers.

Ozturkmen, A. 1994. "The Role of People's Houses in the Making of National Culture in Turkey", *New Perspectives on Turkey* 11: 159–181.
Pagden, Anthony (ed.). 1987. *The Languages of Political Theory in Early Modern Europe*. Cambridge: Cambridge University Press.
Palumbo-Liu, D. 1997. "Introduction: Unhabituated Habituses", in Palumbo-Liu, D. and Gumbrecht, H. (eds.), *Streams of Cultural Capital*. Stanford: Stanford University Press.
Parsons, T. 1937. *The Structure of Social Action*. New York: The Free Press.
——— 1966. *Societies: Evolutionary and Comparative Perspectives*. Englewood Cliffs, NJ: Prentice Hall.
——— 1971. *The System of Modern Societies*. Englewood Cliffs, NJ: Prentice Hall.
——— 1977. *The Evolution of Societies*. Edited and with an introduction by Jackson Toby. Englewood Cliffs, NJ: Prentice Hall.
Parsons, T. and Shils, E. (eds.).1954. *Towards a General Theory of Action*. Cambridge, MA: Harvard University Press.
Past and Present, 152 (1996).
Past and Present, 155 (1997).
Patomäki, H. 2000. "The Tobin Tax: A New Phase in the Politics of Globalization", *Theory, Culture & Society* 17(4): 77–91.
Patterson, Orlando. 1994. "Ecumenical America: Global Culture and the American Cosmos", *World Policy Journal* 11(2): 103–117.
Payton, Robert L. 1988a. *Philanthropy: Four Views*. New Brunswick, NJ: Transaction Books.
——— 1988b. *Philanthropy: Voluntary Action for the Public Good*. New York: American Council on Education, Macmillan.
Pelczar, A. 1996. "Elements of the Background of the Quality Assurance System in Poland", Regional Training Seminar for Quality Assurance in Higher Education: Self Assessment and Peer Review. Budapest, November 11–16.
Penalosa, F. 1981. *Introduction to the Sociology of Language*. Rowley: Newbury House.
Perez Diaz, V. 1998a. "State and Public Sphere in Spain During the Ancient Regime", *Daedalus* 127(3): 251–279.
——— 1998b. "The Public Sphere and a European Civil Society", pp. 211–238 in Alexander, J.C. (ed.), *Real Civil Societies*. London: Sage.
Peri, Yoram. 1998. *Military-Society Relations in Crisis*. Paper presented to the 29th Conference of the Israel Sociological Association, Haifa, February. (Hebrew)
Peters, B. 1993. *Die Integration moderner Gesellschaften*. Frankfurt/M.: Suhrkamp.
Petty, William. (1678) 1899a. "A Treatise of Ireland", in Hull, Charles Henry (ed.), *The Economic Writings of Sir William Petty*. Vol. I. Cambridge: Cambridge University Press.
——— (1672) 1899b. "The Political Anatomy of Ireland", in Hull, Charles Henry (ed.), *The Economic Writings of Sir William Petty*. Vol. I. Cambridge: Cambridge University Press.
Peyrefitte, Alain. 1998. *La société de confiance: Essai sur le origines du developpement*. Paris: Odile Jacob.
Pfau, Thomas. 1990. "Immediacy and the Text: Friedrich Schleiermacher's Theory of Style and Interpretation", *Journal of the History of Ideas* 51(1): 51–73.
Phillipson, Robert H. 1990. *English Language Teaching and Imperialism*. [diss. University of Amsterdam]. Troenninge, Denmark: Transcultura.
Pierson, Donald. 1942. *Negroes in Brazil*. Chicago: University of Chicago Press.
Pierson, G.W. 1956. "The Frontier and American Institutions: A Criticism of the Turner Theory", pp. 47–65 in Taylor, G.R. (ed.), *The Turner Thesis: Concerning the Role of the Frontier in American History*. Boston: D.C. Heath and Company.
Pinker, Stephen. 1994. *The Language Instinct*. London: Penguin.
Pinto, Diana. 1999. "The Third Pillar? Toward a European Jewish Identity", *Golem. Europäisch-jüdisches Magazin* 1: 33–37.
Pirenne, J. 1962. *The Tides of History* (Vol. I). London: George Allen & Unwin Ltd.
——— 1963. *The Tides of History* (Vol. II). London: George Allen & Unwin Ltd.
Plekhanov, G.V. 1956. *The Development of the Monist View of History*. Moscow: Foreign Languages Publishing House.

Pocock, John G.A. 1985. *Virtue, Commerce and History*. Cambridge: Cambridge University Press.
———— 1987. "The Concept of Language and the *métier d'historien*: Some Considerations on Practice", in Padgen, Anthony (ed.), *The Languages of Political Theory in Early Modern Europe*. Cambridge: Cambridge University Press.
Polanyi, K. (1944) 1957. *The Great Transformation*. Boston: Beacon Press.
Popenoe, David. 1994. "The Family Condition of America: Cultural Change and Public Policy", pp. 81–112 in Aaron, Henry J. et al., *Values and Public Policy*. Washington, DC: Brookings Institution.
Porter, Theodore M. 1995. *Trust in Numbers: The Pursuit of Objectivity in Science and Public Life*. Princeton: Princeton University Press.
Portes, A. and Rumbaut, R.G. 1996. *Immigrant America: A Portrait*. Berkeley: University of California Press.
Postman, Neal. 1986. *Amusing Ourselves to Death: Public Discourse in the Age of Show Business*. London: Heinemann.
Prasad, N.K. 1979. *The Language Issue in India*. New Delhi: Leeladewi.
Prince, R.A. and File, K.M. 1995. "Philanthropic Cultures of Mind", in Hamilton, Charles H. and Ilchman, Warren F. (eds.), *Cultures of Giving II: How Heritage, Gender, Wealth and Values influence Philanthropy*. San Francisco: Jossey-Bass.
Public Culture 11(1), a special issue on "Alternative Modernities" edited by Dilip Gaonkar.
Putnam, Robert D., Putnam, Robert Leonardi and Nanetti, Raffaella Y. 1993. *Making Democracy Work: Civic Traditions in Modern Italy*. Princeton: Princeton University Press.
Queiroz, M.I. Pereira de. 1997. *O Carnaval Brasileiro*. S. Paulo: Brasiliense.
Quigley, C. 1979. *The Evolution of Civilizations. An Introduction to Historical Analysis*. Second edition. Indianapolis: Liberty Fund.
Quint, D. 1998. *Montaigne and the Quality of Mercy. Ethical and Political Themes in the Essais*. Princeton: Princeton University Press.
Rabin, Ethan. 1994. "Vilnai", *Ha'aretz*, May 17, p. A5. (Hebrew)
Raday, F. and Bunk, E. 1993. *Integration of Russian Immigrants into the Israeli Labor Market (Research report)*. The Harry and Michael Sacher Institute for Legislative Research and Comparative Law. Jerusalem: The Hebrew University.
Ramirez, Francisco O., Soysal, Yasemin and Shanahan, Suzanne. 1997. "The Changing Logic of Political Citizenship: Cross-National Acquisition of Women's Suffrage Right, 1890 to 1990", *American Sociological Review* 62(5): 735–745.
Rayner, Jeremy. 1988. "On Begriffsgeschichte", *Political Theory* 16(3): 496–501.
Reich, R. 1992. *The Work of Nations*. New York: Vintage.
Reichardt, Rolf. 1985–1996. *Handbuch politisch-sozialer Grundbegriffe in Frankreich 1680–1820*. Munich: Oldenburg.
Reill, Peter Hanns. 1975. *The German Enlightenment and the Rise of Historicism*. Berkeley: University of California Press.
———— 1994. "Science and the Construction of the Cultural Sciences in Late Enlightenment Germany: The Case of Wilhelm von Humboldt", *History and Theory* 33(3): 345–366.
———— 1998. "The Construction of the Social Sciences in Late Eighteenth- and Early Nineteenth-Century Germany", in Heilbron, J., Magnusson, L. and Wittrock, B. (eds.), *The Rise of the Social Sciences and the Formation of Modernity: Conceptual Change in Context, 1750–1850*. Dordrecht: Kluwer.
Reischauer, Edwin O. 1974. "The Sinic World in Perspective", *Foreign Affairs* 52(2): 341–348.
Remennick, L. (forthcoming). *Transnationalism and its Discontents: Russian Jews in Israel of the 1990s*.
Renan, Ernest. 1994. "What is a Nation", in Bhabha, Homi (ed.), *Nation and Narration*. London: Routledge.
Rheinberger, H.-J. 1992. "Experiment, Difference, and Writing: I. Tracing Protein Synthesis", *Studies in the History and Philosophy of Science* 23(2): 305–331.
Rhoades, G. 1990. "Political Competition and Differentiation in the Antebellum United States", in Alexander, J. and Colomy, P. (eds.), *Differentiation Theory and Social Change*. New York: Columbia University Press.
Ricento, Thomas. 1996. "Language Policy in the United States", pp. 122–158 in Herriman,

Michael and Burnaby, Barbara (eds.), *Language Policies in English-dominant Countries: Six Case Studies*. Clevedon, Philadelphia & Adelaide: Multilingual Matters.

Richardson, J. 1998. "Study Warns of Great Divide", *The Australian*, July 28, p. 35.

Richter, Melvin. 1986. "Conceptual History (*Bergriffsgeschichte*) and Political Theory", *Political Theory* 14(4): 604–637.

———— 1987. "*Begriffsgeschichte* and the History of Ideas", *Journal of the History of Ideas* 48: 247–263.

———— 1989. "Understanding *Begriffsgeschichte*: A Rejoinder", *Political Theory* 17(2): 296–301.

———— 1990. "Reconstructing the History of Political Languages: Pocock, Skinner, and the Geschichtliche Grundbegriffe", *History and Theory* 24: 38–70.

Ricoeur, P. 1965. "Universal Civilization and National Cultures", pp. 271–284 in Ricoeur, P., *History and Truth*. Evanston: Northwestern University Press.

Riedel, M. 1972. "Gesellschaft, bürgerliche", in Koselleck, R., Brunner, O. and Conze, W. (eds.), *Geschichliche Grundbegriffe. Historisches Lexicon zur politisch-sozialen sprache in Deutschland*, Band 1. Stuttgart: Klett-Cotta.

Riesman, David, Denny, Reuel and Glazer, Nathan. 1950. *The Lonely Crowd*. New Haven: Yale University Press.

Riley, Jonathan. 1992. "Philanthropy under Capitalism", in Burlingame, Dwight F. (ed.), *The Responsibilities of Wealth*. Bloomington: Indiana University Press.

Ritter, Joachim and Grunder, Karlfried. 1971–1995. *Historisches Worterbuch der Philosophie*, Vols. 1–9. Basel/Stuttgart: Schwabe und Co.

Ritzer, G. 1996. "Globalization, McDonaldization and Americanization", *The Annals of the International Institute of Sociology* 5: 73–90.

Robbins, B. 1998. "Introduction: Actually Existing Cosmopolitanism", in Cheah, P. and Robbins, B. (eds.), *Cosmopolitics*. Minneapolis: University of Minnesota Press.

Robertson. R. 1985. "The Relativization of Societies: Modern Religion and Globalization", in Robbins, T., Sheppherd, W.C. and McBride, J. (eds.), *Cults, Culture and the Law*. Chico, CA: Scholars Press.

———— 1992a. "Globality and Modernity", *Theory, Culture & Society* 9(2): 151–161.

———— 1992b. *Globalization: Social Theory and Global Culture*. London: Sage.

———— 1995a. "Glocalization: Time-Space and Homogeneity-Heterogeneity", pp. 25–44 in Featherstone, M., Lash, S. and Robertson, R. (eds.), *Global Modernities*. London: Sage.

———— 1995b. "Theory, Specificity, Change: Emulation, Selective Incorporation and Modernization", pp. 213–231 in Grancelli, B. (ed.), *Social Change and Modernization: Lessons from Eastern Europe*. Berlin: W. de Gruyter.

———— 1998. "Identidad Nacional y Globalizacion: Falacias Contemporaneas", *Revista Mexicana de Sociologia* 1(enero-marzo): 3–19.

———— 2000. "Globalization Theory 2000+: Major Problematics", in Ritzer, G. and Smart, B. (eds.), *Handbook of Social Theory*. London: Sage.

Robertson. R. and Chirico, J. 1985. "Humanity, Globalization and Worldwide Religious Resurgence: A Theoretical Explanation", *Sociological Analysis* 46(3): 219–242.

Robertson, R. and Lechner, F. 1985. "Modernization, Globalization and the Problem of Culture in World-Systems Theory", *Theory, Culture & Society* 2(3): 103–117.

Robertson, R. and Khondker, H.H. 1998. "Discourses of Globalization: Preliminary Considerations", *International Sociology* 13(1): 25–40.

Rodó, J.E. 1991. *Ariel*. Campinas: Ed. Unicampa.

Rojek, C. and Urry, J. (eds.). 1997. *Touring Cultures*. London: Routledge.

Romero, Sylvio. 1888. *Historia da Literatura Brasileira*. Rio de Janeiro: Garnier.

———— (1894) Doutrina Contra Doutrina. Rio de Janeiro: J.B. Nunes.

———— 1906. *O Brasil Social*. Rio de Janeiro: Typographia do Jornal do Comércio.

———— 1978. *Teoria, Crítica, e História Literária*. Rio de Janeiro: Livros Técnicos e Científicos Editora.

Rorty, R. 1979. *Philosophy and the Mirror of Nature*. Princeton: Princeton University Press.

———— 1989. *Contingency, Irony, and Solidarity*. Cambridge: Cambridge University Press.

———— 1998. *Achieving Our Country. Leftist Thought in Twentieth-Century America*. Cambridge, MA: Harvard University Press.

———— 1999. *Philosophy and Social Hope*. London: Penguin.
Rosdolsky, Roman. 1964. "Friedrich Engels und das Problem der geschichtslosen Völker", *Archiv für Sozialgeschichte* 4: 87–282.
Rosengren, Karl Erik, Wenner, Lawrence A. and Palmgreen, Philip (eds.). 1985. *Media Gratifications Research. Current Perspectives*. Beverly Hills: Sage.
Ross, Dorothy. 1991. *The Origins of American Social Science*. Cambridge: Cambridge University Press.
Rossillon, P. (ed.). 1995. *Atlas de la langue française*. Paris: Bordas.
Rothblatt, Sheldon and Wittrock, Björn (eds.). 1993. *The European and American University Since 1800: Historical and Sociological Essays*. Cambridge: Cambridge University Press.
Roudometof, V. and Robertson, R. 1995. "Globalization, World-System Theory and the Comparative Study of Civilizations: Issues of Theoretical Logic in World-Historical Sociology", pp. 273–300 in Sanderson, S.K. (ed.), *Civilizations and World Systems. Studying World-Historical Change*. Walnut Creek, CA: AltaMira Press.
Rousseau, G.S. and Porter, Roy (eds.). 1980. *The Ferment of Knowledge: Studies in the Historiography of Eighteenth Century Science*. Cambridge: Cambridge University Press.
Rousseau, Jean-Jacques. (1749, 1754) 1986. *The First and Second Discourses*. Victor Gourevitch translation. New York: Harper & Row.
Roxborough, I. 1999. "The Persistence of War as a Sociological Problem", symposium on War and Modernization Theory, *International Sociology* 14(4): 491–500.
Rubenstein, R. 1994. *Comrade Valentine*. New York: Harcourt Brace.
Rubin, Joan, Jernudd, Björn H., Das Gupta, J., Fishman, Joshua A. and Ferguson, Charles A. (eds.). 1977. *Language Planning Processes*. Edited by Joshua A. Fishman, *Contributions to the Sociology of Language*. Hague: Mouton Publishers.
Ruiz, Richard. 1994. "Language Policy and Planning in the United States", *Annual Review of Applied Linguistics* 14: 111–125.
Rüschemeyer, D. 1977. "Structural Differentiation, Efficiency, and Power", *American Journal of Sociology* 83(1): 1–25.
Rushdie, Salman. 1992. *Imaginary Homelands. Essays and Criticism 1981–1991*. New York: Penguin Books.
Russo, Michael. 1983. *CBS and the American Political Experience: A History of the CBS News Special Events and Elections Unit 1952–1968*. Ann Arbor: University Microfilms.
Rustow, D. 1956. "Scandinavia", pp. 169–194 in Neumann, S. (ed.), *Modern Political Parties*. Chicago: University of Chicago Press.
Sabagh, G. 1998. *Future Population Trends and their Implications for Higher Education in the Twenty-First Century: The Case of Eastern and South Asian Countries*. Paper presented at the Seminar on Higher Education in the Coming Century, Tehran, Iran.
Sadki, S. 1999. "400 Algériens passent le bac français á Tunis", *El Watan*, 20 May.
Safran, William. 1991. "Diasporas in Modern Societies: Myths of Homeland and Return", *Diaspora* 1(1): 83–99.
Sahlins, M. 1972. *Stone Age Economies*. Chicago: Aldine.
Said, E.W. 1978. *Orientalism*. New York: Pantheon Books.
———— 1983. *The World, the Text and the Critic*. New York: Pantheon Books.
———— 1993. *Culture and Imperialism*. New York: Knopf.
———— 1994. *Representations of the Intellectual*. New York: Pantheon Books.
———— 1999. *Out of Place. A Memoir*. London: Granta Books.
Sakai, N. 1989. "Modernity and its Critique: The Problem of Universalism and Particularism", in Myoshi, M. and Harootunian, H. (eds.), *Postmodernism and Japan*. Durham: Duke University Press.
Sakamoto, Yoshiyuki. 1995. "A Statistical Research of the Japanese National Character: General Trend of Opinion over Past Forty Years", *Proceedings of the Institute of Statistical Mathematics* 43: 5–26.
Salamon, Lester M. 1987. "Partners in Public Service: The Scope and Theory of Government-Nonprofit Relations", pp. 99–117 in Powell, Walter W. (ed.), *The Nonprofit Sector: A Research Handbook*. New Haven: Yale University Press.
———— 1993. "The Marketization of Welfare: Changing Nonprofit and For-profit Roles in the American Welfare State", *Social Service Review* 67: 16–39.

——— 1994. "The Rise of the Nonprofit Sector", *Foreign Affairs* 73(4): 109–122.

Salamon, Lester M. and Anheier, Helmut. 1996. *The Emerging Nonprofit Sector: An Overview.* Manchester and New York: Manchester University Press.

——— et al. 1998. *The Emerging Sector Revisited: A Summary.* Baltimore: The Johns Hopkins University Institute for Policy Studies, Center for Civil Society Studies.

Salvatore, Armando. 1997. *Islam and the Political Discourse of Modernity.* Reading: Ithaca Press.

——— 1998. "Staging Virtue: The Disembodiment of Self-Correctness and the Making of Islam as a Public Norm", *Yearbook of the Sociology of Islam* 1: 87–119.

Salzmann, A. 1999. "Citizens in Search of a State: The Limits of Political Participation in the Late Ottoman Empire", pp. 37–66 in Hanagan, M. and Tilly, C. (eds.), *Extending Citizenship, Reconfiguring States.* Oxford: Rowman & Littlefield Publishers, INC.

Sanderson, S.K. (ed.). 1995. *Civilizations and World Systems. Studying World-Historical Change.* Walnut Creek, CA: AltaMira Press.

Sandoval, G., Mangahas, M. and Guerrero, L. 1998. *The Situation of Filipino Youth: A National Survey.* Paper presented at the ISA 14th World Congress of Sociology, Montreal, Canada.

Santos, Boaventura de Sousa. 1999. "Toward a Multicultural Conception of Human Rights", in Featherstone, M. and Lash, S. (eds.), *Spaces of Culture: City/Nation/World.* London: Sage.

Sarlo, B. 1988. *Una Modernidad Periferica: Buenos Aires 1920 y 1930.* Buenos Aires: Nueva Visión.

Sasaki, Masamichi and Suzuki, Tatsuzo. 1987. "Changes in Religious Commitment in the United States, Holland, and Japan", *American Journal of Sociology* 92: 1055–1076.

Sassen, S. 1991. *The Global City. New York, London, Tokyo.* Princeton: Princeton University Press.

——— 1994. *Cities in a World Economy.* Thousand Oaks: Sage.

——— 1999a. "Electronic Space and Power", in Featherstone, M. and Lash, S. (eds.), *Spaces of Culture: City, Nation, World.* London: Sage.

——— 1999b. *Guests and Aliens.* New York: The New Press.

Schelling, Thomas C. 1978. *Micromotives and Macrobehavior.* New York/London: Norton & Co.

Schervish, P. 1997. "Inclination, Obligation and Association: What We Know and What We Need to Learn About Donor Motivation", pp. 110–139 in Burlingame, D. (ed.), *Critical Issues in Fund-Raising.* New York: Wiley and Sons.

Scheuch, Erwin K. 1999. "Wider die ökonomisierung aller Lebensbereiche", pp. 137–165 in Beckers, Eberhard et al. (eds.), *Hochschulausbildung im Aus?.* Gießen: Verlag des Professorenforums.

Schieffelin, Bambi B., Woolard, Kathryn A. and Kroskrity, Paul V. (eds.). 1998. *Language Ideologies: Practice and Theory. Oxford Studies in Anthropological Linguistics.* New York and Oxford: Oxford University Press.

Schiff, Ze'ev. 1997. "A Rupture in Security", *Ha'aretz*, November 21, p. b1. (Hebrew)

Schiffman, Harold E. 1996. *Linguistic Culture and Language Policy.* Edited by Crowley, Tony and Taylor, Talbot. J., *The Politics of Language.* London and New York: Routledge.

Schiffman, Zachary Sayre. 1985. "Renaissance Historicism Reconsidered", *History and Theory* 24: 170–182.

Schmidt, S.J. 1989. *Die Selbstorganisation des Sozialsystems Literatur im 18. Jahrhundert.* Frankfurt/M.: Suhrkamp.

Schmitt, Carl. (1926) 1979. *Die geistesgeschichtliche Lage des heutigen Parlamentarismus.* Berlin: Duncker and Humblot.

Schneider, H.K. and Watrin, C. (eds.). 1973. 'Macht und ökonomisches Gesetz', *Schriften des Vereins für Sozialpolitik* 74(2).

Schneider, John. 1996. "Philanthropic Styles in the United States: Toward a Theory of Regional Differences", *Nonprofit and Voluntary Sector Quarterly* 25(2): 190–210.

Scholem, Gershom. 1973. *Sabbatai Sevi: The Mystical Messiah.* Transleted by R.J.Z. Werblowski. Princeton: Princeton University Press.

Scholte, B. 1971. "Discontents in Anthropology", *Social Research* 38: 777–807.

Schooler, Carmi. 1998. "History, Social Structure and Individualism", pp. 32–51 in Sasaki, Masamichi (ed.), *Values and Attitudes Across Nations and Time.* Leiden: Brill.

Schudson, Michael. 1997. "Why Conversation Is Not the Soul of Democracy?", *Critical Studies in Mass Communication* 14: 297–309.

Schulze, Gerhard. 1992. *Die Erlebnisgesellschaft—Kultursoziologie der Gegenwart.* New York: Campus.

Schuman, Howard et al. 1997. *Racial Attitudes in America.* Cambridge, MA: Harvard University Press.

Schumpeter, J.A. (1943) 1994. *Capitalism, Socialism and Democracy.* London and New York: Routledge.

Schwab, Raymond. 1950. *La Renaissance Orientale.* Paris: Payot.

Schwarcz, Lilia. 1993. *O Espetáculo das Raças.* São Paulo: Cia das Letras.

Schwartz, P. and Leyden, P. 1997. 'The Long Boom', *Wired* (July): 115–122.

Schwarz, R. 1977. *Ao Vencedor as Batatas.* S. Paulo: Livraria Duas Cidades.

Science, Vol. 279, March 27, 1998.

Scott, A. 1997. "Introduction", in Scott, A. (ed.), *The Limits of Globalization.* London: Routledge.

Sealander. J. 1997. *Private Wealth and Public Life: Foundation Philanthropy and the Reshaping of American Social Policy from the Progressive Era to the New Deal.* Baltimore: Johns Hopkins University Press.

Seligman, A. (ed.). 1989. *Order and Transcendence.* Leiden: Brill.

Sellers, Charles G. 1991. *The Market Revolution: Jacksonian America, 1815–1846.* New York: Oxford University Press.

Semyonov M. and Lewin-Epstein N. 1987. *Hewers of Wood and Drawers of Water.* Ithaca, NJ: Cornell Institute of Labor Studies.

Sennett, R. 1998. *The Corrosion of Character, The Personal Consequences of Work in the New Capitalism.* New York: W.W. Norton & Co.

——— 1999. "Growth and Failure: The New Political Economy and its Culture", in Featherstone, M. and Lash, S. (eds.), *Spaces of Culture: City, Nation, World.* London: Sage.

Shahrur, Muhammad. 1992. *al-Kitab wa-l-Qur'an: Qira'a mu'asira* [The Book and the Qur'an: A Contemporary Reading]. Beirut: Sharikat al-Matbu'at li-l-Tawzi wa-l-Nashr.

——— 1994. *Dirasat Islamiya al-mu'asira fi-l-dawla wa-l-mujtama'a* [Contemporary Islamic Studies on State and Society]. Damascus: al-Ahali li-l-Taba'a wa-l-Nashr.

——— 1996. *al-Islam wa-l-iman: Manzumat al-qiwam* [Islam and Faith: A Treatise on Values]. Damascus: al-Ahali li-l-Taba'a wa-l-Nashr.

Shannon, T.R. 1989. *An Introduction to the World-System Perspective.* Boulder: Westview Press.

Shapin, Steven. 1994. *A Social History of Truth: Clivility and Science in Seventeenth-Century England.* Chicago: University of Chicago Press.

Shapin, Steven and Schaffer, Simon. 1985. *Leviathan and the Air-Pump: Hobbes, Boyle, and the Experimental Life.* Princeton: Princeton University Press.

Shields, R. 1997. "Flow", *Space and Culture* 1(1).

Shils, E. 1972. *The Intellectuals and the Powers.* Chicago: University of Chicago Press.

——— 1975. "Primordial, Personal, Sacred and Civil Ties," pp. 111–126 in Shils, E. (ed.), *Center and Periphery: Essays in Macrosociology.* Chicago: University of Chicago Press.

——— 1981. *Tradition.* London: Faber and Faber.

——— 1991. "The Virtue of Civil Society", *Government and Opposition* 26(1): 3–20.

Silber, I.F. 1999. "Modern Philanthropy: Reassessing the Viability of a Maussian Perspective", in James, Wendy and Allen, Nick (eds.), *Marcel Mauss: A Centenary Tribute.* Oxford: Berghahn.

Sills, David L. (ed.). 1968. *The International Encyclopedia of the Social Sciences.* New York: Macmillan and Free Press. 17 Vols.; supplement 1979.

Silva, Denise Ferreira da. 1989. "Repensando a 'Democracia Racial': raça e identidade nacional no Pensamento Brasileiro", *Estudos Afro-Asiáticos* 16: 157–170.

——— 1998. "Facts of Blackness: Brazil is not (Quite) the United States . . . and Racial Politics in Brazil?", *Social Identities* 4(2): 201–223.

Silverstein, Michael. 1979. "Language Structure and Linguistic Ideology", pp. 193–247 in Clyne, Paul R. (ed.), *The Elements: A Parasession on Linguistic Units and Levels.* Chicago: Chicago Linguistic Society.

Simmel, G. 1908. *Soziologie: Untersuchung über die Formen der Vergesellschaftung.* Leipzig: Duncker & Humblot.

Simon, C. 1996. "Alger-Tunis, les bacheliers de la 'tchi-tchi'", *Le Monde*, 12 October, P.1.
Skidmore, Thomas. 1993. *Black into White: Race and Nationality in Brazilian Thought*. Durham: Duke University Press.
Skinner, Quentin. 1974. "The Principles and Practice of Opposition: The Case of Bolingbroke versus Walpole", in McKendrick, Neil (ed.), *Historical Perspectives: Studies in English Thought and Society in Honour of J.H. Plumb*. London: Europa.
———— 1996. "From Hume's Intentions to Deconstruction and Back", *Journal of Political Philosophy* 4(2): 142–154.
Sklair, L. 1998. "The Transnational Capitalist Class", in Carrier, J.G. and Miller, D. (eds.), *Virtualism: A New Political Economy*. Oxford: Berg.
Sklar, R. 1979. "The Nature of Class Domination in Africa", *Journal of Modern African Studies* 17(4): 531–552.
Skocpol, T. 1997. "The Tocqueville Problem: Civic Engagement in American Democracy", *Social Science History* 21(4): 455–479.
Skocpol, T. and Rueschemeyer, D. (eds.). 1996. *States, Knowledge and the Origin of Social Policies*. Princeton: Princeton University Press.
Smart, B. 1993. *Postmodernity*. London and New York: Routledge.
Smelser, Neil J. 1959. *Social Change in the Industrial Revolution*. London: Routledge & Kegan Paul.
———— (ed.). 1999. *International Encyclopedia of the Social and Behavioral Sciences*. Amsterdam: Elsevier. 24 Vols.; 2 supplements 2001.
———— 2000. "Die Zukunft der Soziologie: Zentrifugalität, Konflikt, Akkomodation", in Müller, Hans-Peter and Steffen, Sigmund (eds.), *Zeitgenössische amerikanische Soziologie*. Opladen: Leske + Budrich.
Smith, Anthony. 1981. *The Ethnic Revival*. Cambridge: Cambridge University Press.
———— 1998. *Nationalism and Modernism: A Critical Survey of Recent Theories of Nations and Nationalism*. London: Routledge.
Smolicz, J.J. 1990a. "Evaluation of University and College Qualifications in the Philippines", in *Studies in Comparative Education: The Philippines*. Research Paper No. 3. Canberra: Department of Employment, Education and Training.
———— 1990b. "Polarity of Filipino Values", *Asian Migrant* 3(4): 127–132.
———— 1993. "Nation, State and Ethnic Minorities from an Euro-Muslim Perspective", *Muslim Education Quarterly* 11(1): 14–26.
———— 1997. *Non-Government Higher Educational Institutions in Poland*. (unpublished material).
———— 1998a. "Globalisation, Nation-State and Local Cultures", *Political Crossroads* 6(1 & 2): 111–128.
———— 1998b. "Nation-States and Globalization from a Multicultural Perspective. Signopsis from Australia," *Nationalism and Ethnic Politics* 4(4): 1–18.
———— 1998c. *The Iranian Higher Education: From State to Private and Back Under State Patronage*. (unpublished material).
Smolicz, J.J. and Nical, I. 1997. "Exporting the European Idea of a National Language: Some Educational Implications and the Use of English and Indigenous Languages in the Philippines", *International Review of Education* 43(5–6): 507–526.
Smolicz, J.J., Wozniak, A., Smolicz, C., Secombe, M.J. and Uszynska, K. 1993. *In Search of Talent: From Poland to Australia*. Adelaide: Centre for Intercultural Studies and Multicultural Education (CISME).
Smooha S. 1976. "Arabs and Jews in Israel", *Megamot* 22(4): 397–424. (Hebrew)
Soffer, Reba. 1978. *Ethics and Society: The Revolution in the Social Sciences in England 1870–1914*. Berkeley: University of California Press.
Soja, E.W. 1989. *Postmodern Geographies: The Reassertion of Space in Critical Social Theory*. London: Verso.
Sombart, W. (1906) 1976. *Why is there no Socialism in the United States?*. New York: ME Sharpe.
Somers, M.R. 1994. "The Narrative Constitution of Identity: A Relational and Network Approach", *Theory and Society* 23: 605–649.
———— 1999. "The Privatization of Citizenship: How to Unthink a Knowledge Culture", pp. 121–164 in Bonnel, Victoria E. and Hunt, Lynn (eds.), *Beyond the Cultural Turn*. Berkeley: University of California Press.

Sorokin, P.A. 1928. *Contemporary Sociological Theories through the First Quarter of the Twentieth Century*. New York: Harper and Row.
────── 1947. *Society, Culture, and Personality: Their Structure and Dynamics. A System of General Sociology*. New York and London: Harper & Brothers Publishers.
────── 1956. *Fads and Foibles in Modern Sociology and Related Sciences*. Chicago: Regnery.
────── 1957. *Social and Cultural Dynamics*. Boston: Porter Sergeant.
────── 1963. *Modern Historical and Social Philosophies*. New York: Dover Publications.
Soysal, Y. 1994. *Limits of Citizenship*. Chicago: University of Chicago Press.
────── 2000. "Citizenship and Identity: Living in Diasporas in Post-war Europe", *Ethnic and Racial Studies* 23(1): 1–15.
Spivak, G.C. 1989. "Post-Structuralism, Marginality, Post-Coloniality, and Value", *Sociocriticism* 10(10): 3–81.
────── 1994. "Can the Subaltern Speak?", in Williams, Patrick and Chrisman, Laura (ed.), *Colonial Discourse and Post-Colonial Theory*. New York: Columbia University Press.
Spolsky, Bernard, and Shohamy, Elana. 1999. *The Languages of Israel: Policy, Ideology and Practice*. Clevedon: Multilingual Matters.
Sprinkler, M. (ed.). 1992. *Edward Said. A Critical Reader*. Oxford: Blackwell.
Spybey, T. 1996. *Globalization and World Society*. Cambridge: Polity Press.
State Comptroller's Report no. 34, Jerusalem: 1984.
State Comptroller's Report no. 35, Jerusalem: 1985.
State Comptroller's Report no. 39, Jerusalem: 1989.
State Comptroller's Report no. 40, Jerusalem: 1990.
State Comptroller's Report no. 41, Jerusalem: 1991.
State Comptroller's Report no. 45, Jerusalem: 1995.
Steiner, J. 1974. *Amicable Agreement versus Majority Rule: Conflict Resolution in Switzerland*. Chapel Hill: University of North Carolina Press.
Stepan, Nancy. 1982. *The Idea of Race in Science*. Hamden, Conn.: Anchor Books.
────── 1991. *Hour of Eugenics*. Ithaca: Cornel University Press.
Stephenson, N. 1992. *Snow Crash*. New York: Bantam.
Sterling, B. 1989. *Islands in the Net*. New York: Ace.
Stichweh, R. 1984. *Zur Entstehung des modernen Systems wissenschaftlicher Disziplinen: Physik in Deutschland 1746–1890*. Frankfurt/M.: Suhrkamp.
────── 1994. *Wissenschaft, Universität, Professionen: Soziologische Analysen*. Frankfurt/M: Suhrkamp.
────── 1997. "The Stranger—On the Sociology of Indifference", *Thesis Eleven* 51: 1–16.
Stocking, George. 1968. *Race, Culture and Evolution*. New York: Free Press.
Stouffer, Samuel A. (ed.). 1950. *Studies in the Scope and Method of "The American Soldier"*. Glencoe: Free Press.
Street, R.J. and Giles, H. 1982. "Speech Accommodation Theory: A Social and Cognitive Approach to Language and Speech Behavior" in Roloff, M. and Berger, C. (eds.), *Social Cognition and Communication*. Beverly Hills: Sage.
Süddeutsche Zeitung. 2000. 16 May.
Szafran, Maurice. 1990. *Les Juifs dans la politique française*. Paris: Flammarion.
Szalai, Alexander and Petrella, Riccardo (eds.). 1977. *Cross-National Comparative Survey Research—Theory and Practice*. Oxford: Pergamon Press.
Szczepanski, J. 1978. *Systems of Higher Education: Poland*. New York: ICED.
────── 1983. *Sociologiczne zagadnienia wyzszego wykrztalcenia (Sociological Issues in Higher Education)*. Warsaw: PAN.
Sztompka, Piotr. 1993. *The Sociology of Social Change*. Oxford: Blackwell.
Tabory, E. and Lazerwitz, B. 1983. "Americans in the Israeli Reform and Conservative Denominations: Religiosity under an Ethnic Shield?", *Review of Religious Research* 24: 177–187.
Tachau, F. 1963. "The Search for National Identity among the Turks", *Die Welt des Islams* 8(3): 165–176.
Takougang, J. 1997. "Cameroon: Biya and Incremental Reform", pp. 162–181 in Clark, J.F. and Gardinier, D.E. (eds.), *Political Reform in Francophone Africa*. Boulder: Westview Press.

Tarde, Gabriel. (1880) 1903. *The Laws of Imitation*. Translated by Elsie Clews Parsons. New York: Henry Holt.
——— (1901) 1989. *L'opinion et la foule*. Paris: Presses Universitaires de France.
Taylor, Charles. 1990. "Modes of Civil Society", *Public Culture* 3(1).
——— 1993. "Modernity and the Rise of the Public Sphere", *The Tanner Lectures on Human Values* 14.
——— 1994. "The Politics of Recognition", in Taylor, Charles et al., *Multiculturalism. Examining the Politics of Recognition*. Edited and introduced by Amy Gutman. Princeton: Princeton University Press.
Taylor, T., Gough, J., Bandrock, V. and Winter, R. 1996. "A Bleak Outlook: Academic Staff Perceptions of Changes in Core Activities in Australian Higher Education 1991–1996", *Studies in Higher Education*. London.
Tengour, H. 1995. "Le fourvoiement des élites", *Cahiers Intersignes* 10: 67–77.
Teune, H. 1996. "New localisms and old identities in global political economies", *The Annals of the International Institute of Sociology* 5: 107–124.
The Cambridge History of Japan; the nineteenth century. Vol. 5. Cambridge: Cambridge University Press, 1989.
Therborn, G. 1995. *European Modernity and Beyond*. London: Sage.
——— 2000. "Globalizations: Dimensions, Historical Waves, Regional Effects, Normative Governance", *International Sociology* 15(2): 151–179.
Thomas, K. 1978. "The United Kingdom", pp. 41–98 in Grew, R. (ed.), *Crises of Political Development in Europe and the United States*. Princeton: Princeton University Press.
Thompson, E.P. 1968. *The Making of the English Working Class*. Revised edition. Harmondsworth: Penguin Books.
Thomson, D. 1940. *The Democratic Ideal in France and England*. Cambridge: Cambridge University Press.
——— 1960. *England in the Nineteenth Century*. London: Pelican Books.
Tiryakian, E. 1999. "War: The Covered Side of Modernity", symposium on War and Modernization Theory, *International Sociology* 14(4): 473–490.
Tittmus, R. 1970. *The Gift Relationship: From Human Blood to Social Policy*. London: G. Allen & Unwin.
Tocqueville, A. de. 1964. *Oeuvres Complètes, Tome XII, souvenirs*. Paris: Gallimard.
——— (1835) 1969. *Democracy in America* (J.P. Maier, trans.). Garden City, NY: Anchor Books.
Todd, E. 1994. *Le Destin des Immigrés: Assimilation et ségrégation dans les démocraties occidentales*. Paris: Seuil.
Tölölian, Khachig. 1991. "The Nation State and its Others: In Lieu of a Preface", *Diaspora* 1(1).
Tomlinson, J. 1991. *Cultural Imperialism. A Critical Introduction*. London: Pinter Publishers.
——— 1999. *Globalization and Culture*. Cambridge: Polity.
Touraine, A. 1971. *The Post-Industrial Society*. London: Wildwood House.
——— 1992. *Critique de la Modernité*. Paris: Fayard.
Toynbee, A.J. 1965. *A Study of History*. Abridgement of Vols. I–X by Somervell, D.C., 2 Vols. New York: Dell.
Tribe, Keith. 1988. *Governing the Economy. The Reformation of Economic Discourse in Germany, 1750–1840*. Cambridge: Cambridge University Press.
——— 1989. "The Geschichtliche Grundbegriffe Project", *Comparative Studies in Society and History* 31: 180–184.
Tucker, R. 1961. *Philosophy and Myth in Karl Marx*. London: Cambridge University Press.
Tully, James (ed.). 1988. *Meaning and Context: Quentin Skinner and His Critics*. Cambridge: Polity Press.
Turner, B.A. 1975. *Industrialism*. Harlow, Essex: Longman.
Turner, B.S. 1978. *Marx and the End of Orientalism*. London: George Allen & Unwin.
——— (ed.). 1990. *Theories of Modernity and Postmodernity*. London: Sage.
——— 1991. *Religion and Social Theory*. London: Sage.
——— 1994. *Orientalism, Postmodernism and Globalism*. London and New York: Routledge.
——— 2000. "Citizenship and Political Globalization", *Citizenship Studies* 4(1): 81–86.

Turner, F.J. 1956. "The Significance of the Frontier in American History", pp. 1–18 in Taylor, G.R. (ed.), *The Turner Thesis: Concerning the Role of the Frontier in American History*. Boston: D.C. Heath and Company.

Turner, R. Steven. 1987. "The Great Transition and the Social Patterns of German Science", *Minerva* 25: 56–76.

Turner, S. and Turner, J.H. 1990. *The Impossible Science—An Institutional Analysis of American Sociology*. London: Sage.

Turner, T. 1997. "Zaire: Flying High above the Toads: Mobutu and Stalemated Democracy", pp. 246–266 in Clark, J.F. and Gardinier, D.E. (eds.), *Political Reform in Francophone Africa*. Boulder: Westview Press.

Uhlenbeck, E.M. 1994. "The Threat of Rapid Language Death: A Recently Acknowledged Global Problem", in *The Low Countries; Arts and Society in Flanders and the Netherlands*. Vol. 1. Rekkem, Belgium: Stichting Ons Erfdeel.

Ulken, H.Z. 1979. *Turkiye'de Cagdas Dusunce Tarihi*. Istanbul: Ulken Yayynlari.

Urry, J. 1990. *The Tourist Gaze*. London: Sage.

Usher, Arland. 1995. *Journey through Dread*. New York: Devin-Adair.

Ustel, F. 1993. "Turk Milliyetciliginde Anadolu Metaforu", *Tarih ve Toplum* 109: 51–55.

Vakili, Vakil. 1996. *Debating Religion and Politics in Iran: The Political Thought of Abdokarim Soroush*. New York: Council on Foreign Relations.

Van Calcar, Co and Koppen, Jan Karel. 1984. *Cultureel Kapitaal: Op Weg naar een Instrument*. Amsterdam: St. Kohnstamm Fonds.

Van den Berghe, P. 1978. *Race and Racism: A Comparative Perspective*. New York: Wiley.

van Deth, Jan W. and Scarbrough, Elinor (eds.). 1995. *The Impact of Values*. Oxford: Oxford University Press.

van Els, Theo J.M. 1992. *The Dutch National Action Programme on Foreign Languages*. Ministry of Education and Science.

———— 1994. "Foreign Language Planning in the Netherlands", pp. 47–68 in Lambert, Richard D. (ed.), *Language Planning Around the World: Contexts and Systematic Change*. Washington, DC: National Foreign Language Center.

Van Hear, N. 1998. *New Diasporas: The Mass Exodus, Dispersal and Regrouping of Migrant Communities*. London: University College of London Press.

Varis, Tapio. 1984. "The International Flow of Television Programs", *Journal of Communication* (Winter): 143–152.

Vattimo, G. 1988. *The End of Modernity*. Oxford: Polity Press.

———— 1992. *The Transparent Society*. Baltimore: The Johns Hopkins University Press.

Veit-Brause, I. 1980. "A Note on Begriffsgeschichte", *History and Theory* 20: 61–67.

Venn, C. 1999. "Narrating the Postcolonial", in Featherstone, M. and Lash, S. (eds.), *Spaces of Culture: City/Nation/World*. London: Sage.

Verma, Neena. 2000. *The Indo-Trinidadian Revival*. Ph.D. Dissertation, University of Toronto, Department of Sociology.

Vertlib, Vladimir. 1999. "Der zwanzigste April", *Golem. Europäisch-jüdisches Magazin* 1: 38–45.

Veyne, P. 1976. *Le pain et le cirque: sociologie historique d'un pluralisme politique*. Paris: Seuil.

Virilio, P. 1999. *Polar Inertia*. London: Sage.

Voegelin, Eric. 1975. *Enlightenment and Revolution*. Edited by John H. Hallowell. Durham: Duke University Press.

Vogel, Ann. 1994. *Über Mangel, Verlust und Verleugnung von Fremdsprachkompetenz; Eine Analyse des Russischunterrichts in der DDR als Beitrag zur Untersuchung der europäischen Fremdsprachensituation* [unpublished M.A. Thesis]. Amsterdam: ACCESS, University of Amsterdam.

Vogel, Frank E. 1999. *Islamic Law in the Modern World: The Legal System of Saudi Arabia*. Leiden: Brill.

Vycinas, Vincent. 1969. *Earth and Gods*. The Hague: Martinus Nijhoff.

Wagner, Peter. 1994. *A Sociology of Modernity: Liberty and Discipline*. London: Routledge.

———— 1998. "Certainty and Order, Liberty and Contingency. The Birth of Social Science as Empirical Political Philosophy", in Heilbron, J., Magnusson, L. and Wittrock, B. (eds.), *The Rise of the Social Sciencses and the Formation of Modernity: Conceptual Change in Context, 1750–1850*. Dordrecht: Kluwer.

Wagner, Peter, Weiss, Carol, Wittrock, Björn, and Wollmann, Hellmut (eds.). 1991. *Social Sciences and Modern States.* Cambridge: Cambridge University Press.

Wagner, Peter and Wittrock, Björn. 1991a. "Analyzing Social Science: On the Possibility of a Sociology of the Social Sciences", in Wagner, P., Wittrock, B. and Whitley, R. (eds.), *Discourses on Society: The Shaping of the Social Science Disciplines.* Sociology of the Sciences Yearbook XV. Dordrecht: Kluwer.

——— 1991b. "States, Institutions, and Discourses: A Comparative Perspective on the Structuration of the Social Sciences", in Wagner, P., Wittrock, B. and Whitley, R. (eds.), *Discourses on Society: The Shaping of the Social Science Disciplines.* Sociology of the Sciences Yearbook XV. Dordrecht: Kluwer.

Wagner, Peter, Wittrock Björn, and Whitley, Richard (eds.). 1991. *Discourses on Society: The Shaping of the Social Science Disciplines.* Sociology of the Sciences Yearbook XV. Dordrecht: Kluwer.

Wallerstein, I. 1974. *The Modern World-System.* New York: Academic Press.

——— 1979. "Modernization: requiescat in pace", pp. 132–137 in Wallerstein, I., *The Capitalist World-Economy.* Cambridge: Cambridge University Press.

——— 1980. *The Modern World-System II.* New York: Academic Press.

——— 1989. *The Modern World System III: The Second Era of Great Expansion of the Capitalist World Economy.* New York: Academic Press.

——— 1990. "Culture as the Ideological Battleground of the Modern World-System", in Featherstone, Mike (ed.), *Global Culture: Nationalism, Globalization and Modernity.* London: Sage.

——— 1991a. *Geopolitics and Geoculture.* Cambridge: Cambridge University Press/Paris: Editions de la Maison des Sciences de L'Homme.

——— 1991b. *Unthinking Social Science: The Limits of Nineteenth-Century Paradigms.* Cambridge: Polity Press.

——— 1995. "Hold the Tiller Firm: On Method and the Unit of Analysis", pp. 239–247 in Sanderson, S.K. (ed.), *Civilizations and World Systems. Studying World-Historical Change.* Walnut Creek, CA: AltaMira Press.

——— 1996. "Open the Social Sciences", *Items* 50(1): 1–7.

——— 1998. 'The Heritage of Sociology—The Promise of Social Science', *Presidential Address*, 14th ISA World Congress of Sociology, July 26, Montreal.

Walzer, M. 1982. "Socialism and the Gift-Relationship", *Dissent* 29(4): 431–441.

Warren, Mercy Otis. (1788) 1986. Pamphlet "A Columbian Patriot: Observations on the Constitution", excerpts are printed in pp. 272–291 in Kaminski, J.P. and Saladino, G.J. (eds.), *Documentary History of the Ratification of the Constitution.* Vol. XVI. Madison, WI. (1976–): State Historical Society of Wisconsin.

Waters, M. 1995. *Globalization.* London: Routledge.

Watt, W.M. 1991. *Muslim-Christian Encounters. Perceptions and Misperceptions.* London: Routledge.

Weber, M. 1947. *The Theory of Social and Economic Organization.* Translated by A.M. Henderson. New York: Free Press.

——— 1952. *Ancient Judaism.* Glencoe: Free Press.

——— 1958. "The Social Psychology of the World Religions", pp. 267–301 in Gerth, H.H. and Mills, C.W. (eds.), *From Max Weber: Essays in Sociology.* New York: Oxford University Press.

——— 1968a. *Economy and Society*, 3 vols. Berkeley: University of California Press.

——— 1968b. *On Charisma and Institution Building: Selected Papers.* Chicago: University of Chicago Press.

——— 1968c. *Politik als Beruf.* Berlin: Dunker and Humblot.

——— 1970a. "Politics as a Vocation", in Gerth, H.H. and Mills, C. Wright (eds.), *From Max Weber.* London: Routledge & Kegan Paul.

——— 1970b. "Religious Rejections of the World and their Directions", in Gerth, H.H. and Mills, C. Wright (eds.), *From Max Weber.* London: Routledge & Kegan Paul.

——— 1970c. "Science as a Vocation", in Gerth, H.H. and Mills, C. Wright (eds.), *From Max Weber.* London: Routledge & Kegan Paul.

——— (1922) 1976. *Wirtschaft und Gesellschaft*, 5. Bearbeitete Auflage. Tübingen: J.C.B. Mohr (P. Siebeck).

——— 1977. "The Rationalization of Education and Training", pp. 240–244 in Gerth, H.H. and Mills, C. Wright (eds.), *From Max Weber*. London: Routledge & Kegan Paul.

——— 1978. *Die Protestantische Ethik: Kritiken und Antikritiken*. Guetersloh, Germany: Guetersloher Verlagshaus.

Weeks, J. 1998. "The Sexual Citizen", *Theory, Culture & Society* (special issue on Love & Eroticism) 15(3–4): 35–52.

Weinreich, U. 1974. *Languages in Contact. Findings and Problems*. The Hague, Paris: Mouton.

Weinstein, Deena and Weinstein, Michael. 1993. *Postmodern Simmel*. New York: Routledge.

Weissberg, L. 1999. "Introduction. Learning Culture", pp. 7–26 in Ben-Amos, D. and Weissberg, L. (eds.), *Cultural Memory and The Construction of Identity*. Detroit: Wayne State University Press.

Weltsch, Robert. 1946. "Judenbetreuung in Bayern", *Mitteilungsblatt* 19 (May), Tel Aviv.

Werner, Simha. 1999. "Ethics and Morality in the Public Administration: Towards the Third Generation", pp. 131–165 in Kfir, Aharon and Reuveni, Yakov (eds.), *Haminhal Hatziburi Beyisrael: Likrat Sh'not Ha'alpayim (Public Administration in Israel: Towards the 2000's)*. Tel-Aviv: Tcherikover Publishers. (Hebrew)

White, H. 1973. *Metahistory*. Baltimore: Johns Hopkins University Press.

——— 1987. *The Content of the Form*. Baltimore: Johns Hopkins University Press.

Whiteley, W.H. (ed.). 1971. *Language Use and Social Change; Problems of Multilingualism with Special Reference to Eastern Africa*. London: Oxford University Press.

Who's Who, 1998.

Willett, Cynthia. 1998. "Introduction", pp. 1–16 in Willett, Cynthia (ed.), *Theorizing Multiculturalism: A Guide to the Current Debate*. Oxford: Blackwell.

Williams, R. 1977. *Marxism and Literature*. Oxford: Oxford University Press.

Williamson, John B. and Pampel, Fred C. 1993. *Old Age Security in Comparative Perspective*. New York: Oxford University Press.

Winant, Howard. 1994. *Racial Conditions*. Minneapolis: University of Minnesota Press.

Wise, N. 1993. "Mediations: Enlightenment Balancing Act, or the Technologies of Rationalization", in Horwich, P. (ed.), *World Changes. Thomas Kuhn and the Nature of Science*. Cambridge: The MIT Press.

——— (ed.). 1995. *The Values of Precision*. Princeton: Princeton University Press.

Wiseman, J. 1999. "The Continuing Case for Demo-Optimism in Africa", *Democratization* 6(2): 125–155.

Wittrock, Björn. 1993. "The Modern University: The Three Transformations", in Rothblatt, Sheldon and Wittrock, Björn (eds.), *The European and American University Since 1800: Historical and Sociological Essays*. Cambridge: Cambridge University Press.

——— 1998. "Early Modernities: Varieties and Transitions", *Daedalus* 127(3): 19–40.

——— 2000. "Modernity: One, None, or Many? European Origins and Modernity as a Global Condition". *Daedalus* 129(1): 31–60.

Wokler, Robert. 1987. "Saint-Simon and the Passage from Political to Social Science", in Padgen, Anthony (ed.), *The Languages of Political Theory in Early Modern Europe*. Cambridge: Cambrdige University Press.

——— 1998. "The Enlightenment and the French Revolutionary Birth Pangs of Modernity", pp. 35–76 in Heilbron, J., Magnusson, L. and Wittrock, B. (eds.), *The Rise of the Social Sciences and the Formation of Modernity: Conceptual Changes in Context, 1750–1850*. Dordrecht: Kluwer.

Wolf, Eric. 1997. *Europe and the People Without History*. Berkeley: University of California Press.

Wolf, Kurt. (ed.). 1950. *The Sociology of Georg Simmel*. Glencoe: Free Press.

Wolpert, Julian. 1995. "Fragmentation in America's Nonprofit Sector", in Schervish, Paul G., Hodgkinson, Virginia A. and Gates, Margaret (eds.), *Care and Community in Modern Society: Passing on the Tradition of Care to the Next Generation*. San Francisco: Jossey-Bass.

Wood, Gordon S. 1992. *The Radicalism of the American Revolution*. New York: A.A. Knopf.

Wuthnow, R. (ed.). 1992. *Between States and Market: The Voluntary Sector in Comparative Perspective*. Princeton: Princeton University Press.

——— 1994. *Producing the Sacred: An Essay on Public Religion*. Urbana and Chicago: University of Illinois Press.

Yack, Bernard. 1997. *The Fetishism of Modernities*. Notre Dame: University of Notre Dame
     Press.
Yankelovich, Daniel. 1994. "How Changes in the Economy are Reshaping American Values",
     pp. 16–53 in Aaron, Henry J. et al., *Values and Public Policy*. Washington, DC: Brookings
     Institution.
Yeo, Richard. 1991. "Reading Encyclopedias. Science and the Organization of Knowledge
     in British Dictionaries of Arts and Sciences, 1730–1850", *Isis* 82: 24–49.
Young, C. 1996. "Africa: An Interim Balance Sheet", *Journal of Democracy* 7(3).
———— 1998. "The African Colonial State Revisited", *Governance* 11(1): 101–120.
Young, Jock. 1999. *The Exclusive Society*. London: Sage.
Young, Pauline V. 1949. *Scientific Social Surveys and Research*. 2nd edition. New York: Prentice
     Hall.
Young, Robert. 1995. *Colonial Desire*. London: Routledge.
Zelizer, V.A. 1994. *The Social Meaning of Money*. New York: Basic Books.
Zolberg, A.R. 1986. "How Many Exceptionalisms?", pp. 397–457 in Katznelson, I. and
     Zolberg A.R., *Working-Class Formation*. Princeton: Princeton University Press.

LIST OF CONTRIBUTORS

Johann P. Arnason is a Professor at the School of Sociology, Politics and Anthropology, at La Trobe University, Melbourne, Australia

Zygmunt Bauman is an Emeritus Professor of Sociology, at Leeds University, UK

Aysegul Baykan is Assistant Professor in the Department of Sociology, at Koc University, Turkey

Mohamed Benrabah is Maître de Conférence in sociolinguistics and English linguistics, at the University of Grenoble III, France

Eliezer Ben-Rafael is a Professor of Sociology, in the Department of Sociology and Anthropology, at Tel-Aviv University, Israel

Pierre Birnbaum is a Professor of Sociology, at the Sorbonne (Paris I), France

Y. Michal Bodemann is a Professor of Sociology, in the Department of Sociology, at the University of Toronto, Canada

Craig Calhoun is a Professor of Sociology, in the Department of Sociology, at New York University, USA

Dale F. Eickelman is a Professor of Anthropology and Human Relations and Chair of the Department of Anthropology, at Dartmouth College, USA

Shmuel N. Eisenstadt is an Emeritus Professor of Sociology and Anthropology, at the Department of Sociology, at the Hebrew University of Jerusalem, Israel

Eva Etzioni-Halevy is a Professor of Sociology, in the Department of Sociology and Anthropology, at Bar-Ilan University, Israel

Mike Featherstone is the Head of the Theory, Culture and Society Center, at Nottingham Trent University, UK

Denise Ferreira da Silva is an Associate Professor in the Ethnic Studies Department, at the University of Califormia in San Diego, USA

Johan Galtung, is an Emeritus Professor of Peace Studies and founder of the Peace Research Insititute, Oslo, and Director of Transcend: A Peace and Development Network, Norway

Jürgen Heideking was a Professor of History, and Director of the Institute of Anglo-American Studies, at the University of Cologne, Germany

Alex Inkeles is a Senior Fellow at the Hoover Institution, at Stanford University, USA

Elihu Katz is an Emeritus Professor of Sociology and Communication, in the Department of Communication at the Hebrew University of Jerusalem, Israel, and a Professor of Communication, in the Annenberg School of Communication, at the University of Pennsylvania, USA

Karin Knorr Cetina is a Professor of Sociology, in the Department of Sociology, at the University of Bielefeld, Germany

Benyamin Neuberger is a Professor of Political Science, in the Department of Political Science, Sociology and Communication, at the Open University, Israel

Renato Ortiz is a Professor of Sociology, in the Department of Sociology, at the University of Campinas, in São Paulo, Brazil

Roland Robertson is a Professor of Sociology, in the Department of Sociology, at the University of Aberdeen, UK

Masamichi Sasaki is a Professor of Sociology in the Department of Sociology, at Hyogo Kyoiku Univeristy, Japan

Erwin K. Scheuch is a Emeritus Professor of Sociology in the Institute for Comparative Social Research, at the University of Cologne, Germany

Ilana F. Silber is a Senior Lecturer of Sociology, in the Department of Sociology, at University of Bar-Ilan, Israel

Jerzy J. Smolicz is the Head of the Centre for Intercultural Studies and Multicultural Education, at the University of Adelaide, Australia

Bernard Spolsky is an Emeritus Professor of Sociolinguistics in the Department of English, at Bar-Ilan University, Israel

Yitzhak Sternberg is a PhD student in the Department of Sociology and Anthropology, at Tel-Aviv University, Israel

Abram de Swaan is a Professor of Sociology in the Amsterdam School for Social Science Research, at the University of Amsterdam, Holland

Stanley J. Tambiah is a Professor of Anthropology in the Wing of Social Anthropology, at Harvard University, USA

Alain Touraine is an Emeritus Directeur d'Etudes, at the Ecole des Hautes Etudes en Sciences sociales, France

Bryan S. Turner is Professor of Sociology and Head of the Department of Sociology, at the University of Cambridge, UK

Tu Weiming is a Professor of Chinese history and philosophy, in the Faculty of East Asian Languages and Civilizations and Director of the Harvard-Yenching Institute, at Harvard University, USA

Michel Wieviorka is Directeur d'Etude and the Director of the Centre d'Analyse et d'Intervention Sociologique, at the Ecole des Hautes Etudes en Sciences sociales, France

Björn Wittrock is a Professor of Government, and Director of the Swedish Collegium for Advanced Study in the Social Sciences, at Uppsala University, Sweden

.

INDEX OF NAMES

INDEX OF MATTERS